# "You Have Stept Out of Your Place"

# "You Have Stept Out of Your Place"

## A HISTORY OF WOMEN AND RELIGION IN AMERICA

**Susan Hill Lindley**

Westminster John Knox Press
Louisville, Kentucky

*Book design by Jennifer K. Cox*
*Cover design by Alec Bartsch*
*Cover photographs courtesy of the Dictionary of American Portraits.*
*Sarah Winnemucca photograph courtesy of the Nevada Historical Society.*

*First paperback edition*

Published by Westminster John Knox Press
Louisville, Kentucky

This book is printed on acid-free paper that meets the American National Standards Institute Z39.48 standard. ♾

PRINTED IN THE UNITED STATES OF AMERICA

98 99 00 01 02 03 04 05 06 07 — 10 9 8 7 6 5 4 3 2 1

**Library of Congress Cataloging-in-Publication Data**

Lindley, Susan Hill, date.
"You have stept out of your place" : a history of women and religion in America / Susan Hill Lindley. — 1st ed.
p. cm.
Includes bibliographical references and index.
ISBN 0-664-25799-2 (paper)
1. Women and religion—United States—History. 2. United States—Religion. I. Title.
BL2525.L565 1996
277.3'0082—dc20 96-541

*This book is dedicated to my mother and my daughter*

Lois Kathryn Rahenkamp Hill
(1910–1995)

*and*

Kathryn Virginia Lindley

# Contents

# Introduction

In 1965 the Second Vatican Council of the Roman Catholic Church promulgated a decree in which the fathers urged members of religious orders, both men and women, to renew their religious life by returning to the teaching of Christ and the gospel and to the particular purposes of each order's founders. American sisters, already involved in reconsideration of their identity, training, and mission, embraced enthusiastically this official directive to find their roots. The results were often surprising and liberating—and not always pleasing to the male authorities who originally encouraged the search. So, too, other American women, Protestants and Jews as well as Catholics, were prompted by the resurgence of a woman's movement in the 1960s and 1970s to find their religious and female roots.

In an early stage of this historical recovery, students, teachers and scholars focused on famous women—and those who should have been famous. As both a student and a teacher in the 1970s, I experienced this sense of discovery and heard from my students a question familiar to anyone who has taught a course in women's history, "Why didn't anyone ever tell us about Julian of Norwich or Sarah Grimké or Sojourner Truth or Dorothy Day or Henrietta Szold or . . . ?" Fortunately, the fruits of women's studies have gradually spilled into the elementary and secondary schools so that one no longer encounters blank stares at the first mention of Elizabeth Cady Stanton or Harriet Tubman. Recovery of the past also meant finding the negatives: the infuriating, outrageous, sometimes ridiculous things some men have said about woman's nature and roles; the witch-hunts, the legal disabilities, the cultural pressures and restrictions. The negative past for women was real; its exposure and acknowledgment was necessary and healthy and continues to be so for new generations of women. Yet like the Catholic sisters finding in the recovery of their roots a new sense of identity and mission, women in the 1970s and 1980s searched for a usable past, going beyond a few token individual women and women's oppression to reclaim the lives and contributions of our foremothers. The search was important for women and history in general, but it was particularly poignant and critical for American women who identified with the Western religious traditions of Judaism and Christianity. Could one be both a Jew and a feminist, a Christian and a feminist?

By the mid-1990s, women differ in their assessment of the viability of remaining within Jewish or Christian communities, but there is no question that a usable and fascinating past has been recovered. In the last thirty years, research and publication about women have exploded, and one of the most fertile areas of interest has been religion in America. Scholars found that American women have been disruptive and submissive, challenging and supportive. They have been slaves, preachers, missionaries, reformers, critics, and the pillars of home and morality. This work is an attempt to draw together some of the results of that scholarly explosion—monographs, articles, documentary histories, anthologies—and to tell the story of women and religion in America in a single-volume survey text. In telling that story, I have tried to highlight the two-sidedness of a usable past. First, there are the individuals and the movements who stepped out of their culturally assigned subordination in society, family, and church. Sometimes their challenge was radical and direct; at other times, women appeared to accept subordinate or separate spheres and proceeded subtly to expand their limits. The other side is equally important, as researchers have lifted up and valued "ordinary" women and what they did: the Puritan "goodwife" with her quiet but critical contributions to the colony's survival; the Jewish or Polish Catholic immigrant mother preserving for the next generation a religious and ethnic heritage; the black women keeping the church going through their cleaning, cooking, fund-raising, and teaching so that it could be a center and haven for the community.

I have felt both excited and frustrated as I found more material than could possibly be covered in a single volume. Others might have made different choices of inclusion, but I have tried to span a broad geographic, ethnic, racial, and denominational range of American women's religious experiences and contributions. In so doing, I have tried to present the diversity of their voices with integrity. That has meant that although I appreciate the impact of social, economic, cultural, or psychological influences on persons' behavior, I regard these as contributory, not exhaustive explanations. In short, in the absence of strong counterevidence, I have assumed that American women were basically telling the truth about who they were, what they did, and why they did it. It has also meant that I have tried not to let my personal assessments intrude into the story to the point of distortion. Yet I am sure those personal judgments have appeared, and so (as has become the custom in feminist writing, and a good one it is), I should acknowledge explicitly my own location. I am a white, middle-class, Christian "reformist" feminist—that is, someone who is critical of the Church's historical patriarchy and sexism but who embraces that same Church as a source of meaning and hope.

After the sheer relief of completion of a book that has been several years in the birthing, surely the second greatest pleasure of an author is to thank the many people who have helped one in so many ways. I am very grateful to those colleagues and friends who have graciously shared bibliography and insights from their particular area of expertise with me and sometimes read parts of the manuscript: Jane F. Crosthwaite, Richard Grounds,

Joan Gundersen, Evelyn Kirkley, DeAne Lagerquist, Barbara Pitken, Anantanand Rambachan, Barbara Reed, Jan Shipps, and Ann Wagner. My thanks also to Mary Farrell Bednarowski, who read a good part of the manuscript and encouraged me to continue, affirming that "we need" a survey text like this. Needless to say, any errors are a result of my misunderstanding, not their insights. I also want to thank the staff of the Saint Olaf Library, particularly Kirk Moll, Bryn Geffert, and Robert Bruce for research help, and Connie Gunderson for her patience and ingenuity with my many requests for interlibrary loans. My very sincere appreciation, too, to the people at Westminster John Knox press, especially to Alexa Smith, who first encouraged me to submit the manuscript, and to Stephanie Egnotovich, who saw it through to its completion, as well as to Beth Gaede, for her copyediting, and to Nancy Roseberry, for seeing it through production. I am grateful to Kathy Granquist for her patient and meticulous help with proofreading and indexing. The members of the Religion Department at Saint Olaf have been consistently cheerful in the face of my complaints, crises, and triumphs as they assured me that "the book" would finally be completed; and a special thanks to my office-neighbor and church history colleague, Eric Lund, who listened so patiently, so graciously, and so often to stories about a topic well out of his own field. A very special thanks, too, to Erling Jostad, St. Olaf Professor of History with whom I team-taught for nearly twenty years, for his help on the topic of the New Religious Right, his seasoned advice on writing books, and most of all, his friendship and encouragement. Jody Greenslade, secretary of the Religion Department, typed the initial portions from my longhand, taught me how to use a computer, organized and fixed the texts that I, still a computer-beginner, turned out, helped with the index, and through it all offered a ready ear, support, and friendship far beyond the call of professional duty. Finally, I want to express my thanks to my husband John and our children Jonathan, Nathaniel, Kathryn, and Stephen, whose love has kept me going through setbacks and periods of discouragement.

# 1
# *Anne Hutchinson*

In September of 1634, Anne and William Hutchinson and their family arrived from England in the fledgling Puritan colony of Massachusetts Bay. They were warmly welcomed: William was a successful merchant; Anne had skills and experience as a nurse and midwife; most important, both were pious Christians who were quickly admitted to church membership, even though Anne's admission was delayed for a week because of questions raised by the Reverend Mr. Symmes, a minister who had traveled on the ship with them. But probably even he never suspected that the ideas and activities of this devout English matron would nearly tear the colony apart.

Founded in 1630, Massachusetts was to be a godly experiment, a "city on a hill" whose example of the right ordering of a society under God would shine back to the same England that had persecuted the Puritans. The colony's leaders believed that they were a chosen people with whom God had made a covenant. If they obeyed God, they would prosper, but if they were unfaithful, God's favor would be withdrawn. To be chosen was both a blessing and an awesome responsibility. Not everyone in Massachusetts was devout, but at the infant colony's center was a passionate conviction that religion should pervade every sphere of life and that the scriptures provide a clear pattern for a true Christian society.

Anne Hutchinson shared this passionate religious concern. Born in 1591, she was the daughter of Francis Marbury, an Anglican minister. Though no Puritan himself, Marbury was outspoken in his criticism of the established church, particularly the appointment of unworthy ministers by an unconcerned hierarchy. He was imprisoned for his criticisms but later released to take a living at Alford, where he ministered during Anne's childhood, influencing and teaching his eldest child in matters scriptural and theological. In 1605, the family moved to London, but in 1612 Anne married a former neighbor, William Hutchinson, and returned to Alford to start their family of fifteen children. During this time, Anne became a Puritan, influenced especially by the preaching of John Cotton in nearby Boston. Meanwhile, she studied scripture and began the life of inner religious experience that would cause so much dissension later. She became convinced that she could distinguish true preachers from false and, indeed, that there were in England only two of the former: Cotton and her brother-in-law, John Wheelwright. So when Wheelwright was "silenced" by the church authorities and Cotton left for New England in 1633, she turned again to scripture and found there a leading to follow Cotton; the family sailed for New England in 1634.

Not long after they had settled, Anne began holding weekly meetings with a small group of women to study the Bible and go over Cotton's sermons. Soon a second weekly meeting was added, drawing men as well, eventually growing to an attendance of up to eighty people across the whole range of Boston's social spectrum. We have no direct records of these meetings, but it appears from later reports that Anne used them to expound her own insights and to criticize the other ministers, just as she found in her physical and psychological ministry as a nurse and midwife an opportunity to share her religious convictions. By 1636, the colony was divided into two parties: the "Hutchinsonians," including Henry Vane, who had replaced John Winthrop for a time as governor, and most of the members of the Boston church; and their opponents, including Winthrop, most of the ministers, and many of the colonists outside Boston.

The controversy was complicated, for it was manifest in political and personal rivalries, as well as theological disagreements. Cotton was the most prominent minister on the Hutchinson side, and he met with the other ministers in October 1636 to try to clarify the issues; yet there is no question that Anne Hutchinson's theology and activities were the most divisive issues. In October, John Winthrop recorded in his *Journal* his first written reference to her, identifying her as

> a woman of a ready wit and bold spirit, [who] brought over with her two dangerous errors: 1. That the person of the Holy Ghost dwells in a justified person. 2. That no sanctification can help to evidence to us our justification.[1]

Two months later, the ministers summoned Anne to a private meeting at Cotton's house to ascertain her views, although no further action was taken against her at that time. By the end of December, the extent of the controversy can be seen in Winthrop's report:

> Thus every occasion increased the contention and caused great alienation of minds; and the members of Boston (frequenting the lectures of other ministers) did make much disturbance by public questions, and objections to their doctrines, which did any way disagree from their opinions; and it began to be as common here to distinguish between men, as being under a covenant of grace or a covenant of works, as in other countries between Protestants and Papists.[2]

## The Heart of the Controversy

A political power struggle was surely part of the controversy and even intensified over the next year, but at its heart was theology, beliefs that affected both the individual and the community, this life and eternal salvation. Both the "errors" Winthrop had identified in his *Journal* affected the crucial question of the believer's assurance: How can I know whether I am saved? To Anne Hutchinson (and for much of the controversy, John Cotton), God's grace was critical and absolute: Human beings contributed nothing by way of preparation; nor could they look to their upright life (sanctification) even as one tentative sign of justification. Assurance came only through inner religious experience, the direct work of the Holy Spirit. Winthrop and the other ministers, on the other hand, without denying the overwhelming credit to God, allowed that one might prepare for God's grace (though God was not obligated to respond) and that a godly life might be one possible sign of grace in which a believer could find assurance of election.

As the two groups saw each other, the difference was clearly drawn. To the Hutchinson party, the other side was legalistic and slighted the Holy Spirit. It placed too high a value on human effort and encouraged false confidence and hypocrisy—hence, Anne's charge that these ministers preached a covenant of works. Winthrop's side quite reasonably resented that appellation, for even with their slight concessions to human effort, they never denied the lion's share of efficacy in salvation to God's grace. To them, the Hutchinson party appeared immoral, offering a "faire and easie way to Heaven"—no wonder they were popular![3] They gave people an excuse to be lazy and disobedient, undercutting the disciplines of church and state. The consequences of their Antinomian views ("without or against law") could destroy the whole godly experiment, the very purpose of the Puritan colony. Moreover, the Winthrop party felt that the Hutchinson claims for direct experience of the Holy Spirit endangered the authority of not only ministers and magistrates but even of scripture itself. The Hutchinson party found such conclusions as unfair and absurd as the Winthrop party did the charge of works righteousness.

Furthermore, Winthrop and his party were worried that news of the controversy could get back to England, a further danger to the young colony and its mission. So in January of 1637, the General Court called for a fast day in penitent response to religious conditions in Europe and England, to recent natural disasters and Indian attacks (seen by the Puritans as signs of God's displeasure), and especially to "the dissensions in our churches."[4] The afternoon of the fast day, Cotton preached a sermon of reconciliation and then, fatefully, asked John Wheelwright (now in Massachusetts and a firm Hutchinson supporter) to speak. Wheelwright's sermon was *not* conciliatory, and in March he was cited by the General Court for sedition and contempt because of it. His supporters immediately voiced their protest in a petition, insisting he had spoken only of "spiritual," not physical warfare. The actions of neither side during the ensuing power struggle were particularly admirable, and by September a synod of ministers published a list of more than eighty Antinomian "errors" (with some limited dissent by Cotton) and condemned Anne Hutchinson's meetings and theological activities as "disorderly, and without rule."[5] By November, the Winthrop party was in control with a new—and "packed"—General Court. They met; Wheelwright and the leading men of the Hutchinson party were banished, disenfranchised, or both on the grounds of Wheelwright's fast-day sermon and the petition. Technically, the grounds were civil ones: They were a danger to the state.

The court turned last to Anne Hutchinson, "the head of all this faction, . . . the breeder and nourisher of all these distempers."[6] The first charge was that she "countenanced" Wheelwright's sermon and the petition, but the court could not find sufficient evidence for conviction: As a woman, Mistress Hutchinson could not sign the petition, and she had made no public statement. The second charge concerned her meetings, but she continued to defend herself with wit and with counterappeals to scripture, so no conviction was reached. The third charge before the court was that she dishonored the ministers, drawing on the (supposedly) private meeting of the previous December. The argument stretched out at great length, but she held her own and was supported by Cotton's testimony. At this impasse, Anne Hutchinson, fatefully, volunteered information about her religious history, her visions, and her immediate revelations, including a warning that God would curse the court if they punished her. That was enough. She was sentenced to banishment but allowed to remain in the colony over the winter under house arrest, because she was again pregnant. The outcome was not a surprise. Winthrop and his supporters were both prosecutors and judges; the only question about the process was how they would find grounds to convict Anne Hutchinson.

In the spring she faced a second trial, this one by her church. Her previous conviction was, like those of her male allies, on civil grounds: she admitted immediate revelations. These might be false and, unchecked, might include revelations leading to civil violence. The theological charges against her were highly complex, and although she tried valiantly to defend herself without compromising her integrity, the outcome of this trial, too, was a foregone conclusion, especially given (1) the testimony of the ministers who had visited her for what they called "helpful counsel" over the winter and (2) Cotton's defection. She was excommunicated for her heresy and her "lying," and the charge against her by one of the ministers, Hugh Peters, long a bitter opponent, included this revealing statement:

> You have stept out of your place, *you have rather bine a Husband than a Wife and a preacher than a Hearer; and a Magistrate than a Subject.*[7]

The Hutchinson family and other leading members of that party moved to Rhode Island, recently founded as a haven by an earlier dissenter, Roger Williams. Boston tried to reclaim those church members still in good standing, but with little success. The report of Robert Keayne, one such emissary, contains an interesting sidelight, the only recorded comment we have from William Hutchinson, who told the delegates "he was more nearly tied to his wife than to the church, he thought her to be a dear saint and servant of God."[8] In 1642 William died, and Anne moved with those children still at home to the northern side of Long Island Sound, where, in the summer of 1643, she and five of the children were killed by Indians.

## Hutchinson's Impact on American Puritanism

The Antinomian controversy was a critical episode in shaping the development of Puritanism in America; it was also a critical incident in shaping Puritan views on women, and it raises a number of important gender-related questions. Was Anne Hutchinson condemned because she was a woman? Yes and no. The core issues were theological and political (and the two spheres were intimately related for the Puritans). Both parties included persons of both sexes and from all ranks, including ministers. Men were also convicted and banished by the court. Nevertheless, from the point of view of the winners, Anne Hutchinson was the primary problem. Male leaders clearly deplored her influence on other women, and they could find justification for their anger and frustration with her ideas and activities in a long Christian tradition of distrust of women: As daughters of Eve, they were weak of faith and of intellect; they used their wiles to seduce men from truth and piety; scripture clearly enjoined their submission in a godly and well-ordered society. The records of the controversy are filled with comments denigrating Anne and the women Antinomians for their unnatural behavior. Anne Hutchinson was not condemned solely because she was a woman, but her gender made her actions even more offensive, and the Puritan leadership drew far-reaching conclusions from the incident about women and their place.

Was Anne Hutchinson a feminist? For many years, historians accepted the winners' judgment of the "American Jezebel." In the twentieth century, however, she has been portrayed by some as a martyr to religious intolerance or as a heroic defender of women's rights against the patriarchy of church and state. In fact, she was neither a devil nor a saint. Her dissent may have, eventually and obliquely, contributed to the cause of religious toleration in America, but reasoned and principled toleration was no more a central motive of the Hutchinson party than it was of their opponents. They just lost the power struggle. Nor was she a self-conscious feminist in any modern sense. She was pushed over the course of the controversy into defending herself and her actions *as a woman,* especially her right to preach or teach religious matters; to defend women's rights *per se,* however, was not her initial goal. Her primary motivation was religious conviction, as clear and passionately held as that of her opponents. But her beliefs had implications for women in a special way, particularly her emphasis on the primacy of the Holy Spirit and religious experience, as these undercut the traditional authority of leaders of church and state, a male monopoly. Women were not her only supporters, but many were drawn to her cause, and the greater potential of her position for female theological independence may well have been an attraction. Finally, despite the fact that the records of the controversy come from her opponents, their accounts cannot obscure the portrait of a strong, intelligent, and witty woman, a worthy opponent of the best theological minds of her setting.

Did Anne Hutchinson and the Antinomian controversy shape subsequent American Puritan views of women? Perhaps not single-handedly, but decisively. When the early Puritans came to New England, the future was, to a degree, open. They carried with them all the history of Christian misogynism and a tradition of female subordination and spiritual weakness. Yet they also came, most immediately, from a turbulent religious situation in England in which they had been the dissenters, the critics of establishment and tradition. Women played an active and vocal role in English Nonconformist churches in the first half of the seventeenth century, and male Nonconformists alternated between appreciation and suspicion of the women's activities.[9] Puritans also carried, as heirs of the Protestant Reformation, at least a theoretical potential for greater spiritual equality for women. Like men, women were a part of the priesthood of all believers, responsible directly to God for their faith (rather than through the mediation of priests or saints). Women, like men, were encouraged to study the Bible and the state of their own souls. Admittedly, the Protestant reformers did not see such spiritual responsibilities as implying lack of female subjection to male Protestant authorities, but wittingly or not, they had opened a door.

Given that heritage and the circumstances of the New World, with the chance there to shape an ideal, godly society, the Puritans might have modified some traditional views of women. Their guide was scripture, but scripture itself is ambiguous regarding women. As Mary Maples Dunn concludes,

> The people of New England could, if they wanted, find in Paul a situation parallel to their own: a radical spiritual message of equality in tension with social custom. It was not certain how the tension between these two views of women would be resolved in New England, and in this situation, . . . many women engaged themselves in both experiments in church governance and in the discussion of doctrine.[10]

Indeed, Anne Hutchinson herself made extremely effective use in her trial of scriptural precedents more favorable to women and their religious activities.

If the situation for women was open in the early 1630s in the Massachusetts Bay Colony, and if developments could have gone the direction of greater freedom for women (though surely not radical or total equality, realistically), that option was dead by 1637—and largely in reaction to Anne Hutchinson and the Antinomian controversy. Ironically, that reaction might have been less adamant had Anne Hutchinson "merely" challenged the status of women within church and society instead of the theological heart of God's dealings with humanity, election, and authority, both of scripture and within the structures of the godly community. By the time of her church trial, issues of female insubordination were so closely tied to what the Puritan authorities saw as a dangerous and heretical threat to their beliefs, their identity, and their God-given mission that any other woman who stepped out of her place would also be condemned.[11]

# 2
# *Quakers in Colonial America*

When the Puritans' church court pronounced its sentence of excommunication on Anne Hutchinson, one of her supporters, Mary Dyer, rose and left the church with her. Subsequently, she too was excommunicated and banished, and Mary and William Dyer moved to Rhode Island. In the 1650s they returned to England, where Mary Dyer joined the Society of Friends or Quakers. Upon returning to New England, she felt called to witness to her former Puritan neighbors in Boston.

In the meantime, the Puritans decided that Quakers were as troublesome and dangerous as Anne Hutchinson had been, banishing any who arrived in Massachusetts, and in 1658 they passed a law allowing the death penalty for Quakers who would not stay out. Despite her two previous banishments from Boston, in 1638 and 1657, Mary Dyer returned in the summer of 1659 to visit two fellow Quakers currently imprisoned in Boston. Again she was banished; again she returned, and in the fall of 1659 was sentenced to death along with two Quaker men. The men were indeed hanged, and she was literally on the scaffold when she was granted a last-minute reprieve and forcibly removed, one more time, from the colony. The next spring she returned, and this time the sentence of execution was carried out.

Mary Dyer would later be honored as a martyr to religious liberty, and her statue would be placed near Boston Common, but at the time, the Puritan authorities must have viewed her not only as a dangerous heretic, inspired by the devil, but also as an incredibly frustrating woman, who refused to accept either her sphere or her repeated banishments. Even her husband William questioned her sanity. Yet Mary Dyer knew quite clearly what her protest was and why she had to make it. After her sentence of death in 1659, she wrote a letter to the General Court of Boston[1] in which she insisted that she was following God's will and call to her by protesting the wicked and intolerant law of Massachusetts, which restricted the rights and religious freedom of Quakers. Ironically, she was as convinced that their actions were inspired by the devil as the Puritans were that hers were, and, echoing the words of Anne Hutchinson more than twenty years earlier at *her* trial, Mary Dyer warned the Puritans that God's wrath would strike them if they continued these evil ways. Perhaps she was right, at least insofar as the Puritans did suffer considerable infamy in England at the time and in subsequent history for their cruel and intolerant treatment of Quakers.

But what was this Quaker religion that inspired and allowed such radical ideas and actions in a woman like Mary Dyer? The Quakers or Society of Friends arose amid the religious turmoil of mid-seventeenth-century England, out of the same soil as the Puritans. Indeed, they shared the Protestant/Puritan emphasis on the individual's responsibility for his or her own faith and the need for spiritual rebirth. Both groups were also highly critical of the established Church of England, desiring a simpler form of worship and a "purer" membership of "visible saints" or committed Christians. But the Quakers went further with these principles, and they drew far more radical conclusions about the social realities and roles of women and men in this world from their theoretical principles of spiritual equality.

In 1647, George Fox, the founder of the Quakers, ended a troubled spiritual pilgrimage in a religious vision, an experience of Christ as the Light. In that experience was rooted the most distinctive doctrine of the Friends: the "inner light" or "that of God" in every person. The immediate direction of God that can come through the inner light is the ultimate religious authority. Fox and the Quakers honored scripture as inspired revelation, but they also believed that inspiration and revelation were not closed but continued (a position that frightened and infuriated the American Puritans, as can be clearly seen in their treatment of Mary Dyer and Anne Hutchinson, who was, of course, not a Quaker, since she died in 1643, but might be called a kind of "proto-Quaker").

## Women Leaders in Quaker Society

Because of the inner light, Fox and the followers he began to gather asserted from the start a radical, this-worldly egalitarianism, not only of class but of gender. Women were among his first converts, including Elizabeth Hooten, who would go on to be a missionary, and in 1652, Margaret Fell. She was, at the time, an established English matron, the wife of a judge. Judge Fell himself never formally joined the Friends, but he was sympathetic, and their home, Swarthmore Hall, was for some forty years the site of Quaker meetings and the organizational center of the movement. Margaret Fell's own contributions earned her the title of "Nursing Mother" of the Quakers because she served as the group's financial secretary and as a preacher and defender of Quaker ideas, in person and through her pen.

To say that women's religious leadership, including public preaching, was not a popular innovation in mid-seventeenth-century England is a gross understatement. Nevertheless, from the beginning of his ministry, George Fox encouraged and defended it in his action, his speech, and his writings. Margaret Fell, too, defended her own preaching and that of her sisters in an important 1666 tract, "Women's Speaking Justified, Proved and Allowed of by the Scriptures, all such as speak by the Spirit and Power of the Lord Jesus." Freed by the Quaker view of scripture as inspired but neither the final nor the ultimate authority, Fox and Fell argued that Adam and Eve were equal before the Fall; equality was then lost but is restored after spiritual rebirth, and Paul's restrictions on women's speaking do not apply to the regenerate. They also cited such precedents as the women prophets, the woman of Samaria, and the women witnesses of the resurrection.

Thus a reinterpretation of scripture joined with the concept of the inner light, through which God might move any person to speak, to defend a radical new role of religious participation for women. A third element that both encouraged and defended women's preaching was the Quaker rejection of formal priestly authority and their emphasis on lay ministry. True, even some Friends opposed so much female assertiveness, but the views of Fox and Fell were stronger, and many women flocked to the movement and to the role of missionary, including a witness to the American colonies.

Mary Dyer endured the severest punishment of Quaker women missionaries who challenged the New England Puritans, but she was neither the first nor the last to appear in Boston, only to be met with physical humiliation, punishment, and deportation. In 1656, after Mary Fisher and Ann Austin arrived in Boston, male Puritan leaders concluded that the ideas of these women were so dangerous that their books were burned, and they themselves were imprisoned and shortly shipped out to Barbados. Undeterred by such treatment or even Mary Dyer's martyrdom, other Quakers, men and women, continued their witness as missionaries in Massachusetts and, to a lesser degree, other English colonies. Hostility to any Quaker missionary was intensified toward those women who were acting so "unnaturally"; yet more than 40 percent of these early Quaker missionary witnesses were women. (There were twenty-six women among the fifty-nine missionaries who came to America between 1656 and 1663, and twenty-two of them were not accompanied by husbands.)[2] Other colonies were less hostile than Massachusetts, but, with rare exceptions, only in Rhode Island could Quakers find real toleration before the settlement of West Jersey and the founding of the Quaker colony of Pennsylvania in 1681.

Witnessing to the unconverted continued to be one purpose of Quaker missions, but gradually that activity was overshadowed by travel for internal ministry, communication, and encouragement among Quaker societies. Here, too, women continued to play important roles, sometimes traveling with their husbands, but often in pairs of women, married or not. (And Friends did not assume all women should marry.) By the eighteenth century, "Public Friends," as they were called, traveled across the Atlantic in both directions because American Quakers felt called to go to their English brothers and sisters. The "call" was critical; by no means were all Friends engaged in missionary travel. The initial requirement was that the individual have a clear sense of God's leading through the inner light. Like many prophets before them, some Friends denied or resisted the call at first, but they could find no spiritual peace while they did. On the other hand, call was not purely an internal and individual matter; it was to be tested and evaluated by the person's immediate Quaker community, and only when the members were convinced of the call's validity would they issue a "traveling minute" of official approval and authority.

The role of Quaker missionary as an option for women was clearly a radical instance in the colonial period of "stepping out of their place," and decades, even centuries, would pass before other Christian women would be allowed to preach so publicly. Yet equally radical and significant were the roles of religious leadership that developed for Quaker women in the governance of the society through the women's meetings.

Friends had two types of "meetings," which served a variety of functions. First, there were meetings for worship, where both men and women gathered quietly to await the leading of the Holy Spirit. There was no formal liturgical structure or clerical leadership: Those who were inspired by God to speak did, regardless of their gender (contrary to virtually every other contemporary Christian group's public religious practice). But George Fox also developed a system of business or governing "meetings," in part as a communal balance to individual religious experience and in part as a response to the excesses and even fanaticism of a few early Quakers, especially one James Nayler, and the resultant hostility and persecution of Friends by their English neighbors and the authorities. Such business meetings occurred most frequently at the local level; then several local meetings would come together at monthly meetings; monthly meetings from still larger areas, at quarterly meetings; and finally, the most extensive representation, at the yearly meeting. In this theoretically consistent structure, men and women would have separate but parallel meetings. In fact, the women's meetings were not always as strong, not entirely equal to the men's, and in some cases, women's meetings did not even exist, and they were opposed by a number of male Friends. Nevertheless, Fox continued to give them his firm support, as did Margaret Fell, and the Lancashire Women's Meeting, where Margaret and her daughter Sarah were active, was a particularly strong and effective one.

## Women's Meetings

The women's meetings had a number of functions in both England and America as they developed over the next 150 years. First, they provided for the women an opportunity to develop formal administrative skills.

Someone had to run them, so a woman would be appointed as a presiding clerk. Records needed to be kept by a recording clerk in a record book. This seems so obvious, even trivial today, yet it was at the time, as Dunn notes, an "important symbolic act"[3] (not to mention a boon to later historians). As the women's meetings moved into such areas as charitable support of the poor or people in crisis, money was needed. Sometimes it came from the men, but at other times and places, women collected their own, acquiring thereby valuable experience in fund-raising and financial administration. Finally, the women needed space, a place of their own to meet. Generally in England, it was clearly a "lesser" space, a loft or a separate shed, but in America, even the physical space reflected a relative equality of the sexes, because meeting houses were constructed with a large room for joint worship that could be temporarily divided by a partition for separate men's and women's business meetings.[4]

A second major function of the women's meetings was internal discipline of women members, either for inappropriate behavior or absence from meeting. In theory, the women's actions could be overruled by the men's meetings, but in fact, this veto power was not always invoked. Not surprisingly, male Friends were divided between support and disapproval of such female authority and independence.

Charitable activities formed a third important function of the women's meetings, including aid to fellow members in crisis situations, like widows, and help for the poor. Meetings might also issue statements of principle or protest, and as the Society of Friends spread and developed in the American colonies, these included expressions of unusual sensitivity to the human dignity of blacks and Indians, calling for honest treatment by both men and women Quakers.

As the Society of Friends spread and grew in the late seventeenth century and into the eighteenth century, a fourth function of the meetings increased in importance: keeping in touch with other Friends through messages, letters, and traveling ministers. Such communication and support were important not only within a given geographical unit at the monthly and quarterly levels but also throughout the American colonies and back and forth with England. While the support came more *from* the mother country in the first years of the society, the balance was more nearly equal by the eighteenth century. Indeed, not only did the Philadelphia Quaker women send gifts and messages to the general London Yearly Meeting, they protested their English sisters' lack of a London Yearly Meeting of their own and, despite a lack of support from their American brothers, persisted in their opinions until that goal was achieved in 1784.[5]

A final important function of the women's meetings was their role in the supervision of marriage. The Quakers' principled espousal of religious toleration and freedom of conscience did not mean they considered all religious paths equally worthy; they were very concerned to keep children, and hence marriages, within the faith of the society. Thus before a young Quaker woman and man could marry, they had to have the approval of the women's meeting, which would interview them and investigate their background to be certain that they were, indeed, free to marry and were true Friends in their beliefs and actions. Only then could the couple marry, and the ceremony itself would be witnessed and supervised by appointed members of the women's meeting. The men's meetings had a parallel responsibility for marriage within the society, but the initial proposal came to the women, and, in practice, the women often played a more substantive role.

## Quaker Challenges to Colonial Life

In sum, the Society of Friends clearly rejected the absolute male hierarchy asserted in Hugh Peters' second pair of charges against the disruptive Mistress Hutchinson: that she was a preacher rather than a hearer. Although the religious roles and authority of Quaker women were neither absolutely equal nor uncontested within the society, their ability to speak in meeting when led by the Spirit, their roles as traveling ministers, and their participation in church governance through the women's meetings were as significant as they were unusual in colonial times.

Similarly, the Society of Friends challenged the first male/female hierarchy cited at the Hutchinson trial: the authority of husband over wife in marriage. The pattern of marital partnership was set by George Fox and Margaret Fell, who were married in 1669, about a decade after Judge Fell's death. Where a Puritan wife was clearly subordinate to her husband, Quaker husbands and wives were held to be equally responsible in such concerns as the education of children, and their authority in other family decisions was relatively equal. Stepping out of a subordinate place within the family by no means implied a lack of concern on the part of Quaker women for the traditional responsibilities of motherhood and care of the home. Indeed, for them, as for the vast majority of women in colonial America, such concerns took up the largest amounts of time and energy. But being a wife and mother was not the only approved role for a Quaker woman. Like Roman Catholic women and unlike the vast majority of Protestant women after the Reformation's rejection of celibacy, she had a respectable and socially approved alternative. She could remain single and become a teacher or a traveling minister as a young, single woman. Married women, too, might feel called and find the society's approval for traveling ministry, often after most of their children were grown, but not always: sometimes a woman might leave young children in the care of her husband, relatives, or friends, even for extended periods of time.[6] It is likely that, to non-Quaker neighbors, such actions must have seemed shocking and unnatural, but within the society, these women were not only accepted but honored for their dedication and bravery. Motherhood was indeed valued, but not as a woman's only possible identity, and its responsibilities could be overridden for a time by a higher spiritual calling.

The third pair of male-female hierarchical roles that Anne Hutchinson was charged with disrupting—magistrate over subject—was not challenged by Friends in the colonial period. Men were still the active authorities outside the family and the religious arena. Yet, ironically, it was this third sphere—the sphere of politics for the Society of Friends as a whole—that would be undercut after the middle of the eighteenth century in America.

By then, Quakers had found at least relative toleration in most of the American colonies, but it was in Pennsylvania that they achieved the greatest numbers and, significantly, political power. But because of Pennsylvania's policy of toleration, non-Quakers flocked to the colony, too, many settling on its western frontier. Thus tensions arose for those Quakers in positions of political power who had to balance their own pacifist principles with the demands of the English government and of their own nonpacifist subjects. For a time, Quaker authorities evaded the issues by voting funds "for the king" without enquiring too closely into the use of the money, but the French and Indian War brought the crisis to a head, and many Quakers resigned from public office rather than countenance such a blatant compromise of principle.

Meanwhile, the Friends were increasingly concerned about the worldliness of some members. The very real prosperity experienced by many Quakers seemed to undercut the spiritual vitality and discipline of the movement. Thus at the same time as the society's leaders were withdrawing from public roles, there was also a move for internal reform and renewal—for example, stricter exercise of discipline against those who married outside the society. Change and reform merged in a shift toward greater emphasis on humanitarian activities and on being a prophetic voice of witness against injustice. Friends spoke out against war, against dishonest treatment of Indians, and increasingly against slavery. They developed larger ministries in prison reform, care of the poor, and education, even for those who could not pay for it. Such concerns were not, of course, total innovations for Quakers, but the degree of emphasis and of male leadership was new, as men deprived of public governing activities sought new areas for control. Nevertheless, Quaker women continued to participate in the important roles of protest, humanitarian concern, and education.

Not surprisingly, the Friends "backed off" some from the implications of radical gender equality by the eighteenth century. Nor was the equality ever absolute or unquestioned, even within the society; yet the Friends' ideas and actions were extraordinary at the time and are particularly noteworthy when compared to the very different directions of Puritan growth out of similar soil. Even though it was Puritan patterns that came to dominate American culture, the Quaker witness to what might be was not wholly lost.

# 3

# *Puritanism in America*

The violent antipathy of Puritan authorities to women like Anne Hutchinson and Mary Dyer was not a case of simple misogynism. Rather, their attitude was much more ambivalent: Women could be either good or bad, depending not only on their individual piety and morality but also on their acceptance and fulfillment of particular social roles.[1] In the wake of the Antinomian controversy, two contrasting images for women existed side by side in seventeenth-century New England.

On the one hand, the Puritans inherited from Christian history and scripture itself an image of woman as Eve: the weak woman who succumbed to the devil's temptations and lured Adam into the Fall. Subsequent tradition was virtually unanimous in portraying woman as naturally less intelligent, less spiritual, and more carnal than man, not to mention a constant and dangerous sexual temptress. On the other hand, Puritan theology affirmed the spiritual (though not the social) equality of men and women and thus significantly muted the universality of the image of woman as carnal and spiritually inferior—not all women are Eves. But the negative Eve lived on and could emerge sharply when identifying particular women, most dramatically in New England with those women seen as witches.

## Charges of Witchcraft

There were no formal charges of witchcraft in the early years of the New England colonies, but Puritan authorities like John Winthrop implied that Anne Hutchinson and two of her women supporters, Mary Dyer and Jane Hawkins, were witches. The Salem witch trials of 1692 are the best-known instance of Puritan witch hunting in New England, and they involved the largest number of persons, but they were not unique in colonial times. Not only was there a long history of Christian persecution of witches in Europe from the time of the Middle Ages, there were also accusations, trials, and even executions for witchcraft in seventeenth-century New England before Salem. The most intense outbreak before Salem occurred between 1647 and 1663, involving seventy-nine accusations, twenty-three trials, and fifteen executions.[2] Accusations continued after 1663, but with fewer trials and no executions until, in 1688, the events that would culminate in Salem began with charges against the Widow Glover.

Who and what were witches in the eyes of New England's Puritans, and why did they deserve punishment? The greatest concern for most people was the witches' alleged practice of *maleficium,* using supernatural powers to hurt other people or their property. Most Puritans were concerned with results. But there was also concern, especially among the religious leadership, with causes: Witches practiced their harmful powers because they had allied themselves with Satan, and thus they were a spiritual as well as a social threat to the colonies. Ann Hibbens of Boston was one woman executed for witchcraft in 1656, largely because she was convicted of practicing *maleficium* against her neighbors, but her trial was not her first confrontation with the authorities. In 1640 she had been excommunicated from the church for general contentiousness, for disobedience to authorities, including her husband, and for having a bad influence on other church members. Anne Hutchinson's punishment did not entirely prevent other women like Ann Hibbens from challenging male authority or even doctrine, and from being punished for their insubordination, although these were relatively rare cases.[3] But as Carol Karlsen concludes in the case of Ann Hibbens, only when "she was *also* formally accused by her neighbors of supernatural activity and specific malevolent acts was she brought into court on witchcraft charges."[4]

Yet not every New Englander who offended her or his neighbors or who was suspected as the cause of ill fortune was accused of witchcraft. Careful demographic study by recent scholars has provided insight into who was most likely to be identified as a witch.[5] First and foremost, witches were overwhelmingly women, and most of them were middle-aged or older. Accusations were made against persons of high socioeconomic status, but more often, those in lower levels were accused and were more vulnerable once charges were raised. Further speculation about causes of witchcraft charges and the identity of the accused varies widely, and theories range from the socioeconomic-political to the psychological. It is hardly surprising that such varying interpretations should emerge, for the phenomena and events were indeed complex. But why were women especially vulnerable, and why some women and not others? The reasons that hold in European witch hunts, which also disproportionately victimized women, provide a partial explanation for colonial New England's hunts. Much of the power and danger of witches was linked to female sexuality and to women's presumed spiritual or mental weakness (and hence greater vulnerability to Satan). Yet many Puritan women not only were not accused of witchcraft, they were themselves among the accusers, so gender *alone* is an insufficient explanation. A recurrent, distinctive theme that links many New England witches is that these women stepped out of their place. In one way or another, these women refused to accept the male authorities of church, state, and family and their own subordination thereto. As Carol Karlsen has noted,

> They are almost always described as deviants—disorderly women who failed to, or refused to, abide by the behavioral norms of their society. . . . [They presented] challenges to the supremacy of God and challenges to prescribed gender arrangements. . . . Dissatisfaction with one's lot was one of the most pervasive themes of witches' lives.[6]

To the Puritan mind and especially to male Puritan authorities for whom Anne Hutchinson was a vivid memory, the logic was both clear and conclusive. Woman's subordinate role in church, family, and state was not only necessary for the effective functioning of society, and hence the success of the godly community, it was also both natural and ordained by God. Therefore a woman who refused to accept her natural and God-given place must be somehow inspired by the devil. Satan was very real to colonial Puritans, and although Satan's power was not equal to God's, God did permit the devil some freedom to tempt and mislead human beings. (Christians, of course, were to resist those temptations.) Moreover, God could use Satan as an instrument of wrath. Puritans saw in natural disasters or Indian attacks evidence of God's punishment for their laxness and warnings to repent. Similarly, an outbreak of witchcraft was not only evidence of Satan's activity, it might also be, by divine permission, a punishment and a warning.

To see rebellion against subordinate gender roles as an illuminating and contributing element in accusations of witchcraft in New England is not to suggest rebellion was the only cause, or even a self-conscious motive in each individual case. Seeing rebellion against subordinate gender roles as a cause of witchcraft accusations is certainly not equivalent to concluding that all Puritan women were so intimidated by external threats against deviation or by their own internalization of subordination that they were merely weak and helpless victims of patriarchy. For the Puritans had another image of women, the "good woman" who fulfilled the community's social and religious expectations and was honored for her contribution, a contribution that she herself valued. Moreover, to see the gender role assignments for Puritan women as *only* limiting (though they were surely that) is to subscribe to the very patriarchal values that would dismiss the significance of what most women have traditionally been and done. One important part of the story of women and religion in America is the account of women who "stepped out of their place"; an equally important part of that story is the account of women's underrated contributions in their traditional roles. In those traditional roles, Puritan women were not "Eves" but honorable "daughters of Zion."

## Spiritual Equality but Social Subordination: The Place of Women

The single most important role for any person, male or female, in Puritan ideology was that of believer. Beyond that, a woman's most significant role was within the family as a wife and mother. Her familial role had religious as well as social importance, because the Puritans viewed the family as the basic unit of their society, the locus for Christian practice and the education of children in both practical skills and piety. To be sure, Puritans were as convinced that marriage must evidence hierarchical authority, husband over wife, as they were that hierarchical ordering was a necessary and divinely ordained part of every social institution. But if the husband was the final authority, he was not to be a tyrant. Just as the Puritan wife had duties in a marriage, including deference to her husband's rule, so the husband had responsibilities to love, provide, and care for his wife. Love, including sexual love, was not only encouraged, it was expected of both partners, limited only by the recognition that each had an even higher responsibility to love God. The same John Winthrop who called Anne Hutchinson an "American Jezebel" and gloated over the delivery of "monsters" in childbirth to Hutchinson and Mary Dyer as proof of and punishment for their errors was a devoted, appreciative husband to Margaret. Indeed, the letters between them suggest that both were concerned at times lest they love each other more than God.

Within the family, then, the Puritan woman was subordinate to her husband, but subordination precluded neither conjugal love nor a range of activities and responsibilities that contributed to the family and the community. Many of these activities were what the twentieth century might call "secular"—cooking, housekeeping, childcare, neighborly support and charity, and, on occasion, activity as a "deputy husband"[7]—but the Puritan woman also had specific religious responsibilities. Like the father, the Puritan mother was to educate her children in piety, and if his was the final authority, her example and contact with very young children were powerful influences. A Puritan woman might be forbidden to instruct adult males on religion in public, but she could and should teach religion to children and servants in her home.

For most Puritan women, their positions as "Good Wives" and as church members were the social arenas in which they evidenced a religious identity. In church, they should not preach or question male authorities, as John Cotton, once-stung and twice-shy, insisted in 1650, but they need not be absolutely silent: "A woman is allowed to speak in the Church: 1. In way of subjection when she is to give account of her offense. 2. In way of singing forth the praises of the Lord together with the rest of the Congregation."[8] Most Puritan churches agreed with Cotton, although there was at least one exception during the 1640s: John Fiske, pastor of the church in

Wenham, allowed women to testify publicly to their own conversion, one requirement for church membership.[9] Since Anne Hutchinson had used similar arguments, it is hardly surprising that most other Puritan churches preferred a woman to give a private testimony on her conversion, which could be read in church by a man. Yet a lack of opportunity for publicly exercising authority in the churches, while indeed limiting to women, did not mean that women were peripheral to church congregations or that a role in the church was peripheral to a woman's identity. For one thing, full church membership in and of itself was a significant distinction among colonial Puritans. Moreover, women may well have exercised informal and indirect power at times. Ulrich argues convincingly from the indirect testimony of church records that women could be quite influential, albeit through males, in establishing new congregations, especially when the distance to an existing church made it difficult for pregnant women and mothers of young children to travel far or attend frequently. Other records suggest that godly matrons could affect the continued support or the dismissal of a particular minister.[10]

Such informal power and influence on churches was real and may well have existed widely in Puritan New England. Unfortunately, it is difficult to document. Similarly, private prayer, study, and devotion were surely as important to individual Puritan women's religious lives as their public church or semi-public family religious activity, but it is harder to assess and analyze these activities because there are few direct written records from this period by women themselves. Among the exceptions is the famous Puritan poet, Anne Bradstreet. Born in England and raised in a household that combined serious piety with unusual intellectual opportunities for a daughter, Anne Bradstreet came as a young bride to the Massachusetts Bay Colony at its founding in 1630. Although she shared the hardships of the pioneer colony, her membership in one of its first families gave her a certain status and security. She was unique, perhaps, not only in her poetic abilities but in the public recognition her poems received. Nevertheless, the experiences she expressed in that poetry were not atypical: she was a housekeeper, a wife and mother, and a devout Christian. Her poetic portrait of earthly life, its comforts and its sorrows, is neither morbid nor romanticized. She valued domestic comforts and earthly love, and in a poem written after the Bradstreet home burned in 1666, the vivid and homely details of her loss are no less poignant because she reminds herself that true treasures are above. She loved her husband deeply and missed him during his necessary absences, sentiments she recorded in her poetry.

> If ever two were one, then surely we.
> If ever man were lov'd by wife, then thee;
> If ever wife was happy in a man,

Compare with me, ye women, if you can.

. . .

Then while we live, in love let's so persevere
That when we live no more, we may live ever.
—from "To My Dear and Loving Husband"

Nevertheless, in Bradstreet's poetry it is finally the spiritual life and her hope of salvation that are most important, as in the poem "Longing for Heaven."[11]

A pilgrim I, on earth perplexed
With sins, with cares and sorrows vext,
By age and pains brought to decay,
And my clay house mold'ring away.
Oh, how I long to be at rest
And soar on high among the blest.
This body shall in silence sleep,
Mine eyes no more shall ever weep.
No fainting fits shall me assail,
Nor grinding pains my body frail,
With cares and fears ne'er cumb'red be
Nor losses know, nor sorrows see.
What though my flesh shall there consume,
It is the bed Christ did perfume,
And when a few years shall be gone,
This mortal shall be clothed upon.
A corrupt carcass down it lays,
A glorious body it shall rise.
In weakness and dishonour sown,
In power 'tis raised by Christ alone.
Then soul and body shall unite
And of their Maker have the sight.
Such lasting joys shall there behold
As ear ne'er heard nor tongue e'er told.
Lord make me ready for that day,
Then come, dear Bridegroom, come away.

Perhaps for many Puritan women the personal meaning of religion, the satisfactions found within traditional roles, and participation, even informal power, in public religion balanced the very real role limitations the society imposed upon them. At any rate, women continued to join the churches. Indeed, after the middle of the seventeenth century, Puritan church rolls show an increasing proportion of female membership. Significantly more women than men joined the churches. (That imbalance, despite some variations of time and place, would characterize much of American religion from then on.)

Traditionally, religions historians have seen a period of "decline" in late seventeenth-century Puritanism, as the fervor of the founders was lost and New Englanders increasingly sought worldly, not heavenly rewards, and after the Puritan experiment in England failed, undercutting the hopes of the founders that the world would recognize and emulate the "city on a hill." That assessment of decline was shared by and rooted in the views of Puritan religious leaders themselves, as the "Jeremiad" emerged as a typical literary form in the second half of the seventeenth century. It included an idealized picture of the golden age of the founders, a lamentation over present sins and corruption, a warning about current and impending calamities that were the results of God's anger over a broken covenant, and a call for repentance and return to the covenant. Yet a more gender-specific view must qualify that traditional judgment of decline: It was Puritan men who seemed to have lost interest in religion and failed to join the churches as before, and it was, of course, those same men who controlled public institutions.

Why did women continue to join a church that so clearly insisted upon their subordination? Some scholars have suggested that the expectations for believers, especially lay people, involved less psychological dissonance for women than for men. A dominant image in Puritan theology was the analogy of marriage with the relationship between the believer and God. From one perspective, the metaphor says something of Puritan views of marriage: It was clearly "good," a potential source of joy, a fitting comparison to the human being's most important relationship. Similarly, the metaphor suggests that the believer's relationship with God could be one of trust, joy, and fidelity, balancing some views of Calvin and the Puritans as gloomy and repressive people whose theology was based primarily on fear. Nevertheless, in both cases there was a clear hierarchy: God and the husband are the authorities; the believer and the wife are to be obedient, submissive, and dependent. For women, this was no problem, because they played the same role in each pair. But it may have been more difficult for some men to accept the necessary psychological shift from socially sanctioned dominance and independence to submissiveness, obedience, and subordination. Furthermore, after the colony's early years, Puritan religious leaders had developed a stronger insistence on ministerial authority within the church, limiting lay power. Thus a Puritan layman was faced with a twofold shift—submission to God and to the clergy—if he joined the church.[12]

Like any psychological explanation, this interpretation must remain tentative and selective; clearly, some laymen did join churches. Furthermore, one could argue, as does Ben Barker-Benfield, that it was precisely because men could exercise authority over women (in family, church, and state) and thus identify with the dominant side of hierarchy in these spheres that they could accept a theological position of submission and helplessness vis-à-vis God. "Perhaps [male Puritan leaders] could sustain their espousal of passive, feminine qualities only by reminding themselves of how active, masculine and Christ-like they really were by way of their relationship to those beings they construed as unmitigatedly dependent, that is, to women."[13] On the other hand, one could argue that acceptance of a "female" model for the role of believer by some Puritan laymen in the churches, and certainly by the clerical leadership, is evidence that distinct sex roles did not mean to Puritans that men and women had fundamentally different *natures* as human beings. Virtues, and in certain circumstances, behavior, were not rigidly gender-specific.[14] Nevertheless, male psychological dissonance and female psychological congruence may provide one reason for higher proportions of female church membership.

Another explanation may have been the growing role divergence that developed in seventeenth-century Puritanism. In an increasingly complex and prosperous colonial society, men simply had more options and more varied public concerns than women and hence were less likely to need church membership to establish a successful identity. Although in theory the Puritan husband continued as the religious head of the family, public distractions and demands may have encouraged a husband's tendency to let his wife take care of religious as well as domestic concerns at home.[15] More specifically, Barbara Epstein has argued that economic concerns were behind the decline in male church membership.

> The real weakness of Puritan ideology was that it was incompatible with trade relations. . . . As the market system developed . . . it presented New Englanders, especially men, with opportunities for profit that required the aggressive self-assertion and pursuit of self-interest that Puritanism condemned. It was largely trade that drew New Englanders, especially men away from church membership and church attendance.[16]

Finally, women's unique biological experiences may help to account for their higher levels of church membership. In the more settled Puritan society of the second half of the seventeenth century, conversion and joining the church were seen as most appropriate for adults, specifically, with the life change marked by marriage and parenthood. While these affected both sexes, marriage and motherhood was a more comprehensive role identity for women, and it brought to their immediate attention the possibility of mortality. Women could expect to be pregnant soon and frequently; women sometimes died in childbirth; infants and young children were also vulnerable to death. Both the status of adulthood and the concrete awareness of mortality should, Puritans believed, turn one's attention to the state of his or her soul and its eternal destiny. The realities and potential consequences of childbearing made the concern especially immediate for women and may have hastened their conversions.[17]

Even as they lamented decline, Puritan ministers of the late seventeenth century were aware that women continued to join the churches. As a result, they too speculated on the reason for the apparently greater incidence of female piety, drawing conclusions not unlike more modern theories. For one thing, women had fewer distractions; they simply weren't as busy as men (at least from the male perspective!) As Cotton Mather, one of the most prominent ministers of his time, wrote, women "have more *Time* to employ in the more immediate Service of [their] Souls, than the *other Sex* is owner of. [They] are ordinarily more within the *House,* & so may more mind the Work within the *Heart,* than *we.*"[18] Mather further concluded that the curse of Eve had been turned to a blessing for women.

> God Sanctifies unto them their Fear of Death. . . . They are in Deaths often; This prepares them to Dy, and this teaches them to Live. The Dubious Hazards of their Lives in their Appointed Sorrows, drive them the more frequently, to commit themselves into the Hands of their Only Savior. They are Saved Thro' Childbearing; inasmuch as it singularly obliges them to *Continue in Faith, and Charity, and Holiness, with Sobriety.*[19]

Benjamin Colman, another leading Boston divine at the turn of the eighteenth century, disagreed with Mather in other areas but concurred on the significance of women's childbearing.

> The Curse pronounc'd upon our first Mother Eve, turn'd into the greatest Blessing to Your Souls. Your frequent Returns in Your own Apprehension towards the *Gates of Death,* by which we all receive our Life, suitably lead you to a returning serious tho'tfulness for your souls and of Your Spiritual State.[20]

What is critical to note here, however, is that Mather and Colman are suggesting that the *experiences* unique to women may make them more pious, more likely to take religion seriously. They are *not* proposing that female nature itself is more spiritual than male nature. Women are not inherently or naturally more pious than men. In another century, American religion would take that step, reversing the historic Christian view that women are, by nature, more carnal and *less* spiritual than men, but that is not what these Puritans were saying.

## Portrait of a "Good Wife"

Ministerial literature of the late seventeenth and early eighteenth centuries noted the increasing proportion of women church members and proposed possible explanations for that phenomenon. It also provided a broad, perhaps a little idealized, portrait of a good Puritan woman. These portraits appeared most frequently, though not exclusively, in funeral sermons, so a certain amount of idealization is to be expected, even as the pattern was presented as a goal for which living women could strive.[21] The most important characteristic of a good woman was her piety, a piety that went beyond mere external performance of religious duties (prayer, reading the Bible, church attendance) to internal attitudes of love and delight in things of religion. Thus far, female piety was no different from male piety, and in that sense, men and women were perceived as spiritual equals. The difference came in the ways or arenas in which piety was exercised. A woman's piety was essentially private or confined to the domestic sphere. She might, indeed, converse with her neighbors on spiritual topics or, occasionally, write, as did Anne Bradstreet. Mather even encouraged appropriate religious writing, noting that, while scripture required "That the Woman may not speak in the Church, yet our God has employ'd man[y] women to Write for the Church . . . ."[22] Still, a woman would not teach, let alone preach, publicly in church or share in church government. She would not challenge the male religious authority of her husband or minister. She could, however, and should be a teacher at home to her children and servants; she should also teach by example and pray for others. In such ways, she might even influence adult males, including her husband, but she should not challenge their authority directly.

A good woman also demonstrated her virtue by fulfilling her domestic roles, and a favorite Puritan text was Prov. 31:10–31, a description of the good wife. This passage, and the Puritans, stressed virtues of love and support of her husband, neighborly charity, good household management, successful motherhood, and wisdom. (One thing conspicuously absent in the list of desirable qualities of a good wife is physical beauty, as Mather noted in *Ornaments,* where Proverbs 31 was his text.[23]) In other words, if Puritans assigned women to particular spheres, they also acknowledged the value of what women did there. That domestic sphere in the close-knit Puritan economy included neighbors, as well as immediate members of a biological family, and neighborly charity was a Christian duty for women as well as men. Puritans' understanding of their covenant with God had a strong element of social responsibility and corporate identity. As John Winthrop said in "A Modell of Christian Charity," a classic summary of Puritan self-understanding written aboard the *Arbella* as they were about to begin their new colony,

> every man [must] afford his help to another in every want or distresse. . . . [and] performe this out of the same affeccion, which makes him carefull of his owne good according to that of our Saviour Math. [7:12] Whatsoever ye would that men should doe to you. . . . Lastly, when there is noe other meanes whereby our Christian brother may be releived in this distresse, wee must help him beyond our ability, rather than tempt God. . . . [24]

In the colonial period, formal organizations for benevolence (care of the sick, widows, orphans, and others in unfortunate circumstances) were few and far between, and those that existed were almost always organized, administered, and supported financially by men. Nevertheless, women were active in many areas of informal benevolence and neighborly charity. As good Christians, they visited the sick, helped neighbors in crisis with labor or material goods, and maintained the domestic hospitality so crucial in a new settlement. They might also "take in" orphans or children from poor and distressed families as apprentices or servants. Although Puritan women did not have the formal structure of the Quakers' women's meetings as a base for charitable activity, their informal functioning in such benevolence was not only accepted but expected.

Puritan appreciation of good women was genuine, but it was also based on the assumption that spiritual equality was compatible with continued social subordination. That view, not the Quakers' attempt to translate spiritual equality into greater social equality, dominated colonial American culture. Yet the tension would remain between a theoretical spiritual equality and the actuality of limited and subordinate roles, and so eighteenth-century women in America would continue to step out of their place not so much by dramatic protest as by building on accepted female roles. Those roles were not abandoned, but were challenged by expansion, since women were also spiritual beings for whom God's renewed call was even more authoritative than the norms of social order.

# 4
# *Religious Diversity in Colonial America*

Well before the arrival of European Christians, "American" religion was markedly diverse, with its many distinct Indian nations and tribes. By the seventeenth century, the New World was even more religiously pluralistic, adding significant representations of European Christians, Catholic and Protestant, and unwilling immigrants from Africa. English settlers dominated the thirteen coastal colonies, but French Huguenots, German Lutherans, Dutch Reformed, and Scotch-Irish Presbyterians had substantial populations, and the founding policy of religious toleration in Pennsylvania provided a refuge for free-church groups like Mennonites and Dunkers. In other parts of the New World, Spanish Catholics preceded the English by a century, and French Catholics paralleled English settlement in the seventeenth century. This chapter looks at the religious experiences of women in four other large colonial groups: Anglicans, Catholics, Native Americans, and African Americans.*

## Anglican Women

While Puritans were the dominant religious group in New England and Quakers in Pennsylvania, the Church of England was the established church (effectively and sometimes legally) in the southern colonies and had a sizable presence in every colony by the mid-eighteenth century. The three groups were alike in being white, Protestant, and English, but the Anglicans differed from their Puritan and Quaker neighbors in two important ways. First, there were simply fewer women, proportionately, in the southern colonies during the seventeenth century. Second, Anglicanism was the established church in England (except for the relatively brief period under Oliver Cromwell). Thus Anglicans had no background of dissent, no disability based on religious conviction, no need to protest or seek

*Throughout this book, I have used interchangeably both "blacks" and "African Americans" and "Indians" and "Native Americans," since neither scholars nor other persons in these groups themselves are unanimous in preferring one name over the other.

greater religious freedom in the colonies. In short, most of them lacked the passionate and consuming religious fervor that so moved many Puritans and Quakers. But that does not mean Anglicans were indifferent to religion, either in their concern for the stabilizing and moral influence of religion as a public institution or as a matter of personal meaning and devotion.

The religious experiences of Anglican women were both like and unlike those of their Puritan and Quaker sisters. They produced no famous rebels or dissenters, at least none who left significant footnotes in history, but their religious roles and lives were quite similar to the "good women" of the Puritans, despite very real theological differences between the groups. They had no formal roles of leadership or governance in the institutional church, but they were faithful and active members. Occasionally an Anglican woman took extraordinary steps to promote or preserve her church, as when Mary Taney of Maryland wrote in 1685 to the Archbishop of Canterbury, pleading for funds to establish an Anglican church and help to support a minister in Maryland—funds ultimately granted by the king from his own resources.[1] Another woman who approached public authorities in defense of her faith, however, was less successful. In 1708, Ann Walker, an Anglican, appealed to a Virginia council to prevent her Quaker husband from raising their children as Quakers. Virginia authorities had no love for Quakers, but they were still unwilling to undermine the husband's familial authority, and they denied Ann's petition.[2] Unfortunately, there is no conclusive evidence on whether or not women significantly outnumbered men in church attendance or membership,[3] but it seems likely that their proportionate numbers were at least equal to men and quite possibly greater by the end of the colonial period.

The most important sphere for Anglican women's religious experience was the family. Female roles and subordination were not a major theme of sermons,[4] but that may be, in part, because they were so little challenged, and the popular devotional and advice literature of the eighteenth century clearly inculcated submission and wifely obedience.[5] Yet the family was an extremely important social and economic institution, offering a broad scope for women's talents and contributions, as well as a lot of hard work. The family also had important religious functions, as important as the Puritan family's, albeit in somewhat different ways. A characteristic of Anglican parishes in the South was their great geographical size, in contrast to parishes in both the mother country and Puritan New England. Anglican clergy conducted services in churches, but they also had to travel to reach remote parts of their parishes, and that meant staying and conducting services in the homes of parishioners. The difficulties of travel and geography, combined with personal preference, meant that baptisms, weddings, and funerals were typically held at home for most of the colonial period, and the home was woman's sphere, under her control in very practical ways.[6]

Anglican women, like Puritan women, were expected to take a major role in religious education of children. Where the family's socioeconomic status was higher, the mistress of the household also instructed slaves and servants. So long as such teaching was "private" (i.e., in the domestic sphere) and a woman did not presume to teach adult white males, including her husband, it appeared not to contradict the society's understanding of biblical prohibitions. Within the home, in family prayers and devotions, even adult white males could be influenced religiously by example, or by tactful and indirect means. Like Puritan women, too, Anglican women engaged in the informal benevolence of neighborly charity, even though formal and organized charity was the responsibility of male church wardens and vestries. Finally, religion was to Anglican women, as it was to Puritans and Quakers, a source of personal strength, comfort in the face of loss, interest, and identity. A few women were able to leave written records in diaries and letters as evidence of their religious concerns, but there is no reason to doubt that many of the far greater number of illiterate or unremembered women shared similar experiences. The theological content of religion varied among the colonists, with Anglicans tending to a more "rational piety that stressed moderation, repentance and salvation;"[7] and female colonists themselves took these differences very seriously, as do historians. But women across theological lines shared a central religious role in the family and a practice of piety that provided them with meaning and identity.

## Roman Catholic Women

The Catholic presence in the original thirteen colonies was a relatively small one, particularly when compared to Catholics in nineteenth-century America. Most English Catholics settled in Maryland, although in the eighteenth century, the tolerance and geographical proximity of eastern Pennsylvania encouraged Catholic settlement there, and there were small clusters of Catholics in other colonies. Like Puritans and Quakers, they experienced disabilities in England because of their religion, although the Stuart kings were relatively tolerant and the Catholic response was less confrontational, keeping a lower profile. Thus religious freedom was not a primary cause of colonial Catholic emigration, even though Maryland, under Catholic proprietors, provided such freedom at various time periods. But because of the Protestant majority even in Maryland, there were also periods of legal intolerance, when that "low profile" continued to be an effective response to Protestant hostility.

The Catholic community in Maryland was relatively small, tightly knit, and well-to-do, with a significant representation among the landed gentry. Family interests, Protestant distrust, and a scarcity of priests gave English colonial Catholicism a "domestic" form. Most services were held in homes, and the emphasis was on personal devotions rather than participation in public services. Such family-centered religion did not mean women held formal, institutional authority in the church, nor does it mean that religion was "feminized." It does mean that circumstances highlighted women's religious roles and contribution.

> Women occupied a special place in the Catholic community. Not only was the mother of the family the principal instructor in religion, but she was also the chief cook, who saw to it that fast days were observed; the parish devotional societies that developed in the eighteenth century were primarily female in membership. This central place of women may also be seen in penal legislation passed by the Maryland Assembly; the lawmakers recognized the important place of the mother in the religious training of children and were intent upon reducing this influence when Protestant children were left with a Catholic Mother.[8]

Far more significant numbers of Catholics came to the New World from France and Spain. Even though French and Spanish Catholicism was not part of the original thirteen colonies, its story is part of a broader American religious history in the colonial period, important in its own right and providing a valuable comparison with English colonization. Furthermore, both Spanish and French Catholics would become part of the United States through annexation of territories where they had settled and through immigration, bringing with them their own cultural and religious traditions.

France, England, and Spain all had distinctive motives and methods for colonization, but they shared some assumptions and goals. None questioned their own superiority as white, Christian Europeans or their right to "discover" and settle the lands already populated by Native Americans. In each case, they publicly proclaimed their goals to convert the "heathen," although English efforts were far feebler than those of Spain and France. Even when establishing missions was a significant and, for many missionaries, a very sincere goal, it was always mixed with motives of conquest and economic exploitation.

Perhaps the most significant difference between the religious experiences of Roman Catholic women in the English colonies, on the one hand, and in the French and Spanish settlements, on the other, was the availability of two respected roles for French and Spanish women. From the early centuries of Christian history, Roman Catholicism provided for women an honorable alternative to marriage and motherhood: a celibate religious vocation. True, the choice was rooted in a dualistic world view that equated women with the less spiritual, more carnal half of reality, and the choice came at a cost. When women chose the life of celibacy, they were perceived as denying their very nature as women and becoming more like men, though never with equal male authority and prerogatives in church and society. Nevertheless, for hundreds of years, a religious vocation provided Christian women with an alternative, and sometimes the possibility of *relative* autonomy, education, and even spiritual equality with men.

English colonial Catholics never denied this alternative in theory, but in fact, relatively few young women joined orders even in the eighteenth century, and they typically returned to Europe to do so.[9] In contrast, women's religious orders were important in New Spain and New France. The Catholic Reformation in Spain had included a reform and renewal of women's orders, with a consequent impact on Spanish America. The earliest convents had been founded in Mexico and South America by the middle of the sixteenth century, and orders spread rapidly during the next hundred years, not only as a result of sincere religious devotion but also because they served a social function: to provide a place for "the offspring of impoverished conquistadors or unsuccessful settlers" when socially appropriate marriages were problematic. As a result, Spanish convents in the Americas "became the enclave of the socio-ethnic elite formed by women of Spanish descent."[10] While poor white women, having no dowry, could not join the full, formal orders, they had an alternative in discalced branches of some orders. Eventually orders were founded for Indian women, and the Third Orders were opened to all women, regardless of race or economic status. Thus almost all Catholic women had some option of a religious vocation, even though the range of choices remained stratified by class and color. Spanish orders stressed enclosure and a life of piety, prayer, and devotion, separated from worldly concerns. "Within convents, women had a special world of their own, with inspiring models, such as the Virgin Mary and the female saints. They also had a certain degree of personal independence and security, as well as the respect and status granted to them as the chosen brides of Christ."[11] In addition, they had more opportunities for education than their noncloistered sisters. Eventually, some of the sisters used that education to teach others, as convents in the eighteenth century began to sponsor schools for young girls. With that one exception, however, Spanish American orders for women focused on the cloistered life, inner spiritual development, and prayer.

In contrast, the religious orders for women in New France were involved in forms of missionary and charitable service. Marie of the Incarnation shared with male French missionaries the dream of converting the Indians and thus founded a school for girls, including Indians, in Quebec in the 1640s. Marguerite Bourgeoys opened schools in Montreal in 1657. Jeanne Mance began a hospital in Quebec in the seventeenth century. Marguerite D' Youville ran a hospital in Montreal in the eighteenth century "and opened it to all the destitute of society: the elderly, orphans, and prostitutes, as well as wounded soldiers."[12] For the founders and for the women who joined them, such service was in addition to, not a replacement for, personal devotional life and discipline. Traditionally, religious historians have neglected the experiences and contributions of women religious in New France in favor of the exploits of male explorers, missionaries, and martyrs, yet the women provided an important network for female identity, support, and services. Indeed, their world was sufficiently attractive that a number of New England Puritan women who were captured by Indians during the colonial period and ended up in New France chose to stay there, despite deeply rooted Puritan antipathy to both France and Roman Catholicism. Marriage to French men was an option for some, but others became nuns and participated in the sisters' missions of service, even when they could have returned to New England.[13]

Like their sisters in New France, the French nuns who came to New Orleans during the colonial period were involved in apostolic service. Members of the Ursuline Order, they took over a hospital, cared for orphans and "fallen women," established a boarding school for paying pupils, and ran a free day school that was also open to blacks and Native Americans. The Ursulines were able to support themselves and offer these services in part because they also received the income from a plantation, complete with slaves, and kept some blacks themselves as boarders and servants.[14]

The role of women religious was an important option for Catholic women in New Spain and New France, but most became wives and mothers. Their lives and their religion were shaped by differences in culture, in theology and religious practice, in social, economic, and political systems. Being Catholic and French or Spanish gave women, as well as men, an identity different from being English and Protestant. Nevertheless, their identities were also shaped by being women in a patriarchal society, especially by their roles in the family, and from that perspective, they were similar to the English women of the thirteen colonies. Their duties were domestic; they were especially involved in the religious education of their children; they found comfort and personal meaning in religion despite their exclusion from governance of church or state. Regardless of individual rank or economic position, Spanish, French, and English Catholic women in colonial America shared in the immigrants' dominance of the New World, a dominance rooted in a common Christian and European heritage. The situation was very different for Indian and black women.

## Indian and Black Women

To try to tell the story of the religious experiences of black and Indian women in colonial America involves several layers of difficulty. First, sources from the women themselves are rare indeed; most contemporary observations come from white, and usually male, observers. Even those who tried to be relatively sympathetic could not overcome a cultural blindness that assumed the truth and superiority of white European Christian ways and dismissed native peoples as heathen. European males' insensitivity to what others might understand as "religion" was compounded in the case of native women, since what women thought and did was by definition unimportant. Second, although in both Africa and pre-Colombian North America the native peoples existed in many different tribes, each with distinctive religious, cultural, and historical identities, white observers who were perfectly well aware of differences among Christians tended to overlook similar differences in tribal peoples.

Despite such real limitations, some recovery of the story is possible, as are some tentative generalizations. Certainly Indian and black women shared a similar experience in the American story: oppression, exploitation, devaluation, and invisibility. Yet that reality did not mean they were merely passive victims; there were also rebels and those who resisted capitulation to white ways. In addition, there were similarities in the religious and cultural backgrounds of the tribal heritage—matters of worldview and perception that transcended specific practices—not only within each group but in some ways between blacks and Indians. Both African and Native American traditions saw reality as integrated. They did not draw clear lines between "natural" and "supernatural," between the spiritual and material worlds. Thus "religion" was an integral part of their culture and daily life, not a separated sphere or activity. (Indeed, that may be one reason white observers had such difficulty recognizing black or Indian religion, for they could seldom transcend their own definitions and expectations.) While both blacks and Indians may have acknowledged a supreme High God or Great Spirit, they also believed in many lesser divinities and spirits who were intimately involved with human life and nature. Medicine, magic, and religion were closely interrelated, and thus healers were also religious authorities. In short, the tribal heritage of both blacks and Indians was characterized by integration of all aspects of life and reality.[15]

While there were differences among various tribes on the roles of women and men, it appears that in most Indian and African groups, women could take roles of religious leadership. Especially an older woman might occasionally hold a position as religious leader and source of wisdom for both men and women. Women as well as men might be gifted with powers of healing and magic. In Indian religion, young women as well as young men participated in the vision quest, "probably . . . the single most common attribute of North American Indian religions."[16] There were distinctive male and female activities, complementary if separate. Here the contrast with much Christian practice is striking, not only because some women could achieve broad religious authority (Christianity has occasional female saints), but because even when the sexes were separated and women were excluded from male religious activities or rituals, they had a parallel religious sphere in which they could exercise formal and official leadership roles, acknowledged and respected by both men and women.[17]

For both Africans and Native Americans, contact with Christianity was thrust upon them, not a result of their own initiative. In that encounter, the desire and the ability to retain the traditional culture and religion varied. Conversion of the Indians was a major, though of course not the only, concern of Spanish and French Catholics in the New World. For English colonists, despite protestations on both sides of the Atlantic, serious missionary activity was sporadic and short-lived, with a few notable exceptions. For their part, Indians had the benefit of tribal unity and support in resisting conversion and maintaining tribal ways. Even when they were pushed from their traditional lands, they generally were relocated as a group. Many rejected the missionaries' attempts to change and "save" them. Some were so fully converted to Christianity and the white European culture that was seen as inseparable from it that they had to break from or were rejected by their Indian community. A third alternative in the encounter between the two cultures was syncretism, a selective adaptation of Christian ideas, symbols, or practices to traditional Indian religion.

But why would Indians want to convert? Sometimes they had little choice because the military power of the conquerors enforced the efforts of the missionaries. Sometimes the attraction was novelty, sometimes prosaic but critical needs like food and protection. A further attraction was sacred power, when Christian rituals or sacred objects appeared to possess strong "magic," especially since the concept was a familiar one in their own traditions. Father Christien le Clercq, a French seventeenth-century missionary, told of an encounter with an old Indian woman who had obtained some rosary beads, which she regarded as a source of great power. The Frenchman tried, without success, to discount such "superstition" and instruct her in a "purer" form of Christianity. His account also contains a telling comment on the white male's view of female religious leadership:

> It is a surprising fact that this ambition to act the patriarch does not only prevail among the men, but even the women meddle therewith. These, in usurping the quality and the name of *religieuses,* say certain prayers in their own fashion and affect a manner of living more reserved than that of the commonality of Indians, who allow themselves to be dazzled by the glamour of a false and ridiculous devotion.[18]

Not all Catholic missionaries were as scornful as this one of Indian ways, though most assumed that any learning in the encounter between the two religions was a one-way street. Nevertheless, the response of syncretism, of selective acceptance of Christian rituals, objects, and beliefs while retaining traditional religion, was far more common among Indians than the Christian goal of total conversion.

Blacks experienced even more disruption than Indians from their traditional culture and religion. Not only were they forcibly removed from Africa, but the horrors of the "middle passage" and the circumstances of the slave trade and the slave system in North America separated most slaves from their tribal communities and even families, as well as from their land. The question of how much African heritage slaves were able to retain has been hotly debated by scholars for decades, with extreme positions of "a great deal" and "almost none" represented.[19] The most reasonable conclusion seems to be somewhere in the middle: Blacks in colonial America did retain or adapt some African practices and basic assumptions of their traditional worldview, but they also experienced significant trauma and disruption.

Retention of African tradition may have been easier in seventeenth-century colonial America in part because conversion of Africans to Christianity was not a high priority for English settlers. Indeed, many colonial Christians went beyond indifference to outright hostility toward conversion, largely because owners feared that conversion and baptism would necessarily lead to emancipation because one should not hold a fellow Christian as a slave. Even when colonial legislatures passed laws specifically stating that baptism was not a cause for emancipation, most slave owners were reluctant to make any effort to convert their African slaves, for they still regarded blacks as less than fully human. As the secretary of the eighteenth-century Anglican association, the Society for the Propagation of the Gospel (S.P.G.), founded in part to evangelize blacks and Indians, reported

> the greatest Obstruction [to conversion of blacks] is, the Masters themselves do not consider enough, the Obligation which lies upon them, to have their slaves instructed. Some have been so weak as to argue, the Negroes had no Souls; others, that they grew worse by being taught, and made Christians: I would not mention these, if they were not popular Arguments now, because they have no Foundation in Reason or Truth.[20]

Nevertheless, some English colonial Christians tried to instruct and convert Africans to Christianity. These efforts were more prevalent in the North (partly, perhaps, because there were fewer blacks there) and among the small population of "free" blacks.

North and South, black women were more likely to convert to Christianity than men.[21] Perhaps they were responding to the attention of white Christian women, for whom religious education of servants and slaves as well as children was acceptable—indeed, expected—unless hostility to evangelism of slaves was stronger than the call to convert them in a given setting. An early eighteenth-century S.P.G. missionary noted the work of two white mistresses:

> Mrs. Haige and Mrs. Edwards, who came lately to this Plantation [Carolina], have taken extra-ordinary pains to instruct a considerable number of Negroes, in the principles of the Christian Religion, and to reclaim and reform them. [Their success in instruction convinced the missionary to baptize fourteen blacks.] I doubt not but these Gentlewomen will prepare the rest of them for Baptism in a little time; and I hope the good example of these two Gentlewomen will provoke at least some Masters and Mistresses, to take the same care and pains with their poor Negroes.[22]

Mistresses as well as masters were formally encouraged by church authorities to give religious instruction to their black slaves. Unfortunately, there is no conclusive evidence to show whether white women were more conscientious in such efforts than white men, or whether black women responded more often than black men to female instruction, but this may have been so. Or perhaps, as "DuBois (and, more recently, Alex Haley) [have] conjectured . . . African women usually made the initial breakthrough to 'accept' Christianity, hoping their conversion would benefit them and their families."[23] Nevertheless, there were proportionately few conversions of blacks to Christianity before the Great Awakening, and blacks who did convert were never accepted as full equals to whites, even in the churches.

Occasionally, an individual woman of color who became a Christian achieved a degree of honor and even fame in white society. Two of the best known were Kateri Tekakwitha and Phillis Wheatley. Kateri Tekakwitha's mother was a Christian Algonquin who was captured by the Iroquois and married to one of their chiefs. Tekakwitha was born in 1656 but orphaned as a young child and raised by an uncle. She was attracted to Christianity through the activities of French missionaries, requested instruction, and was eventually baptized in 1676. The response of her own people to her conversion was quite hostile, so the next year she escaped to the French community of Sault Saint Louis, near Montreal. In 1679, she took a formal vow of virginity, the first Indian Christian woman to do so, living a life of such intense piety and penitence that she died in 1680. The admiration that she aroused during her lifetime from both Indian and French Christians endured and increased after her death. As an eighteenth-century biographer, Father Cholenec, concluded,

> God did not delay to honor the memory of this virtuous girl by an infinite number of miraculous cures, which took place after her death, and which continue to take place daily through her intercession. This is a fact well known, not only to the Indians, but also to the French at Quebec and Montreal, who often make pilgrimages to her tomb.[24]

Phillis Wheatley was brought from Africa on a slave ship and purchased in 1761 by a wealthy Boston merchant, John Wheatley, as a servant for his wife Susanna. At the time, Phillis was probably about seven or eight years old. Her experience as a slave was hardly typical. Not only was she made virtually a member of the family and freed shortly after her master's death, she was given a thorough education, to which she responded with obvious intellectual ability, and she began in her teens to write poetry. She also converted to Christianity, joining the church in 1770, and religion was a major theme of her poems and letters. Her gifts attracted considerable attention, which increased after a visit to England in 1773, where a volume of her poems was published. Soon after her return, her mistress and, a few years later, her master died, as did public attention. She married John Peters, a free black, in 1778 and bore three children, but her husband provided little support, her health deteriorated, and she died in poverty in 1784.

Phillis Wheatley's personal gifts, intelligence, and talent were real enough, but she was seen in her own time as particularly exceptional because of her race. Her book, *Poems on Various Subjects, Religious and Moral,* included a letter from John Wheatley describing her education, and the affirmation of eighteen of Boston's most prominent men that she was, truly, the author of the poems. For those in revolutionary Boston with moderate anti-slavery sentiments, here in the person of a young black girl was proof that blacks were not necessarily or naturally inferior in mental or religious capacities. Yet Phillis Wheatley was viewed as an exception and her fame was purchased at the price of repudiation of her African cultural and religious heritage, in the eyes not only of her contemporaries but of some more recent scholars who believe she "sold out" her blackness for white acceptance.[25] It is true that she was a sincere, devout Christian of her day and thus rejected African religion as paganism, but she did not subscribe to views of inherent black inferiority.

> 'Twas mercy brought me from my *Pagan* land,
> Taught my benighted soul to understand.
> That there's a God, that there's a *Saviour* too;
> Once I redemption neither sought nor knew.
> Some view our sable race with scornful eye,
> "Their colour is a diabolic die."
> Remember, *Christians, Negroes,* black as *Cain,*
> May be refin'd, and join th' angelic train.
>
> —On being brought from Africa to America[26]

Nor did she accept slavery, for herself or for other blacks. She saw it as unreasonable, unchristian, and an affront to God.[27]

No doubt both Kateri Tekakwitha and Phillis Wheatley were exceptional persons, deserving their place in history. Nor is there any reason to

# 5
# *The Great Awakening*

Beginning in the second quarter of the eighteenth century, the English colonies in America were swept by a wave of religious excitement and revivals known as the Great Awakening. It was not uniquely American, for similar events and ideas appeared on the other side of the Atlantic, notably the Wesleyan revival in England and the Pietist movement in Germany. Yet the Great Awakening had a particular impact on America insofar as it affected all parts of the colonies at one time or another, and it produced a figure, George Whitefield, the "Grand Itinerant," whose fame stretched from New England to Georgia.

The earliest manifestations of the Great Awakening in America occurred in the middle colonies under the preaching of a Dutch Reformed pastor, Theodore Frelinghuysen, and a New Jersey Presbyterian family, William Tennent and his sons, Gilbert, John, and William Jr. In the 1720s and 30s, they criticized the churches and especially other ministers for their formalism, their laxness in enforcing moral standards, and most important, their failure to experience true piety and spiritual regeneration. If ministers were, in Gilbert Tennent's terms, "unconverted" and "pharisees," how could they lead their flocks to conversion and true piety? The Tennents' preaching lit the fires not only of revival but also of controversy and even led to splits in the churches. Meanwhile, in the Connecticut River Valley of Massachusetts, the brilliant Puritan preacher and theologian Jonathan Edwards experienced a revival harvest in his church in Northampton and the churches of nearby towns. There had, indeed, been some "harvests" under his grandfather and predecessor in the Northampton Church, Solomon Stoddard, but the revivals of 1733–35 were of such major scope and out of what Edwards saw as such unlikely and dry material that he could only attribute them to a mysterious outpouring of God's grace.

The Great Awakening in its full-fledged and widespread form was triggered in the late 1730s and 1740s by the preaching tours of George Whitefield. Already well known in England as a preacher and close associate of John Wesley, Whitefield visited Georgia briefly in 1738, where he became interested in sponsoring an orphanage. His subsequent tours were undertaken in part to raise support for that venture, but the orphanage was soon overshadowed by Whitefield's dramatic and effective revival preaching. He arrived in Philadelphia in 1739 and swept through New England and back to the middle colonies and the South in 1740, while Gilbert Tennent followed him to New England in 1741. Whitefield and Tennent were functioning as itinerants, traveling rather than located ministers. At first Whitefield was welcomed by local ministers and properly invited to preach; some later itinerants failed to observe expected proprieties and were far less welcome. Moreover, the publication of a fiery sermon by Tennent on "The Dangers of an Unconverted Ministry" and of certain rather derogatory portions of Whitefield's journal infuriated some leading New England clergy, so that the Great Awakening produced there, as it had in the middle colonies, both revivals and a bitter and prolonged controversy that split churches.

As important as itinerants like Whitefield were, the efforts of local preachers and concerns within local congregations were at least as important to the spread of evangelical religion and revivals. This was true in New England; it was perhaps even more true in the South. Though Whitefield did preach in the South, the religious change of evangelical awakening there came more slowly and later. Indeed, it was, as historian Sydney Ahlstrom suggests, "not so much a revival as . . . an immense missionary enterprise."[1] In the South, it was especially the Presbyterians, the Separate Baptists, and the evangelical Anglicans (and proto-Methodists) who revived and spread evangelical religion in the second half of the eighteenth century. Whether or not their work was technically part of the "Great Awakening," it certainly continued themes and results of a movement that significantly affected the face of religion in colonial America.

To the supporters and participants of the Great Awakening, its most important results were the revitalized religious life and the assurance of eternal salvation that came from conversion. But the Great Awakening also resulted in the founding of colleges, in humanitarian and missionary efforts that were the fruit of conversion, in real church growth but also controversy and division, and in broad social and cultural changes. At the beginning, the most public divisions and controversies were within the ranks of the clergy. But in the revivalists' very criticism of their colleagues, they presented an invitation to laypersons to take more personal responsibility for their own religious lives and to assume more power in the churches, an invitation many were quick to take up. The hierarchy of clergy over laity was one part of the established social order with its hierarchies of class, race, and gender, a social order upheld and reinforced by colonial churches. Thus the invitation to challenge a particular hierarchy, that of the ministers, not only undermined that structure but also opened the door to other challenges. Particularly in the South, the crucial distinction between converted and unconverted provided an alternative way of viewing persons' status and worth in society. As Donald Mathews notes, "The Evangelical call to come out of the world, a call to create new social distinctions on the basis of religious commitment, was clear and unmistakable."[2]

Not only did the Great Awakening contribute to the undermining of clerical authority and a consequent increase in the power of the laity, but the central message of the revivals also had a democratizing effect. What counted was a person's religious experience of conversion and inner regeneration, not formal education or lengthy religious instruction. The very emotionalism of revivals, which was to its critics one of the Great Awakening's most dangerous faults, was to its supporters a valid emphasis on the "heart" and the affections in religion. If, then, the Great Awakening was, at least in part, a movement that challenged traditional social hierarchies and structures, if the critical religious distinction is an experience of God's grace in conversion that can come to any person, regardless of education or social status, we might expect the Great Awakening to have had a particular impact on white women and African Americans.

## The Impact on African Americans

In the case of blacks, the impact of the Great Awakening was clearly major. For the first time in the English colonies, large numbers of African Americans were converted to Christianity. This was true among blacks, slave and free, in the North, and particularly striking in the South. Leaders of the Great Awakening like Whitefield invited and commended the response of black people to the revival message. Yet they were not the first white clergy to seek to evangelize blacks, slave and free; S.P.G. missionaries and Puritans had tried for two or three decades, but with only modest success. It was the particular religious approach and experience of the Great Awakening in the South during the last third of the eighteenth century that significant numbers of blacks found accessible and meaningful. In a revival, conversion was an immediate response to powerful and emotional preaching, whereas white Puritan or Anglican clergy insisted on a long period of religious instruction and testing for black converts. The revivals also placed less emphasis on understanding complex theological doctrines. Instead, the key was the sinner's repentance and immediate experience of God's grace in conversion. Particularly in the South and on the frontier, blacks were able to incorporate elements of traditional African religion—singing, dancing, the "ring shout"—into the lively and emotional setting of the revival and religious worship. "The powerful emotionalism, ecstatic behavior, and congregational response of the revival were amenable to the African religious heritage of the slaves, and forms of African dance and song remained in the shout and spirituals of Afro-American converts to evangelical Protestantism."[3]

Finally, the religion of the Great Awakening provided a relatively more egalitarian Christianity to black converts, not only in the conversion experience itself but also in the churches that formed as a result of the revivals. In those churches, laypeople as well as clergy had a significant role in enforcing church discipline, and a black person might appeal to that court for the justice that was nearly impossible to attain elsewhere.[4] Furthermore, since religious authority, even preaching, was more a function of one's religious experience than of formal training or social status, blacks could occasionally lead and counsel whites.[5] Yet the racial egalitarianism promoted by the Great Awakening should not be exaggerated. There was an appeal across race, class, and gender lines in the call of revival leaders for conversion; there was, sometimes and in some places, greater equality among church members; there were instances, rare but with symbolic importance, of black men preaching to whites. But the realities of racism remained, and ultimately the efforts of black converts with fellow blacks were of more importance than instances of interracial preaching or qualified fellowship.

## The Impact on Women

The impact of the Great Awakening on white women and on black women *as* women is more ambiguous than the movement's religious significance for colonial African Americans. On the one hand, the Great Awakening in New England, where women had outnumbered men as church members for decades, actually increased the *proportion* of male members. Yet women still outnumbered men in these churches, and the southern forms of the revival seemed to attract more women than men.[6] Nevertheless, women did not participate in the Great Awakening in dramatically greater or smaller numbers than men. Nor does the actual experience of conversion as perceived by participants appear to have been radically different for women than for men. Drawing on numerous contemporary conversion accounts from New England, Barbara Epstein concludes that men and women reported very similar experiences. They "followed the same patterns of conversion, spoke of the same kinds of sins, and described their experiences in similar language."[7] At most, there were subtle differences: Women were more critical of themselves, not just for particular sins, but for their essentially sinful nature.[8]

Other scholars have seen the Great Awakening as significant for the story of women and religion in America, not because of distinctive participation levels or perceptions by colonial women themselves, but because it emphasized a religious style that came to be especially associated with women. Conversion was most deeply a matter of the "heart," not the "head"; it was the sinner's affections—unworthiness, guilt, gratitude, joy—that testified to the genuineness of his or her conversion.[9] To be sure, colonial Christians did not make a head-heart separation primarily along gender lines or even see the two as rigidly distinct or antagonistic. It was not until the nineteenth century that a clear gender division, with a positive assessment of heart over head, emerged in some manifestations of American religion, but it is possible to see roots of what some scholars have called the "feminization" (not merely in numbers, but in style) of American religion in the first Great Awakening.

## Expanded Roles for Women

The Great Awakening also gave a fresh impulse to and further justification for expanded religious roles for women. The central experience of God's grace in conversion not only assured the individual of salvation, it also propelled him or her to witness of that experience to others and to join a community of like-minded persons where the new life in Christ could be shared and cultivated. Significantly, it was the experience of grace that gave authority, not formal theological training, thus opening a door for women as well as black men. Few Christians in the eighteenth century approved of women's preaching in public, and even the acceptance of black men as preachers was relatively rare, but there were other ways a person could testify to her or his faith, even in semipublic settings. In some Baptist churches in places like Rhode Island and Virginia, women were permitted to take part in business meetings and even vote. Occasionally Baptist women exercised a vocal public role, praying or exhorting in religious meetings. Like their Quaker sisters, these Baptist women, such as Martha Marshall, met with criticism and opposition to their speaking from fellow religionists, but, again like early Quaker women, they also found acceptance and support in congregations and from some influential male allies. (Martha Marshall was the wife of Daniel Marshall and the sister of Shubal Stearns, two of the most prominent leaders of the Baptist wing of the Evangelical Revival in the South.)[10]

The Methodist movement was also an important component of the evangelical revival in America after the middle of the eighteenth century, bringing with it the unusual openness of John Wesley and the early Methodists in England to a greater religious voice for women. (Technically, there was no separate Methodist Church in America until after the Revolution, and John Wesley himself lived and died an ordained Anglican priest. Nevertheless, there was an identifiable Methodist *movement* within the Church of England in both England and America in the latter half of the eighteenth century.) John Wesley's views were rooted first in the example and continuing influence of his remarkable mother, Susanna. The wife of an Anglican clergyman, Susanna took very seriously her responsibility for intense and systematic religious instruction for each of her numerous children. Then in the winter of 1711–12, during the absence of her husband and the presence of a rather ineffective curate, she found herself leading a Sunday evening society and "family" prayers for over two hundred people. The curate complained to the absent priest; the priest rebuked his wife; she replied in defense of what she had done and, while agreeing to obey if he insisted, left Samuel Wesley in no doubt of the risk he ran by invoking husbandly authority.

> If you do, after all, think fit to dissolve this assembly, do not tell me that you desire me to do it, for that will not satisfy my conscience: but send me your *positive command,* in such full and express terms as may absolve me from all guilt and punishment for neglecting this opportunity of doing good when you and I shall appear before the great and awful tribunal of our Lord Jesus Christ.[11]

Samuel Wesley did not insist, and Susanna's early example and continuing counsel were very influential in her son's greater acceptance of women's leadership in early Methodism. The effectiveness of Methodist women in England and, eventually, America further confirmed the Wesleyan practice.

Neither among the Methodists and Baptists nor among Puritan converts in the Great Awakening were women given full religious equality as preachers, but they did find broader opportunities for other kinds of religious leadership and influence. An obituary for Hannah Hodge, a Philadelphia Puritan converted by George Whitefield, not only tells of her long-term religious influence and leadership, but also notes, "After the first impressions made by Mr. Whitefield, four or five godly *women* in the city, were the principal counsellors to whom awakened and inquiring sinners used to resort, or could resort, for advice and direction."[12] Devereux Jarratt, a prominent minister of evangelical Anglicanism in the eighteenth century, credited his religious awakening to the mother in a home where he was boarding, one Mrs. Cannon. In his view, God used her nightly reading of sermons "to draw out my attention, and fix it on the subject [of religious experience], in a manner unknown to me before."[13] Mrs. Cannon did not presume to preach, to expound herself on scripture and theology, reading instead from a male authority; nevertheless, the family devotions reflected her initiative and effective leadership.

Women in the Great Awakening continued to build on their accepted religious roles within the family. Clergy wives provided practical support and spiritual examples for their husbands, from the Baptist women of the southern frontier who opened their homes to traveling preachers and revivals—and "held the fort" while their own itinerant husbands were gone on the Lord's work—to Sarah Edwards, whose own spiritual life was used as an inspirational example in a published account by husband Jonathan. Particularly in the South, women also took the initiative in joining and promoting the new evangelical religion in the face of apathy or even outright opposition from men, using their powers of persuasion and secure in their sense of following a divine call that overrode their usual deference to male authorities.[14]

## Sarah Osborn

A striking example of women's religious leadership in the Great Awakening is found in the life of Sarah Osborn of Newport, Rhode Island. Born in England in 1714, she emigrated to the New England colonies in 1722, married at eighteen, and was left a widow with a young son before she was twenty. She turned, successfully, to schoolteaching to support herself and her child. She remarried in 1742, but her husband's business failures and precarious health forced her to return to teaching. In the meantime, after a period of spiritual struggle, she was converted and joined the First Church of Newport in 1737. Influenced by the preaching of Whitefield and Tennent in the early 1740s, she agreed to lead a young women's religious society, which met in her home for the next fifty years, despite periods of greater or diminished interest. When another wave of revivals hit Newport in the 1760s, not only was her Female Society rejuvenated, but Sarah Osborn expanded her role in religious leadership as others sought her spiritual counsel. She began teaching a group of African Americans on Sunday evenings, and eventually the Osborn home became the site of evening gatherings every day except Saturday, although Sarah herself did not lead the young men's group.

Sarah Osborn's activities and her own spiritual life are detailed in an extended correspondence with a nearby minister, the Reverend Joseph Fish. Begun when Fish's daughters were pupils in Osborn's school, their exchange of letters continued for many years. At first, her tone was quite deferential to a "spiritual father," but over time she gained self-confidence, giving as well as seeking spiritual advice and opinions. Fish had been very supportive of her Female Society, but he raised some questions about the extent and appropriateness of Osborn's activities in the 1760s, although it is not clear whether these were more his own concerns or reflections of criticisms he had heard from others in Newport. Osborn responded with a spirited defense. The blacks came to her freely, she reported; she was teaching them to read and the results of their meetings could be seen in improved morality as well as spiritual renewal. Nor did she in fact or in intention usurp the role of the male ministers, she argued: "I only read to them [the blacks] talk to them and sing a Psalm or Hymn with them. . . ."[15] She insisted that her religious work had not meant she had slighted her female duties at home or her school teaching; rather, it was a source of great spiritual satisfaction and refreshment. Most important, she believed that she was following God in her work and that God was using her for good, and besides, she concluded with a touch of irony, no male leaders had been willing to take her place in this work.

> I am rather as a Servant that Has a Great work assigned Him [i.e., Herself], and However ardently He may wish it was in Superior Hands, or that His Master would at Least Help Him, yet if He

> declines He dares not tell Him, well if you dont do it your self it shall go undone for I will not, but rather trys to do what He can till God in his providence point out a way for it to be better done.[16]

Fish appears to have accepted Osborn's defense, for their correspondence continued, as did her religious meetings. Indeed, a few years later, she and her Female Society were instrumental in calling Samuel Hopkins, a disciple of Jonathan Edwards and leading Puritan divine, to the pulpit of the First Church. Hopkins, in his turn, greatly admired Osborn, publishing *Memoirs* of her life and editing selections from her profilic writings on spiritual and biblical topics.

Sarah Osborn was perhaps exceptional, but she was not unique among colonial Puritan women. While she was careful not to appear to usurp male leadership roles, she read widely and wrote extensively on religious matters, supported the revivals of the Great Awakening, and attracted many of her contemporaries to her religious meetings. Her Female Society not only provided women with a space for mutual support and development, anticipating similar groups in the Second Great Awakening, but also clearly influenced her own church's direction. Many women, inspired by their own religious experiences during the Great Awakening, tried to bring others to God's grace in conversion. The domestic circle was an obvious and immediate place to begin, but women felt called by God to witness to persons beyond that sphere when opportunity arose. Most did not set out consciously to challenge social propriety or traditional authorities, but if these were set against what they perceived as God's will, then divine authority clearly superseded human conventions or clergy who preached false religion.

The Great Awakening is an important movement in the story of women and religion in America because they were, as persons, active participants in it in numbers at least as great as men. It was particularly important for black Americans as a group, precipitating a major increase in conversion to Christianity in the colonial period and, in some instances, relatively greater equality in the church. It is less clear whether the movement had a distinct impact on black women *as women*. The impact of the Great Awakening on white women as women was real, if not dramatic. It provided expanded religious roles for women, which were numerous, public, and striking enough to elicit criticism from certain male religious authorities. That criticism, however, was not limited to women but included discomfort about the expanded power and roles of white laymen, the uneducated, and social inferiors, servants and slaves, for the movement challenged traditional established hierarchies. One can almost hear the growing level of outrage in the tone of Charles Chauncy, the most prominent critic of the Great Awakening in New England: "Indeed young *Persons,* sometimes *Lads,* or rather *Boys:* Nay, *Women* and *Girls,* yea *Negroes,* have taken upon them to do the Business of Preachers."[17] And as real as the criticism was, there were also men and women who supported and appreciated women's expanded religious activities.

Not only was there appreciative response to women's expanding religious roles, but those roles were rooted in precedents that had gained broad social acceptance. For decades before the Great Awakening, Christian women in colonial America had been allowed and expected to be concerned about their own spiritual state, to be respected for their piety, to converse within a private circle and even to write on religious matters, and to offer religious instruction in the home to children and "lesser" males like servants and slaves. Indeed, while there is no widespread or conclusive evidence that white colonial women were more involved and more successful teaching blacks than were men, impressionistic evidence and particular instances suggest that this may have been the case in schools or societies, or within the household. Not only did Sarah Osborn work with blacks, but a group of white women in New York opened a short-lived school for black women in 1712.[18] Anne Wager, an Anglican, ran a school for young blacks in the 1760s and early 1770s in Williamsburg, Virginia, with a heavy emphasis on religious instruction.[19] The importance of the Great Awakening was to increase such accepted roles and their visibility, as well as to provide a further theological justification for women's religious activities through a renewed emphasis on the authority of the individual's conversion experience.

Finally, insofar as the Great Awakening was, in part, a challenge to traditional social and religious hierarchies, women, too, received some encouragement to step out of or at least to expand their place. It did not produce significant, self-conscious female protest on a wide scale, perhaps because most women converts were reasonably satisfied with what they could do, especially since criticism of their activities, though present, was by no means universal. Furthermore, it may be that because the Great Awakening itself already divided churches and communities, female converts found their primary identification with the new religious community, and the solidarity of interest needed there overrode the gender identification that might have led to further questioning of women's roles.

# 6
# *The Ideal American Woman*

Victory in their rebellion against England and the establishment of a new nation were decisive political changes for colonial Americans; they also brought significant changes for American religion. The American Revolution was understood by colonial leaders as part of sacred history, of God's dealings with humanity. The war itself was a time of testing, and analogies between America (Israel) and England (Egypt) were frequently invoked. Victory was a sign of God's help and approval, but it also brought heavy responsibilities to the newly created nation as a whole to be a "city on a hill" to the rest of the world.

The most immediate church-related problem to face the architects of the Constitution was the matter of establishment: should there be a state church? The weight of Western tradition and European example was on the side of establishment: A state church was necessary to ensure social harmony and to inculcate morality in the citizens. Yet there were arguments, both principled and pragmatic, against a federal establishment of religion. Given the diversity of religious groups in the colonies, no single one could claim national dominance and therefore state favor. Moreover, an anomalous alliance of Free Church leaders, like the Baptist Isaac Backus, and Deists, like Thomas Jefferson, distrusted state churches and argued for religious freedom on principle. Thus the new Constitution and its Bill of Rights embodied a radical experiment: a nation without an established state church. By not establishing a state religion, the nation's founders were not disputing the crucial role of religion in ensuring a stable and virtuous society. Rather, they believed that the churches could still fulfill that function without legal establishment and federal support. Churches thus became voluntary associations, dependent on the free choice of the people for affiliation and financial support. (There were lingering establishments at the state level in Connecticut and Massachusetts, but their days and influence were numbered.)

In the late eighteenth century, disestablishment was seen as radical, even risky. America was a democracy and hence its "rulers" were its citizens. If the experiment were to succeed, these rulers must be wise and virtuous, and conventional wisdom stated that religion was the source of morality in the people. Could the churches, now voluntary associations, not only support themselves as institutions on that basis but also perform the function of shaping a virtuous citizenry? The question was a serious one for church leaders as the nation moved toward a new century, especially with the growth of unchurched populations in the original settlements and on the frontier. Heavy Roman Catholic immigration in the nineteenth century added to the Protestant establishment's fears, since its leaders regarded Catholicism as little better than irreligion and, moreover, a threat to democracy because of Catholics' supposed loyalty to a foreign power, the pope. The fate of America as God's chosen nation, in the eyes of Protestants, depended on reaching the unchurched and containing Catholic influence.

The Revolution also affected American women. While they had no formal role in government (and, indeed, were widely presumed to have no interest or competence in politics) and were not involved directly in the war as soldiers, women were drawn into political concerns. Boycotts against England in the years before the war depended on women's cooperation not to buy or use goods like tea or imported cloth and to produce homespun. As controversy heightened, some "Daughters of Liberty" expressed public, if anonymous, political views in writing. Once fighting began, it was women who were left to run and defend the homestead while their husbands were absent. Because the war was fought on American soil, it came, in many cases, literally to their doorsteps. Even if women had wanted to avoid matters considered beyond their sphere, they simply could not do so.

These experiences and the talk of equality and natural rights that was so central to Revolutionary ideology caused at least a few women to consider their own position. Abigail Adams's caution in a letter to her absent husband, John, to "Remember the Ladies" as the founding fathers created a new nation is the most famous request for a change in women's rights, and her political interests were as great as her practical contributions to the patriots' cause. But other individual women, familiar with Enlightenment theory and caught up in the dramatic changes of war and nation-founding, also raised questions about the extent to which natural *human* rights applied to women. Judith Sargent Murray boldly asserted women's equality in intellect in one of the earliest American defenses of women's abilities and rights and even proposed a drastically different reading of the Fall, used for so long as justification for women's subordination and proof of their inferiority.

> It doth not appear that [Eve] was governed by any one sensual appetite; but merely by a desire of adorning her mind; a laudable ambition fired her soul, and a thirst for knowledge impelled the predilection so fatal in its consequences. Adam could not plead the same deception; assuredly he was not deceived; . . . he was

> influenced by no other motive than a bare pusillanimous attachment to a woman![1]

Thus the combination of the Revolution and the intellectual atmosphere of the Enlightenment resulted in a small but significant voice defending greater equality for women. But by and large, these radical minority views were either ignored or deflected. Even those involved made no serious, sustained call for equal political rights, nor were they concerned to promote women's leadership in the institutional churches. Rather, they focused their energies in calling for better education for women *so that* women could better fulfil their particular role in the new nation: Republican Motherhood.

## From "Good Wife" to "Republican Motherhood": An Evolution in Image

The ideal image for American women that emerged from the Revolutionary period was Republican Womanhood or Republican Motherhood.[2] If America's existence, growth, and success as a democratic nation and an example to the rest of the world were dependent on the virtue and contributions of its citizens, what were those citizens' responsibilities? For men (specifically, white, propertied men) the answer was clear: at minimum, an informed and intelligent vote; when events or personal abilities so dictated, military or government service. But women were also citizens, desirous of contributing to America's welfare. The idea of their voting, fighting, or governing was seen as either laughable or outrageous, but they could contribute indirectly. Thus an Abigail Adams could see her efforts in running the farm in John's absence and her own acceptance of that absence as a very real contribution, freeing John for public service. It was a sacrifice for a higher cause that she freely accepted. (It is important to note that, in the ideal, the wife's sacrifices to free her husband's time and energy were made so that he could, in turn, serve a cause larger and higher than self, not simply so he could achieve personal fulfillment or private economic gain.) After the war, of course, only a few husbands would be called to services that demanded such immediate, practical sacrifice. What all American women could and should do was to be Republican Mothers, to raise their sons to be virtuous and intelligent citizens and their daughters to be equally virtuous and intelligent Republican Mothers in their turn.

In order most effectively to raise such sons and daughters, a woman herself had to be educated, and her own virtue had to be an informed one. Thus the men and women who promoted more and better education for women emphasized that such education, far from threatening women's traditional domestic roles and duties, would enhance those responsibilities and make women more capable of fulfilling them effectively and intelligently. It was a functional argument, not one based on women's own interests or abilities or personal fulfillment; nonetheless, it was both sincere and, in its time, pragmatic. Education for women, enabling subsequent education by women as mothers, should therefore combine intellectual, domestic, and religious training, and would result in political benefit for the nation.

The role of the Republican Mother was not simply imposed upon women by men anxious to keep women in their place and deny their rights. It was promoted and embraced by women, for it justified education for them, encouraged their political and intellectual interests, commended them for what was in actuality a major part of their lives in the family, and assured them that they could make an important contribution to the public good and America's millennial future. One can recognize all this and yet still see that Republican Motherhood deflected arguments for women's equality as persons and citizens and reinforced the limitations of the domestic sphere as woman's "place" and family duties as her reason for existence.

As an image and ideal, Republican Motherhood represented both continuity with and change from the colonial ideal of the "Good Wife." Expectations that women should be religious, should function primarily within the family unit rather than in the public world, should be concerned parents responsible for rearing pious, moral, contributing children by teaching and example, and should be appreciated for their socially valuable contribution were nothing new. Both the Good Wife and the Republican Mother were to exhibit wisdom in general and a reasonably high level of knowledge in a particular field. For the Puritan Good Wife, that area was religious; for the Republican Mother, political. Of course, in neither case was it expected that she would attain an intellectual level equivalent to male experts, let alone exercise public leadership. Nevertheless, learning was encouraged at "appropriate" levels and made her better able to fulfill her duties.

While there was continuity between the ideal image of the Good Wife and that of the Republican Mother, there was also some shifting of emphasis and context in the image. For the Republican Mother, the goals and motivations of the ideal mother were more overtly political, a response to the new political situation, even as the political role for women remained indirect. In addition, the responsibility for rearing moral and informed children was more gender-specific, the mother's particular function, rather than a common parental one. Because a woman's role as mother was at the center of the post-Revolutionary image, there was proportionately less attention given in portraits of the ideal woman to other roles and functions, roles that had been more evenly balanced in the image of the Good Wife. Nevertheless, we must be careful not to separate too sharply "political" and "religious" spheres or functions. Colonial Christians, especially

Puritans, had not done so, and the rhetoric of the Revolution clearly tied together the religious and the political in its vision of America's role and destiny. Disestablishment meant to the founders that government would not aid a state church and that the principle of religious liberty would be upheld, but the founders assumed that social harmony and a moral citizenry were critical to national success. Voluntary churches should be one institutional source of moral values; other institutions like schools should also help to shape virtuous and patriotic citizens. Beyond and behind these were mothers, with an influence that was earlier, more universal, and more continuous for future citizens than even churches or schools. As Linda Kerber notes, "Motherhood was discussed almost as if it were a fourth branch of government, a device that ensured social control in the gentlest possible way."[3]

## The "True Woman": The Nineteenth-Century Ideal

Republican Motherhood was a transitional image between the colonial Good Wife and the nineteenth-century ideal, which emerged as incredibly pervasive and influential: the "True Woman." In 1966 historian Barbara Welter published a now-classic study of the image and ideal of nineteenth-century American womanhood, "The Cult of True Womanhood, 1820–1860."[4] Drawing upon an enormous range of popular literature, Welter paints a portrait of the True Woman that emerged from both male and female writers by means of her four "cardinal virtues." A True Woman is pious, pure, submissive, and domestic.

Women are naturally religious, moral, virtuous, or so said the conventional wisdom of the nineteenth century. When that assertion is compared with the assumptions about woman's nature that pervaded Christian thought even into the seventeenth century, the reversal is dramatic. Those daughters of Eve who had been seen as weaker in faith and spiritual qualities by their very nature had undergone a 180-degree change to become naturally pious and moral. Yet the change was not, in fact, immediate. It was prepared for in the ideology of late seventeenth- and early eighteenth-century church leaders, especially Puritans, when they tried to account for women's greater participation in the churches and suggested that the particular experiences of women as childbearers made them more open to the call to conversion and the consolations of religion. The distinction is subtle but extremely important: Puritan leaders like Cotton Mather allowed only that a woman's experiences, not her nature, might make her more religious; nineteenth-century writers completed the reversal of tradition by positing substantively different natures for men and women.

A similarly dramatic reversal occurred in perceptions of women's sexuality. Instead of being the naturally carnal gender, the tempting Eves who constantly threatened men through their insatiable lust, women (at least good or "true" women) were distinctly asexual, naturally pure, and it was men whose sexuality was so rampant and hard to control. To be sure, while popular images of which gender is more sexual changed, the traditional double standard of sexual conduct did not; if anything, it was even stronger in nineteenth-century America. Men, after all, could hardly help themselves and were dependent on women's purity and self-restraint, whereas women not only knew what men expected of them but had few sexual urges themselves, anyway.

The True Woman was to be submissive. In particular, she was to accept her subordination to her husband. This "cardinal virtue" was nothing new. Women had always been on the lower side in hierarchical pairings in Western tradition, a reality perceived as right, natural, and divinely ordained since the first human couple. Even in America, after all, it was the traditional hierarchies of the Puritans, not the radical challenges of the Quakers, that dominated. The compensation held out to women for their acceptance of subordination was the promise of "female influence," a power that could only be exercised gently, subtly, and in private. Surely no True Woman would desire any other, unfeminine, source of power. The rhetoric of the nineteenth century may have been more effusive, and at times submission seemed to be equated with total passivity, but the substance of female subordination represented no dramatic change from dominant Christian tradition.

Finally, the True Woman was domestic. On the one hand, this fourth virtue was again nothing new. Most women had for centuries been primarily involved in household tasks and the bearing and nurturing of children. Yet the domesticity of nineteenth-century America was far more than a simple division of labor. Not only was the content of domestic work undergoing a change, but the emotional investment in qualitative domesticity was significantly intensified as the home took on moral as well as functional characteristics. The home became a distinct and self-contained *sphere,* virtually the only appropriate sphere for women, and the only place a True Woman could be really happy.

Thus the nineteenth-century image of the True Woman was both continuous and discontinuous with previous ideals or expectations. Some roles, such as subordination or domestic concerns, had a long heritage; other characteristics represented fairly dramatic changes. It was the insistence on rigid separation by gender, however, that was distinctive in nineteenth-century imagery, the assumption that men and women have radically different natures and should function in radically different spheres most of the time. (Men were, of course, present in homes, but it was not their natural habitat. Churches remained, at least in theory, a desirable setting for both sexes and the one place outside the home where respectable women would appear, though not, of course, as leaders.)

## Sources of the Cult of True Womanhood

Why did the cult of True Womanhood, with its idealized and distinctively female sphere of domesticity, arise and flourish in popular perceptions of nineteenth-century Americans? One major cause was social and economic change. America in the nineteenth century began an accelerating process of urbanization and industrialization. The changes were, of course, more rapid in some geographical areas than in others. They occurred at different times in different parts of the nation, and many years would pass before even a simple majority of Americans lived in cities. Nevertheless, this was the direction in which the country was moving. For men, the changes meant that more often their "work" would be physically separated from the home, in offices or factories. Work for such men was a separate sphere in a way that it had not been for farmers or small craftsmen. Furthermore, the public sphere was also the domain of politics (another male preserve), so that insofar as male Americans found their work and identity in political and economic activity, their setting would be a separate, public, male sphere. Furthermore, the economic and political enterprises of the male sphere were so crucial and time-consuming that men could rationalize their lack of attention to traditional religious duties as a result of busy-ness. Interestingly enough, the idea that men were too busy for religious concerns was not new in the nineteenth century. Cotton Mather had cited women's greater leisure as a possible explanation for their greater piety, and in 1765, the Reverend James Fordyce wrote to a young woman, "The situation of men lays them open to a variety of temptations, that lay out of your road. The bustle of life, in which they are generally engaged, leaves them often but little leisure for holy offices."[5]

At the same time that many men began to leave the home for their productive activities, the range and variety of productive tasks within the home began to diminish. Homes in an agricultural or small-craft economy were centers of production for the staples of survival like food and clothing. With increased industrialization, such products and services could be obtained elsewhere. Hence the range of productive activities in the home that had characterized the role of the Puritan Good Wife was narrowed, and the woman's direct economic contribution to the family's survival also diminished. In an economic sense, she was more thoroughly and exclusively dependent upon her husband as "breadwinner." What remained were her role as provider of personal service and comfort for that husband/breadwinner and her role as mother. Because the wife's range of roles had diminished at the same time that her husband was more often physically absent from the home, what had been in colonial ideology a parental responsibility became largely a maternal role: child rearing.

The practical social and economic changes that made motherhood the key role for American women were reinforced by ideological changes. As noted before, the central contribution of the ideal Republican Mother, *her* duty as a citizen of the new nation, was to raise intelligent and virtuous children who were prepared to take on their gender-defined roles as citizens in their turn. In addition, the nineteenth century saw a shift in broad cultural perceptions of children and their basic natures. The colonial Puritans had seen children (like all human beings) as fallen and sinful, and the resultant task of parents to be one of breaking their willfulness and inculcating habits of obedience, but nineteenth-century theory began to move toward an assessment of childish nature as basically innocent and therefore malleable, highly dependent on early influence and training. The logic appeared to be both clear and inexorable to many nineteenth-century Americans: America's success, not just in a material sense but as a divinely chosen example for the world, was dependent on the intelligence and virtue of its citizens. Today's children would be tomorrow's citizens, and their characters were to be shaped by those persons who spent most time caring for them and educating them by precept and example: mothers. Because so much depended on that role, American women had an awesome privilege and responsibility, and naturally that role should be a woman's central concern.

Finally, the pervasiveness and popularity of the cult of domesticity was in part a response to a pace of social change that could be frightening. When so much of the public sphere was changing, the home and the woman who presided over it seemed to be the one stable element left, the place where traditional values could be preserved and upheld. By its very separation from the public world, the home came to be seen as a refuge, a haven, a pillar of stability. Thus the private-public split that was beginning to characterize American society took on heavy emotional and value-laden overtones. On the one side was the public world of economic progress, of politics, of men. Characterized by change and competition, it was at least amoral, sometimes (regrettably but necessarily) immoral. On the other side was the home, the private world of women that served, ironically, as both support for and haven from the public sphere, the center of harmony, peace, stability, morality, and, increasingly, religion (which was often inconvenient or irrelevant to the public sphere.) Is it any surprise that the guiding spirit of that private world, she whose natural place it was, was also expected to be naturally pious and pure?

### The Impact of the Cult

Such a private/public split in nineteenth-century American society, like the image of the true woman, is a construct, necessarily oversimplified. Historical generalizations can be illuminating, but their limitations must also be kept in mind. First, the economic and social changes that precipitated two distinct spheres were real, but they were neither universal nor immediate. Second, there was a significant "space" between the two rigidly defined spheres, neither the purely domestic female world nor the male public world of commerce, war, and politics. Religion *was* part of the woman's domestic sphere, but it was also part of this middle ground shared by men and women, as was charitable or benevolent activity. Finally, the achievement of True Womanhood was not equally available, attractive, or meaningful to all American women. Though the values assigned to domesticity were pervasive, the men and women who most actively promoted a cult of domesticity were primarily white and Protestant, with roots in New England and the Northeast, and thus a limited sample of Americans. Their cultural dominance and access to popular publications gave them disproportionate influence that should not be underestimated, but it was not unlimited. Women themselves could be selective, accepting and promoting values like piety and personal concern for others, but sometimes ignoring or challenging restrictions on their activities.

Furthermore, the cult of domesticity was simply not feasible for many poor women, especially immigrants and women of color, who had few opportunities to enjoy the private sphere and relative leisure assumed to be available for the ideal True Woman for domestic duties. Significant numbers of American women *had* to enter the public sphere of employment as factory workers or domestics. Black women slaves had still less control over their own personal lives, let alone economic security. Even the white, middle-class Protestant women who helped to create as well as support the image were sometimes unmarried or widowed. Thus the degree to which diverse groups of American women shared the values of True Womanhood varied. Black women, Catholic, Lutheran, and Jewish immigrant women, women living in the South or on the western frontier had distinctive traditions and beliefs that shaped their values and self-understandings. Neither their values nor their situations were a neat fit with the cult of domesticity in its more extreme or idiosyncratic form. In short, the image of woman's nature and sphere assumed by proponents of the cult to be "universal" simply wasn't. Many American women faced practical social and economic barriers that precluded their achievement of True Womanhood. Many did not share its assumptions and values or the ways those values were presumed to be manifested in women's lives.

Certainly there were points of concurrence and contact between the dominant ideology and the lives and values of other groups of American women. Yet even these reasons behind practices and values were not necessarily the same as the causes that produced the cult of True Womanhood among middle-class, white Protestants in the Northeast. At these points, reinforcement rather than imposition of values is a more useful model for understanding the impact of the cult. For example, the model of Evangelical Womanhood that arose in the American South was largely congruent with the image of the True Woman, but as Donald Mathews has shown, it came from a different context, one in which evangelicals moved from being dissenters to shapers of southern culture.

> To supplant the sinful power of the aristocratic ideal of womanhood, Evangelicals began to shape a model of behavior and ideals which was peculiarly the possession of women and was based on their unique contribution to the ideal community. This emphasis on, indeed *commitment* to "women's sphere" therefore came out of the early Evangelical perception of the cosmic conflict between the church and the world.[6]

Indeed, the critique of "ornamental" ladies was shared by evangelicals in other parts of the nation, including the Northeast. To them "usefulness" was a key to the notion of admirable Christian womanhood and should, perhaps, be added as a fifth "cardinal virtue." Thus the context in the Northeast, where evangelicals were a solid part of the "establishment" and where the beginnings of industrialization and urbanization helped to account for the rise of a cult of domesticity, may have differed from a southern or frontier setting, but evangelicals in all areas rejected those notions of female passivity and practical uselessness that were present in some images of true womanhood.

In a second example, many Catholic and Lutheran immigrants brought with them to America very traditional religious and social views on the relationship of men and women. Once in America, they were often concerned to preserve their distinctive ethnic and religious identity, to avoid excessive "Americanization." One way to do so (but by no means the only one) was to maintain the home as a religious and ethnic center where traditions could be preserved and passed on. If immigrant mothers in particular worked outside the home, it was as a last resort, far more a matter of financial necessity than of personal preference. Thus, if submission to male authorities and a view of the home as the desirable center for women's activities characterized an ideal for these immigrant women, it was more a result of inherited traditions and resistance to assimilation than a matter of conformity to dominant American ideology.

The contrast between a homogeneous image and a complex, diverse reality helps to explain the apparent paradox of women in America at this time. Nineteenth-century America saw both a pervasive image of true womanhood within a cult of domesticity *and* the flowering of women's activities and a women's rights movement. Women were stepping out of their place with a vengeance! As influential as it was (and it was indeed influential), not only did the cult of True Womanhood fail to reflect the experiences and values of many women in America, but there was ambiguity and tension built into the cult itself. On the one hand, it was very limiting for women, confining them to a narrow sphere with restricted roles that were presumed to be natural and sufficient for all women, regardless of class, race, or personal talents and inclinations. Women were valued and commended only to the extent that they served others (men and children), and they had identities only in relation to those others. Yet the cult of domesticity was a two-edged sword, for in practice it also provided a common space for women, a space in which they could exercise power as they found common identities and causes. It provided validation for what large numbers of women actually did most of the time. In other words, the cult could be both prescriptive and descriptive. The myths of motherhood can be seen, cynically, as a male method of palming off on women the parental role for which they themselves no longer had time or interest and a way of making sure women did not interfere in the male world. But they can equally, and fairly, be seen as a construct of women themselves, a way of insisting on the importance of women's contribution, even the indirect control of national destiny by women. Eventually, American women would use the cult's ideology combined with the virtue of "usefulness" to break its limits and expand woman's sphere. To see how this was done, we must turn from images and ideals to the actions of women in nineteenth-century America, especially in that institution that formed an uneasy bridge between private and public spheres: religion.

# 7
# *The Second Great Awakening*

The constitutional disestablishment of religion presented Protestant church leaders with a twofold challenge. Could the churches, voluntary organizations bereft of state support, continue to exist and even grow in the new nation? And could they promote the piety and morality, grounded in religious belief, that were so crucial for the success of the American experiment? Most church leaders concurred in the broad cultural assumptions about Republican Motherhood. Female citizens would make their distinctive contribution to national morality and hence national success by raising pious, intelligent, virtuous, and responsible children. But male church leaders were by no means ready to depend only on women to respond to the challenges, and thus they set about promoting revivals all across the new nation, revivals that, they hoped, would revitalize the religion of nominal Christians and bring the unchurched into the Christian fold. The result was what historians have called the Second Great Awakening in the waning years of the eighteenth century and approximately the first three decades of the nineteenth century, that is, from about 1795 to 1830. By the end of this Great Awakening, the first challenge at least had been clearly met with success: Churches had been able to thrive and spread as voluntary institutions.

## Women's Central Role

The Second Great Awakening cut across denominational lines and was particularly manifest among Congregationalists, Presbyterians, Methodists, and Baptists. Indeed, it propelled these last two groups to numerical dominance among Protestants. It cut across geographical boundaries from the southwestern frontier to the "burned-over district" of western New York (so named because the fires of religious excitement swept it so often), to New England and the eastern seaboard. Its most effective form was the revival, from the wilder camp meetings of the frontier to the more restrained but equally consuming revivals of New England, and in all cases, American women played a central role in the awakenings. Most simply, women were a critical part of the Second Great Awakening because they outnumbered men as converts and church members, continuing the pattern begun in the colonial period. Even when the relative proportion of male converts increased during a time of particular excitement in a specific place, women still formed the numerical majority.[1] But why did women experience conversion and join the churches more frequently than men? For one thing, there was precedent in American religion since the late seventeenth century, and the cultural expectations of the nineteenth century, the assumption that women were naturally more religious than men, reinforced that precedent. More precise explanations of women's higher participation, however, vary, underlining the complexity of motives among individuals and groups at different times and in different places. In a study of the New England phase of the Second Great Awakening, Nancy Cott suggests that these young women were experiencing economic and social changes that disrupted their identity formation. Daughters had made an economic contribution to families by spinning and weaving, but that activity was moving from families to factories, sending those daughters out of the home into factories—or into schools to teach—to earn money. At the same time, a shortage of eligible males and a greater emphasis on romantic love raised uncertainties about marriage. As a result, these young women found in conversion a way to shape their lives and identities; and in church groups, a supportive community.[2]

Alternatively, Martha Blauvelt argues that young women's responses to conversion may have been rooted in their recognition of the contrast between the expectations for single and married women. The unmarried young woman had greater freedom and fewer responsibilities than her married sister. "As women approached maturity and marriage, the frivolity of their youth no longer seemed appropriate, but sinful, and they became particularly susceptible to the revival's evangelical message. . . . Conversion was the means through which women adapted to their culture's demands that they submit to both God and man."[3] Yet the female conversions of the Second Great Awakening may just as well be evidence of women's self-assertion, even in the face of male disapproval. Ryan suggests, given the numbers of solitary female converts in her study, "that by joining a church independently of relatives many women exercised a degree of religious autonomy during periods of revival."[4] Donald Mathews's study of evangelical religion in the South also supports the idea that conversion could be a form of female self-assertion. Especially, though not exclusively in the South, a fair number of husbands opposed their wives' religious activities, and women were faced with choosing between the authority of their male "heads" or, as they perceived it, of God. For many, the latter had the greater claim and gave them the strength to defy the former. (Mathews does note one extraordinary case of both submission and perseverance. Sarah Moss was converted, but her husband refused to let her join the church, so she waited forty years until he died and then applied for church membership![5])

It seems clear that women who were converted during the Second Great Awakening were a complex group of human beings with diverse situations and motives, and no single sociological or psychological theory can fully "explain" their actions. Nevertheless, conversion and subsequent church membership provided a common experience for many American women, even beyond the personal, religious significance for the individuals involved. The churches, or more broadly, religious interest, gave women a respectable sphere outside the home for peer support and meaningful activity. At the same time, religion reinforced women's role as guardians of religion in the home, giving that role eternal as well as temporal importance. Indeed, it was as wives and mothers that converted women could make their first contribution to the cause of revivals. Without denying the leadership role of ministers, all converts were expected to testify to what God had done for them, to witness to others so that they, too, might seek conversion. For women, the closest others, whose well-being was both a deep concern and a responsibility, were members of their families, and within the family they could exercise that gentle and tactful influence that even the most conservative clerics allowed them. Ryan's careful study of successive revivals in and around Utica suggests the effectiveness of wifely/motherly influence. Records of conversion and church memberships include numerous individuals with no obvious family religious connection, but they also include significant numbers of husbands and children of previously converted women. The evidence of data reinforces the dominant cultural image of the mother as the effective religious leader and initiator in the family.

Women sometimes took more public roles in revivals, praying aloud in mixed gatherings and even occasionally preaching. Women preachers did exist in the early nineteenth century, but they were rare and most often found among some Baptists or Methodists on the frontiers. Furthermore, occasional female preaching and exceptional female preachers are not the same thing as equal and formal religious leadership for women. The famous camp meeting of the southern frontier, so crucial to the Awakening there, was actually more organized than fascinated and condescending contemporary observers realized, and the role of women in the camp meetings illustrates the possibilities and the limits of female participation. In a typical camp meeting, the major role of leadership and preaching was restricted to white men, and participants were separated by race and gender to hear the preaching. But there were lesser roles of religious leadership that could be exercised during the course of the meetings by white women and black men and women. As new converts, they could give formal, public testimonials about their experience to the meeting. They could also function as "convert exhorters," working directly with individual sinners under conviction, that is, in the process of conversion. Sinners under conviction were encouraged to come forward to the "anxious seat" or "glory pen" where races and genders did mix. In that setting, female (and black) exhorters, "good singers," and "praying persons" mingled with and exercised religious authority for sinners, even white males.[6] Thus frontier revivals opened some greater roles of public religious authority for women converts, but they also clearly retained limits on women's activities.

A few women preachers were also found on the frontier of western New York in the early nineteenth century. So when Charles Grandison Finney, the most famous revivalist of the Second Great Awakening, included women's public prayer and speech in mixed gatherings as one of his "new measures" to promote revivals, there was precedent for such female activity. Nevertheless, the practice was discouraged by evangelical leaders in the more settled East. Like other new measures and, indeed, Finney himself, it was accepted only reluctantly and gradually because of his unarguable success. Despite opposition, then, some women were able to pray, exhort, or testify publicly in the wake of the Second Great Awakening, and in so doing, not only contributed directly to the revivals but also set an important precedent for women's public religious leadership.

Yet women's activities "behind the scenes" were at least as important to the success of the Awakening and the expansion of women's religious roles. Nineteenth-century evangelical Protestants believed firmly in the power of prayer, and women could most certainly pray, in private as individuals and in the company of other women in prayer meetings. Such gatherings represented one of the earliest—and culturally, least problematic—forms of women's associations. The fellowship and support women found in a setting outside the domestic sphere was surely valuable, but so was their formal purpose, prayer—to the women themselves and to revival leaders like Finney. Finney was convinced that fervent and directed prayer, often by pious women, prepared a community for a revival, complemented its progress, and extended its impact. To those involved, intercessory prayer was an active service, and they believed in its importance and efficacy. Nor did women confine their religious activities to church membership, the immediate family, or female prayer societies; they also joined together in a range of formal and informal associations. The earliest of these, like female prayer societies, were directly "religious" in the sense of being closely related to the churches and focused on specifically "religious" goals: encouraging conversions, developing the spiritual life of converts, and supporting local churches and a missionary effort to "unchurched" or "under-churched" sections of America. Women and men both formed associations and raised money to support traveling ministers and to provide Bibles and devotional tracts to spread "true" (i.e., Protestant) Christianity.

## Benevolence and Conversion: Traditions and Change

### Maternal Associations

One type of religious association that grew directly out of the Second Great Awakening was specifically female: the maternal association. Founded in Maine in 1815 by Ann Louisa Payton, a Congregational minister's wife, maternal associations spread through New England and New York to the frontiers of Ohio, where Lydia Finney, first wife of the prominent revivalist, played an active leadership role in the Oberlin Maternal Association.[7] These groups of mothers met for mutual support and common, purposive prayer. In one sense, there was nothing new about women's seeking the support and advice of other women about their common experiences and responsibilities as mothers. (Indeed, we find "parenting" classes and support groups thriving in the late twentieth century!) Yet these nineteenth-century groups were new in their degree of formal structure, the specific and organized methods proposed, and the national, even eternal destinies that were perceived to depend on maternal success. Members agreed to shape their concern through systematic religious duties that included "praying for each child daily, attending meetings semi-monthly, renewing each child's baptismal covenant regularly, reading systematically through the literature on the Christian education of children, setting a pious example to children at all times, and spending each child's birthday in prayer and fasting."[8] By the 1830s, mothers' magazines were established to extend and reinforce the network, but the goal remained to focus intensely on the critical responsibility of a Christian mother for the religious destiny of her own children.

For some female converts, the maternal associations were the major, if not the exclusive, focus of their contribution to the Awakening. Other women, without denying maternal religious concern as one element of their response to conversion, participated in other associations designed to shape a more Christian and moral America. In both cases, maternal concern seemed to produce the desired results in at least some children. Ryan has documented the kinship ties in the successive revivals of upstate New York, but there is no reason to suppose that those results could not be duplicated elsewhere if records were available. The very prevalence of the stock figure of the pious mother in nineteenth-century sermons, folklore, and literature testifies to real roots in American experience, however standardized or even caricatured that figure became. The thoughtless male sinner, brought face to face with his desperate situation by personal crisis or a relentlessly convincing preacher, who then recalled with both shame and gratitude the patient prayers and instruction of his pious mother, was a literary truism not only because it fit American cultural ideology but also because it was frequently based on genuine experiences.

## The Sunday School Movement

The Sunday school movement was another religious response to the Second Great Awakening that was important for women, particularly younger, single women. By teaching Sunday school classes, they found an activity that fulfilled their need for useful action and yet was eminently respectable, dealing as it did with religion and children. They also found a like-minded and supportive peer group in other teachers and their students, since a special focus in the early decades of the nineteenth century was teen-aged girls. As teachers, they could pass along their own values of Evangelical Womanhood, and numerous deep and long-term friendships grew out of these relationships, even outlasting physical separation. For some young women, Sunday school teaching was a "bridge," preparation for a religious career as a writer, a minister's wife, or a missionary teacher. In the first half of the century, few women held administrative leadership roles, but by the second half of the century, women expanded their roles within and their goals for the movement.[9] By the twentieth century, "religious education" would become a formal and paid professional role for women in the churches, with its roots stretching back for more than a century.

## Charitable Organizations

Women's Bible and tract societies, Sunday schools, and groups formed to raise funds to support poor but pious male seminary students and missionary-ministers to unchurched regions like the frontier were often collectively identified as "home missions." Still another form of home missions was charitable and benevolent work for the "less fortunate." Neighborly concern was nothing new for religious women in America, having strong roots in colonial times among various religious groups. While women's benevolent activity was increased by the revivals of the Second Great Awakening, such activity was not simply and universally dependent on the revival impulse. What was new in the nineteenth century was the degree of formal organization involved in female benevolence. Colonial Quaker women were an exception in having a formal organizational base for charitable functions in their women's meetings, and when, late in the eighteenth century, Quaker men in places like Pennsylvania turned from public political service to the philanthropy of organized benevolence, taking over Quaker women's activities, the women began to form their own societies.[10] But most colonial women's charity was unstructured, the informal response to immediate, local need. With the dawn of the nineteenth century, however, non-Quaker women began to found and manage formal benevolent organizations. For example, in 1822 women of the "pioneer elite" in Rochester, New York, formed the Female Charitable Society to help the "sick poor."[11] The women of Petersburg, Virginia, organized and ran a Female Orphan Asylum starting in 1812 as part of their traditional concern with poor relief.[12] The actions of the women of Rochester and Petersburg were not unique, isolated examples, and they are further significant because there was so little male opposition to the new groups. Indeed, many men of the early decades of the nineteenth century were quite willing to leave such forms of poor relief to the women. As Suzanne Lebsock notes, "The asylum was an affirmation of women's role as friend in need; the founding of an orphanage was not so much a rejection of woman's sphere as it was an attempt to give institutional form and public importance to its most positive features."[13]

These early charitable organizations were sponsored primarily by women of the "established," relatively affluent classes and were associated with a sense of Christian duty, and they are important evidence that benevolent activity was not solely a result of the Second Great Awakening or found only among those denominations most directly influenced by the revivals. Nevertheless, the revival impulse and the expectation that one's conversion would bear fruit greatly accelerated the growth of women's benevolent work as part of home missions. The Second Great Awakening also modified charitable work through its millennial expectations. Where traditional charitable activity tended to assume that the "poor would always be with us" and that the better-off members of society had a moral and religious obligation to aid the "deserving" poor (like widows and orphans), the evangelicals inspired by the Awakening were convinced that, in America at least, the poor could be converted, as well as helped, and thus escape from poverty. As Carroll Smith Rosenberg puts it in her study of the New York City mission movement, "Coinciding with an increasing commitment to egalitarian social arrangements, this new pietism led Americans to declare a religious war upon the poverty of their cities. The victory they expected would bring both the conversion of the urban poor and, they believed, of necessity, an end to poverty itself."[14] The city missions of New York and other urban centers designed to convert and aid the poor were by no means exclusively a female activity, but women were actively involved in the work, from raising funds to acting as "friendly visitors" door to door among the poor, distributing Bibles, tracts, and material aid, and sharing a personal, if sometimes condescending, concern.

The benevolent activities of home missions, then, continued a deep-rooted tradition of neighborly charity as a Christian duty, but they added new elements of formal organization for women and, in the cases of groups inspired by the revivals, a millennial justification and urgency that tied conversion and benevolence together. The women involved posed no major challenge to social structures or male spheres, but they did gain important experience in public skills like fund-raising and administration. Contact with the poor also raised the women's consciousness about social conditions. Later in the century, women in home missions would begin to raise more radical questions about social and economic structures and their own female roles. Throughout the century, these women were thus not only stepping out of their place by expansion, taking on some "male" roles in the service of an appropriately female concern; they were also bringing some of their own "female" values of personal concern, neighborly charity, and nurturing into the public sphere, which, they believed, needed more of those values. In a sense, they were bringing a part of woman's culture with them as they moved into an expanded sphere, thereby affirming elements of their "woman's place" as broadly significant and desirable for the society as a whole.

Conversion in the Second Great Awakening provided for many nineteenth-century American women both a sense of religious assurance and reinforcement of dominant cultural values. Since one of those values was active usefulness, the expected fruit of conversion, women were propelled into a wide range of activities. But it was not expected that each woman would respond in the same way. As Anne Boylan notes, "One could select one's own level and style of commitment to the ideal, whether it be devotion to family and home, teaching Sunday School once a week, engaging in numerous benevolent activities at once, or becoming a full-time missionary."[15]

## The Continuation of Traditional Women's Roles

At the same time that nineteenth-century American women showed fruits of their conversion and culturally assigned religious role in a range of new and expanding activities, challenging the limits of women's sphere, they also continued to provide prosaic but critical behind-the-scenes support for local churches. Supportive work at the local level was shared by women in virtually every Protestant denomination, whether or not they were directly affected by the Second Great Awakening. Such "hidden" roles and work by women involved, of course, church attendance, frequently more faithful than that of men. Women sang in choirs and taught Sunday school classes. They gathered in groups to raise money and to socialize. Whether in the more settled East or on the advancing frontier, women's financial contributions were significant for a church's well-being or even survival; the contributions could also be a way of exercising real if indirect power in churches at a time when few women had the formal power of a vote in congregational organizations. In Julie Roy Jeffrey's study of frontier women, she quotes one minister's tribute, which could surely have been echoed by many others: "As is always the case, in the infancy of Christian efforts, we have been greatly indebted to the ladies of our congregation for material aid. By their sewing society &c. they have furnished fuel and lights and kept up repairs."[16] Sometimes the women responded to clerical or male lay leaders' requests for aid, but sometimes they had their own ideas about what was most needed and where they would provide funding. L. DeAne Lagerquist notes a similar pattern among immigrant Lutherans on the frontier:

> As women were seldom allowed to vote in church meetings, they used their money as a means of making their voices heard. What the women would pay for could be done; what the women wanted they could pay for. Their dollars gave women a way of influencing the decisions of the congregation and the church at large.[17]

Such a system had its limits, to be sure, but these women of independent ideas and resourcefulness were quite willing to go beyond gentle, private influence, shaping their churches by using their power of the purse. As Leonard Sweet concludes,

> Congregations may have left the maintenance of church buildings in the hands of men, but fundraising for new buildings, as well as mission and outreach, was largely left to the women. For small, struggling churches, the presence of a women's society often made the difference between life and death, between surviving and thriving.[18]

Women's attendance and contributions of time and money were needed even by long-established churches in the East, but on the frontier, women also played a critical if unsung role in establishing churches and maintaining a reasonably continuous religious life when male clergy were scarce. They led prayers or read sermons when a missionary preacher or itinerant was unavailable; they taught the Sunday schools whether a male minister was there or not.[19] Joan Gundersen's detailed study of a frontier Episcopal parish in Minnesota reveals a determined group of women who used their financial resources, control of social opportunities, and persuasion to establish and shape the church, all the while maintaining a public front of male leadership. The Ladies Social Circle formed with the goal of founding a parish and raised funds by providing some of the few social occasions available in frontier Northfield. Men could and did attend their meetings, as "honorary members (at double the women's dues)," but only women could "vote, conduct meetings, and hold office."[20] The vestry, of course, was all male, though not very active, and the women recruited a man as token head of their fund drive, but a contest between the women and the Seabury Mission under Bishop Whipple over the site where a church would be built suggests how much real power the women had. All Saints Church rose, not on the site selected and purchased by the male hierarchy, but on the lot the women wanted. The experience of All Saints, where women effectively began and ran the parish for its first few decades, may not have been universal, but neither was it unique.[21]

To recognize the importance of women's activities in the ongoing life of local churches is not to slight the contribution of male leadership, especially as ministers and missionaries. The women themselves highly valued the regular services and preaching of a minister. Although some male church leaders opposed any form of women's organization as at best frivolous and at worst a disruption of a God-given natural order,[22] most recognized, if sometimes condescendingly, the real worth of what the women did. Thus traditional church histories with their dominant male, clerical focus need to be balanced with an awareness of the very real, if often prosaic, contributions of church women. Female activities were important to the churches and to the women themselves, both because they filled women's spiritual needs and because church-related women's groups often functioned as a bridge between the domestic and public spheres. In their church groups, women practiced basic but crucial skills like public speaking and writing. They learned how to organize a group; run a meeting and keep the group's records; raise, account for, and spend their own money. They found broader interests in the world outside their homes. Eventually, many of these women would move on to other causes and activities—and not always ones that were as unarguably respectable and appropriate for women from a nineteenth-century cultural perspective as church work was.

## The Minister's Wife

Similarly neglected by traditional church histories yet critical in the lives of churches was another female figure: the minister's wife. In his study of the minister's wife in nineteenth-century America, Leonard Sweet concludes that marriage to a minister was "one of the most coveted careers available to American women."[23] In that setting, she moved beyond earlier Protestant models of "the Companion" or "the Sacrificer" to become a genuine "Assistant" or even "Partner" in her husband's ministry, particularly in a parallel leadership role as the head of the women's groups and activities in the church.[24] The most famous ministers' wives of the era, like Elizabeth Atkinson Finney and Catherine Booth, were publicly active alongside their husbands in promoting revivals and new forms of evangelical religion, gaining widespread recognition and appreciation for their efforts at the time (though less often remembered by subsequent historians.) But scores of other ministers' wives played equally active and crucial roles at a local level. It was they who frequently took the lead in founding and running various women's groups, from prayer societies, maternal associations, and missionary societies, to groups promoting a range of charitable and benevolent causes. They functioned as effective pastors by visiting potential converts, the sick and bereaved, and other church members. Such calls were time-consuming and purposive, not simple social occasions for women with too much leisure, and indeed, as Sweet concludes, "Women came to dominate evangelistic, pastoral, and social visitation because of clerical default."[25]

There were, of course, drawbacks to the role of minister's wife. Congregations came to see them as automatic, unpaid labor; they were often expected to set a perfect example of female piety, industry and modesty, fulfilling church and domestic demands with minimal income, since ministers and their wives were presumed to be above crass material concerns. Not every minister's wife in the nineteenth century enjoyed the position or could maintain the idealistic hopes with which she began. Some, surely, resented congregational assumptions that they would take the lead in every church-related female activity, regardless of personal inclinations or talents, or other demands upon them. Nevertheless, the position as a minister's wife was actively sought and welcomed by many young women as a religious vocation, a way to translate their faith into action, to serve God and the church. They could draw upon a certain prestige as wife of the minister to speak or pray in public and to lead women's groups. They could also, usually, count on a level of husbandly support for their religious interest and activities that many other women could not. While few of them openly challenged the theories of female subordination or separate spheres, many in fact expanded through their own actions ideas of what women could appropriately do.[26]

The Second Great Awakening in America confirmed the ability of churches to survive and grow on a voluntary basis. Significant numbers of Americans experienced conversion and joined the churches—but they did not stop there, for it was assumed that one's conversion had results not only in eternal salvation but also in temporal fruits. In America, such fruits most commonly took the form of associations, which attracted both men and women. Some societies had an obvious, specifically religious function, like Bible and tract societies, or continued traditional forms of charity. Others turned their attention to broad "moral" concerns through an explosion of reform groups in the first half of the nineteenth century. Women's participation in these reforms will be traced in a subsequent chapter, but their concern, like male reformers', was often rooted in the Awakening's revivals. First, however, we will trace women's participation in the foreign missionary movement, an extraordinarily popular cause that cut across denominational and geographical lines. The missionary crusade combined evangelical activity with moral concerns and, indeed, underlines the artificiality of making too sharp a distinction between religion and humanitarianism in nineteenth-century America.

# 8
# *The Foreign Missionary Movement*

In October of 1800, a small group of Baptist and Congregational women, led by Mary Webb, met to found the Boston Female Society for Missionary Purposes and began a movement that, by the end of the century, would involve more women than "all areas of the social reform and women's rights movement combined."[1] Foreign missions achieved that astonishing scope because they cut across denominational and geographical lines; by the dawn of the twentieth century, virtually every Protestant group in America supported some form of women's missionary society.

## Early Groundwork in the Missionary Movement

The earliest women's missionary groups arose in the context of the Second Great Awakening along with the prayer circles and maternal associations that provided organized female outlets for religious activity, and they often combined interest in both "home" and "foreign" missions as the fruit of conversion. Over the course of the century, some Protestant women's groups continued to link home and foreign missions, but more typically, women's support for evangelization of the "heathen" overseas was channelled through distinctive foreign missionary societies. The women's missionary movement of the nineteenth century increased the practical and public skills of the women involved, developed their global interests and ties, gave them a power base in the churches, and provided a distinctive Protestant religious vocation for women. Before the Civil War, women's interest in foreign missions was concentrated primarily in the Northeast among those denominations most immediately affected by the Second Great Awakening. The women usually worked through and under male boards, and most women in the field were the wives of male missionaries. In the second half of the century, however, women's missionary activity increased dramatically both in sheer numbers and in geographical and denominational range. Separate women's boards were formed at the regional and national levels, and significant numbers of single women joined their married sisters overseas.

Mary Webb's Boston Female Society for Missionary Purposes was soon followed by other small, local groups. Their most popular form was the "cent" or "mite" society: women who pledged to give, out of their own, often limited means, a cent a week for the cause of foreign missions, intentionally evoking the biblical precedent of the widow's mite. It was a highly effective tactic, for it allowed almost every woman to feel she could make a difference and also raised substantial sums. Male religious leaders and missionary boards generally welcomed the money and approved of such evidence of female piety, but they still had reservations about women engaging in inappropriately independent activity. The women soothed and reassured them that no challenge to male headship was intended and that their fund-raising would by no means cut into general missionary contributions (which it did not)—and then proceeded with the interests and activities that would ultimately result in precisely the unwomanly behavior the men feared. In their small groups, the women learned how to run meetings, keep records, and raise money. To spread the word on missionary needs and organizational techniques among local societies, the women sent representatives, wrote letters, and published appeals in missionary journals. The female societies also promoted education about missions and the lands to which their hard-earned mites would go to spread the gospel. Thus even in the first phase of women's participation in foreign missions, when no serious challenge to male control was raised, the seeds of organizational skills and education were sown. As R. Pierce Beaver concludes:

> Given the lack of cultivation from the headquarters of the boards and societies, the want of integration into mutually sustaining national and regional organizations, the denial of representation and influence in the making of missionary policy, and even the denial of women's right to lead and speak in their own meetings in some instances, it appears most remarkable that the women persisted in raising funds, praying, stimulating general interest, and educating themselves and their children. What kept the women going decade after decade . . . is the role the missionary wives were playing in the enterprise overseas.[2]

## Missionary Wives

From its earliest days, the American Board of Commissioners for Foreign Missions (ABCFM) not only sent wives with their male missionaries, but publicly justified its reasons for doing so. The male missionary needed a wife for himself and for the example he would set for those to whom he preached. Thus the first and most important responsibility of the missionary wife was to comfort, help, and support her husband so that he could concentrate on his work of evangelism. Second, while the husband was, of course, to be head of the family, the missionary wife was more immediately involved in establishing and overseeing the Christian family household that would serve as an example to the "heathen." Finally, she had a role, as time permitted, to work with and teach the native women and children, her more direct missionary calling.

Not only did women in the missionary societies agree with the male boards about the value of the missionary wife, they also identified with her, and with no one more than Ann Hasseltine Judson, one of the first and quite possibly the most famous and revered missionary wife of the nineteenth century. Born in 1789, Ann Hasseltine was a typical daughter of Puritan New England in her roots, in her conversion in 1806 while attending Bradford Academy and her subsequently joining the Congregational church, and in her early career as a teacher. But when she agreed to marry Adoniram Judson and accompany him onto the foreign mission field, her life took a dramatic turn. Shortly after their marriage in 1812, they set sail for the Orient with another young missionary couple, Harriet and Samuel Newell. During that voyage, Ann and Adoniram became convinced through their Bible study that Christians should be baptized as adults, not infants, a decision that was surely a serious theological issue for them and that had major repercussions for their sponsoring denominational boards, but that had little impact on Ann's broad influence and appeal for Protestant women engaged in the cause of foreign missions.

Tensions with the British at their original destination in India led the Judsons to establish their mission station in Burma, where both plunged into language study. While Adoniram worked on a mammoth project of Bible translation and corresponded with the mission boards on official business, Ann fulfilled a direct missionary calling by writing short tracts and catechisms and teaching the women. She also wrote letters home to be published in missionary journals, which had an enormous influence on American women in their combination of the familiar and the exotic. On the one hand, her readers could identify with her piety and her sorrow at the loss of an infant son, an all-too-familiar experience; on the other hand, Ann described a culture and customs that were utterly foreign to her readers and evoked their sympathy and renewed efforts on behalf of the women. She was convinced that non-Christian women not only faced the perils of eternal damnation, but also that their pitiful condition in this world was largely due to the absence of Christian values and respect for womanhood.

Health problems forced Ann to return to the United States in 1822, and during her recuperation she continued to spread and popularize the missionary cause in her speaking and writing. In 1823 she rejoined Adoniram in Burma, but a year later they were caught in the British-Burmese War, Adoniram was imprisoned, and Ann spent the next two years alternately ministering to her husband and his fellow missionary-prisoners and appealing to and bribing Burmese officials. The hardships that she endured and her courage and enterprise came out later, but at the time, a blackout on news intensified concern at home for the heroic missionaries and their fate. Ann and Adoniram both survived, and when the war ended, they reestablished their mission, but Ann's health had been broken and she died on October 24, 1826, followed a few months later by the daughter she had borne during the Judsons' ordeal. Ann's death only increased her already considerable fame and status as a heroine, now a martyr to the cause of Christian missions. Within three years of her death, James D. Knowles published her biography, based heavily on her own writings. It was frequently reprinted, and numerous other accounts of her life continued to appear throughout the nineteenth century, making her an extraordinarily well-known figure and dramatically increasing interest and support for foreign missions among Protestant women in America.[3] The news sent home by missionary wives not only enlivened and encouraged local missionary societies in their work, it also served as an important means of recruiting young women to follow their example.

A particularly fertile field for such recruitment was found among young women taking advantage of expanding educational opportunities for women in the first half of the nineteenth century at schools like Mount Holyoke. The history of Mount Holyoke in its first decade demonstrates clearly the close interrelationship of evangelical religion, teaching, and foreign missions. Mary Lyon is best remembered, and justly so, for her contribution to women's education by founding Mount Holyoke, but she was herself personally pious and fostered frequent revivals among her students. She insisted that female education had a broader purpose than pure self-cultivation. (We need not doubt Lyon's sincerity in noting that her tactics were also eminently practical. She would have had far less success in raising money had she not emphasized the good that educated women would do for their families and their society within their culturally acceptable roles.) Young educated women often became teachers, a "natural" extension of their maternal instincts and qualities of patience and nurturance (and they were far cheaper to employ than their male peers), and even if they married after a few years, their skills would transfer to their next role as mothers. But Mary Lyon was also deeply committed to the cause of foreign missions. As Elizabeth Alden Green concludes, "Next to the Seminary itself, this was the cause closest to Mary Lyon's heart. Foreign missionaries had been her particular heroes since childhood."[4] Lyon contributed generously to the cause herself and encouraged her students and teachers to do so as well in periodic missionary subscriptions, paralleling the methods and motivations of the female "cent" societies. Consequently, a disproportionately high number of Mount Holyoke students and teachers in the 1840s married missionaries and left for the field, often as a result of on-campus visits and recruitment by missionaries. The young women's response to a challenge that combined adventure and self-sacrificing idealism nearly always meant marriage to a missionary, and Mount Holyoke by no means discouraged a little matchmaking among suitable partners for the sake of the cause. Indeed, Mary Lyon's own niece Lucy Lyon, a teacher at Mount Holyoke before she left for China, felt compelled to protest to a friend, "I did not accept [Edward Lord's] hand *merely* because he was to be a missionary."[5]

Some of these missionary wives died fairly soon after they reached their station and were extolled as martyrs in the grand cause. Others spent their lives in the field. Still others followed several careers in a lifetime, like Susan Tolman, who graduated from Mount Holyoke in 1845, taught there until 1848 when she married Cyrus Mills, and served with him in China and Hawaii for fifteen years, after which Susan and Cyrus went to California and founded Mills College.

The vast majority of missionary wives undoubtedly set out with high hopes and dedication, and while some were successful, others were not. Some suffered mental or physical breakdowns, and even for many who retained their health and sanity, the realities of mission life fell short of their idealistic dreams and expectations of service. The greatest obstacle was sheer time. The missionary wife (known as an "assistant") who pictured herself working alongside her husband discovered that, once children began to arrive, she had little time and energy for evangelism or service to native women, since of course the full responsibility for running the household and caring for the children fell on her shoulders. Those same children sometimes presented her with a cultural dilemma as well. How could she prevent her sons and daughters from being influenced by the "impure" and immoral practices and ideas of the natives? Only by her own constant supervision, which then left her little time to convert and uplift those same natives. As Jane Hunter notes of missions in China, "women worked hard to recreate an American home environment, to educate their children according to American standards, and to keep them as free as possible from the opportunities, as well as the corruptions, of their Chinese surroundings."[6] Some American women were more open to different cultures than others and thus experienced less tension between their perceived duties as mothers and as missionaries, but rare indeed was the missionary for whom the obvious "superiority" of American, Christian ways was not a given. And even a relatively greater openness to a foreign culture and its influence did not obviate the real, practical problem of time.

It was thus clear after a few years of experience that the direct work of many missionary wives for the cause would be sporadic or limited, however dedicated they were. It was also evident that the effectiveness and even access of male missionaries to native women was severely restricted by time and cultural mores. Finally, most American Protestants, especially women, became convinced that no foreign nation could be Christianized if the women and therefore the home, that crucial building block of a Christian society, were not reached. But the obvious solution of sending single women as missionaries to devote full time to the service ran into a wall of male opposition. To most male leaders, it was inconceivable that a woman could sustain the hardships of travel, residence, and work in an "uncivilized" land without the protection and guidance of a husband, and if one misguidedly believed that she could, then her qualities of true womanliness were surely suspect. Exceptions might be made for a single woman who could travel and live with a married couple, but such exceptions were reluctantly and rarely made. Helen Barrett Montgomery in her classic overview of the American women's missionary movement tells the story of the Reverend David Abeel, an American missionary in China, who in 1834 stopped in England on his way home to plead for single women missionaries. A British society was formed, but when Abeel preached the same message in the United States, while a few women responded positively, "[t]he innovation was so stoutly resisted by the denominational Boards that at their urgent request the new organization was given up and woman's work for woman in heathen lands postponed for thirty years or more."[7]

## Single Women

Nevertheless, there were a number of women, unmarried or widowed, who became missionaries before the Civil War. Charlotte White, a widow, was in 1815 the first single woman sent overseas by the ABCFM, but much to the board's relief, she married a missionary before she even got to Burma. Betsy Stockton, a black woman, was sent to Hawaii in 1823 as a "domestic assistant" and conducted a school there for two years. Others followed, steadily if not rapidly. Some were quite successful and stayed in the field for many years. One of these was Fidelia Fiske, who shared with many missionary wives a background at Mount Holyoke but who was atypical in being single. Responding to a missionary appeal for teachers at a seminary in Oroomiah in Persia, Fiske sailed in 1843 and over the next fifteen years built a successful boarding school for girls. Because of health problems, she returned to Mount Holyoke in 1858 and spent the last six years of her life working with students there and promoting the cause of missions through visits and lectures.

Other single women missionaries lasted only a brief time at their destinations before dying, leaving, or marrying. Most were connected with a missionary family for the sake of protection and propriety (often with a result unintended by the mission boards, as the single woman was perceived by native people as the missionary's second wife!), and most were involved with teaching women or children and visiting women in their homes, since these functions were regarded as appropriate for women and could not easily be fulfilled by men. But there were even exceptions among the exceptions: single women who worked alone and engaged in the "male" work of evangelizing both sexes and organizing churches, like Eleanor Macomber, who worked among the Karens in Burma, and Mary Sharp, who worked mainly with men of the Kroo tribe near Monrovia.

Sometimes, too, a missionary wife became single through the death of her husband after she had arrived in a foreign land, and she continued their work on her own as a widow. Such was the case of the second Mrs. Judson, Sarah Boardman. She began her missionary career in the conventional fashion, by marrying a male missionary, and the two set out for Burma in 1825. The same Burmese War that was the arena for Ann Judson's heroic endeavors delayed the Boardmans' mission activity, but eventually they began work in the rural areas among the Karen tribe. When George Boardman died in 1831, his widow determined to carry on his work of evangelism, as well as hers of teaching, which she did until 1834, when she married fellow missionary Adoniram Judson. Her missionary career as wife, widow, and then wife was, like Ann Judson's, a popular one with American supporters of missions and proof that women could work on their own when called upon to do so.

Thus in the decades before the Civil War, American women laid important groundwork in the missionary movement. A substantial number entered the field despite all obstacles as full-time, single, career missionaries.[8] More fulfilled their sense of calling as "assistants" to their missionary husbands and sometimes made considerable contributions on their own. Many American Protestant women, inspired by letters and accounts by the women missionaries, organized, raised funds, and spread the word. But it was the last four decades of the nineteenth century that saw a real explosion of women's missionary activity, both at home and abroad. When Helen Barrett Montgomery celebrated "Fifty Years of Woman's Work in Foreign Missions" in 1910, she was by no means ignoring the pioneer societies and missionaries, but she recognized the organization of the Woman's Union Missionary Society in 1861 as the movement's "coming of age." Soon after the Civil War, other women followed this example by forming separate women's boards or auxiliaries in the denominational bodies.

## The Formation of Separate Women's Organizations

What prompted this shift in structure and activity and the creation of separate women's boards? Some of the motives had been building for years. In general, male boards liked the money that the women raised but resisted anything more than token representation of women in their deliberations. It was a power issue: Women wanted more say in how the money they raised was spent—who was sent where and to do what. Moreover, the women resented the male boards' refusal to provide adequate financial support for the single women missionaries they did send, especially compared to the salaries of single men.[9] Second, there was a broad perception among the women that the male boards and missionaries neglected foreign women and their needs in favor of more traditionally male activities like founding churches, preaching, and trying to reach the native men. The women had no quarrel with the value of these male concerns, but they felt strongly that reaching and serving foreign women was at least as important a part of the work. They believed that work with women could be best done by women for practical, cultural reasons, and they identified with their "heathen" sisters and their needs in this world as well as the next. In short, the women were perfectly willing to accept a division of labor, as long as they had the resources to fund and control their own work.

Developments in women's education contributed to the change. As noted above, new institutions like Mount Holyoke and its less famous sisters produced a significant number of women who entered the mission field, and even more who stayed home but retained a strong interest in supporting the movement. Education also occurred in literally hundreds of small, local mission societies, as women heard speakers, read letters from the field, subscribed to missionary journals, and held study groups on the work and conditions in China or India or Africa or Burma. At a basic level, such study expanded the women's horizons, a not inconsiderable contribution, but the learning had another purpose: the women were expected to act on the basis of that knowledge by prayer, fund-raising, and further dissemination of the message. Furthermore, as teaching expanded as a female career and as a critical element of maternal responsibility in the United States, it seemed obvious that women had a natural function and duty to teach in foreign lands as well. Finally, women's experience in the Civil War acted as an important trigger to the formation of separate women's mission boards. Many women on both sides of the conflict had served as nurses and on the Christian Commission. Many had been forced to manage farms or businesses in their husbands' absence. The women discovered that they could act independently and effectively for a cause, and they did not forget the lesson but turned their skills to the object of evangelization of the world.

The actual form of the women's organizations varied. The earliest, the Women's Union Missionary Society, was ecumenical, while other groups were limited to a particular denomination, like the Congregationalists, who organized in 1868, or the Methodists, in 1869. Some, like Methodists or Quakers, were independent. Others, like the Congregationalists, operated in cooperation with the general (i.e., largely male) denominational board.

Some, like the Episcopalians, were clearly designated as auxiliaries under male control. Yet even in the last case, women were able to develop in fact, if not in theory, a fair degree of power and autonomy to enact policies and in day-to-day activities.[10] Not surprisingly, women's organizations were slower to form and achieve recognition among groups in southern Protestantism or midwestern Lutheranism, and the male opposition was stronger. Southern Methodist women won support for a Woman's Missionary Organization by 1878, and the Southern Baptist women organized in the 1870s and 1880s, but as Beaver comments, "Social conservatism, backed up by some degree of theological argument, restrained the women of the Presbyterian Church in the United States beyond the bounds of reason."[11] They had no denomination-wide organization until 1912! Despite continued male grumblings (and to be fair, with strong support from individual men), the women persisted, gaining respect for their patient tactfulness and their unarguable success.

While there were very real differences among the women's missionary boards, they shared some techniques and ideology. As Montgomery noted in 1910, "Perhaps the most distinctive contribution of the Women's Societies to missionary administration has been their demonstration of the power of small offerings frequently collected from large numbers of contributors."[12] (Men tended to target large gifts.) Not only did the women's approach raise significant sums, it also gave to the many contributors a real sense of pride and ownership in the cause. Montgomery notes the simple and flexible organization of the women's groups as a second source of their success, and points, third, to the women's development of "the light infantry of missionary literature"[13]—leaflets, stories, poems, and inexpensive journals that appealed to women and children. The journals provided field reports, practical tips on organizing, and stories about individual women missionaries, which functioned as a kind of Protestant version of lives of the saints insofar as they were hagiographic in tone and served as inspirational patterns to which readers might aspire. Such literature, with its emphasis on personal stories and concrete conditions, was enormously prolific, popular, and effective. Virtually every women's group had its journal, and the women leaders were not above adding pressure to the journals' intrinsic appeal to swell subscription lists. As a result, the women's magazines throve when other denominational periodicals struggled or required subsidy.[14] And like the women's societies themselves, the journals provided for the women who produced them experience in valuable skills like writing and editing for publication.

Women's missionary literature contributed to a common ideology of the movement. Detailed in its pages in reports from the field were numerous accounts of the deplorable, pitiful condition of "heathen" women. Footbinding in China, suttee in India, and female infanticide were the most dramatic instances of female oppression related with horror to American women, but equal stress was placed on native women's seclusion and subservience to husbands, fathers, and mothers-in-law. Child marriage, polygyny, easy divorce for men, and the helpless condition of divorced, abandoned, or widowed women were deplored. Women's lack of education and of access to health care were detailed to arouse American women's sympathy. The appeal was clearly humanitarian, and if missionaries were guilty of exaggerating the conditions, they did not invent them. American Protestant women then perceived their own situation as far better and their limitations minor by comparison. And they further concluded that the reason for the contrast was, quite simply, Christianity. From their nineteenth-century perspective, only Christianity elevated and enlightened women and sanctified marriage and the home. Thus while the women of the missionary movement were unquestionably and sincerely devoted to evangelization, to saving heathen souls from certain and eternal damnation, they were at least as deeply concerned to bring what they saw as the benefits of Christianity to the earthly lives of foreign women.

The ideology of the women's missionary movement thus existed in symbiotic relationship with the dominant images of women in nineteenth-century America. As the vast majority of white Protestant women in America embraced some version of the cult of True Womanhood or Republican Motherhood, they felt it to be both a privilege and a responsibility to extend their roles and values to those foreign women who, it seemed to them, were the victims of oppression and degradation. Having accepted their own role as guardians of home, piety, and virtue, they argued that no heathen nation could be Christianized without a firm basis in Christian homes, and American cultural ideology conceded that these were women's spheres. Hence, heathen women must be reached, and reached by women missionaries sent by American women. As an article in *The Heathen Woman's Friend* put it in 1869, "Christian civilization does little for a nation until it has lifted woman from the condition of a thing to the dignity of a sister and a wife. You cannot evangelize a country until you convert the women."[15]

## Field Work

This ideological connection of women and Christianity not only provided commonality for the movement, it also shaped women's missionary work in the field. Nevertheless, it is important not to draw too sharp a distinction between "spiritual" and "humanitarian" concerns either as motivation for American women missionaries or as activities in foreign lands. During the nineteenth century and into the early twentieth century, there was significant diversity among missionary women, and their reasons for going were also diverse.

## Evangelism

Virtually all women missionaries shared with other American Christians sincere convictions that without conversion, "heathen" men and women would be damned, that the soul of every person was equally valuable in the eyes of God, and that they, as Christians, had a duty to spread the gospel. Most felt a clear and particular call from God to the work, whether that call came in a dramatic moment or developed gradually but firmly over a period of time. For single women especially, missionary work was an avenue to a full-time religious career, when preaching and ordination were effectively closed to Protestant women in America, but without the divided loyalties and responsibilities of the missionary wife. In that sense, becoming a missionary functioned for Protestant women as the alternative of a religious vocation did for Roman Catholics. Humanitarian motives were widely significant, especially as stories of women's oppression were returned from the field or experienced firsthand by the missionaries themselves. Finally, the sheer sense of adventure held out by foreign missionary work, as well as the possibility that a woman could do something significant with her life and use her skills to the fullest in what was often called a "larger life," cannot be ignored as motivations.

Women's missionary activity combined "spiritual" and "humanitarian" concerns in different proportions, and few would have viewed them as antithetical. In the broadest sense, there was a shift over the century from a more narrowly defined evangelism to greater emphasis on "uplifting women,"[16] but even an early pioneer missionary wife like Ann Judson expressed concern for the conditions of foreign women without the influence of Christianity, and the great majority of later missionaries saw in their educational or medical work opportunities for evangelism.

Evangelism was a basic activity for female as well as male missionaries. A few women engaged in open, formal, direct evangelism like that done by the men, preaching and establishing churches, but they were rare and had to endure strong opposition. One of the most famous was Charlotte Diggs "Lottie" Moon, who would become something of a Southern Baptist saint. Born in an old Virginia family in 1840, she helped her mother run the family plantation during the war and taught in southern schools afterward, but in 1873 she went to China to a Southern Baptist mission. During the rest of that decade she learned the language and taught in the mission schools of Tengchow, but she became frustrated with city life and the narrow scope of her teaching. She turned instead for the next decade to the more direct evangelism of itinerating in small, rural villages of Shantung Province, founding a church in Pingtu. After a furlough home, she returned to Tengchow, working there until her death in 1912.[17]

Much more frequently, women missionaries' evangelistic efforts were personal, informal, or indirect, focused on foreign women. Women missionaries had some access to these foreign women, when male missionaries did not, though even women missionaries faced cultural and linguistic barriers that limited their effectiveness. One branch of their evangelism came to be called "zenana" work, a Hindu term that was used popularly by missionaries for all forms of female seclusion. While women's boards supported and women missionaries attempted such personal evangelism throughout the movement, it was both slow and labor-intensive, and thus not very "cost effective," although there were always hopes that reaching upper-class women had a potential for broader impact. The other focus for female evangelism was poor women, to whom access was sometimes easier and for whom Christianity could represent material help as well as (or at times, more than) spiritual benefits.

## Education

More typically, evangelism was furthered along with or through education, the most widespread and effective form of women's missionary activity, and one that seemed eminently compatible with current American cultural and religious ideology. On the one hand, virtually all Protestant missionaries placed a high value on basic literacy because reading the Bible was so central to their understanding of Christianity. On the other hand, American society widely accepted the teaching of children as a natural role and duty for women. Thus women missionaries, married and single, founded and taught in day schools for local children. Even such basic educational endeavors were complicated by the need to learn the language and the problems of attracting pupils on a sustained basis, but the hope was that children so reached might influence their families and be more open to conversion as adults. Of course the Bible (or parts of it) in the appropriate native tongue was a basic text, but the missionary teachers also wrote and used brief, simple catechisms and stories to encourage basic literacy while making religious and moral points. Women founded boarding schools, especially for girls, in the hopes that more sustained and pervasive influence of the teachers would result in more effective evangelism and the formation of "Christian character." In both cases, day schools and boarding schools, instruction in Christianity and literacy was central, but the schools usually provided additional training in domestic skills and exposure to subjects like arithmetic or geography. The boarding schools, for obvious reasons, could provide a more extended curriculum, and over time the schools came to include forms of teacher or medical training for young native women, who could in turn function in roles similar to those of the American missionary women. Some schools, as well as individual women missionaries, became involved in training native "Bible women" as further agents of Christianization.

While the largest number of American women missionaries were involved in educational activities, their degree of success varied widely. Some made little impact, hindered by linguistic and personal inadequacies and cultural resistance, and they experienced a high degree of frustration. Others failed to realize the high hopes and expectations for dramatic change with which they began but took satisfaction in modest achievements. And a few, like Isabella Thoburn, were markedly successful and saw schools they founded and nurtured thrive on a reasonably permanent basis. Born in 1840, Isabella Thoburn had considerable teaching experience in the United States before she was sent to India in 1869 by the newly formed Methodist Women's Foreign Missionary Society as one of its first two missionaries. From 1869 until her death in 1901, she returned to America on three furloughs to regain her health and promote the missionary cause, but she spent the rest of her life in India. In 1870, she started a day school for girls in Lucknow. The next year she moved it to Lal Bagh (Ruby Garden), an estate purchased by the Methodists from a government official, and added a boarding school. In 1874, she also took on the leadership of a girls' school in Cawnpore, and in the meantime, she continued to teach classes for poor girls and to supervise the training of "Bible women." The Lal Bagh school expanded, adding a department for teacher training and becoming first Girls High School and finally the Lucknow Women's College.

## Health Care

The third major focus of women's missionary activity was health care, again with combined evangelistic and humanitarian goals. Offering rudimentary health care and instruction in hygiene to native women from the early days of the movement was clearly perceived by the missionaries as another way to attract attention for evangelism, but it was also a response to genuine need. Moreover, it was clear that cultural mores restricted the care male missionary doctors could offer to native women (even if they had the time), and thus female physicians were needed. The missionary "call" of Ida Scudder, who worked in India in the first decades of the twentieth century, provided an unusually dramatic example of the need. The daughter and grandaughter of medical missionaries herself, she was determined not to follow in their footsteps until the night that three men—a Brahmin, a Muslim, and another high-caste Hindu—sought help from the Scudders for their wives in difficult labor. Ida was willing to aid her physician-father but not confident about working alone. None of the men, however, would accept a male doctor in those circumstances, and all three women died. Ida therefore returned to the United States for training in order to become a medical missionary to India.[18] Thus, the growing availability of medical training for women in the United States and the founding of women's missionary boards willing to send and support female physicians in the field added a new missionary role for women. Isabella Thoburn, a teacher discussed above, was one of the first two women sent abroad by the Methodist women in 1869; the other was a newly trained physician, Clara Swain. By the end of the century, she had practiced medicine among Indian women, trained other women as doctors and nurses, founded in 1874 the first hospital for women in India, and served as physician for the women and children of the royal family, a position she used to promote better health care and conditions for Indian women and children. Few female missionary physicians achieved the fame or impressive accomplishments of a Clara Swain or an Ida Scudder, but they did make important contributions of a humanitarian nature, and most also perceived themselves as evangelists. They operated dispensaries and hospitals, and they trained some native nurses and physicians to extend the scope of health care. If they could never begin to meet the full need of the countries in which they served, they at least made a difference for a considerable number of people. They were supported and honored by American women in the missionary movement, and some discovered a professional bonus in the work. "The woman doctor found a far more interesting practice, an opportunity to perform operations, to study rare diseases, and to escape a professional life as a poorly paid listener to female complaints, her probable lot had she remained at home."[19]

## The Significance of the Women's Missionary Movement

Recent research has amply demonstrated the historical importance of the nineteenth-century women's missionary movement in the stories of American religion and American women, and it has also shown that the movement involved genuine diversity in its programs and personnel, as well as common techniques and ideologies. Still, there are key questions about its significance and impact. First, were American women missionaries agents of cultural imperialism, perhaps even more than men? Second, how was the women's missionary movement related to the cause of women's rights and feminism in nineteenth-century America? Third, what impact did American women missionaries have on the women of other lands; did they achieve their goals?

### Cultural Imperialism

Undoubtedly American missionaries, including women, were agents of cultural imperialism, and some scholars have argued that the women, given the nature of their work and focus, were even more effective (or guilty) than men. As Shirley S. Garrett notes:

> It is fair to say that basic education, practical training, moral guidance and gymnastics in the open air at an early hour pervaded the curricula of mission schools in the late nineteenth century, reflecting the contemporary values of middle-class America. Such aims appeared vastly less important than economic imperialism or gunboat diplomacy. Yet they struck at the nerve endings of society, for behind this genteel orientation was a philosophy that collided with the values of feminine upbringing in Asian societies.[20]

But to deal with the question of cultural imperialism, we must deal with different levels or types of influence pursued by women missionaries.

Much missionary literature focused on certain blatant abuses of women from a humanitarian perspective, in particular, suttee in India, footbinding in China, and female infanticide. The practices did exist and the missionaries were genuinely appalled at such basic violations of human rights, although missionaries tended to exaggerate their incidence, even if subconsciously, to make their point and elicit American support for missions. And American Christian missionaries made a substantial contribution toward legal restrictions and practical limitations on such practices. Nevertheless, Christian missionaries tended to overlook or slight indigenous efforts for reform, especially in their reports home. In part, this may have been a practical tactic, but it was also due to the missionaries' blindness to resources *within* an indigenous religious tradition for reform of such abuses, based on the missionaries' general dismissal of these traditions as nothing but unenlightened paganism and their conviction that *only* Christianity promoted true respect and uplift for women.[21] This missionary blindness was unfortunate and unfair; it was also understandable. Very few nineteenth-century Christians could so transcend their historical context as to question the absolute truth and superiority of Christianity, especially if by doing so, they seemed to undercut the whole purpose of their missionary work and the very real dedication and sacrifice it demanded.

Second, the missionaries wanted to impress upon the societies to which they came certain broad moral and cultural values. For women missionaries, this related in particular to the institution of marriage and the family: monogamy, family structure, and child-rearing practices, including female education. Not only did they assume the superior morality of middle-class, Protestant American standards and hence have little tolerance for alternative cultural arrangements, it was that very domestic ideology that formed the core of their distinctive missionary calling as women. There is no question that American Protestant women were cultural imperialists at this level, but it is more difficult to try to judge their assumptions and activities from some cross-cultural, normative perspective. Is monogamy an absolute good, or is it culturally relative? Is polygyny socially functional in some societies? Are there situations where wives and widows clearly suffer in variant cultural patterns set for family life by particular religious or cultural systems? Should girls as well as boys have access to education? If so, of what type? How does female education enhance or hinder girls' lives in the culture or tradition in which they must live? American women missionaries lost little sleep over such questions, since to them the answers were clear. The twentieth century observer, however, may find it harder to draw a line between desirable goals of cultural sensitivity and acceptance, on the one hand, and encouragement of basic human rights and dignity, on the other.

Finally, American missionaries were often cultural imperialists with regard to artifacts and social customs like dress. Some missionaries appeared to assume that certain styles of Western music, dress, or manners were indispensable parts of a Christian gospel that was indistinguishable from Western civilization. In retrospect, this level of cultural imperialism on the part of American missionaries, along with an obliviousness to alternative forms of culture and civilization, is the least defensible and most parochial. Yet it was also the type of cultural imperialism most likely to be modified, at least for those persons who stayed on a mission station for many years. As Barbara Welter concludes:

> The ethnocentric attitude and national and religious absolutism of [American missionaries] cannot be denied. In almost every case, however, if they remained in the field any length of time, there was identification with and sympathy for some aspects of the host culture. Missionaries were far more sensitive to the societies in which they worked than is generally believed.[22]

And some greater cultural sensitivity filtered back to the women supporters of the movement in small but significant ways, such as when the title of the Methodist women's missionary journal was changed in 1896 from *The Heathen Woman's Friend* to *Woman's Missionary Friend.*

Regardless of different levels and degrees of cultural imperialism, it was clearly a part of the missionary movement and thus posed a real dilemma for the potential convert to Christianity. Too often, such a person had to choose between the new religion and his or her own tradition or culture. Some accepted Christianity, perhaps because they were convinced of its superiority or they had little to lose, but for others the price of cultural repudiation was too high. And some converts were able to keep both, to adapt selectively from the Christianity and Western culture offered by the missionaries and still to keep ties with their own cultural traditions and identity. Just as there were differences among the missionaries' imposition of cultural imperialism, so there were differences in its effect, and thus the fairest assessment lies somewhere between the hagiography of the early missionary historians and the blanket, cynical condemnation of the movement's severest critics.

## Women's Rights and Feminism

A second key question concerns the relationship of the women's missionary movement to women's rights and feminism in nineteenth-century America. A number of scholars have argued that the women's missionary movement actually retarded the cause of women's rights at home by ignoring or even repudiating its goals and tactics. With rare exceptions, women whose central concern was missions did not openly support woman suffrage or press for equal leadership with men in the churches. This may have been, in part, a tactical necessity: In order to get anywhere, particularly in more conservative denominations or areas of the country like the South, women had to assure a fearful male leadership that women's missionary organizations were not the first step toward "radical" feminism and women's rights. Public concessions to male fears did not, however, mean the women were above using social expectations to advance their cause. Elaine Magalis tells the story of a Methodist women's missionary meeting at which a few stubborn male clerical monitors had to be put out by a policeman so the women could respect the conventions and not address a mixed audience. "Later Mrs. Butler had an argument with Dr. Durbin . . . about the meeting. A collection had been taken, even though the women had promised to refrain from raising funds at public assemblies. Mrs. Butler asserted, presumably with a straight face, that the meeting was not public since no men had been present."[23] Yet the disclaimer of interest in women's rights was not simply a political tactic, for many of the women themselves opposed what they perceived as radical and unwomanly demands. A widespread image of the women's rights movement, however unfair, was of women, loud and strident in their public posture, selfishly concerned with their own advancement to the detriment of husband, children, and less fortunate neighbors. It was that image of "women's rights" that Elvira Yockey, a founder and leader of women's missionary work in the Reformed Church, repudiated in an address at the women's triennial meeting:

> The unwomanly aggressiveness which some feared was entirely absent. There was no spirit of self seeking, no effort to adopt masculine methods, or usurp masculine prerogative, but only an intensely earnest desire to have some part in the evangelization of the world. This earnestness, as is usually the case in the best type of womanhood, went hand in hand with a persistence that admitted no denial.[24]

The women of the missionary movement were frightened of being associated with that "radical" image. Undoubtedly they had internalized to some degree the cult of True Womanhood or an Evangelical Womanhood that presumed women are normatively and naturally self-sacrificing, and thus they found it difficult to proclaim publically or perhaps even to recognize in themselves legitimate ambition and desire for self-fulfillment. Perhaps they were also insisting, indirectly, that women's traditional roles were valuable and valid, not activities to be despised or repudiated.

Those who see tension between the women's missionary movement and women's rights not only cite direct opposition, however, but also point to deflection of nineteenth-century women's energy from women's rights to missions and to the underlying ideology of women's missions as significant. Women's work for women was, after all, predicated on two assumptions: first, that women are naturally suited to the domestic roles of creating a Christian home and nurturing children and so influence society profoundly but indirectly; second, that American women are far better off than their "heathen" sisters because of Christianity's purported respect for womanhood. That perceived contrast meant that many women in the missionary movement failed to see much to criticize in their own lives and society. Joan Brumberg makes this argument:

> Materials geared to developing women's overall conception of the emancipatory nature of Christianity versus the oppressions of the ethnic religions were pervasive. . . . Having established an angle of double-vision, the mass of American women came to use cross-cultural information to support rather than challenge gender and family arrangement in their own country . . . [and hence were] generally skeptical, if not downright hostile, to the emergence of an indigenous feminist political movement and its critique of sexual subordination at home. Rather than examine their own social relations, the bulk of American Protestant women sought to define themselves by what they were not.[25]

Or as Marjorie King concludes more succinctly, "Missionary women exported femininity, not feminism."[26] There were real ideological tensions between those proponents of women's rights whose basic premise was that men and women are equal as persons and should therefore have equal rights and opportunities in society, and those nineteenth century women, many of whom supported foreign missions, who accepted a gender-based division of spheres and roles.

Thus there is much truth in the charge that the women's missionary movement failed to give direct support to issues of women's rights like suffrage and deflected women's concern from the United States scene by accepting cultural roles and contrasting their status with the greater oppression of women in other lands. That assessment, however, is too one-sided. In part, the problem is rooted in how one defines feminism. If it is to include only direct and immediate challenge to male prerogatives, clearly "stepping out of woman's place," then the missionary movement was conservative, not feminist, despite the occasional challenges of women missionaries on the field who demanded voice and vote in meetings of the missionary boards there. But if one includes what has been called "soft" feminism, stepping out of women's roles by both accepting and enlarging them, then the contribution of women in the foreign missionary movement is a significant and complementary one for "women's rights." Women at home gained valuable experience in skills of organization, administration, fund-raising, speaking, and writing. Their women's boards gave them an important power base in the churches. The example of women missionaries who functioned as ministers on the field in everything but name would be used as a pragmatic argument in the fight for ordination. While not all women missionaries were either happy or successful, there were many, especially single women, for whom a missionary career represented greater global awareness, independence, self-fulfillment, and a self-confident sense that they were doing valuable work in a significant cause. Whatever their rhetoric of selflessness and sacrifice, they were, in fact, finding the enlarged opportunities for women promoted in the women's rights movement.

## The Impact on Women of Other Lands

The third question is perhaps the hardest to answer: What impact did the women missionaries have on women in foreign lands? Certainly the women of the nineteenth-century American missionary movement did not achieve their stated goals on a large scale; they neither evangelized the world nor uplifted Asian and African womanhood through Christianity. They did achieve their goal and convert some women who became part of the small Christian churches in countries like India or China, and if those churches made little impact on the religion of such nations as a whole, they were nonetheless meaningful for the individuals involved in them. American missionaries contributed to ending or limiting practices like footbinding, suttee, and female infanticide, even if they themselves took too much credit for these reforms. They established schools, orphanages, clinics, and hospitals that endured and grew, although the institutions proved not to be as effective instruments of evangelism as their founders had intended. The largest area of women's missionary activity, female education, had mixed results, and not always the ones the missionaries hoped for. Many schools were short-lived and ineffectual. Some of the boarding schools especially trained girls in Western ways and for a career in teaching, medicine, or as wives of upper-class, influential men, and a good number of the prominent Asian women of the twentieth century were educated in mission schools. The schools also reached some poorer women. As Shirley Garrett notes, "Female missionary education was to be sharply criticized in the following years and there is certainly much to criticize, but for the very poor women it was a lifeline, possibly not very important to society as a whole but crucial to them."[27]

Some contemporary scholars, when assessing the impact of women's missionary work, stress both the limits of missionary influence and the unintended, "secular" nature of the differences they did make by providing services and alternative female role models.[28] Products of their own class and cultural ideology, the women missionaries reinforced class structures and gender-defined spheres as much as they challenged them.[29] Yet even what Jane Hunter calls "the missionary message of U.S. domesticity," as tied as it was to cultural imperialism, could have dramatically different results in different situations. In China, she concludes, "the message of Christian domesticity preached by missionary women was less transformative than the force of their own example."[30] But in South Africa, the same missionary message on domesticity and "the notion of the inviolable Christian home was itself potentially revolutionary and liberating for black women . . . [as it later gave them] an ideological tool in their struggles against labor policies which split families."[31]

While it is important to address such key questions about the significance of the American Protestant women's missionary movement, it is not surprising that the answers are mixed, even ambiguous. Not only were there important variations among individuals and groups over a long period of time and in different mission stations, there are also significant differences in the perspectives and normative assumptions that scholars bring to their assessments of topics like feminism or cultural imperialism. Nevertheless, the missionary movement was a crucial component in the development of women's roles in nineteenth-century American religion within the context of culturally dominant white Protestantism. The women involved in general accepted a domestic identity as "their place," but their work at home and abroad greatly expanded that place through public activities and increased global awareness.

# 9
# *Reform Movements*

The Second Great Awakening proved that churches could survive and thrive as voluntary associations. It also helped to fuel an explosion of reform groups in antebellum America. Important manifestations of the reform spirit were found within nonevangelical churches like the Unitarians as well, for whatever their theological differences, they shared the evangelicals' tremendous optimism about the future of this new nation, convinced that voluntary associations could change society for the better as active, committed individuals worked together. The various reform societies formed a continuum with the "home missions" of the churches, and there was considerable overlap of personnel, but they may be viewed as distinctive insofar as the reform societies were more clearly directed at changing a particular social structure or pattern: sexual conduct, drinking, slavery, prisons. Reformers generally insisted that change came by individuals converted and won to a cause, but they sometimes addressed structural issues and institutions like the saloon or slavery, recognizing that environment can enhance or obstruct personal change. While traditional charity and benevolence sought to ameliorate social problems, reform societies confidently expected to eliminate them.

Women with a broad range of religious backgrounds worked for reforms, but they soon found they faced a double challenge. Like their male counterparts, they had to convince others to join them in a particular cause, but they discovered that they also were forced to defend their right as women to step out of their place to act and organize in a public way. Thus, women reformers shared with women in church groups and charitable activities the obstacles of male opposition to public action, but the men's oppositon was intensified when the cause was controversial. Supplying Bibles to the unchurched or protecting female orphans was one thing; denouncing slavery or the sexual double standard was quite another.

Women and men worked for numerous reforms during this period, including education for the handicapped, care of the insane, and prison reform, but in this chapter, I focus on three areas in more detail: sexual behavior and prostitution ("female moral reform," as it was known);

temperance; and antislavery. All three emerged as public issues in the antebellum period but continued, sometimes with a slightly different focus or new tactics, after the Civil War. All three were distinctly "religious" from the point of view of their participants in the sense that advocates were directly motivated by theological convictions and causes were perceived as clear-cut moral issues, *sins* against both God and neighbor. Many reformers worked from an institutional church base, and even when their more radical and controversial demands elicited criticism from clergy or established churches, the reformers often claimed that it was they, not their opponents, who most truly followed the "pure religion of Jesus." Finally, all three movements sooner or later raised questions about women's rights. Some women reformers became radicalized, rejecting those culturally imposed gender expectations that blocked their action and denied them public responsibilities and rights. Others conceded a gendered division of human nature and spheres of responsibility but insisted that it was their very characteristics and concerns as women that justified their reform activity. By the end of the century, the division between "radical" and "soft" feminism had blurred considerably in the rhetoric and actions of women reformers. But before turning to our three key reforms, it is necessary to look briefly at still another important cause that helped to make women's reform groups possible and effective: female education.

## Women's Education

Women's education was one of the earliest and most basic reforms involving women in antebellum America, a reform associated closely with three pioneering educators: Emma Willard, the founder of Troy Female Seminary; Mary Lyon, the founder of Mount Holyoke Seminary (later College); and Catharine Beecher, whose contribution lay less in the endurance of any of the particular schools she began than in her widespread efforts as a publicist and organizer in the cause of female education. In the early decades of the nineteenth century, promoting more sustained and intellectually rigorous education for women was perceived by many Americans as quite radical, judging by the amount of ridicule and opposition encountered by its advocates, but in retrospect, the movement and Willard, Lyon, and Beecher themselves appear fairly traditional. The idea that women need more and better education in order to best fulfill their duties of training moral and intelligent citizens was an integral part of the ideal of Republican Motherhood. The pioneer educators drew upon these ideological roots at the same time that they firmly and publically accepted women's traditional nature, roles, and spheres. As a consequence, some historians have tended to dismiss them as essentially "antifeminist."[1]

Nevertheless, their efforts were unintentionally subversive to tradition. When members of a socially suppressed group—whether defined by gender, race, or class—gain access to education, the door is opened for other challenges to the status quo. Both the premises and the consequences of better female education carried radical implications for women in nineteenth-century America, despite the vociferous assurances by women like Willard, Lyon, and Beecher that their primary goal was to make women better able to fulfill their culturally assigned roles. In the first place, the educators insisted that women have intellectual capacities as great as those of their brothers but simply had lacked the opportunity to develop them. They thus promoted rigorous intellectual standards in their schools and criticized female ignorance and the frivolity that they believed was a product of contemporary "finishing schools" for young women.

Second, these three pioneers intentionally carved out a "profession" for women: teaching. To be sure, teaching was seen as an extension of woman's natural role as nurturing mother, and a fair share of public acceptance of women teachers was based on the pragmatic justification that they could be paid less than men. Indeed, for many young women, teaching was very much a temporary profession, filling a few years before they married. Yet neither the young women themselves nor the pioneer educators saw the temporary nature of the profession as a waste, for they assumed that the same knowledge and skills would be exercised in the role of motherhood. And there were young women for whom teaching was not a stopgap but a lifelong career, by choice or by necessity. Catharine Beecher was particularly insistent that such "woman's work" be respected and called a "profession."

> Most of the defects which are continually discovered and lamented in present systems of education may be traced, either directly or indirectly to the fact, that the formation of the minds of children has not been made a profession securing wealth, influence, or honor, to those who enter it. . . . [Other professions are honored; they have a long period of training and stiff requirements.] But to *form the mind of man* is deemed so simple and easy an affair, that no such preparation or precautions are required.[2]

Religion, specifically the evangelical Protestantism of the Second Great Awakening, was an intrinsic part of both sides of early female education, the traditional and the potentially radical. Willard, Lyon, and Beecher were all devout Christians, and they used explicit religious justifications openly in their appeals for support. Moreover, religion was a pervasive influence at their schools, both as part of the regular curriculum and in the periodic revivals they fostered on campus. Curricular study of religion and revivals were also part of many male colleges at the time, but the religious influences at the women's schools included acceptance of woman's natural and divinely ordained spheres and her nature as deeply directed by a call to sacrifice self for others' good. Thus the challenge to traditional ideas and mores was more subtle. Religion could give a young woman justification for resisting family pressures and demands on the basis of a "higher" duty, as she directed her sacrificial "nature" to groups in the broader society she perceived as needing her help, rather than solely to the demands of a biological family.

As in Republican Motherhood, women's contribution as teachers was frequently articulated in terms of the nation's moral and religious needs, and teaching was explicitly defended as a religious vocation, not only appropriate to women but best fulfilled by them. When Catharine Beecher accompanied her father Lyman, the famous revivalist, to Cincinnati in 1832, she shared his conviction that the fate of the American experiment depended upon Christianizing and civilizing the West, countering the baleful influences of "infidelity" and Roman Catholicism. But she saw the work she and her father did as complementary: Where Lyman insisted on the need for trained Protestant preachers, Catharine spent the next two decades arguing for the crucial missionary work of women as teachers. "It must be shown," she wrote, "that teachers are needed as much as ministers, that teachers' institutions are as important as colleges, that it is as necessary to educate and send forth 'poor and pious young women' to teach, as it is 'poor and pious young men' to preach."[3]

Both Troy and Mount Holyoke, as well as Zilpah Grant's Ipswich Female Seminary, produced an extraordinary number of teachers in their early decades, and while the majority remained in more settled areas of the nation, a significant minority undertook "home missions" through teaching in the South or on the frontier.[4] Sponsoring boards for frontier teachers often insisted that applicants testify to their personal conversion experience or required supporting letters from their ministers with applications.[5] Once settled on the frontier, pioneer teachers organized Sunday schools, as well as "secular" ones, and, ironically, "found themselves departing from the very norms they expected to maintain. In the absence of permanent churches, they took on religious responsibilities [like public prayer] themselves."[6] Like their sister-graduates who followed a call to the foreign missions field, these young women found in their teaching an adventure, a career, and a religious vocation.

## Sexual Behavior and Prostitution

"Female moral reform," as the movement was euphemistically designated, had roots in the Second Great Awakening and traditional charity and became distinctively a women's reform cause. In 1830, a young Presbyterian minister, John R. McDowell, began work as a city missionary in New York City. Incensed at the plight of New York's prostitutes and public tolerance of their existence, he recruited support from women and a few prominent male reformers to protest the immorality and to establish a halfway house for prostitutes, hoping to convert and reform them. His support quickly evaporated, however, when he published a sensational and controversial "Magdalen Report" suggesting that prostitution was widespread in the city and that many customers were respectable, even prominent men. Undeterred, he continued his campaign and found new support among New York's Christian women, recently fired to action by Finney's urban revivals. Convinced that the "fallen" could be converted to Christianity and a moral, respectable life, Finney's followers were equally certain that society could and must be purified by Christian action. Christians should not accept gross public sin as inevitable. In 1834, the women founded the New York Female Reform Society, with Lydia Finney as its first director, and took over *McDowell's Journal,* renaming it the *Advocate for Moral Reform.* Through visiting speakers and the pages of their journal, the women of the New York Female Reform Society spread the word and enlisted the support of women throughout the Northeast, so that by the end of the 1840s over four hundred auxiliary societies had been formed.[7]

Female moral reformers had several distinct but related goals. One was to rescue, convert, and reform prostitutes. To this end, at first they continued to support McDowell in his efforts and hired two more men to assist him, but they soon began using female volunteers as visitors and then hiring women like Margaret Prior, later a women's rights leader, to do the work. They founded a "House of Reception" where repentant prostitutes could be converted and trained in a more respectable profession, but it was not a notable success. As Carroll Smith-Rosenberg concludes, "Despite such pious efforts . . . few prostitutes reformed; fewer still appeared, to their benefactresses, to have experienced the saving grace of conversion."[8] Nevertheless, the women continued their work of visitation, and while they never gave up hope for conversions, they became more involved with immediate material aid and efforts to find employment opportunities for those women, whom they perceived primarily as victims. They believed that most prostitutes did not choose their way of life but had been tricked by unscrupulous, unfeeling men, seduced and abandoned. With their virtue lost and with few avenues for respectable employment, they were, at worst, ignorant and weak, more sinned against than sinners.[9]

Sympathetic, if condescending, to the prostitutes, the women reformers refused to condemn them as sinful "fallen women" when their male patrons, especially men who came from the same "respectable" classes as the women reformers themselves, were ignored or excused. Thus a second goal of the movement was to expose and attack the sexual double standard. The women denounced this moral inequity. They called upon other women to exclude male offenders from respectable society, and no longer implicitly to condone such male behavior. They published the names or initials of male customers observed when missionaries or volunteers visited brothels, defending this controversial tactic in the *Advocate*.

> We think it proper even to expose names, for the same reason that the names of thieves and robbers are published, that the public may know them and govern themselves accordingly. We mean to let the licentious know, that if they are not ashamed of their debasing vice, we will not be ashamed to expose them.[10]

Organized prostitution was a less immediate reality for the small-town or rural women who joined the society than it was for women in New York and other cities, but they shared the concerns of their urban sisters. They worried about the fate of young men and women exposed to temptation in growing urban centers without the restraint and protection of family and church. They sympathized with the innocent victim of seduction. They, too, experienced and deplored the double standard, and they told their stories in letters to the *Advocate*. If some reports were exaggerated or vindictive, they could still be based in real abuses. Rural or urban, the women of the Female Moral Reform Society shared a broad goal of social change: moral purity for both men and women. True to the millennial spirit of the revivals, they believed that widespread conversions were possible and that society could be reformed as a consequence. Part of that reformation meant raising men to standards of sexual purity presumed to be natural for women and inculcated by Christianity, since prevention was even more important than rescue. "The tactic of preference, women moral reformers agreed, was to educate children, especially young male children, to a literal adherence to the Seventh Commandment. This was a mother's task."[11]

## Manifestations of Feminism

The Second Great Awakening had already emphasized the crucial religious and moral power of mothers and spawned numerous "mothers' associations." What was controversial in female moral reform was the women's willingness to speak out on "indelicate" subjects and their overt attack on male hypocrisy. By the standards of their day, these women were stepping out of their place and intruding on the male sphere. Indeed, some scholars have seen in the female moral reform movement the earliest manifestations of nineteenth-century feminism. The women refused to play merely a backstage role but insisted on running the movement themselves and preferred hiring women as visitors and editorial staff for the *Advocate*. Spurred by their concern for the economic plight of the prostitute, the women argued for more and better-paid employment opportunities for women who had no husband or father to support them. At times they intruded into the male sphere of politics by petitions, the one form of political action in which they could engage formally. Finally, the women's attack on the double standard has been seen as a covert expression of hostility to men and their power and a protest against female helplessness. Carroll Smith-Rosenberg found two dominant themes over the years in the letters and articles in the *Advocate*.

> The first was an angry and emphatic insistence upon the lascivious and predatory nature of the American male. Men were the initiators in virtually every case of adultery or fornication—and the source, therefore, of that widespread immorality which endangered America's spiritual life and delayed the promised millennium. . . . Women saw themselves as having few defenses against the determined male, his will was far stronger than that of women. . . . letters often expressed a bitterness that seems directed not only against the specific seducer, but against all American men.[12]

The second theme was a call to women for united action. Women thus could have an impact, calling men to live up to the very standards and characteristics they assigned to, and then commended in, women.

There was a real tension here. On the one hand, these women reformers clearly assumed that women were naturally more moral than men, especially in matters of sexual purity, thus endorsing the image of the cult of True Womanhood. On the other hand, they refused to accept that gender division when it excused male immorality or prevented their own work for reform. All Christians, after all, were called to a single high standard. The movement occasionally flirted with the radically egalitarian, feminist implications of the latter position, most notably when the *Advocate* published in 1838 an article by the Quaker abolitionist, Sarah Grimké. Grimké rejected any biblical interpretation or religious tradition that restricted women's moral agency and autonomy. "The first duty, I believe, which devolves on our sex now," she wrote, "is to think for themselves. . . . Until we take our stand side by side with our brother; until we read all the precepts of the Bible as addressed to women as well as to man, and lose . . . the consciousness of sex, we shall never fulfill the end of our existence."[13] Grimké was too radical for the vast majority of the *Advocate*'s readers in her criticisms of the clergy, male interpretations of the Bible, and women's traditional roles.[14] Most readers preferred instead to affirm women's more pious, pure nature and to use that assumption to justify their atypical public action in a cause that, they believed, defended women's values. If that meant, as Mary Ryan has argued, that "[i]n the end they used their social power to create a moral code which exacted particularly stringent sexual repression from their own sex,"[15] few women in nineteenth-century America saw that as a problem or were ready to embrace the radical egalitarianism of a Sarah Grimké.

The fervor and visibility of the Female Moral Reform Society declined after the 1840s, especially in its rural auxiliaries, but the *Advocate* continued to be published and the New York group was transformed into the

American Female Guardian Society with a greater focus on social service.[16] Like most other reform movements in midcentury, it was overshadowed by the immediate crises of slavery and war, but its issues and its women workers emerged again in the postwar crusade for moral purity.

## The Purity Crusade

The "purity crusade" of the last four decades of the nineteenth century continued the double focus of the female moral reform movement in its attack on prostitution and its campaign to purify society by changing individuals and imposing social controls.[17] Numerous abolitionist leaders took up a new, but in their view, related cause in the years after the Civil War: the "white slavery" of prostitution. The ensuing years saw a series of battles between the new abolitionists and the advocates of regulation. Regulation of prostitution, to the new abolitionists, smacked of compromise with what was clearly a sin, and they would no more countenance half-measures and tolerance for "white slavery" than they had in the case of black slavery, for both involved the selling of human beings. At the same time, purity crusaders insisted on the importance of prevention through moral education societies. Like their antebellum sisters, the women of the movement attacked the double standard and promoted the efficacy of maternal education to change and purify society. Their definition of "purity" was decisively shaped by the gender-based definitions of the cult of True Womanhood. Purity—and spiritual superiority—were in stark contrast to "animalistic" lust and carnality. The True Woman merely tolerated sex as a concession to her husband's regrettably lower needs and as a means to the good of procreation. Seemingly unaware of the logical contradiction in which they involved themselves, women both affirmed the "purity" of asexuality as distinctive and natural for women and hoped to change men's carnal nature by early education or conversion. Promoters of the purity crusade, male and female, thus bought into a largely negative assessment of sexuality. Purity became "a denial of sensuality, an ascetic ideal. . . . Like Christian ascetics before them, social purists believed that the control of sexual passions was basic to religious personality."[18] In their suspicion of sexuality, purity crusaders drew upon a deeply rooted Christian tradition. They also appealed to nineteenth-century understandings of "scientific 'laws of health.'"

> Purity reformers, borrowing from philosophical vitalism and mechanism as it suited their purposes, claimed sex energy as a God-given trust. Hence, sexual intercourse was for procreation only—its vital and religious function. Furthermore, they encouraged moderation, for energies expended in sex were lost to other channels of expression—especially work. The energy system, considered finite and, in accordance with Newtonian physics, running down, had to be conserved.[19]

Support of the purity crusade included a virtual "who's who" of women's rights in nineteenth-century America: Elizabeth Blackwell, Susan B. Anthony, Julia Ward Howe, Lucy Stone, Mary Livermore, Antoinette Brown Blackwell. Frances Willard drew the influential Women's Christian Temperance Union into the cause. Not everyone in the purity crusade operated from an overtly religious base, but ministers frequently joined forces with women to combat regulation, and Unitarians, Friends, and Episcopalians were particularly early and prominent in their support of purity reform.[20] The crusade had several specific goals. The denial of regulation and the eradication of prostitution were central, but reformers also worked to raise the legal "age of consent" for female intercourse. "Women reformers recognized in low age of consent laws [seven in Delaware, ten in several other states] a persistent threat to family purity and a bar to woman's social and spiritual advancement. Furthermore, the extremely low age permitted the recruitment of scarcely adolescent girls into the brothels."[21] Prison reform, especially the indiscriminate mixing of offenders and the lack of prison matrons, was seen as another related cause, as were the working conditions for women in the cities and the lack of protection for female travelers.

The purity crusade was a widespread and complex movement, one that is not easily categorized as simply conservative or progressive. Based in a vision of a "better" American environment, it promoted both the censorship of an Anthony Comstock and the cause of urban labor. It was in part religious, an attack on violations of the Seventh Commandment; in part, humanitarian as it sought to aid and protect economically and socially vulnerable women. In part, it was an exercise in social control as its leaders sought to shape society in accordance with their own essentially middle-class understanding of moral behavior and admirable character, of family structure and cultural taste, using coercion and censorship, if necessary, to achieve their goals. And it was most certainly a woman's reform, however ambiguous its legacy. If the movement over the course of the nineteenth century used and reinforced cultural stereotypes about women's nature and roles and thus deflected the cause of feminism, it also gave women a forum for expression of their legitimate grievances and an arena for public action. "Soft" and "radical" feminists made common cause in their anger at the double standard of sexual conduct and its detrimental effect on women, for in fact women were socially, economically, and sexually more vulnerable than men.

## Temperance

Women's involvement in temperance reform followed a pattern more similar to the women's foreign missionary movement than to female moral reform; that is, women participated in temperance groups in the antebellum period but in a supportive or auxiliary role. Only after the Civil War did temperance become a women's reform movement in the sense of having independent women's organizations and leadership. Yet temperance was like female moral reform insofar as both movements began with a specific focus on a single issue but broadened to a range of social concerns by the end of the century.

Temperance was not seen as either a religious or a moral issue by most colonial Americans, even religious leaders; indeed, liquor flowed freely as a normal part of ordination celebrations. A few voices were raised in protest against intemperance in the late eighteenth century, particularly among Quakers and Methodists, but widespread interest came in the nineteenth century, like so many other reforms, in the wake of the Second Great Awakening. Ministers like Lyman Beecher played prominent roles in this early phase of the movement, and the goal was moderation, not total abstinence. By the 1820s and 1830s, divisions appeared within the movement: Should reformers advocate temperance or complete abstinence? Should they concentrate on individual change, symbolized by signing a pledge and achieved by moral suasion, or were legislative means to control the liquor trade necessary? In the 1840s, a new temperance group, the Washingtonians, emerged, made up of former drinkers who had changed their ways and tried to convince other drinkers to do the same. By the mid-1840s and into the 1850s, the movement shifted its tactical emphasis from primary reliance on persuasion to more political and legislative solutions.

The shift of tactics had a significant impact on women's involvement in the movement. In the earlier phases, women were encouraged to participate through their "moral influence" especially within the family and through fund-raising, but not to take roles of public leadership. Given the central emphasis on moral suasion and individual change at the time, such a nonpublic role could be accepted by women as an important contribution to the cause, one that was eminently consistent with the other religious and domestic roles for women that came out of the Awakening. Women also could join parallel or auxiliary groups like the "Martha Washington" societies of the Washingtonians, signing the pledge themselves and providing moral support and material aid for the reformed drunkard and his family.[22] The Order of the Sons of Temperance, another group organized in the 1840s, also had a female auxiliary, the Daughters of Temperance. But as the focus of the movement shifted more and more to political tactics and legislative goals, the importance of the women's temperance activities was undercut, for political action was seen as inappropriate and, indeed, impossible for women.

The situation became increasingly frustrating for the women. Most women believed—and indeed, most male temperance leaders conceded—that it was men who had problems with drinking and women who were especially the victims of its effects. The shift to more political tactics then exacerbated the women's sense of powerlessness, and for some women raised the logical, if radical, question of woman suffrage. Women like Susan B. Anthony, Elizabeth Cady Stanton, Lucretia Mott, and Lucy Stone, all of whom were active in temperance reform, found in their exclusion from action and leadership one more impetus to espouse directly women's political rights. In the mid-nineteenth century, their position was still seen as too radical by most women, but more women were prepared in their frustration to challenge "what they considered a more galling and restrictive ban: that against public speaking by women."[23] Women protested that restriction dramatically at temperance conventions. In 1852, Susan B. Anthony was an official delegate to a temperance convention in Albany but was denied the right to speak, so she and some other women left to organize their own society and convention. At that convention, Anthony and Stanton issued a strong call for women's rights, but most of the women present could not endorse so radical a stance. Instead, they agreed to admit men as full members, the men took over, Anthony and Stanton withdrew, and the organization foundered.[24]

New York City was to be the site of a "World's Temperance Convention" in 1853, but women were not to be allowed to speak or to help run the proceedings, so some critics dubbed it the "Half World's Temperance Convention" and organized an alternative meeting. Nevertheless, Antoinette Brown, who would later in that same year be the first woman ordained by a mainline Protestant church, attempted to address the "World's" convention, only to be drowned out by the audience. A disgusted Horace Greeley summarized the convention in an editorial in the New York *Tribune:*

> First Day—Crowding a woman off the platform.
> Second Day—Gagging her.
> Third Day—Voting that she shall stay gagged. Having thus disposed of the main question, we presume the incidentals will be finished this morning.[25]

If concern for temperance propelled a few women into women's rights, most were marginalized as the movement focused on political tactics, and the movement as a whole was overshadowed by the coming of war. Only after the war did women claim a public and dominant role in temperance reform with the "Woman's Crusade" of 1873–74.

### The Woman's Crusade

In December 1873, Dio Lewis, a popular lecturer, precipitated the crusade in the small towns of Ohio. Traditionally Hillsboro is credited with being the birthplace of the crusade,[26] as Lewis challenged his female audience to take action against the evils of the saloon by telling the story of his mother's experience many years before. Distressed by her husband's drinking, she and some friends took action by confronting the local saloon owner with prayer and a successful plea to close the saloon. Indeed, this incident was not unique. There had been several instances during the 1850s when women took direct action against the liquor trade, marching on a local saloon, even destroying property in their protest.[27] Later the women shifted their tactics to the spiritual and psychological coercion of prayer in saloons. Thus historian Jed Dannenbaum concludes that "the Crusade was not the beginning but rather the climax of the social movement, and . . . must be considered within the context of the decades of female activity that preceded it."[28] Nevertheless, the crusade that began in Ohio in 1873 caught fire and achieved an unprecedented degree of participation and publicity.

The morning after Lewis's lecture, the women of Hillsboro met at the Presbyterian church for prayer and organization. They then proceeded as a group to the local saloons, singing hymns and praying as they went, with the objective of persuading the owners to sign a pledge that they would no longer sell liquor. A few days later, a similar action was begun in another small Ohio town, Washington Court House, again in response to Lewis's lecture. Once begun, the crusade spread rapidly through newspaper coverage, word of mouth, and visits from crusaders. By the summer of 1874, over nine hundred cities and towns had experienced crusades. They were most numerous and most successful in the small towns of the Midwest, but there was crusade activity in other parts of the country and in urban centers. In each local crusade, women could draw support and inspiration from the examples of other communities, as well as from each other, and positive reinforcement was necessary, for they also encountered active opposition, even physical violence from unsympathetic crowds or saloon owners who tried to humiliate or intimidate them. Some women, surely, were discouraged, but others persisted with renewed dedication, seeing in their own suffering an experience of testing, purification, and identification with Christ.[29]

The Woman's Crusade was clearly religious, both in its motivations and its practical implementation. Most, although not all, of the women involved came out of an evangelical Protestant tradition. They saw themselves as soldiers, at war against sin, whose weapons were prayers and hymns as they appealed to saloon owners to "convert" to Christian temperance. Churches provided not only personnel but organizational centers for the movement. As Ruth Bordin concludes, "Every meeting of which we have any record at which Crusades were organized and launched took place in Protestant churches."[30] Many ministers supported the crusaders and preached temperance sermons, although others were critical, not of temperance as a cause, but of the "unwomanly" tactics of the crusaders. Male support was one important element in the success of local crusades, but it was the women who engaged in "frontline" action, and as the crusade spread, the women could draw directly upon existing church and missionary women's networks.

Why did so many women respond and participate, especially when crusade activities were for many of them a significant break with traditional expectations for female behavior? Temperance had long been seen as a woman's cause insofar as it was assumed that the vast majority of drinkers were men and that women were the victims of abuse and neglect by drunken husbands, yet powerless legally and economically. By law, an intemperate husband could squander his wife's property (if she had any), as well as his own wages, on drink, and a mother did not have legal rights to her children. Moreover, a significant impetus of the crusade was the women's fear that even good middle-class, Christian, nondrinking husbands and sons might be tempted by the saloons and fall into alcoholism and ruin. That fear was based in fact: Liquor was more widely available after the Civil War, legal regulations frequently went unenforced, and while not every woman who marched had immediate personal and familial experience with drunken males, enough had lost a husband or son to alcoholism that the threat was very real to them.[31] However unusual the public, confrontational tactics may have been for many women, the issue at stake fit squarely within woman's sphere as moral guardian of home and family. Other scholars have emphasized less conscious motives for the crusade: (1) middle-class women feared loss of economic security and status if their breadwinners drank; (2) the crusade gave them an opportunity to express antagonism to men and a male culture; (3) it was an attempt at social control by a middle class that felt increasingly threatened by a growing immigrant, working-class population that failed to share middle-class values and standards.[32]

Regardless of the mix of stated and unconscious motives behind the Woman's Crusade as a whole or for individual women, the events were a watershed in the American temperance movement. Thousands of women got involved in the attempt to close down saloons, and in many cases they succeeded, if only temporarily. In the long run, the crusade did not stop either drinking or the liquor trade, but it did generate extensive publicity for the cause. More important than the crusade's impact on saloons were its effects on the female crusaders. Bordin argues:

> What gave the Crusade its thrust and its real importance was that these women were experiencing power. . . . The Crusade had an emotional impact equivalent to a conversion experience and moved these women to feminist principles, whether they recognized them or not. . . . [it] was a liberating force for a group of church-oriented women who could not have associated themselves directly with the equal rights or suffrage movements.[33]

Even before the crusade itself ended, women began to shape a more structured and permanent organization that would ensure them a prominent place in the temperance movement, a work that culminated in November of 1874 when the Woman's Christian Temperance Union (WCTU) held its first national convention.

## The WCTU

As an organization, the WCTU was arguably the most important, permanent result of the Woman's Crusade. In the last quarter of the nineteenth century, it was "both the leading temperance organization and the leading women's organization in the United States . . . [and] the major vehicle through which women developed a changing role for themselves in American society."[34] In part, its success was due to a structure that was strong at both national and local levels, giving women a prominent voice through national leaders and a means to address the particular concerns and interests of the local community. In part, it succeeded because it ultimately embraced a wide range of positions and perceptions of women, from an evangelical domesticity that was compatible with the cult of True Womanhood to radical socialism. Not surprisingly, its members did not always agree, but they were united in a conviction that women should have a distinct, important, and public role in shaping American society.

Who were the women who joined the WCTU? Some already had substantial experience in reform or public work, like Annie Wittenmyer, the union's first president. A widow, she had been active in Methodist foreign missions, served on the Sanitary Commission during the Civil War, and had experience as an editor. Many others were drawn directly from the Woman's Crusade, although not every woman who had marched and prayed immediately joined the WCTU. Still others had no particular background in organized, public activity, beyond the women's work in a local congregation, perhaps. Virtually all of the women were "religious," and the large majority were white, middle-class evangelical Protestants. These were the women who were gathered in cities and towns, who had benefitted from better and more widespread female education, and who had a reasonable amount of leisure time to devote to voluntary activity, thanks to industrialization and the availability of domestic servants. The matter of "leisure time" for middle-class women was one contributing cause of the growth of the WCTU, but it was not a sufficient cause. Not all middle-class women got involved, and the WCTU included some working-class, immigrant, and black women. Yet black and immigrant women never formed more than a small minority of Union membership, and not simply because they lacked the leisure time of white, middle-class, American-born women. In some cases, they belonged to a religious or ethnic group that did not share the evangelical Protestants' view of drinking as a sin. And the WCTU itself was ambivalent in its treatment of immigrants. On the one hand, they were approached as women who shared female roles and concerns that cut across class lines and thus could be recruited and organized. On the other hand, they were part of the group that was perceived as a problem, foreigners who did not share "American" patterns and values. The WCTU was, at times, condescending and bigoted; it sometimes endorsed racist and nativist sentiments as a way of arguing that white, Protestant women should have more political power. (Similar attitudes and tactics were unfortunately also evidenced by the women's suffrage movement by the end of the century.) Yet some WCTU leaders, notably Frances Willard, repudiated such bigotry publicly.[35]

The years from 1874 to 1879 were a time of modest growth for the WCTU as its leaders, with limited financial resources, worked to recruit members, publicize the cause, and develop an effective organization. Initially, the WCTU was strongest in the East and Midwest, with very little support in the Far West and much slower growth in the South, where male opposition to *any* public role for women was pervasive. Bordin quotes one woman from Tennessee on the obstacles women faced even in an arguably "moral" cause like temperance: "The prejudices of the Southern people are all against women doing anything in public, and especially opposed to the woman's Temperance Crusade. Particularly is this true of our ministers. They quote St. Paul, and tell us we are wonderfully out of our places."[36] From the beginning, the WCTU was strictly a women's organization. Men could attend as guests, speak occasionally, and give money, but they could not vote or take leadership positions. Perhaps the women thereby implicitly accepted a continued gender-division of spheres. Perhaps they also feared that if men were admitted as full members, they would take over, as they had earlier in the temperance movement.

The 1870s also saw a struggle between two early leaders, each of whom had a different vision of the WCTU. One was Annie Wittenmyer, older and more conservative, who endorsed a single-minded focus on "gospel temperance" and the use of moral suasion to achieve reform and was quite skeptical of the appropriateness or effectiveness of political means. The other was Frances Willard, one of the most extraordinary persons of the nineteenth century. Although she was elected corresponding secretary at the Union's first convention, she was a relative newcomer to the temperance cause. Her own background was in education; she was younger than Wittenmyer and more open to the women's movement and political means. She supported at least limited suffrage for women but was in a distinct minority with that position. She thus came up with a slogan that was surely a stroke of political genius—"home protection"—and tied it to the vote. By so doing, she "did not demand suffrage as a right, but only as a means of promoting what her supporters saw as moral and proper, the protection of home from the evils of the liquor traffic."[37]

Frances Willard was thus a prime example of the nineteenth century woman who "used" the cult of True Womanhood to advance women's rights. This does not mean she was simply an opportunist or a hypocrite; she *did* support temperance, and she appears to have accepted an image of women as naturally more pious, chaste, and moral than men. But she also wanted women to become more independent and active in the public sphere. She was shrewd enough to perceive what methods and arguments would work to bring along more timid or conservative women toward her vision. Finally, she was an unusually charismatic speaker and leader who inspired great personal devotion in others. By 1879, she had developed a sufficient following to be elected over Wittenmyer as president.

Willard's election was a turning point for the WCTU, but it did not constitute an overnight reversal of direction. There had been some support among members for political means, particularly the petition, during the 1870s. Furthermore, as some women at the local level embarked on missions of gospel temperance like visiting prisons, they encountered for the first time conditions that spurred them to think about broader reforms. Nevertheless, Willard's leadership was critical. She spent an incredible amount of time in the 1880s on speaking tours, and as a result, the WCTU grew dramatically all over the country. Meanwhile, she promoted a "Do Everything" policy that linked temperance to a wide range of social reforms. There was always a delay between what the national WCTU, and especially Willard, called for and its acceptance by most of the rank and file, and some members never agreed with Willard's more radical proposals. But many women did change their views, and Willard's leadership and the organization provided important space and support for women who wanted to pursue change.

One of the most significant contributions of the WCTU was to make woman's suffrage respectable for those women who had formerly perceived it as a threat to religion and the sanctity of the home. But Willard and some chapters or members of the WCTU moved into several other reforms, linking them to home protection and temperance. The move was possible in part because the women began to pay attention to and analyze the *causes* of drinking. In its early days, the WCTU shared several middle-class American assumptions, including the idea that poverty was a result of vice, laziness, and especially intemperance. By the late nineteenth century, Willard and many of her followers had drastically revised that assumption, arguing that intemperance might instead be the result of poverty. If so, social conditions had to be changed, and legislation enacted, in order for the curse of the saloon and intemperance to be banished from American society. Thus members of the WCTU worked for prison reform, especially for women prisoners. They joined the purity crusade, linking prostitution not only with drinking but also with economic and social conditions that left poor women with few respectable options for employment and self-support. Some promoted the kindergarten movement, an institution more like day care or Head Start than the kindergartens of the twentieth century, since it was "specifically designed for the children of working mothers who would otherwise be forced to leave their children alone in locked rooms."[38] Meanwhile, temperance was increasingly pursued by political means. The WCTU promoted, with significant success, compulsory temperance education in public schools, and for a period in the 1880s, Willard was able to effect a formal alliance between the WCTU and the Prohibition Party.

Finally, Frances Willard allied herself openly with the cause of labor, joining the Knights of Labor and, in 1889, the Socialist Party. On these points, she was not able to bring most WCTU members with her, but she had modest support. Her reasoning and arguments followed lines similar to those she had used to promote woman's suffrage; that is, these organizations were rooted in a defense of home and family. Working men and women needed relief from long hours and unsafe, unhealthy working conditions so they would not repair to the saloons for temporary enjoyment and oblivion. Single women needed a sufficient wage to resist the temptations of prostitution; men needed wages enough to support their families and reasonable work hours so they could spend time with their families. In short, Frances Willard became a proponent of the Social Gospel.

By the early 1890s, the WCTU entered a period of slower growth, if not decline. In part, this was due to Willard's withdrawal from active leadership in the movement, largely for reasons of exhaustion and ill health, as well as her friendship with Lady Henry Somerset, which kept Willard in England. In part, the Union was hurt by internal divisions over its political position and the building of a large WCTU Temple in Chicago, divisions exacerbated by personal rivalries. In part, women were finding other bases for their allegiance and interest, from the General Federation of Women's Clubs and the Association of Collegiate Alumnae to the National American Woman Suffrage Association and settlement work. When Willard died in 1898, the WCTU backed away from her radical vision and "Do Everything" policy to revert to a narrow and relatively conservative focus on prohibition. Nevertheless, the WCTU had made a difference. Its members had taken the religious and cultural values and roles assigned to women and used them as justification for public action and social reform. They had founded and supported specific agencies that gave structure to neighborly Christian outreach in a complex, urban, industrialized society. And the women had expanded their own sense of power and identity as they, in large or small ways, stepped out of their place in support of a cause they believed in.

## Antislavery

For many antebellum reform leaders, opposition to slavery was a logical part of their vision of a moral, Christian society, and they spoke, wrote, and organized for that cause as they did for temperance or home missions. Yet antislavery aroused far more controversy and resistance, not only in the South but for many northerners, too, who considered it dangerous and radical. The issue split communities, reform societies, churches, and ultimately the nation itself. The most uncompromising wing of the movement, identified with William Lloyd Garrison, was the immediate soil of an explicit women's rights movement in the United States and was extremely important historically, despite the relatively small numbers of persons involved. Yet any description of women, religion, and slavery must also include the stories of women in the more moderate antislavery movement, a brief discussion of southern women and slavery, and an account of the involvement of some northern women with the newly freed black people.[39]

A few lonely voices, from prominent Puritan ministers like Samuel Hopkins to Phillis Wheatley, were raised during the colonial period to protest a system that treated human beings as property. The Society of Friends was the earliest religious group in America to provide a consistent (though not unanimous) protest and to attempt to set their own house in order. Antislavery was not a popular cause for most of the first half of the nineteenth century, but it could be discussed even in the South in the early decades. Political and economic interests, which had existed for some time, joined with the growing fear that bordered on paranoia about slave rebellions to silence any southern dissent by the 1830s, and southern hostility was reinforced by reports of the words and actions of radical northern abolitionists.

Radical abolitionists were a relatively small wing of the antislavery movement, and they aroused almost as much opposition in the North as in the South, yet among them are found some of the most dramatic stories and famous names. Garrison published his first issue of the *Liberator* in 1831, announcing his fervent conviction that slavery was a sin and thus no compromise was possible with individuals or institutions that supported or even tolerated it. He included not only men but also women in his appeal, and among those who responded were two prominent Boston Unitarians, Maria Weston Chapman, who helped to organize the Boston Female Anti-Slavery Society in 1832, and Lydia Maria Child, who in 1833 published *An Appeal on Behalf of That Class of Americans Called Africans,* notable not only because it was "the first anti-slavery work to be published in book form" in America and written by a woman, at that, but also because Child attacked northern racism as well as southern slavery.[40] Meanwhile in Philadelphia, Quakers led by Lucretia Mott founded the Philadelphia Female

Anti-Slavery Society in 1833. Like the Boston group, it included black women as well as white, and it supported the Garrisonian position. Like their male counterparts, the women spoke, wrote, and organized, emphasizing moral suasion as the preferred means to attack the evils of slavery, although they also came to use the petition to try to move politicians to enact such legislative restrictions as were within their power.

### Sarah and Angelina Grimké

Living in Philadelphia at the time were two sisters from a wealthy South Carolina family whose opposition to slavery had driven them north, where they joined the Quakers. But Sarah and Angelina Grimké did not join the Philadelphia Female Anti-Slavery Society at first, both for personal reasons and because they were part of the Orthodox Friends, not the Hicksite group of James and Lucretia Mott. As Sarah and Angelina became interested in the radical abolition of the Garrisonians, they encountered serious disapproval from their Orthodox Quaker Society. Frustrated, they finally agreed to go to New York and work with the American Anti-Slavery Society. As its agents, they embarked on a lecture tour in New England that precipitated them into contemporary notoriety and a dramatic place in the history of women's rights, as well as antislavery. The Grimké sisters were not exactly unknowns when they began their New England tour in 1837. Angelina had written a letter of support to Garrison in 1835, which he promptly reprinted in the *Liberator,* and in 1836 she had published her *Appeal to the Christian Women of the South*. In the same year, Sarah had written an *Epistle to the Clergy of the Southern States.* As repentant members of a slave-owning family who could speak of the evils of the institution from personal observation, the two sisters seemed ideal candidates to arouse sympathy for abolition and to help organize more antislavery societies, and Angelina was a particularly gifted speaker. At first they addressed only women, but soon men began to attend their lectures, and they drew large, mixed audiences—and considerable controversy. In July of 1837, the Congregational ministers of Massachusetts issued a "pastoral letter" in which they decried the divisiveness of abolitionism and the attacks of the radicals on churches and ministers, and specifically denounced the activities of the Grimké sisters.

> We invite your attention to the dangers which at present seem to threaten the female character with widespread and permanent injury. The appropriate duties and influence of women are clearly stated in the New Testament. Those duties, and that influence are unobtrusive and private, but the sources of mighty power. When the mild, dependent, softening influence upon the sternness of man's opinions is fully exercised, society feels the effect of it in a thousand forms. The power of woman is her dependence, flow-

> ing from the consciousness of that weakness which God has given her for her protection.
>
> We appreciate the unostentatious prayers of woman in advancing the cause of religion at home and abroad; in Sabbath-schools; in leading religious inquirers to the pastors for instruction; and in all such associated efforts as become the modesty of her sex. . . . But when she assumes the place and tone of man as a public reformer . . . she yields the power which God has given her for her protection, and her character becomes unnatural. If the vine, whose strength and beauty is to lean on the trellis-work, and half conceal its cluster, thinks to assume the independence and the overshadowing nature of the elm, it will not only cease to bear fruit, but fall in shame and dishonor into the dust.[41]

Appealing to nature and to divine law, the pastors set clear limits on women's sphere and activities, and the bulk of public opinion was with them. Sarah and Angelina Grimké rejected those limits; Angelina, in a series of letters in the *Liberator*, and Sarah, in a book that became a classic of women's rights, *Letters on the Equality of the Sexes*. Both sisters had consistently based their opposition to slavery on religious and biblical principles, and Sarah began at the heart of the debate, challenging a male biblical interpretation that limited women, in terms that would mark religious debate into our own time. Citing Genesis 1, she insisted that men and women were "both made in the image of God; dominion was given to both over every other creature, but not over each other," and that equality was taught by Jesus, who made no distinctions based on gender in the duties of his followers. "Men and women were CREATED EQUAL; they are both moral and accountable beings, and whatever is *right* for man to do, is *right* for woman."[42]

Restrictions on their freedom to follow what they understood as God's call to speak for the slave led the Grimké sisters directly into consideration of their own rights as women and a principled defense of human rights, and they were supported by radical abolitionists like Garrison and Abby Kelley, a young Quaker who was an uncompromising advocate of the rights of blacks and women. But other abolitionists disputed the connection or, even if they agreed in principle that both women and slaves were oppressed, feared that a public connection of the two causes would hurt the antislavery movement. By 1840, the movement split partly over the use of political tactics, as Garrisonians took a "come-outer" position, thus rejecting alliance with any religious or political body that condoned slavery. Blanche Hersh contends, however, that the public role of women in the societies was "the more explosive" issue,[43] and when Abby Kelley was appointed to a committee of the American Anti-Slavery Society, she was not accepted and the movement divided.

The year 1840 saw another dramatic antislavery event that would have direct consequences for the women's rights movement: a World Antislavery Convention in London. Among the American delegates were a few women, including Lucretia Mott, but the convention refused to seat them. As a compromise, the women were allowed to observe the proceedings silently from a screened-off gallery, where they were joined in protest by a few sympathetic men like Garrison and Charles Remond, a black delegate. Elizabeth Cady Stanton was there, too, the young bride of a male delegate, and her conversations with Lucretia Mott led ultimately to the Seneca Falls Convention in 1848.

While historians can trace a direct line from abolition to women's rights, in the nineteenth century the connection provoked controversy and contradiction. Women like Lucretia Mott and the Grimké sisters were powerfully driven by a sense of religious call into positions and activities that evoked widespread condemnation by the churches, and many of the leaders of the feminist abolitionists ultimately separated from the institutional churches and orthodoxy.[44] To them, the connection of the rights of the slave and the rights of women seemed obvious and equally important, yet many saw no such relationship, or even if they conceded one, insisted that the sin of slavery took moral and tactical precedence. John Greenleaf Whittier chided the Grimké sisters in 1837: "Is it not forgetting the great and dreadful wrongs of the slave in a selfish crusade against some paltry grievance of [your] own?"[45] The issue of tactical precedence emerged again in the aftermath of the Civil War and split the women's rights movement. Stanton and Susan B. Anthony had put their work for women's rights on hold during the conflict, but they refused to accept the Fourteenth Amendment's extension of suffrage only to black men, whereas other women's rights leaders like Lucy Stone and Lucretia Mott conceded with Wendell Phillips that this was "the Negro's hour." The dilemma was an agonizing one for those involved, and its outcome filled with irony. The government gave black men a formal right to vote, but black male suffrage was rapidly undermined in the South by legal and extralegal means, and the women's rights movement born in abolitionism was, by the end of the nineteenth century, using racist arguments to try to get the vote for white women.

Women were broadly involved in the antislavery movement, if most eschewed the public efforts and explicit women's rights position of the radicals. They formed local antislavery societies or auxiliaries and tried to use culturally acceptable methods of influence and moral suasion within their families and the evangelical churches. Their justifications for their concern tended to be religious and, increasingly, rooted in their perception of slavery as inimical to family values and Christian morality. The slave system respected neither the virtue of black women nor the holiness of marital and maternal ties; as such, it was incompatible with Christianity.

Angelina Grimké set the precedent for an antislavery appeal to women as women in her 1836 *Appeal to the Christian Women of the South*. Lack of political power was no excuse for inaction, she argued: "I know you do not make the laws, but I also know that *you are the wives and mothers, the sisters and daughters of those who do. . . .*" Women could read, pray, speak and act, and they should be the ones to introduce the subject by petition to legislatures, for women would be "the most likely to introduce it there in the best possible manner, as a matter of *morals* and *religion,* not of expediency or politics."[46] Themes of female influence within the family and female moral superiority, however, were minor notes in Grimké's 1836 appeal. The themes were much clearer in the single most influential publication of the antislavery movement, which damned slavery especially for its effects on the black family, *Uncle Tom's Cabin* by Harriet Beecher Stowe.

### Harriet Beecher Stowe

As a member of the prominent Beecher family, Harriet had long been exposed to a range of antislavery views from the sympathy of Lyman and Catharine for colonization in the 1830s to the more ardent antislavery of her brother Edward. Two particular events, one public and one private, appear to have triggered her decision to use her pen in service of the cause. In 1850, the Fugitive Slave Act was passed, forcing Northerners to choose between active support of the slave system or breaking the law. Edward and his wife Isabella, then living in Boston, were incensed: Edward denounced the law from the pulpit, and Isabella wrote to her sister-in-law, "Hattie, if I could use a pen as you can, I would write something that will make this whole nation feel what an accursed thing slavery is." Harriet's children recalled her reaction: "I will write something, I will if I live."[47] For Harriet, public indignation was reinforced by private pain. In 1849, she lost a beloved young son to cholera, and she later wrote to a friend:

> It was at his dying bed and at his grave that I learned what a poor slave mother may feel when her child is torn away from her. In those depths of sorrow which seemed to me immeasurable, it was my only prayer to God that such anguish might not be suffered in vain. There were circumstances about his death of such peculiar bitterness, of what seemed almost cruel suffering, that I felt that I could never be consoled for it, unless this crushing of my own heart might enable me to work out some great good to others. . . . I allude to this here because I have often felt that much that is in [*Uncle Tom's Cabin*] had its root in the awful scenes and bitter sorrows of that summer.[48]

Stowe combined the public and the personal issues in a dramatic scene early in her novel. Eliza, a slave woman, has learned that her kindly but improvident master plans to sell her son, Harry, and, desperate, she flees north across a half-frozen Ohio River, arriving exhausted at the home of Mr. and Mrs. Bird. Traditional and domestic, Mrs. Bird normally does not meddle with the male world of politics, but she quizzes her senator-husband on implementation of the recent Fugitive Slave Act in Ohio. Learning that he supports it, she is horrified. "It's a shameful, wicked, abominable law, and I'll break it, for one, the first time I get a chance; . . . I don't know anything about politics, but I can read my Bible; and there I see that I must feed the hungry, clothe the naked, and comfort the desolate; and that Bible I mean to follow." Eliza subsequently tells her story, and confronted with a concrete instance of the effect of slavery on a family, both Senator and Mrs. Bird help her to escape. Just before Eliza leaves, Mrs. Bird gives Harry some of the lovingly preserved clothes of her own dead son.[49]

*Uncle Tom's Cabin* was as controversial and complex as it was influential when it was first published, and it has elicited a wide range of assessments ever since. There is no single character stereotype for Northerners or Southerners, blacks or whites, men or women, and Stowe touched upon virtually every current antislavery argument in its pages, including the indictment that slavery treats human beings as mere property. Nevertheless, one of its most consistent themes is the evil of slavery as a destroyer of families. If many of Stowe's female characters are more sensitive to that evil and, at times, more religious than any of the male characters except Uncle Tom, the author's goal was to convert more Americans of both genders to those "female" values through dramatic portrayal of a sinful system. In the last chapter of the book, Stowe makes her religious purpose clear, when she insists that the dramatic scenes and characters of her fictional work are rooted in fact. She appeals specifically to "generous, noble-minded men and women, of the South" and to "mothers of America" in particular to empathize with slave mothers. She reminds northern Christians that they, too, are guilty of inaction and complicity and ends on an apocalyptic note:

> A day of grace is yet held out to us. Both North and South have been guilty before God, and the *Christian Church* has a heavy account to answer. Not by combining together, to protect injustice and cruelty, and making a common capital of sin, is this Union to be saved,—but by repentance, justice, and mercy: for, not surer is the eternal law by which the millstone sinks in the ocean, than that stronger law, by which injustice and cruelty shall bring on nations the wrath of Almighty God![50]

However sincere Stowe's hope that Christians, especially Christian women, of the South would act to end slavery, it was clearly unrealistic. By the 1850s, public criticism in the South of slavery as a system had long been impossible. Evangelical Christians defended slavery as biblical as well as a necessary social system in the South, though ministers were willing at times to criticize its abuses, especially the failure of owners to respect marriage and family ties among slaves and to provide blacks with the light of the gospel. Southern white women surely shared the racism of their husbands and fathers, and an individual mistress could be as cruel and inhumane as a master. Nevertheless, while southern women voiced almost no public protest against slavery as a system, there is some indication that they were more critical of slavery than men were. Historian Ann Scott suggests that "there was widespread discontent with the institution of slavery" among white women and notes that twenty-four Virginia women petitioned the legislature to abolish slavery *after* the Nat Turner rebellion.[51] More often, women expressed their criticisms of the morality of slavery in letters or diaries, and for many, their opposition was more practical than principled: Slaves made a lot of work for conscientious mistresses, and women deeply resented the double standard that condoned their husbands' sexual exploitation of black women and undermined their own marriages.[52] Yet whatever the reservations of some white women about slavery, the vast majority deeply resented the attacks of an outsider like Harriet Beecher Stowe,[53] and when war came, they supported the Confederacy in their prayers, actions, and sacrifices. Their ties of race and class were clearly stronger than any sisterly identification with black or northern women.

## The Main Issue: Slavery

The primary focus of antislavery reform was just that: opposition to slavery as a system. A few abolitionists, particularly in the more radical wing, criticized northern racism and tried to proclaim and act on social equality of the races, only to be met with consistent ridicule or hostility. These same few radicals often saw a relationship between issues of black rights and women's rights and, in some cases, pacifism or nonresistance.[54] But for most reformers, the issue was slavery, and thus the legal proclamation of emancipation brought a feeling of premature but understandable euphoria and a sense of accomplishment. Northern women who sympathized with the antislavery cause continued to express their concern by supporting the northern war effort, joined by other northern women who had never participated very actively in the antislavery movement. After the Union victory, many of these women shifted the focus of their concern, now newly confident of the abilities to work and organize that they had discovered during the war. Some continued the fight for women's rights; some turned to foreign missions, temperance, or the neoabolitionism of the purity crusade. But there were some women who continued to respond to the needs of black people in direct ways. Laura Haviland, a radical Methodist widow who had traveled for the underground railroad, worked for The Freedmen's Aid Commission during the war and later with free blacks in Kansas. In 1862, Quaker Lucy McKim accompanied her father to the Sea Islands off South Carolina to work with the former slaves there. "A trained musician, [she] was deeply impressed by the songs of the slaves and committed them to musical annotation. Her work led to the publication of a book, *Slave Songs of the United States,* in 1857."[55] Other Quaker women, especially from the Midwest, went south alone or with their husbands to teach and aid the former slaves.

### Postwar Missionary Efforts

After the war, the largest group of women to continue direct reform work with blacks were the northern teachers who went south under the auspices of various missionary organizations, especially The American Missionary Association. In many ways, they were like the young women who set out as foreign missionaries. They saw their work as a religious call, in this case to serve former slaves who would need more than formal emancipation to become responsible members of society, and their particular contribution would be teaching. As Jacqueline Jones notes in her study of northern teachers in Georgia, "The Freedmen's teachers derived justification for their work from the ideology of evangelical abolitionism. Slavery was a sin against God and man; it denied the black person the ability to function as an independent moral being."[56] In the crusade for black education in the South, men were involved, most often as superintendents and administrators, but the vast majority of the teachers were young, unmarried northern women. Indeed, the "Yankee school marm" would become a stock character of southern culture, idealized by Northerners and ridiculed and vilified by Southerners. The teachers were not advocates of women's rights and generally accepted their position subordinate to the male leadership of the movement, though with occasional protests, but they saw in this work an opportunity to live out a vocation of evangelical usefulness.

Most of their time was engaged in teaching, and blacks of all ages were intensely eager for education, making substantial sacrifices to seek it. Basic literacy skills were an important component of their teaching, but the northern missionaries were equally concerned with moral instruction, hoping to instill values of piety, sobriety, self-control, thrift, and hard work in their pupils. They distributed physical relief when they could. They taught Sunday schools and tried to organize temperance societies. Like foreign missionaries, the northern teachers can be criticized for cultural insensitivity and condescension. Too often, they neither understood nor valued the blacks' religious expressions or cultural "ethos of mutuality."[57] The help they offered was genuine and, in the circumstances of the postwar South, a practical necessity, and blacks appreciated the aid at the same time they resented some of the "strings attached." Moreover, the northern teachers underestimated the forces of white Southerners to keep blacks "in their place" through political and economic means, as well as by sheer terrorism.

Nevertheless, if the white women teachers were still racist, and they were, they were less so than the majority of white Americans, north or south. They endured physical hardship, southern white hostility and intimidation, and discouraging conditions as they tried to act out a commitment to serve others. If they were unable to effect broad, long-range changes in the South, they achieved some limited success at a personal level and continued in a small but direct way the efforts of antebellum antislavery reformers. Only a few northern white women teachers, like Joanna P. Moore, remained in the South after the mid-1870s, and northern efforts were channelled especially into black normal schools and colleges, not primary education. Yet, as Evelyn Brooks Higginbotham has demonstrated, some northern church women continued to act on their concern for southern blacks throughout the rest of the nineteenth century. White northern Baptist women cooperated with black Southern Baptist women during the 1880s and 1890s to fund and support schools, including "mothers' training schools." The northern Baptist women kept alive an awareness of the plight of southern blacks through their journals and speakers in the North, and they spoke out publicly against lynching and other racial violence. As Higginbotham concludes:

> The role of women's missions proved a noteworthy exception to the betrayal of blacks' hopes for equality and justice during the late nineteenth century. As the white South structured a segregated society and sanctioned, either explicitly or implicitly, the violence perpetrated upon black communities, evangelical religion in the form of organized women's missions fostered bonds of interracial cooperation in an effort to uplift the quality of black life in the South. Notwithstanding its imperfections, interracial cooperation between black and white Baptist women did find concrete ways to offer hope and opportunity.[58]

Despite such exceptions, many northern reformers "forgot" the problems of black people as they turned to challenges arising from urbanization, industrialization, and immigration. Meanwhile in the South, where the vast majority of African Americans continued to live, even the rather limited Christian concern or charity of whites to slaves and free blacks in the antebellum period virtually disappeared, as southern whites moved to rebuild their society and enforce white control and rigid segregation. Only at the very end of the century would some Christian women of the South turn to any organized, religiously inspired, and still circumscribed concern for the well-being of their black neighbors.

## Conclusion

The relationship of women, religion and reform in nineteenth-century America is an extremely complex issue. So many women were involved in so many different causes at different times, and their mix of motivations varied, as did their level of activity and commitment. Consequently, historical generalizations must be qualified even as they illuminate women's story. "Religion" was clearly related to reform for American women. It provided the motives, means, and locus for much early reform, yet "religion" in the form of clergy, biblical injunctions, and institutional churches sometimes opposed or restricted women's reform work. As a result, some women backed away from a given cause. Other women moved away from "religion," at least in its orthodox and institutional forms. Still others redefined the content of their faith and its implications for action, reinterpreting the Bible as they did so.

The fit of women's reform work with "feminism" or the cult of True Womanhood is equally ambiguous. Some reformers explicitly rejected notions of appropriate female spheres, insisting that all persons as persons have public rights and moral responsibilities. Others embraced notions of women's special nature and spheres, yet insisted the "female" values should be more widespread in the public sphere, and that if women had to undertake "unwomanly" actions to protect the world that had been assigned to them, so be it. The challenge that faced these nineteenth-century women was formidable: to claim self-fulfillment for women without condoning egotistical selfishness; to affirm the human being's social connectedness and care for neighbor without endorsing denial and sacrifice to the point of self-negation; to demand that women be respected as full persons, with rights and opportunities enjoyed by men, without thereby implicitly embracing a male system and male values that denigrated women's traditional activities and concerns.

As white, middle-class, Protestant women sought to change the lives of individuals and the shape of their society through various reforms, there were surely elements of social control involved. The women could be condescending and insensitive to cultural patterns and values of other Americans whom they sought to save. In some cases, neither their methods nor their solutions were ones that would elicit approval in the late twentieth century. Nevertheless, the women *acted* on their convictions and made a difference, for American society and for themselves, and the issues they addressed are still serious challenges: racism, alcohol abuse, and the results of a sexual double standard.

# 10
# *Women's Religious Leadership in the Nineteenth and Early Twentieth Centuries*

On September 15, 1853, the First Congregational Church in Butler, New York, witnessed a milestone in the history of Christianity as Antoinette Brown became the first woman formally ordained to the ministry. From the perspective of the late twentieth century, this historic first appears as a central event in the story of women's leadership in the Protestant churches of nineteenth-century America. Yet that appearance can be deceptive, not only because of Brown's own subsequent career and because rare indeed were the nineteenth-century sisters who followed in her footsteps, but also because full, formal ordination was not the dominant concern of women religious leaders in the nineteenth century. On the one hand, women clearly exercised religious leadership in the churches through their foreign missionary societies and women's groups and, more informally, in their homes. On the other hand, even considering the question of formal leadership and power in the churches outside of separate women's organizations, women's preaching was a greater concern than formal ordination. Finally, the issue of laity rights for women and the Protestant deaconess movements contribute to the complexity of the issue.

## Preaching and Ordination

Acceptance of women's preaching was not only a necessary foundation for the cause of women's ordination, it was a more significant issue in nineteenth-century American Christianity. Yet the meaning of the assertion that a particular woman "preached" is slippery. In one sense, there was female preaching in colonial America: Quaker women were led by the inner light to testify in meetings and become missionaries; a few Baptist women prayed and exhorted publicly during the First Awakening; near the end of the eighteenth century, two extraordinary women, Jemima Wilkinson and Mother Ann Lee, pushed beyond the bounds of Christian orthodoxy on the basis of personal inspiration and preached, successfully enough to attract substantial followings, male and female. But it was in the nineteenth century that more individual women emerged as pioneers and role models. Clearly within a tradition of evangelical Protestantism, they raised no heterodox challenges beyond their insistence that women, as well as men, might be called by God to preach the gospel directly and publicly to mixed audiences.

Jarena Lee (b. 1783) resisted her call to preach at first, as would so many of her successors, and then had it rejected in 1811 by Richard Allen, leader of the African Methodist Episcopal Church. Yet the call returned when her husband died, and by 1818, Allen was more supportive, and Lee began a very successful itinerant ministry as an "official travelling exhorter," if not a formally licensed preacher.[1] Salome Lincoln (1807–1841), identified by her biographer as "The Female Preacher," shared the experience of a call initially resisted, but finally began to preach in 1827, though her itinerant ministry took her more often into homes than churches, until her marriage in 1831 curtailed her ministry.[2] But it was Phoebe Palmer whose arguments and example as a female preacher made a significant impact on mid–nineteenth-century America. Unlike Lincoln or Lee, Palmer combined the roles of wife and preacher, defending her activities in print, as well as in person, to wide audiences.

## Phoebe Palmer

Like many other female religious leaders in American history, Phoebe Palmer was largely neglected by scholars until recent years, yet she made several significant and related contributions to American Protestantism in the nineteenth century. A prominent leader of the resurgent Holiness tradition, she reemphasized Wesley's doctrine of sanctification and articulated it in her distinctive "altar theology." Through her writings and especially through her famous "Tuesday meetings" in the Palmer home, she influenced thousands of believers, including several prominent male church leaders. She herself led numerous revivals in the United States, Canada, and Great Britain. Finally, in *The Promise of the Father,* she not only defended her own actions as a woman preacher and encouraged other women not to deny God's call but also produced one of the longest and most comprehensive works on women's preaching yet to appear.

Born on December 18, 1807, Phoebe Worall grew up in a devout Methodist family. On September 28, 1827, she was married to Walter Clarke Palmer, a physician who shared her Methodist faith and was both a partner and supporter of his wife's ministry throughout their marriage. The couple's early happiness was marred by the death of their first three children in infancy, and Phoebe came to see these deaths not only as personal tragedies but also as tests sent by God, for she feared that she had let earthly love for her family replace the love of God in her heart and her Christian duty of evangelism. Thus she was deeply troubled about her own faith even when she and her sister, Sarah, combined two women's prayer meetings in 1836 to meet in the Palmer home, beginning what would become the famous Tuesday Meetings for the Promotion of Holiness. Finally, on July 26, 1837, Phoebe had her own theological breakthrough and experienced "entire consecration."

Phoebe Palmer was well within the Wesleyan tradition in her desire to receive a "second blessing," that is, sanctification, by which the believer is not only accounted righteous through the merits of Christ (i.e., justification) but actually made holy in this life. Her problem, she later reflected, was in expecting the experience to be dramatic, distinguished by clear *feelings* of grace or renewal. For her, the theological breakthrough was to recognize that willingness to dedicate everything to God and subsequent faith in God's promises of acceptance, found in scripture, were more important than feelings.[3] The seeds of her distinctive "altar theology" were present in that 1837 experience. First, the believer had to dedicate everything to God, to lay all upon the altar (Rom. 12:1). (For Palmer herself, this meant dedicating especially her family, that even her love for Walter and their children must be given to God.) But having done so, rather than worrying about whether God would accept the sacrifice and looking for decisive feelings of sanctification, the Christian was to believe God, believe the clear promise in scripture: "I will receive you" (2 Cor. 6:17). The altar, which is Christ, then sanctifies the gift (Matt. 23:19). As Palmer's biographer, Charles Edward White, summarizes her theology:

> Because she knew she was continually presenting herself to God as a living sacrifice, "lay[ing] all upon the altar," and because she knew that the altar sanctifies the gift, she could know with syllogistic certainty that she was sanctified. This scriptural logic put an end to her doubts and finally gave her the assurance she had sought so earnestly.[4]

In 1839, men began to attend the Tuesday meetings, including prominent Methodist leaders like Thomas C. Upham and, later, Nathan Bangs, both of whom were convinced by her and subsequently provided valuable support, defense, and publicity for her. The Tuesday meetings grew and continued, at least when the Palmers were in town, for the rest of Phoebe's life. In the meantime, she became involved in a number of humanitarian endeavors, notably the Five Points Mission in New York, as a necessary fruit of faith. She promoted Holiness doctrine in her writings, including the very popular work, *The Way of Holiness,* first published in 1843 and going through some fifty reprintings by 1867,[5] and her editing of the journal, *The Guide to Holiness.* She also promoted her ideas in person through her work as a sought-after and highly successful revivalist. During the 1840s, she began to preach at summer camp meetings, sometimes with Walter and sometimes alone. In 1853, the Palmers made the first of several preaching tours into Canada, crowned in 1857 with a major revival in Ontario. Returning to New York, she was a central figure in the remarkable urban revivals of

1857–1858. The next year, Phoebe and Walter went to the British Isles to further the revival and Holiness cause. She continued to write, travel, and preach until illness limited her schedule in the early 1870s and finally prevented her work for the last few months of her life before she died on November 2, 1874.

Charles White's assessment of Phoebe Palmer, the revivalist, acknowledges not only the sheer numbers of revivals she led but also her contributions to revivalism as a major movement in American religion.

> One positive contribution is that by preaching holiness she helped to balance the relative emphasis on justification and on sanctification in the American church. Her second contribution is negative. While she helped to bring a much needed balance into the American church by preaching holiness, the way in which she preached entire sanctification tended to devalue the doctrine. Her third contribution, however, was beneficial. She systematized and organized lay-people to work with urban revival campaigns. Her contribution marks the transition between the clergy-centered crusades of Charles G. Finney and the lay-oriented campaigns of D. L. Moody.[6]

One might well add a fourth contribution: her direct influence on and encouragement to the women who attended her Tuesday meetings or revivals or who read her works. Among them were Amanda Berry Smith, Catherine Booth, and Frances Willard, all of whom would become important advocates in the cause of female preaching.

Despite Phoebe Palmer's success as an evangelist, her right as a woman to preach did not go unchallenged in her own day, and so in 1859, she published *Promise of the Father; or, A Neglected Specialty of the Last Days* as both apologia and challenge. Underlying her arguments were two theological convictions. First, if the sanctified believer did not testify publicly to what God had done, God would revoke the gift; for women, as well as men, response to God's call in public witness was not a matter of preference but a necessity. Second, Palmer was convinced (as were many other American Christians) that she was living in the "last days," and that it was critical that the church neither neglect nor repress the gifts of the Spirit, even or especially when they are bestowed on women.

Palmer's initial defense was based in scripture, both because the Bible was so central in her own religious experience and theology and because biblical prohibitions so frequently formed the basis of attack from opponents of women's preaching. To her, the key passage was the account of Pentecost in Acts 1 and 2.

> When the founder of our holy Christianity was about leaving his disciples to ascend to his Father, he commanded them to tarry at Jerusalem until endued with power from on high. And of whom

was this company of disciples composed? . . . here were both male and female disciples: . . . they are waiting for the promise of the Father.

And did all these waiting disciples, who thus with one accord continued in prayer, receive the grace for which they supplicated? It was the gift of the Holy Ghost that had been promised. And was this promise of the Father as truly made to the daughters of the Lord Almighty as to his sons?—See Joel ii, 28, 29. . . . Where the Spirit was poured out in answer to the united prayers of God's sons and daughters, did the tongue of fire descend alike upon the women as upon the men? How emphatic is the answer to this question.

"And there appeared unto them cloven tongues, like as of fire, and it sat upon *each of them*."[7]

*All* of the company, Palmer insisted, proclaimed the Word. Furthermore, she argued, to preach and to prophesy meant essentially the same thing in early Christianity, and the gift of prophecy to individual women is attested to in both Old and New Testaments and was recognized well into the third century.

In arguments that would be repeated frequently in the debate over women's preaching and ordination, Palmer took on the key negative passages. Paul's prescription that women should be silent in the church (1 Cor. 14:34–36) was particular to that situation (else it contradicts his own directions of women being veiled *when* they prophesy in 1 Corinthians 11). Moreover, churches clearly do not follow that command of silence literally. The prohibition of women's teaching in 1 Timothy 2:9–15 is linked and confined to women's usurping authority, not to any and all teaching, and, Palmer concluded, "Women who speak in assemblies for worship, under the influence of the Holy Spirit, assume thereby no *personal authority* over others. They are instruments through which divine instruction is communicated to the people."[8]

Palmer further argued that the success of women who have preached is testimony to the authenticity of their actions; God has blessed their evangelistic efforts with abundant fruits of conversion. She cited not only her own extensive experiences as a revivalist but those of other women as well. Repression of female gifts, she warned her ministerial opponents, retards the growth of the church and the coming of God's kingdom and imposes an untenable burden on Christian women.

We believe that hundreds of conscientious, sensitive Christian women have actually suffered more under the slowly crucifying process to which they have been subjected by men who bear the Christian name than many a martyr has endured in passing through the flames. We are aware that we are using strong language; but we do not use it in bitterness, but with feelings of deep humiliation before God that the cause of truth demands the utterance of such sentiments.[9]

Throughout her writings, Palmer could be sharply critical of men, especially clergy, who repressed and rejected women's religious gifts. Her advocacy of women's preaching in public to mixed audiences was a radical stance at the time, yet it was not based on a theory of women's rights. Rather, it was rooted in her theology and in a prophetic tradition of religious leadership whereby it is God's call, not human customs or church traditions, that authorizes preaching. Thus Palmer did not advocate either ordination or sacramental ministry for women, nor was she particularly supportive of other issues of women's rights in her day. She accepted and valued the domestic role of wife and mother as natural and divinely sanctioned for women, subordinate only to every believer's first duty to God. Happily married herself, she lacked sensitivity to the woman for whom obedience to a husband might mean not only repression of God's call to testify but also suffering for the woman herself and her children at the hands of a drunken or abusive husband.[10]

## Antoinette Brown

It was Palmer's younger contemporary, Antoinette Brown, who not only sought formal ordination but was also more closely allied to a self-conscious women's rights movement. She was born on May 20, 1825, to a New England family with deep Puritan roots and grew up in the religious ferment of the "burned-over district" of New York. Her interest in religion, attested in her public profession of faith and by her joining the local Congregational church at age nine, was hardly unusual for a young woman of her circumstances and background. Her desire to become a minister, however, (not a teacher or even a foreign missionary, but a minister) most decidedly was unusual, as was her decision that she would therefore need a theological education. After teaching for a few years and saving her money, she entered Oberlin College in 1846, graduating from its "literary course" (the approved route for women students) a year later. At the time, Oberlin offered unusual educational opportunities for women, but even radical Oberlin was not prepared to train women, as it did men, for public speaking, a restriction roundly protested by Brown and her friend Lucy Stone. The school was even less ready to endorse Brown's desire to enroll in the theological course. Brown insisted; Oberlin resisted; finally a compromise was reached by which she took the theological courses but received no formal recognition: no student license to preach, no degree. When assigned an exegesis paper on Paul's strictures against women preaching, Antoinette Brown argued that "Paul meant only to warn against 'excesses, irregularities, and unwarrantable liberties' in public worship."[11] While her paper was published in the *Oberlin Quarterly Review*, her insistence that Paul's words were limited to particular historical conditions, typical of the line of argument taken by advocates of women's preaching in the nineteenth century, was an argument rejected by most male theologians. Nevertheless, Brown achieved what she wanted from Oberlin, the theological education that was, for her, a necessary preparation for ministry.

For the next two years, Antoinette Brown used her skills as a public speaker on the lyceum circuit to support herself and became involved in temperance, abolition, and women's rights, but she also preached whenever she could, usually at the invitation of a liberal male minister. Then in 1852, a small Congregational church in South Butler, New York, invited her to become their pastor. Despite the small salary they offered, Brown moved there in the spring of 1853 and took up preaching and pastoral duties. By summer the church's board decided to recognize her status with public, formal ordination, and on September 15, 1853, that historic "first" occurred. Luther Lee, a radical Wesleyan Methodist minister Brown knew through her reform work, agreed to preach an ordination sermon, "Woman's Right to Preach the Gospel." Taking as his text Galatians 3:28, he concluded, "If the text means anything, it means that males and females are equal in rights, privileges and responsibilities upon the Christian platform."[12] His sermon went on to cover the biblical ground that had already been raised by defenders of women's preaching from Margaret Fell to Sarah Grimké and would become familiar in debates for the next century and beyond: the example of prophetesses in Old and New Testaments, especially the women at Pentecost; Paul's recommendation of Phoebe as *diakonos* in Romans 16:1, misleadingly and inconsistently translated at that time as "servant"; denial that 1 Corinthians 14 and 1 Timothy 2 imply absolute and universal prohibitions on women, since they are neither consistent with other biblical examples nor followed literally by the churches. Lee's conclusion is especially interesting, insofar as he included not only Brown's call but also her theological education as grounds for her fitness for preaching and ordained ministry.

> We are not here to make a minister. It is not to confer on this our sister, a right to preach the gospel. If she has not that right already, we have no power to communicate it to her. Nor have we met to qualify her for the work of ministry. If God and mental and moral culture have not already qualified her, we cannot, by anything we may do by way of ordaining or setting her apart. . . . All we are here to do . . . is . . . to subscribe our testimony to the fact, that in our belief, our sister in Christ, Antoinette L. Brown, is one of the ministers of the New Covenant, authorized, qualified, and called by God to preach the gospel of his Son Jesus Christ.[13]

Yet Antoinette Brown did not remain long in the position she had dreamed of and worked so hard for. The job itself was exhausting, and she had little outside support, for she was caught between the majority of

Christians, who opposed women's preaching and ministry, and her friends in the women's rights movement like Lucy Stone, who were critical of the Bible and the organized Christian church. Most significant, she had begun to question some tenets of orthodox Calvinism, especially infant damnation. Self-doubt was followed by a physical breakdown, and she resigned her position in July 1854.

Over the next decade, Antoinette Brown resumed her public speaking and reform work. She married Samuel C. Blackwell in 1856 and through the 1860s and 1870s combined domestic and maternal responsibilities with serious study. Beginning in 1869, she published several books on philosophy and science and resumed more active public work as their five daughters grew older. Her study helped her come to terms with her own religious convictions, and in 1878 she formally joined the Unitarians and resumed preaching, though she was unable to find a full-time parish. In 1903, she helped to found a Unitarian Society in Elizabeth, New Jersey, preaching there once a month as "minister Emeritus," and in 1908, Oberlin belatedly awarded her the honorary theological degree, doctor of divinity, and formally listed her as a member of the theological class of 1850.[14] Unlike many of her coworkers for women's rights, Antoinette Brown Blackwell lived long enough to cast her vote in 1920 and died the following year on November 5.

## Other Women in the Pulpit

Phoebe Palmer, as a prominent female preacher and revivalist, and Antoinette Brown, as an ordained minister, however brief her career, were significant nineteenth-century pioneers, and if they were not typical, neither were they unique. Other women became ministers, formally or effectively, at home or on the foreign mission field. Writing in 1889 in defense of women in the pulpit, Frances Willard estimated "that there were in the United States five hundred women who have already entered the pulpit as evangelists, and at least a score (exclusive of the 350 Quaker preachers) who are pastors, of whom several have been regularly ordained. The denominations that have ordained women are the Methodist, Baptist, Free Baptist, Congregational, Universalist and Unitarian."[15]

Why were these groups open to women ministers, however rarely? For Quakers, the tradition was as old as the Society of Friends itself, and Quaker women were the most numerous group in female ministry in the nineteenth century, often combining religious leadership and preaching with reform work or foreign missions.[16] In Congregational and Baptist churches, the key advantage for women ministers was polity. Because the local congregation was the final authority in such decisions, a woman had only to convince a local parish to accept her, rather than waiting upon the agreement of regional or national boards or bishops. Even so, few women followed Antoinette Brown's historic example in the nineteenth century, and by 1900, there were fewer than forty women ministers in Congregationalism.[17]

Unitarians and Universalists occupied a position at the liberal end of the theological spectrum in American religion, and both produced outstanding early feminists in women like Judith Sargent Murray, Margaret Fuller, and Lydia Maria Child. Neither group, however, was wedded to a literal interpretation of the Bible that could be used to cite as universal and eternal Paul's negative comments on women. There was still plenty of opposition even in these groups to women's religious leadership, but there was also enough openness to allow several Unitarian or Universalist women to become ordained. Indeed, depending upon how ordination is defined, some have argued that it was Olympia Brown, not Antoinette Brown, who was the historic "first" ordained woman in America.[18] Born in 1835 in Michigan, Olympia, like Antoinette, encountered serious opposition to her desire to gain a theological education and become a minister, although Olympia had an encouraging encounter with Antoinette while Olympia was a student at Antioch. After graduating from Antioch, Olympia enrolled in the theological school at St. Lawrence University in New York, graduated, and was ordained by the St. Lawrence Association in June 1863. Unlike Antoinette, however, Olympia served in several regular pastorates in Weymouth, Massachusetts; Bridgeport, Connecticut; and Racine, Wisconsin for a quarter of a century, and was also an important leader in the women's rights movement.[19]

The question of women ministers in Methodism is particularly problematic. On the one hand, a tradition of women's religious leadership goes back to the founding of the Methodist movement in England and was continued in America. The rise of the Holiness movement and the example of Phoebe Palmer encouraged women's preaching, whether or not the women had official status. But the issue is complicated by several factors. Methodists had numerous leadership roles, including class leaders, exhorters, and evangelists, as well as preachers and fully ordained ministers. Licenses to preach might be formal or informal, oral or written, local or general. Different Methodist bodies, north and south, had different practices. Thus it is clear that Methodist women did preach in the nineteenth century, sometimes with an official license. The first may have been Maggie Newton Van Cott, who after gaining recognition as a traveling evangelist was granted an official license to preach by the New York Conference of the Methodist Episcopal Church in 1869, an action that led to immediate controversy. Amanda Way received a local license from the North Indiana Conference in 1871. Historian Janet S. Everhart has argued that at least fourteen women had local preacher's licenses in the 1870s, and that the growing numbers of such women may have helped to precipitate in 1880 the General Conference's explicit rejection of ordination for women and revocation of the local preaching licenses some women already had.[20] Despite continued controversy and the arguments of as prominent a leader as Frances Willard, the General Conference of the Methodist Episcopal Church, North, only allowed women local ordination in 1924 and full conference membership in 1956.[21]

## Basic Arguments about Women's Preaching and Ordination

Controversy within some denominations in the nineteenth century, first over women's preaching and then over ordination with its attendant status and pastoral and sacramental responsibilities, continued into the twentieth century. Some arguments were new, but others reiterated the main lines of debate so frequently raised earlier.[22] For Protestant Christians, the Bible was a central battleground. Advocates of female ministry cited Genesis 1:26–28, where both male and female are created in the image of God, and the example of prophetesses in the Old Testament. Opponents countered with the Creation and Fall accounts of Genesis 2 and 3 as evidence of woman's lower status in the order of creation and her guilt in the Fall, with the consequent punishment of subordination. From the New Testament, supporters noted Galatians 3:28, the women witnesses to the resurrection and at Pentecost, women leaders in the early church like Phoebe and Priscilla, and Paul's concession that women might pray or prophesy when veiled in 1 Corinthians 11. Opponents cited instead 1 Corinthians 14 and 1 Timothy 2 as decisive. It was not these passages that were historically conditioned or exceptions, they insisted, but rather the prophetesses and women leaders, whose example set no precedent for modern women. Moreover, passages like Ephesians 5 showed that the social hierarchy of husband over wife was part of the divine order.

Neither side seemed likely to convince the other on scriptural grounds alone, and other areas of debate were explored. Those favoring women's preaching frequently cited a sense of divine call, superseding all earthly authorities. They argued pragmatically from women's success and the church's need for effective evangelism, as well as from the example of successful women missionaries who functioned as ministers in everything but name. Opponents also drew on historical and social arguments, especially what they saw as the inevitable conflict of the duties of a minister with a woman's primary role as wife and mother, and indeed, with her very nature. In response, advocates like Frances Willard turned the argument around, insisting that, if anything, woman's nature made her a more suitable and effective minister than a man.[23]

The wisdom of arguing women's special qualifications for ministry can be questioned, in terms of both substance and tactics. Such an argument appears to accept the cult of True Womanhood with its assumption of a female nature, often epitomized in motherhood, that ultimately limits women's options and basic humanity.[24] It may have contributed to further "feminization" of American religion at a time when many male church leaders felt personally threatened by women's power in the churches, and alarmed at the continuing decline in men's church attendance and the lack of a strong, masculine image to attract talented young men to the ministry. Yet the charge that motherhood and ministry (and, indeed, most other public work) were incompatible was so pervasive that it could hardly be ignored. Over and over, the testimonies from women ministers that Willard solicited for her book included protestations that their children were not neglected. As one wrote, "As for me, I shall go on standing as an unwelcome and unanswerable fact before opposers. And, at the end of their profound arguments and fearful prophesying, I will still point to my five blessed boys, and meekly inquire, 'Have they gone to ruin?'"[25] The tactics of those who advanced special female qualifications for ministry were similar to those of reformers who "used" the cult of True Womanhood to expand women's spheres. "If women are so naturally moral and virtuous, all the more reason they should vote to protect their homes and balance the corruption of male politics," they insisted. The extent to which the arguments of these nineteenth-century feminists were based on genuine convictions about female nature and roles and the extent to which they simply exercised shrewd political judgment is nearly impossible to determine in retrospect.

As important as questions of women's preaching and ordination were for some groups in nineteenth-century America, other denominations had not yet even reached the point of debate. In many cases, the battle for laity rights for women had to be fought first, before ordained leadership was even thinkable. Could women speak and vote at congregational meetings? Could they serve as delegates to regional or national conventions? Could representatives from the women's church groups, particularly the missionary boards, speak publicly at national conventions to report on their work? For Presbyterians, Lutherans, Episcopalians, and Methodists and Baptists in the South, the answer to these questions was a resounding negative until well into the twentieth century, although sometimes what was forbidden at national conventions was permitted in local churches.[26]

The whole issue of laity rights for women was complicated by the women's missionary movement. As women in various denominations finally won the right to form distinct women's organizations, they established a sphere for activity and power that was within the churches at local and national levels, but also separate. These groups were extremely important in giving women experience in leadership, in building their skills and confidence, and in forming a power base. Yet they also may have retarded the push for laity rights and ordination simply because the women had enough to do in these separate spheres. When the male leadership in several denominations effected a merger of the women's boards with the general boards in the early twentieth century, frequently co-opting the women's power and voice at anything more than a token level, they precipitated an unintended and ironic consequence. Women and some of their male supporters turned with renewed interest to the issues of laity rights and ordination for women.[27]

## The Deaconess Movement

A final component of women's leadership within Protestant churches in the second half of the nineteenth century was the deaconess movement, because the deaconess presented an alternative model for female ministry. Modern revival of a female diaconate occurred in Germany when a Lutheran pastor, Theodore Fliedner, and his wife, Fredericke, founded an institution at Kaiserswerth. They began with a home for a few female prisoners, recently released, but the institution grew rapidly to include work with the poor and sick, a hospital, and training especially for nurses, as well as a mother house for the active deaconesses and a home for retired deaconesses. The Fliedners saw their work as a Christian response of mercy to the suffering, as well as a particular vocation for unmarried women. Over the next half century, the Kaiserswerth model was widely copied in Europe, not only among Lutherans, but within other Protestant denominations as well. Similarly in America, the Protestant groups that attempted to reestablish a female diaconate looked to Kaiserswerth as an inspiration, whether or not they were Lutheran. There were modest attempts by Presbyterians and some other smaller groups to revive the office of deaconess, but the major success in America came with Lutherans, Episcopalians, and Methodists.[28]

### Lutheran Deaconesses

The first attempt to establish a female diaconate in America was made by a young Lutheran pastor, William Passavant, of Pittsburgh. Passavant had visited Kaiserswerth in 1846 and was convinced that such work could be equally valuable in America. He gained Fleidner's support, and in 1849 four German deaconesses arrived to staff the hospital that would become the Pittsburgh Infirmary. The next year a motherhouse and organization, the Institution of Protestant Deaconesses, were established, and the first American deaconess was consecrated. But Passavant's experiment did not prosper as Kaiserswerth's had. Few American women were attracted to the work, and some of the European sisters whom Passavant had recruited left. There was little substantive support from the Lutheran church, and there was widespread suspicion of a movement that seemed so "Romish." Passavant himself lived long enough to see more successful establishments of Lutheran deaconesses toward the end of the century, but the initial experiment, though historically notable, was essentially a failure.

A more successful deaconess movement grew within German and Scandinavian Lutheranism in America in the last two decades of the century. In 1884, a wealthy Lutheran layman, John D. Lankenau, brought seven German deaconesses to Philadelphia to staff the German Hospital there. Two years later, a motherhouse was begun as a community for the women and a means of training American recruits. It was overseen by a male pastor or rector and an "Oberin" or "head sister." Work was expanded to include an orphan's home, a girls' school, and a kindergarten, but the hospital and nursing remained the central concern of the deaconesses. Changing times, good organization, and a wealthy patron, as well as close ties and support from the German-American community and the Pennsylvania Ministerium of the Lutheran Church, helped the Philadelphia institution to succeed where the Pittsburgh one had not. As historian Frederick Weiser notes, "By 1916, the Philadelphia Motherhouse of Deaconesses had eighty-two sisters of whom fifty-nine were consecrated. It was the most successful [Lutheran] deaconess institution in America in terms of numbers of members and varieties of service."[29]

Meanwhile, Norwegian-American Lutherans also ventured into the deaconess experiment. In 1883, Sister Elizabeth Fedde came from Norway to Brooklyn in response to a call from her brother-in-law. She began "outdoor" relief immediately, visiting the poor and sick in their homes, but she soon moved to found a hospital and a deaconesses training program. Before Fedde returned to Norway in 1896, she spent a year in Minneapolis, helping to found a home and hospital there. Three deaconesses from Minneapolis helped to organize a third Norwegian Lutheran deaconess center in Chicago in 1891, which, despite controversy and splits in the early years, ultimately became the largest of the Norwegian sisterhoods.[30] As with the German groups, nursing and hospitals were the dominant work of Norwegian-American deaconesses, but some also were involved in social work, and a significant number trained to serve on the foreign mission field.

Swedish-American Lutherans began deaconess work in Omaha in 1889 under the leadership of E. A. Fogelstrom, first with a children's home and then a hospital, and smaller branches were established in St. Paul, Minnesota (1892), and Axtell, Nebraska (1914). In 1893, Passavant's institution was revived in Milwaukee with a hospital, motherhouse, and training program. Finally, in 1895 the General Synod, representative of Lutherans with longer American ties and roots, moved to establish its own center for a female diaconate in Baltimore. American Lutherans in the late nineteenth century were divided by theological and ethnic differences, and so were their respective deaconess movements. Nevertheless, when the Philadelphia group called in 1896 for a conference of evangelical Lutheran deaconess motherhouses, all but the Brooklyn group accepted the invitation, making it "the first inter-Lutheran agency" in America.[31] Over the next twenty years, the group held twelve conferences to deal with organizational matters and to study, define, and publicize the diaconate. Out of the papers presented, a picture of the distinctive form and concerns of the Lutheran branch of the deaconess movement in America emerges.[32] While some Lutheran deaconesses were involved in various forms of social work or foreign missions and some served as parish assistants, the vast majority worked as nurses in institutional homes and hospitals.[33] The women's ministry was emphatically characterized as a "ministry of mercy, *not* of the word," undertaken in the spirit of the Christian love and charity that is a result of justification. Lutheran deaconesses were not a challenge to male church leadership, nor were they expected to try to change social systems and structures.[34] Finally, Lutherans saw their deaconesses as distinctive (and superior) to other forms of the diaconate in American Protestantism because of the centrality of the motherhouse ideal. It was to be a school, a church, and a home, a family with the rector and Oberin as parents, a religious congregation but "differ[ing] from the average congregation in the sincerity with which it exercised its faith because its members differed from the average Christian in the totality of their commitment, in the exclusive nature of their concentration on the life in Christ."[35]

## Episcopal Sisterhoods

Something like a deaconess order appeared first among American Episcopalians in the form of "sisterhoods." The first, the Sisters of the Holy Communion, was founded in 1845 by Anne Ayres and influenced by Kaiserswerth. Like deaconesses, sisters were to live together and carry on a ministry of mercy, especially nursing. Over the next decades, a number of such groups were founded in the United States or transferred from England. By 1880, "six major sisterhoods were at work in the Episcopal Church. For the next two decades, they grew slowly but steadily and gradually acquired responsibility for many institutions."[36] In some cases, the groups used the term "deaconess," and much of their work was essentially the same as the work of some sisterhoods. But other sisterhoods followed a more classical monastic pattern of an ordered religious life with less emphasis on active service. While many American Protestants thought the deaconesses smacked of Rome (and often they did), despite efforts by advocates of the diaconate to distance themselves from a Catholic model, the sisterhoods raised even more suspicion. In addition, there was a tendency to confuse or even conflate the two roles, a problem that retarded official approval of a female diaconate by the Episcopal Church's General Convention. Although small deaconess groups had been formed and functioning since midcentury with the encouragement and supervision of individual priests and bishops, it was not until 1889 that the General Convention passed a deaconess canon, "the first national recognition of women's ministries in the Episcopal Church."[37]

The women's ministry was to be centrally one of *service*, and that definition cut two ways. On the one hand, it distinguished the deaconess from those Episcopal sisterhoods whose focus was more on a disciplined religious life in a semimonastic tradition;[38] on the other hand, it reassured male church authorities that the deaconess was not the female equivalent of a male deacon. She was not to exercise authority in the church; she had no liturgical functions, as deacons did; whereas he was ordained, she was set apart; she must be single. And the diaconate for women was most emphatically not a step toward priesthood, as it was for the vast majority of male deacons.[39] As long as such distinctions were observed, and the women were clearly under male clerical control, their work was welcomed. Yet while women acceded to the strictures laid down by the General Convention and male clergy, their own perspective was rather different. As Mary Donovan notes:

> The clergy saw the deaconess as a religious extension of the ideal of true womanhood—a woman who would be pious, pure, submissive, and domestic, who would simply substitute obedience to the priest or bishop for obedience to a husband. Contrastingly, the women saw the deaconess as a professional church worker—trained in Scripture and theology as well as housekeeping and nursing—who would exercise a vocation of service to the Lord Jesus Christ through the institutional Church. The deaconesses were trained (generally by other deaconesses) to be initiators; the clergy expected them to work as directed.[40]

The women's concern for theological education and professional standards was reflected in the high priority given to the establishment of training schools for deaconesses after official sanction was granted in 1889. Schools were founded in New York and Philadelphia by 1891, and their curricula involved substantial academic work and practical training, including but not confined to nursing. In contrast to the Episcopal sisterhoods and the Lutheran deaconess training institutions, these schools were not clearly tied to a single location or institution, and many of their graduates were sent out to work in foreign missions or parishes, especially those in urban areas concerned with social outreach.

### Deaconesses in Methodism

The deaconess movement was a moderate success in American Lutheran and Episcopal churches, but in Methodism it achieved its greatest visibility and participation. Much of that success must be credited to Lucy Rider Meyer (1849–1922) and the Chicago Training School that she founded. Lucy Rider was an extraordinary woman who, before she married Josiah Shelley Meyer in 1885 and with him began the Chicago school, taught for a year in a Quaker freedmen's school in North Carolina, earned a degree from Oberlin, prepared to go to the foreign mission field as the wife of a medical missionary until her fiancé died, studied chemistry at Massachusetts Institute of Technology and taught it at McKendree College in Illinois, and served as the field secretary and an author for the Illinois Sunday School Association.

Like many other deaconess establishments, the Chicago Training School had a modest beginning, opening in October of 1885 in a rented house with the Meyers and only a handful of students but high hopes. Yet it grew rapidly. In 1886, the Meyers purchased a lot and built a home for the school, a deaconess order and home were established, and they developed a training school for nurses associated with Wesley Hospital. The earliest students' work was primarily house-to-house visitation for evangelism and practical help, but soon the school's graduates were leaving for the foreign mission field or to help establish deaconess homes and training institutions in other cities—Cincinnati, Minneapolis, New York, Boston, Detroit—to continue a twofold ministry of nurse and visiting evangelist/helper. Meyer herself was a creative and successful publicist and fund-raiser for the cause. She began publishing *The Message* (later *The Deaconess Advocate*) in 1886 and was able not only to call upon a number of wealthy donors but also to tap many small gifts, especially from women, through the "nickle [sic] Fund," chain letters, and the "Do-Without Band." Her campaigns brought in money and occasional recruits, inspired by her descriptions of the critical needs among the urban poor and her vision of the diaconate as a religious vocation both appropriate for women's skills and a challenge to their faith. She met the inevitable critics by pointing out that all the workers, including herself, were unsalaried, receiving only room, board, and a small personal allowance. She soothed Protestant fears of Roman Catholicism by pointing to the biblical and apostolic roots of the order and to the differences between Protestant deaconesses and Catholic nuns, as the former did not take permanent vows. Deaconesses did wear a uniform, but it was less cumbersome than the nun's habit, and it served practical purposes. It was economical and timesaving, and its uniformity prevented distinctions based on the sisters' different economic backgrounds. Furthermore, the uniform became a form of protection when the deaconesses went about their work in the cities. "Our uniform protects us as with a coat of mail. Such a *sentiment* has gathered about it that the very roughest men revere a woman who has it on."[41]

Credit for the success of the deaconess movement in American Methodism must surely also be given to other leaders and supporters, male and female, as well as to the deaconesses themselves. Indeed, in the latter part of the nineteenth century, a rivalry arose within Methodism between

Meyer and her supporters, who felt the deaconesses should work under the supervision of the church's conferences, thus gaining status and support, and a group led by Jane Bancroft Robinson, who wanted the movement controlled by the Women's Home Missionary Society to prevent men from taking over. The controversy was a real one and continued well into the twentieth century;[42] nevertheless, Meyer's role in the movement was central. As historians Catherine M. Prelinger and Rosemary S. Keller conclude, "During Meyer's 34 years of leadership, at least 5000 women were consecrated into the deaconess order. She and her graduates have been credited with founding more than 40 major Methodist institutions, including hospitals, orphanages, and homes for the elderly."[43]

## The Impact of the Deaconess Movement

How, then, do we assess the relationship of the deaconess movement to women's religious leadership in the churches? Was its impact positive or negative? On the one hand, church bodies granting women approval for this ministry at the national level may have deflected the push for laity rights, "approved" preaching, and ordination for women. The same year the Methodist General Conference recognized the office of diaconate for women, 1888, it refused to seat four elected, female lay delegates. (Eight years earlier the conference had ruled that women could not be ordained or licensed as local preachers.) When Presbyterians, Lutherans, and Episcopalians gave formal recognition to a female diaconate, they were most emphatic that this was a distinctive office of service and neither parallel to nor a step toward male church offices and authority. The very words used to describe how the deaconess's position was acknowledged were carefully chosen: "set apart" or "consecrated." Some women leaders spoke of deaconesses as ordained, and even a few men supported the use of the term for deaconesses, giving them a kind of clerical office, but they were rare exceptions.[44] For the vast majority of the churches' male leadership, and, indeed, for many women, the ministry of a female diaconate was acceptable precisely because it was one of service. Its spirit and its practical work were congruent with a prevailing image of woman as nurturer, whose natural virtues of self-sacrifice, patience, and humility were eminently suited to the needs of the poor, especially women and children, whether in the growing and troublesome urban centers of the United States or on the foreign mission field. Safely confined to women's "natural" sphere, deaconesses appeared to pose little threat of invading male turf or usurping male prerogatives of authority and leadership.

Nevertheless, the office of deaconess did give women official status within the church. Virtually every supporter of the movement asserted the biblical and early church roots of the office, with Phoebe as a kind of patron saint. In part, these arguments were a response to Protestant critics who thought the deaconess was too much like a Catholic nun, but they also strengthened the case for a legitimate, biblical office for women in the church's formal structure. Moreover, the training schools established in the last quarter of the century provided a degree of professional training and status for women; the diaconate was, for many, a bridge to professional positions in church work that would be further developed in the twentieth century. The schools provided theological education for women who were barred from most theological seminaries or who, perhaps, could not afford to attend college, since most of the deaconess training institutes were fairly inexpensive and many offered forms of financial assistance. Deaconesses addressed serious needs in their nursing, social service, and missionary work. Beyond such services, these women often found and cultivated a real sense of sisterhood in their communities, looking to other women as role models and support networks. Finally, the answer to the question of whether the impact of the deaconess movement on women's rights and religious leadership was positive or negative must be "both." Whether it was more positive or more negative may depend on whose perspective is weighted more heavily: the views of male church authorities, or the self-understandings of the women involved.

The female diaconate continued to be a viable ministry for Protestant women for the first few decades of the twentieth century, and while it was never a major movement, neither was it negligible. After the 1920s, however, it showed marked decline for a number of reasons. Some churches continued to debate the clerical status of the deaconess and her role in the church. Protestant prejudice about the diaconate's "Catholic" flavor continued, as did lingering public suspicions of women who voluntarily chose to reject women's happiest and most natural role in marriage. At the same time, the diaconate had limited appeal to women in twentieth century America as other options appeared. Professions like social work and nursing grew, as did lay careers like religious education in the church itself. Moreover, these positions were salaried, whereas the deaconess only received a modest living allowance. By the mid-twentieth century, the growing possibility of full ordination for a woman who felt called to a religious vocation as a lifework made the more restricted and subordinate office of deaconess both unattractive and unnecessary.

Yet for a half century, the deaconesses made a significant contribution through the questions they raised, as well as the work they did. Conservative male church leaders may have hoped that sanctioning a female diaconate would defuse and deflect more radical questions about women's rights in the churches and society and direct female energy into an appropriate womanly, subordinate sphere of service. For at least some deaconesses, however, their practical work experiences among the urban poor pushed them into that liberal wing of American Protestantism known as the Social Gospel.

# 11
# *The Social Gospel*

In the last quarter of the nineteenth century, the Social Gospel movement arose among American Protestants. In one sense, it was nothing new: love and service to others as a fruit of or complement to faith was a theme as old as Christianity, and many Christians in nineteenth-century America were active in humanitarian and reform work, believing that such activity was a necessary result of genuine conversion. Yet the Social Gospel was more than this. Its advocates had been shaped by the new forms of biblical criticism and nineteenth-century liberal theology. Liberal theology's themes that the kingdom of God is the center of Jesus' teaching and that all people have worth and dignity because they are created in the image of God were especially important to the Social Gospel. The problems of growing urbanization and industrialization, the conflict of labor and capital, and the poverty and apparent irreligion of inner city populations were particular concerns of the movement's leaders. Thus the Social Gospel was distinguished, on the one hand, from general charity and humanitarian work by the religious motivation behind its ideas and activities and its insistence on connecting social ideals with the kingdom of God, at least partially realizable in this world.

On the other hand, the Social Gospel moved beyond traditional Christian charity in its recognition of corporate identity, sin, and salvation, along with individual sin, faith, and responsibility. Few of the movement's leaders questioned the importance of conversion, but they also insisted that structural social changes were imperative. Social, economic, and political systems could be identified as evil and might thwart the most well-meaning and sincere attempts of their victims to change. In particular, Social Gospel leaders questioned the nineteenth-century assumption that poverty, at least of able-bodied males, was simply the result of laziness or vice. Nineteenth-century wisdom allowed that some of the poor, namely widows, orphans, and the handicapped, were not personally responsible for their state and hence were deserving of charity. Practitioners of Christian charity, however, rarely raised questions about the social structures that produced poverty, whether the poor were "deserving" or (undeserving) "paupers."

Traditional scholarship on the Social Gospel focused almost exclusively on men, the male clergy and theologians who were viewed as the movement's leaders, but recent revisionist historians have addressed the issue of women and the Social Gospel from two perspectives. First, how did the movement's acknowledged leaders view women? Second, and ultimately more important, how did women participate in the Social Gospel?

## Male Leadership Views about Women and Their Roles

The men who led the Social Gospel movement, from Washington Gladden to Walter Rauschenbusch, generally shared the views about women's nature and roles common to liberal Protestants of their day. Few Social Gospel leaders supported women's suffrage in the nineteenth century, but neither were they among the most conservative forces who insisted on woman's full submission and silence in all phases of church life. By the twentieth century, some, like Lyman Abbott, continued to oppose women's suffrage, but others like Rauschenbusch, the movement's most prominent leader, accepted and endorsed the vote for women.[1] They praised women's faithful attendance and activities in the churches and especially their religious influence in the home. Like the vast majority of middle-class Americans of their day, they simply assumed the natural piety of good Christian women. To them, far more pressing concerns were the relative scarcity of male church members and the popular image of religion as a "feminine" activity. By the latter part of the nineteenth century, not only did women significantly outnumber men in church membership, as they had for decades or even centuries in some churches, but the male leaders of the Protestant denominations began to identify such "feminization" of religion as a serious problem. Thus a conscious purpose of male Social Gospel writers was to appeal to men and to present an image of Christianity as manly and heroic.[2]

It was not that Social Gospel leaders didn't want women to be religious or active in home and church. Rather, because they so fully accepted the prevailing cult of True Womanhood, they simply assumed that women would be "religious" under normal circumstances. As a result, the leaders' own images of women fell into familiar stereotypes. Most admirable was the good Christian woman, the wife and mother whose spheres of activity were home and family, whose power was exercised indirectly as inspiration, influence, and example. Male writers also portrayed women, especially those of the working class, as victims who were exploited in factories and shops, or seduced or forced by economic necessity into prostitution. Social Gospel men sympathized with these women, deplored their situation, and supported protective legislation and economic action to limit or eliminate female labor outside the home. The men's sharpest criticism was directed at three types of women, all of whom departed in some way from the cardinal virtues of a True Woman: notorious women whose radical ideas had led them into atheism or heresy, like Elizabeth Cady Stanton or Mary Baker Eddy; society women whose lives were lazy, extravagant and frivolous and who exploited their own sisters as domestic servants; and young women whose idea of emancipation was to ignore traditional standards of womanly modesty and shun the role of motherhood.[3]

The tendency of male Social Gospel leaders to see women in stereotypes and in social roles, rather than as individual persons, was rooted in their view of the family. While these men held positions across a spectrum from moderate to radical on political and economic analyses and proposals, they were virtually unanimous in their reverence for the family and the mother's role in the home. Rauschenbusch was typical in his assessment that the family was "the most Christian" section of the social order, that its current ideal state was a product of Christianity, and that it was the key to building a Christianized society, as well as a pattern for other social relationships because of its principles of cooperation and self-sacrifice. This ideal family in turn depended on the mother, and motherhood was praised more highly and assessed with more awe than any other human institution, not excluding the church. Again, Rauschenbusch is typical: "As for the word 'mother'—that carries a mystic breath of sweetness to which we all do homage."[4] Thus, a Christian society depended on the home and family in an idealized, middle-class American form, and these in turn depended upon mothers. Concurrently, Social Gospel men were convinced that marriage and motherhood were the natural fulfillment for every woman. It was inconceivable to most of them that a normal woman would choose voluntarily to remain single; such a status could only be the result of misfortune or dire economic necessity.[5]

This romantic singlemindedness about woman's nature and roles as inherently different from those of men shaped the Social Gospel men's approach to women. They were genuinely distressed at the economic, physical, and sexual exploitation of working women. They recognized the overwhelming odds against the poor maintaining in the inner cities a minimally decent home, where the family's most basic needs of nutrition, health, and safety could be met, let alone a middle-class ideal home. Thus they supported changes to protect women who had to work, married or unmarried, but in the long run, they preferred solutions that would support the ideal home as they perceived it: sufficient wages and job security for the working man to support a family and the elimination of temptations like the saloon. The romantic ideal also meant that most male Social Gospel leaders paid relatively little attention to middle-class women who were attempting as deaconesses, settlement workers, or teachers to promote a Social Gospel. The men by no means condemned the activities;

they simply did not take women seriously as equal partners in dialogue and work in the movement to build a Christian society. The role of women was to be the pillars of the home.[6] However radical some Social Gospel spokesmen were on a range of political, economic, social, or theological issues, they were not radicals about women and their roles. They assumed the family and woman's role within it was basically good, and change was needed only to correct abuses and conditions that prevented the family from functioning as it should. For most of the male leaders, women did not play a central role as thinkers or actors in the movement. But rather than concluding, therefore, that women were not part of this historical movement, we must instead look to what women themselves were thinking, writing, and doing.

Women's participation in the Social Gospel was both easier and more difficult than the men's participation. On the one hand, there were broad cultural assumptions and long-standing traditions, shared by women and men, about woman's nature as self-sacrificing and nurturing, particularly suited to caring for weaker members of society. As long as women preserved propriety and did not neglect their families, they were commended for works of charity and service to the unfortunate. Thus the step from charity to reform and a social gospel seemed a natural one to some women, especially when their experiences revealed the inadequacy of charitable aid and individual regeneration. On the other hand, their duties as wives and mothers prevented most women from undertaking full-time work in the church and religious reform, and there was widespread prejudice against women's becoming too public or radical in their actions, especially if those actions impinged on the male turf of politics and economics. Even women who did not marry had few formal options for careers within the church: They might become foreign missionaries or officers in various missionary societies; by the end of the nineteenth century, they could become deaconesses or teach in religious training schools. With rare exceptions, they could never aspire to ordained ministry or teaching in a theological seminary. Yet these were the dominant career choices of the Social Gospel movement's acknowledged male leadership. Thus a woman who was convinced that her faith led her into a social gospel would either have to express her interest through part-time voluntary activities, if she were married, or if she were single, she would have to find an alternative career path, not the ordained ministry that was so obvious a choice for her like-minded brother.

## Vida Dutton Scudder

Without a base in pulpit or seminary classroom, few women became theorists of the Social Gospel. The most notable exception was Vida Dutton Scudder, one of the few women acknowledged even briefly in traditional Social Gospel histories, generally in the context of her work on various church boards, her association with the settlement movement, and her connections with the "left-wing" of the Social Gospel and its leaders, especially W.D.P. Bliss. Scudder was born in 1861 in India, but her missionary father drowned while she was still an infant, and she and her mother returned to an extended family in New England that was both long established and reasonably affluent. As she grew up, she traveled and studied in Europe, as well as in Boston, culminating her education at Smith College and a year's postgraduate work at Oxford. Shortly after her return from England, she accepted a teaching post in the English department of Wellesley College, a position she would retain until her retirement in 1928. Yet Scudder had been radicalized at Oxford, in part through contact with John Ruskin, and as much as she loved the English literature she taught and wrote about, she also used her teaching position to promote social Christianity. Her favorite course was "Social Ideals in English Letters," and she later wrote:

> I first offered it in spite of administrative disapproval and departmental indifference. . . . I was never allowed, perhaps for good reason, to include it in our carefully organized majors; but in spite of handicaps, it was often largely elected, and more alumnae thank me for it than for any other course I ever taught; they tell me that its worth to them grows with the years.[7]

Nor did Scudder's attempt to influence her students end in the classroom. She was a founding member of the College Settlements Association (CSA), begun in 1887, which eventually supported three main settlements (in Boston, New York, and Philadelphia), as well as chapters on college campuses. Although she herself was never a permanent settlement resident, she spent what time she could at Denison House in Boston, continued to be active in the governance of the CSA, and recruited her students for the movement. She was convinced that the experience would have a lasting influence even on those young women who went on to marriage or other careers, and thus it would make a contribution to social change as important as the direct work settlements could do with the urban poor. Scudder's 1903 Social Gospel novel, *A Listener in Babel,* is set in an urban settlement, and it served as a vehicle for her to explore theological, political, and social issues with a keen eye for their complexity.[8]

Another product of Scudder's interest in settlements was a growing understanding of labor issues and particularly the problems of working women, and she was one of the organizers of the Women's Trade Union League in the early twentieth century. Her concerns had been expressed and reinforced by her direct association with the radical wing of the Social Gospel movement. In 1889 she joined with fellow Bostonian and Episcopalian W. D. P. Bliss as a charter member of his Brotherhood of the Carpenter, an Episcopal mission in Boston that espoused socialist principles. In the 1890s she became a member of the interdenominational Society of Christian Socialists and an Episcopal group, the Christian Social Union. Scudder continued to claim an explicit Socialist identity in the twentieth century, joining the Socialist party in 1911 and writing later in her autobiography, "the ultimate source of my socialist convictions was and is Christianity. Unless I were a socialist, I could not honestly be a Christian. . . . "[9] It was not that Scudder's Christianity was subordinated to her socialism—indeed, she recognized that socialism was imperfect—but she believed it was the system most likely to advance the kingdom of God in her own time. In her 1912 book, *Socialism and Character*, she argued that not only were socialism and Christianity compatible but that only radical structural change of society to a system like socialism could provide an environment in which *all* persons could hope to develop "character," religious virtues.[10]

Vida Scudder found a further outlet for her Social Gospel concerns through membership on boards that promoted awareness of social justice in her own Episcopal Church. She helped to found its Church Socialist League in 1911 and served as one of its vice presidents, and in 1918 she helped to organize the Church League for Industrial Democracy. Such groups gave her an opportunity to work with male Episcopal leaders, even though that church still denied her, as a woman, formal voice and vote in its deliberations. The Society of the Companions of the Holy Cross (SCHC), however, was an all-woman's group in which Scudder found sisterly support and a platform for social concerns. Founded in 1884 by Emily Malbone Morgan, the SCHC emphasized a blend of spirituality and action in the world for its members, with a special concern for working women. Scudder joined in 1889, serving as its director of probationers from 1909 to 1942 and, unofficially, as leader of its radical, activist wing. She encouraged other women from the settlement movement, like Helena Dudley, Ellen Gates Starr, and Mary Simkhovitch, to join the Society. Despite the reservations of some members about the wisdom of public action by the society as a whole, Scudder and her supporters were able to pass petitions in 1907 and 1916 to the General Convention of the Episcopal Church calling for more social action.[11]

Vida Scudder clearly belongs in the circle of leadership of the Social Gospel for her ideas and activities. Her writings display the movement's characteristic theological notes of concern for corporate identity and systemic analysis, still rooted in a profound personal piety. Hers was an Anglo-Catholic spirituality rather than the evangelical piety of a Walter Rauschenbusch, but for both of them, the personal and the public, spirituality and social activism, were integrally related. Unlike most of her male colleagues, however, Scudder displayed a very real gender-consciousness in her writings and actions.[12] Few other women in the Social Gospel were as theologically sophisticated as Scudder, but they shared her special concern for women's needs and potential. Theirs was, in most cases, a "pragmatic social gospel"[13] focused on action rather than theory or constructive theology. But they were not unaware of theology, especially the Social Gospel's distinctive concern for the kingdom of God and the resultant stress on corporate identity and social structures in need of redemption. For many women, those theological insights came as a result of reading or hearing the movement's male leadership. These women appreciated the insights of male theologians and were clearly shaped by that theology. But the women's consciousness was also raised as a result of their own experiences. Even women who did not begin their work with a fully developed Social Gospel theology had a strong religious motivation, the desire to show their faith in action and to be useful, and they were aware of the particular problems of urbanization, industrialization, and immigration: the challenge of the cities. The question then was where could they go, what could they do *as women*?

## Women's Roles in the Social Gospel Movement

For some, the answer was home missions work, either through a particular denomination or through an ecumenical Protestant group like the WCTU. Although some women found full-time careers in such work, it was an especially important option for women who had to combine their concerns with the responsibilities of home and family. For some women seeking a church-related career of social action, the emerging deaconess movement was an alternative, and the settlement house movement attracted other women fired by religious and social concern. Finally, women supported the Social Gospel with their pens. In articles for religious journals and in books, they described their own experiences and the urban conditions they encountered in their work. Some used the novel as a vehicle to popularize their concerns, and although none of the women achieved the fame of novelist Charles Sheldon, some had a better grasp of the complexity of urban and labor problems and paid more attention to women's contributions and needs.[14] The dominant purpose of the women's writing was to encourage others, especially church members, to understand modern urban conditions, to recognize the challenge the conditions posed for Christians, and to address the needs with their time, money, and talents.

When suggesting that women who found alternative careers to ordination should be viewed as part of the Social Gospel movement, it is important to be clear about those claims. By no means did all the women who were active in home missions or as deaconesses endorse a distinctive Social Gospel. Many of them never took the step from humanitarian, individual, charitable aid to the questioning of structures. Like the Salvation Army's work with the cities' poorest, many of the women's efforts were sincere and valuable; they simply were not part of the Social Gospel. But other women took that step and thus should be included in the Social Gospel movement. Neither should all settlement work be identified directly as part of the Social Gospel. Most settlements, in self-conscious distinction from city missions or "institutional" churches,[15] were not involved in evangelism, and not all settlement workers were personally religious. Yet many women were driven by religious faith into the work, seeing settlements as complementary to churches in advancing the kingdom of God.[16]

### Frances E. Willard

In 1976, Ronald C. White Jr. and C. Howard Hopkins published a revisionist look at the Social Gospel,[17] including under "Neglected Reforms and Reformers" a section on Christian women and politics. Their focus was on a single figure, a woman well known in American history but not traditionally associated with the Social Gospel: Frances E. Willard. Yet Willard was both personally religious and socially and politically radical, especially through her alliance with the labor movement and socialism in the late 1880s. Under her leadership as president, the Women's Christian Temperance Union moved from a narrow focus on temperance to endorsement of women's suffrage—"For Home Protection"—and urban reform. The WCTU thus provided Protestant women with a national platform from which they could voice their views as women on social and political issues, as well as "a vast grass-roots organization that worked for charitable and political solutions to social problems."[18] To be sure, Willard herself and her more radical supporters tended to be more progressive than much of the union's rank and file membership, but theirs was the articulate voice of leadership, and their example and endorsement provided space for local groups to move into social reform. Thus some women used their WCTU base to work for prison reform, labor reform legislation, kindergartens for working mothers, and centers for educational and vocational training. Some women who began with a conviction that drunkenness was the problem came, through observation and experience, to see intemperance as a result of urban conditions that required broader institutional and structural reform. For these women, even if they were a minority of the WCTU's members, work under the Union's auspices was a way to act on a social gospel.

### Southern Methodist Women

Many Protestant women who did home missions work through their denominational groups, not only in the East and Midwest but even in the

South, also found themselves acting on a social gospel. In part because of its general social and religious conservatism, in part because there was less urbanization and industrialization there, the late–nineteenth-century American South has been seen as largely outside the Social Gospel movement. White's and Hopkins' revisionist volume challenges that generalization by citing recent work on male religious leadership,[19] while other historians have suggested that the Social Gospel found a voice in the South particularly among Methodist women.[20] The women involved did not constitute a majority among Methodist women, let alone southern women as a whole, yet their voice was not historically insignificant. The work of the Women's Home Mission Board began modestly with raising money to repair parsonages, but by the 1890s the women expanded their focus, despite suspicion and opposition from the church's male leadership. Their special focus was the home, which they saw (as did most male Social Gospel leaders) as the crucial foundation for a Christianized society. But they soon discovered, as had their northern sisters, that social and structural barriers prevented the poor from maintaining stable Christian homes and bringing up children to be productive citizens and Christians. Thus the Methodist women began to support kindergartens and better public education. They criticized industrial exploitation of children, especially in the textile mills, and called, albeit with little result, for more restrictive labor laws. They established boarding homes, worked with "fallen women," and deplored the plight of female domestic servants. They enthusiastically promoted temperance. In short, some southern Methodist women did move from charity to questioning structures and systems.

In part, their changing ideas resulted from observations and experiences, but these Methodist women were also directly influenced by the Social Gospel. In 1894, the Central Committee of the Women's Parsonage and Home Mission Society suggested a reading course for its members, and the first two books on their list were Josiah Strong's *Our Country* and Washington Gladden's *Applied Christianity*, followed in subsequent years by other writings of acknowledged Social Gospel leaders.[21] The center of the Social Gospel message that they heard, believed, and acted on was the kingdom of God. As McDowell notes, "Taking their cue from advocates of social Christianity such as Walter Rauschenbusch, the women stressed the importance of extending Christ's kingdom on earth."[22] As they moved into the early decades of the twentieth century, these Methodist women insisted that individual evangelism and active service to make this world more like God's kingdom were essential and complementary parts of Christian faith.

Southern Methodist women also supported the work of training schools and deaconesses as part of their Christian response to urban problems. Before southern Methodists formally created a women's home missions group, Laura Askew Haygood founded Trinity Home Mission in Atlanta for evangelism and outreach to the poor in 1882. In 1892, Belle Harris Bennett, who had visited Lucy Rider Meyer in Chicago and observed her training school, founded Scarritt Bible and Training School in Kansas City. At first, Scarritt focused on recruiting and training women for the foreign mission field, but it soon began to train home missionaries as well. After 1902, when the General Conference of the Methodist Episcopal Church, South, approved a female diaconate, deaconesses were trained at Scarritt for a variety of roles, including city mission work in Wesley Houses.[23] Bennett herself went on to a long and productive career as president of the Woman's Board of Home Missions and as an effective advocate of women's laity rights in southern Methodism.[24]

## Social Gospel in the North and Midwest

Although there were some deaconesses in the South by the early decades of the twentieth century, the movement there was not as successful or widespread as it was in the North and the Midwest. While not all deaconesses developed a Social Gospel consciousness, a good many, especially among Methodists and Episcopalians, did develop such a consciousness as a result of their work. If the early deaconesses began their work in the inner cities with traditional Protestant assumptions about poverty and with goals about individual evangelism and charity, many soon discovered the gross inadequacy of individual charity and the need for broader changes, including challenges to political and economic systems, in the environment in which the poor lived. They began to gather data systematically and to ally themselves with urban reformers. Results of the women's experiences in the form of new social methods and theories were incorporated in the deaconess training schools, just as sociology began to find a place in some male Protestant seminaries. Deaconesses tried to publicize the conditions they discovered and the solutions they advocated to the broader church through speeches, journals, and books. If these works were seldom as intellectually and theologically sophisticated as those of the Social Gospel's male leadership, they definitely moved from individual charity to recognition of corporate guilt and calls for structural change. Hoping to produce a change of heart and action in their readers, deaconesses painted vivid pictures of real families and their conditions. Isabelle Horton (1853–1933) was a deaconess trained at Lucy Rider Meyer's Chicago school who went on to work at the Halstead Street Institutional Church in that city. In 1904, she published *The Burden of the City* for the northern Methodists' Woman's Home Missionary Society In a section entitled "Field Notes," she presents the observation by a typical deaconess of a specific family: the filth and over-crowding; the sickness of the babies for whom milk is an expensive luxury; the overworked mother, and the father too sick to work even if he could find employment; the valiant but pathetic efforts of an eleven-year-old to care for her younger siblings. She concludes:

> You think of Hercules and his Aegean stables. But Hercules needed for his task floods of water, and pure air and sunshine, and broad, free spaces. You wonder what even his strength would avail here; and suddenly you realize that to save this one family you have to face all the problems of the modern city. The health commission, the landlord question, the pauperizing influence of alms-giving, faulty education, labor and wage problems—all are concerned in the condition of things in this one cellar.[25]

Thus Horton encouraged cooperation with other groups working for urban reform and praised the work and "Christlike spirit" of Jane Addams, even as she expressed her own preference for a combination of evangelism and social service.[26] She repeatedly insisted that city workers should be wary of imposing their own theories or plans without sufficient careful study of concrete conditions, but she did not shy away from radical challenges to the system that produced poverty, drunkenness, and insecurity.

> If this be true—if under the present system a "righteous distribution" of profits is impossible, let the "moral forces" be brought to bear, though the system be destroyed. Or if "destroyed" savors too much of revolution and anarchy, let us say replaced by a new system which shall not set a man's best self and his business interest over against each other; one in which one man's success shall not mean the failure of hundreds of his weaker brothers, but in which his gain shall mean the good of all.[27]

Just as male Social Gospel theologians insisted that both individual conversion and structural changes were needed to Christianize the social order, so deaconesses too saw evangelism and social service as equally important in their work and appealed directly to their fellow church members to respond out of Christian commitment. What deaconesses lacked in theological sophistication when compared to the leading men of the movement, they made up for in an activism that was lived out among the cities' poor. As Mary Agnes Dougherty argues, if male leaders like Rauschenbusch who insisted they were a few voices in the wilderness before 1900 had paid attention to the deaconesses, they might have felt less lonely, and if a historian like Robert Handy had been similarly alert, he might have been less likely to conclude that Social Gospel leaders were "not so much activists as they were preachers, proclaimers, and educators."[28]

### The Settlement Movement

Finally, when assessing women's role in the Social Gospel, we must consider the settlement movement, not because settlements consistently combined evangelism and social service as deaconesses and home mission workers did—many, including the most famous ones like Hull House, self-consciously did not—nor because all settlement workers saw themselves as part of the Social Gospel. But while many settlements eschewed evangelism among their neighbors for reasons of principle and pragmatism, some settlements were associated with churches,[29] and many early workers were religiously motivated and personally pious. Allen Davis, in his classic study on settlements, argues that the most successful settlements were non-sectarian but also admits the crucial importance of religious motivation in the movement's early years, citing a 1905 poll by W. D. P. Bliss of 339 settlement workers: 88 percent were active church members, and "nearly all admitted that religion had been a dominant influence in their lives."[30]

Thus the settlement movement as a whole should not be cavalierly baptized as religious or as simply a branch of the Social Gospel in a kind of church-historical imperialism, but neither should it be ignored as if it had been a purely secular social and political phenomenon in American history. Some settlements were religiously affiliated. Many settlement leaders and residents were motivated by religious convictions. Numerous Social Gospel leaders, men and women, promoted and participated in settlement work. For some of those women, like the young college students recruited by Vida Scudder and the College Settlement Association, the settlement experience was a short-term one, before they moved on to other careers or marriage. Other women, like Helena Stuart Dudley (1858–1932), found in the settlements themselves a career and long-term commitment that was effectively a religious vocation. Along with Scudder, Dudley was a founder of the College Settlement Association and became the head of the association's Denison House in Boston from 1893 until 1912, working closely with the labor movement of her day. She was also a lifelong member of the Society of the Companions of the Holy Cross.[31]

Did women participate directly in the Social Gospel movement? They did, and their ideas and actions spanned a theological and political spectrum from moderate to radical, just as male leaders' did. While the women shared certain beliefs and methods with the men, they made their own distinctive contributions. Like the male leaders, the women believed that the kingdom of God was a central theme of Jesus' teaching and optimistically hoped they could bring American society closer to that ideal through social action. They saw in the emerging problems of the nation's cities the key challenge to the churches of their day and promoted systemic reforms, not just traditional charity. Like many male Social Gospelers, the women had little patience with debates over fine points of doctrine and felt that a life of service inspired by Christ was a better test of Christian faith than adherence to a particular creed, although they continued to affirm the importance of individual conversion and personal devotion. These women generally shared the men's admiration for the Christian home as the foundation of society. They did not, however, therefore conclude that their own contribution was limited to being admirable wives and mothers. Some sought full-time careers as single women. Others, although married, insisted on extending their natural concerns for home and children to the homes and children of the poor, and if that meant challenging their own traditional roles, as well as economic and political structures in the "male sphere," they were willing to do so. As a consequence, the women were sometimes quite critical of what they perceived as male systems, and they were impatient with what they saw as unwarranted male restrictions on their activities. Few, however, were overtly hostile to men in general, with the possible exception of seducers and liquor magnates. Rather, the women were more likely to sympathize with drunken husbands or with employers as victims of the system, and they wanted to work with men for common goals.

Most women in the Social Gospel were more activists and publicists than theologians or theoreticians. That activism focused especially though not exclusively on the needs of women and children. These middle-class Protestant women established kindergartens and day nurseries. They argued for more restrictive child labor legislation. They deplored prostitution but recognized the social and economic realities that fostered it and tried to save young women in the cities by sponsoring boarding houses and employment bureaus and by condemning the grossly inadequate wages paid to women. In their activities, whether part-time or full-time, many of these women also found the personal satisfaction of meaningful work and a sense of sisterhood with each other and with the women they tried to serve. Like the women who became foreign missionaries, they were sometimes condescending and culturally insensitive toward their immigrant neighbors, unconsciously assuming the superiority of white, Protestant, middle-class values, yet they also saw firsthand the real survival issues of poor families and tried to do something about them. In sum, women were indeed an important part of the movement, complementing and extending its work through their ideas and activities, even as they expanded their own horizons as women.

# 12

# *Native American Women and Religion in Nineteenth-Century America*

Princess or squaw: most white Americans in the nineteenth century, to the degree that they even considered Native American women, pictured them in one of those two stereotyped images. The former was indeed a positive, if overly romanticized, image, a legacy of Pocahontas, its archetype, but one that bore no more relation to reality than did the myriad legends, stories, poems, and plays produced about Pocahontas to that woman herself. Moreover, the image and those Native American women who were presumed to exemplify it were seen as admirable precisely because they were helpful to whites and had accepted a significant degree of white culture. From a white point of view, these women were the exceptions whose finer qualities of intellect and morality enabled them to understand, appreciate, and embrace an obviously superior white, Christian civilization. Thus there was little attempt to understand the complex motivations that might have been present in such women and their choices.

The "squaw" was a negative image, eliciting a mixture of revulsion and pity. Most whites assumed that all Indians were inferior—ignorant, degraded savages and heathen—and furthermore, that the women were mistreated by the men, who regarded them as slaves, "beasts of burden," forced to do all the tedious drudgery while the lazy men ruled over them. Even if the Indian woman was not sexually loose by choice, she was victimized by polygyny, or her sexual favors could be bought, sold, or given away by male relatives. Such assumptions then reinforced a widespread perception that only Christianity raised women to a position of honor and respect.

Although widespread, such images had little or no connection to the reality of Native American women. In part, this was due to white misunderstanding of what they did observe. For example, that an Indian woman might walk behind a man was not an expression of subservience but for her own safety, because he then responded first to danger or attack. The polygyny that was common in many Native American tribes and assumed by whites to be evidence of female degradation was perceived differently by Native American women. As Katherine Weist notes, "Seen in the context of women's labor, polygyny was important to the women for the assistance they gained in the household duties and the pleasure they derived from working with other women."[1] White observers concluded that Indian women were little better than "beasts of burden" because they saw eastern tribes in which women performed the "male" work of farming, "male" by their European culture patterns, while the "lazy" men sat around and did nothing. They failed to understand a gendered division of labor whereby women were more immediately involved in the agricultural work of gathering and/or raising of plant food, while men's work was in hunting and war. Nor was the division simply a "practical" one, for it was rooted in religious perceptions and a worldview in which men drew upon those spiritual powers involved in the necessary taking of life, while women were linked, through their activities and their biology, to spiritual powers of creating and nurturing life. Crossing the two kinds of spiritual power—doing the work appropriate to the other gender—could be dangerous to those involved and counterproductive to successful undertakings.[2] Cultural misunderstanding was exacerbated for the many white Americans who had little or no firsthand contact with Native Americans. Written sources available to them were problematic. Race or gender or both served as filters between Native American female reality and recorded account. Most of the records written by Native Americans were by men, and even those could not avoid problems of translation. Moreover, Native American people could be justifiably reluctant to speak candidly about their lives and beliefs.[3]

Stereotyped white images also took little account of the great diversity among Indian tribal groups. Added to intrinsic differences present among tribes before the arrival of whites were the differences that came as a result of white contact, in different degrees and at different times for various tribes. Internal differences within a particular tribal group were often increased by white contact, as tribal members chose or were forced into different responses to white culture, including white religion. Nevertheless, despite real diversity among Native American peoples, there were also some commonalities among Native American women, in their roles and their religion in particular, beginning with the fact that religion was integral to all of life, not a separate sphere of experience. Of course, there were some especially sacred objects, places, times or actions, but religion pervaded daily life as well, because no sharp line was drawn between natural and supernatural.

## Beliefs and Rituals

Some tribal groups identified "a pervasive spiritual power" or a high god or goddess, but in most cases a wide range and variety of spiritual beings, male and female, were more immediately active in the daily life of the people.[4] Many of these figures were identified with animals or with mythic founders of the tribe (or both), who set the tribe in its particular land and taught the people how to live. The stories about these figures were told and retold by both men and women, shaping the identity, values, and actions of the tribe in a religious oral tradition that was as authoritative for Native Americans as written scriptures were to Christians. Maria Chona, a Papago woman, affirmed, "I knew all about Coyote and the things he can do, because my father told us the stories about how the world began and how Coyote helped our Creator, Elder Brother, to set things in order."[5] These beings were very much part of present reality; they might be helpful or harmful and so should be honored, placated, or even avoided, but always respected. Pretty-shield, a Crow woman, tells numerous stories of encounters by herself and others with "Persons," spirits sometimes in human and sometimes animal form, who may be dangerous or protective, but whose warnings and instructions are ignored at one's peril. She herself and others in her tribe often had a particular animal who was their "medicine," a kind of guiding spirit or source of authority. "My grandmother's name was Seven-stars . . . and her medicine was a chickadee," she said. She then recounted the story of her grandmother's defense of a chickadee as a young girl; later the bird returned and instructed her grandmother in a vision. Pretty-shield's own medicine was the ant, discovered in her "medicine dream" shortly after the death of an infant daughter. A Person appeared and spoke to her, standing beside an anthill.

> "Come here, daughter." Again I walked toward her when I did not wish to move. Stopping by her side, I did not try to look into her face. My heart was nearly choking me. "Rake up the edges of this ant hill and ask for the things that you wish, daughter," the Person said; and then she was gone. Only the ant hill was there; and a wind was blowing. I saw the grass tremble, as I was trembling, when I raked up the edges of the ant hill, as the Person had told me. Then I made my wish, "Give me good luck, and a good life," I said aloud, looking at the hills. . . . now, in this medicine dream, I entered a beautiful white lodge, with a war-eagle at the head. He did not speak to me, and yet I have often seen him since that day. And even now the ants help me. I listen to them always. They are my medicine, these busy, powerful little people, the ants.[6]

Vision quests as means of finding a special spirit guardian were common to many Native American tribes. While Pretty-shield's medicine dream came to her after she was a mature woman, the more typical time for a structured quest was around puberty. The vision quest was especially common and important for young boys, but in some tribes, girls, too, made vision quests, sometimes as part of the rituals surrounding the onset of menstruation, a crucial social and religious rite of passage that was marked in virtually every Indian group. Details varied among the tribes, but most included a period of isolation, care and instruction from other women, and ultimately celebration at her change in status.[7] In many but not all tribes, women continued to withdraw from community activities during their menstrual periods, at which time they might have particularly close contact with creative spiritual powers or pose a potential spiritual danger to others in the tribe, such as men engaged in preparation for war or the hunt. Maria Chona remembered the ways in which her experience at puberty was both like and unlike that of her brothers: Girls are "very dangerous" at that time, she reported. "It is a hard time for us girls, such as the men have when they are being purified. Only they give us more to eat, because we are women. And they do not let us sit and wait for dreams. That is because we are women, too. Women must work."[8]

Activities at a significant point in the life cycle, such as coming of age, were examples of the ritual that was so central in Native American religious life. Birth, marriage, and death, too, were occasions marked by distinctive rituals in virtually every tribe, although the particular forms might vary. Childbirth was generally an all-female affair, when older women or relatives assisted the new mother, sometimes in a special location, but other early rituals, such as naming the child, could involve both men and women. The honor of naming was given to different persons in different traditions, and a name might be changed for a serious reason. Waheenee, a member of the Hidatsa tribe, tells how the name first given her was changed because she was sickly. "We Indians thought that sickness was from the gods. A child's name was given him as a kind of prayer. A new name, our medicine men thought, often moved the gods to help a sickly or weak child."[9] Among the Omaha, choosing a permanent name was delayed until the child was about four, when he or she went through a ceremony known as "The Turning of the Child." The mother brought her child to the tent, but he or she entered alone with a new pair of moccasins. Other adults sang the songs and pointed the child in the direction of each of the four winds, put on the moccasins, and announced his or her new name.[10]

Like the ritual surrounding birth and naming, the particular forms for marriage and burial varied widely among different tribal groups, but all had ways of marking the solemn occasion to launch persons on the next stage of life's journey, be that the married life of adults or a form of continued existence after death. Virtually every Native American tribe believed in some form of afterlife that all would reach in time, although some spirit-journeys might be longer than others. Few, if any, however, had a concept of eternal punishment, which was a point of major conflict or puzzlement when Indians were confronted by Christian missionaries. Sarah Winnemucca, a Piute Indian who gained fame as a reformer and defender of her people, embraced a nominal Christianity, but expressed her distress at this strange Christian belief.

> When I was a child in California, I heard the Methodist minister say that everybody that did wrong was burned in hell forever. I was so frightened it made me very sick. He said the blessed ones in heaven looked down and saw their friends burning and could not help them. I wanted to be unborn, and cried so that my mother and the others told me it was not so, that it was only here that people who did wrong and were in the hell that it made, and that those that were in the Spiritland saw us here and were sorry for us. But we should go to them when we died, where there was never any wrongdoing, and so no hell. That is our religion.[11]

Rituals were also associated with recurrent times in the yearly cycle, like harvest or the buffalo hunt, as well as with special events like a war party or crises like illness. Maria Chona told how the Papago tribe all moved in midsummer to a Cactus Camp for the work and ceremonies that would ultimately bring down the rain. When the cactus fruit was finally ripe, the women picked it, boiled down the juice, and made liquor. All the adults joined in the singing, the hospitality, and the drinking, "[m]aking themselves beautifully drunk, for that is how our words have it. People must all make themselves drunk like plants in the rain and they must sing for happiness."[12]

Ritual response to a crisis of illness or injury frequently came from an especially authoritative figure, a medicine man or woman or a shaman. At times this involved herbal medicine, but at least as important were the practitioner's close connection with the spirit world and his or her resultant understanding of the disharmony that caused the illness. Carolyn Niethammer suggests that women exercised both forms of healing:

> Some early medicine women specialized only in natural curing; others used both natural and supernatural means to cure patients who came to them. The knowledge of herbal medicines was not confined exclusively to the women in the early tribes, but generally women seemed to be more familiar with various herbal potions and brews. Women who practiced medicine were usually middle-aged or older—partly because by this age a woman was no longer busy caring for small children, and partly because older women were free of the taboos associated with menstruation.[13]

Nevertheless, such a distinction should be drawn cautiously since lines between natural and supernatural were more a white construction than a Native American one. The same close connection of the medicine person with the spirit world meant that these leaders were sources of wisdom, explaining the significance of signs and events and giving a community direction in times of need. In some tribes, the same spiritual power that worked positively in a shaman could function malevolently in a witch; such figures were feared, shunned, punished and sometimes even executed.[14] Nevertheless, the negative figure of the witch was less common than the positive one of medicine person, and women were not identified as witches simply because they as women tried to exercise authority.

## Gender Roles

In many, if not most, Native American groups, women could be religious leaders of some sort, yet it is fair to say that women exercised such leadership for a tribe as a whole, rather than within particular female spheres and activities, less frequently than men. As a young girl, Maria Chona seems to have had the special gifts, dreams, and abilities that would have marked her as a religious leader, but the elders of her family discouraged her from becoming a medicine woman because of her brother's prior claims. "'That cannot be,' said my father. 'We have one medicine man in the house and it is enough.'"[15] Yet her special religious calling was deferred, not denied entirely, and later in life she rediscovered special spiritual powers, especially healing, and took over her brother's position after he died. She explained, "[H]e taught me many cures [in his last illness]. 'Now you must stand in my place,' he said. And he told all the people, 'I am going to die but she will take care of you.'"[16]

In religion, as in tribal life generally, men and women had some areas of common participation and interest and shared the values and expectations—the "ethics"—that were passed on from parents to children by story, example, and training. Among those values was a strong concern for the survival and well-being of the group, and the individual's identity was shaped by the community's needs and by association with an extended family or clan. It would be inaccurate to suggest that Native American tradition had no place for individualism,[17] but in comparison with dominant white values in nineteenth-century America, Native American men and women were much more inclined toward communal values and corporate identity.

Yet there were also separate gender spheres and responsibilities in tribal life. Women had primary responsibility for care of the home, whether that was the relatively permanent structure of groups like the Pueblos in the Southwest, the longhouses of the Iroquoian peoples, or the earth lodges and tepees of Plains Indians. In many cases, female care also meant female construction and ownership, so that in the area of property rights, at least, many Native American women were well in advance of their white sisters at the time. Women were in charge of childcare on a day-to-day basis, though men shared in the education and love of children. In general, women gathered and/or raised plant food, while men supplied meat from the hunt, but the extent of those roles varied, given the location and resources of different tribes. Where agriculture formed a larger part of subsistence, men as well as women spent substantial time in cultivation, and women took part in such critical events as the buffalo hunt among Plains tribes by helping the men to prepare, physically and spiritually, and by transforming the animals taken into meat, clothing, and the tools and utensils of daily life.

Because of their contributions to the food supply, women in some tribes "owned" the food. As with female ownership of the home, this meant women had significant economic power, though ownership was seldom seen in white terms of private property. As Niethammer notes,

> Although women had absolute control of the food supply in many societies, it did not give them license to withhold provisions from those who were hungry. Quite the contrary, for most Indian cultures highly valued generosity and hospitality not only as requirements of sociability but also as a necessary form of welfare and unemployment benefits. For those families who had more than enough to eat, food was not only nutrition but a road to popularity as well. One of the main reasons for gaining wealth was to be able to share and win friends by one's generosity, and the status of a woman in a community depended to a large extent on the manner in which she chose to distribute the extras in the family larder.[18]

The requirements of status may have been one reason for polygyny in some tribes; that is, the hospitality that was assumed to accompany higher status demanded the time and contributions of more than one wife. Hospitality was not the only justification, however, and few Indian women seem to have regarded polygyny as a source of oppression.[19]

Like the hunt itself, war was predominantly a male activity, with women's participation generally confined to sending out and welcoming back the warriors (by no means an insignificant role, practically and ritually). Yet the division of labor by gender that characterized Native American life should not be perceived rigidly. For example, Sarah Winnemucca insisted that among the Piutes, when a first child is born, "the father goes through the labor of piling the wood for twenty-five days, and assumes all his wife's household work during that time. If he does not do his part in the care of the child, he is considered an outcast."[20] Waheenee, the Hidatsa woman, described at length a hunting party composed of several young couples who left the tribal base for an extended period, although once out, the women made camp, cooked, and helped to prepare the meat and skins while the men actually hunted the buffalo.[21] And if war was primarily a male activity, it was not exclusively so; there were women warriors in some tribes, accepted and admired as such.[22] It is clear from Prettyshield's account that women warriors existed and that they were exceptions. On the one hand, she was insistent that "Sign-talker," as she called Linderman, should record the presence of Indian women who fought with General Crook in the Battle of Little Big Horn. Yet she also made it clear that war was more a necessary sorrow than a desirable role for women of her tribe: "I cannot tell you about the fighting itself. That is a man's business. Our men were always fighting our enemies, who greatly outnumbered us. Always there was some man missing, somebody for us women to be sorry for."[23]

Finally, both men and women had opportunities for creative expression as they made the clothing, blankets, utensils, and tools that were practically necessary for daily life but that were also works of beauty and self-expression, and frequently of religious significance, too. Sheer enjoyment, as well as solemnity, could characterize ritual occasions, and Indian children had toys and games. Sometimes these were shared by boys and girls, but more often they were enjoyed with others of the same sex, at least in part because most Native American groups discouraged excessive or unsupervised interaction among young men and women. When describing her own girlhood, Waheenee seems a little bemused by white obtuseness: "White people seem to think that Indian children never have any play and never laugh. Such ideas seem very funny to me. I have seen children at our reservation school playing white men's games. . . . We Indian children also had games. I think they were better than white children's games."[24]

## The Impact of White Culture and Christianity

When attempting to understand Native American society and to compare and contrast it with white social structures regarding gender roles and equality, modern scholars have frequently raised issues of matrilineal and/or matrilocal social structure, especially among the Iroquois. Such structures characterized some, but not all, Native American groups and may have supported female religious and other leadership roles, but they should not be perceived therefore as evidence of "matriarchy."[25] Rather, they underline the variety within Native American traditions, a variety also evident in the roles, activities, and customs affecting men and women. Even a modest acquaintance with those differences explodes the derogatory image of "the squaw," yet it should not be replaced with a romanticized equality shaped by twentieth-century presumptions and values. Neither an undifferentiated equality nor a rigid hierarchy is an appropriate model for most Native American societies. Rather, a better model is one of complementarity, where distinctive roles for men and women are presumed, some movement across gender lines is accepted, and there are significant areas of commonality in culture and in religion in particular.

Native American women who had significant life experience of traditional tribal ways before major intrusions of white culture and who were as old women able to recount those experiences to whites perceived that complementary model as both accepted and acceptable. To them, white culture brought no great boon of increased respect and opportunities for women, whatever white missionaries may have believed. The women may have accepted the inevitability of change that was the result of greater contact with white culture, but they also expressed regret at the passing of the old ways. Looking back, Waheenee concluded:

> I am an old woman now. The buffaloes and black-tail deer are gone, and our Indian ways are almost gone. Sometimes I find it hard to believe that I ever lived them. My little son grew up in the white man's school. He can read books, and he owns cattle and has a farm. He is a leader among our Hidatsa people, helping teach them to follow the white man's road. He is kind to me. We no longer live in an earth lodge, but in a house with chimneys; and my son's wife cooks by a stove. But for me, I cannot forget our old ways. Often in summer I rise at daybreak and steal out to the cornfields; and as I hoe the corn I sing to it, as we did when I was young. No one cares for our corn songs now. Sometimes at evening I sit, looking out on the big Missouri. The sun sets, and dusk steals over the water. In the shadows I seem again to see our Indian village, with smoke curling upward from the earth lodges; and in the river's roar I hear the yells of the warriors, the laughter of little children as of old. It is but an old woman's dream. Again I see but shadows and hear only the roar of the river; and tears come into my eyes. Our Indian life, I know, is gone forever.[26]

It was circumstances of time and geography that allowed some nineteenth-century Native American women fully to experience traditional ways for at least a part of their lives. For others, the disruptions of white contact and the changes and choices it required came sooner. Of course, some Native American tribes in what would ultimately become the United States had considerable contact with whites during the colonial period. Spanish missionaries attempted to plant Roman Catholic Christianity among the Pueblos in the Southwest during the sixteenth and seventeenth centuries. At first, little sustained missionary work accompanied the Spanish settlement of St. Augustine in 1565, but Franciscan efforts in Florida in the last quarter of the sixteenth century and through the first half of the seventeenth were significant. French Catholics went among the Huron in areas of the northern United States and Canada from the seventeenth century on, as the English began to colonize the east coast. While the English were far less interested and less effective missionaries than their Spanish and French counterparts, they made some efforts to convert and educate the indigenous peoples they encountered, and their colonization and growth made white contact and disruption of traditional tribal ways inevitable sooner or later.[27] But United States nationhood and the dawning of the nineteenth century accelerated the pace of interaction, forcing confrontation with white culture on more and more Native Americans.

## Extermination, Removal, and Assimilation

Independence meant to the government of the United States that Indians were regarded or needed less than in pre-Independence days as separate nations who could be military allies. The Louisiana Purchase turned eyes westward for national expansion and settlement. White Americans saw three options for the Indians (who were seldom asked for their opinions on the matter): they could be exterminated, removed, or assimilated. There were surely Americans who favored the first alternative, but it was hardly one that could be presented so baldly as a respectable public option, certainly not by the churches and professing Christians. Removal was a more attractive option, based on the premises that the two societies could not live together because of vast cultural differences and that there was plenty of "empty space" out west. Unfortunately, the theory failed to take account of certain complications. First, the west was not uninhabited, and when a tribal group that had lived in the East was removed further west, it might displace another tribe from its own ancestral lands, causing considerable intertribal friction; nor did the tribal ways and the religious significance of the land that had developed in one geographical area easily translate to a new area. Advocates of removal also underestimated the speed, extent, and sheer rapacity of white exploration and settlement over the course of the nineteenth century. Finally, even without such complications, implementation of a policy of removal and reservations was problematic: dishonest agents; broken treaties; whites who ignored laws and boundaries with impunity; even faulty surveys and records and lack of communication were ongoing and disastrous realities. Yet a reservation system continued to have its defenders, including whites who considered themselves to be friends to the Indian, and who were aware of some of the problems and saw in the system a way to protect Indian rights to *some* land where they could continue traditional ways. Others, like Christian missionaries, at times defended the reservation system as a temporary expedient because they deplored the results of "bad" white influence on simple, impressionable Indians.

Ultimately, most Christians, missionaries and those self-consciously concerned with Native peoples, endorsed the third option: assimilation. To assimilate meant, quite simply, that Native Americans would adopt white culture and white religion; they could then become a part of American society. That the price for Indians of their acceptance was denial of their traditions and identity was not seen as a serious obstacle or even loss. Underlying such insensitivity, however, were a practical judgment and a related, relatively unquestioned premise. If Indians did not adapt, they could not survive. The process of "civilization," it was assumed, was simple, linear, and progressive, and white (especially Protestant) culture was the highest point reached thus far. Thus even sympathetic missionaries rarely questioned that the Indians were "uncivilized," lower on some evolutionary scale of progress, or that they would benefit from white culture, just as their "heathen" souls must be saved by Christian evangelism.

It was the perception not only of missionaries but of the government as well that Christianity and civilization were related, even inseparable. Thus the missionary activities of the churches to Native Americans were usually implicitly endorsed and were sometimes directly supported by the government. Missionaries would establish not just churches but schools and carry white civilization to the Indians, thus making assimilation a viable option. For the first two-thirds of the century, government support of Christian missions was indirect, as missions were planted within existing states and, by the 1830s, expanded into the West, home of the Plains Indians. Missionaries to the Plains preached, founded schools, and made some converts, but their impact was modest. Other aspects of white contact were far more devastating to the Indians. New diseases decimated tribal populations, and an increasing pace of white settlement forced tribes to give up more and more land and become more and more dependent on the government, a government that through malice or neglect or dishonest agents seldom delivered on its promises. Missionaries and church leaders were well aware of problems and were important critics of government policies and personnel and defenders of the Indians, even during the Dakota War of 1862. Along with other reformers, they persuaded Washington that its Indian policy was a disaster and a new approach was needed.

## Grant's "Peace Policy"

The result was the changes of 1869 known as Grant's "Peace Policy." The Board of Indian Commissioners was created to oversee Indian affairs, and its volunteer members were to be moral, well-to-do churchmen, who presumably would neither permit dishonesty nor be tempted to financial gain at the expense of their charges. Christian churches were given the power to control reservations and nominate Indian agents who would be better qualified and more honest than past ones. Given the premise that Indians must be civilized if they were to survive and the expectation that churches and their representatives were the most qualified instruments for the task, the policy looked plausible. Unfortunately, it did not work. Division of responsibility among Christian denominations was made with little attention to their historic contribution, current situation, interests, or resources. Thus Roman Catholics, despite a history of missionary activity, were virtually excluded. Serious denominational rivalries developed, causing internal problems, wasting time and resources, and, not incidentally, setting a bad example for Indians of the nature of the "one, true religion." Nor was it easy to find enough missionaries, let alone honest and competent agents. Within two decades, churches lost their formal powers and the "Peace Policy" was replaced by the forced acculturation of the General Allotment or Dawes Act of 1887. Each Indian would receive a certain amount of land (depending on gender, age, and family status), and the rest of a tribe's reservation land would be available for white settlement. Many reformers, including some Native Americans, supported the concept, not simply or necessarily because they endorsed acculturation but because it was, minimally, a way to protect what land remained to Indians from continual illegal white encroachment and government changes. The ultimate result, however, was a massive loss of Indian land in those areas where allotment was enforced.[28]

## Evaluating Christianity's Role

With historical hindsight, it is hard to avoid asking whether there was not a better alternative than extermination, removal, or forced acculturation. While Christian churches in general and missionaries in particular were by no means the only players in white-Indian relationships in the nineteenth century, they did have a significant role. Could a more moderate program of assimilation have worked better, had there been more cultural humility and sensitivity on the part of white Christians? Or was the clash of cultures in increasingly confined space inevitable, especially given the disparity of power and resources (not to mention human greed)? Not only was Christianity imbedded in a particular cultural system, but Native American religions, too, were intrinsic parts of cultures that were interdependent wholes. So were the missionaries in one sense correct, if not right? That is, did the inherent clash of cultures require a major cultural break if an Indian converted to Christianity?

Before that question can be addressed, the recognition that religion is indeed an intrinsic part of a cultural system needs to be qualified. Native American culture and religion were not static; Indians had already adapted some white imports, like the gun and the horse among Plains tribes. Such changes were integrated into existing patterns, and, even more important, they were a matter of choice, not forced acculturation. Second, there were important differences among Christian missionaries in their approaches. Some, like Roman Catholics and Episcopalians, were more willing to adapt Christian ideas and practices to existing Native American ones, to condone a kind of syncretism or to offer elements of tradition that were more attractive and adaptive to Native Americans.[29] Finally, widespread and effective resistance to white acculturation probably would have required the kind of united front on the part of Native American tribes that simply did not exist in the nineteenth century. Long-standing intertribal suspicions, even enmity, did not disappear with the arrival of whites. Not only could (and did) whites play up such rivalries to their own advantage, but Native

Americans, too, sometimes sought white support against a threat from a traditional tribal enemy.

Thus Native Americans evidenced a range of responses to white culture and to Christianity in particular. White Christians in the nineteenth century were convinced that those Indians who responded positively to them were the good and intelligent ones, while those who resisted were not only pagan but backward and ignorant. Some later historians, quite rightly deploring not only the dishonest treatment by whites but also their religious and cultural imperialism, have reversed the assessment: those Indians who converted to Christianity were weak or even traitorous, while those who resisted assimilation by refusing to give up traditional ways, using force if necessary, were strong and admirable. Neither generalization in its extreme form does justice to the complexity of the historical situation or acknowledges that Native Americans could have a range of reactions and make a variety of choices and still have integrity and deserve respect. Thus I began with a glimpse of Native American women's traditional ways and religion and will now turn to women's religious ideas and choices as Native Americans confronted white Christianity, especially in the form of missionaries.

## The Impact of the Missionary Movement

The central goal of Christian missionaries was conversion, saving the souls of heathen who would otherwise be eternally damned. To the most culturally powerful white Americans, Christianity meant Protestantism (Protestant missionaries tended to see Catholic efforts as little better than heathenism itself), and the Bible is central in Protestant Christianity. To read the Bible, a person must be literate; hence schools are necessary. And schools require the kind of social, economic, and political system that will support them: civilization. Not only were schools central to Protestant missionary efforts, but the most desirable schools, in their view, were boarding schools, which could remove young Indians from the harmful influences of tribe and parents and shape their values and character, at the same time the children were instructed in reading, writing, and religion. Schools often included instruction and student participation in manual labor along gender lines considered appropriate by whites. For many Indian children, the experience was not a happy one. The language, the religion, the child-rearing philosophies, the gender roles themselves were frequently opposed to Native American cultural traditions or religious beliefs.[30] Thus Indian boys were to learn to be farmers, regardless of whether or not that was a traditional male role in their tribal culture, and schools for Indian girls inculcated not only Christianity but a particular vision of appropriate female domesticity and the skills needed for it. As one missionary wrote:

> The object of the Dakota Home is to train up housekeepers for future Dakota homes. Hence our effort is to train them into the knowledge and habit of all home work, and to instill in them the principles of right action, and cultivate self-discipline. They learn to cook and wash, sew and cut garments, weave, knit, milk, make butter, make beds, sweep floors, and anything else pertaining to house-keeping, and they can make *good* bread.[31]

### Mary Riggs and Sue McBeth

Missionaries who were designated as such by salary and title were usually men, especially in the first half of the nineteenth century, but as in the case of foreign missions, women had a role as "missionary wives" who would not only support their husbands but exemplify true Christian womanhood, establish a true Christian home, and possibly teach school as well. Stephen and Mary Riggs went in 1837 as missionaries to the Sioux (Dakota) under the auspices of the American Board of Commissioners for Foreign Missions, and Stephen later wrote an account of their experiences in *Mary and I: Forty Years with the Sioux.* (Although Stephen is identified as author, a significant portion of the work consists of lengthy quotations from Mary's diary and letters.) In an introduction, S. C. Bartlett praises Mary, particularly her education, her bravery and patience, her teaching of Indian children, and concludes, "But it was the chief test and glory of her character to have brought up a family of children, among all the surroundings of Indian life, as though amid the homes of civilization and refinement."[32] Yet it is evident from Mary's diary and letters that she saw herself as a part of the mission. Neither she nor Stephen questioned the benefits of white civilization and Christianity, and she did her part to teach women and children and to commend and encourage the "good" Christian Indians. Like Stephen, too, she could be critical of whites, whether of the dishonesty of agents or the practice of military officers who "kept" an Indian woman in addition to a legal wife.[33]

Unlike Mary Riggs, whose direct missionary activity was subordinate to her responsibilities as Stephen's wife, Sue McBeth was a full-fledged missionary herself. Sent by the Presbyterians to the Nez Perce tribe in the American Northwest in 1873, she devoted her life to the tribe until her death in 1893. McBeth was atypical insofar as she was directly involved in training (male) native ministers to carry on the work, but she shared the assumptions of the vast majority of Protestant ministers that total conversion to Christianity was necessary, that Native American religion was nothing more than heathenism, and that Christianization had to include the total acceptance of white culture, from matters of dress to appropriate sex roles. Like the women who went into the foreign mission field, Sue McBeth saw the establishment of "Christian and civilized homes" as a key to success, and native women as the foundation of Christian homes. In an 1884 letter, she wrote:

> In the building up of that home after God's plan . . . the wives and mothers, as well as husbands and fathers need to be taught the duties of their "several places and relations"—as God has revealed them. The mother is even more important than the father perhaps—because she has so much to do with training the children in the new way—or leading them on in the old.[34]

Sue McBeth and Mary Riggs were typical of white Protestant women in the nineteenth century, whether missionary wives or missionaries themselves, members of mission boards, or women reformers who turned their attention to Native Americans in the decades after the Civil War, insofar as they all believed the values of the cult of True Womanhood were a necessity for Native American women. Therefore, they assumed that Native American women must change.[35] The feminine virtues and female gender roles of the cult of True Womanhood were tied to an emerging social, economic, and political system that emphasized separate gender spheres, where men had power and women had "influence." That system was in many ways very different than the ones found among most tribes. Thus, ironically, women missionaries and reformers failed to see that most Native American women shared at least three of the "cardinal virtues" of the cult—piety, purity, and domesticity—because those qualities were not expressed in white cultural terms. Native American women were surely religious, but they were not Christian. In addition, contrary to white stereotypes, they were not promiscuous even though their sexual patterns and marriage practices were different from white ones. And most Native American women were "domestic" in the sense of being centrally occupied with childrearing and making a home, including gathering and preparing significant parts of the food supply. In a further irony, it could be argued that the one "cardinal virtue" that was not shared by those Native American women, whom Christian women thought they were "uplifting," was submissiveness. In many tribes, women had an important political voice and significant economic and personal power and independence as a result of their domestic roles of literally creating homes and producing food.

## Catharine Brown

While many Native American women saw little to attract them to white Christianity and culture, there were women who converted, who accepted white education ambivalently or sought it enthusiastically. Catharine Brown, a Cherokee woman, was one of these.[36] Born in northern Alabama around 1800, at the age of seventeen Catharine Brown sought admission to a missionary school in what is now Chattanooga. Within a few months of her arrival, she began to express an interest in Christianity and was ultimately baptized and admitted to the Presbyterian church. After completing her education, she served for a little less than a year as a teacher in a school for girls in the settlement where her family lived. She then went to live with a missionary family to continue her own studies, but her health began to fail and she died of consumption in July 1823. Before her death, however, she was very active and relatively successful in persuading her family and friends to accept Christianity and in forming a women's missionary group. Judging from the letters and diary entries printed in her *Memoirs*, her religious and cultural conversion was all that any missionary could have wished. Her language and theology could be those of a white evangelical Protestant, except that it was "her" people who were living in pagan darkness.

While the rapidity and thoroughness of Catharine Brown's conversion were not typical, there is no reason to doubt her personal sincerity, and her choice can be seen as one end of a spectrum of Native American responses to Christianity. Moreover, the Cherokees had been among the most willing to accept Christianity and white cultural patterns, and their exemplary acculturation included acceptance of white gender hierarchies and cultural roles. At the very time Catharine Brown was embracing Christianity, other Cherokee women were unsuccessfully protesting their loss of social, economic, and political power.[37] We might wonder whether the sense of importance and identity Catharine Brown discovered in her role as a Christian was in part compensation for the loss of women's traditional importance in her tribe. The tragic experience of the Cherokees was thus an early, clear, and ironic exposure of the false promises of acculturation. As Henry Bowden writes, "By 1828 the Cherokees had reached a pinnacle of successful acculturation. . . . Their place in American life seemed to be secure. Then two events occurred in quick succession to dispel that illusion. In 1829, Andrew Jackson became president, and whites discovered gold in northern Georgia."[38] The Cherokees were "removed," despite the efforts of some white reformers and church leaders to protest such treatment, and embarked on the famous "Trail of Tears."

## Native-American Conversion

Assimilation carried a high cultural price, and even then it did not assure protection. Removal, however, offered Native Americans only a temporary security. Sooner or later, virtually every tribe would be faced with substantial white contact, including the efforts of Christian missionaries, and at least some of the tribes' members would embrace a form of Christianity. Why did some convert? There is no single, simple answer. At times, the primary attraction may have been pragmatic: Food, shelter, or protection were offered as benefits to those who expressed a willingness to hear about Christianity. In some cases, where guidance through dreams and visions was a deeply rooted spiritual tradition, the dreams and visions themselves could be seen as the source of a divine directive toward the new religion. In some situations, the magic and power of the white god appeared to be stronger and hence more attractive than those of tribal spirits, especially when other circumstances had disrupted or nearly destroyed the old coherent culture. In the aftermath of the Dakota War, missionaries among the prisoners and their families in the camps made a significant number of converts. Stephen Riggs' description of the situation is plausible, despite his own theological bias:

> Their own gods had failed them signally, as was manifest by their present condition. Their conjurers, their medicine men, their makers of *wakan*, were nonplused. Even the women taunted them, by saying, "You boasted great power as *wakan* men, where is it now?" These barriers, which had been impregnable and impenetrable, in the past, were suddenly broken down. Their ancestral religion had departed. They were unwilling now, in their distresses, to be without God—without hope, without faith in something or some one.[39]

Virginia Driving Hawk Sneve proposes a similar explanation, though from the perspective of a late twentieth-century Native American Christian; she is thus less inclined than Riggs to dismiss Dakota religion entirely. Christianity, she argues, was seen as a way of sharing the power of the whites' god without necessarily abandoning all former beliefs. It could also fill a religious and cultural void created when changes made the traditional ways no longer possible. She also suggests why women were likely to convert before men:

> To the Dakota, a man was destined to be a warrior and hunter. To refuse to fight or hunt and agree to plow the land was a sign of weakness. The male who voluntarily submitted to these shameful things—which he must do to become a Christian—made great personal sacrifices in the face of degrading ridicule from his people. Women became the first converts, for their acceptance of Christianity did not mean an abandonment of their former role as wife and mother.[40]

Stephen and Mary Riggs also found that women were earlier and more numerous converts and that male converts were taunted for joining a "woman's" group,[41] suggesting that, among some tribes at least, Christianity may have been initially more attractive or less problematic for women than for men.

Still another motive for conversion may have been the attractions of white culture and particularly formal education, for both intrinsic and practical reasons. Education meant exposure to Christian beliefs and practices, and the Native American who wished to pursue further education found the path easier when he or she embraced Christianity, nominally or fully. Whether or not individual Native Americans who actively sought white education were convinced of the superiority of white culture, or parts of it, they could recognize the value of education as a source of the critical tools needed to function in white social and political power structures in order to defend the tribe from very real threats of exploitation and destruction. Two Native American women, Sarah Winnemucca and Susette La Flesche, are women who made such a choice: Both learned white ways and appeared to accept white values and religion to the point that they qualified as "Indian princesses" in white imagery. Yet each also used her position and ability to try to defend her own people from white threats to their well-being or even survival. Their choices were never easy ones; each woman had to balance the pain of real loss in her traditional identity with the potential or perceived gain that accommodation to white culture might bring to her and her people.

## Sarah Winnemucca

Sarah Winnemucca, whose Indian name was Thoc-me-tony or "Shell-flower," was born around 1844, a member of the Piute tribe in western Nevada. Her own family, especially her grandfather, known as Truckee, was quite friendly to the whites who began to arrive. Her grandfather told her of a mythic time when the white boy and girl could not get along with the dark boy and girl, so their parents reluctantly separated them, but that he now hoped for healing and reconciliation.[42] Truckee served with John Frémont in California and throughout his life tried to work peacefully with whites and to convince his family to share his perceptions. As a young girl, however, Sarah was more resistant, aware that too many whites did not return her grandfather's good faith. Nevertheless, she learned the whites' language and ways through a visit to California, a period when she lived with a white family, and a brief stay at a school run by Roman Catholic sisters, until parents of its white students insisted on her removal. The linguistic skills and familiarity with white culture that she gained would serve her later as she worked as an interpreter and tried to intercede with white authorities for her people.

Despite Truckee's sanguine hopes, white treatment of the Piutes was anything but peaceful and friendly. During the 1860s, '70s, and '80s, the Piutes were repeatedly relocated. First some were placed near their Nevada lands but subjected there to white encroachment and violence, and then later as the tribe was further divided, some were sent unwillingly to Malheur Reservation in Oregon. Piutes were caught up on both sides of the Bannock War, and in its aftermath, were forced to move over the mountains in winter to Yakima Reservation in Washington, despite Sarah's services to the army and the fact that some Piutes had opposed the Bannock rebellion. Over these years, Sarah Winnemucca became a go-between and advocate, desperately trying to protect her people from exploitation and mistreatment and to find some land where they could survive, be together, and enjoy a degree of long-term security.

Sarah Winnemucca began her role as an official interpreter in 1866 when she and her brother Natchez were called to Fort McDermitt to explain the current Indian unrest. They described its cause as white encroachment and violence. The army authorities were sympathetic, and a large group of Piutes was taken in at the fort and given protection and the means of survival. As a result of this and her subsequent experiences in the Bannock War, Sarah Winnemucca was convinced that, in general, the military was a safer and more honest resource for her people than were either government agents or missionaries.

> Have not the Indians good reason to like soldiers? There were no Custers among the officers in Nevada. If the Indians were protected, as they call it, instead of the whites, there would be no Indian wars. Is there not good reason for wishing the army to have the care of the Indians, instead of the Indian Commissioner and his men? The army has no temptation to make money out of them, and the Indians understand law and discipline as the army has them; but there is no law with agents. The few good ones cannot do good enough to make it worth while to keep up that system. A good agent is sure to lose his place very soon, there are so many bad ones longing for it.[43]

The only agent she knew who was an exception was Samuel Parrish, agent at the Malheur Reservation to which some of the Piutes were removed in 1872, where she agreed to be his official interpreter in 1875. From Sarah's accounts of his speeches in *Life Among the Piutes,* Parrish was clearly paternalistic and convinced that his "charges" had to fully adopt white ways of farming, but he was at least honest and tried to help the Indians to survive. Unfortunately, he was soon replaced. As Sarah writes, "It was because they said he was not a Christian, and all the reservations were to be under the Christian men's care."[44] His replacement, as she repeatedly and bitterly notes, was indeed a "Christian" man who cheated and violently mistreated the Indians, finally driving a frustrated Sarah from the reservation.

She had no better luck with higher government authorities, even when she, her father, and her brother were summoned to Washington in 1880 as a result of her public lectures in California, lectures in which she denounced dishonesty and immorality in the agents' treatment of the Piutes.

The three of them met with Secretary of the Interior Carl Schurz and even with President Hayes, and they left believing they had gained some help for the Piutes, but it never came. When a campaign was launched to discredit her, she received support and defense from military leaders like General O. O. Howard, and in 1883 she returned to the East for a lecture tour, where she met Elizabeth Palmer Peabody and Mary Mann in Boston. These New England Unitarians and reformers took up her cause, helping her to spread her story through lectures and in her book and to circulate a petition to Congress, citing the peaceful and friendly history of the Piutes and asking the government to

> restore to [the Piutes] said Malheur Reservation, which is well watered and timbered, and large enough to afford homes and support for them all, where they can enjoy lands in severalty without losing their tribal relations, so essential to their happiness and good character, and where their citizenship, implied in this distribution of land, will defend them from the encroachments of white settlers, so detrimental to their interests and their virtues. And especially do we petition for the return of that portion of the tribe arbitrarily removed from the Malheur Reservation, after the Bannock war, to the Yakima Reservation on Columbia River, in which removal families were ruthlessly separated, and have never ceased to pine for husbands, wives, and children, which restoration was pledged to them by the Secretary of the Interior in 1880, but has not been fulfilled.[45]

Sarah Winnemucca was thus a Native American advocate of a policy that was widely supported by reformers in the late nineteenth century but that was later discredited for its ethnocentrism and its disastrous effects on Indian landholding. Yet her support grew out of her own experiences of the arbitrary removal and white encroachment suffered by the Piutes, with no help from Indian agents or missionaries. Severalty and citizenship seemed to promise them a legal security they had lacked for decades. Nor did she see how her people could survive without adapting to white ways like farming and without gaining sufficient education to function in the white system. Sarah Winnemucca's acculturation was selective: She spoke in her public lectures of the traditions of the Piutes, as well as the wrongs they had suffered, and she wrote a brief article in 1882 about her tribe's ways before contact;[46] and when she taught in an Indian school in Nevada for a few years toward the end of her life, she stressed appreciation for tribal customs and stories, as well as for learning English and white skills. Perhaps in part because of her experience with the ostentatiously Christian and thoroughly reprehensible agent who replaced Parrish, she never embraced more than a nominal Christianity, preferring instead to write in her book about the "Spirit-Father."

## Susette La Flesche

When Susette La Flesche was born in 1854, she was in a sense already a part of both white and Native American worlds, as both of her parents were. Joseph La Flesche was the son of a French trader father and an Indian mother, although there are conflicting records as to whether his mother was a Ponca or an Omaha.[47] Susette's mother was Mary Gale, the daughter of a white army physician, John Gale, and Nicomi, a Native American. Despite their dual heritage, Joseph and Mary identified with the Omaha tribe, and Joseph was eventually adopted by and succeeded Big Elk, one of their major chiefs. He used this position to try to persuade the Omahas to adapt to the white world, not because he rejected the value of traditional ways but because he was convinced adaptation was the only way the Omahas could survive the floods of white settlement and white power. Other leaders and factions in the tribe disagreed, neither accepting his leadership nor trusting his proposed directions for their people.

The Omahas' situation in the middle of the nineteenth century was a precarious one. The population was declining rapidly, due largely to white encroachment and disease. The tribe was torn by internal divisions, exacerbated by the government's preference for dealing with the "paper chiefs" it created rather than traditional ones. There had been a significant loss of land thanks to a series of treaties, culminating in 1854, when the Omahas gave up their traditional hunting grounds and were moved to a reservation of some 300,000 acres near their traditional enemies, the Sioux. In that same year, Susette La Flesche was born.

Although some Omahas under her father's leadership were moving to adopt certain white practices, Susette's early life on the reservation gave her considerable experience of traditional ways: living in an earth lodge; observing one of the tribe's last buffalo hunts; taking part in the traditional ceremony of "The Turning of the Child" when she was about four, at which time she received her tribal name, Inshta Theumba or Bright Eyes. But she also attended the mission school on the reservation, where she learned English and was exposed to Christianity. When the school closed, one of the teachers arranged for her to continue the education she hungered for at the Elizabeth Institute in New Jersey. Upon graduation, she returned to the reservation in 1875 and, after experiencing considerable frustration with white bureaucracy, was finally able to get a government appointment as a teacher there.

Joseph La Flesche had tried to help his people to bridge the two cultures in two ways: through his work on the reservation, where he encouraged the people to take advantage of white educational opportunities and to adopt a white economic system of farming and trades; and through his role as a spokesman with white authorities. Two of Susette's younger sisters continued his work at the local level. Rosalie took over her father's position after his death as an emotional and practical center of the tribe, taking a leadership role in economic development, promoting education, and serving as a go-between for the members of the tribe and various local white authorities. Susan went away to school and ultimately earned a medical degree from the Woman's Medical College in Philadelphia in 1889. She then returned to the Omahas, serving as physician first at the government school and finally for the entire tribe. Susette's early position as a teacher had set a similar course until dramatic events in 1879 thrust her into national prominence, and she became a public spokesperson to publicize government mistreatment of the Indians.

The Ponca, a tribe closely related to the Omahas (White Swan, a chief, was Joseph La Flesche's half brother), had ceded large tracts of land to the government in return for what they believed would be a secure reservation near the Niobrara River. But the government later assigned that same territory to their traditional enemies, the Sioux, and forcibly removed the Poncas to Arkansas, ignoring their distress and their request to be returned to their own land or at least to be allowed to join their relatives on the Omaha Reservation. When the son of Standing Bear, one of the chiefs, died in a malaria epidemic, Standing Bear and a small party started north to bury his son in their traditional lands. They made it as far as the Omaha reservation, when he was arrested for leaving Indian territory without permission. Local white sympathizers, including local clergy and a journalist named Thomas Tibbles, took up the cause and filed a court case, resulting in a landmark decision that an Indian was indeed a legal person. Tibbles then arranged a lecture tour to publicize the Poncas' mistreatment and to raise money to finance an extended legal battle on their behalf, and Susette La Flesche was made one of the party, since her facility with English enabled her to act as Standing Bear's interpreter.

"Bright Eyes," as she was designated in the tour's publicity, not only served as an interpreter for Standing Bear but gave her own addresses and interviews, detailing the wrongs done to the Poncas and, indeed, to many Native American tribes, and appealing for restitution and legal protection of Indians' rights. The tour generated considerable public sympathy, as noted reformers took up the Ponca cause; it also met considerable opposition from a government very slow to admit and rectify its errors. During the group's stay in Boston, Susette La Flesche met Henry Wadsworth Longfellow, who is said to have concluded, "This is Minnehaha." Whether Susette La Flesche, "Bright Eyes," was flattered or distressed by the association, it had mixed consequences for her public image and for the cause to which she was dedicated. Identification with such a popular, romantic figure probably helped to ensure her own acceptance and generate more public sympathy for the wrongs of America's native peoples, but it also locked her into a stereotype. As Green concludes, "Indeed, Susette was never able to establish herself before the public as a separate entity apart from the Indian Maiden."[48]

Later, during a tour of England, Bright Eyes was billed as the Indian "princess," despite her protests that the title was inappropriate because "the Omaha had no system comparable to European royal position by inheritance."[49] Sarah Winnemucca, too, was widely identified as an Indian princess when she began her public crusade for justice for the Piutes. While both women probably imbibed some of the expected gender values of white culture, they were also shrewd enough to perceive the usefulness of the "Indian princess" image in moving their audiences to support of Native American rights, just as a Frances Willard or a Jane Addams could use the cult of True Womanhood to argue for the extension of female rights.

Bright Eyes fit the image: not only were her education and command of English impressive, but she was beautiful and demonstrated an appropriately female "refinement of manners," as noted over and over in newspaper accounts. Few of her white admirers could perceive or appreciate the tensions involved for the woman who was torn between two worlds, living in and attracted by elements of them both, yet never fully satisfied or accepted by either. This duality included her religious identity as well. Susette, like most of the other members of her family, eventually joined the Presbyterian church. She taught a Sunday School class along with her regular classes at the reservation school. In short, she became an accepting if hardly a publicly fervent Christian. Yet she was unwilling to dismiss the traditional values, rituals, and beliefs of her people as worthless "heathenism," so her own faith was a selective blending of elements from both sources that she saw as compatible and valuable.[50]

Susette La Flesche's marriage to Thomas Tibbles in July 1881 seemed to tip the balance in her identities toward the white world. For a time, both continued to push for the government reform that would culminate in the Dawes Act, but later her own interests were submerged as Tibbles turned his attention to Populism, and her husband's estrangement from several members of her family was a source of personal pain. Susette kept up contacts with her family and the reservation as well as she could despite repeated moves. She also attempted to preserve some of the Omahas' tribal traditions and values through her writing and illustrations, though in a more modest way than her half brother Francis, a noted anthropologist. She died in 1902, having lived long enough to see some of the detrimental effects of the Dawes Act. Yet the allotment policies for which she fought in the 1880s appeared to her to be the best, if not the only, way to save some Indian land and protect the tribes from constant white encroachment and repeatedly broken treaties.

## Helen Hunt Jackson

Among those who heard Standing Bear and Bright Eyes in Boston was a woman who would become one of the best-known Indian reformers of her age: Helen Hunt Jackson. Born in 1830, Jackson was atypical of nineteenth-century reformers in that she had not been involved in other causes before she heard about the government's mistreatment of the Poncas, but once she had, she became totally involved in the cause. She arranged lectures, she wrote letters, and she began the research that two years after she had heard Standing Bear and Bright Eyes would result in a landmark protest work, *A Century of Dishonor.*[51] The book told not only the Poncas' story but those of several other tribes as well, and it ended with a chapter on "Massacres of Indians by Whites," countering the prevalent prejudice that only "savages" perpetrated such acts on innocent, peaceful whites. Jackson paid to have a copy of the book sent to every Congressman, "bound in blood-red cloth. . . . Embossed on the cover were the words of Benjamin Franklin: 'Look upon your hands! They are stained with the blood of your relations.' "[52] She then turned her attention to the plight of the California Mission Indians, another group in immediate danger of losing their land, and was able to get an appointment as an official government agent to help find permanent homes for them. Frustrated by the conditions she discovered among the Indians and the agents who were supposed to help them, the unwillingness of the government to respond quickly and constructively, and a continuing public apathy to the injustices, she decided to write a novel self-consciously patterned on *Uncle Tom's Cabin* in the hopes that it would arouse similar public indignation. Unfortunately, *Ramona,* published in 1884, was received by most of the public more as a romantic love story than as a protest novel demanding action.[53] Jackson died in 1885, but her crusade for the California Mission Indians was carried on by some of the reform groups she had helped to inspire, notably the Women's National Indian Association. Ironically, their goals were more sweeping than hers had been, because she was not particularly concerned with massive acculturation and conversion of the Indians to evangelical Protestantism, as was the WNIA. As Valerie Mathes concludes:

> The reformers who carried on her legacy were imbued with evangelical Protestant Christianity and strongly anti-Catholic. Jackson, on the other hand, was not driven by evangelicalism and did not appear to be anti-Catholic. . . . Jackson's Indian legacy therefore had an ironic twist. Interested primarily in preserving the land base for future generations of the California Mission Indians, she opened the door to reformers who were much more divisive and destructive of Indian culture.[54]

With her central focus on legal protection of the Indians and their land and her willingness to respect Indian culture and traditions, Helen Hunt

Jackson had more in common with Sarah Winnemucca and Susette La Flesche than she did with most of her white sister-reformers and, indeed, the public governmental policy of allotment and acculturation that prevailed at the end of the nineteenth century. Hoping to help the California Mission Indians, she created in the character Ramona a fictional Indian princess, perhaps unwittingly reinforcing that stereotype for white Americans.

Nevertheless, the complex lives of Native American women like Sarah Winnemucca and Susette La Flesche who had to make hard personal and cultural choices as they tried to bridge the two cultures, as well as the accounts of women like Maria Chona, Waheenee, and Pretty-shield, expose the gross inadequacy of "princess" and "squaw" to encapsulate the roles and religion of Native American women in the nineteenth century.

# 13

# *African-American Women and Religion in Nineteenth-Century America*

The reality and consequences of racial difference shaped the lives and religion of black women in the nineteenth century more than any other factor. Slavery in the first half of the century and continued racism in both the North and the South after the Civil War affected not only the economic and political status of African Americans but also the structures and experiences of black religion, black gender relations, and families. Hence the religion of black women was in very basic ways shared with black men and incontrovertibly different from the religion of white women, and in this chapter I begin with a brief overview of the common black religious experience. Yet at the same time, there were ways in which the religious experiences, activities, and obstacles encountered by black women were similar, though never identical, to the experiences, activities, and obstacles faced by white women, especially within evangelical Protestantism. Thus the story of black women and religion at this time is related to but distinct from the story of black males' religion and of white females' religion. It is a story that has its own internal diversity and complexity, just as other groups' stories do.

## The African-American Religious Experience

The Great Awakening of the eighteenth century significantly increased the numbers of African Americans who embraced an evangelical Protestant Christianity, but it was not until the first half of the nineteenth century that substantial numbers of enslaved black Americans became Christian, either as members of Christian churches or through less formal but pervasive influence. The revivals and camp meetings of the Second Great Awakening were decisive, but they were supplemented by a more formal and systematic effort known as the "plantation mission." Missionaries and church leaders reminded slave owners of their Christian duty to convert the "heathen" and reiterated the argument that Christianity made blacks "better" (i.e., more docile, honest, and obedient) slaves. The arguments were not new; they had been voiced, if not widely heeded, by colonial missionaries. But the increasing criticism by abolitionists of slavery as immoral and unchristian made southern slaveowners more sensitive to the need to justify slavery as a positive good. They responded by insisting that the Bible did not condemn slavery, and that Africans in their native land might have been free but were doomed to everlasting damnation, whereas their current status as Christian slaves not only held out the promise of eternal salvation but also protected, through a benevolent, paternalistic system, the childlike Africans who could never have survived on their own in America.

## Slave Religion

Despite the efforts of white southern church leaders and slaveowners to limit and shape the Christianity offered to the slaves, they could not prevent blacks from finding and embracing a Christian faith very different from one whose central text was "Slaves be obedient to your masters" and whose only reward was freedom in heaven. That owners were reluctantly aware that Christianity could be a two-edged sword was evident in the increasing restrictions on slaves who gathered without white supervision, even for religious services. Restrictions were also placed on allowing slaves to learn to read the Bible for themselves, especially after a series of slave uprisings that culminated in Nat Turner's rebellion in 1831; the rebellions had been led by men who identified with biblical heroes and articulated religious justifications for their resistance.

The slave religion that emerged in the antebellum South was a complex mixture. One element was the "visible institution," the public forms of organized worship and preaching approved by white owners, and the controlled instruction by masters (or frequently, mistresses) that emphasized heaven as the reward for obedience and white-defined morality in this life. Far more significant for the slaves themselves was the "invisible institution," the informal, often secret religion of the slaves that included both activities and a crucial theological perspective. Despite the threat of severe punishment, blacks continued to hold secret meetings, often at night in the slave quarters or in the "hush harbors" of the woods. There they were free to be themselves, and the Christian message that echoed in prayer, preaching, and song was a very different one: hopes for freedom were not confined to heaven, and the white insistence that blacks' slavery was God's will because of their innate inferiority was firmly rejected. Not Ephesians 6:5 but Exodus was a central text, an assurance that a God of justice did not condone their enslavement and would ultimately lead them to freedom.

It was that conviction of their own worth and God's justice that slaves retained not only in their secret meetings but in the public religious activities where visible and invisible blended in rhythms of worship. Sundays were important, often a day off from field work when worship provided the opportunity for self-expression and a chance for community contact. The periodic revivals and camp meetings, especially after harvest, were a social and religious experience for blacks as well as whites. Baptisms, weddings, and funerals acknowledged the religious significance of universal human transitions, and they offered a break from the monotony of slave life and affirmed black humanity and dignity. As Albert Raboteau notes, "Baptism, the central Christian symbol of spiritual death, rebirth, and initiation was a memorable occasion for the slaves. Accompanied by song, shouting, and ecstatic behavior, baptism—especially for Baptists—was perhaps the most dramatic ritual in the slave's religious life."[1] While some masters forbade any slave marriages, some allowed weddings between two slaves to be celebrated by a clergyman. Other slave marriages were marked by the custom of "jumping the broomstick," though in almost every case, the slaves realized that even church-sanctioned marriages could be broken up at the whim of an owner. Funerals, too, were very important, and if forbidden by a harsh master, might be held in secret. African traditions were sometimes incorporated into funerals, because some blacks believed the soul of the deceased would return to Africa. Moreover, a proper burial affirmed that the one who had died was a person of worth and dignity, not a piece of property to be disposed of.

Within the slave community, the black preacher emerged as a central figure. A few were privileged; most were watched closely as potentially dangerous sources of leadership and could be severely punished for the "wrong" kind of preaching. Confined to a white-approved message (or double entendres) in public, preachers came into their own in secret meetings, expressing hope for God's deliverance and freedom in *this* life as well as offering hope and consolation in heaven. Many black preachers were skilled orators, using vivid biblical imagery and dramatic delivery in a lively service with free congregational response in shouting, music, and dance. Some preachers learned to read the Bible, especially in the earlier decades of the century, but even those who could not read knew their Bibles well.

Biblical imagery, along with influence from evangelical Protestant hymns and adaptation of African song, dance, and rhythmic patterns, produced one of the most distinctive forms of slave religion, the spiritual. Whatever their sources, spirituals gained form and identity in the black experience, where they were communal and active. Subsequently scholars have debated their meaning, some emphasizing their protest and coded messages, while others focused on the religious elements of hope and consolation in suffering, a way for slaves to escape, even temporarily, the oppressive reality of their current existence. In fact, spirituals could easily have been both protest and consolation, holding a whole complex layering of meanings for different persons at different times as they helped slaves to develop and retain the sense of self-worth, identity, and dignity denied them by whites. "Canaan" could mean *both* the North, with a promise of earthly freedom, *and* heaven, a future after death when loved ones would be reunited and where the somebodiness of the slave and the ultimate justice of God would be vindicated.

## Religion among Free Blacks

While slavery existed in the North in the colonial period, it was never practiced to the same extent as in the South, and by the nineteenth century northern blacks were technically free. Many were Christian and most belonged to "mixed" churches, yet blacks were almost never treated as equal members, especially as their numbers grew. They were relegated to the sides, back, or galleries of the churches during services and denied full membership privileges, a situation that finally led to some formal splits in the churches and the founding of all-black denominations like the African Methodist Episcopal Church under Richard Allen and the African Methodist Episcopal Zion Church. These Methodist-born groups were the first to be independent on the denominational level, but separate black churches among Presbyterians, Episcopalians, and Baptists also emerged in the North, and there were even a few all-black churches in the South dating back to the late colonial period.

Emancipation was perceived by many African Americans as the divine deliverance for which they had longed, but their hopes were dashed as southern whites regained power and northern concern was diverted to other issues after a brief period of "reconstruction." In the difficult decades between the Civil War and World War I, the black church played a crucial role in the black community. After the war, southern churches split along racial lines. Meanwhile, all-black northern churches like the A.M.E. and A.M.E. Zion moved south and reaped significant harvests of converts. The churches' work built on the existing dominance among black Christians of those evangelical Protestant denominations that had been most successful in the Second Great Awakening, so that the vast majority of black Christians by the end of the century were either Methodist or Baptist, and it was their form of black religion that came to be regarded as most typical. Still, there were African Americans in other Christian bodies, sometimes in "mixed" congregations and sometimes in separate black churches within predominantly white denominations like the Presbyterian or Episcopal churches. Although these churches never accounted for more than a small minority of black Protestants, they produced important leaders, both men and women, for the black community. In addition, there were black Catholics during the colonial period in areas that would eventually become part of the United States. Blacks, both slave and free, were part of Spanish settlements in Florida and California. The areas around New Orleans and Mobile included substantial numbers of black slaves and of the mixed-race groups known as "free people of color," many of whom came from Haiti. Approximately 20 percent of the Catholics in Maryland were black at the turn of the nineteenth century.[2] Given these concentrations, it is not surprising that the two religious orders for black women founded in the antebellum period were in Baltimore and New Orleans.

### *Religious Orders for Women*

The first order for women of African descent, the Oblate Sisters of Providence, was founded in Baltimore in 1829 by a French priest, Father Joubert, and four black women, who were refugees from Haiti. One of the four, Elizabeth Lange, became their first superior. The sisters founded a school for black girls and served as nurses during a cholera epidemic in 1832. Although they lost support after Joubert's death—at one point, Samuel Eccleston, Bishop of Baltimore, is said to have proposed "that there was no need for black religious and that they might do well to disband and become domestics"[3]—they regained support by the late 1840s and ultimately founded other communities. Their primary focus was education, but they also ran orphanages for black children, and it was the Sisters' Chapel that "was the focal point of worship for the Black Catholic community of Baltimore until 1857."[4] A second order, the Sisters of the Holy Family, was founded in New Orleans by Henriette Delille and Juliette Gaudin in 1842. (A third woman, Marie-Jeanne Aliquot, supported them but could not be a member of the order, since she was white and the others were free women of color.) The sisters were dedicated to education and to service of poor blacks and slaves—visiting the sick, establishing a hospice and an orphanage, and providing material help as they could. Like the Oblate sisters in Baltimore, the black sisters in New Orleans provided heroic nursing service in an epidemic, an outbreak of yellow fever in 1853. Though few in number, black sisters in the nineteenth century made an important contribution to the double minority of black Catholics.

### *Black Churches' Roles in the Black Community*

Nevertheless, by far the greatest number of black Christians in the nineteenth century were either Baptist or Methodist, and the vast majority lived in the South. The religious role of black churches remained central, as did distinctive forms of black worship and meaning, but the churches served other crucial functions for former slaves. They provided identity and a social center for the black community, setting and enforcing moral standards.

They were centers of economic cooperation and one of the few places where blacks could exercise political functions. They supported the education that was critical to hopes of progress by the black community. The ministry emerged as one of the few leadership roles permitted to black men in the South, and the black preacher was often the leader and spokesman for the local black community. Although formal ministry in black churches was generally confined to men, black women were equally important in the support, functioning, and survival of black churches.

Part of the reason for male resistance to female leadership in the churches was rooted in the destructive mix of racial and gender roles and images that emerged under slavery. In the dominant culture of the antebellum South, the two traditional and conflicting images of woman were split along racial lines. White women were Mary: pure, virtuous, submissive, and venerated on their pedestal; black women were Eve, perceived by whites as naturally carnal, loose, and available. The slave system itself both produced and rationalized that white perception: Black female slaves were sexually exploited by white men and had few ways to resist for themselves, and black men had few ways to protect their wives, sisters, and daughters. In their turn, black men were given a double, and impossible, cultural message: The ideal male is the strong protector and support of his Christian family, but you will not be allowed to achieve this, not only at the economic level but also at the point of defending your women from white males' rape; you are, thus, only a "boy." Similar messages of economic restriction and personal powerlessness continued in the postwar South, combined with white paranoia about black men's supposed hypersexuality and insatiable lust for white women. (It is worth noting that the horror frequently expressed by southern whites about miscegenation—or "mongrelization"—applied only to legal marriage or the union of a black man and a white woman.)[5] Yet white cultural images were largely divorced from black realities, and black women themselves had little say in the development of white gender projections. Despite the truly adverse circumstances of slavery, many black men and women took marriage vows very seriously, as evidenced in the number of newly freed slaves who searched long and hard for spouses and family members from whom they had been forcibly separated.[6] Even if, as some scholars have argued, black men's later insistence on male prerogative and familial and church hierarchies structured by gender were largely adapted from white culture,[7] it is still reasonable to suspect that many black women, fully aware of destructive white cultural messages and the limited possibilities for leadership available to their husbands, brothers, and fathers, were willing to support the men's formal leadership in the only public institution controlled by blacks in the postbellum South, the church.

## The Experience of African-American Women

The realities of race meant that the religious experiences of African-American women could never be identical to those of white women. Nevertheless, there were points of contact for the two races in the evangelical Protestantism with which most black Christians were associated.

### Conversion

Foundational in that religious experience was conversion, the recognizable change of heart that made possible a person's ultimate salvation by the grace of God and that was expected to result in a change of life. Indeed, referring to W. E. B. DuBois's classic essay on slave religion, Albert Raboteau has suggested that conversion be added as a fourth distinctive characteristic to DuBois's three, "the preacher, the music, and the frenzy." "The experience of conversion was essential in the religious life of the slaves. For the only path to salvation lay through that 'lonesome valley' wherein the 'seekers' underwent conversion, an experience that they treasured as one of the peak moments in their lives."[8] For evangelical Protestants, slave or free, black or white, male or female, conversion followed a typical pattern: a period of anxiety over one's salvation; recognition of one's own sinfulness and helplessness; and finally an experience of God's grace and pardon. Actual conversion might occur in a dramatic moment, often during a revival meeting but sometimes alone, and it might be accompanied by a visionary experience, but the preliminary stages could last for weeks, months, or even years. Jarena Lee, a free black born in 1783, recounts a period of some four years in which she was anxious about the state of her soul but unable to find the resolution of conversion, meanwhile being beset by direct and vivid temptations from Satan. Then, three weeks after she heard Richard Allen preach, she was converted during a sermon.

> The text was barely pronounced, which was: "I perceive thy heart is not right with God" [Acts 8:21], when there appeared to *my* view, in the centre of the heart *one* sin; and this was *malice,* against one particular individual, who had strove deeply to injure me, which I resented. At this discovery I said, *Lord* I forgive *every* creature. That instant, it appeared to me, as if a garment, which had entirely enveloped my whole person, even to my finger ends, split at the crown of my head, and was stripped away from me, passing like a shadow, from my sight—when the glory of God seemed to cover me in its stead.[9]

From the point of view of the converted, the greatest significance of conversion was religious: instead of being damned, the converted one was forgiven by God and gained hope of salvation. But for many black women, conversion had other important consequences. In a culture that placed black females at the bottom of a hierarchy of human value, conversion gave black women a sense of increased self-esteem, personal worth, and dignity rooted in God's validation of their humanity. A related result was the ability to face and deal with white racism in ways that were constructive and liberating rather than personally destructive. Studying the religious experiences of five black women in the nineteenth century, Jean M. Humez concludes that their conversions "suggest that one of the most necessary, emotionally transforming results of 'getting religion' for a black woman was learning to face and control the debilitating repressed anger and fear provoked by living with white racism."[10] A strong sense of confidence rooted in the assurance of God's presence and protection was another result of conversion. Amanda Berry Smith, a famous evangelist and missionary, wrote in her autobiography, "though I have passed through many sorrows, many trials, Satan has buffeted me, but never from that day have I had a question in regard to my conversion. God helped me and He settled it once and for all. This witness of God's spirit to my conversion has been what has held me amid all the storms of temptation and trial that I have passed through."[11] That sense of divine protection encompassed not only spiritual but physical dangers as well. Harriet Tubman's extraordinary courage on her raids into the South for the Underground Railroad was based in part in her conviction that she was an instrument of divine Providence and that a guardian angel accompanied her on those trips, and other black women similarly saw God's hand in their escape from white violence.[12]

## Preaching and Evangelism

For black and white women who were part of the Holiness movement in American Methodism, conversion was followed by a second turning point of sanctification, which was followed for some black women by a third call: to spread the gospel through preaching. These women often report initial resistance and reluctance to respond even to a vivid and visionary call of God to preach, due to an awareness of public disapproval, to fear that the call was the work of Satan rather than God, or to a sense of personal unworthiness. Struggle was a frequent theme of conversion accounts, as the sinner resisted the need to give up worldly pleasures, but the struggle was intensified for women with the call to preach. Like white women who experienced a similar call, they ran into serious opposition from male church authorities. Nevertheless, they found no spiritual peace until they accepted what they understood as God's definite and unequivocal call. Jarena Lee's experience was typical as she first approached Richard Allen (he allowed for some female exhortation and prayer meetings):

> But as to women preaching, he said that our Discipline knew nothing at all about it—that it did not call for women preachers. This I was glad to hear, because it removed the fear of the cross—but no sooner did this feeling cross my mind, than I found that a love of souls had in a measure departed from me; that holy energy which burned within me, as a fire, began to be smothered.[13]

For the next eight years, Lee only exhorted occasionally, meanwhile marrying a pastor, but after his death, she felt the call renewed. This time, she received Allen's permission and later his commendation for her work and had a successful career as an itinerant evangelist.

In her autobiography, Jarena Lee defended her preaching on the same three basic grounds that were cited by other nineteenth-century women, black and white. First and most important was God's direct call, an authority higher than any human institution or cultural expectation. Second, she pointed to the results: sinners turned to God as a result of her work; could the church afford to lose them as the price of silencing women? Third, knowing how Scripture was cited to prevent women's preaching, she pointed to biblical precedents for her work, like the women who were the first to proclaim Christ's resurrection. Despite Richard Allen's support of Jarena Lee, despite her success in winning souls and the activities of other women associated with the African Methodist Episcopal Church throughout the nineteenth century, including the extraordinary fame and success achieved by evangelist Amanda Berry Smith, male A.M.E. Church authorities continued to resist female religious leadership, making small progressive concessions only as these were forced upon them. In 1848 and again in 1852, a group of women known as the Daughters of Zion petitioned the General Conference for formal preaching licenses; the all-male body refused.[14] In 1868, the General Conference allowed an official female office, but a clearly limited and subordinate one, the stewardess, and not until 1884 did the Conference agree to license women as local preachers. Even then, the action seems to have been motivated largely by a decision that "to exert some control over preaching women was better than official refusal to acknowledge their widespread existence."[15] Finally in 1900, the Conference sanctioned another official but subordinate role for women, the deaconess. The positions of stewardess and deaconess were not equal to the male roles of steward and deacon, and neither they nor the woman's functions as exhorter, missionary, or evangelist were seen as the "first step" toward ordination, as were comparable roles for men.

Throughout the nineteenth century, the African Methodist Episcopal Church, like most white evangelical Protestant churches, reluctantly accepted the female preaching it could not prevent but drew the line at ordination, which would have made women the equals of men in the church's institutional structure. Only in the mid-twentieth century did the

A.M.E. Church grant full ordination to women, at about the same time as the Colored Methodist Episcopal Church. Despite the examples of some colonial Baptists who allowed women to preach and sanctioned the role of deaconess, and despite the congregational polity that, in theory, would have permitted a local congregation to ordain a woman, virtually all of the black Baptist churches that emerged in the nineteenth century excluded women from preaching and religious leadership. Only the African Methodist Episcopal Zion Church, under the leadership of Bishop James Hood, granted formal ordination to women by the end of the nineteenth century. In 1894, Julia Foote was ordained a deacon; Mary Small was ordained deacon in 1895 and elder in 1898; Julia Foote also was ordained elder in 1900. These women thus became the first to achieve full ordination in any American Methodist body, black or white; no other Methodist church would grant full ordination to women for another half-century.[16]

Why would black male church leaders have been so reluctant to grant leadership roles to black women, when they themselves, unlike white male ministers, had experienced the pain of exclusion and discrimination, though on grounds of race rather than gender? Did not the religious and cultural heritage of Africa provide precedent for women in roles of religious leadership? Yet after the Civil War, black men, including ministers, more and more adopted the patriarchal assumptions of white culture in general and of the white churches in particular.[17] Perhaps they saw these patterns as personally desirable or advantageous, or as inseparable from Christianity. Or perhaps they hoped (in vain) that white society would be more likely to accept and respect black communities and churches that conformed to its values. At any rate, in public black male church leaders cited theological and biblical arguments very similar to those given by white Christian opponents of women's preaching or ordination. Finally, the conflicting and destructive gender images and expectations for black men and women that were rooted in slavery joined with the economic and social realities of the postwar South to produce what C. Eric Lincoln and Lawrence Mamiya call "the complex problem of black male identity in a racist society. If the ministry was the only route to even a shadow of masculinity, the inclusion of women seemed very much like a gratuitous defeat for everybody."[18] In any case, most black women in the churches accepted the restriction of formal religious leadership to men, but there were some who, despite being at odds with church and culture, felt convinced of a divine call to preach that would not be silenced.[19]

## Traditional Support for the Church

Even if few black women sought ordination, the black church was still critically important to women and the women were critically important to the church, often in ways that paralleled the contributions of white Protestant women to their churches. Black women were members and fund-raisers; they found mutual support as they banded together for common purposes and were frequently led by the minister's wife. Sara Allen, wife of Richard, left few records of her own work, much of which was typical for that role, like organizing a "sewing circle to repair the tattered clothing of many of the church's travelling preachers."[20] She was also, however, an active worker for the Underground Railroad and was revered as "Mother Allen" in African Methodism.[21] Throughout the century, the wives of ministers (or bishops, in African Methodism) often provided female leadership at local, regional, and national levels, forming women's societies like the United Daughters of Allen in the A.M.E. Church to promote missions and reform and to provide for the welfare of the black community.

Money raised by women was critical to the survival of black churches, most of which were poor. The example of the women's sewing society of the "most famous black church in Memphis, Beale Street Baptist," which raised a good part of the money needed to build the church itself,[22] was duplicated over and over in churches large and small. One of the earliest Sunday schools in the United States was founded by a black woman, Catherine Ferguson, who in 1793 opened a Sabbath school for poor children in New York City. If anything, the education provided by black churches—largely by black women—was even more critical than the Sunday schools and other church-related teaching of white Protestant women, since black children's educational opportunities in general were neglected, restricted, or denied by white society. Teaching, singing, cleaning, cooking, organizing, raising money, sewing, doing whatever needed to be done—black women were, not only in the nineteenth but well into the twentieth century, what Theressa Hoover has called the "backbone" and the "glue" of black churches.[23]

### Missions and Reform

For black women as for white Protestant women, home and foreign missions were important concerns, and as the nineteenth century progressed, the interest of black American Christians in Africa was especially poignant and immediate. As black Baptists and African Methodists developed their own missionary interests and programs, the support of black church women was critical. While official church boards were male-dominated, women banded together at the local level to raise money and to provide approval and moral support for the cause. By the end of the century, they had formed women's boards or auxiliaries at the regional and national level, with a special concern for African women and children and with financial support often directed to women missionaries, married or single.[24] The pattern is very similar to the story of white Protestant women and foreign missions.

Unlike white women's missions in the nineteenth century, however, black women (like black men) were primarily devoted to work in Africa, although there were some African Americans involved in foreign missions to other parts of the globe. One of the earliest unmarried women sent out by the American Board of Commissioners for Foreign Missions (ABCFM) was a black woman, Betsy Stockton. Although she did not hold full missionary status, being called instead a "domestic assistant," she was sent to Hawaii in 1823 and conducted a school there for two years. Amanda Berry Smith left the United States for England in 1878 and sailed for India the following year, where she worked closely with Methodist bishop James Thoburn, who had nothing but the highest praise for her personal qualities and her gifts as a preacher. In seventeen years in Calcutta, he noted, "I have never known anyone who could draw and hold so large an audience as Mrs. Smith." Her faith was of "a standard of purity and strength rarely witnessed in our world. . . . As she left the country, she could look back upon a hundred homes which were brighter and better because of her coming, upon hundreds of hearts whose burdens had been lightened and whose sorrows had been sweetened by reason of her public and private ministry."[25] By the beginning of 1882, however, Smith was in Africa, mainly Liberia and Sierra Leone, where for the next eight years she worked as a missionary—evangelizing, establishing Sunday schools, and promoting the Holiness movement and temperance—before returning to the United States in 1890.

As it had for Amanda Berry Smith, Africa held a special attraction for other black Americans interested in foreign missions. Indeed, the return of some American blacks to their homeland was an interest shared by blacks and whites in America throughout the nineteenth century, but with very different perspectives and justifications. The American Colonization Society, the conservative wing of the antislavery movement, promoted the return of free blacks to Africa in the first part of the century, but it was opposed by black leaders like Richard Allen, not because he rejected freely chosen return by American blacks but because he perceived the underlying racism of the movement, whose goal was to rid American society not only of the sin of slavery but also of the "problem" of free blacks. White American Protestants who promoted sending black missionaries to Africa perceived the hand of providence in slavery as the means by which Christianity could be spread not only to those Africans who were brought to the United States but also through those who, now Christian, returned to their "heathen" brothers and sisters with the gospel. Mission boards like the ABCFM hoped that black missionaries would be especially effective with others of their race; moreover, they believed that African Americans would be less subject to African disease and could better sustain the African climate. Black Christian leaders in America shared some motivations and assumptions with white Christians. They, too, generally dismissed the traditional religions of Africa as pagan or nonexistent and took for granted that Christianity and "civilization" (defined in white Western terms) would be blessings for the "Dark Continent." But their religious conviction was accompanied by a special sense of duty to Africa and hopes for a kind of racial vindication. Walter L. Williams concludes:

> By bringing Christianity and Westernization to Africa, the black missionaries thought they had the key to redeeming the continent. If they could convert and educate the indigenous people, they were sure that Africa would begin a rise in "civilization" and world respect. This new rise, they felt, would improve the status of black people all over the world, including those in the United States.[26]

Moreover, while white proclamations about God's providential use of slavery included a note of guilty rationalization, similar beliefs in black leaders arose out of an anguished wrestling to discern some theological meaning in the undeserved suffering of slavery. Surely a just God would not have allowed so much evil without some ultimate intention of good. Perhaps that good was to be the redemption of Africa through those of her sons and daughters who had been refined in the fires of suffering.[27] Thus both white mission boards and black Protestant churches in America sponsored black missionaries to Africa during the nineteenth century, often in conjunction with colonization efforts.[28]

Unfortunately, many black missionaries still encountered racism on the mission field. Not only did some white missionaries continue to assume the innate racial inferiority of Africans, even after they were converted to Christianity and adopted forms of white civilization, but the black American missionaries themselves were discriminated against. There were occasional exceptions, white missionaries who worked comfortably with their black counterparts and freely acknowledged their contributions, but others refused to believe that American blacks could be anything but subordinates and displayed deep-seated personal prejudice. Reflecting on her own experience in Africa, Amanda Berry Smith criticized the attitudes of white mission boards and of some—not all—white missionaries.

> I suppose no church or society ever gave a salary to a colored man, no matter how efficient he was, as large as they give to a white man or woman, no matter how inefficient he or she may be in the start; and I think they are generally expected to do more work. . . . I have known some white missionaries who have gone to Africa, who were just as full of prejudice against black people as they are in this country, and did not have grace enough to hide it; but seemed to think they were in Africa, and there was no society that they cared for, and that the black people had but little sense, so they would never know if they did act mean and do mean things.[29]

Black women missionaries shared with black men the problems of racism, yet in other ways, they were like white women missionaries. Most black women who went to mission fields before the last few decades of the nineteenth century went as "assistants," wives of male missionaries who nevertheless saw a role for themselves in the work. Not until the later years of the century did many single black women—women like Nancy Jones, Maria Fearing, and Sarah Gorham—undertake the work as full-fledged missionaries. Other women continued to accompany missionary husbands. For example, the well-known educator Fanny Jackson Coppin accompanied her husband, Levi, who was appointed the first bishop of South Africa in 1900, uniting the A.M.E. Church in America with the Ethiopian Church in South Africa.[30] Most of the women shared with other American missionaries, male and female, black and white, the conviction of the superiority of Christianity and Western civilization, although some came through experience to express more appreciation for African culture. Fanny Jackson Coppin admitted that before she left America, she had dismissed the existence of serious religion in Africa, but she found more than she expected.

> [Coppin] therefore felt that the major role of missionaries was to improve on the African ethical, spiritual, and moral life: "Our religious training is, in a sense, but an explanation of [Africans'] own religious impulses." Seemingly dedicated to preserving the indigenous culture, she asserted that it was the task of missionaries to structure religious training around patterns that already existed.[31]

Coppin was also active in humanitarian work and education, and in this she was typical of black women missionaries, married or single. A few, like Amanda Berry Smith, were directly involved in preaching to large groups, but most black women, like their white missionary sisters, were encouraged to keep to appropriate women's work, especially education, health care, and informal evangelism and humanitarian work with women and children, including orphans. African-American women felt a special bond with the native women and, like their white counterparts, believed in the importance of education and the Christian home as bases for effective, long-term change. Like white women missionaries, too, they were sometimes insensitive to variant cultural patterns and gender roles.[32] Although the women were sometimes frustrated by limits imposed upon them, they generally accepted the roles seen as appropriate for women, genuinely convinced of the roles' importance and aware that the roles were often neglected by the male boards and missionaries. They believed that God had called them, personally and specifically, to the work. If necessary, they were willing to sacrifice to follow that call, as in the case of Maria Fearing.

Born a slave in 1838, Fearing struggled to get an education and taught for many years before she heard the call to Africa in 1894. When the Presbyterian Board rejected her application because of her age, she proceeded to raise the money for passage herself so she could go, which the Board "allowed," finally appointing her as a regular missionary after she had been in the Congo for two years![33] While relatively few African-American women served as foreign missionaries in the late nineteenth and early twentieth centuries, those who did contributed significantly to the work they believed in. Moreover, they were supported financially and emotionally by a much larger number of women back home in the church missionary societies, who, in turn, learned more about their homeland from the missionaries.

### Benevolent and Reform Activities

Preaching, foreign missions, and traditional supportive work for the churches by no means exhausted the religious interests and activities of African-American women in the nineteenth century. The evangelical Protestant conviction that conversion should result in fruits was joined in black women with acute awareness of the desperate needs of their people, and thus they became involved in a range of benevolent and reform activities that were frequently church-based and almost invariably motivated or justified by religious faith. If it is hard for the historian to distinguish clearly for white nineteenth-century women among activities labeled "church work," "benevolence," and "reform," it is even more problematic to separate these for black women, given the restricted resources available to blacks and the centrality of the church in the African-American community.

Well before the Civil War, free black Christian women were actively involved in a range of charitable and educational activities designed to help their communities, even when the women themselves had few financial resources. In the postbellum South, the women of the rapidly proliferating black churches joined together to raise money and to provide and sponsor basic services for their communities. Kathleen C. Berkeley cites as one example among many the work of the Daughters of Zion of Avery Chapel, an A.M.E. church in Memphis, who joined together to hire a physician to care for church members, realizing how racism and poverty made such care hard to attain otherwise. Black churchwomen from every class and Christian denomination were active in benevolent and humanitarian work, from the black Catholic sisters who ran schools and orphanages, to well-known leaders like Harriet Tubman, who in her later years worked to establish a home for old and poor blacks, and Amanda Berry Smith, who moved to Chicago after her return from Africa and founded a school and orphanage. Countless women's church groups supported benevolent work, not because they themselves in most cases were particularly well-to-do, but because there were so few other resources for social services for African Americans. In the later nineteenth century, some of this collective female activity moved from its largely working-class base in the churches to the colored women's clubs, led by educated middle- and upper-class black women. Yet even there, the leadership acknowledged the "self-help" activities of working class women, encouraged their groups to affiliate with the women's clubs, and "carefully nurtured [their] relationship with the traditional institution associated with benevolence in the black community—the black church."[34]

### *Antislavery*

Black women were also active in the range of reform activities in nineteenth-century America that moved beyond charitable benevolence or even self-help into attempts to change social structures. For obvious reasons, the reform that claimed most attention from freeborn blacks and ex-slaves in the first half of the nineteenth century was antislavery. Although traditional histories of abolitionism have focused on the white male leadership of the movement, and more recently, on black men and white women, black women were also active and passionate participants in the cause. Two exceptions to this general historical neglect were ex-slaves, Sojourner Truth and Harriet Tubman. Their contributions are sufficiently familiar not to require treatment at length here. Harriet Tubman worked on the Underground Railroad, and Sojourner Truth was a highly effective speaker for abolition and women's rights. Her "Ain't I a Woman?" speech not only silenced the white male clerical critics at an 1851 Women's Rights Conference in Akron, Ohio, but has become a classic in the modern feminist movement. Both women were deeply religious with a close, even mystical sense of divine presence and guidance in their work.

Free black women in the antebellum North were also active in antislavery, although only a few can be mentioned here. Maria Stewart, born in 1803, burst onto the public stage in Boston in 1831, the first American woman to give public speeches that have been preserved. Widowed in 1829 after only three years of marriage, she experienced a religious conversion the next year and credited that event with her determination to devote herself to "the cause of God and my brethren." She denounced slavery as a sin and addressed a special plea to the men and women of her race, rejecting any thought of inherent racial inferiority and calling upon blacks to develop their full potential.

> Many think, because your skins are tinged with a sable hue, that you are an inferior race of beings; but God does not consider you as such. He hath formed and fashioned you in his own glorious image, and hath bestowed upon you reason and strong powers of intellect.[35]

Despite her connections with the radical wing of the movement under Garrison (her speeches were printed in *The Liberator*), Stewart left Boston in

1833, at least in part because of criticism of her "unwomanly" behavior. In her farewell address, she defended her public actions on the basis of God's call and cited the biblical precedents that would become common in nineteenth-century women's religious defenses of their actions.

> Soon after I made this profession [of faith], the Spirit of God came before me, and I spake before many. When going home, reflecting on what I had said, I felt ashamed, and knew not where I should hide myself. A something said within my breast, "press forward, I will be with thee." And my heart made this reply, Lord, if thou wilt be with me, then will I speak for thee so long as I live. . . .
>
> I believe, that for wise and holy purposes, best known to himself, he hath unloosed my tongue and put his word into my mouth, in order to confound and put all those to shame that have rose up against me. . . .
>
> What if I am a woman; is not the God of ancient times the God of these modern days? Did he not raise up Deborah . . . Esther . . . Mary Magdalene . . . the woman of Samaria . . . [and the] holy women [who] ministered unto Christ and the apostles? . . . If such women as are here described have once existed, be no longer astonished then, my brethren and friends, that God at this eventful period should raise up your own females to strive, by their example both in public and private, to assist those who are endeavoring to stop the strong current of prejudice that flows so profusely against us at present. No longer ridicule their efforts, it will be counted for sin.[36]

Sarah Parker Remund was another free black northern woman who spoke publicly for antislavery. Born in 1826 in Salem, Massachusetts, the sister of Charles Remund, a prominent black male abolitionist, she joined him on the antislavery lecture circuit in 1856, but in 1859, her contribution took a different, but complementary turn: she went to England. When the Civil War broke out, she remained there, lecturing in England and Ireland to oppose English recognition of the South and to continue to raise the moral question of slavery. Slavery was wrong, finally, because all persons are created by God and equal in his sight and because Jesus had specifically identified himself with "the least of these, my little ones."[37] For a while after the war, Sarah Remund returned to the United States and worked with her brother and Frederick Douglass for universal suffrage, but she later returned to England and then to Florence, where she became a physician.

The contributions of free black women to antislavery were not confined to the few who risked public lectures. Many were active in the formation of antislavery societies, organizing, writing, and raising money, like the women of the Forten family in Philadelphia. James Forten, though a descendent of slaves, had fought in the Revolutionary War and by the early nineteenth century was one of the wealthiest blacks in the country. An ardent opponent of both slavery and colonization, he contributed his ideas and substantial funds to the radical wing of abolitionism, and the Forten home was for decades a center of antislavery. His wife, Charlotte, and their daughters Margaret, Harriet, and Sarah, were founders of the Philadelphia Female Anti-Slavery Society in 1833 (along with Lucretia Mott and the black Quaker educator, Sarah M. Douglass), and all three daughters continued to be active in antislavery and education. The Forten women's influence pushed the Philadelphia antislavery organization "to reflect a black abolitionist perspective, a perspective equally dedicated to the abolition of slavery and to the triumph of racial justice in America . . . their female Society went far beyond reflecting the views of well-meaning ladies; it emerged as an aggressive, persistent force for change in the Philadelphia area."[38]

### *Education*

For black women in antebellum America, ending slavery was the single most critical reform, but they were fully aware of other problems facing African Americans, from lack of political and economic power to inferior education to continued racism even within the antislavery movement. A significant number of black men, as well as black women, supported women's rights, including suffrage, and education was a high priority. In part, that commitment was rooted in a hope (a genuine one, however naive it may seem in retrospect) that if black people proved themselves, they could counter the common southern insistence on innate racial inferiority and be accepted by white society as equal, worthy human beings. Thus it is hardly surprising that northern blacks were quick to respond to a call for teachers for the newly freed slaves of the South.

The usual picture of the northern teacher who went south after the Civil War is of a young, white woman, as indeed many were. Nevertheless, black men and women also heeded the call of groups like the American Missionary Association (AMA). As was true with white volunteers, the men generally held administrative and supervisory positions, and women were teachers. Like their white sisters, black women teachers often cited a sense of divine call in their applications, but they also were moved by a strong sense of racial solidarity and duty. They experienced many of the same physical hardships, bureaucratic frustrations, and subtle or blatant sexism that white teachers did, but with a further important difficulty: racism, not only from white southerners but also from their white supervisors and fellow teachers. Sara G. Stanley was one such teacher, a graduate of Oberlin who emphasized in her application to the AMA both her sense of God's call and her feeling for her fellow African Americans. She was sent to Norfolk, Virginia, where a school founded by a black woman, Mary Peake, was designated as the AMA's first institution in the South. Stanley expected hard work, but she was frustrated and distressed by the racism she encountered among her white fellow workers, so she wrote to the AMA protesting their attitudes and actions as contrary to the Christianity they professed and presumed to teach to their students. Stanley's experience was not unique, and it surely added to all of the other problems that northern teachers faced in the South, yet their contribution was still a significant one.[39]

Education in the postwar South was indebted to northern teachers and administrators, black and white, who answered the call for help, whether their stay was short or long. But the project was not simply one of North-helping-South. Education was a central concern in northern black communities, and southern blacks from all economic levels worked hard, often at considerable sacrifice, to educate themselves and their children. Some individual women who were able to gain an education dedicated their lives to making such opportunities possible for other African Americans. Lucy Craft Laney, the daughter of an ex-slave and Presbyterian minister, was born in Georgia in 1854 and took advantage of increased educational opportunities during Reconstruction. After her graduation from Atlanta University in 1873, she taught school and then, with significant aid from the Women's Home Missions Board of the Presbyterian Church, opened a school for black children in Atlanta. Frances Jackson Coppin was born a slave in Washington in 1837, but an aunt purchased her freedom. She attended Rhode Island State Normal School and graduated from Oberlin in 1865, became a teacher and later principal of the Institute for Colored Youth in Philadelphia, and had a highly successful career as an educator before she accompanied her husband, Levi, to South Africa. Linda Perkins calls Coppin "one of the most influential Black educators and community leaders in the nineteenth century. . . . Driven by a deep religious devotion to helping her race through education, Fanny Coppin by the end of the century, headed one of the most prestigious Black academic institutions in the nation. . . ."[40] Anna Julia Cooper was born into slavery but benefited from the education supported by American Protestants in the postwar South, in her case the Episcopal St. Augustine Normal School in Raleigh, North Carolina. She, too, graduated from Oberlin and became a teacher and principal for many years at the M Street High School in Washington, D. C.[41] Other black women joined Laney, Coppin, and Cooper in the nineteenth century in a female educational tradition that was carried forward into the twentieth century by women like Mary McLeod Bethune and Nannie Helen Burroughs. For these pioneer black women educators, religion was a critical source of inspiration and continuing support, and their work was, in the fullest sense of the term, a ministry. Yet to their notable public contributions must be added the work of thousands of women who taught their children at home, in Sunday schools, and in low-paid teaching jobs; theirs, too, was a ministry.

*Anti-lynching*

While black women were involved with other reform causes in the nineteenth century, like moral reform or temperance, these were less central for them than antislavery and education. Toward the end of the century, a third cause of special concern to black women emerged: lynching. In Memphis on March 9, 1892, three black men were lynched, an event that had become common in the late nineteenth-century South, generally justified by the claim that the victims had raped or otherwise offended white women. But this time a young black woman journalist who had been a friend of the three men refused to accept that judgment. Ida B. Wells in a column in the *Memphis Free Speech* revealed the real reason for the lynching—that the black men's store was taking business away from white storeowners. Wells then began to research other cases of lynching, exposing the lack of foundation for the usual sexist and racist justifications. In a column on May 21, 1892, she cited statistics from cases she had studied and concluded, "Nobody in this section of the country believes the old threadbare lie that Negro men rape white women. If Southern white men are not careful, they will overreach themselves, and public sentiment will have a reaction. A conclusion will then be reached which will be very damaging to the moral reputation of their women."[42] Fortunately Wells was in New York when her exposé was published, for a mob attacked her newspaper office, and Wells herself was threatened with death if she ever returned to Memphis. Settling in the North, she continued to be a leader in the anti-lynching cause, an active promoter of black women's clubs, and a radical and outspoken supporter of civil rights and woman's suffrage.

The events in Memphis in March 1892, inspired another black woman to enter the public sphere. Mary Church Terrell, like Wells—although sometimes at odds with her—became a leader of the black women's club movement. Many such groups of black women throughout the nation emerged with the purpose of promoting both racial uplift and women's progress.[43] The clubs provided an alternative and complementary female institution to the women's societies within the black churches that had long worked to serve the material, educational, and emotional needs of black people. Not only did the clubs continue that church-based work, but they also provided role models and experience in leadership for black women as they moved into the twentieth century.

The relationship of church work and reform activities for black women in the nineteenth century was a very close one. While it would be presumptuous to argue that every black woman who sought leadership in reform or benevolent groups did so because she was denied ordained ministry in the black churches, the deep religious convictions of so many of these women justify identifying their careers as what Lincoln and Mamiya call "sublimated paths to ministry," where community service and reform or political activities "stemmed from a moral concern to uplift the race that was deeply rooted in religious motivations." Thus they conclude, "Probably many of these women and many unnamed others would have become ordained as clergy if that were an option available to them, because the Black Church and their Christian beliefs were the central values of their lives."[44]

## The Politics of Respectability

That religion and racial uplift were central concerns of leaders in African-American communities in the late nineteenth century is clear. More debated is the extent to which these black men and women "bought into" dominant white cultural values in the churches themselves and as they promoted "racial uplift." Some scholars have argued that black churches and other groups dedicated to racial uplift did adopt certain white cultural values, either because they saw them as intrinsically desirable or because they hoped thereby to gain acceptance and greater opportunities in a white-dominated society. Within the black churches, this was manifest in the male leadership's resistance to women's preaching and ordination, as mentioned earlier. Daniel Payne, an A.M.E. Church bishop and one of the most influential black leaders of the nineteenth century, not only opposed women's preaching and ordination but also endorsed "woman's central role . . . of domestic educator"[45] in an 1885 book, *A Treatise on Domestic Education*. Stressing the critical educational role of the family, Payne insisted that both parents should be involved in education but also that the wife was to be subordinate to her husband and that her particular charge was to be "the natural molder of character." "There is a sense . . . in which the mother is the special teacher and educator of her own child, and every mother ought to be conscious of this truth because it is only the mother having this consciousness who diligently performs her duty as a mother."[46] Yet like so many white feminists of the nineteenth century, Payne argued further that the crucial nature of the mother's educational role necessitated women's own education, and he was a strong supporter of black women educators like Fanny Jackson Coppin.

As black male clergy adopted some prevalent white cultural values and gender images, so too did the female leadership of the black women's clubs. William Jeremiah Moses argues that this was especially true in sexual morality. "The black women's club movement saw its primary work as encouraging the masses of peasant poor to adopt the Victorian morality of the middle classes. They hoped that a dramatic change in the sexual behavior of the masses would make them more acceptable to the white-American mainstream and would ease interracial tensions."[47] While Moses concedes that there were sharply differing views within the black women's club movement, including a more radical wing represented by women like Ida B. Wells-Barnett, and that even leaders like Mary Church Terrell who advocated domestic feminism *also* worked for political and economic reforms, he still concludes that the dominant tone of the National Association of Colored Women was "conservative rather than radical; and its attitudes toward fundamental American institutions was admiring, rather than critical."[48]

## Blacks' Perspectives on a "Politics of Respectability"

Evelyn Brooks Higginbotham presents a more complex and sympathetic analysis of the motives and goals of those black women leaders, in club or church work, who promoted a "politics of respectability." These women did accept the culturally dominant assumption of "essentialism"—that is, that men and women are different by nature—and stressed the need for individual change in manners and morals, particularly in the areas of hard work, sexual morality, and temperance. They were so deeply concerned with white perceptions and misperceptions of black character and behavior that at times they were insensitive to alternative cultural patterns among poor blacks, and their rhetoric could contribute to a conclusion that blamed blacks, especially black women, for their own victimization. Nevertheless, the "politics of respectability" promoted by black women leaders also protested structural racism, encouraged self-esteem and achievement for both men and women, provided some common ground for cooperation with white women reformers, and self-consciously countered the false and debilitating image of the black woman as morally loose and carnal.[49] Furthermore, if the cult of True Womanhood and the feminization of American religion[50] are seen as typical of white culture and gender images in the nineteenth century, applying either concept to black women and black churches at that time is problematic. While a few well-to-do black women and men may have seen in full-time female domesticity a sign of social and economic achievement, for the vast majority of black women, any ideal of staying at home full-time was a practical impossibility; without the women's economic contribution, few poor black families could have survived. A little higher on the economic scale, many black women found professional careers in teaching and nursing and, more often than white women, continued those careers after marriage. Other black women whose husbands' positions released them from the stark necessity of paid employment found active careers in voluntary church and humanitarian work for their race. Thus the cult of domesticity in its most extreme and limiting form simply does not fit black women in the nineteenth century.

Nor was black religion markedly "feminized." Far from being marginalized (along with women) into a private sphere, the ministry remained a prestigious and powerful position for black men. Similarly, black churches were not only religious institutions but also centers for community building, socializing, and economic, political, and educational activities for both men and women. Yet while most black churchwomen accepted the formal leadership of black male clergy, they did not therefore necessarily endorse female images or roles that were simply passive and subordinate. Black Baptist women in the last decades of the nineteenth century argued on biblical grounds against a passive, silent role for women in the churches and in the broader society. Women leaders accepted and valued women's roles in the family, but they also insisted on the importance of public activity for women, "defining themselves as both homemakers and soldiers."[51] Turning to the Bible, they cited figures like Deborah and Huldah to show that women could "combine humility and grace with aggressive zeal and strong intellect" and that "marriage need not negate public leadership for women."[52] While the women seldom pressed for female ordination or equal representation in the church's governing structures, they did challenge gendered character stereotypes and develop their own female spheres for significant action without repudiating traditional female roles.

A similar combination of "traditional" and "radical" can be found in the work of a prominent black female educator and Episcopalian, Anna Julia Cooper, whose book, *A Voice from the South*, was published in 1892. On the one hand, she, like so many evangelical Protestants of her day, was convinced that Christianity elevated women and that women, with their distinctive characteristics that complemented male traits, made a unique contribution to civilization by shaping the characters of their children. On the other hand, she deplored the cultural limits placed on women's self-development and education and the lack of appreciation for their contributions. Cooper repeatedly insisted on drawing specific attention to black women, arguing that their voices and concerns were neither subordinate to nor adequately represented by either black men or white women. Thus she took black men to task for their sexism, remarking that "while our men seem thoroughly abreast of the times on almost every other subject, when they strike the woman question they drop back into sixteenth century logic."[53] At the same time, she was severely critical of the white women's movement and of the emerging labor movement in the North for their racism and class-consciousness. She found it hard to sympathize with the plight of northern white laborers or white "working girls" in comparison with the lot of so many poor black women.

> But how many have ever given a thought to the pinched and downtrodden colored women bending over wash-tubs and ironing boards—with children to feed and house[,] rent to pay, wood

> to buy, soap and starch to furnish—lugging home weekly great baskets of clothes for families who pay them for a month's laundrying barely enough to purchase a substantial pair of shoes![54]

Anna Julia Cooper identified and decisively rejected racism and sexism in the America of her day, especially since black women were victims of both at the same time, and their needs and voices were widely ignored. Thus she repeatedly and explicitly lifted up the unique concerns of black women. Progress for blacks that included only men, gains for women that were restricted to whites were ultimately inauthentic and un-Christian. Yet Cooper could also sound a more hopeful note. Sharing the assumption of many Americans of the age that the nation had a special, divinely directed role in the development of civilization and that their own era was a turning point, she denied that race was a "problem" and embraced American diversity. African Americans, she insisted, had distinctive and invaluable contributions to make; so, too, did women. Cooper thus rejoiced in the special potential of black women, even while she deplored their past and present double-oppression.

> To be alive at such an epoch is a privilege, to be a woman then is sublime. . . . To be a woman in such an age carries with it a privilege and an opportunity never implied before. But to be a woman of the Negro race in America, and to be able to grasp the deep significance of the crisis, is to have a heritage, it seems to me, unique in the ages.[55]

14

# *Roman Catholic Women in Nineteenth-Century America*

In 1820, the Roman Catholic Church in the United States had fewer churches than any other denomination; by 1850, it was the single largest denomination in America.[1] The major source for that growth was immigration that by the end of the century would make Catholics one of the most ethnically and economically diverse churches in America. Women, of course, were part of that diversity: the wealthy, socially prominent Catholic lady who traced her English roots to the colonial period; the young Irish girl working as a domestic servant in the 1850s to support herself or help her family; the Italian mother recently arrived in New York, striving to preserve her family, her religion, and her traditions in the face of desperate poverty; the Hispanic woman of the Southwest whose world was changed not by her own emigration but by the currents of war and American territorial expansion. In addition, Roman Catholic women had a unique position among American Christians, for their tradition provided not one but two respectable roles for women: wife and mother; and the honored single life of a religious sister. Finally, Catholic women shared an experience of mistrust or even outright hostility from the dominant Protestant culture. Nativism was at times more virulent, at times more muted, and Catholic women with greater economic security and longer roots in America were less affected than recent immigrants who were perceived as "foreign" in culture, values, and religion and hence a threat to the great American experiment. Women religious were often particular targets of nativism, yet they eventually earned Protestant respect for their selfless service. The story of Catholic women in America, themselves a diverse group, thus contains both continuity and conflict with the dominant Protestant culture.

## The Roman Catholic Experience in America

Whatever differences Roman Catholic clergy in America may have had with their Protestant brothers, the image of the ideal woman was not one of them. Catholic priests and bishops, prominent laymen, and, to a large degree, laywomen fully endorsed the cult of True Womanhood or domestic ideology that saw woman's natural, divinely appointed sphere as home and family. If anything, the domestic ideal was promoted even more fervently and longer by Catholic religious leaders than it was by Protestants. (Catholic clergy, of course, continued to praise the choice of a religious life for Catholic women, but even there the qualities and duties of sisters were presumed to be essentially feminine and maternal.) The more negative traditional image of Eve had not disappeared from Roman Catholic thought by the nineteenth century, but it was muted, more typically associated with irreligious women and those females unnatural enough not to find fulfillment in maternal roles, or, somewhat inconsistently, with the threatening sexual temptation to men represented even unintentionally by presumably asexual women. Good Catholic mothers were Mary: pious, pure, self-sacrificing, patient, and submissive to male authorities. Catholic expressions of the image were legion, but one of the most popular was Bernard O'Reilly's *Mirror of True Womanhood*. First published in 1876, it had gone through seventeen editions by 1892. O'Reilly both praised women for their natural virtue and piety, their self-sacrifice in domestic roles, and their charity to the less fortunate, and warned of the dangers to female character and civilization itself posed by "modern" notions of women's rights. "No woman," he wrote, "animated by the Spirit of her Baptism . . . ever fancied that she had or could have any other sphere of duty or activity than that home which is her domain, her garden, her paradise, her world."[2]

Yet just as it is misleading to assume that the image of the "True Woman" in Protestant culture accurately or comprehensively reflected the actual lives of Protestant women across class, geographical, ethnic, and racial lines, so too we must move carefully from the rhetoric of domestic ideology to the experiences of all Catholic women. In its typical and most limiting form, the cult of True Womanhood was inherently class-biased. Immigrant women surely valued home and family and their roles therein, but few had the luxury of full-time domesticity, and their own ethnic traditions about female roles within the family did not necessarily fit an American cultural ideal. Furthermore, middle-class Catholic women, like their Protestant sisters, found ways to use or reinterpret the image to expand their concerns and activities, even as they insisted they agreed with the ideal. Female education, literary activity, and church and benevolent work could all be defended as compatible with women's "natural" roles and yet at the same time subtly undercut restrictive definitions of female domesticity.

## Education

Throughout the nineteenth century, some male Catholic leaders were highly suspicious of female education,[3] but most supported the "right" kind, education that would prepare women for their future duties as good

Catholic mothers. The early leaders of American Catholicism under Bishop John Carroll were vitally concerned to promote Catholic education in the new nation. Carroll's highest priority was to establish male colleges and seminaries to educate American-born priests for the church, but the second educational priority of Catholic leaders in the early nineteenth century was academies for young women, which would provide "the moral and religious training of their pupils as future American mothers."[4] Catholic women shared this concern for education in the faith. They also concurred with their Protestant sisters that if woman's primary contribution to society was to be "Republican Motherhood," she would have to be educated herself in order to fulfill her role most effectively. Catholic female academies were usually founded and run by women religious, but laywomen worked with the sisters, provided financial support as they could, and sent their daughters to be educated, as often they themselves had been. Catholic female academies, and later women's colleges, have been criticized for their class bias, their conservatism, and their acceptance that training women for motherhood or recruiting future women religious were their only legitimate goals, yet education often opens doors and leads to results not intended by its initial supporters.

Several Catholic women used their education to launch careers as writers and became the "lady novelists," whom James Kenneally calls "unwitting innovators" in the nineteenth century. Writing did not take women out of the private sphere to express and, in some cases, support themselves; moreover, the message they propounded was thoroughly supportive of women's spiritual and domestic roles and hence acceptable. Yet if these writers reinforced traditional notions of the ideal woman as pious and domestic, they concurrently undercut presumptions of female weakness and passivity. In his study of Catholic novels in the nineteenth century, Kenneally concludes that female characters in novels by male authors were, indeed, weak and passive. "However, in the writings of Catholic women, including those most supportive of the 'cult of true womanhood,' females were the stronger characters, frequently shaping their own destiny and in a way superior to base men whom they enabled and redeemed."[5]

Promotion of female education and the writings of women novelists fell largely within acceptable cultural bounds for women and paralleled similar activities among the white Protestant women who were part of the cultural establishment. Yet Protestants and Catholics differed significantly on one point: Catholic educators and writers also supported a self-conscious Catholic identity. Female academies were needed to produce not just good mothers but knowledgeable *Catholic* mothers. Catholic women novelists promoted domesticity and traditional moral values, as did their Protestant counterparts, but they also wanted to explicate and defend the Catholic faith and counter Protestant errors and misrepresentations. As Kenneally notes, "These novels often taught dogma by means of lengthy disputations between a Catholic and a Protestant. Usually the Catholic was young, sometimes a religious, and always well versed in Scripture and apologetics."[6] Not surprisingly, she almost invariably won the debate.

## Charitable Activities

Church work and charitable activities were generally approved by the dominant culture as being within woman's appropriate sphere. Thus, many Protestant women joined such organizations and found personal fulfillment outside the domestic circle, in some cases moving on to more challenging reforms. Roman Catholic laywomen, too, were mainstays of the churches through their attendance and support, but they were less directly involved in charitable activities for most of the nineteenth century than either Protestant women or Catholic laymen. The most important charitable agency in nineteenth-century American Catholicism was the St. Vincent de Paul Society, whose formal membership was confined to laymen (though female financial support was always welcomed). Direct female involvement in charitable work was more typical of women religious than of Catholic laywomen. Nevertheless, some middle- and upper-class Catholic laywomen engaged in charitable activities during the first three-quarters of the nineteenth century. Often this work was coordinated with that of the sisters, as laywomen worked as volunteers or raised or donated funds. Catholic women who were both devout and relatively wealthy, like the Parmentier women of Brooklyn, donated substantial time and money to charitable and philanthropic causes. Sylvia Parmentier emigrated from Belgium to the United States with her husband Andre in 1824. After he died, she and her daughters Adele and Rosine supported a range of charitable causes from orphanages to missions to sailors, Indians, and blacks. They also supported the educational work of the Sisters of St. Joseph, leaving them property for a school.[7]

For most of the nineteenth century, the Roman Catholic approach to benevolent activity was traditional charity; while it surely responded to real needs among the poor, it seldom challenged the structures and systems of society. Few Roman Catholics, male or female, were actively involved in the various reforms of the day, at least partly because many reforms were so overtly Protestant. The one exception was temperance, which Dolan calls "the most enduring reform movement that Catholics sponsored in the nineteenth century."[8] By 1872, Catholics formed their own temperance society, the Catholic Total Abstinence Union of America, and some Catholic women joined that group, but there was still significant opposition in the Catholic hierarchy to such "public" reform work for women. Thus Debra Campbell concludes that the attraction of the WCTU over the CTAU for many Catholic laywomen may have been not only its "more socially acceptable" constituency but also "the warm welcome they received and the freedom from worry about what the priests and bishops were thinking."[9] Not only did Catholic laywomen become active temperance supporters in the last decades of the nineteenth century, they also became more immediately involved in citywide charitable organizations designed to meet the needs of new immigrants and, in a few cases, the settlement movement.

It was not, however, the activities of middle- and upper-class Catholic laywomen or development of an ancient tradition of works of mercy that fueled the most radical Catholic social activity at the end of the nineteenth century. Rather, it was the immediate needs of the far larger number of poor and working-class Catholics that drew them, and finally the church, into labor reform. But to tell that story, we need first to return to the single most significant factor shaping and challenging the Catholic Church in nineteenth-century America: immigration.

## Immigration and Ethnic Identity

Irish immigration to the United States began early in the nineteenth century but became a flood during the 1840s because of the potato famine in Ireland and continued throughout the century. German Catholics, too, came throughout the century, looking for land or work or to escape religious persecution at home. After 1880, a "new" kind of immigrant, especially Italian and Polish Catholics, began arriving in large numbers from southern and eastern Europe. In the meantime, many French Canadians had moved into New England, seeking work in its textile factories, and Mexican Catholics in the Southwest became part of the United States church after the nation took over that territory in 1848. These were the six largest ethnic Catholic groups of the nineteenth century, but others, like Slovaks, Czechs, Bohemians, Lithuanians, and Ukrainians, came from eastern Europe.[10] Some immigrants stayed in the cities, while others headed to farms in the Midwest, and Mexicans, of course, were "here" already. All these groups shared some experiences—poverty and Protestant hostility—and most had ambivalent feelings about the changes they were experiencing, with hope for a better life mixed with regret at leaving their homes. But the various groups also had distinctive traditions, despite a common Roman Catholic faith.

Catholic faith was central to the identity of most immigrants, but it was a faith tied to the distinctive ethnic traditions they had left. Ethnic identity was symbolized and reinforced by devotion to a particular saint, like St. Patrick for the Irish or St. Stanislaus for the Polish, or to a particular manifestation of Mary, like the Virgin of Guadalupe for Mexicans, or the Madonna of Mount Carmel, who came to America with Italian immigrants and grew to be the center of the Italian Catholic community from her home on 115th Street in Italian Harlem.[11] Ethnic loyalty was frequently stronger than common Catholic identity, so internal tensions were sometimes more immediate than divisions with the more distant Protestant majority, and parishes were organized by nationality (often coinciding with urban neighborhood) more than strict geography. Ethnic tensions were also evident in the relationship of different Catholic immigrant groups with the American church and its hierarchy.

To be sure, the institutional church in America tried to be extremely supportive of new arrivals, both in the persons of priests, who helped them in practical ways like finding jobs, and of sisters, who provided them with schools, medical care, and other social services. But relations were not always smooth. It was not that the hierarchy was insensitive to ethnicity, assigning a French priest to an Irish parish or placing German sisters among English-speaking midwestern Catholics. There were surely cases of Catholics from one group misunderstanding or denigrating the traditions of another, but there was also the practical problem of too few institutional resources to fill the needs of a rapidly expanding and diverse Catholic population. The hierarchy also faced a continuing dilemma: how to promote sufficient "Americanization" among immigrants to allow them to survive and function in their new home and to defuse Protestant suspicions, without letting the immigrants become so Americanized that they left the church—a dilemma shared in practical ways by the immigrants themselves and their descendants.

Among immigrant groups, Catholic faith might or might not be closely identified with the institutional church. For Irish Catholics, the church and its services were central and the relationship between pulpit and pew a comfortable one, especially as the Irish came to dominate the American hierarchy by the later nineteenth century. Similarly, the parish was the center of Polish Catholic life, and there was a strong tradition of respect for the clergy. On the other hand, Italian and Mexican Catholics were more suspicious of the institutional church, and its services and parish life were not as critical for their own practice of Catholicism. Italian and Mexican Catholics inherited a tradition of anticlericalism rooted in the identification of the church with the ruling classes, so their approach to American institutional Catholicism was cautious. Moreover, as Colleen McDannell notes:

> Italian and Mexican immigrants found an American Catholicism thoroughly steeped in Irish ways. The state of one's Catholicism was measured by attendance at mass, respect for the priest, and participation in parish activities. The Italian and Mexican preference for communal religious celebrations (the *festa* or *fiesta*), their elaborate rites of passage (baptisms, weddings, funerals), and their emotional devotion to the saints had little in common with the more restrained Irish. While the Irish were willing to follow their educated clergy and lay leaders, Italian and Mexican immigrants

> chose to continue the religious traditions brought from their villages.[12]

Thus it is important to try to understand how the people themselves defined and understood their faith and its relationship to the formal leadership and institutional forms of the church. It is also helpful to be gender specific, for even among groups like Italian and Mexican Catholics, men were most likely to be alienated from or critical of the faith and the church. For most immigrant women, especially in the first generation, the Catholic Church and Catholic faith were extremely important in their lives and identities. Indeed, the dominant form of Catholicism that emerged in America over the course of the nineteenth century, which Jay Dolan calls "devotional Catholicism," was in some ways "feminine." Catholic women made up the majority of church members; they attended services more faithfully than men and often joined the female devotional sodalities associated with the parish. The characteristics promoted by the church for the laity were those identified in the nineteenth century as natural for women: emotionalism and sentimentalism, docility and obedience to authority, represented by the church's hierarchy and clergy.[13] Yet we should not conclude that certain religious values and activities were simply imposed on immigrant women by the church's hierarchy or by American culture. Particular familial and religious roles for women were part of the ethnic heritage of many immigrants and were embraced and endorsed by women themselves. Religious devotion to God and especially to Mary and the saints, expressed through private prayers, novenas, festivals, and ubiquitous domestic shrines with their candles, pictures, and statues, helped Catholic women preserve their identity and provided a source of comfort, strength, and meaning in a world that was often harsh and bewildering. When resources in a new land were inaccessible or seemed foreign and ineffective, women could turn to a long tradition of folk religion in which miracles were accepted and expected, and Mary and the saints granted healings and other favors. As one Italian immigrant woman put it, "The Madonna is the mother of us poor women. She helps us all the time. In the old time there were more miracles than now, but I see lots of miracles—in Chicago, too. The Madonna and the Saints, they all the time make miracles to help me out. I all my life keep the good faith and the strong religion, that's why."[14]

## Women and the Family

The female identity of most immigrant Catholic women was shaped primarily by their roles within the family, and the family was at least as important as the church as a locus of religious identity and practice. In their turn, the Catholic Church and ethnic religious tradition invested women's roles with divine authority. The family as a religious center more important than the church is especially clear among Italian Catholics, where what Robert Orsi calls the "domus" (including the extended family, the physical location of home, and a source of meaning, values, and identity) dominated the life and defined the faith of Italian Harlem. The family was equally central to Mexican Catholic faith, again where there was a strain of suspicion of the institutional church, but family was also a religious center among those groups that had closer ties to the institutional church and that saw the parish as locus of religious practice.

Typically, responsibility for the family's spiritual, as well as physical, well-being and the maintenance of family-centered religion fell on women. In this cultural expectation, immigrant Catholic women were like their more established Catholic sisters and Protestant women. In 1865, William Henry, bishop of Natchez, wrote in Catholic terms, but his general perception of the spiritual role of the mother (and his excusing of fathers from more active roles in their children's religious education) could be paralleled in Protestant pronouncements.

> If the mother is not Catholic, what will ever supply for [the children] those early impressions of Catholic piety which it is the mother's place to give? How can the father, engaged all day in his out-door business, teach his children their prayers, give them their first lessons in Catholic faith, and train them from infancy in Catholic practices, to invoke the sweet names of Jesus and Mary, to make the sign of the cross, to love and fear their Guardian Angels, to cherish their medal, to recite the first lessons of the Cathechism, to love and imitate the Infant Jesus at Bethlehem and Nazareth? And without these things, the innocent years of childhood are a blank in the Christian life, which after-piety may atone for, but it never can supply, but which more probably will make it impossible for any structure of piety to be built where the foundations have been so neglected.[15]

Yet even as immigrant women shared with other American women the central role expectation of religious nurturer of children, they preserved and passed on particular ethnic identities and values through their education of children and attention to family shrines and religious festivals. Not just Italian and Mexican but also Irish, German, and Polish Catholic homes had their family shrines, with rosaries and candles, pictures and statues of Jesus, Mary, and favorite saints. Crucial stages of human and family life—birth, coming of age, marriage, death—were marked by sacraments and by religio-familial celebrations, and religious festivals took on a particular ethnic flavor, even literally in their foods. Italians gathered in Harlem starting on July 16 for the festival of the Madonna of Mount Carmel. For Mexican women, Holy Saturday was the occasion for a special healing ritual in the home. Polish women prepared special dinners for Christmas Eve and marked K + M + B (for the three wise men) on their doors with chalk on Epiphany to protect their homes from evil.[16]

Unless they chose the alternative of joining a religious order, the vast majority of Catholic women in America found their identity within the family, just as church tradition and American Catholic clergy said they should. But to what extent were those roles restrictive for women, particularly since the family pattern advocated as natural and divinely given was patriarchal? Women did lack the freedom of movement and the range of choices assumed by men. Wives were expected to obey their husbands, and although the high standard of sexual purity theoretically applied to both sexes, in practice young women were held to it far more strictly and punished far more harshly if they fell. Rosa, the Italian immigrant, for example, is forced into an unwelcome marriage and stays despite her husband's physical and mental abuse of her and her children, because of the pressure of tradition and because she recalls the words of her priest in Italy: for a wife to disobey her husband is sinful. Yet women exercised real power in their families, the church, and the community. They generally accepted their familial roles and took pride in the importance of their contributions. The role of religion in women's lives was complex: it reinforced their submission and restrictions, but it could also provide an escape, literally and emotionally. The same priest whose advice to Rosa about wifely submission contributed to her entrapment also provided her with a justification for disobedience that she recalls when she finally leaves her abusive husband. "'God gave the man the right to control the woman when He made him stronger, Rosa,' said Don Domenic. 'It's a sin for the wife not to obey. Only when the husband wants his wife to sin against God and the Madonna she must not obey him. Remember that, Rosa.'"[17] Firmly convinced that her husband's insistence that she live in and manage a brothel he has purchased will endanger her soul and those of her children, she takes those children and runs away. Orsi's analysis of women in the domus of Italian Harlem reveals a similarly complex mix of women, power, restrictions, and religion. When the burdens and expectations that accompanied the power of women in the domus grew overwhelming, the women could turn to other women and, even more, to the Divine Mother for help and understanding. The feast of the Madonna was dominated by women, divine and human, celebrating their roles and contributions. Yet that very celebration reinforced the limits of female roles and sent a double message about female power. As Orsi concludes:

> The festa reproduced characteristic modes of relationship in the community between powerful women and those subject to them. Though the people loved the Madonna, they also feared her enormous and potentially capricious power. . . . This was, of course, the same kind of power men and women claimed that the significant women in the community—their mothers, married aunts, the

> healers, and comari—wielded; it was the domus-centered and absolute power which these women were compelled (and taught by devotion) to wield. . . . Once a year, women were educated into the nature and limits of their power at a celebration of a woman of power.
>
> At the same time, however, women were also expected to atone at the festa and before the symbol of their power precisely for the power the community claimed was theirs. Women almost exclusively bore the penitential burden of the devotion. They alone bartered their suffering to free a member of their domus from pain or misfortune. They alone were dragged down the main aisle of the church, licking the stones that paved the way to the throne of the Madonna. The festa was the time of the exaltation but also of the degradation of the women of Italian Harlem; given the structure of the life of the domus and the assumptions of the community about the role of women, degradation and exaltation could not be separated. Even as it was affirmed and revealed in a sacred setting, women were called upon to pay for their possession of the power which they had no choice but to accept.[18]

## Women, Economics, and Labor

A second important issue is the degree to which the roles of women among Catholic immigrants were influenced by the American cultural ideal of True Womanhood. There were surely similarities—woman's role in the home, exaltation of motherhood, female purity and submission—but was the congruence a direct result of American cultural influence? McDannell argues that it was, at least in part and in some cases. "Irish women, many of whom had had no contact with Victorian domestic ideology before leaving Ireland, learned from their Protestant mistresses how a 'good' woman acted and what a 'good' family looked like." And Irish women tried to replicate those values as they moved into the middle class.[19] Thus, McDannell argues, the domestic ideology promoted by male clergy and Catholic literature was a product of the Irish and the Catholic elite in America. How much that ideal influenced poor Catholic women and other ethnic Catholic communities is another question. Although some of their beliefs about female roles and qualities may have coincided with aspects of an American cult of True Womanhood, the source of those beliefs was at least as much the traditions immigrants brought with them as American influence. Furthermore, in some very important ways, the cult of True Womanhood was both irrelevant and impossible for most Catholic immigrant women, who lacked the financial means to enjoy full-time domesticity. Quite simply, immigrant Catholic women had to work outside the home (or bring work into it) if they and their families were to survive.

Here, again, Catholic ethnic groups differed. Irish Catholics drew a cultural distinction between single and married women: married women were not to work outside the home or even be involved in volunteer activities, though they might take in lodgers or do piecework at home, but single women had significantly more freedom and were expected to work for pay, often as domestic servants, to support themselves and to contribute to the family's economic well-being. Many German Catholics took up farming in rural areas, but those who stayed in the cities demonstrated patterns similar to the Irish regarding women's employment. Italian Catholics showed similar resistance to mothers working outside the home, but single Italian women were more likely to seek jobs in factories than as domestic servants, since the latter job would separate them more from their families. Single Polish women often sought factory work, but after marriage, they either took in lodgers or piecework. Unlike their Irish, German, or Italian counterparts, however, Polish married women also found work as "domestics" but in the better-paid cleaning jobs in offices, schools, churches, and hotels. French Canadian immigrants as families, including women, found work in the mills of New England, but they tended not to enter domestic service, while Mexican American women, often the most economically disadvantaged, were forced into whatever unskilled labor they could find, including farm work, domestic service, and work in garment or food-processing plants.[20]

Most middle-class Catholic married women did not seek paid employment outside their homes, though single women and widows might have to or choose to do so, seeking work in "female" professions like teaching. Over time, the children and grandchildren of Catholic immigrants moved into the middle class, so that their women, too, looked for work that was more personally and financially rewarding. But as some immigrants moved slowly up the economic ladder, newer arrivals replaced them at the bottom, and regardless of differing ethnic patterns of female employment, the base reality for poor immigrant women was the same: they had to work for pay, inside or outside the home, and that meant that they experienced firsthand the deplorable conditions, instability, and inadequate pay of the working class in late nineteenth-century America. It is thus no surprise that many Catholic women supported and even led the labor movements of their day.

### Leonora Barry

Among prominent early women labor leaders were several Irish Catholics, including Leonora Barry and Mary Kenney O'Sullivan, both of whom saw no inconsistency between their commitment to the cause of labor and their identity as good Catholic women. Leonora Kearny was born in Ireland in 1849 and came with her parents to the United States in 1852. She married William Barry in 1871 but was left a widow ten years later with two children to support. She began working in a hosiery mill and soon learned how bad conditions were and how little she could earn—sixty-five cents for her first week's work—so she joined the Knights of Labor, an organization open to women, as well as men, that was especially attractive to Irish Catholics. She rapidly rose to a leadership position and in 1886 was elected the head and general investigator for the Department of Women's Work. One major part of her job over the next four years as she traveled widely was to investigate working conditions. What she found was appalling: charges for sewing machines and thread taken out of the woman's already meager wages; unhealthy, dangerous working conditions; petty harassments and fines, like the Newark corset factory where a worker who was one minute late was "locked out and fined two hours pay 'for wasted time.'"[21] Barry wanted to do more than investigate; she wanted to organize women workers. In this effort, however, she was less successful, encountering hostility from male workers and apathy from many women. Some Catholic clergy criticized her, but she refused to be intimidated or to give up her faith. When one priest called her a "Lady Tramp" and criticized the Knights as immoral, she defended the society and her right as "an Irishwoman, a Catholic and an honest woman" to serve the cause of labor.[22] In 1890, Barry married again and withdrew from active labor work, believing that married women should work outside the home only in cases of stark economic necessity; however, she continued to be active in Catholic charity organizations and in support of temperance and women's suffrage.

### Mary Kenney O'Sullivan

Mary Kenney O'Sullivan was born in the United States in 1864, though her parents had come from Ireland. Like Barry, she had to enter the labor force after the death of a male breadwinner, in this case her father, who died when she was fourteen, leaving her to support herself and her invalid mother. She found work at a printing and binding company in her hometown of Hannibal, Missouri, and moved with it to Iowa; but she lost that job when the company failed, and so moved on to Chicago. Continuing to work as a binder, she joined the Ladies' Federal Labor Union No. 1703 and helped organize the Chicago Bindery Workers' Union. In the meantime, she met Jane Addams and became convinced that the settlement workers were genuinely sympathetic to working women. In 1891, she became the first woman general organizer for the American Federation of Labor, but she soon left the post, frustrated by the lack of support from male union members and leaders, who regarded women merely as temporary workers who would quit to marry, and who believed women were too passive and weak anyway to be effective union members (although John O'Sullivan, whom Kenney met in Boston, was an exception). After a brief return to Chicago and Hull House, Mary Kenney went back to Boston to continue her labor work and, in 1894, married John O'Sullivan. The couple lived at the settlement Denison House and had four children. Unlike Leonora Barry, however, Mary O'Sullivan continued her work for the labor movement during her marriage and after John's death in 1902.

Mary O'Sullivan's ties with the settlement movement and her labor experience came together in 1903, when she helped to found the Women's Trade Union League, the "first national body dedicated to organizing women workers."[23] The WTUL's hope to bring women together across class lines was reflected in its two types of membership: women workers, many of whom were Catholic or Jewish; and "allies," sympathetic middle-class women, largely Protestant, whose experience in reform work and the settlement movement led them to embrace the cause of working women. Its first priority was to organize women, but the league also supported investigative work, public education, and lobbying for laws to protect workers. Though hurt at times by internal tensions and its ambivalent relationship with a class-biased women's movement and a sexist labor movement, the league nevertheless made significant contributions to women workers in the first decades of the twentieth century.

Most American Catholic leaders did not initially approve of either the labor movement or women's working outside the home. In the last years of the nineteenth century under the leadership of men like Cardinal Gibbons, however, they became more supportive of labor, not only as they, like American Protestant leaders in the Social Gospel movement, became more aware of the justice of labor's complaints but also because so many Catholics were workers and would be lost to a church that failed to understand their needs and support their cause. Catholic leaders also came to recognize, if grudgingly, that Catholic women were in the labor force by necessity. While they continued to advocate a living wage for male workers as the ultimate solution, so that women would not have to work and could stay in their preferred roles at home, they conceded that short-term reforms were necessary, especially to protect the health, safety, and purity of single women workers, future Catholic mothers. Their focus was primarily on single women; it was assumed that a woman could and should quit work when she married, and this would be possible if the husband and father received more pay.

## Women's Suffrage

Catholic concern for labor, including qualified support for women workers, was widespread by the turn of the twentieth century, but Catholic attitudes toward women's suffrage were mixed. Despite internal divisions between conservatives and liberals on other matters, the majority of

Catholic bishops and priests in nineteenth-century America agreed that woman suffrage was an affront to divine law and the natural order and a threat to family and society. Much of this opposition was no doubt rooted in a tradition of conservative views on women's roles and abilities, reinforced by an American cultural ideology of domesticity. Yet Catholic religious leaders also feared the women's movement, and suffrage in particular, because it was associated with Protestantism. The alignment was overt in Massachusetts in the 1880s, as Protestant women joined with nativists in a battle over the public schools. Massachusetts women had been given the school franchise in 1879, and in an 1888 election,

> Independent Women Voters, a nativist association . . . along with the WCTU, the other nativist groups, and a good many Boston ministers, exhorted women to register, vote, and save the public schools. Protestant women responded, and the candidates of the Committee of One Hundred [a nativist group with its own slate for school board] were swept into office on the strength of the largest feminine vote in Boston history.[24]

Nativist appeals were widespread in the women's suffrage movement over the next decades (as was overt racism, especially in the South). It was argued, for example, that it was unfair and potentially disastrous for the country that ignorant and illiterate foreign men could vote when moral, educated, white Protestant women could not! Such arguments, however, could cut both ways. Finally, despite the disapproval of the Catholic hierarchy, some Catholic women did vote in the school elections, and in succeeding years, more Catholic leaders reluctantly accepted women's suffrage as a practical necessity to protect Catholic interests and values.

Catholic opposition to woman suffrage came not only from the male hierarchy; some prominent Catholic women were leaders of female antisuffrage forces. After the Civil War, Ellen Ewing Sherman and Madeline Vinton Dahlgren used their pens and their socially prominent positions in Washington to attack woman suffrage, arguing that it was un-Christian and smacked of socialism, that it would damage woman's finer nature and undermine both family and nation. They even circulated petitions to Congress, apparently untroubled by any incongruity between their actions and the ideals they promoted. As Kenneally concludes:

> Like antifeminists for the next century Sherman and Dahlgren were enmeshed in a mass of contradictions, using political means to protect women from political burdens and assuming a public role to proclaim that the major responsibility of females lay in the privacy of their home. Moreover, neither woman was a traditional housewife adhering to the virtue of domesticity.[25]

In the early twentieth century, Katherine Conway, another prominent Catholic woman, denounced women's suffrage and glorified woman's private home influence, though she herself was single, a successful author and professional journalist, serving as editor of an important Catholic paper, the Boston *Pilot,* for three years. Thus some female Catholic opposition to women's suffrage came, however incongruously, from well-educated, middle- and upper-class women who justified their own public activities by using them to support traditional values of the home and women's role therein. They were joined by many working-class Catholic women who also opposed the ballot for women or who were simply too absorbed in the struggle for survival to pay attention to what they saw as a concern of middle-class Protestant women.

Yet other Catholic women embraced the cause of suffrage, even when it brought them into conflict with their own church. Most were by no means radicals but middle-class women who, like many Protestant advocates of women's rights, publicly endorsed woman's separate spheres and distinctive nature and argued that women should vote because they were more moral and would use the ballot to clean up politics, promote reform, and eliminate public policies that hurt home and family. (One Catholic woman, Lucy Burns, was an exception and among the most radical supporters of women's rights, using confrontational tactics and working with Alice Paul and the Woman's Party in the last years of the struggle.) Further important support for suffrage came from Catholic women leaders in the labor movement like Leonora Barry and Mary K. O'Sullivan, who saw the franchise as a way to help the cause of working women. One of the most effective of these women was Margaret Foley, who had worked in factories and joined the Boston branch of the WTUL before she was hired as an organizer by the Massachusetts Woman Suffrage Association in 1902. A devout Catholic, Foley repudiated charges that suffrage was necessarily associated with irreligion and immorality, and she concentrated her organizational efforts among working-class Catholic women, for whom hers was a credible voice because she shared their religion and knew firsthand the practical problems they faced. To Foley, woman suffrage was not an end in itself but a means to broader social goals, particularly the protection of women, children, and workers.[26]

Arguments from Catholic women themselves, particularly those in the labor movement, helped to convince more Catholic clergy of the need for women's suffrage, so that by the twentieth century, many priests and bishops were more sympathetic, including prominent leaders like Bishop John Spaulding of Peoria, Archbishop John Ireland of St. Paul, and Bishop Bernard McQuaid of Rochester, New York. Karen Kennelly argues that not only was there no official Catholic position on the issue, but it is difficult to discern the relative strength of the sides. "The most one can conclude from the record of the day is that a spectrum of views on the woman question was represented, with those against woman suffrage often receiving more publicity than those for it as the campaign for a federal amendment waxed and waned."[27] Once female suffrage was achieved, Catholic opponents accepted the inevitable. They still worried about "radical" associations and implications of the women's movement, especially its connection with evils like divorce, birth control, and the immodesty represented by make-up and women's fashions in the 1920s, so they urged Catholic women to maintain traditional womanly values and use their votes to promote moral government and to protect home and family.

## The Roles of Women Religious and the Women's Movement

The relationship of the Catholic Church, and of Catholic women in particular, to the women's movement in nineteenth-century America was a complex one, shaped not only by a relatively conservative religious tradition but also by factors of class, ethnicity, and religious identity. Nevertheless, in general Catholic women were less involved with feminism than were Protestants. One reason for their lack of interest in increasing female options may have been the presence within the church of a long-standing and honored alternative role: women who did not choose a primary identity as wife and mother could seek educational and vocational fulfillment as a religious sister. As Eileen Brewer argues,

> No other women in America so fully controlled their own destinies or lived in a world so radically separate from men as did the nuns. The convent provided an extraordinary alternative for those dissatisfied with the options available to women in outside society and might partially explain the absence of middle-class Catholic women in reform movements.[28]

An alternative role as nun was both important and problematic for Catholic women.

### Historical Overview of European Orders

European traditions, cultural conditions, and church law all affected nuns in nineteenth-century America, not only those who came from Europe but also those orders founded or joined by American women. A central element of the church's law that proved especially problematic for sisters in America was the tradition of enclosure. In the early Middle Ages, women religious, at least those leaders drawn from the upper classes, enjoyed a significant amount of freedom and power as abbesses, learned women, mystics, and missionaries. But in 1298, Pope Boniface VIII imposed total enclosure and solemn vows on all women religious in the bull "Periculoso." The pope's stated justification for these limitations was his distress that

> certain nuns, who, having slackened the reins of decency and . . . shamelessly cast aside the modesty of their order and of their sex, sometimes gad about outside their monasteries in the dwellings of secular persons, and frequently admit suspected persons within the same monasteries, to the grave offence of Him to whom they have, of their own will, vowed their innocence, to the opprobrium of religion and to the scandal of very many persons. . . . [29]

There were surely genuine abuses by nuns in the twelfth and thirteenth centuries, especially by those upper-class women who, contrary to the pope's assumption, had not truly entered the convent willingly but were placed there by families for various political, economic, and social reasons. Nevertheless, the church's long-standing suspicion that women were by nature weaker in faith and more carnal than men and a fear that women were dangerous temptations to men who were pursuing a religious vocation also stood behind the pope's insistence that nuns must be absolutely separated from the world.[30] Insistence on strict cloistering was reiterated after the Council of Trent, and in 1566, Pope Pius V's "Circa Pastoralis" decreed that all women religious must take solemn vows of poverty, chastity, and obedience. Unlike simple vows, solemn vows are irrevocable and thus have not only a spiritual but an economic impact, for they prevent the women from having any claims to property, past, present, or future. "Parents and relatives wanted religious women firmly settled in solemn vows. They were loathe to have them remain at home after their parents' death with the disposition of an inheritance at their command, nor did they want them returning from their communities to claim their share in inheritances."[31]

Nevertheless, Catholic women were drawn to communities that emphasized apostolic service, as some male orders like Franciscans and Dominicans did. Angela Merici founded the Ursulines as a noncloistered community in the sixteenth century. St. Vincent de Paul and Louise de Marillac founded in 1633 the Daughters of Charity to serve the poor. Other local congregations of women who emphasized service and took simple vows continued to exist, but they did not enjoy full, official church status and support, and restrictions could be imposed from above, as they were for the Ursulines after Merici's death. Finally in 1749, Pope Benedict XIII in "Quamvis Justo" expressed papal toleration for apostolic sisterhoods that were not enclosed and whose members took simple vows, but such groups still did not have full status or formal approval. Not until 1900 would such women's congregations be considered "true religious" by Rome, and even their tolerated-but-second-class status in the nineteenth century involved close, detailed regulations about the women's contact with the outside world.

## European Orders Try to Survive in America

Ambiguous status was one problem for sisters in nineteenth-century America, the vast majority of whom were active, not fully cloistered. A related difficulty was the contrast between the American situation and the European society in which most of the orders for women had been founded. In Europe, nuns who chose to do so could follow a strictly enclosed and contemplative life, for the orders that survived were financially secure through long-standing endowments and church support. The American church did not have that kind of financial resource, and its hierarchy saw far more need for active sisters who could teach and perform other critical works of mercy than for "unproductive" contemplatives. Finally, there were often serious cultural clashes between Americans, Catholic and non-Catholic, and the European sisters who came to the United States as missionaries, and few of the European orders that could not or would not adapt survived.

The pattern was set in the early decades of the nineteenth century, when of twelve communities of women in America, the six founded or largely staffed by Americans survived, while only one of the European communities, the Religious of the Sacred Heart brought to St. Louis from France by Philippine Duchesne, was ultimately successful. (Another European order, the Ursulines of New Orleans, was well established when it came into the United States through territorial expansion.)[32] One factor that immediately affected the early communities was economic survival; since they did not have the endowments of European houses, they had to find ways to support themselves. Some farmed, raised sheep, bound books, sold needlework, or did whatever else they could to earn money, but the most typical source of funds was one that fit well with the concerns of the hierarchy for the young American church: teaching. Most of the early orders opened schools for middle- and upper-class girls. Not only was this a service in itself, but the pupils' tuition enabled the sisters to support themselves and also teach poor children for free, although the two populations were generally served by separate schools. A second source of economic stability showed one way sisters adapted readily to the American environment: they acquired slaves to do the hard manual labor. As Ewens notes, "Seven of the eight communities of this period which survived acquired slaves through dowry, inheritance, gift or purchase."[33]

Survival was not, however, simply a function of economic support. Sisters also had to work out compromises between European rules and American conditions. When a community like the Sisters of Loretto in Kentucky tried to "do it all" under the austere Belgian priest, Charles Nerinckx—to combine farming and teaching with continued strict and full observance of a European rule, especially rules for dress and demands of prayer and penance, with no concessions to American climate or conditions—it literally killed them. For example, fifteen sisters under the age of thirty died between September 1823 and September 1824.[34] The first indigenous American sisterhood, founded in 1809 by a widowed convert, Elizabeth Seton, also had to adapt to survive. At first French priests and male advisors tried to pattern her group on the Daughters of Charity, but Seton herself and the influential Archbishop John Carroll recognized the need for adaptation in rules and the impracticality of having the women serve only the poor when they had no endowment. Instead they became the Sisters of Charity with modified rules, teaching both the wealthy and the poor.[35]

The example of Elizabeth Seton and her Sisters of Charity illustrates well the fact that the conflict over adaptation did not divide along consistent lines, as male clerics both opposed and supported change. Sometimes it was a male bishop or priest who refused to give dispensations from a rule that did not fit American conditions and needs. Sometimes it was the European motherhouse of an order that resisted, and American sisters had to break with that motherhouse to survive and follow what they understood as their calling. In such cases, the understanding and support of American clergy were welcome. At other times, American priests and bishops were so concerned with what they perceived to be the needs of the church that they pushed changes when the sisters themselves did not want them, or interfered unnecessarily in the internal affairs of the community, and then the authority of the European motherhouse could give the sisters ammunition to resist unwanted change and interference that, they believed, would destroy their identity and mission. Most sisters truly wanted to serve the American church and its people; indeed, they had joined an order or come to America as missionaries to do just that. They also valued, however, their particular spiritual identity and practices and the traditions in which they were rooted. Thus the issue was not only who was supporting change and why but also the nature of the modifications. Unquestionably, some adaptation was critical to the sisters' survival in America, but, as Mary Ewens notes, the problem was

> to distinguish between those things which were essential to the life and spirit of a community and those which were merely a part of an earlier culture whose usefulness had disappeared when the culture itself changed. Thus when the Poor Clares, whose aim was a strictly contemplative life, took on the work of teaching, they completely altered the character of their community and doomed it to failure. But when the Visitandines and Religious of the Sacred Heart changed the schedules of classes found in their European rules to fit American needs, they were only facilitating the success of the work to which they had always been devoted.[36]

During the 1830s, 40s, and 50s, Catholic immigration to the United States increased dramatically, and at the same time some thirty-nine new congregations of women religious were either formed in America or came from Europe to help meet the needs of the rapidly expanding American church. Thus, as existing orders either adapted and survived or disappeared, the new ones encountered some of the same issues that earlier ones had: economic survival, modification to American conditions, and relationships with male clergy, who were sometimes extremely supportive and sometimes extraordinarily frustrating. While law, tradition, and the formal structures of authority in the church tended to favor male bishops, abbots, or other superiors when conflicts arose, the women religious had advantages of their own. Not only could they appeal to their motherhouses, but they had the very practical advantage of being in short supply in a situation of heavy demand. As Ewens notes, "they could and did vote with their feet, or threatened to, when the occasion warranted it. There was always another bishop, just over diocesan borders, who needed the services the sisters provided."[37]

### *Internal Ethnic Tensions*

Increasing Catholic immigration made the services of women religious valuable and necessary, but it also contributed to growing ethnic tensions, both within the American Catholic Church and with Protestant Americans. Some of the internal tensions affected sisters in very practical ways. For example, French nuns whose own command of English was limited had a hard time teaching that language in the schools they staffed. Sometimes the clash was more cultural than linguistic, as European sisters were shocked and distressed at American customs, while American Catholics deplored the class-consciousness of the sisters, who neither shared nor approved of American values of freedom and independence. Mother Theresa Gerhardinger, founder of the School Sisters of Notre Dame, wrote long letters back to her male superior after she arrived in America in 1847. She fully realized the need for strong, active sisters—"We cannot use sisters and young ladies who desire only to live a quiet, retired conventual life, those who cannot be employed in school; unless they bring with them considerable funds. . ."—but she feared the influence of English language and customs on her German order ("May God preserve us from this!") and deplored American children's lack of manners and the failure of parents to discipline them.

> Children attend one school today, another tomorrow, just as they please. If they are corrected they do not come back; learning they often consider recreation. All they want to do is eat cookies, taffy, and molasses candy, a cheap sweet. . . . They laugh and jeer at priests. . . . They do not manifest the slightest eagerness to learn German. . . . One of the reasons the children do not want to study is the fact that their minds are filled with concern for boys. . . . Clothing, too, is immodest.

Yet through her complaints and frustrations, Gerhardinger was sufficiently perceptive to realize that American Catholics were no more likely to change than she was, concluding, "I feel less capable of being a superior here than in Europe, and I must take steps to resign: otherwise I shall spoil everything. Sisters Caroline and Seraphina have a calling for America; their views are opposite mine, and I am sure the Lord will assist them when they are in a position of authority."[38] Sisters Caroline and Seraphina were indeed more successful in adapting to American culture, establishing schools, and serving Catholic children, but they, too, encountered problems, from poverty to Protestant hostility to persuading their motherhouse to agree to necessary adaptations in their rule, though in that matter they were supported by male clerics.[39]

### *Protestant Hostility*

Tensions within the American Catholic Church between Europeans and Americans or among ethnic groups might limit the sisters' satisfaction and effectiveness, but Protestant hostility, manifest in the emerging nativist movements of the 1830s, 1840s, and 1850s, was even more disturbing. Protestants who feared that the growing numbers of Catholic immigrants presented a threat to America's special destiny found in nuns a focus for attack. While some well-to-do Protestants sent their daughters to the sisters' academies because they believed the academies were the best schools available, other Protestant leaders dismissed the nuns' assurances that they would respect the religious differences of their pupils and were convinced that nuns were secretly subverting Protestant faith in vulnerable children. The distinctive habits of women religious made them an easy target for verbal and physical harassment, to the point that many sisters chose to wear "secular" clothes when they were traveling outside their convents (and received relatively easy dispensations for that particular change in their rules.)

The most virulent Protestant attacks on religious sisters came in the wake of a wave of sensationalist exposés by "escaped nuns," culminating in Maria Monk's *Awful Disclosures of the Hotel Dieu Nunnery of Montreal*, published in 1836. Though Monk herself was thoroughly discredited—she had actually escaped from a Montreal asylum for wayward girls—her "account" sold some 300,000 copies before the Civil War and continued to be printed thereafter.[40] Like supermarket tabloids of the late twentieth century, the accounts were ludicrous and wildly popular, for they seemed to confirm the worst suspicions of American nativists about the Catholic Church and nuns in particular. The revelations struck at two basic cultural values of Protestant Americans, freedom and the natural roles of women. Innocent young girls, the accounts claimed, were trapped or lured into convents and then held against their will. The girls were forced to suffer deprivation and disgusting penances or, worse, seduced by lascivious confessors and priests; the illegitimate babies that followed were then murdered and buried in convent cellars. Some aspects of the stories were rooted in reality: penance was part of the sisters' spiritual lives, and even modified enclosure rules, symbolized in walls and grates, limited nuns' contact with family members as well as the outside world. To Protestant critics, such practices seemed inconsistent with Catholic insistence that sisters joined and remained in convents voluntarily. But the denunciations of the exposés went far beyond the realities of penance or enclosure. Moreover, the very concept of women religious was incomprehensible to many Protestants. Surely no normal, natural woman would voluntarily give up hope of marriage and motherhood to immure herself in what was, in effect, a prison; thus Catholic nuns must be either immoral and unnatural tools or innocent and unwilling victims of a fanatical church.

However unreasonable or unjustified the exposés may have been, they had very real and tragic consequences, as convent property was vandalized and sisters themselves were attacked. The most infamous incident occurred at an Ursuline convent, Mount St. Benedict, in Charlestown, Massachusetts, in August 1834. Rebecca Reed, a young woman who had been dismissed by the Ursulines after six months in the novitiate, was circulating accounts of her "escape" when a second sister, Elizabeth Harrison, left the convent for a short time for health reasons. She soon asked to return, but nativists in Boston were convinced she was being detained by force, and they demanded that she be freed. The sisters allowed a group of selectmen to tour the convent and speak with Harrison on Monday, August 11. Their report exonerating the nuns was to have been published the next day, but on Monday night, a mob gathered at the convent to "free" Harrison, forced their way in, set the convent on fire, and even dug up the bodies of sisters in the convent cemetery.[41] Fortunately, all the sisters escaped, and responsible civic and Protestant church leaders publicly deplored the mob action. Nevertheless, exposés by supposed ex-priests and ex-nuns continued to appear, because they were financially rewarding and they fit nativist prejudices, and sisters in other parts of the nation continued to suffer harassment and physical attack.

## Apostolic Work

Nativism was a serious problem for sisters, but in the middle decades of the century some Protestant Americans came to respect the Catholic sisters as inflammatory rumors were replaced by firsthand observation of their apostolic work. Education was a central concern for the great majority of congregations, which had by then established a two-tiered system: day schools or boarding schools, called academies, for paying pupils; separate free schools for the poor. Protestant parents who could afford the tuition often chose to send their daughters to the sisters' schools, were pleased with the results, and defended the nuns against nativist attacks.

### *Orphanages*

A second important area of service entered by many congregations was the establishment of orphanages. Like the free schools for the poor, orphanages were a response to genuine human need, and the work of the sisters in both earned respect from their Protestant neighbors. Catholic church leaders encouraged the sisters to staff orphanages for Catholic children in particular because they feared that public or Protestant-sponsored institutions tried to convert their charges from Catholicism. Yet in both schools and orphanages, the presence of boys was an issue. Some congregations taught only girls, while others accepted young boys into their schools up to the age of nine, ten, or twelve. Orphanages run by sisters included boys until 1845, but then the Sisters of Charity, who ran most of the country's Catholic orphanages, sought closer affiliation with the French Daughters of Charity, whose rule did not allow sisters to care for male orphans over the age of five. Some Sisters of Charity in New York then founded a new community, with the hearty endorsement of Bishop Hughes, while other institutions for orphans of both sexes were taken over by different congregations.

### *Nursing*

Nursing was a third important area of service for many sisters, both through home visits and the establishment of hospitals, but it was their nursing services in times of crisis that inspired a dramatic turn in public attitudes toward Catholic women religious. Cholera and yellow fever epidemics broke out periodically in American cities, especially in 1832–34, 1849–50, and 1855, and in each case, the sisters performed heroic and selfless work for the sufferers, rich or poor, Catholic or non-Catholic. When the epidemic subsided, formerly suspicious and hostile Protestants had developed respect and even affection for these Catholic women.

What happened on the local level became national with the coming of the Civil War. Ewens estimates that 640 of 3200 Civil War nurses were sisters, a number disproportionate to their presence in the population. Despite the then recent work of Florence Nightingale, nursing outside a woman's own home had a low image, and the sisters had far more practical experience than any other group of women. At first, some Protestants were hostile or fearful of the sisters, but as the conflict wore on, the nuns earned enormous respect for their skill, patience, and selflessness. Political and military leaders from Union and Confederacy paid tribute to them. A testimonial from the *Chicago Tribune* in December 1861, is typical:

> The Sisters of Mercy have taken hold of the hospitals in Jefferson City as nurses for the sick there, and will certainly, as far as they command the means, replace the horrible filth, and squalor, and wretchedness that filled them at my first visit, with a gentle, cheerful, abiding care and purity, and peace. Pray permit me, Standing so far from these women in ecclesiastical and theological ideas, to testify to their beautiful, holy and unselfish devotions wherever I have found them in our hospitals, East or West. The doctors can find nowhere else such perfect nurses—quiet as Quakers, yet cheerful and chatty whenever the undying womanly instinct is touched. . . . They give, asking nothing again, what no money can purchase. [42]

Sisters tried to fulfill emotional and spiritual as well as physical needs of their patients, though they were sufficiently aware of Protestant suspicion to be careful to avoid unwelcome proselytism. Nevertheless, they responded with spiritual comfort and instruction in Catholic doctrine when asked, and in some cases even baptized dying soldiers who requested the sacrament.[43] (Catholic tradition allows "even a woman" to baptize in emergency situations when a priest is not available.) Surely there were Americans after the Civil War who continued to dislike and distrust nuns, and greater public respect for Catholic women religious had already been growing gradually due to their service in teaching, orphanages, and nursing, especially during epidemics; still, the Civil War remains an important turning point for Catholic sisters in America.

In the decades between the Civil War and the turn of the twentieth century, Catholic immigrants with even greater ethnic diversity continued to pour into the United States. Existing congregations added new missions, and some fifty-nine new foundations were established. Because so much of the practical burden of serving the immigrants fell on the sisters, and because sisters in fact outnumbered not only priests but also male religious, the women were often the most immediate representatives of the church in the daily lives of immigrants. Contact came in two major areas: education and social services, especially for the poor.

### *Education*

Education had long been central to the work of nuns in America, but changes within the American church's policy and in the broad field of education raised new issues for teaching sisters. The first two plenary councils of the American church, held in 1852 and 1866, encouraged the founding of parochial Catholic schools but did not require them. At the Third Plenary Council in 1884, however, parochial schools were made obligatory, despite the continued opposition of a few bishops. Many of the church's leaders perceived, quite accurately, that the public schools were in effect Protestant or ignored religion, and neither was seen as a desirable alternative for Catholic children. Moreover, parochial schools could preserve not only the Catholic religion of immigrant groups but also their ethnic traditions and identity, and sometimes their language. Other Catholic leaders like John Ireland preferred to work out some kind of compromise with public schools, if possible, for they believed that Americanization was ultimately in the best interests of the immigrants, and they wanted to maintain good relationships with America's Protestant majority.

There were also practical problems in implementing the decision of the 1884 council. The Catholic population split over the issue, sometimes along ethnic lines. And even among Catholics who supported parochial schools in principle, lack of money was a very real obstacle, especially in parishes composed largely of poor immigrants. Thus the service of women religious as teachers was critical, not only because of their experience and their Catholic faith, but because they were, frankly, cheap. Teaching sisters were paid significantly less than women who taught in public schools, and they received less than male teaching religious, despite the fact that both groups had taken vows of poverty![44] Thus the needs of the American Catholic Church as a whole, perceived and articulated by its hierarchy, affected the educational mission of women religious. Some congregations continued to maintain their female academies, and these convent schools attracted the daughters of middle- and upper-class Catholic families to an education that emphasized Catholic piety and loyalty, along with cultured gentility. The values promoted by the nuns who ran such schools influenced the church as a whole through the schools' graduates, some of whom became nuns in their turn and taught in parochial schools, while others became writers or entered social service professions. "Most importantly," concludes Brewer, "married alumnae brought the ideals of the convent school into the home and instilled them in their children."[45] Women's congregations also tried to maintain the free schools that served the poor, but more and more, efforts and personnel were funnelled into parochial school teaching. At the same time, local bishops and even parish priests assumed greater control over female congregations, seeing parochial schools as under their authority. Inevitably, clashes occurred over a congregation's constitution on matters like teaching boys or regulations of the sisters' daily lives, and conflict over matters of power and authority were exacerbated by the issues' implications for the allocation of scarce financial resources.

The Third Plenary Council had also encouraged the establishment of normal schools to train Catholic teachers, because the bishops recognized the need to maintain or increase the level of Catholic education in the United States. For much of the nineteenth century, many Catholic schools were regarded as at least as good or better than public schools. (Indeed, especially in rural and frontier areas, the line between public and private was not always clear; when Catholic sisters were the only teachers available, they might be paid by the state.) But as the public school movement grew and spread, it was accompanied by more concern for teacher qualifications, and this development posed a dilemma for teaching sisters. Even if their congregations' constitutions put no obstacles in the way of their formal training, the financial realities and pressing needs of parochial schools did. Too often, there was neither the time nor the money to allow novices to finish their own educational training before they started to teach. When some sisters sought higher education, they found that Catholic universities would not admit women, while some bishops forbade their attendance at "secular" schools.[46] Gradually some greater opportunities for continuing education, like extension courses or summer school, were developed for the sisters, but overall, it was difficult for them to keep up with the increasing professionalization of public education.

Although parochial school teaching was a central concern for women religious in the later nineteenth century, it was by no means their only work. Many communities continued to found and staff orphanages, hospitals, shelters for the poor, and homes for the aged, works of mercy that filled a real need of the time. But sisters involved in nursing began to encounter problems similar to those of teaching sisters. As Ewens notes, "Though Catholic nursing communities had for centuries been considered the leaders in their field, they failed to adapt to the rapid changes in hospital administration and technique which revolutionized the nursing profession in the decades following the Civil War."[47] Part of the problem lay in the congregations' rules. For example, the habits and headdresses worn by some sisters were seen as breeding grounds for germs, and some congregations did not permit sisters to work with maternity cases or allow them to study anatomy and physiology. By the time of the Spanish-American war, nursing sisters were still praised for their self-sacrifice and devotion, but their professional skills compared unfavorably with nonreligious nurses.[48]

### *Social Service*

The problems posed for women religious in the later years of the nineteenth century were real ones, whether they came from local bishops and priests, their own constitutions, or increasing professionalization in fields in which they traditionally had served. Those problems should not, however, obscure the worth of the sisters' contributions, for the sisters continued to provide the majority of Catholic social services to their compatriots. In addition, some congregations responded to human needs wherever they saw them, disregarding if necessary church law or traditions that would have impeded their work. Thus some twelve Catholic infant homes and maternity hospitals were opened before 1900, "despite Rome's statement that work of this kind was unsuitable for consecrated virgins."[49] The

Order of Sisters of the Good Shepherd operated homes for delinquent girls and prostitutes, like the one in Minnesota. Arriving in St. Paul in 1868, the nuns developed a penitent program and a house for prostitutes, some of whom were sent there by court order, some by families, and some of whom came voluntarily. In any case, and no matter how often they returned, the nuns never turned them away. The sisters also developed two alternatives for those who wished to stay: the Consecrates, who lived as a semi-religious group and helped at the house but were not bound by solemn vows or enclosure and could leave at any time; and a cloistered, contemplative option, the Order of Saint Mary Magdalen. Although relatively few women stayed with these groups permanently, they were a rare and positive alternative. In her study of prostitutes in the American West, Anne M. Butler concludes:

> To an observer the entire situation appeared inconsistent and impossible. How could a prostitute of coarse, sexual raucousness submit to the life of silent, chaste discipline? If spiritual motivations, which were personal and private, were removed from the equation, more similarities existed than were first evident. . . . [Both were communities of women located, though for different reasons,] at the outermost rim of society. . . . [The new life offered] a stability and security seldom found among prostitutes. Convent life brought an end to physical and sexual mistreatment from customers. In addition, Magdalens found a niche in life where they could live without sanctimonious condescension from associates who had never participated in prostitution. Other Magdalens, retreating from identical experiences, cast no stones; among the Magdalens' protectors, the Good Shepherd Sisters, no apologies were necessary. For prostitutes who understood all too well that the end of the road came quickly, a life of cloistered security presented an option.[50]

Most of the sisters' work was directed to fellow Catholics, though in times of crisis especially, they made no distinctions among sufferers, and their schools attracted non-Catholics as well. Yet there were also groups of sisters who tried to respond to the needs of African Americans and Native Americans during the nineteenth century. The Oblate Sisters of Providence and the Sisters of the Holy Family, orders for black women that served black people, have been discussed in the previous chapter of this work, and other congregations of sisters also offered education to blacks, although they sometimes incurred the wrath of the white community and had to desist. Some nuns who came to the United States hoped to serve as missionaries to the Indians, but both their opportunities and successes were limited. Toward the end of the century, a wealthy Philadelphia heiress, Katherine Drexel, determined to dedicate her fortune and, at the direct suggestion of Pope Leo XIII, her own life to blacks and Indians. She went through a novitiate with the Sisters of Mercy and in 1891 founded an order, the Sisters of the Blessed Sacrament for Indians and Colored People. Her sisters staffed and her money helped to support a number of schools, missions, and other services for blacks and Native Americans. Yet black Catholics were always a small minority among both Catholics and black Christians, and Catholic missionary work among Native American peoples was like white Protestant missions: sincere, well-intentioned, and often self-sacrificing, but ultimately insensitive to Indian culture. Attempts were made to begin congregations of Indian sisters, but unlike the black sisterhoods, they did not survive, and the few Indian Catholic women who felt drawn to the religious life joined white orders.[51] As Dolan concludes, "What limited positive influence the church had on the quality of Indian life was, in the final analysis, far outweighed by the destruction that resulted from the disintegration of American Indian life."[52]

What, then, was the relationship of Catholic sisters in nineteenth-century America to dominant cultural images of women and to the church of which they were a part? At a practical level, they were atypical, permanently single by choice, not by default, at a time when the vast majority of women married, and society assumed that all but the most eccentric single women would seek fulfillment in woman's natural roles of marriage and motherhood if they had the chance. (Whether the single women themselves felt that way is quite another question. Certainly some sisters felt that voluntary celibacy was personally as well as spiritually preferable to the married state. For example, a missionary sister in New Mexico "believed that her calling had saved her from a traditional woman's lot. When she met poor mothers of five or six children cooking for twenty to forty men at a mining camp, she wrote, 'Oh! How often I thanked the good God for saving me from such a fate.'"[53])

On the other hand, the predominant image of sisters promoted by the church was still a maternal one, a spiritual motherhood and ideology of nurturing. Like the True Woman, sisters were to be pure, pious, and submissive, and, if they were not strictly cloistered contemplatives, as few in America were, their activities were to be domestic, "female" ones: teaching, caring for the sick, the elderly, and children. Indeed, some priests and bishops assumed that nuns would care for the domestic needs of male religious like cleaning and laundry. The founder of Notre Dame, Father Edward Sorin, recruited nuns not only to teach in a female academy but also to "'look after the laundry and infirmary' of the priests and students—even though the nuns might have to walk six miles."[54] When Samuel Mazzuchelli, an Italian Dominican missionary priest, founded a boys' college in southwestern Wisconsin, he requested the help of some sisters, noting, "We shall be in need of some good persons to keep school to the girls of this parish, and to do all the sewing and mending of our house which will be considerable this winter."[55]

Church authority in the form of law and traditions and in the persons of the male hierarchy reinforced culture in definitions of the nuns' spiritual motherhood and structural subordination. Dolan assesses their status as "Catholic serfs, having fewer rights and fewer options than priests, brothers, or lay people."[56] Yet if the functional status of sisters was low, the choice of a religious life was still perceived and respected as a spiritually higher vocation, and the church in America could never have expanded as it did and served its recurring waves of immigrants without them. Sisters were subordinate and obedient, but they were not servile and passive. They pushed for changes they thought were necessary to fulfill their apostolic calling, and they resisted demands of male authorities when they believed changes would compromise their spiritual or congregational identity. Individual sisters, women like Mother Austin Carroll and Mother Joseph Periseau, compiled records of accomplishment that rivalled those of the church's male heroes.

Born in Ireland in 1835, Mother Austin Carroll joined the Sisters of Mercy, where she gained experience in teaching and service to the poor. In 1856, she came as a missionary to Rhode Island to continue similar work; she served as a nurse during the Civil War and in 1869 led a group of sisters to New Orleans. An incredibly energetic and effective leader, by the time she died in 1909, she and her sisters had established sixty-five schools, fourteen convents, thirty-eight libraries, and nine residences for the poor.[57] She also pushed the sisters' work in new directions, like prison ministry, and she herself worked on death row and interceded with prison officials for better conditions for women prisoners. She established a shelter, training school, and employment bureau for immigrant women. She was a prolific author. Not surprisingly, she had her share of confrontations with male church officials, who complained to Rome about her insubordination, but after years of investigation, she was ultimately exonerated.[58]

Esther Pariseau was born in 1823 and as a child learned skilled carpentry in her French Canadian Catholic father's carriage shop. In 1843, she joined the recently founded Sisters of Providence in Montreal, whose special vow was to serve Christ in the persons of the poor. When the Bishop of Nisqually in Oregon territory recruited Sisters of Providence to work on that frontier in 1856, she, as Mother Joseph of the Sacred Heart, led the group of five nuns on the long journey by ship and across the Isthmus of Panama to Vancouver, Washington. The group soon founded a school, took in orphans, and started a hospital. By the time of her death in 1902, she and her congregations had expanded dramatically, founding some seven academies, five Indian schools, two orphanages, a home for the elderly, and eleven hospitals.[59] In Mother Joseph's case, "building" these institutions had a very literal meaning. Not only did she and her sisters found and staff them, she used her considerable skills as a carpenter and architect to work on them and supervise their construction. As was true for so many groups of Catholic women religious, money was always in scarce supply, so Mother Joseph personally undertook numerous begging tours throughout the Northwest, braving frontier conditions from floods to wolves to raise money to support the sisters and their institutions. Mother Joseph's contributions are now recognized as she is one of the five women, and the only nun, in Statuary Hall at the United States Capitol.[60]

Mother Austin Carroll and Mother Joseph of the Sacred Heart were by no means unique, as congregational histories of women religious in America attest. If few nuns in nineteenth-century America were formally identified with the women's movement, they nevertheless exemplified some of its goals. Their identities were defined by neither husbands nor children but realized instead within a sisterhood of women. They pursued lifelong careers in a variety of fields. Their lives and work in America made changes in the church's views of nuns inevitable, however slow they were in coming.

# 15
# Jewish Women in Nineteenth-Century America

If Roman Catholics were a relatively small group in America until the massive nineteenth-century immigrations, Jews were an even tinier minority in the colonial period, and their numbers, too, were dramatically augmented by waves of immigration from the mid-nineteenth to the early twentieth century. Nevertheless, Jews were present from the day in 1654 when a group of refugees from Brazil arrived in New Amsterdam. Theirs had been a long and circuitous journey, not only as individuals but as a people.

## The Diaspora

In the year 70 C.E., Roman forces put down a Jewish uprising in Palestine and, fatefully, destroyed the Jerusalem temple and with it, the cultic part of Jewish religion that focused on ritual sacrifices at the temple under the direction of priests. Another Jewish rebellion in the second century ended in defeat at the hands of the militarily superior Romans and the expulsion of the remaining Jews from Jerusalem, although small communities of Jews continued to live in other parts of Palestine. Jews thus became a people in exile, and centuries would pass before they again had a homeland of their own. The Jewish dispersion or *diaspora,* however, did not begin with the Roman defeats; sizable communities of Jews had been living outside Palestine for many years. Judaism continued, but it now focused on synagogues as centers for worship and study and on the leadership of the rabbi. Over the next five centuries, rabbinic scholars in Palestine and especially in Babylonia completed the Talmud, a massive commentary on Jewish law that incorporated the Mishnah, a codification of oral commentary on the Torah, and the Gemara, further commentary on the Mishnah. The Talmud would then shape Jewish practice for centuries. Originally, the rabbi was primarily a scholar and teacher of the law, as well as a judge, due to his learning and expertise. Over time, he also became the spiritual head of a Jewish community. Jewish settlements spread from the Middle East and the Roman Empire's cities throughout Europe, developing their own traditions: the Sephardim in Spain and

Portugal and the Ashkenazim in Central and Eastern Europe. Often actively persecuted by their Christian neighbors, the best that Jews could usually hope for was benign neglect or grudging toleration.

That limited toleration ended in Spain in 1492 when the Spanish succeeded in expelling the last of the Moslems from their territory. The Spanish then turned to the Jews, offering three choices: conversion to Christianity, expulsion, or death. A few years later, Jews were also expelled from Portugal. Jews fled to other parts of Europe, particularly Holland, which was at the time relatively more tolerant than most nations; when the Dutch captured Recife from the Portuguese rulers in Brazil, a sizable community of Jews moved to the New World. But when Portugal recaptured its territory, it reinstituted persecution of the Jews, and some of those who fled ended up in New Amsterdam, the first Jewish settlers in what would become the United States.

## Protecting the Tradition

Over the years of exile, Jews developed a coherent, comprehensive, and conservative religious and cultural tradition as a means of survival in the face of persecution and pressures for assimilation. In that tradition, gender roles were clearly defined and divided. The male sphere was the synagogue, and the highest achievement for a male Jew was to be a religious scholar; the female sphere was the home. Both spheres were crucial to Jewish identity and survival, but if in theory they were to be separate and equal, in fact women's sphere and women themselves were subordinate. Women were excused from numerous commandments or *mitzvot,* especially time-related ones, under the argument that their domestic duties prevented them from such things as regular attendance at synagogue services. Women were not counted in the *minyan,* or quorum of ten adult males needed for public worship, and they could not speak or lead in services. They were allowed to attend services at the synagogues, and many women did so, especially on the Sabbath and holidays, but they were separated from male worshipers, usually seated in a balcony behind a screen so they would not distract the men. Given the division of spheres, it was assumed that most women did not need to learn Hebrew to study the law or even to learn to read at all.[1] Thus during the services, the women would often be led in prayers by a *zogerke,* a woman who was able to read the Hebrew of the prayers for the synagogue service.

In terms of marriage, only a Jewish man could initiate a divorce, and in theory he could do so for the most frivolous reason. In fact, divorce was discouraged and, while the rabbis could not change the law which made divorce exclusively a male prerogative, they did attempt to make it more difficult for a man to divorce his wife, and they tried to respond to the painful situation of a wife whose husband had disappeared (which might or might not have been at his own choice, especially during times of persecution).

Effective exclusion from the male world of the synagogue and unequal marriage laws did not mean, however, that women had no religious roles or made no contribution to Jewish religious life and survival. Not only were women expected to worship only Yahweh and keep many of the commandments in the same way that men were, the home was an important setting for religious ritual as well as a center for the transmission of Jewish identity from one generation to another, and women had particular commandments (*mitzvot*) of their own, especially connected to home and family. As part of her responsibility to prepare the house and food for the Sabbath, she separated a small portion of dough, said a blessing, and threw it into the oven before baking the Sabbath bread (*hallah*). She had the honor and duty of lighting special candles on the eve of the Sabbath (*hadlaqah*). Women had the practical responsibility for seeing that the dietary laws of *kashrut* were followed, even though a male rabbi was the ultimate authority on these laws (and rabbis were known to cite the practice of their mothers or of the wives of famous rabbis). Finally, women were responsible to visit the *mikvah* or ritual pool seven days after the conclusion of their menstrual periods; during menstruation and until she had been to the *mikvah*, a woman was to have no physical contact with her husband, and she was responsible for making sure that neither she nor her husband violated cultic purity. Laws about ritual impurity of women at such times, or *niddah*, continued even when other laws about cultic purity associated with sacrificial worship at the temple became inoperative.

Jewish attitudes toward sexuality, particularly female sexuality, were ambivalent. On the one hand, the laws of *niddah* and a strong postbiblical tradition enjoining female modesty, lest a woman tempt a man to lust or distract him from his worship or study, suggest a negative view of female biological and sexual functioning. Yet Judaism was never as affected by a spirit-matter dualism as Christianity was. Celibacy was regarded as a misfortune, not an ideal. Marital sex was viewed very positively, not only for procreation but for pleasure, so that along with the laws of *niddah*, Jewish tradition had laws of *onah*, which required a man to offer sexual intercourse to his wife at regular intervals (the frequency depending on his occupation) and to be concerned for her pleasure.[2]

Whatever ambiguity had developed about female sexuality in particular, Jewish assessments of home and family were overwhelmingly positive. As long as women accepted the division of spheres and fulfilled their female roles, keeping the good Jewish home that enabled their husbands and sons to pursue their spiritual responsibilities, they were warmly and genuinely respected. As with the colonial Puritans, it was only the deviant woman who stepped out of her place who drew scorn or disapproval.

Women developed a rewarding ritual and spiritual life that did not exclude the public worship of the synagogue but was primarily a more private and home-centered spirituality. During the Middle Ages, a Yiddish literature aimed particularly at women developed among Ashkenazic Jews. It included prayers known as *tkhines,* which sanctified the special women's *mitzvot,* crucial events in her family's life, special holidays like *rosh hodesh* (the festival of the new moon), and visits to the cemetery. *Tkhines* often invoked the matriarchs, Sarah, Rebecca, Rachel, and Leah, as well as other biblical heroines with whom Jewish women could identify, not just the male figures referred to in synagogue services.[3] Thus the vast majority of Jewish women accepted their roles and found pride and satisfaction in their contributions; they understood quite well that what they did was critical to Jewish survival in a frequently hostile world.

## Judaism in Early America

When the small band of Sephardic Jewish refugees arrived in New Amsterdam in 1654, Peter Stuyvesant was less than welcoming, for reasons of religious prejudice and fear that they might become a drain on the young colony, but Jews in Amsterdam put pressure on the Dutch East India Company, and they were permitted to stay. Before the end of the century, Jews in New York had formed a congregation, and Jewish women contributed money and sewing for the first house of worship, built in 1729. Slowly other Jews, both Sephardim and Ashkenazim, arrived during the colonial period, though the Sephardic ritual dominated in the colonial and early national periods. By the time of the American Revolution, there were organized Jewish communities in New York, Rhode Island, Pennsylvania, and South Carolina; Jews were scattered in other parts of the colonies also, but their numbers were still very small—two thousand Jews, at most, by 1800. If they did not enjoy full legal toleration and social acceptance, they enjoyed greater political and religious freedom and economic opportunity than Jews in most of Europe.

Nevertheless, their small numbers were often problematic for the Jews, and it was not always easy for them to remain observant. Jews formed functioning congregations when they could, and the home remained a potential center for Jewish practice and identity, but no rabbi came to the United States before the nineteenth century. Another serious problem for Jews who wanted to preserve their religion and their culture was intermarriage, whether caused by the attractions of acculturation or the scarcity of suitable Jewish marriage partners, and Jews who married Gentiles were frequently lost to the community. Toward the end of the eighteenth century, Rebecca Samuel wrote to her parents in Germany about the difficulties of remaining observant and resisting acculturation in Petersburg, Virginia. While she was grateful for the lack of persecution and the economic opportunities in America, she felt isolated and was particularly concerned for her children.

> Dear parents, I know quite well you will not want me to bring up my children like Gentiles. Here they cannot become anything else. Jewishness is pushed aside here. [Those Jews who did live in Petersburg she scorned for their nonobservant laxity.] . . . You can believe me that I crave to see a synagogue to which I can go. The way we live now is no life at all. We do not know what the Sabbath and the holidays are. On the Sabbath all the Jewish shops are open, and they do business on that day as they do throughout the whole week. But ours we do not allow to open. With us there is still some Sabbath. . . . My children cannot learn anything here, nothing Jewish, nothing of general culture. My Schoene [my daughter], God bless her, is already three years old; . . . . I have taught her the bedtime prayers and grace after meals in just two lessons. I believe that no one among the Jews here can do as well as she.[4]

Rebecca's family soon moved to Richmond, where there was a larger Jewish community.

By no means were all Jews in America in the colonial and early national period wealthy, but some families did prosper, among them the Gratz family of Philadelphia, and Rebecca Gratz was possibly the best known Jewish woman of her time (and is believed to be the prototype for Rebecca in Sir Walter Scott's *Ivanhoe*). Born to a prominent Philadelphia family in 1781, Rebecca never married but spent her life caring for the family home, her unmarried brothers, and a sister's orphaned children, in an active literary circle, and in a range of charitable endeavors.[5] While she had social and literary friends among her Christian neighbors and was close to the Christian women married by two of her brothers, she was herself a devout and observant Jew. Like Christian women of her time and class, she accepted the home as a centrally important sphere for women but was able to extend that sphere through the charitable and benevolent associations in which she was active. She worked with Christians in some of these endeavors like the Philadelphia Orphan Asylum, but other groups were specifically Jewish, like the Female Hebrew Benevolent Society she helped to found in 1819.

Rebecca Gratz is best remembered for her establishment of a Hebrew Sunday school in 1838, serving as its president for a quarter of a century and establishing a successful movement that was nationwide by the 1880s. Although she may have been influenced by contemporary Christian Sunday schools, by concern for the education of poor children, and by a perception that immigrants would need to be "Americanized," she insisted on the Jewish character of the school, recognizing that those who did not know their heritage were most likely to lose it to Christian missionary work. Some acculturation or Americanization was good and necessary, but not when it meant sacrificing Judaism. In an 1858 report on the school, she wrote:

> As Israelites in a Christian community, where our youth associate and compete with their fellow-citizens in all the branches of the arts and sciences, it is essential they should go provided with a knowledge of their own doctrines—that they should feel the requirements of their peculiar faith, and by a steadfast, unobtrusive observance of them, claim the respect of others, and the approbation of their own consciences. As descendants of the great nation to whom God entrusted his Holy Law, which was to enlighten all the people of the earth, and the living witnesses of His sacred Legacy, the Jews ought to be among the purest and wisest of the sons of men, and the most faithful adherents to their religious duties; therefore it is incumbent on them to 'teach their children diligently.'[6]

In addition, Gratz's Sunday school broke with tradition and opened a new role for women by allowing them to teach classes of both boys and girls, and she herself was an important role model for other Jewish-American women who wanted to combine a Jewish identity with a greater public role.[7] A descendent of a colonial Jewish family, practicing traditional orthodoxy in the Sephardic rites, she lived to see the Jewish population in America explode with the first major wave of Jewish immigration, which came in the mid-nineteenth century. These Jews dramatically increased the proportion of Ashkenazic Jews from central Europe; they also brought a new perspective on Jewish religion and tradition.

## The Rise of Reform Judaism

Many of the Ashkenazic Jews who began to stream into the United States in the 1840s came from Bavaria. Fleeing restrictions, persecution, and poverty, they practiced a traditional orthodoxy. But Jews also came from Germany, where many had been influenced by the emerging Reform movement, and through their leaders they shared this perspective with other immigrants. The setting of America itself, with its religious freedom and voluntarism, encouraged change, and eventually all these immigrants would come to be identified as "German" Jews, though not all of them embraced Reform Judaism. The Reform movement in Germany was a response to the Enlightenment and the "emancipation" of the Jews starting in the eighteenth century. Certain legal and political restrictions on Jews were lifted because they were incompatible with enlightened modern thought, so Jews were able to participate more as citizens and to seek "secular" education themselves. Prominent Jewish scholars embraced Enlightenment philosophy and principles of universalism, and some even converted to Christianity—as did some prominent Jewish women. Indeed, for those among the Jewish elite who could afford it, "secular" education was even easier for daughters than for sons, since in traditional Judaism, their education had been minimal, while young men still had the option and obligation of Hebrew religious studies.[8]

Emancipation was a welcome step, insofar as it lessened the persecution, discrimination, and scorn that had been the lot of Jews for centuries in Europe. Yet ironically it also undermined the sense of cohesion and clear identity that were products of the isolation of Jewish communities. Thus the Jewish Reform movement arose in the nineteenth century with a twofold purpose. On the one hand, it embraced much of modern Enlightenment thought and values and was embarrassed by those "Oriental" aspects of traditional and Talmudic Judaism that seemed backward and superstitious. On the other hand, Reform leaders were disturbed that many Jews were becoming so assimilated and secularized that they were lost to the faith. The leaders therefore attempted to shape a Judaism that would be free of what they saw as unnecessary and rigid traditionalisms but that would retain Judaism's enduring spiritual values, based in Hebrew Scriptures more than the Talmud, and thus draw back "modern" men and women to Judaism.

The status of women in Judaism was not the central concern of liberal rabbis. Nevertheless, it was one issue they addressed, both because affirmation of equal rights for women seemed a consequence of enlightened principles and because they feared the loss of more prominent Jewish women to Christianity.[9] Thus in Breslau in 1846 at the third in a series of conferences of liberal rabbis, they received a report suggesting changes in the legal status of Jewish women. The report insisted, "For our religious consciousness . . . it is a sacred duty to express most emphatically the complete religious equality of the female sex. . . . It is thus our task to pronounce the equality of religious privileges and obligations of women in so far as this is possible."[10] It then proceeded to suggest six specific changes in the legal, religious status of women:

1. Women were to observe all *mitzvot,* including the timebound ones from which they had traditionally been exempt.
2. Women had the same obligations toward children's religious education as men.
3. A religiously mature woman could make a religious vow that could not be invalidated by her husband or father.
4. The man's traditional morning prayer, thanking God that he had not been born a woman, was abolished.

5. Girls and women should participate in religious instruction and public worship, and could thus be counted in the *minyan*.
6. Thirteen was to be the age of religious maturity for both boys and girls.

These six changes by no means covered every legal disability suffered by Jewish women; nevertheless, they were a significant move toward greater religious equality—and responsibility—for women. Yet the impact of Breslau should not be overestimated: the rabbis themselves simply received the report at the end of a long conference. A theoretical call for change is one thing, but implementation is another, and concern for women was not at the top of the Reform rabbis' agenda, although a few congregations in Germany instituted some of the new measures. Moreover, legal changes were not accompanied by sociocultural changes in women's roles, so Jewish tradition merged with outside cultural influences, continuing to see woman's "natural" roles as wife and mother and her sphere as the home.[11]

## Reform Stirrings in America

Even if the changes were limited and their implementation slow, they were brought with Reform Judaism to America, where further developments affecting women's religious lives would occur. In fact, there had already been some Reform stirrings within American Judaism that were largely manifest in changes in worship practices, producing most notably a split in a Charleston congregation in 1824 and the organization of a Reform congregation in Baltimore in 1842. It was the wave of "German" immigration, however, and particularly the leadership of Isaac Mayer Wise (1819–1900) that fueled the growth of Reform Judaism in America. Born in Bohemia, Wise briefly served congregations there and then emigrated to the United States in 1846, where he became the leader of a Jewish congregation in Albany and began to institute modest changes in worship. That congregation split, with Wise leading the breakaway group, but in 1853 he accepted a call to the Bene Yeshurum congregation in Cincinnati, where he remained for the rest of his life. His Reform sympathies became evident in various practices, such as mixed seating in family pews in the synagogue, the use of an organ and of vernacular prayers for parts of the service, and preaching in English, and he encouraged the growth of other Reform congregations through his travel, advice, and the two newspapers he founded: the *American Israelite* in English, and *Die Deborah* in German. Wise also produced and published an American ritual, Minhag America, and was instrumental in bringing together thirty-four Reform congregations in the Union of American Hebrew Congregations in 1873 and in founding Hebrew Union College in Cincinnati in 1875 to train Reform rabbis. In 1885, Wise presided over the conference of Reform rabbis who produced the "Pittsburgh Platform" as a statement of Reform Judaism. The platform emphasized the enduring value of Judaism's ethical monotheism but expected change in many traditions and practices as consistent with modern civilization. It also rejected many traditional practices, even parts of the Mosaic law, and the hope of a return of Jews to Palestine. It saw Judaism as a religion, not a nation or people, was open to other religions and modern scientific developments, and encouraged concern for social justice.[12]

Thus by 1885, Reform Judaism had emerged as a dominant, organized, and widely popular form among American Jews, but that dominance must be qualified in three ways. First, many Jewish people and congregations were neither sympathetic nor formally allied with the Reform movement, fearing that its compromise of tradition and accommodation to American and Christian ways had gone too far. Second, there were differences among Reform congregations, from those whose changes were more modest than Wise's to even more radical Reform congregations in the East led by David Einhorn. Third, by 1885 a second major wave of Jewish immigration from eastern Europe, which was very Orthodox, had begun. These new arrivals would ultimately outnumber the "German" Jews and their Reform movement, and to them we will return later.

## Reform Judaism's Impact on Women

Obviously, Jewish women as Jews were affected by Reform Judaism, but what was its impact on Jewish women as women? Some of Reform's changes in practice, championed by Isaac Wise, had immediate and direct impact on women: the shift in synagogue seating from a separate women's gallery to the mixed seating of the family pew, the introduction of mixed choirs, services of confirmation for both boys and girls. Use of the vernacular in parts of the service and in sermons made congregational worship more accessible for women, who generally did not understand Hebrew. In the area of marriage, the double-ring ceremony, with a less passive role for the bride, was introduced, and Reform leaders advocated the authority of civil law for divorce, rather than the traditional religious laws. Wise, indeed, was more radical in his proposals than many of his Reform colleagues and than the congregations themselves. He supported the religious education of women and opened Hebrew Union College for their attendance. In an 1876 statement, he credited the presence of women for an increased level of decorum in services and urged that women be allowed to be voting members of congregations and serve on their boards. Wise even advocated women's suffrage and the possibility of female ordination as rabbis, though neither these nor female synagogue membership would take place for some time.

Yet Reform's changes for women, like Jewish emancipation in Europe, was a two-edged sword. Greater integration into the synagogue and its services surely enhanced that aspect of women's religious lives, even though they were not allowed to take formal leadership roles or to assume full membership privileges. (Neither were women in most Christian churches at the time. Moreover, like many Christian ministers of the day, Reform rabbis were grateful for the increased presence of women at synagogue worship at a time when many male Jews had more pressing outside interests that precluded regular attendance.) But Reform also eliminated many of the traditional rituals and practices, like the laws of *niddah* and *kashrut*, that had shaped women's Jewish lives and identities through personal observance. As Ann Braude wryly notes, "With some significant exceptions, the shapers of Reform Judaism found that male religious practices were rational and essential, while female religious practices were temporal and superstitious."[13] For some American Jewish women, the price of Reform was too high: what was gained in the synagogue was lost in the home as a ritual religious center.

From another perspective, however, the home's religious significance grew as American ideals affected Reform and Orthodox women alike. While few German Jewish immigrants were wealthy and women worked alongside their husbands in stores or businesses, as these families moved up a socioeconomic scale—and many did rapidly—they adopted middle-class ideals of domesticity. Unless driven by economic necessity, a woman should stay at home, and be responsible for the spiritual and moral education of her children. A division of spheres was part of Jewish tradition, but the division's particular nineteenth-century forms were also shaped by the cultural values of white American Protestants, especially the notions that women are by nature more pious than men and that they have a special genuis in promoting morality and spirituality. Wise's 1876 statement urging women's synagogue participation reveals a telling, if unconscious, combination of justifications.

> We need women in the congregational meetings to bring heart and piety into them. We must have women in the boards for the sake of the principle. We must have women in the school-boards to visit the Sabbath-schools, and to make their influence felt. We must have women in the choir committee, because they understand music better than men. But, all other considerations aside, the principle of justice, and the law of God inherent in every human being, demand that women be admitted to membership in the congregation, and be given equal rights with man; that her religious feelings be allowed scope for the sacred cause of Israel.[14]

Women deserve justice as equal human beings, yet women possess a distinctive nature. Most Jewish women accepted the division of spheres and natures, as did their Christian sisters, and they continued subtly to expand the female sphere at the same time that they accepted their special roles as guardians of the home and pillars of morality.

### *Jewish Women Outside the Home*

Throughout the nineteenth century, Jewish women stepped out of the home into various voluntary charitable and benevolent societies. Their contributions were real ones, valuable in and of themselves, but they also gave women the opportunity to expand their minds and their awareness of and activity in the larger public world in "appropriate" ways. Synagogues, in turn, depended not only on women's attendance but on their fund-raising and their service as teachers for children. Yet few Jewish women got directly involved in the more radical reform causes of the day like abolition or women's rights. In part, this was due to awareness that they were still a small community whose acceptance from Christian neighbors might be jeopardized by controversial positions. In part, Jews recognized that Christian evangelical advocates of some radical causes, including the women's movement, were frequently anti-Semitic. In part, traditional Judaism's expectations of feminine modesty and roles remained powerful deterrents.[15] (Ernestine Rose was a notable exception—and a woman who rejected the Orthodox Judaism into which she was born.)

Another acceptable outlet was the literary society and writing. Two women of the nineteenth century achieved widespread recognition as poets, Penina Moïse and Emma Lazarus. Moïse was born in 1797 to a well-to-do Sephardic family in Charleston, but her mother's death and her father's business reverses forced her to leave school to help support and care for the family. Nevertheless, she continued to study on her own, became part of a literary circle, and began writing poetry, which was published not only in Charleston but in other major newspapers and *Godey's Lady's Book*. In 1833, a book of her poems was the first such to be published by a Jew in the United States. Moïse remained an active and faithful Jew, and many of her poems were written in English and used as hymns in her moderately "Reform" congregation in Charleston; some are still in use today. In her later years, she became blind, but she still opened a school after the Civil War and continued to write poetry by dictating to her niece.

Although Moïse and her work are largely forgotten, Emma Lazarus (1849–1887) achieved wide and lasting fame when her poem, "The New Colossus," was inscribed on the base of the Statue of Liberty. She, too, was born into an affluent Sephardic family and showed an early interest and ability to write poetry. In her younger years, Emma Lazarus's Judaism was relatively nominal, although her family belonged to a prominent New York Sephardic congregation and she herself had some literary and historical interest in Judaism. It was events in Europe and contact with Russian Jews fleeing the persecution and pogroms that evoked in her a passionate concern for the Jewish people and a more self-conscious Jewish identity. She attacked Christian anti-Semitism, defended the cause of east European Jews, and celebrated the heroes of Jewish history and the integrity of Jewish religion in both poetry and prose. She also worked to raise support for the immigrants' plight among her more settled, Americanized, and comfortable Jewish compatriots, calling upon them in a series of articles in the *American Hebrew* in 1882 and 1883.

> The fact that the Jews of America are civilly and religiously emancipated, should be, I take it, our strongest impelling motive for working towards the emancipation of our oppressed brethren. . . . We must help our less fortunate brethren, not with the condescending patronage of the prosperous, who in self-defense undertake to conceal the social sores of the community by providing a remote hiding place for the outcast and the beggar, but with the keen, human sympathy of men and women who endeavor to defend men and women against outrage and oppression, of Jews who feel the sting of every wound and insult inflicted upon their bloodkindred.[16]

Lazarus helped to found the Hebrew Technical Institute in New York to provide education and job training for newly arrived immigrants. Moreover, she became an early and outspoken advocate of Zionism, hoping that Palestine could serve as a safe and permanent refuge for Russian Jewish victims of persecution. Although her voice lived on, her intense work came to an early end, for she died at the age of only thirty-eight.

## Orthodox Judaism

Who were these "Russian" Jews who began pouring into the United States in the 1880s? They were not all natives of Russia, any more than the "German" Jews were all German, but came from throughout eastern Europe. The assassination of Czar Alexander II in 1881 triggered a new wave of pogroms and persecution throughout Russia and especially within the Pale settlement to which most Jews were confined,[17] as did newly restrictive laws against the Jews in places like Romania and Austro-Hungary. Over the next four decades, some two million east European Jews poured into the United States, seeking relief from repression and better economic opportunities. Due both to the conditions from which they fled and to their own cultural values, eastern European Jewish immigration was very family oriented: proportionately more women and children emigrated than in any other contemporary ethnic group. Some came from urban areas to which they had been drawn by industrialization, especially after the turn of the century, and some had been influenced before they left not only by industrialization but by the movements of Haskalah (Jewish enlightenment) or socialism. Yet a great many of these Jews from eastern Europe lived in small towns or *shtetls,* practicing a traditional way of life and religion that had been relatively unchanged for centuries.

This traditional, orthodox Judaism included clear divisions between the spheres of men and of women. The most highly respected role for a man was to be a Talmudic scholar, and the synagogue was the sphere in which men most clearly expressed their religious identity. Woman's cultural and religious sphere, on the other hand, was the home, where she was expected not only to maintain Jewish customs but also to enable the religious development of husband and sons. If a woman was fortunate enough to be married to a scholar, she was not only allowed but expected to be the family's major breadwinner, for the marketplace, the provision of economic support, was considered an extension of the home sphere. That way she could free her husband for religious duties and study. Because a woman's own place in the community and in an afterlife depended on her husband's religious achievements, it was considered an honor and a privilege to be married to a scholar. As Mary Antin noted of the Jewish society of her childhood, here was the one exception to the class divisions that generally governed marital choices.

> One qualification only could raise a man above his social level, and that was scholarship. A boy born in the gutter need not despair of entering the houses of the rich, if he had a good mind and a great appetite for sacred learning. A poor scholar would be preferred in the marriage market to a rich ignoramus. In the phrase of our grandmothers, a boy stuffed with learning was worth more than a girl stuffed with banknotes.[18]

Not all adult Jewish males were scholars, however, and those who were not were indeed expected to provide economic support for the family. Nevertheless, here, too, Jewish women often contributed to such support by helping in a store or business or by selling various goods in the marketplace.

Religion was a central part of these Jewish women's identities, even if their place in the synagogues was limited, for their piety was rooted in the home and family. They faithfully kept the women's *mitzvot* and maintained kosher homes. Preparation for the Sabbath and other religious holidays was largely a female function, and women could take great personal satisfaction in the way they preserved Jewish practice on such occasions. Such preparation was a great deal of work, on top of other domestic or economic responsibilities, yet women enjoyed not only the religious significance of these occasions for themselves and their families but also the break they provided from the daily struggle to survive. Bella Chagall, in a memoir of her early life in Vitebsk, Russia, where her father was a rabbi and her mother ran the family store, describes her mother's joy in the Sabbath:

> The last to leave the shop is mother. She tries all the doors once more to see that they are locked. . . . Now her soft shoes slip into the dining room. In the doorway she halts for a moment: the white

> table with the silver candlesticks dazzles her eyes. At once she begins to hurry. She quickly washes her face and hands, puts on a clean lace collar that she always wears on this night, and approaches the candlesticks like a quite new mother. With a match in her hand she lights one candle after another. All the seven candles begin to quiver. The flames blaze into mother's face. As though an enchantment were falling upon her, she lowers her eyes. Slowly, three times in succession, she encircles the candles with both her arms; she seems to be taking them into her heart. And with the candles her weekday worries melt away.
>
> She blesses the candles. She whispers quiet benedictions through her fingers and they add heat to the flames. Mother's hands over the candles shine like the tablets of the decalogue over the holy ark. . . .
>
> I hear mother in her benedictions mention now one name, now another. She names father, the children, her own father and mother. . . .
>
> "May the Highest One give them his blessing!" concludes mother, dropping her hands at last. . . .
>
> "Good shabbes!" mother calls out loudly. Her face, all opened, looks purified, I think that it has absorbed the illumination of the Sabbath candles.[19]

Growing up in the shtetls, girls did not join their brothers in learning Hebrew or active study at the *shul*. They might learn to read Yiddish, but their primary education in work, in religious practices, and in piety came from their own female relatives, in preparation for the time when they, too, would marry and raise a family. Traditionally, marriages were arranged through a matchmaker, and girls were expected to bring a dowry. Indeed, a well-to-do family might consider it such an honor for a daughter to marry a promising young scholar that they would be prepared to support him through his studies. On the other hand, a poor young woman may have seen in emigration a desirable alternative to an unwelcome marriage or to prospects that were limited because she lacked a dowry.[20] Most Jewish women in the *shtetls* accepted the role divisions and female limitations, knowing the value of their own contributions and finding identity in female companionship, but some young women occasionally resented their second-class status. Bella Chagall tells of her frustration at being excluded from the *sukkah* (a special hut constructed for the Feast of the Tabernacles) and her satisfaction when a rainstorm drove the men indoors,[21] and Mary Antin as a child resented the special considerations and educational opportunities given to boys but unavailable to her simply because of her sex: "There was nothing in what the boys did in *heder* [Hebrew school] that I could not have done—if I had not been a girl."[22]

## Immigration to America

A great many east European Jews who left their homes ultimately came to the United States. It was often a reluctant departure, necessitated by poverty or persecution, and while they hoped to find greater toleration as well as greater economic opportunities in the New World, they felt the pain of losing the familiar and apprehension about a strange, new land: would they be able to preserve their religion there? Sometimes whole families left together; at other times, a father or an older brother or sister might go first alone, hoping to earn money quickly and thus be able to bring other family members to America. These immigrants did, indeed, escape severe persecution and oppression, but they found that Americans, too, were prejudiced and that the streets were not paved with gold. Most settled in urban centers, especially New York City, seeking out neighborhoods where other Orthodox Jews congregated and finding work wherever they could.

In some ways, the transition was easier for Jewish women than for Jewish men. The most immediate challenge faced by new arrivals was basic support, food and shelter, for few had been able to bring much in the way of resources with them. Men who were scholars found that not only were their skills no source of economic support, they were not even particularly respected by their new neighbors, and the culture scorned the "lazy" man who could not or would not support his family. Most Jewish immigrant women, on the other hand, were used to contributing to the economic support of the family and were already very skilled at "making do" and stretching limited resources to care for and feed their families. Young women found work in the factories and contributed their meager earnings toward the family's income. Married women's working outside the home for others was frowned upon, yet they found numerous ways to supplement the family income: they took in boarders or piecework, became pushcart vendors or peddlers, or spent long hours helping in a family store or business.

There was another, subtle way in which the transition may have been easier for women than for men. While numerous synagogues were founded in places like New York's Lower East Side, they did not serve as centers of learning as much as they had in the shtetls, nor was the prestige and authority granted to rabbis and scholars as great as it had been in Europe. Women's religious identities were more easily transferred and maintained, even when they underwent some adaptation. As Sydney Stahl Weinberg notes:

> The religious observances and customs of women, rooted in the home and tradition, could be practiced as easily in America as in Europe, while the obligations of men, focused on biblical texts and commentaries studied in the synagogue, found stonier soil in the

> United States. . . . while the *mikvah* all but disappeared from the American scene, and many younger married women abandoned the *sheitel* [a wig worn by married women], the great majority kept kosher homes, lit candles on the Sabbath, and maintained their ritual celebrations of holidays in the home. Many were able, as their husbands were not, to observe the Sabbath by not working outside the home.[23]

Yet in other ways, the immigration experience was more difficult for women. Pressures of poverty and cultural change took their toll on family life, and if a husband divorced or, worse still, deserted his wife, she could have a desperately hard time finding enough work to support herself and her children. Some help was available from groups like United Hebrew Charities, and aid to widows or abandoned women and their children formed a major item of their budgets. Even so, Paula Hyman concludes, "The statistics are likely to understate the scope of the problem, for many deserted wives sought assistance from public charity with great reluctance, some only years after their husbands left them."[24] Other Jewish women were driven to prostitution by poverty and the lack of either decent jobs or community and family support. Yet despite real problems and stresses, the family remained a crucial center for identity, stability and survival for east European Jewish immigrants.

## Americanization and Education

Related to issues of survival, both in its basic sense of food and shelter and in the sense of religious and cultural identity, was the question of Americanization. Immigrants recognized that some adaptation to the new setting was unavoidable, yet many of the first generation hoped to keep change to a minimum, fearing that adaptation would undermine religious and cultural loyalty. On the other hand, sons and daughters often saw new and attractive possibilities that had been unknown in Europe and pursued them, despite parental disapproval and fears. Customs like arranged marriages were resisted or discarded; "American" clothing, entertainment, and freedom seemed far preferable to the "backward" ways of an older generation. Indeed, the very values that many Jews brought with them, as well as the stark necessities of survival, contributed in different ways to an inevitable Americanization of the next generation. While some children, especially older daughters, had to find work in the textile factories, others, especially sons and younger daughters, benefited from the educational opportunities in America that permitted them to move out of poverty and yet also distanced them from their "foreign," traditional, Orthodox parents.

If the traditional reverence for male religious scholarship was weakened in America by necessity and cultural pressures, it was to a degree replaced by passion and respect for education in general, for both boys and girls.

Not only did parents sacrifice to give at least one child an education, so, too, did older siblings. Although Mary Antin and her older sister were separated by only two years, Frieda's lot was the workshop so that Mary, an obviously gifted child, could continue in school. Anzia Yezierska, in her semiautobiographical novel, *Bread Givers,* tells not only of the grinding poverty of an immigrant family whose father was a scholar but also of the blighted hopes of three older sisters, sent out to work and then married off by a traditional father who ignored their own wishes. The youngest daughter, Sarah, rebels and determines to "make herself for a person," working her way through high school and college until she becomes a teacher. As a group, Jewish immigrants rose from poverty faster than most, though newcomers arrived to fill the places at the bottom of the socioeconomic ladder, and as they moved into the middle class, they adopted American cultural expectations.

> The full-time housewife thus appeared sooner in immigrant and second-generation Jewish communities than among other immigrant groups. Jewish women experienced more rapid mobility than other immigrant women, but their experience of mobility was vicarious and left them dependent on their husbands for their status. The decision to work outside the home was not left to the women themselves.[25]

## Factory Work and the Labor Movement

Education was desirable but simply not possible for many first-generation Jewish immigrant women. Economic need drove them into the factories, where the meagre pay, long hours, and terrible working conditions pushed many women into the young labor movement. For example, some 80 percent of the workers in the New York shirtwaist industry were women, and young Jewish women made up two-thirds of that number and were instrumental in the "Uprising of the 20,000" in 1909. Not only had the women endured bad conditions, unfair practices, sexual harassment, and pay cuts in the shirtwaist factories, when they struck, those on picket lines suffered verbal abuse, physical violence, and arrest. When the workers met in November and debated whether to call a general strike, it was a young Jewish woman, Clara Lemlich, who grew impatient with delay, rose, and moved in Yiddish for an immediate, general strike. Her call was cheered, and the crowd responded with a traditional Hebrew oath—"If I turn traitor to the cause I now pledge, may this hand wither from the arm I now raise"—and began "women's most significant struggle for unionism in the nation's history."[26] After nearly a year, the companies gave in to many of the unions' demands (and formalized, with union consent, lower pay for women workers), but the unions were forced to compromise on some health and safety regulations. It was a fateful compromise, for in

March 1911, the worst industrial fire in the nation's history took place in the Triangle Shirtwaist Factory. Young Jewish women were heavily represented among its victims, including 146 people who died because the company had ignored safety regulations, failing to provide fire escapes and locking the workers in (so they would not take unauthorized breaks or steal things!) Thus the women could not get out of the wooden building's top floors when a fire broke out. Some tried to jump out the windows and were killed by the fall, while others died from the heat and smoke. A horrified public helped finally to force legislation to increase safety regulations and ensure their enforcement.

While a few Jewish women who came to America had been involved in radical political and labor movements in Russia, most went into factory jobs out of economic necessity. They not only came to represent numerical strength in the American labor workforce, but they were also typically among the more militant workers, facing with loyalty and bravery the intransigence of employers, frequently unsympathetic courts, and public apathy. Most worked to support themselves and contribute to family income, hoping to leave the factory after a few years to marry. Yet in the meantime, they gained a measure of independence and self-assurance from the work. Even if most of their earnings went to the family budget, they were able to keep a little for their own expenses, and their status as wage earners gained them respect and a certain degree of freedom from parental control in such matters as the use of free time to attend evening lectures and meetings, even unchaperoned.[27]

While most young Jewish women were part of the rank and file, leaving the factories and the unions after a few years, a number of prominent women labor organizers and leaders were Jewish, like Rose Schneiderman and Pauline Newman, both of whom came with their families from eastern Europe before 1900, worked in the factories, and rose to leadership in union organizing. Women organizers received little help or recognition from male union leaders, who shared the broadly held male cultural presumption that women should stay at home, if possible, and who argued that since most women left to get married, they were only temporary workers and thus not good union material. Male unions supported unequal pay and gendered job divisions. They failed to see the sexual harassment suffered by women workers as a serious concern. Even union benefits were unequally applied. Alice Kessler-Harris notes the example of a capmakers' strike where "married men got strike benefits amounting to six dollars a week, but women, even those who supported widowed mothers and young siblings, got nothing."[28] Thus women labor leaders turned to the Women's Trade Union League for help. Unquestionably, the middle- and upper-class women reformers, the "allies" in membership of the WTUL, delivered significant aid, supporting the women garment workers' strikes and even joining the picket lines. Yet there were often tensions between the working-class Jewish women and the middle-class reformers, tensions generated not only because of religious and class differences but also over tactics and the relative importance of goals like women's suffrage. Through the early decades of the twentieth century, women like Newman and Schneiderman, devoted to the cause of working women, were torn between the WTUL and the male-dominated labor movement. Both worked for a time as organizers for the International Ladies Garment Workers' Union, but Schneiderman ultimately cast her lot with the WTUL, and Newman went to work for the Joint Board of Sanitary Control.

While some second-generation Jewish women retained the Orthodoxy of their parents, for others the attractions of Americanization, education, and upward mobility weakened their loyalty to traditional beliefs and practices. Similarly, many Jewish women active in the unions found socialism and the cause of labor a more compelling faith than the strict Orthodoxy of their ancestors, though these women drew upon a deeply rooted prophetic concern for justice that was also a part of their religious heritage. Some women broke with Orthodoxy by working on the Sabbath, failing to follow traditional *mitzvot* for women and other religious rituals, or rejecting formal affiliation with a synagogue, yet still identifying themselves with Jewish people and culture. In her study of east European Jewish immigrant women, Weinberg used forty-six oral histories as well as written sources and found that many women did not so much reject Judaism as simply modify their understanding of what was necessary to Jewish female identity.

> Although forty of their mothers had maintained kosher homes, only about a third of the younger immigrant women did, and a few more lit candles on Friday night. Only one wore a *sheitel*. However, more than 80 percent celebrated the major Jewish holidays, and all considered themselves to be good Jews, even the one woman who also claimed to be an atheist. Only one woman married a non-Jewish man.[29]

## The Growth of Women's Organizations

Nor was change in a Jewish female identity an issue faced only by immigrant women of east European Orthodoxy; "German" Jewish women, too, were forging new female roles and understandings in the last years of the nineteenth and early decades of the twentieth century. Indeed, it was the very waves of east European immigrants that precipitated some of the changes in these women's religious activities.

Jews in America, men and women who traced their roots back to the colonial period as well as those who came during the middle decades of the nineteenth century, were not initially welcoming to the huge numbers of east European immigrants, despite their being fellow Jews. Their culture appeared foreign and backward to established Jewish Americans, epitomizing much that the "German" Jews had tried to eliminate for themselves and in the eyes of Christian neighbors. They feared that so many poor, "ignorant" (in terms that Americans valued), and "strange" foreigners would rekindle anti-Semitism and undercut the acceptance from other Americans that German Jews had worked so hard to achieve. They also feared that the needs of the immigrants would drain the resources of established institutions and philanthropy. Nevertheless, whatever their fears and personal feelings, the German Jewish communities did respond to the needs of their co-religionists, providing a great deal of material and personal aid. They met immigrants at the docks; tried to help them find family members, shelter, and jobs; and offered classes in English and vocational skills in an attempt to see that the immigrants became Americanized as quickly as possible. From the point of view of the German Jews, Americanization was both necessary and desirable.

Immigrants did not always see it the same way. East European immigrants were often distrustful and scornful of American Jews, who didn't keep the Sabbath properly, ignored traditional practices like keeping a kosher home, and held no esteem for the traditions of Talmudic scholarship. In short, German Jews seemed to them little better than Gentiles—Jews who had sold their birthright for the pottage of acceptance, and they resented the condescension and cultural insensitivity of their benefactors. Still, the aid German Jews offered was welcome and substantial. Indeed, the scope of the need was so great that existing charitable organizations, largely male-run, turned to Jewish women for help in fund-raising and the provision of volunteers. The women, in their turn, soon came to direct their efforts especially to immigrant women and children. Like the white Protestant women of the foreign missionary movement, Jewish women thought that male boards tended to neglect the particular needs of women and children and that they, as women, had a greater understanding and sensitivity to those needs. They met immigrant women as they arrived in the United States, comforted the children, helped women traveling without an adult male to find family members or fiancés and to negotiate the entrance bureaucracies, and made sure that young women were not victimized by pimps or procurers upon arrival. Through their organizations, German Jewish women followed up with new arrivals, using "home visits" to check on their well-being and to help them adjust to America and find available resources for social services. In time, some Jewish women adopted the more "scientific" methods of an emerging social work profession and became involved with the settlement house movement, especially in New York, working in both nondenominational establishments like Lillian Wald's famous Henry Street Settlement and specifically Jewish institutions like the Educational Alliance.

Concern for east European Jewish immigrants was a major cause of the expansion of Jewish women's organizations, but there were other factors that spurred their development. In the late years of the nineteenth century, many Reform congregations founded temple sisterhoods. Like their Christian counterparts, these congregation-related groups of women performed a wide range of functions from fund-raising to care and beautification of religious buildings to charitable work. They also provided a female space where women developed skills of organization and speaking and discovered their common goals and identity. Yet the groups were distinctively and self-consciously Jewish: like the Sunday school movement begun by Rebecca Gratz, they promoted Jewish education of children to counter overt Christian evangelism or more subtle pressures to assimilate, and they worked to combat anti-Semitism. Furthermore, the sisterhoods continued the process through which American Jewish women became more active in the synagogues, for while they clearly accepted and supported the value of the home as women's particular sphere and contribution, they were unwilling to remain excluded from the traditionally male sphere of the synagogue. Rather, they believed, both were necessary to female Jewish identity.

Although temple sisterhoods began to appear in the last years of the nineteenth century, they did not organize nationally until 1913, when the National Federation of Temple Sisterhoods was founded for Reform congregations. Five years later, the National Women's League of the United Synagogue of America was founded in Conservative Judaism, that movement that emerged in the twentieth century with its center in the Jewish Theological Seminary of New York. Conservative Judaism would try to walk a middle way between Reform and Orthodoxy, drawing adherents from both of those streams.[30] In the meantime, however, the first national group for Jewish women, the National Council of Jewish Women (NCJW), had been founded. In 1891, Hannah Greenbaum Solomon (1858–1942), a prominent Jewish woman from Chicago, was asked to organize a Jewish Women's Congress to be part of the 1893 World's Columbian Exposition in Chicago. The task was formidable, as Solomon recalls in her autobiography:

> Not only were there no organization lists available . . . there was not even a federal organization. The problem of establishing contacts was a poser that gave me the utmost concern. [She finally wrote to leading rabbis in the United States, asking for the names of women who might contribute to the Congress.] Then, when I received a response from each of these spiritual leaders, all of whom proved most genuinely interested and cooperative, I wrote ninety letters (all by hand, and each one personal) to the women whose names had been suggested.[31]

After much planning, Solomon had a program set and speakers committed. She was then approached by male Jews involved in the Congress of Religions who solicited the women's cooperation, but since their idea of cooperation did not include women on the program, the Jewish women declined their offer.

### Jewish Women's Congress

The Jewish Women's Congress was a decided success. The speakers included a number of prominent Jewish women and represented a wide range of interests and positions on Judaism from Reform to traditionalist. The opening prayer and a subsequent address on "Woman in the Synagogue" were given by Ray Frank (1865–1948), already famous as the first American woman to preach at Jewish services. A California journalist, Frank had preached at two Rosh Hashanah services and one on Yom Kippur eve in Spokane, Washington, in 1890, and her fame had spread quickly. After the 1893 Congress, Frank studied at Hebrew Union College, continued to receive invitations to speak and even an offer to assume spiritual leadership of a Chicago congregation (which she declined), but after her marriage in 1901 to Simon Litman, she ended her public career. Although Frank was deeply committed to Judaism, her 1893 address, like her life, appeared to be ambivalent about Jewish women's roles. On the one hand, she insisted that qualified women could be rabbis or congregational leaders, just as women were prophetesses in biblical times, but she also indicated that she had no personal interest in such a role, accepted a gendered division of natures and spheres, and insisted that the home was woman's "noblest work."

> What matter whether we women are ordained rabbis or not? We are capable of fulfilling the office, and the best way to prove it is to convert ourselves and our families into reverent beings. . . . Nothing can replace the duty of the mother in the home. *Nothing can replace the reverence of children, and the children are yours to do as ye will with them.*
>
> Mothers, ye can restore Israel's glory, can fulfil the prophecy by bringing the man-child, strong love of the Eternal, to his Maker.[32]

Another speaker, Mary M. Cohen, sounded similar themes in her address, "The Influence of the Jewish Religion in the Home." Not only was Judaism intimately bound up with the home, she insisted, but its domestic, material practices were in no way spiritually inferior to those in the male realm of the synagogue.[33] Other speakers, without rejecting the value of women's traditional domestic contributions, endorsed expanding roles for women: Julia Richman (1855–1912), a famous New York educator, spoke on women as wage earners and the particular problems of east European Jewish immigrants, and defended a woman's right to choose single independence over marriage at any cost.[34] Finally, congress organizers Hannah Solomon and Sadie American used the meetings as a forum to call for the formation of a national organization of Jewish women, the National Council of Jewish Women (NCJW). Over the next few years, local chapters were organized in most major cities, and in 1896, the first national meeting of the NCJW was held, with Hannah Solomon as its first president.

## National Council of Jewish Women

Although many of its members came from Reform congregations, the NCJW actively encouraged the participation of all Jewish women, including those with more traditional or Orthodox views.[35] Indeed, one of the organization's purposes was to encourage dialogue among Jewish American women. Another goal was to encourage women to study Judaism, for the sake of their own spiritual development and informed religious identity, and so that the women might more effectively pass the faith to their children in their homes and through Sabbath school teaching. Third, the council encouraged and subsequently became very active in a wide range of philanthropic and reform work, with a particular emphasis on the needs of east European immigrants. One issue of special concern to the women of the NCJW was quite controversial: "white slavery." Neither the problem nor calls for reform were new in late nineteenth-century America, but many male Jewish leaders were reluctant to acknowledge its existence in their own communities, for Jews had always been proud of their strong family traditions and morality, and they feared a backlash of anti-Semitism if the ancient traffic in vice were identified with the new waves of Jewish immigrants. Nevertheless, the NCJW women, under the leadership of Sadie American, insisted that the problem was a real one, working with the women involved and promoting awareness and reform.[36]

Because not all members of the NCJW came from Reform congregations, they did not necessarily share the concern of Reform Jewish women to expand the religious roles and rights of women in the synagogue. Nevertheless, the NCJW provided support and a forum for those who did. In 1895, Rose Kohler, daughter and grandaughter of famous Reform rabbis and active in the NCJW's work for religious schools, addressed a New York meeting of the council and decried the continued exclusion of women from formal synagogue membership and suffrage.[37] In 1895 Rosa Sonneschein, another advocate of reform, founded a journal, the *American Jewess*, as "a feminist platform advocating women's social, political, communal, and religious emancipation."[38] By no means seeking emancipation from Judaism—Sonneschein was distressed that American Jews were so lax in their Sabbath observance—she nevertheless insisted upon the need for women's equality, including the vote in both the synagogue and the nation. The *American Jewess* folded after four years, but the campaign for expanded religious rights for women would continue.

### Hadassah and Jewish Distinctiveness

The National Council of Jewish Women compiled an impressive record of work and continued to be an important voice for Jewish women's concerns, but there were other voices raised and other organizations formed by Jewish women in the late nineteenth and early twentieth centuries. Especially important was Hadassah, a Zionist organization for women founded in 1912 by Henrietta Szold (1860–1945). The daughter of a prominent Baltimore rabbi, Szold became a writer and a teacher, actively involved in Jewish education and scholarly and editorial work with the Jewish Publication Society. Although she was moderately supportive of Zionism in her earlier years, it was a trip to Palestine in 1909 and her reaction to conditions there that made her dedicate the rest of her life to that cause, dividing her time between the United States and Palestine. Szold gave extraordinary service to the cause of Zionism and the people of Palestine, and Hadassah ultimately became "the largest of all the Zionist groups and the largest Jewish woman's organization in the world."[39]

The existence and growth of Hadassah is an important reminder that however much the religious experiences of Jewish women in America may have paralleled those of their Christian sisters, they were also distinctive, shaped internally by an ancient tradition and externally by the Jews' cultural status as outsiders. As Jews gained acceptance from Christian Americans, at different times for different groups, Jewish and Christian women found they could work together across religious lines for a common cause like suffrage. While only a few Jewish women, notably Maud Nathan, achieved national prominence in the suffrage campaign of the early twentieth century, many were active at the local level. Middle- and upper-class Jewish women supported the women's movement and suffrage in particular, even as they were wary of its anti-Semitic tendencies,[40] and working class women were drawn in even greater numbers than their Catholic sisters to work for the female vote as a means to support the cause of labor and their own needs as working women.[41]

Within their own religious communities, Jewish women, like their Protestant sisters, expanded their visibility and activities through women's organizations. They provided direct support to congregations, engaged in charitable and benevolent work, and developed a female space for identity, cooperation, and activity that was compatible with cultural expectations about women's nature and spheres. Cooperation with Christian women in certain areas of common concern would have the further effect, Jewish women hoped, of increasing Christians' understanding of Judaism and thus decreasing anti-Semitism. Yet as much as Jewish women's groups may have functioned in similar ways to those of Christian women, they also maintained a clear, self-conscious Jewish identity. The educational work promoted by Jewish women was designed not only to equip children for survival and success in America but also to instill in them an understanding of their own faith that would help them resist unwelcome assimilation or even conversion. Like the True Women of Christian America, Jewish mothers felt a strong sense of responsibility to pass on patriotic, moral, and religious principles to their children in the home, but it was a Jewish identity and a Jewish future that they hoped to preserve and protect.

In the light of diversity within American Judaism, especially after the arrival of east European Jewish immigrants, the balance between stepping out of and preserving their place was particularly delicate for Jewish women. Many found the atmosphere of America with its religious freedom and its openness to change supportive of their desire to expand their religious roles and responsibilities into areas previously reserved for men. Yet at the same time, so much of Jewish traditional identity in general, and women's Jewish identity in particular, was associated with rituals in the home that other Jewish women were wary of losing a deeply rooted and meaningful domestic female piety for the sake of a dubious and partial emancipation and equality. At what point might elimination of Jewish ritual practices threaten to undermine not only their female identity but their Jewishness and that of their children? Thus, stepping into places formerly denied them did not mean, for most Jewish women, rejecting the traditional sphere of the home and their influence as wives and mothers; rather, they followed the route of change by gradual expansion.

# 16

# *Alternative Religions in Nineteenth-Century America*

Most women in nineteenth-century America found their religious identity in traditions with ancient roots: Christianity in its various Protestant or Catholic forms; Judaism; the traditional tribal religions of African or pre-Columbian peoples as these were affirmed, rejected, or blended with the dominant Christianity of white America. Yet other Americans took advantage of an atmosphere of ferment, experimentation, and formal principles of religious freedom to break from the mainstream in search of new religious alternatives. Such sectarian groups typically incorporated much of Christian tradition but claimed a new and higher truth, often involving a significant new revelation, scripture, or authoritative leadership. These groups appealed to both men and women. They frequently challenged social and economic as well as religious orthodoxy. And in their vision and working out of new truths, some of them offered new ideas about women in the context of religious leadership, marriage, and economic roles and activities. Some were ephemeral and short-lived. Others endured for many years before they faded from the American scene. A few survived and grew to become established religious groups of the twentieth century. In this chapter, I focus on four manifestations of sectarian Christianity that hold particular interest for the story of women and religion in America: the Shakers; the Oneida Community; the Church of Jesus Christ of Latter-day Saints; and the Church of Christ, Scientist. In none of the four was an explicit feminism the primary motivation or goal, yet each offered some significant theological challenge to traditional notions of God or of woman's nature or roles.

## The Shakers

Although born in England, the United Society of Believers or Shakers developed concurrently with the history of the United States: Ann Lee and a small group of her followers landed in New York in 1774. The exact origins of the group are debated by scholars, but they may have been influenced by the French Camisards, whose influence spread to England in the eighteenth century.[1] James and Jane Wardley were early leaders, but it was one of their converts, Ann Lee, who emerged as the spiritual founder of the Shakers. The poor and illiterate daughter of a Manchester blacksmith, Ann Lee was deeply distressed about her own sinfulness before joining the society. In marriage she had suffered through four pregnancies, only to have all of her children die as infants.[2] Like other members of the group, she was imprisoned for her disruptive behavior, and during a period in prison in 1770 she experienced a vision in which God revealed to her that the original sin of Adam and Eve was sexual intercourse and that she, Ann, was to be a special messenger of God to her age. Four years later, she and eight companions fled to the United States. Although her husband Abraham Standerin was one of the eight, he later left her permanently when she continued to refuse to have marital relations. By 1780, the small band had regrouped at Niskeyuna, New York, and began to grow, gaining important recruits, including Joseph Meacham, in the aftermath of a revival. These early Shakers encountered significant hostility because of the strangeness of their religious beliefs and practices. In addition, during the Revolutionary War their American neighbors branded them as traitors or spies because of their pacifism and British nationality. Ann Lee died in 1784, and leadership was assumed by James Whittaker, one of her companions from England. At his death in 1787, Joseph Meacham took over as leader.

The early Shaker movement in America was not highly organized. Rather, it was a religion marked by personal experience, ecstatic worship, and fluidity in ideas and practices. After the accession of Meacham to leadership, the Shakers moved into a period of institutionalization. One of Meacham's early acts was to appoint Lucy Wright as co-leader in a pattern that became typical of Shakers thereafter. Each Shaker community was led by two elders and two eldresses who were the spiritual heads of the society. Their work was complemented by two deacons and two deaconesses, who were in charge of the temporal affairs of each settlement, although the leaders of the New Lebanon, New York, community held the highest authority. These leadership roles were self-perpetuating through appointment, and strict obedience was expected from members. Eventually, each community or village was divided into "families" representing different levels of membership (e.g., leaders, children and the elderly, probationary members) and with different responsibilities.

Under Meacham, the first meeting house was erected for worship, which became more organized and orderly. Singing, which had in the earliest period been personal, spontaneous, uncoordinated, and often wordless, was regularized in community songs and hymns that frequently summarized Shaker doctrine. Similarly, the ecstatic movements of early individual Shakers as they were seized by the spirit were replaced by structured but still lively dances called "Holy Order" by Meacham. Although its forms changed, dancing remained a central part of Shaker worship, as fascinating and unusual to outside observers as it was meaningful to its Shaker participants.

After Meacham's death in 1796, Lucy Wright became the effective head of the society, although male successors to Meacham were elected, and it was under her direction that the next significant stage of expansion occurred. The society began publishing works that summarized Shaker beliefs for both external and internal audiences, a means of both proselytism and self-defense against public misunderstanding based on ignorance or the "exposés" of former members. Wright sent Shaker missionaries into parts of the American frontier that had been affected by the revivals of the Second Great Awakening, reaping a harvest of converts among those who were disappointed with the results of revival, and establishing new communities.

Upon joining a community, a new member had to confess his or her sins and agree to abide by the rules of the society. Celibacy was required, and to minimize sexual temptations, men and women were strictly separated in most of Shaker life, from work to sleeping quarters to seating at meals. Men and women even used separate entrances to Shaker buildings. From Meacham's time on, Shaker communities practiced a kind of primitive Christian communism, with individuals retaining only a minimum of necessary personal possessions. Following Mother Ann's injunction to "put your hands to work and your hearts to God," labor was not only a necessity but a sacred duty. Each Shaker was to learn a trade or craft, and all were expected to help in the daily life of the community. Simplicity in all aspects of life was stressed. Indeed, it was the combination of craftsmanship and simplicity manifest in Shaker crafts, furniture, and architecture that so attracted outsiders in their own day and since.

In 1837, a distinctive stage of Shaker development known as "Mother Ann's Work" began when a group of young girls experienced a kind of spirit possession that was manifest in visions, trances, and ecstatic behaviors. The behaviors spread to other communities and more broadly within communities, including men as well as women, leaders as well as more peripheral members. Individuals received "spirit messages" and gifts from the supernatural world. Some messages were personal ones of reassurance or admonition. Others (especially those received by leaders) were more general directives and reminders for the society. Early messages came primarily from Mother Ann and Jesus Christ. Later they were received from other Shaker leaders who had died, from God the Father and Holy Mother Wisdom, and even from historical figures like George Washington or groups like native Americans, Chinese, and Eskimos. Sometimes the spirit gifts took the form of new songs or symbolic drawings. By 1847, Mother Ann's Work had effectively ended.[3] During this period, Shaker membership reached its peak of about 4000 members in some eighteen villages.

Thereafter, their numbers gradually declined, although a few small groups survived into the late twentieth century.

## The Distinctiveness of Shaker Ideas and Practices

Shakers were thus one of the most successful and enduring religious communitarian groups in American history. Their ideas and practices were also among the most distinctive. Three in particular have been fascinating to scholars of women and religion: female images of the divine, views on sexuality and marriage, and female leadership. Not only were the Shakers founded by a woman, but their theology included an affirmation that the Godhead was dual, male and female, God the Father and Holy Mother Wisdom. Furthermore, Shaker theology asserted that just as Jesus Christ had revealed the male aspect of the Godhead, so Ann Lee was the incarnation of its female aspect. Whether or not Ann Lee saw herself as, or her earliest followers believed her to be, a savior and incarnate manifestation of the divine is ambiguous, and evidence can be cited on both sides. It isn't clear whether the *early* Shakers associated God's second coming with a collective (that is, with the formation and growth of their group) or with a particular individual, Ann Lee.[4] By the early nineteenth century, however, Shakers clearly regarded Ann Lee as God's second incarnation. The period of Spiritualist revival further enhanced the roles of women leaders like Ann Lee and Lucy Wright and drew the female aspect of godhead, Holy Mother Wisdom, into greater prominence, even as presumed divine gender characteristics mirrored cultural ones. "Holy Mother Wisdom possessed all the traits of an ideal mother, the Eternal Father those of a male counterpart. Each filled conventional roles—the loving, tender mother and the stern, potentially wrathful father. Yet both had the capacity for love and justice, mercy and power."[5]

Ann Lee's vision and subsequent preaching formed the basis for the distinctive Shaker practice of strict celibacy as part of a person's separation from worldly sins and desires and subsequent striving for perfection. (The requirement of celibacy did not immediately undermine Shaker growth, since they actively sought converts. Furthermore, there were children in Shaker villages, either the natural offspring of converts or orphans taken in and cared for by the community. Many of these children ultimately left the Shakers, but some remained as lifelong members.) In addition, celibacy encouraged the believer to focus on God and salvation and promoted, for both men and women, loyalty to the group as a whole over individual concerns or familial attachments. But celibacy also had practical consequences and potential benefits for women: freedom from the debilitating physical and emotional consequences of frequent childbearing and the time-consuming activities of motherhood. Moreover, celibacy and strict sexual separation among the Shakers contributed to the development of women's leadership. Certainly Ann Lee's early status established a precedent, but her immediate successors were male until Joseph Meacham appointed Lucy Wright as co-minister. As Marjorie Procter-Smith notes, "Although it is conceivable that Meacham's decision to appoint eldresses and deaconesses was motivated by a commitment to the principal of equality between the sexes, it is certain that pragmatic requirements of a mixed celibate community demanded a distinct set of leaders for Shaker women."[6] Whatever Meacham's mix of motives, the precedent he set, along with the effective early leadership of Lucy Wright, opened a door for female leaders, and nineteenth-century Shakers prided themselves on the sexual equality that they believed their communities embodied.

Nevertheless, the equality of women with men in Shaker communities was qualified. At a practical level, Shakers retained a traditional and gendered division of labor: women took care of "indoor" domestic tasks (including cleaning the brothers' rooms and doing their laundry), whereas men were involved in a wider range of activities, especially outdoor work and traditionally male jobs.[7] Men were also in charge of most of the economic responsibilities for the community, especially as trustees who dealt with the outside world. In part, such a traditional division of labor by gender may have been a necessary consequence of Shaker insistence on strict separation of the sexes, but it also reflected cultural values of the day.

Shakers' acceptance of traditional understandings of woman's nature and spheres was further reflected in their worship and theology. Although women participated in hymns and dancing, they seldom led worship services or preached. Thus the new opportunities for vocal participation during Mother Ann's Work by a believer who received a spirit message may have been especially welcome to women; as with the role of prophetess, immediate divine direction superseded normal restrictions on women's speaking. Furthermore, as Procter-Smith suggests, it may not have been purely coincidental that the figure of Holy Mother Wisdom became newly prominent during Mother Ann's Work, for women were the ones who "spoke" for her, and her divine power legitimated their own.[8] And while the Shaker God was dual, characteristics and images associated with the Father and the Mother reflected traditional gender assumptions. Nor was the lengthy Christian tradition that viewed women as carnal, subordinate, and more guilty for the Fall entirely overcome:

> While the images of the Daughter of God and the Mother of the New Creation are both powerful and positive, the image of the Bride of Christ reinforces and justifies patriarchal marriage patterns of dominance and submission, and the image of the "Second Eve" is made powerful at the expense of the rest of womankind, which must bear the onus of causing the Fall. And all the images are interlocking. The Daughter of Zion is the one anointed to raise

> women from their sin and misery, to be the second Eve; the Mother of All Living is mother because she is the obedient spouse of her Lord and Head, Jesus Christ.[9]

Despite such ambiguities, the Shakers offered much that was positive and unusual for nineteenth-century American women. Moreover, by the end of the century, the society had become increasingly feminized. Women constituted the vast majority of members. Their economic contributions were critical to the group's survival. They exercised considerable power for the society as a whole, not just the women members, and moved into leadership roles previously reserved for men, like writing theology and being trustees. And they were outspoken advocates of women's rights.[10] Being a Shaker was not every American woman's notion of the ideal female life, but for more than two hundred years, some women embraced it as a meaningful alternative. Near the end of a long life, Eldress Polly Reed, a Shaker artist and member of the Lead Ministry who had joined a Shaker community by herself at the age of eight, wrote, "A Shaker life has been mine to enjoy from early childhood, & I have never regretted the choice I then made."[11]

## The Oneida Perfectionists

Like the Shakers, the Oneida Community founded by John Humphrey Noyes rejected traditional monogamy, yet at first glance, Oneida's solution makes the community look like a polar opposite of Shakerism. In fact, there were many similarities between the two groups. Both shared a sense of millennial expectation and saw in their own times and their religious and social innovations the beginnings of the kingdom of God on earth. Both separated themselves from American society and practiced economic communism. Both criticized American materialism and individualism, promoting instead the good of the group. Both modified the roles and status of women. While Shakers insisted on celibacy, however, the Oneida Community practiced a system known as "complex marriage." Though vilified by its opponents as "free love," complex marriage was not simple promiscuity. Rather, like the Shakers' celibacy, it was a system whose challenge to traditional Christian monogamy was rooted in both theology and practical considerations as these came together in the extraordinary person of its founder.[12]

Born in Brattleboro, Vermont, in 1811 to a fairly prosperous and prominent New England family, John Humphrey Noyes graduated from Dartmouth College and began to study law. In 1831, however, he was converted in a revival by that famous ex-lawyer, Charles Grandison Finney, and determined to become a minister. He studied first at Andover Seminary, where he joined a group known as "The Brethren," who practiced a kind of mutual criticism for moral improvement, a practice Noyes would later institute in his own community. Finding Andover otherwise insufficiently religious, Noyes transferred to Yale in 1832 and at the end of the school year received a license to preach. Meanwhile, he was attracted by theological perfectionism, and on February 20, 1834, he publicly declared himself to be free from sin. He did not mean, he insisted, that he was therefore faultless and beyond the need for improvement: "I do not pretend to perfection in externals. I claim only purity of heart and the answer of a good conscience toward God."[13] Noyes insisted that spiritual perfection was a biblical demand, possible in this life for Christians since the second coming of Christ had already occurred in the year 70 C.E. Despite a tendency toward theological perfectionism at Yale at the time, church authorities could not condone Noyes's blunt and open avowal and so revoked his license to preach, but Noyes attracted some followers, including a young woman named Abigail Merwin.

For the next several years, Noyes led an itinerant existence, starting in 1834 in New York City, where he experienced great psychological turmoil and, apparently, a break-through mystical experience. He then traveled in New England while he developed his views and attempted to convert others to them. In 1837, Abigail Merwin married another man. A private letter in which Noyes expressed his feelings was published without his permission, and its closing passage became infamous, branding him as an advocate of "free love."

> When the will of God is done on earth, as it is in heaven, *there will be no marriage.* The marriage supper of the Lamb is a feast at which *every dish is free to every guest.* Exclusiveness, jealousy, quarreling have no place there . . . . In a holy community, there is no more reason why sexual intercourse should be restrained by law, than why eating and drinking should be—and there is as little occasion for shame in the one case as the other. . . . I call a certain woman my wife. She is yours, she is Christ's and in him she is the bride of all saints. She is dear in the hand of a stranger, and according to my promise to her I rejoice. My claim upon her cuts directly across the marriage covenant of the world, and God knows the end.[14]

Eventually, Noyes settled in Putney, Vermont; he married Harriet Holton in 1838. Over the next six years, Harriet suffered through five difficult pregnancies and births, with only one surviving child, an experience that influenced Noyes's ideas on marriage and sexuality. Meanwhile, he had converted a small group of friends and family to theological perfectionism, and they began to practice "biblical communism" of property. In 1846, they instituted "complex marriage," an organized system in which each woman was considered the wife of every man and vice versa. For Noyes, it was the logical outcome of the rejection of all exclusivity by purified Christians. People in Putney, however, did not see it that way: Noyes was charged with adultery and arrested. He fled Vermont in 1847, and the next year the rest of the Putney group joined him and a few other sympathizers in Oneida, New York.

At first, times at Oneida were economically hard, but when Sewell Newhouse, the inventor of a highly successful small animal trap, joined the group in 1848, the community began to prosper, making those traps and expanding to other industries, as well as pursuing agriculture. Noyes maintained firm control as a divinely inspired leader, but he also actively wrote and published his ideas for a world he hoped would see the light and follow Oneida's example.

## Complex Marriage

The system of complex marriage practiced for more than thirty years at Oneida was rooted in Noyes' millenialist perfectionism. Individual salvation from sin was to be accompanied by establishment of the kingdom of God on earth, in which neither the private property of capitalism, which promoted greed and selfishness, nor the "private property" of marital exclusivity and a man's "ownership" of his wife would be tolerated.

> In the kingdom of heaven, the institution of marriage which assigns the exclusive possession of one woman to one man, does not exist. Matt. 22:23–30. "In the resurrection they neither marry nor are given in marriage." . . . Christ, in the passage referred to, does not exclude the sexual distinction, or sexual intercourse, from the heavenly state, but only the world's method of assigning the sexes to each other, which alone, creates the difficulty presented in the question of the Sadducees. Their question evidently referred only to the matter of *ownership*. . . . In the kingdom of heaven, the intimate union of life and interests, which in the world is limited to pairs, extends through the whole body of believers; i.e., *complex* marriage takes the place of simple. . . . The abolishment of worldly restrictions on sexual intercourse, is involved in the anti-legality of the gospel. It is incompatible with the state of perfected freedom towards which Paul's gospel of "grace without law" leads, that man should be allowed and required to *love* in all directions, and yet be forbidden to *express* love in its most natural and beautiful form, except in one direction.[15]

The system of complex marriage as developed at Oneida was highly organized. If a man wished to have intercourse with a woman, he asked her directly or through a mediator, but she had the right of refusal. Special or exclusive attachments were forbidden, and an "ascending and descending hierarchy" of spiritual progress shaped choice of partners, as those lower in the scale were encouraged to couple with persons above them. In practice, this usually meant that young men were initiated by older women, and young women by older men. Furthermore, an integral part of the system was what Noyes called "male continence," a practice developed by Noyes to separate what he saw as two distinct parts of intercourse, the (superior) amative function of spiritual communion and pleasure, and the propagative function, which should occur only when conception was desired.[16] Traditional monogamy, Noyes argued, was especially unfair to women, for not only did it make them the property of men, it left them unable to resist male advances that often resulted in debilitating, frequent pregnancies. No woman should have to suffer as Harriet had in the early years of their marriage. In male continence, the man refrained from ejaculation, thus preserving the vital force of his own semen and preventing his partner from becoming pregnant, without denying the mutual pleasure of communion in intercourse. Noyes insisted that men could easily learn the technique, and apparently most of those at Oneida did, for in a twenty-year period after 1848 during which male continence was practiced, "community records show only twelve unplanned births in a group numbering approximately two hundred adults, equally balanced between the sexes, and having frequent sexual congress with a variety of partners during that time."[17] In 1869, the Oneida Community began a new phase, an experiment in "scientific breeding" they called "stirpiculture." Although "amative" intercourse and complex marriage continued for most of the community, "propagative" intercourse was reinstituted in particular cases for the purpose of producing "superior" offspring. Couples could apply to a committee, which also had the power to suggest pairings. Given the Oneida community's underlying assumptions about eugenics and spiritual superiority, it is perhaps not surprising that older male leaders and especially Noyes himself were disproportionately represented as fathers.

## Oneida's Contributions to Women

What did Oneida offer to women in particular? For those who were convinced enough of the truth of Noyes's ideas to overcome traditional sexual morality and join the community, Oneida provided a significant alternative to monogamy: sexual variety and satisfaction without the risks of frequent pregnancy. Nor were Oneida's innovations in sex roles confined to complex marriage, for it was one of the few American communitarian experiments that did not consistently assign work along traditional gender lines. The women of Oneida were encouraged to develop their interests, sharing outdoor and industrial labor with men. In part to facilitate such work, the women adopted a modified "Bloomer" dress and cut their hair.

> Early in the summer [of the first year at Oneida], . . . some of the leading women in the Association took the liberty to dress themselves in short gowns or frocks, with pantaloons, . . . and the

> advantage of the change soon became so manifest that others followed the example, till frocks and pantaloons became the prevailing fashion in the Association. The women say they are far more free and comfortable in this dress than in long gowns; the men think that it improves their looks; and some insist that it is entirely more modest than the common dress.
>
> Another new fashion broke out among the women in the following manner. The ordinary practice of leaving the hair to grow indefinitely, and laboring upon it by the hour daily, merely for the sake of winding it up into a ball and sticking it on the top or back of the head, had become burdensome and distasteful to several of the women. [Having resolved to their own satisfaction that such a fashion did not contradict the spirit of Paul's instructions in I Corinthians 11, the women cut their hair, and the fashion] . . . soon prevailed throughout the Association, and was generally acknowledged to be an improvement of appearance as well as a saving of labor.[18]

Women at Oneida were encouraged to venture into other "male" areas, from outdoor sports like baseball or swimming to bookkeeping and higher education. Such breaks with cultural gender expectations were frequently justified through criticism of "effeminacy," an image of women as delicate, unhealthy, passive, and more concerned with fashion than usefulness. Men and women worked together on special projects, like "bees" to gather a strawberry harvest or increased industrial work to fill a large order. They shared recreational opportunities like croquet, concerts, and plays.[19] Women also took part in "mutual criticism," Oneida's rotating system of discipline that functioned to defuse tensions and provide social control. A small group of community members would meet formally with a particular person, expressing their views on the subject's strengths, weaknesses, and specific needs for change and growth. The subject was to remain silent during the criticism but at another time might serve as critic, just as his or her critics would became subjects in their turn.

Yet female equality was neither thoroughgoing nor an end in itself at Oneida. Some Oneida women were above some men in the "ascending hierarchy," but they were not among the community's top leaders, and they seldom spoke at the "evening meetings" that were a key part of Oneida's religious and communal life. Almost all the "housework," from cleaning and childcare to sewing and laundering the men's clothes, as well as their own, was done by women. Nevertheless, Oneida's system at least provided women with a choice of alternative occupations, and even within the traditional domestic tasks, which demanded a high proportion of women's time, the practice of frequent rotation of jobs provided a certain level of variety. Furthermore, Noyes's theology and biblical interpretation continued to assume that men were superior to women in a Pauline order of creation, and that the sexes have essentially different, if complementary, natures, although men and women were both encouraged to avoid extremes of masculinity and femininity and to cultivate instead positive traits presumed to be natural to the other sex. Noyes, and apparently most of the men and women at Oneida, sympathized with many of the criticisms about the treatment of women made by the women's rights movement of their day, but they believed that its methods and solutions were misguided in setting women *against* men and rejecting female roles and nature. (Whether or not "man-hating" was a fair characterization of the nineteenth-century women's movement is another question. Fair or not, it was an image held by many men and women of the day.)

Outsiders' reactions to Oneida were mixed. Many of their immediate neighbors admired their peaceful and apparently happy life and appreciated their economic contributions: Oneida developed a reputation for honesty and high quality products; it also hired significant numbers of outsiders for domestic and industrial work. But other Americans, especially the clergy, were scandalized by the group's "immoral practices" and pressured public opinion and the government to "do something" about the group. Yet external pressures were ultimately less significant than internal ones in precipitating the community's break-up. Noyes himself was aging, and no single leader appeared capable of taking his place. Instead, several competing factions had developed within the group. Furthermore, the stirpiculture experiment seems to have increased tensions and resentment about complex marriage among some of the younger members, and young men who had been sent off to Harvard or Yale for further education began questioning the community's theology and religious foundations. By 1879, Oneida formally and publicly gave up the practice of complex marriage, and on January 1, 1881, the community was disbanded and replaced by a joint-stock company. John Noyes himself moved to Niagara Falls with a few faithful followers and died there in 1886.

## The Mormons

The Church of Jesus Christ of Latter-day Saints, or Mormons, shared with the Shakers and Oneida a strong millennial sense, belief in continuing revelation through a modern prophet, a demand that followers "come out" of a less enlightened and sinful society, and a rejection of traditional monogamy, basing its alternative, polygamy, on theological grounds. That alternative of polygamy, decried by contemporary critics as barbaric and demeaning to women, and a strictly all-male priesthood might seem to indicate at first glance that nineteenth-century Mormonism had little to offer women searching for wider roles in society and religious leadership. Yet closer study suggests that the Mormons, like the Shakers and the Oneida Community, present a complex picture of women and sectarian religion.

The Church of Jesus Christ of Latter-day Saints was born in the volatile atmosphere of the "burned-over district" of New York when Joseph Smith (1805–1844), a young man dissatisfied with both his prospects and the religious alternatives around him, claimed to have received a divine revelation and discovered a set of "golden plates." With the help of a set of "seer stones," Joseph translated the plates into the *Book of Mormon* before they were swept away by an angel. In 1830, the *Book of Mormon*, containing both a complex account of ancient civilizations in America and definitive answers for most of the theological controversies agitating American Protestants at the time, was published, and the church was formally organized with Smith at its head. The group grew rapidly, and a branch formed in Kirtland, Ohio, to which the New York believers moved in 1831. Despite continuing growth, the young Mormon church was forced to move again in the wake of economic problems and non-Mormons' hostility, finally ending up in Nauvoo, Illinois, where Smith was able to get unusual power and autonomy for his community through a charter that gave them political control and their own militia.

Through the early 1840s the Mormon settlement in Nauvoo prospered, but their neighbors' opposition grew proportionately, fueled by Smith's grandiose claims of power and by rumors that they were practicing "spiritual wifery" or polygamy. When defectors and dissidents within Nauvoo established an opposition press and Smith suppressed it, public anger exploded. Joseph Smith and his brother Hyrum surrendered to the authorities, but a mob attacked the jail where they were being held and lynched them on June 27, 1844. In the wake of this blow, some small groups, including the members of Smith's family who repudiated polygamy, headed in different directions. The dissident Smiths ultimately founded the Reorganized Church of Jesus Christ of Latter-day Saints, but most of the Nauvoo Mormons regrouped under the leadership of Brigham Young and began their trek toward Utah and the Great Salt Lake, where they would be beyond the reach of hostile American neighbors.

Although the Nauvoo period lasted for only a few years, it was extremely important in the formation of the Mormon Church. Joseph Smith consolidated his role as continuing source of divine revelation and organized the theology and authority structures that were critical to his vision of a new, millennial order. The theology and structures would be carried on and further developed by Brigham Young after Smith's death. Among the changes instigated at Nauvoo was the extremely controversial practice of polygamy, even though it was not publicly acknowledged until 1852. Smith presented the practice as the subject of a formal divine revelation in 1843, although it had begun secretly before that time. While Smith cited the precedent of Hebrew patriarchs and insisted it was necessary for those who would achieve the highest level of celestial marriage in the afterlife, even his close associates like Brigham Young were initially offended by the suggestion. Emma Hale Smith, Joseph's wife, never truly endorsed it, though she reluctantly accepted her husband's secret marriages to other women,[20] and many of the women approached by Smith or his close associates were equally shocked but ultimately came to accept the new system, due to family pressures, economic need, or religious conviction.

Once they were established in Utah Territory, Mormons were able to practice polygamy publicly for several decades, an experiment that Foster calls "the largest, best-organized, and most controversial venture in radically restructuring marriage and family life in nineteenth-century America."[21] While outsiders consistently expressed the most vehement opposition and condemnation, convinced that Mormon women were victims who had been deluded or cowed into submission, some Mormon women themselves were publicly outspoken in defense of the system. Why? The primary reason was religious conviction. As one Mormon woman, herself a plural wife, explained:

> I am sure that women would never have accepted polygamy had it not been for their religion. No woman ever consented to its practice without great sacrifice on her part. . . . The principle of Celestial Marriage was considered the capstone of the Mormon religion. Only by practicing it would the highest exaltation in the Celestial Kingdom of God be obtained.[22]

Mormons believed in two kinds of marriages, temporal unions and marriages "sealed" for time and eternity. Only men and women thus sealed would enjoy the continued joys of the afterlife, and the highest kingdoms were reserved for men with plural wives and their children.

It would be as unrealistic to assume that every Mormon woman was unequivocally content with polygamy as it would be to accept the assessment of contemporary critics that they were all miserable victims of male Mormons' lust and tyranny.[23] Indeed, the majority of Mormon marriages were monogamous,[24] and there were undoubtedly strains and jealousies in some plural households. Nevertheless, the system held out some compensations for women that could reinforce theological conviction. Not only did plural marriage mean a higher position in the world to come, it also generally carried higher status in this life, because it was male Mormon leaders who practiced plural marriage most frequently and had the most wives. Since Mormon men were expected to demonstrate their financial ability to support an additional wife and her children before they married again, plural marriage represented for some women economic security as well as the status and companionship of a family, an especially attractive option for immigrant converts who came to Utah from Europe or eastern America. Plural marriages, at their best, provided women with the close companionship of other women in an extended kinship system. They also allowed wives to divide domestic duties. Considering that many

Mormon men were absent for long periods of time on missionary travels, such emotional and practical help could be very valuable. Moreover, having husbands who were absent on missions, involved in church business, or dividing their time among several wives meant that these pioneer women developed considerable economic and emotional independence. While family and children were seen as women's most important concerns, the frontier culture of Utah demanded that women take on additional roles outside the home, and the male Mormon leadership encouraged such female initiative.

## Women's Roles and the Female Relief Society

Only male Mormons could exercise the formal religious leadership of the priesthood. Yet women participated in religious expressions like "spiritual gifts" and female temple ordinances, and they organized their own sphere of church activity through the Female Relief Society in ways strikingly similar to developments in other religious groups in nineteenth-century America. It is not surprising that a group convinced it was experiencing a new dispensation would be marked by gifts of the Spirit—dreams, visions, speaking in tongues—and these appeared by the Nauvoo period, manifest in women as well as men. While such ecstatic experiences diminished over time amidst warnings that they not be misused, the gift of healing continued to be exercised by women throughout the nineteenth century, most often for families and other women, especially those about to undergo childbirth. While some male leaders were critical, others supported the women as long as they distinguished such healings and blessings as believers from the temple healings and blessings of the male priesthood. Not until the early twentieth century were these women's spiritual functions eliminated in favor of exclusively male priesthood administration.[25] Furthermore, women not only received temple ordinances like baptism, endowment, healing, and sealing in celestial marriage, they also administered certain temple ordinances to other women.[26]

In addition to the limited exercise of religious leadership through spiritual gifts and female temple ordinances, Mormon women developed their own church organization, which formed a significant female power base in the nineteenth century. The Female Relief Society was begun by Joseph Smith in March 1842 with the somewhat ambiguous charge that it would be "under the priesthood after a pattern of the priesthood."[27] Emma Hale Smith was named president by her husband; she chose two associates, and Eliza Snow was its secretary. The primary purpose of the early organization was, as its name implies, charitable work, but it also provided a setting for the exercise of women's spiritual gifts and for veiled sparring between Emma and Joseph, who frequently addressed its meetings, over the new doctrine of polygamy.[28] The Relief Society was disbanded in 1844 amidst mounting tensions in Nauvoo. Local groups began to appear again a decade later, but it was not until 1869 that a central organization was re-established by Brigham Young and put under the presidency of Eliza Snow, who had been a plural wife of Joseph Smith and later of Brigham Young.

The most powerful woman in Mormonism in the second half of the nineteenth century, combining personal gifts with access to male leadership, Eliza R. Snow (1804–1887) was simultaneously president of the Relief Society and the head of female temple officiators. Under her direction, the Relief Society established local and regional branches throughout the church. Though loyal and deferential to the male priesthood, the women's group was organizationally and financially independent. The women continued informal charitable work but also moved into more institutionalized forms of care, supporting hospitals, promoting the education of nurses, and sponsoring early women physicians, summer camps and schools for preschool children. The society offered classes for its members in a range of cultural, literary, and practical areas, and promoted the exchange of ideas among Mormon women through its meetings and through a journal, the *Woman's Exponent,* which was founded in 1872. Though approved by the Mormon priesthood, the paper was financed, run, and written by women and covered topics from literature to theology to politics.

The *Woman's Exponent* functioned as a platform not only for the defense of Mormon beliefs, polygamy in particular, but also for women's rights. Decades before their eastern sisters, women in Utah territory received the right to vote in 1870. Female suffrage was applauded, and its loss through the Edmunds-Tucker Act of 1887 was protested in the pages of the journal, where readers could also find criticism of America's double sexual standard, unequal pay and education for women, and the image of the fashionable but helpless "lady."[29] Despite serious differences on polygamy, Mormon women leaders made common cause with the more radical wing of the women's movement under Elizabeth Cady Stanton and Susan B. Anthony and sent delegates to national meetings.

By the end of the nineteenth century, Mormon women regained the vote, but the Mormon church had officially given up the practice of polygamy as the price of statehood. As the church moved into the twentieth century, the activities and independence of women were sharply restricted, and the single ideal of motherhood replaced the wider range of roles available to pioneer Mormon women. Various forces were at work in the change: Mormons lost the isolation that permitted their distinctive marital patterns and strengthened their unity; new patterns of control within the church emerged; and the influences of American culture were more immediate and attractive. Nevertheless, a combination of religious fervor for a new order, a frontier setting, and even the system of polygamy had for a time given Mormon women significant role options and independence to balance their religious subordination. Although polygamy was emotionally difficult for many Mormon women, it provided for others a setting that encouraged female bonding and independence. As a Mormon woman defending polygamy in an 1874 issue of the *Woman's Exponent* wrote:

> Is there then nothing worth living for, but to be petted, humored and caressed, by a man? That is all very well as far as it goes, but that man is the only thing in existence worth living for I fail to see. All honor and reverence to good men; but they and their attentions are not the only sources of happiness on the earth, and need not fill up every thought of woman. And when men see that women can exist without their being constantly at hand, that they can learn to be self-reliant or depend upon each other for more or less happiness, it will perhaps take a little of the conceit out of some of them.[30]

## Christian Science

Mary Baker Eddy and the Christian Science that she founded (or as she preferred to put it, "discovered") holds particular interest for the study of women and American religion. Unlike the Shakers, the Oneida Community, and the Church of Jesus Christ of Latter-day Saints, the Church of Christ, Scientist, never advocated or practiced a systematic communal existence as an outgrowth of its theology. It did, however, offer women an androgynous vision of God, new roles for religious leadership, and the authority of a female founder, Mary Baker Eddy.

Born on July 16, 1821, in New Hampshire, Mary Baker was the youngest child in a substantial New England Congregationalist family. The dominant concerns of her maturity were prefigured in her childhood: she showed an early interest in religion, while her health was sufficiently fragile that much of her education occurred at home. In 1843, she married George Washington Glover and moved with him to the South, but he died less than a year later, leaving her a pregnant and penniless widow. She returned home to New Hampshire where her son was born, but her health was so poor that he was given to a foster family. Despite continuing health problems, in 1853 she married again, this time to Daniel Patterson, an itinerant dentist. The marriage was not a happy one: Patterson was frequently absent—at first, for his profession, and then as a Confederate prisoner during the Civil War. They were poor, and Mary's health deteriorated even further. In the course of her search for a cure, she met Phineas Quimby, an advocate of the mental basis for ill health and therefore of natural healing such as he believed Jesus had done, and she enjoyed an immediate recovery. Converted, Mary began lecturing on his theories, but when

Quimby died in 1866, she was devastated, emotionally and physically. A few weeks later, she slipped on the ice, hurt her back, and was, she reported, given up as a hopeless case by physicians. Yet three days later, she was miraculously healed after reading Matthew 9:2. (Later critics were more skeptical about the nature of her injury and cure, citing the physician who treated her. Nevertheless, the event was clearly decisive for her, and her account was accepted by her followers.)

Mary Patterson concluded that it was up to her to take up her mentor's work as a teacher and healer, and she spent the next decade in wandering poverty and obscurity while refining her own ideas. By 1875, she founded a Christian Scientists' Home in Lynn, Massachusetts, and published the first edition of *Science and Health*. In 1877, having divorced Patterson in 1873 for desertion, she married Asa Gilbert Eddy. Now her movement began to grow rapidly, not only through her publications, including literally hundreds of editions of *Science and Health* to which she added in 1883 a *Key to the Scriptures*, but even more as a result of her extraordinary skills as a teacher, conceded even by her critics. The Church of Christ, Scientist was formally organized in 1879, followed a few years later by the Massachusetts Metaphysical College, with Mary Baker Eddy as the central figure in both. But in the late 1880s, she began to withdraw into seclusion, emerging only rarely thereafter. These years were marked by considerable controversy, often rooted in conflict with defecting students, rivals, and public critics, and by obsessive fear of "Malicious Animal Magnetism," a destructive mental energy focused on her by her enemies. Yet she was able to consolidate and maintain absolute personal authority, and she established a solid and lasting institution under the "Mother Church" in Boston. Mary Baker Eddy died in 1910, a very powerful and wealthy woman.[31]

## Developments for Women

That Christian Science as a new and enduring religious group was founded by an American woman is in itself significant. (Another modern religious body, the Seventh Day Adventists, was also founded in the nineteenth century by a woman, Ellen Gould Harmon White, but beyond the unique prophetic authority of White herself, that group presented no major challenges to traditional views on God or women's religious activities.) Christian Science, however, offered further developments for American women. Eddy viewed God as dual: male and female, father and mother. As she wrote in *Science and Health*, "The ideal man corresponds to creation, to intelligence, and Truth. The ideal woman corresponds to Life and Love. We have not as much authority, in divine Science, for considering God masculine, as we have for considering Him feminine, for Love imparts the clearest idea of Deity."[32] Whether Eddy was influenced by Shakers on this point is unclear. Also debated is whether she saw herself, as Ann Lee may have and as Lee's followers surely did, as a second incarnation or messiah. While Eddy publicly repudiated such a claim, there is evidence in her writings and the evaluations of her early followers that she at times saw herself in a uniquely revelatory role. She argued that a woman must reveal the motherhood of God and complete the full spiritual truth of Christianity.[33] Clearly, for Eddy, women were not inherently inferior but were at least equally in the image of dual-gendered Deity. Indeed, in Eddy's interpretation of Genesis, it was the much-maligned Eve who was "first to abandon the belief in the material origin of man and to discern spiritual creation. . . . This enables woman to be first to interpret the Scriptures in their true sense, which reveals the spiritual origin of man."[34] Here was the foundation of Eddy's theology, developed from the germs of Quimby's thought: the premise that all reality is spiritual, and that the objective world of the senses and matter—and hence sin, disease, and death—is ultimately unreal.[35]

Not only did Christian Science offer to the women attracted to its message an androgynous image of God and a unique revelatory role for a woman, it also provided opportunities for religious leadership in two ways. First, as Christian Scientist societies developed, they were structured with a parallel male-female leadership in the official readers, whose task was to read from the Bible and from *Science and Health*. (No personal elaboration or "sermon" was permitted for readers of either gender.) Second, women found careers within the church as missionaries of Eddy's message and as healing practitioners, a potential means of economic support and independence. Since matter is ultimately unreal, to overcome ill health, a person must simply recognize that unreality; healing is a mental discipline that once understood can be used effectively for self and others. Eddy's ideas here fit into a nineteenth-century medical world that was both diverse and divided, with the emerging "scientific" (and male-controlled) medicine challenged by a range of "natural" and spiritual treatments, from water-cures and Grahamite diets to mesmerism and spiritualism.

Mary Baker Eddy's relationship to the formal women's rights movement of her day is ambiguous. On the one hand, she offered women religious and economic independence from men, attacked the male power structures of church and medicine, promoted legal and economic equality for women, and gave at least a qualified endorsement to woman's suffrage. Yet women's rights were not her primary concern. Like many women of her age, she accepted an image of women as naturally spiritual, pure, nurturing, self-effacing, and essentially more moral than men.[36] Nor did she propose changes in marriage patterns. While she suggested in chapter 3 of *Science and Health* that marriage would disappear in the final spiritual consummation, she heartily endorsed monogamy, chastity, and traditional sex roles in this world: "Man should not be required to participate in all the annoyances and cares of domestic economy, nor should woman be expected to understand political economy."[37]

Mary Baker Eddy was by no means the only woman in late nineteenth-century America whose public pronouncements were sometimes at odds with her personal activities, for she promoted domesticity while pursuing an independent and successful career. But in her case, the contrast was especially striking at two points. She extolled motherhood and its educational influence, even as she had effectively abandoned her own child to others' care. Moreover, she was unwilling to share with other women the significant religious power and leadership that she, as a woman, had obtained. True, Christian Science offered women the qualified religious leadership of being readers or healing practitioners, but they were never permitted to challenge or share Eddy's own prestige and position. Not only was her personal authority and control of the church absolute, she filled the next positions in its central executive structure with men, and any potential female rivals who arose, most notably her disciple, Augusta Stetson, were ruthlessly cut off. Stetson continued to protest her loyalty to Eddy, although she was never reinstated, and maintained her own following among a dissident group of Christian Scientists in New York. Within the structure of Christian Science, women might indeed appreciate the theological innovations of its female founder, but there was little room for further explorations or prominent leadership of their own.

## Summary

### Female Imagery of God

Shakers, Oneida Perfectionists, Mormons, and Christian Scientists were neither the only forms of sectarian religion nor the only utopian communal experiments in America during the nineteenth century, but they raised a number of important issues for women and religion, some of which were reflected in other sectarian or communal groups of the time. Out of a critique of exclusively male images of God, feminist theology in the late twentieth century has rediscovered precedents of female imagery from a variety of sources, including passages in Hebrew Scriptures and medieval mystics like Dame Julian of Norwich, and hence has focused on the Shakers and Christian Science with their prominent belief in God as mother as a counterpoint to the traditional view of God as father. Less frequently noted is the Mormon concept of a mother in heaven, partly because the image was more muted in Mormon theology and practice, partly because the heavenly mother was as clearly secondary in the Mormon theology as were women themselves in the Mormon church. As Linda P. Wilcox notes, "The idea of a Mother in Heaven is a shadowy and elusive one floating around the edges of Mormon consciousness."[38] Nevertheless, the concept existed from the early days of Mormonism, a logical consequence and necessity of a system in which procreation and parenthood transcended earthly life and continued on the celestial plane. The idea was endorsed, if hardly emphasized, by early leaders like Brigham Young and was enshrined in a popular hymn by Eliza Snow: "In the Heav'ns are parents single? No, the thought makes reason stare! Truth is reason; Truth eternal Tells me I've a mother there."[39] A few other groups like the Rappites or Zoarites posited an androgynous deity or pre-Fall human, but the image did not imply greater respect or equality for women, whose female nature and existence remained tied to the Fall.[40]

Female imagery for God in some cases supported increased religious leadership for women, as in Shakerism and Christian Science, but it was neither a sufficient nor a necessary condition for such female leadership. Indeed, in Christian Science, leadership for women other than Mary Baker Eddy was limited, and in other groups founded or led by women, notably the Seventh Day Adventists and the Amana Inspirationists, who flourished after the Civil War, the authority of the female leaders, Ellen White and Barbara Heinemann, respectively, was unique, based on their individual roles as divinely inspired prophets.[41] Having a female founder or leader did not necessarily mean that other women in a religious group received equal authority or opportunities along with men, let alone instead of them. Yet another movement in mid-nineteenth-century America, the Spiritualists, did offer consistent leadership roles to women.

## Spiritualism

While the particular nineteenth-century manifestations of Spiritualism are generally traced to upstate New York and the "rappings" of the Fox sisters starting in 1848, neither the sisters nor their methods dominated the development of Spiritualism in midcentury. Rather, the central role was taken by the trance medium, usually a woman, who gave spirit-inspired addresses to large audiences at a time when few women dared to take the public platform. Mediums could be so daring both because they were "overpowered" by a higher authority, not claiming it in their own persons, and because their characteristics and actions fit so well with dominant cultural images of women's nature. As Ann Braude writes:

> Spiritualism embraced the notion that women were pious by nature. But, instead of concluding that the qualities that suited women to religion unsuited them to public roles, Spiritualism made the delicate constitution and nervous excitability commonly attributed to femininity a virtue and lauded it as a qualification for religious leadership. . . . Mediumship allowed women to discard limitations on women's role without questioning accepted ideas about woman's nature.[42]

Thus Spiritualism gave many women a significant and central role as religious leaders and authorities, but even there, the leadership was qualified, for speakers on Spiritualist platforms "observed a rigorous sexual division of labor": though women spoke under the direct influence of spirits, men presided, ran meetings, and lectured in a "normal" state.[43] Like Shakerism and Christian Science, Spiritualism made a form of religious leadership available to the many, not just the few, yet while several individual Spiritualist women attained considerable power and fame as mediums, the very fluid and individualistic nature of the movement precluded the emergence of a single, authoritative founder or leader, male or female.

## Leadership

Neither Oneida Perfectionists nor Mormons offered women prominent leadership roles in the central organization, but at Oneida, neither male nor female community members approached the religious authority of the community's charismatic founder. Noyes, like other founders of sectarian religious groups, never proposed to give his followers equal access to leadership, being convinced that he had unique insights and special divine authorization. While the Mormon theological leadership of the priesthood remained exclusively male, nineteenth-century Mormon women did develop their own spheres of activity. Especially in the early period, Mormon women exercised religious authority through spiritual gifts and healings, for, like the spiritual gifts of Shaker women during Mother Ann's Work and the activities of trance mediums in Spiritualism, immediate spirit direction superseded normal church structures or cultural limitations. Furthermore, the Mormon Female Relief Society paralleled in many ways the women's church, mission, benevolent, and reform groups in mainline Christianity. If the Mormon women's sphere within the church's organization was ultimately subordinate to a male power structure, it functioned with sufficient independence to provide women with genuine opportunities for expression and leadership.

## Marriage and Sexuality

Not every sectarian religious or utopian communal group of nineteenth-century America attempted to modify traditional monogamous marriage patterns, but those that did proved consistently fascinating to both their contemporaries and to subsequent historians. The most common alternative practice was celibacy, a long tradition in Christian history, although not one generally practiced in mixed-gender communities. While most Protestant Americans had serious reservations about principled celibacy, whether practiced by Catholic priests, monks, and nuns or by communal groups like the Shakers, the arrangement elicited a grudging if uncomprehending toleration from the wider public. Far greater hostility was aroused by groups who proposed a system that allowed sexual intercourse outside the bounds of legally and religiously sanctioned monogamy. Oneida's complex marriage and Mormon polygamy horrified most Americans, as did the "free love" supposedly promoted by Spiritualists and a few socialist communities. With a few exceptions, what Spiritualists and socialists advocated was not actually "free" love in the sense of unbridled promiscuity or orgies, but was rather an insistence that unions be based on "spiritual affinity" and true love, coupled with support for easier availability of divorce for persons caught in unhappy marriages.[44] Some principles and goals, if not methods, of sectarian or communal sexual practices were, in fact, shared by leaders in the women's rights movement who sympathized with the plight of women who had few alternatives once married, to continual sexual availability to their husbands and the consequent physical and emotional risk of frequent pregnancies. The celibacy of the Shakers, the complex marriage of Oneida, the principles of Spiritualism, and even, in its way, the polygamy of the Mormons all offered women an escape from the prospect of too many unwanted pregnancies at a time when birth control was neither respectable nor reliable.

Although the practical results for female reproduction were similar, if not identical, among these groups, the underlying assessments of sexuality were quite different. For hundreds of years, Christianity had adopted a modified spirit-matter dualism that viewed sexuality and intercourse as the epitome of the "lower" half of that dualism, especially typical of woman and tolerated within marriage for its procreative results. By the nineteenth century, women had "changed sides"—that is, it was they who had naturally pure and asexual natures and men who could barely control their lust—but the generally negative assessment of sexuality (as clearly distinct from motherhood) continued. Celibate groups like the Shakers took the tradition to one logical extreme. While they exempted redeemed women from the greater guilt of Eve and a natural association with the carnal side of dualistic reality, they insisted that both men and women, to be saved, must abandon the intrinsic sinfulness of sexuality. Mary Baker Eddy resolved the tension in a different but equally extreme way: by denying the very reality of the material, the "lower side" of dualism for both men and women. Sexuality was not so much a real evil to be avoided as something that in an ultimate sense did not even exist. Whatever concessions she made to monogamous unions in this life, marriage and sexuality had no place in the consummation of a spiritual kingdom. On the other hand, Spiritualists, Oneida Perfectionists, and Mormons, despite the differences in their respective proposals, presented theological bases for a more positive view of sexuality. As radical individualists, Spiritualists criticized traditional marriage when it justified a husband's authority over and unrestrained sexual access to his legal wife, but they approved the sexual contact freely chosen by men and women in the context of love and spiritual affinity.[45] Noyes celebrated the "amative" function of intercourse and explicitly endorsed female sexual pleasure as legitimate, and Mormons pictured a heaven in which marriage and procreation continued beyond the bounds of death.

## A Mix of Views

Finally, while sectarian groups raised issues of women's rights beyond those of women's religious leadership, marriage, and sexuality, no group's "advanced" views in one area necessarily correlated with "advanced" views on other topics. Thus, Shakers provided a theological breakthrough with their understanding of a Mother God and significant religious and community leadership roles for women, but they were quite traditional in their assignment of work roles by gender, while Oneida, without a female image of the divine or particular opportunities for female religious leadership, encouraged women to take on "male" tasks and to adopt a freer style of dress and shorter hair. The Oneida community as a matter of principle broadened cultural perceptions of appropriate jobs for women, but in the Mormon pioneer experience, this broadening was a matter of practical necessity, although the results were enjoyed by women of both groups. Health reform was an issue of broad and immediate relevance to American women of the nineteenth century, involving changes in dress and activity as well as issues of diet and "natural" medical treatment, and was promoted in one way or another by groups from the Seventh Day Adventists and Spiritualists to Oneida Perfectionists and Christian Scientists. Although Noyes and his Oneida Community, including its female members, questioned the value of women's voting, Mary Baker Eddy and Shaker leaders gave suffrage at least a qualified endorsement in the latter half of the nineteenth century, and Mormons and Spiritualists were firm and consistent supporters.

The alternative visions of sectarian Christianity are an important chapter in the story of women and religion in America, first, because they were real religious choices that attracted many women; second, because they raised possibilities for new views of women's religious leadership, marriage patterns, and women's rights. Each group offered elements that would prove attractive to late twentieth-century feminists, yet none provides a complete or consistent model for contemporary feminist concerns. That was, after all, not their goal. For all their radicalism, feminism in a full or abstract sense was not the top priority of any of these groups. The changes for women that they promoted, whether modest or radical, arose within broader visions of theological conviction and social change, and the groups took advantage of the relative freedom and fluidity of nineteenth-century America to put those ideas into practice. Even while they encountered hostility and misunderstanding, they shared with the wider society a firm conviction that, fueled by religious conviction, progress and change in this life as well as the next were thoroughly possible.

# 17

# A Nineteenth-Century Feminist Critique of Religion

In conjunction with the publication of the *Woman's Bible,* Elizabeth Cady Stanton posed two questions: "1. Have the teachings of the Bible advanced or retarded the emancipation of women? 2. Have they dignified or degraded the Mothers of the Race?"[1] While Cady Stanton's own conclusions were clear—the Bible and organized religion had been more a hindrance than a help to women's emancipation—the responses to those questions that were published in an appendix to the *Woman's Bible,* many from leading women of her day, displayed a range of opinions. Twentieth-century historians, too, have differed over the question of whether religion helped or hurt the cause of women. In Cady Stanton's own day, however, few Americans were willing publicly to attack the Bible and Christianity in as radical and sweeping a way as she did. Even women who criticized particular interpretations of key biblical passages or who chafed at exclusive male control of formal church leadership seldom denounced the Bible or the Christian church as a whole. Far more commonly, they insisted that, rightly understood, the Bible justified woman's equality. Like the vast majority of American Christians, they held as an article of faith that Christianity elevated and increased respect for woman, although there was significant disagreement about what the practical results of that elevation should be. While many Americans, male and female, feared that woman's high and respected position would be irretrievably damaged by removing women from their pedestals, their natural and divinely ordained spheres (an opinion frequently endorsed by clergy), others found commitments to both women's rights and Christianity to be compatible.

Nevertheless, throughout the nineteenth century a few voices were raised that not only rejected traditional religion but also criticized churches for their complicity in preventing woman's advancement at the same time as they exploited the credulity and devotion of their female members. In this chapter, I focus on a few prominent women who combined support for women's rights with a radical critique of institutional religion: Frances Wright, Ernestine Rose, Margaret Fuller, Elizabeth Cady Stanton, and Matilda Joslyn Gage.

## Frances Wright

Frances Wright was born in Scotland in 1795 to rather radical parents, but they died when she was only two years old, so she and her younger sister Camilla were raised by an aunt and a grandfather. These relatives provided her with the comforts of affluence and an extensive private education, but the young Fanny had little sympathy for their conservatism. As young adults, Fanny and Camilla went to live with a great-uncle, James Mylne, a college professor at Glasgow whose liberal sympathies they found more congenial, and Fanny's political radicalism and religious skepticism were further developed. She later recounted that her interest in America as a republican beacon of hope for the world was aroused at this time, and in 1818, the two sisters left for an extended visit to the United States, where their connections and wealth assured them of a warm welcome and the freedom to travel extensively. Returning to England, Fanny Wright published in 1820 her *Views of Society and Manners in America,* which, despite some criticisms of slavery, presented a highly positive picture of this new nation. Over the next few years, she developed friendships with Jeremy Bentham and Lafayette, and she and Camilla followed the French hero to America again in 1824.

Once in America, Fanny Wright more openly denounced slavery and investigated the experiments of the socialist radical, Robert Owen, activities that both lessened the high regard with which an American public had previously responded to her book and that led in 1825 to her establishment in Tennessee of a racially mixed communitarian experiment called Nashoba. The experiment was idealistic—her idea was that its black members would through labor in the community eventually earn their freedom—but it was never particularly successful in either recruitment or production. After Fanny left for Europe to restore her health, accompanied by Robert Dale Owen (the son), defections further undermined the colony's fragile existence, as did publicity about an alliance between her Scottish overseer and a mulatto woman and Nashoba's endorsement of "free love."

Despite Nashoba's failure, Fanny Wright returned to America and embarked on a series of public lectures. For most Americans, the impropriety of a woman addressing mixed public audiences was exacerbated by her uncompromisingly radical views on religion, women, and race, and Fanny Wright gained notoriety as "The Great Red Harlot of Infidelity." In the winter of 1829–30, at considerable personal expense, she took the blacks from Nashoba to be freed in Haiti. She also got pregnant during the trip and so, after returning briefly to the United States, left again in 1830 for Europe, where her daughter was born. Eventually she married the baby's father, Phiquepal D'Arusmont, but the remainder of her life was not particularly happy. Her beloved sister Camilla died. She quarreled with or became estranged from many old friends. The marriage was not very successful, and ultimately both her husband and daughter turned against her before her death on December 13, 1852.[2] Nevertheless, later leaders of the American women's movement would honor her for her pioneer work in the cause of women's rights, despite (or in a few cases, because of) her religious radicalism and "immoral" ideas.

## A Daughter of the Enlightenment

Fanny Wright was convinced that traditional religions, including Christianity, were intrinsically irrational, had produced overwhelmingly harmful effects for humanity, and impeded human progress. In the spirit of a true daughter of the Enlightenment, she insisted that knowledge must be based on facts, which may be ascertained by the senses and arranged by the human mind. Hence religion, with its conflicting traditions and claims of supernatural occurrences, cannot be tested and validated by the individual's reason and thus does not qualify as knowledge. Nor did she allow for religion even the utilitarian benefit of promoting morality: "so far from entrenching human conduct within the gentle barriers of peace and love, religion has ever been, and now is, the deepest source of contentions, wars, persecutions for conscience sake, angry words, angry feelings, backbitings, slanders, suspicions, false judgments, evil interpretations, unwise, unjust, injurious, inconsistent actions."[3] Morality, rather, was a rule of life to be developed by rational individuals through experience and proper education in a republican setting that recognized the individual worth of every human being.

Wright did not single out Christianity as theoretically worse than other religions—indeed, she had an occasional good word for Jesus as a man, and she was convinced that he would have been estranged and appalled by the religion practiced in his name[4]—but she was deeply distressed by its growing influence in America in the wake of the Second Great Awakening. Wright was particularly bitter in her denunciations of the clergy, or "priestcraft," insofar as they encouraged people to waste their time and money on church buildings and missionary endeavors. (Wright would have preferred that support go to "Halls of Science.")[5] She also believed the clergy thwarted free inquiry and reason in the interests of the establishment: "the hired preachers of all sects, creeds, and religions, never do, and never can, teach any thing but what is in conformity with the opinions of those who pay them."[6] Wright's attack on religion was not generally gender-specific; that is, she did not single out biblical statements or Christian traditions about women as her central critique. But she did believe that the power of priestcraft was particularly detrimental for women, since women had fewer opportunities for education than men and thus were more credulous and susceptible to clerical influence.

> I will ask if two professions do not now rule the land and its inhabitants? I will ask, whether your legislatures are not governed by lawyers and your households by priests? And I will farther ask, whether the deficient instruction of the mass of your population does not give to lawyers their political ascendancy; and whether the ignorance of women be not the cause that your domestic hearths are invaded by priests?[7]

Fanny Wright's views on women were rooted in the same commitment to principles of reason, republicanism, freedom, and the importance of the individual that underlay her critique of traditional religion; that is, women have the same natural rights and deserve the same opportunities as men because they are equal human beings. Yet while this philosophical justification was central, she also appealed to men's self-interest to, for example, support female education, arguing that such women would make better partners in happier marriages and better mothers for the next generation.[8] Wright occasionally argued from the stance so common in the nineteenth century that women deserve more rights because of their superior female nature. This argument appeared most notably in her last work, *England the Civilizer,* where she attacked "the male principle" that had dominated history. The female instinct, she argued, worked for "the conservation, care, and happiness of the species. . . . the female instinct assumes a character commensurate with the wider range of the human faculties, and originates, sustains, and promotes the whole scheme of progressive civilization." Yet men and their governments withheld the benefits of the female principle from civilization by "forcibly circumscribing all the holy influences and lofty aspirations of woman within the narrowest precincts of the individual family circle . . . by forcibly closing her eyes upon the claims of the great human family without that circle."[9] Nevertheless, the dominant justification in Wright's arguments for women's rights was women's status as equal persons, not a special female nature.

Fanny Wright was not alone in the first half of the nineteenth century in her passionate commitment to better education for women, for women's own sake and for the good of humanity, although few would have endorsed her proposed solution: government-run and -supported boarding schools for children from the age of two on, so that a rising generation would not be tainted by the superstitions and prejudices of their parents. But Wright's ideas on sexuality and marriage were horrifyingly immoral to most Americans of her day. Well before even the more radical leaders of the women's rights movement would add more widespread access to divorce to their list of changes needed by women, Fanny Wright went further, endorsing sexuality as "the strongest and . . . the noblest of the human passions" and questioning the marriage tie itself as an external, cultural, and frequently immoral imposition on men's and women's freedom. And as if that were not enough to send pulpit, press, and public into a frenzy, she suggested miscegenation as a potential solution to the race problem![10]

Such ideas ensured that Fanny Wright would be widely vilified in her own day as a threat to religion, morality, and civilization itself, to the point that her name became an "ism"—Fanny Wrightism—used as a scare word to stifle further consideration of her ideas. In addition, her personality may have contributed to her unpopularity, for she could be abrasive and insensitive. She was so supremely self-confident of the rational and self-evident truth of her own views that she could hardly imagine the possibility of good faith dissent. Yet it may be that without that self-assurance, Fanny Wright could never have championed the ideas she did nor withstood the opposition she encountered.

At the Tenth National Woman's Rights Convention, held in New York in May 1860, Ernestine L. Rose commented:

> Frances Wright was the first woman in this country who spoke on the equality of the sexes. She had indeed a hard task before her. The elements were entirely unprepared. She had to break up the time-hardened soil of conservatism, and her reward was sure—the same reward that is always bestowed upon those who are in the vanguard of any great movement. She was subjected to public odium, slander, and persecution. But these were not the only things she received. Oh, she had her reward!— . . . the eternal reward of knowing that she had done her duty; the reward springing from consciousness of right, of endeavoring to benefit unborn generations.[11]

## Ernestine Rose

Though fifteen years younger than Wright, Ernestine Rose was also a pioneer of the American movement for women's rights, as well as a radical critic of traditional religions. Like Wright, Rose was born in Europe, was influenced by the Enlightenment and Robert Owen, and came to America with high expectations for freedom and democracy, but in other ways, the early experiences of the two women were significantly different.

Ernestine Potowski was born in Pietrkow, Poland, in 1810, the only child of a pious and respected Jewish rabbi. Perhaps because she had no brothers, her father allowed her to begin the study of Hebrew as a young child, though he did not really approve of female education or of Ernestine's iconoclastic questions. As her biographer reports, she was "a rebel at the age of five; at the age of fourteen she was a heretic."[12] She questioned her father and her faith about traditional doctrines and practices, especially those that limited female aspiration and implied female inferiority. The crisis came after her mother's death when Ernestine was sixteen:

without her knowledge, her father arranged a marriage for her to a man nearer his own age, promising as a dowry the inheritance Ernestine had received from her mother. She not only refused the marriage, she took her case to a Polish court, won, gave the inheritance to her father anyway, and left home in 1827. She went to Berlin, where she managed to support herself as well as further her education, and after brief stays in other parts of Europe, she came to England where she met Robert Owen, whose political philosophy and religious free thought she embraced as her own. In 1836, she married William Rose, a silversmith and fellow disciple of Owen, and the couple left for America to settle in New York City.

In America, Ernestine Rose quickly became involved in the antislavery cause and the beginnings of a women's rights movement, working specifically in New York for the passage of an act to restore the property rights of married women. Under the English common law that prevailed in the United States at the time, a married woman had virtually no legal rights: she could not own property in her own name or make contracts; she had no legal rights of guardianship for her children; nothing prevented a man from expropriating any property his wife had before their marriage or any of her earnings thereafter; and he could apprentice a child away without her consent. Given her own experiences, the need for change seemed to Ernestine Rose painfully obvious, but it was twelve years after the act was first introduced in 1836 that it finally passed in 1848. The cause was not a popular one, and Rose recalled that it took her five months to obtain five signatures on a petition.

Although Ernestine Rose was not present at the historic meeting in Seneca Falls in 1848, she was closely associated with the woman's rights movement thereafter; she served as an officer and speaker at numerous conventions and was an active, popular, and effective lecturer on behalf of the cause. As those who worked with her later recalled, "Those who sat with her on the platform in bygone days, well remember her matchless powers as a speaker; and how safe we all felt while she had the floor, that neither in manner, sentiment, argument, nor repartee, would she in any way compromise the dignity of the occasion."[13] Like Fanny Wright, Rose's primary justification for her work was woman's status as a human being, who thus deserved equal rights as a matter of simple justice. As president of the national convention in Philadelphia in 1854, she said:

> There is one argument which in my estimation is the argument of arguments, why woman should have her rights; not on account of expediency, not on account of policy, though these too show the reasons why she should have her rights; but we claim . . . our rights on the broad ground of human rights; and I for one again will say, I promise not how we shall use them.[14]

Thus she had little patience for those who feared that any changes would destroy woman's finer influences and character.

> It is high time . . . to compel man by the might of right to give woman her political, legal and social rights. . . . She will find her own sphere in accordance with her capacities, powers, and tastes; and yet she will be woman still. . . . Away with that folly that her rights would be detrimental to her character—that if she is recognized as the equal to man, she would cease to be woman![15]

Like most women's rights supporters, Ernestine Rose was also active in abolitionism and hoped that the obvious justice of the causes and the women's active work in the Women's Loyal National League during the Civil War would be rewarded with the extension of suffrage to both women and African Americans at the war's close. Such was not to be the case, and the women's movement split between those who refused to support the vote for black men while it was still denied to all women and those who cautioned patience to women in recognition of "the Negro's hour." Rose joined with Stanton and Anthony to establish the National Woman Suffrage Association, favoring the former position, but she and William left for Europe shortly thereafter, returning only briefly to the United States. William died in England in 1882, and while Ernestine survived him by ten years, her grief at his death and her own poor health prevented her from much further active work.

## Rose and Religion

Ernestine Rose was also like Fanny Wright in her religious views, though in her case it was an inherited Judaism rather than Christianity that she rejected. In part, that rejection was gender-related, rooted in her experiences as a young girl who was told that her options were more limited and her nature inferior to man's, and she later viewed the clergy and their appeals to the Bible, especially the second creation account and Paul's strictures on women, as obstacles to woman's advancement. While she was aware that other leaders in the movement saw the Bible as a potential resource for women's equality, she resisted the inclusion of formal religious positions in women's rights platforms. Interpretations of the Bible were too many and too varied, she thought, for it to be a firm support, and despite a few, commendable exceptions, the clergy remained a major source of opposition to the woman's cause. She also believed women should not exclude potential supporters by a kind of religious test.[16]

Ernestine Rose criticized religion for its effect on women, but she was also repelled by the apparent irrationality of religious beliefs. Human nature, she insisted, was essentially good, and because ignorance was the problem, knowledge would be the answer to humanity's improvement:

"Knowledge not of what sort of beings we shall be hereafter, or what is beyond the skies, but a knowledge pertaining to *terra firma,* and we may have here all the power, goodness, and love that we have been taught belongs to God himself."[17] As a self-proclaimed "infidel," she was active in the religious free-thought movement of the mid-nineteenth century, writing frequently for its journal, the *Boston Investigator,* and speaking at annual celebrations of the birthday of Thomas Paine. Ironically, it was anti-Semitic comments in that free-thought paper in October of 1863 that caused Rose to break her usual silence about the Jewish faith she had inherited but rejected. Despite her personal beliefs, she responded angrily to what she saw as unfair and unjustified attacks on a people who had "suffered barbarous treatment and deadly persecution," who shared the same human nature as everyone else, and whose religion was no worse than any other. She concluded, "Then let us as Infidels . . . not add to the prejudice already existing towards the Jews, or any other sect."[18] The editor replied, Rose sent a counterreply, and the controversy continued for weeks, though to no clear-cut resolution. Nevertheless, as Yuri Suhl concludes, "the readers must certainly have benefitted from an extended discussion on Jews in which not only their religion but many other aspects of their life were presented by Ernestine in their proper historical perspective."[19]

Although Ernestine Rose drew her share of hostile criticism for her political and religious views, she was never as thoroughly vilified as Frances Wright. In part, this was due to the fact that she appeared on the American scene later than Wright, but she also posed less of a challenge to contemporary sexual mores: she explicitly repudiated "free love,"[20] and her long and happy marriage to William shielded her from one form of scandal and personal attack.

## Margaret Fuller

Both Frances Wright and Ernestine Rose were born in Europe and emigrated to America, where they became pioneers in the support of women's rights; Margaret Fuller, a third feminist critic of religion in the mid-nineteenth century, reversed the pattern. She was born in Cambridgeport, Massachusetts, in 1810, the eldest child of Margaret and Timothy Fuller. Her father early took charge of her education, and she began studying Latin at the age of six as part of a rigorous classical course that might not have been atypical for a bright, well-to-do boy but was highly unusual for a girl, however intellectually gifted. Reciting her lessons late at night to a demanding father led to nightmares and personal problems, which Margaret later detailed in an autobiography, concluding, "I had no natural childhood."[21] Most of her education occurred at home until 1823, when her father decided she needed the company of girls her own age and more training in "feminine" skills and graces, so he sent her to a boarding school. The experience was not particularly happy, despite the interest and sympathy of a kind teacher, and by 1824 Margaret returned home to participate actively in the intellectual life of Cambridge, meeting a number of young prototranscendentalists then at Harvard. But in 1833, her father moved the family to a small farm in Groton, where much of Margaret's time was taken up by helping her mother and teaching her younger siblings. When her father died in 1835, she became effectively the head of the household; she had to give up a much-desired trip to Europe and find a way to earn money, so she became a teacher, first at Bronson Alcott's Temple School and then in Rhode Island.

In 1839 she returned to Boston and for the next several years actively participated in the transcendentalist movement, developing a close friendship with Emerson, visiting Brook Farm, and editing the transcendentalist journal, the *Dial*. Her account of a summer's trip to the West, recorded in *Summer on the Lakes,* drew the attention of Horace Greeley, who offered her a job on his New York *Tribune*. In New York, away from the highly intellectual atmosphere of Boston, her social and political interests broadened considerably as she developed her skills as a journalist. In the summer of 1846, her longtime dream of going to Europe was realized. She and her friends, Marcus and Rebecca Spring, toured the British Isles, where Margaret was well received and met many of the leading figures of the age, including the Italian political rebel, Mazzini. When the American group went to Italy, Margaret became deeply involved in the political and revolutionary climate of Rome. She also met a young aristocrat, Giovanni Ossoli, whose sympathies were nevertheless with the radicals. They became lovers, she got pregnant, and in September 1848, their son was born in the small Italian village of Rieti. (Margaret Fuller was at great pains to keep the scandal of her pregnancy secret, and there is considerable controversy over when, or even if, she married Ossoli. They were probably not married before the child was born, given complications with his family, but they may have been later. She certainly, if belatedly, introduced him to friends and family as her husband, and he openly and legally acknowledged his paternity.)[22]

Margaret returned to Rome during the turbulent times of hopeful rebellion, brief independence, and then siege, working as a nurse and administrator in a hospital and sending reports back to the *Tribune*. When Rome fell to the French, she and Ossoli fled, retrieved their son, who had been left in Rieti, and moved to Florence. Fearing that they had no future in Italy, they left for America, but a relatively peaceful voyage ended tragically just off the coast of Fire Island, New York: the ship was wrecked, and Margaret, her husband, and her child were drowned on July 19, 1850.

## Fuller's Contributions to Women

Women's rights were not Margaret Fuller's central focus, nor did she participate in the organized movement that was just beginning while she was in Italy. Nevertheless, later leaders honored the pioneering work she did during her transcendentalist period. At one level, her contribution was one of personal example, a living refutation of sweeping claims that women were incapable of serious intellectual development. Even her critics acknowledged that her intellect was formidable. Her more specific contributions, however, were in the "Conversations" she conducted with Boston women from 1839 to 1843 and in an article she wrote for the *Dial,* "The Great Lawsuit," later expanded into *Woman in the Nineteenth Century.* Fuller's purpose in the Conversations was to earn money by doing something she enjoyed and was very good at, but she also wanted to help other women develop their ability to think seriously and independently, away from the constraining presence of males. As Paula Blanchard notes in her biography of Fuller,

> Margaret hoped to induce them to systematize their thought and express themselves boldly as they had never been asked to before. She hoped to sharpen their thinking habits, but beyond that, and more important, she hoped to bring them to an understanding that their inadequacies were not innate, but were the result of superficial education and the attitude of self-depreciation instilled by social custom.[23]

Thus the content of the Conversations, which was not particularly radical, was ultimately of less importance than the experience and encouragement offered to women to think for themselves.

Fuller developed a similar theme of female self-reliance in *Woman in the Nineteenth Century,* published in 1845. Women need education, but they need to learn from other women and, even more, from themselves—not simply to depend on men to teach them.[24] They need and deserve freedom for self-development as individuals, mentally and in their choice of a life's vocation. That vocation might very well be consistent with the roles approved by society and filled by many women, but for Fuller, the point was that it would be freely and intelligently chosen and that it would not be imposed on those women for whom it was not a congenial choice. In a famous passage, she wrote:

> But if you ask me what offices [women] may fill, I reply—any. I do not care what case you put; let them be sea-captains, if you will. I do not doubt that there are women well fitted for such an office, and, if so, I should be . . . glad to see them in it. . . . I have no doubt, however, that a large proportion of women would give themselves to the same employments as now, because there are circumstances that must lead them. . . . The difference would be

that *all* need not be constrained to employments for which *some* are unfit."[25]

In addition to equal educational and vocational opportunities, women deserve equal legal and political rights. Fuller drew specific attention to the legal disabilities of married women, but she also implicitly endorsed suffrage, and she exposed the inherent class bias of those who argue that legal rights are incompatible with woman's "higher" calling as moral influence and guardian of the home. "Those who think the physical circumstances of Woman would make a part in the affairs of national government unsuitable, are by no means those who think it impossible for negresses to endure field-work, even during pregnancy, or for sempstresses to go through their killing labors."[26] Addressing sexual morality, Fuller called for higher views of marriage as intellectual and spiritual partnership, unions based on mutual love and common ideals, and she, like the advocates of female moral reform, did not shrink from discussing the "indelicate" subject of prostitution, a problem rooted in inadequate educational and economic opportunities for women, the double standard, and male hypocrisy.

Fuller's primary justification for change was woman's equality as a person, answerable to God and not men, who therefore deserved greater opportunities and fewer restrictions so that she might develop her potential for her own sake and for the progress of humanity, not proximately for men, that she might serve or please them better. At times, however, Fuller seemed to ascribe distinct psychological natures and a kind of complementarity to the sexes. Woman's nature was more intuitive, spiritual, and, as she put it, "electrical." Man (a term she sometimes used generically, especially when capitalized) was an ideal, composed of two halves. Neither half had yet developed as it could, but women had been even more artificially retarded, and until they were freed to be themselves, further progress toward the ideal was stifled. Yet having posed a general or theoretical difference of nature, Fuller immediately qualified that assertion for individuals. Neither the ideal male nor the ideal female is incarnated in pure form. "Male and female represent the two sides of the great radical dualism. But, in fact, they are perpetually passing into one another. . . . There is no wholly masculine man, no purely feminine woman."[27]

Fuller's struggle to reconcile equality and complementarity on a theoretical level was mirrored in her life. Her gifts and ambitions were ones her society labelled masculine, and for much of her life, she believed that the practical price she must pay to fulfill them was celibacy, even while she privately expressed her longing for marriage and children. When she finally became a wife (legally or effectively) and mother in Italy, some of her contemporaries exulted in her belated discovery of her own femininity, her "true" nature as a woman. They (and some later historians) felt vindicated: her previous identity was obviously the result of misguidance or repression. Fuller herself leaves no doubt that she was deeply fulfilled by love and motherhood, but she did not, therefore, repudiate the rest of her identity. She had every intention of continuing her career in some way, for what she sought for herself and painfully modeled for later women was not the choice of either "masculinity" or "femininity" but the individual woman's potential to embrace both.

In her own way, Margaret Fuller made a significant contribution to the young cause of woman's rights, even though the movement was not her primary, lifelong concern. But was she also a radical critic of religion? Her attacks on organized religion were far less sweeping than those of Wright or Rose, though she shared some particular concerns with those women. She disliked narrow sectarianism; she deplored the effects of "priestcraft" on women but felt they would decrease as female intellectual powers were freed and developed; she excoriated Christians who failed to practice Christ's principles, especially toward African Americans and Native Americans.[28] As an adult, she recalled her childhood sense of disaffection from the cold rationalism of her father's Unitarianism, and she seldom participated in formal religious services. But the decision was a personal one; she had no objections to others' participation as long as it was not narrow or exclusive.

Fuller's own religion was compatible with, although not comprehended by, a broad transcendentalism: belief in a divine spirit manifest in a wide range of forms; a highly positive view of the basic goodness and potential progress of human nature in harmony with and inspired by that spirit. In 1842, she wrote "Credo," which appears to be, until the end, a fairly orthodox personal statement of belief:

> I believe (*in my own way*) in [Old Testament leaders and prophecies and the need for a Redeemer and an Atoner] . . . I believe Jesus came when the time was ripe, that he was peculiarly a messenger and son of God. I have nothing to say in denial (of) the story of his birth. . . . [She accepts the truth of Jesus' miracles, resurrection, and ascension.] . . . But when I say to you, also, that though I think all this really happened, it is of no consequence to me whether it did or not, that the ideal truth such illustrations present to me, is enough. . . . For myself, I believe in Christ because I can do without him; because the truth he announces I see elsewhere intimated; because it is foreshadowed in the very nature of my own being. But I do not wish to do without him. He is constantly aiding and answering me. Only I will not lay any undue and exclusive emphasis on him.[29]

Similarly, while she herself felt no need for the forms of the church, she would not deny them to others, nor did she see their disappearance as either likely or necessary. Indeed, paradoxically, she looked forward to a time "[w]hen all can use and learn from [the forms and props of religion], yet feel able to do without them, [and then] they will depart no more."[30]

The differences between Margaret Fuller's critique of religion and those of Wright and Rose can be traced not only to differences in personal experience but also to broad philosophical influences. Wright and Rose were, intellectually, daughters of the Enlightenment and saw religion as basically irrational and hence untrue (not to mention an obstacle to woman's advancement). Fuller was a Romantic, not only in her appreciation for intuition, creativity, and spirit, but also in her willingness to find truth in a wide variety of forms, inspiration in a diverse group of historical and religious heroes and heroines. To orthodox, traditional Christians of her day, her solution may have appeared more subtle but no less serious or shocking than the attacks of Wright or Rose. Her views clearly undermined the literal authority of the Bible, and she questioned the exclusivity and the historical facticity of Christianity. Fuller knew "how wide the gulf [was] that separates me from the Christian Church,"[31] and there was sufficient public criticism of her unorthodoxy that her brother felt obliged to protest, in an introduction to a posthumous edition of *Woman in the Nineteenth Century*, "Surely, if the Savior's test, 'By their fruits ye shall know them,' be the true one, Margaret Ossoli was pre-eminently a Christian. . . . Abhorring, as all honest minds must, every species of cant, she respected true religious thought and feeling, by whomever cherished."[32]

## Elizabeth Cady Stanton and Matilda Joslyn Gage

There was no Fuller-like ambiguity in Elizabeth Cady Stanton and Matilda Joslyn Gage when these two leaders of the radical wing of the women's movement expressed their views on religion in the closing decade of the nineteenth century. By then, both women had concluded that the influence of Christianity on women was overwhelmingly harmful; that impact was why they rejected the church. Moreover, they shared a number of similarities in their personal lives and in their lifelong devotion to the cause of women's rights.

Both women were born to well-to-do families in upstate New York, Elizabeth Cady in 1815 and Matilda Joslyn in 1826. Each was encouraged by her father to pursue a more rigorous education than was typical for girls, in part, perhaps, in recognition of intellectual talent, but also because Matilda was an only child, and Elizabeth's only surviving brother died when he was twenty and she tried to fill his place for her grieving father. Both married, Matilda to Henry H. Gage in 1845, and Elizabeth to Henry Stanton in 1840. As a new bride, Elizabeth accompanied her abolitionist husband to the World's Antislavery Convention in London, where she met

Lucretia Mott, another delegate. Impressed by the older woman's ideas and example, and appalled by the exclusion of women delegates from voice and seat at the convention, Cady Stanton and Mott agreed that a convention for women's rights was needed, though it would be another eight years before that historic event took place in Seneca Falls, New York. Matilda Joslyn Gage was not present then, though she did attend and speak at the National Woman's Rights Convention in Rochester, New York, in 1852, but the active participation of both women was limited in the early years by the time-consuming responsibilities of motherhood: Gage had four surviving children, while Cady Stanton had seven.

Only as their children grew could the two women devote more consistent energies to the cause: Cady Stanton, as a major theoretician, writer, and popular and effective speaker; Gage, as an organizer, writer, and editor. When the movement split after the Civil War, both joined that National Woman Suffrage Association (NWSA), which was formed in protest of the subordination of the vote for women to the immediate concern to enfranchise black men. Both worked actively for the NWSA during the 1870s, and together with Susan B. Anthony, Gage and Cady Stanton compiled and edited the first three volumes of the massive *History of Woman Suffrage* (volumes 1 and 2 were published in 1881; volume 3, in 1886.) Neither Cady Stanton nor Gage had much sympathy for the rival, more conservative, suffrage group, the American Woman Suffrage Association (AWSA), and thus they initially resisted Anthony's proposals to merge the NWSA with the AWSA, but when the union took place in 1890, Cady Stanton accepted the presidency of the new organization, while Gage broke with it and founded her own, more radical group, the Woman's National Liberal Union.

By this time, Gage was thoroughly convinced that the Christian church was the greatest obstacle in the way of women's rights, and she feared the growing influence of Frances Willard and her WCTU in the movement, for Gage saw their endorsement of religious legislation as a threat to the separation of church and state. Three years later, she published her major work, *Woman, Church, and State,* an expanded version of themes she had sounded for years. Cady Stanton was scarcely less hostile to organized religion, but she was willing to retain a formal association with the new National American Woman Suffrage Association (NAWSA) even as her energy and attention shifted to her own culminating attack on religion, the *Woman's Bible,* for which Gage was a member of the revising committee. Both women had by then followed in the footsteps of Fanny Wright and Ernestine Rose, becoming professed "free thinkers." They saw that position, as Wright and Rose had, as integrally related to the rights of women as persons. Yet ironically, the free thought movement of the late nineteenth century was itself divided over the issue of female suffrage, and a prominent argument of the "antis" was their fear that giving the vote to women would increase the political power of the priesthood, to which most women so credulously and irrationally submitted.[33] While Cady Stanton and Gage rejected such arguments, they were not without their own prejudices in regard to suffrage, prejudices that were equally inconsistent with a pure theory of human rights. Their attacks on Judaism and Christianity, especially the Roman Catholic Church, because of these religions' treatment of women too easily led to what sounded like broad anti-Semitic, anti-Catholic, and anti-immigrant bigotry. Nor was this a new development for Cady Stanton. Her anger that female suffrage was sacrificed to the cause of black male votes surfaced in the racist rhetoric she used in 1869 to call for a sixteenth amendment to grant women the vote.

> If American women find it hard to bear the oppressions of their own Saxon fathers, the best orders of manhood, what may they not be called to endure when all the lower order of foreigners now crowding our shores legislate for them and their daughters. Think of Patrick and Sambo and Hans and Yung Tung, who do not know the difference between a monarchy and a republic, who can not read the Declaration of Independence or Webster's spelling-book, making laws for Lucretia Mott, Ernestine L. Rose, and Anna E. Dickinson.[34]

Stanton was not, of course, alone in her sentiments. Through pragmatism or prejudice, many proponents voiced elitist and racist appeals to justify female suffrage. But Anthony and the younger generation of activists who dominated the movement after 1890 were finding new strength in an alliance with the same religious women whose influence the free thinkers feared. In that situation, few welcomed the radical critique of religion offered by Gage and Stanton. Matilda Joslyn Gage died in 1898, isolated and generally repudiated and forgotten by the movement to which she had devoted so much of her life. Cady Stanton maintained an honored position as elder stateswoman, but her direct influence on the movement was significantly diminished, and she died in 1902.[35]

## Critiques of Religion

Earlier in her career, Elizabeth Cady Stanton had identified other causes, like the family or legal restrictions, as the greatest problem for women, but by the last quarter of the nineteenth century she and Gage came to see religion, specifically the Christian church, as the greatest obstacle to woman's advancement. At an 1878 convention of the NWSA, both supported a series of controversial resolutions attacking religion:

> *Resolved,* That as the first duty of every individual is self-development, the lessons of self-sacrifice and obedience taught woman by the Christian church have been fatal, not only to her own vital interests, but through her, to those of the race.

> *Resolved,* That the great principle of the Protestant Reformation, the right of individual conscience and judgment heretofore exercised by man alone, should now be claimed by woman; that, in the interpretation of Scripture, she should be guided by her own reason, and not by the authority of the church.
>
> *Resolved,* That it is through the perversion of the religious element in woman—playing upon her hopes and fears of the future, holding this life with all its high duties in abeyance to that which is to come—that she and the children she has trained have been so completely subjugated by priestcraft and superstition.[36]

### *Woman's Bible*

Despite harsh attacks from without, especially from Christian clergy and the AWSA, and dissent within the NWSA itself, Gage and Stanton continued their critique of religion, proposing resolutions at succeeding conventions but also turning to other means to express their concerns. Encouraged by the growth of science, biblical criticism, and free thought, and by a new revision of the biblical text by male scholars in 1881, Cady Stanton conceived the idea of the *Woman's Bible* and began to recruit women scholars to serve on a committee and write commentaries on parts of the Bible pertaining to women. While over twenty women were listed as members of the revising committee and several other women contributed commentary, the bulk of the work of organizing and writing for the project was done by Cady Stanton herself.

Volume 1 was published in 1895 and covered the Pentateuch. In her introduction, Cady Stanton asserted that both the Old and the New Testaments had been used to keep women in a separate and subordinate sphere.

> The Bible teaches that woman brought sin and death into the world, that she precipitated the fall of the race, that she was arraigned before the judgment seat of Heaven, tried, condemned and sentenced. Marriage for her was to be a condition of bondage, maternity a period of suffering and anguish, and in silence and subjection, she was to play the role of a dependent on man's bounty for all her material wants, and for all the information she might desire on the vital questions of the hour, she was commanded to ask her husband at home.[37]

Not only did Cady Stanton reject all of these teachings, she questioned the divine inspiration of the scriptural writers. She did not, however, reject the Bible in toto: she agreed with some of its ideas and particularly approved the example and teachings of Jesus, but she had no sympathy either for those passages that condemned women or with the Christians who insisted that these applied to contemporary practice. To Stanton, the truths of the Bible that were valid for nineteenth-century Americans were so not because of the Bible's intrinsic divine authority but because they accorded with immutable natural laws, whose content was, to her, self-evident. Thus she commended the first Creation account (Genesis 1) for showing the "simultaneous creation of both sexes, in the image of God"—and for thereby endorsing a dual-gendered godhead and rejecting the concept of man's dominion over woman.[38] (Cady Stanton reflected her belief in a dual-gendered deity, as well as a shrewd, practical awareness of all to whom thanks are due, in her preferred table grace: "Heavenly Father and Mother, make us thankful for all the blessings of this life and ever mindful of the patient hands that oft in weariness set our tables and prepare our food. For humanity's sake, Amen.")[39] On the other hand, she rejected the second creation account (Genesis 2 and 3) as an unscientific, unconvincing attempt to denigrate woman, arguing instead that Eve showed a commendable desire for wisdom. Indeed, in an 1869 article in *The Revolution,* Cady Stanton had argued (a little tongue-in-cheek, perhaps) that Eve, far from being the source of human misery, had through her inquisitiveness opened the door to subsequent human knowledge and progress. Without her act, "Moses and Aaron, Samson and Solomon, Columbus, Newton, Fulton and Cyrus Field, would have been to this hour listlessly sunning themselves on the grassy slopes of Paradise, ignorant of the laws of their being and everything beyond their own horizon."[40]

Not all biblical women were commendable: Sarah, given her treatment of Hagar, and Rebekah and Rachel—with their greed, pettiness, and dishonesty—were hardly admirable moral examples. Despite a few glimmers of "true, grand, and beautiful" sentiments, like the golden rule and the Ten Commandments, Cady Stanton found most of the Pentateuch uninspiring, with its image of a jealous, wrathful, and violent God. She concluded, "Indeed the Pentateuch is a long painful record of war, corruption, rapine, and lust. Why Christians who wished to convert the heathen to our religion should send them these books, passes all understanding. It is most demoralizing reading for children and the unthinking masses. . . ."[41]

Volume 2, published in 1898, covered the rest of the Old Testament and the New Testament. Here, Cady Stanton found several admirable, strong women, such as Deborah, Ruth, Huldah, Vashti, and Esther, but she was outraged by the treatment of Jepthah's daughter, innocently sacrificed to fulfill her father's rash and foolish vow. "We often hear people laud the beautiful submission and the self-sacrifice of this nameless maiden. To me it is pitiful and painful."[42] Cady Stanton frequently returned to this theme: women have been taught for too long to sacrifice themselves for others; what they need is self-development. Thus she particularly liked the parable of the wise and foolish virgins.

> Now, to my mind, there is nothing commendable in the action of young women who go about begging funds to educate young men for the ministry, while they and the majority of their sex are too poor to educate themselves, and if able, are still denied admittance into some of the leading institutions of learning throughout our land. It is not commendable for women to get up fairs and donation parties for churches in which the gifted of their sex may neither pray, preach, share in the offices and honors, nor have a voice in the business affairs, creeds, and discipline, and from whose altars come forth Biblical interpretations in favor of woman's subjection. . . . such are indeed like the foolish virgins. . . . The wise virgins are they who keep their lamps trimmed, who burn oil in their vessels for their own use, who have improved every advantage for their education, secured a healthy, happy, complete development, and entered all the profitable avenues of labor, for self-support, so that when the opportunities and the responsibilities of life come, they may be fitted fully to enjoy the one and ably to discharge the other.[43]

Cady Stanton's reading of certain stories and parables may have been culturally heterodox but not overtly heretical; however, other of her comments were more radical. Not only did she view the Bible as a whole as a human, not a divinely inspired, product, she also questioned the doctrine of the virgin birth, viewing it as "a slur on all the natural motherhood of the world."[44] In addition, she denied the unique divinity of Jesus (although she admired his human example and teachings), virtually dismissed Paul's authority, and questioned the whole idea of original sin and the consequent need of a redeemer.

> The real difficulty in woman's case is that the whole foundation of the Christian religion rests on her temptation and man's fall, hence the necessity of a Redeemer and a plan of salvation. As the chief cause of this dire calamity, woman's degradation and subordination were made a necessity. If, however, we accept the Darwinian theory, that the race has had a gradual growth from the lower to a higher form of life, and that the story of the fall is a myth, we can exonerate the snake, emancipate the woman, and reconstruct a more rational religion for the nineteenth century, and thus escape all the perplexities of the Jewish mythology as of no more importance than those of the Greek, Persian, and Egyptian.[45]

The *Woman's Bible* created a sensation, going through seven printings in six months.[46] But while some readers praised it, others' reaction was decidedly hostile, even within the suffrage movement. At the annual convention of the NAWSA, a resolution was introduced disassociating the organization from the *Woman's Bible*. Several leaders opposed such a step, and Susan B. Anthony made an eloquent plea for toleration. She reminded those gathered that they had never before yielded to calls to censure an unpopular religious position or to repudiate an unorthodox woman like Ernestine Rose, and she warned that such action could set a dangerous precedent against freedom of thought and speech. Nevertheless, the resolution passed, for too many of those present either were personally offended by Stanton's views or feared that appearing to condone them would hurt the cause of suffrage.

Elizabeth Cady Stanton's major religious work focused on the Bible itself (although her commentaries ranged into historical and contemporary women's issues), for it was the Bible that was so often quoted as the ultimate and uniquely divine authority for woman's subordination. In contrast, Gage's most fully developed critique focused on a longer and broader historical view of Christian practice and influence. Gage revised an address she had given at the 1878 convention and printed it, first in *The National Citizen*, which she edited, and then in the first volume of the *History of Woman Suffrage*. Then in 1893, she published a much more extended version in her book, *Woman, Church and State*. She challenged even more thoroughly than Cady Stanton the contemporary assertion that Christianity elevated woman, for Gage found virtually nothing of value to woman in the Bible or the historical church. On the contrary, she insisted that it was the church, controlling and allied to the state under patriarchy, that was responsible for woman's degradation. In a breathtakingly broad survey of laws and practices over time and place, she reiterated her contention that a greedy, immoral priesthood had dominated the state and forced women in particular into virtual slavery of mind and body. In chapters devoted to celibacy, canon law, "marquette" (the medieval practice whereby a lord claimed marital rights over every new bride), and witchcraft, Gage argued that not only had male rulers, spiritual and temporal, denied all power to woman and labelled her as inherently inferior and sinful, they had hypocritically promoted a double standard of sexual and moral behavior.

## *The Matriarchate*

Things had not always been thus, Gage insisted. Influenced by the work of anthropologists like Johann Jacob Bachofen, Gage argued that an ancient matriarchal period had preceded the rise of patriarchy in the world's civilizations. But where Bachofen saw the development from matriarchy to patriarchy as progress, Gage portrayed it as fall. Not only had an ancient matriarchate existed, but it was a kind of golden age of peace and harmony. Under the matriarchate, it was women who were rulers and deities, men who were inferior.

> Never was justice more perfect, never civilization higher than under the Matriarchate. . . . Under the Matriarchate, monogamy was

> the rule; neither polyandry or promiscuity existed. . . . The Patriarchate under which Biblical history and Judaism commenced, was a rule of men whose lives and religion were based upon passions of the grossest kind, showing but few indications of softness and refinement. . . . During the Matriarchate all life was regarded as holy; even the sacrifice of animals was unknown. The most ancient and purest religions taught sacrifice of the animal passions as the great necessity in self-purification. But the Patriarchate subverted this sublime teaching, materializing spiritual truths, and substituting the sacrifice of animals, whose blood was declared a sweet-smelling savor to the Lord of Hosts. Both infanticide and prostitution with all their attendant horrors are traceable with polygamy,—their origin—to the Patriarchate or Father-rule, under which Judaism and Christianity rose as forms of religious belief. . . . The sacrifice of woman to man's baser passions has ever been the distinguishing characteristic of the Patriarchate.[47]

After hundreds of pages of examples of the horrors endured by women under patriarchy, Gage ends her work on a hopeful, even apocalyptic note. Despite the continued opposition of the church and its clergy to claims of female freedom and equality, women, Gage believes, are awakening to their situation, their potential, and the nature of their oppressors.

> Looking forward, I see evidence of a conflict more severe than any yet fought by reformation or science; a conflict that will shake the foundations of religious belief, tear into fragments and scatter to the winds the old dogmas upon which all forms of christianity are based. . . . it will be the rebellion of one half of the church against those theological dogmas upon which the very existence of the church is based. . . . During the ages, no rebellion has been of like importance with that of Woman against the tyranny of Church and State; none has had its far reaching effects. We note its beginning; its progress will overthrow every existing form of these institutions; its end will be a regenerated world.[48]

### *Underlying Views on Women*

Like Wright, Rose, and Fuller, Elizabeth Cady Stanton's most typical argument for women's rights was rooted in a view of women and men as persons first, equally human and thus deserving of equal rights and opportunities, though all four women occasionally seemed to endorse a view of distinctive (if not superior) female nature. Thus Cady Stanton sometimes embraced a kind of complementarity of the sexes, and if nothing else, she was politically astute enough to realize the strength of appeals to the particular virtues and insights of motherhood and to exploit her own matronly appearance and experience as wife and mother of seven to counter the image of the feminist as frustrated, unfulfilled spinster.

In contrast, Gage's views of the matriarchate and her analysis of the world's history under patriarchy suggest that for her, the balance tipped the other way: while she sometimes spoke of the equal rights due to all persons (but withheld from the majority of humanity for most of its history by the rulers of church and state), her more basic view was one of women's natural superiority to men. Women were not only more peaceful than men, they were also more spiritual, more moral, and more "pure" than lustful and animalistic males; it is the rebellion of women that will "regenerate" the world. Thus Gage, unwittingly and ironically, seemed to agree with the more conservative suffragists whose influence on the movement she feared. Their dominant argument for suffrage became not woman's natural rights as an equal with man but her superior and distinctive morality; woman would use the vote to clean up politics and to protect the higher goods of home, family, and religion. In short, Gage accepted and projected onto the matriarchate the values and assumptions of Victorian womanhood, even as she explicitly rejected the Christianity that promoted them so widely in that time and culture.[49]

## Summary

In their critique of religion in general and Christianity in particular, Elizabeth Cady Stanton and Matilda Joslyn Gage both continued and moved beyond the themes sounded by the earlier voices of Fanny Wright, Ernestine Rose, and Margaret Fuller. All five were critical of the leading "personnel" of the church, the clergy, and deplored the influence of "priestcraft"—that is, a narrow, authoritarian, sectarian leadership—on women in particular. They realized that it was women who by and large were the most faithful members and supporters of the churches, and thus they urged women to learn, to think for themselves, to exercise the freedoms supposedly granted to all Americans to throw off the shackles of superstition. Too much of women's time and of the money they raised was "wasted" on established churches. It would be better for a woman to direct time and money to her own education or to improving the conditions of others in this world.

The five women were further frustrated by the opposition of many clerical leaders to specific changes in women's roles and rights, from education to legal protections for married women to the vote. To them, the crime of the church and its Bible was not just teaching woman's inferiority and subordination but getting women to internalize that assessment and accept their "guilt." Thus they urged other women to reject, as they had, appeals to a literally interpreted Bible as a divine and hence unquestionable authority decreeing woman's silence, subordination, and powerlessness. For Wright and Gage, the rejection was virtually total, while Fuller and Stanton conceded that some forms of Christianity or some individual Christian leaders supported women's demands for greater opportunities in church, state, and society.[50] Yet other nineteenth-century women identified themselves as both Christians and proponents of women's rights, and they, too, criticized particular interpretations of the Bible and rejected the opinions of conservative clergy. What finally distinguished Cady Stanton and Gage as "radical critics" was their skepticism that the church could be reformed from within, their refusal to accept individual voices of clerical support as a substitute for the churches' official pronouncements and actual practices, their conviction that overall, Christianity, far from elevating woman, had oppressed her, and their mature conclusion that patriarchy and sexism (to use a more modern term) were basic, not peripheral, to the Bible and Christianity.

Thus these feminist critics went beyond attack on the clergy and interpretations of certain biblical passages to question the basic content and message of Christianity. Addressing women in particular, they repudiated self-sacrifice as a theological and moral good (and one that was, in practice, urged selectively along gender lines) and promoted self-development instead. It was this radical, direct challenge to cultural as well as theological assumptions about woman's role and nature that contributed to the contemporary perception that feminists were "selfish." Yet none of the five women promoted a purely egotistical individualism; all were active in reforms of one type or another and expected women (and men) to contribute to the good of humanity. They simply believed that women could do so with more integrity and more effectiveness if they were first allowed the opportunity to develop as full persons, unrestricted by legal barriers or cultural expectations that defined women through roles of service and subordination.

These women critics further attacked the content of Christian doctrine in their rejection of original sin and the Fall. Gage and Cady Stanton were the most explicit here, arguing that without a Fall, not only were women freed of the traditional guilt of Eve, but that there remained no logical necessity for a divine Savior. But a similar conclusion was implicit in the earlier ideas of Wright, Rose, and Fuller. While Wright and Rose were more directly daughters of the Enlightenment and Fuller was more immediately indebted to Romanticism, all three shared a high view of human nature and a conviction of the possibility, even inevitability, of human progress. Yet these radical critics were not the only women to question the doctrines of Fall and original sin or their consequences. Several of the sectarian groups covered in the previous chapter modified or denied the Fall,[51] many liberal Christians endorsed a basic goodness in human nature, and even the nineteenth-century evangelical heirs of Calvinism qualified their understanding of human depravity to exclude the possibility of the damnation of innocent infants and children. Nevertheless, the attack of the radical critics was more overt, and the implications they derived from their denial of the Fall, notably rejecting the necessity of a Savior, went too far for most American Christians to accept.

The religious questions of these nineteenth-century radicals reemerged in the last third of the twentieth century. Debates over women's ordination in certain branches of Protestantism once again brought interpretations of key biblical passages, as well as the nature of the Bible and its authority, to the fore. Advocates of goddess religion and/or an ancient matriarchy rediscovered a foremother in Gage. With the reprinting of *The Woman's Bible* and *Woman, Church, and State,* feminist theologians of the late twentieth century found that many of their questions, criticisms, and even solutions had been voiced by Stanton and Gage a century ago.

# 18

# *Women's Religious Leadership in the Twentieth Century*

## Movement in the Mainline

The passage of a constitutional amendment for woman's suffrage in 1920 was a landmark in women's pursuit of equality in America. To be sure, the vote was not the panacea that some of its more exuberant supporters had predicted, but it was a real as well as a symbolic victory, a cause that united women across classes, races, and cultural perspectives. Contrary to some traditional interpretations, women did not immediately "relax," suspending any and all efforts for further change until the resurgence of a woman's movement in the second half of the century, but other diverse issues, more specific to particular classes and groups of women, claimed their attention. Some of the issues were "religious" ones, but religion itself was becoming less central in American culture during the twentieth century. Not only was there a marked increase in religious pluralism (although, as we have seen, religious pluralism was a fact in America from its earliest days), but there was more emphasis on individual preference in religion, and religious identification was not necessary for social and cultural respectability. In the meantime, other authorities, particularly science (natural and social), widely and effectively challenged religion's position. The issue was not so much a decline in church or synagogue membership—in fact, that peaked in America in the late 1950s—but how central and identity-defining religion was for Americans. As women gained more access to the public sphere—more options for self-expression, professional work, and useful service—many did not "need" religion as much to find an identity and work, volunteer or paid, outside the domestic sphere.

Nevertheless, "religion" in an expanding variety of forms was still important to American women. Many women continued to focus on activity and leadership within the institutional churches and synagogues. Women made significant gains in the nineteenth century in finding a public voice and spheres of power, but they were still far from achieving equality with men, especially in the formal structures of the denominations. For some groups, notably among mainline Protestants and the less traditional branches of Judaism, the twentieth century saw a slow but definite progress, culminating in formal access to ordained ministry at the same time that women continued to define distinctive spheres through their own religious organizations. For others, particularly more conservative Protestant groups, there seemed to be a move backward from the gains of the previous century, despite a handful of famous exceptional women who exercised religious leadership for men as well as women. Finally, there were those groups—notably Roman Catholics, Eastern Orthodox, Orthodox Jews, and some Protestants—who continued to defend traditional and generally subordinate spheres and images of women. I turn to these latter two in the next chapters; in this chapter I sketch the story of those groups in which women had, by the end of the twentieth century, gained formal opportunities for equal religious leadership.

## Women's Mission Boards

During the latter half of the nineteenth century, many women's mission boards emerged as critical centers of women's activities and power within the churches, whether the boards were formally separate or functionally so as auxiliaries. But in the early decades of the twentieth century, attempts occurred in some Protestant denominations to merge the women's boards with general church mission boards. Part of the larger historical context of the proposed mergers was widespread concern that religion in America had become dangerously feminized: that is, that women dominated the churches numerically and that religion itself was perceived as a feminine concern. The situation was by no means a new one. Women had long constituted a majority of members in many of the Christian churches in America, but it was not until the last years of the nineteenth century and the early decades of the twentieth that the matter caused conscious and public consternation among male religious leaders. In the nineteenth century, American men were reasonably content with a cultural system that affirmed the man's public economic and political roles and assigned religious activity largely to women. But that configuration was less acceptable and more threatening when, as Gail Bederman has argued, "the Victorian gender system had begun to lose coherence in the face of a cultural reorientation connected to the growth of a consumer-oriented, corporate culture."[1] One male response to the perceived problem of feminization was an active attempt to attract men back to the pews and to change religion's image. Thus in 1911 a broad coalition of mainline Protestant groups launched the Men and Religion Forward Movement, "the only widespread religious revival in American history which explicitly excluded women."[2] Religion was presented as "manly," associated with sports and business success, and church activities were promoted that would appeal to men, while female power in the churches could be countered.

In that context, gender rivalry and resentment was one element of, though not a comprehensive explanation for, the move to merge mission boards. Male leaders who endorsed change feared that women had erected a rival or parallel church, an organization that competed with the larger denominational body for funds and duplicated its resources and administration. As R. Pierce Beaver has pointed out, some of the men's charges were more justified than others. The claim that women's support of their own mission work diminished their general giving was especially unfair, because the women consistently promoted (and got) "double-giving" from their members. Men also resented the claim that the women were more "efficient" and able to keep administrative costs down. Here the men's resentment was justified, for much of the women's administration was done by professional volunteers who could afford to work with little or no pay. In addition, women's boards kept costs down by paying relatively low salaries to single women missionaries and offering meager retirement programs to them.[3]

Needless to say, proposals for merger were also presented in a more constructive light: merger would lead to increase in efficiency, integration of efforts, and, given the symbolic significance of women's suffrage, an acceptance of men and women working together as equals. Helen Barrett Montgomery, in her classic work, *Western Women in Eastern Lands,* addressed the proposal. Noting that women were certainly not willing to accept a change that left them as mere collectors of money that men would then decide how to spend, she admitted that the vision of men and women working together on a single board was attractive—but then wondered if it were realistic. "In the first place, are men ready for it?" she asked. "Are they emancipated from the caste of sex so that they can work easily with women, unless they be head and women clearly subordinate?"[4] Montgomery was skeptical, and she was not convinced that consolidating boards and giving up the distinctiveness of the women's work were wise ideas. On the first point, at least, she proved prophetic: In very few instances were the men who wanted integration actually willing to accept women as equals on the boards specifically or in the churches in general, despite the designation of token board positions in some cases.

### Varied Responses to Merging Boards

In fact, however, there were differences among denominations on the issue of merging of women's boards. In some cases, the women's boards never had all that much power to begin with. Lutheran women, particularly in the Midwest, were slower than other Protestant women to develop women's organizations at all, even prayer or Bible study groups, and with few exceptions, while their mission organizations evidenced strong interest and financial support for missions, they developed little autonomy in terms of organization or financial control until nearly the middle of the twentieth century. The Episcopal women's missionary organizations were organized by the late nineteenth century, but they were clearly auxiliary and not represented on the General Board. At times, they did in fact exercise some autonomy in the direction of funds, but to do so, they had to raise enough money for their own projects *and* those determined by the General Board.[5] When women finally got representation on the Board of Missions, it was at a token level.

Presbyterian women in the South, like Lutherans, were fairly late in organizing: into the 1880s, women's groups beyond the local level were opposed as "unscriptural, unPresbyterian, and unwomanly."[6] By 1910, when other women's boards were celebrating a half century of mission work, southern Presbyterian women "were humiliated to discover how poorly the work of their scattered groups compared with the efficient work of other denominations; to find that theirs was the only important evangelical denomination in America with no department of women's work, and with no systematic promotion of the missionary program of the church among its women."[7] Thus in 1912, the southern Presbyterian Church appointed a woman "superintendent" to oversee a new department, the Woman's Auxiliary of the Presbyterian Church in the United States, but it was not until the 1920s that Hallie P. Winsborough, the president of the Women's Auxiliary, was permitted to read her own report to the General Assembly.

A third group, the Mennonite Church, was also fairly late in developing distinctive roles for women, like teaching Sunday school and occasionally speaking at Sunday school conferences, and it was not until 1911 that local "sewing circles" were brought together by Clara Eby Steiner as the Mennonite Woman's Missionary Society. Despite modest attempts to enhance female administration of their own work and interests, Mennonite women accepted their subordinate status in the church, and by 1928, the General Board effectively took over the women's work, rejecting any executive role for women and even renaming the society the General Sewing Circle Committee of the Mennonite Board of Missions and Charities.[8] The point in such groups was not that women either lacked interest or failed to make serious contributions to the work of foreign and home missions, but simply that they were unable to establish even a modest amount of autonomy for themselves as women in the work.

On the other hand, women's groups in some other denominations were able to resist takeover and retain or even increase their autonomy, or were able to achieve a reasonably high degree of equality in a merger. Reorganization among the Disciples of Christ did indeed include the subordination of the distinctive Christian Woman's Board of Missions, but the new United Christian Missionary Society of 1919 gave unusually equal representation to women, 50 percent on the Board of Managers and the Executive Commission, and women continued to serve in high executive positions.[9] The northern Baptist women merged their own regional foreign missionary groups but maintained a parallel agency in the Woman's American Baptist Foreign Mission Society, coordinated with the general denominational mission board. Not until the middle of the twentieth century was a merger effected, and at least initially (if not subsequently), women had equal or even greater representation in the new body.[10] Northern Methodists also successfully resisted the pressures for merger during the early decades of the twentieth century, and when the Methodist Episcopal Church North, Methodist Episcopal Church South, and Methodist Protestant Church themselves merged in 1939, the women maintained their independent base. As R. Pierce Beaver notes;

> This Woman's Division of Christian Service was related to the entire mission program of the church without destroying the independence and initiative formerly exercised by the Woman's Foreign Missionary Society of the Methodist Episcopal Church. This is most remarkable in view of the trends prevailing at that time and the strong central organization of the church. It is said to be due solely to the determined opposition of the women to attempted subordination and thorough integration.[11]

Not only did the Methodist women retain their autonomy through the first half of the twentieth century, in various forms it has continued into the present through the Women's Division. In a recent study, Theressa Hoover argues that, rather than being an outdated holdover, the Methodist women's group may be a successful and necessary mutant, a base and voice for women in a church where women are still far from equal in real power. "The real question," she asks, "is not why is the Women's Division still hanging on as a resourceful women's organization within United Methodism, but how can other churches afford to be without our equivalent? Practically speaking, without an organizational base how can their women maneuver for greater authority and exert significant leverage on behalf of women, children, or any other group?"[12]

Black Baptist women, like their white Baptist sisters in the North, managed to maintain the functional autonomy of their recently created national group, known as the Woman's Convention (WC), through the early decades of the twentieth century. In the 1880s, black Baptist women began to form state conventions, bringing together the work of local church groups. A central early goal was the support of education, especially schools for and controlled by African Americans themselves, though the women also supported foreign missions and other causes. When the National Baptist Convention (NBC) was created in 1895 as a vehicle and voice of black nationalism, pride, and repudiation of white racism, women were firm supporters of what would be by far the largest denomination among African Americans and one of the largest Christian groups in America. But while there had been strong black women church leaders and some token female representation on the boards of the groups that came together in 1895 to form the NBC, women were not given equal voice in its public deliberations, let alone the leadership and decision-making structures of the NBC. In 1895, the women expressed some dissatisfaction with their subordinate role and got an auxiliary, but the NBC's male leadership dissolved it a year later.

Finally in 1900, the Woman's Convention was founded with the support of some male Baptist leaders and the work of outstanding women like S. Willie Layten, Virginia Broughton, and Nannie Helen Burroughs. As Evelyn Brooks Higginbotham notes, "Burroughs, more than anyone else, embodied the Baptist women's independent spirit. . . . Her long leadership of the convention (from 1900 until her death in 1961) was fraught with tension around the issue of women's recognition and power within the denomination."[13] Burroughs's concern for autonomy was shared by her constituents, most of whom came from the working poor, though the leadership of the WC was drawn from what Higginbotham calls "the Female Talented Tenth" of educated, middle-class black women. Over the next decades, the WC both supported and depended on its hundreds of local chapters, raising money for foreign missions, establishing the National Training School for Women and Girls and a settlement house in Washington, D.C., bringing black women together at its annual conventions, and speaking out boldly against racism in American society. If the deepest concern of these black Baptist women was racism, and they stood solidly with their brothers on that ground, they occasionally formed alliances with white Baptist women for the sake of common goals and to protest sexism in the black churches, even though they did not press for female ordination.

Thus women in some denominations maintained the power of their organizations through the early decades of the twentieth century, and others, like Lutherans, southern Presbyterians, or Mennonites, lost little in mission board mergers, mainly because they had little power or autonomy in the first place. For still other Protestant women, mergers represented a clear setback in independence and control. The Methodist Episcopal Church, South in 1910 merged not only the women's and general boards but also the home and foreign mission boards into one Board of Missions. Women continued to have a Woman's Missionary Council under the General Board and were promised up to one-third representation on the Board of Missions as part of the integration. Belle Bennett, the strong president of the Woman's Missionary Board, publicly and graciously accepted the inevitable, but privately, she held no illusions that true equality of power would result. "I am a unionist," she commented, "but I did not believe in the union of the Woman's Board with the General Board on the basis which we were compelled to accept. I accepted what they gave, fearing something worse—complete subordination."[14] Similarly, the three Woman's Boards of Missions of the Congregational Churches were merged under the Committee on Missionary Unity in 1924. Again, the ostensible reason for the change was organizational efficiency, and women were granted minority representation on the larger board, but the net result was a loss of real power.

The merger of the northern Presbyterians' boards is a particularly clear case of takeover despite female resistance. Under the able leadership of Katharine Bennett, the Woman's Board was extremely effective in raising money and interest and had gradually developed more and more autonomy in its administration, so that by 1915 it was formally incorporated and could thus receive legacies in its own right. It was distinct from the Board of Home Missions and directly responsible to the General Assembly, and in 1916, Katharine Bennett became the first women to give her own formal report to the Assembly. But in 1920, the Presbyterian Church in the U. S. A. initiated plans for widespread reorganization. The Woman's Board was taken over by 1923, although women were given minority representation on the new boards and maintained some control over funds they raised and some of the schools and hospitals they supported. The women were not, however, content, and in 1927, in response to a previous request by the General Assembly, Margaret E. Hodge and Katharine Bennett presented a report on *Causes of Unrest among the Women of the Church.* The authors praised the work the women had done before the merger, stated clearly the resentment many women felt at the arbitrary treatment they had received during reorganization, and hinted at future conflicts, now that the women's separate sphere had been effectively coopted.

> So long as there was a service into which they could put their strength and affection, the women were willing to ignore the disabilities that faced them in general church work, although similar disabilities had been removed in other activities. But when the church, by action taken by the men of the church with but the slightest consultation with the women, and then only as to methods, decided to absorb those agencies which had been built up by the women, the by-product of such decision was to open the whole question of the status of women in the church. Then women faced the fact that their sex constitute about *60 per cent of the membership of the Presbyterian Church,* but that a woman as an individual has no status beyond a congregational meeting in her local church, and that the long developed and carefully erected agencies which she had cherished could be absorbed without a question being seriously asked of her as to her wishes in this matter. . . . It should not surprise anyone that among thinking women there arose a serious question as to whether their place of service could no longer be found in the church when a great organization which they had built could be autocratically destroyed by vote of male members of the church without there

> seeming to arise in the mind of the latter any question as to the justice, wisdom, or fairness of their actions.[15]

Thus one result of the mission board takeovers was both unintentional and ironic: Many women who had been content with the activities and autonomy of their separate sphere began to raise broader questions about the role and status of women in the churches. Ultimately, of course, the goal would be ordination, but first for many groups was the issue of laity rights. And in the meantime, women continued to form and to function through distinctive women's organizations, including the interdenominational group, Church Women United, and to explore alternative roles of nonordained leadership in the churches.

## The Expansion of Female Laity Rights

Some more liberal denominations, like the northern Methodists, had begun to grant more laity rights and representation to women by the late nineteenth century. For other denominations, the mission board takeovers prompted renewed concern that women have a broader and more official voice in church policy making. Belle Bennett, the leader of the southern Methodists who had accepted the takeover gracefully if not happily, turned her attention to grassroots campaigns for female laity rights. In a speech before the 1910 General Convention, she described the request as "neither unwomanly nor unreasonable" and, like the advocates of woman's political suffrage, argued on the grounds both of women's rights and of a kind of complementarity that the church needs the distinctive perspective of women. She emphasized the tradition of women who spoke out for the poor and the outcast, especially the women and children who lacked homes and protection by men.[16] Ten years later, in 1920, southern Methodist women gained religious suffrage.

Often the change came about over a long period of time and varied significantly among parishes and synods or dioceses within a denomination, as with Lutherans and Episcopalians. In a few rare instances, especially among Danish Lutherans, women were allowed to vote on congregational matters by the last decades of the nineteenth century, but the majority only began to gain such rights over the first half of the twentieth century. By the 1950s, many (but not all) of the Lutherans in the synods that would ultimately form the Evangelical Lutheran Church in America had the vote, but even then, few women held congregational offices.[17] For Episcopalians, too, the pattern of voting and serving in offices at the parish and diocesan level varied. In the early 1900s, an occasional parish, especially on the frontier, might allow women to vote, but it was the second quarter of the twentieth century and beyond before female laity rights became widespread. As Mary Sudman Donovan notes, "As late as 1961, women served on vestries in only 31 of the 104 dioceses and they were elected as delegates to only 47 diocesan conventions." Not until 1970 were women seated as deputies in the General Convention of the Episcopal Church in America, a development more vigorously resisted by male lay delegates to that body than by the male clergy.[18]

Neither the takeover of women's missions boards, when these occurred, nor the gradual expansion of female laity rights meant that women's groups within the churches ceased to function, though over the course of the twentieth century they did face certain organizational problems at the local level and beyond. As groups proliferated—circles, ladies' aid societies, missionary and benevolent societies, altar guilds, and so forth—the relationships among them could sometimes produce tensions, rivalries, or dissipation of efforts, even as the range of groups allowed women choices in their relationship to the church and other women. Organizational questions were also raised at the regional or national level, not only in terms of the relationship of the women to general (largely male) boards or councils but also internally among the women's groups and between national leadership and grassroots constituency. Often the older women leaders found that younger women had less time for and interest in church work as the younger women's opportunities, professional and volunteer, in the broader society expanded. Nevertheless, even as women in the twentieth century entered more spheres of the life of the society and as organized religion became less central in the identity of many women, large numbers of women still found in church work an important source of meaning, activity, and female fellowship. Women's groups in the churches tended to focus in three areas. Both foreign and home missions continued to be very important to some women, even as the focus of much Protestant missionary work gradually changed and as the functional autonomy and power of the separate mission associations were lost in some cases. Sometimes a group at the local level would merge with the church's general women's society; sometimes the fund-raising that had been so much a part of the missions tradition expanded into benevolent activities in the local community as well. A second key focus was study, especially of the Bible, and personal spiritual development. Finally, the women's groups continued to provide the lion's share of the prosaic but critical support for individual churches: cooking for church suppers, funerals, and weddings; cleaning and caring for the church's physical structure; supplying the bulk of Sunday school teachers; providing fund-raising—so often essential to the expansion or very survival of a congregation—through bazaars, church socials, and other occasions.

## Ecumenical Cooperation: The United Council of Church Women

At the same time, Protestant women continued a successful tradition of ecumenical cooperation, begun in the mission, benevolent, and reform groups of the nineteenth century. Among the most notable was the United Council of Church Women (UCCW), which was founded in 1941, bringing together the National Council of Church Women, the Council of Women for Home Missions, and the Committee on Women's Work of the Foreign Missions Conference. In 1950, the UCCW became the General Department of United Church Women of the National Council of Churches of Christ, a relationship that was not always satisfying or productive for the women, even though they supported the general ecumenical work and approach of the NCC. Thus in 1966, the women decided to resume an autonomous national existence, pulled out of the NCC (without too many hard feelings), and became Church Women United (CWU). Over the years, this women's organization supported a very wide range of activities for women at both the local and national level, including the sponsorship of three distinctive occasions: the World Day of Prayer in Lent, May Fellowship Day, and World Community Day.

The purpose of the UCCW, set forth in its first constitution, was specifically Christian and ecumenical: "to unite church women in their allegiance to their Lord and Savior, Jesus Christ, through a program looking to their integration in the total life and work of the church and to the building of a world Christian community."[19] The group developed a reputation for taking rather liberal social positions, even when compared to parallel male ecumenical bodies. Not surprisingly, the UCCW in its early years was active in war relief and was subsequently a strong supporter of the United Nations. It was also a relatively early and firm voice in favor of racial integration. For example, when a Washington hotel refused to accept reservations from black women delegates to a UCCW board meeting in 1945, all the women left the hotel and stayed in Washington homes instead.[20] During that same decade, the national leadership only recognized state councils that were racially integrated.[21] On other issues like peace, global justice, and hunger, the UCCW and its successors took progressive stands and followed pronouncements with substantive work. The women were also quite open in issues of membership and cooperation; indeed, one cause of their tension with the NCC during their period of organizational cooperation was the women's inclusion of Unitarians on their boards, and when they were reorganized as Church Women United, the organization was open to both Roman Catholic and Eastern Orthodox women, worked cooperatively with Jewish women's groups on common social concerns, and encouraged ecumenical dialogue. To be sure, that the UCCW or CWU leadership took a particular position on race or McCarthyism or global justice did not mean that all the rank and file agreed with those stands, let alone actively worked to make changes. The same divergence between leaders and rank and file was true for denominational boards or the NCC. Nevertheless, the work and formal positions of the women were significant and might have posed an interesting and ironic question for someone like Elizabeth Cady Stanton, who had concluded that the support of individuals within the churches for women's issues did not outweigh the failure of those same denominational bodies to take formal, official stands in favor of women's rights.

## Vocational Opportunities

Work in organizations like the UCCW and its successors allowed some twentieth-century women to make a significant voluntary or professional contribution to the church without being ordained (though some later leaders were also ordained). Other women found a genuine, though nonordained vocation within the churches as missionaries or deaconesses, although the latter option attracted fewer women as the twentieth century progressed than it had around the turn of the century, in part because women had broader professional options by then, including "secular" social work, in part because of the ambiguous status and low pay of the female diaconate. In addition, women entered church work in newly developing professional and staff positions: in church music, as parish workers or church secretaries, and particularly in the field of religious education.

### Education

Religious education as a distinctive field emerged in the early twentieth century, especially at the University of Chicago. Dorothy Jean Furnish identifies three factors in that emergence: the impact of biblical criticism beyond professional scholars; the influence of the philosophy and methods of John Dewey; and the impact of liberal theology with its emphasis on growth and Christian living, rather than the revivalist tradition of conversion and personal salvation.[22] (To be sure, not all the women who found a career in religious education embraced liberal theology. Henrietta Mears (1890–1963) opposed biblical criticism and emphasized individual conversion and yet had a very successful career as a religious educator, developing a widely used "Gospel Light" curriculum.) Nor was religious education initially a female-dominated field. In the early decades, there were roughly equal numbers of men and women in the work, but as Furnish notes, "due to the effects of the depression, by 1938 only 26 percent of the directors [of religious education (DREs)] were men. Women were willing to work for less money, and thus began the myth that it was inherently a woman's profession. . . ."[23] Nevertheless, while men could be DRE's (and were often preferred by male pastors), the position was particularly significant for women because it fit the image of women as nurturers and teachers, and it did not require ordination. The field attracted black and white women, whose duties might include direct teaching in a congregation, training Sunday school and other teachers, youth work, and writing curricula, as well as staff work at the regional or national level in denominations. Furthermore, seminaries began to admit women, often to a special course for religious education, if not the full course required for ordained ministers.

A few women found religious careers teaching in parochial schools (especially Lutheran ones), in colleges and, finally, in seminaries. In 1939, Georgia Harkness, a theologian and social activist, was appointed to a position in applied theology at Garrett Biblical Institute and thereby became "the first woman to teach in a major theological seminary in the United States in a field other than Christian education."[24] Thus many women found expanding options and satisfying careers in the churches, whether as missionaries, deaconesses, leaders of women's groups, teachers, DREs, or members of local and national church staffs, yet women's options and frequently their status remained limited as long as they were denied formal ordination.

## Ordination

The real push for female ordination in most American denominations came in the twentieth century, even though a few denominations had broken the ordination barrier in the nineteenth century. Nineteenth century "firsts" did not, however, mean that women were ordained in large numbers or were able to find parish positions easily. For example, while the Unitarians had ordained several women in the nineteenth century, starting with Olympia Brown in 1863, by 1959, of 539 ministers listed in the Unitarian Yearbook, only six were women, one active and five retired.[25] Congregationalists, who claimed the first ordained woman in Antoinette Brown (1853), had ordained only a total of 100 women three-quarters of a century later.[26] Nor did the formal opportunity in a given denomination necessarily mean women were encouraged or even accepted as ministers. For example, in the early 1930s, a Chicago Congregational advisory board counseled a female seminarian:

> We are your friends. It is because we know so well the frustration awaiting any woman in the ministry that we are urging you to enter related work. We are trying to protect you not only from heartbreak but also ridicule. Think of the sensationalism of women evangelists. No matter how earnest you would be, no one would believe your sincerity. And consider our obligation to protect the

> dignity of the profession. . . . There's only a slight chance you'd get a church and little promotion or professional advancement if you did.[27]

Their comment was probably realistic if discouraging, for many women, as well as men, in the churches opposed female ordination, and in the nineteenth century just as a brave few had felt called to preach and argued their case, so in the twentieth century, some women (and a few men) continued to work for formal changes in mainline Protestant denominations to permit women's ordination.

Before turning to Protestant denominations whose polity makes female ordination a national or regional issue, we should note the situation of Protestant groups like Baptists and Disciples of Christ who, like the Congregationalists, follow congregational polity, that is, who recognize the autonomy of the local congregation. These groups have ordained women, generally in their more liberal branches or areas of the country. Thus, for example, Disciples of Christ and northern Baptists have a substantial number of ordained women, but women pastors are very rare, though theoretically possible, among Southern Baptists. Despite the strength and leadership of individual black Baptist women and the autonomy of the Woman's Convention of the National Baptist Convention, the NBC and the other major black Baptist conventions have been quite resistent to female ordination. As C. Eric Lincoln and Lawrence Mamiya note:

> While there is no specific policy against the ordination of women in any of the black Baptist denominations, the general climate has not been supportive of women preaching and pastoring churches. However, in recent years there has been a small minority of black clergymen who have sponsored women candidates for ordination in their associations. The Baptist principle of congregational autonomy has been helpful in these cases since the independence of each church and pastor cannot be challenged by any denominational authority.[28]

In a few cases, widows have replaced their husbands as Baptist pastors, and there are some female clergy in the Progressive National Baptist Convention (PNBC).[29]

### *Methodists*

The story of female ordination among American Methodists is complicated not only by differences among its branches before the 1939 merger and by racial divisions within Methodism but also because of the range of Methodist offices, from local licenses to preach through full membership in the General Conference. Two important Methodist bodies broke the female ordination barrier before 1900. As noted in chapter 13, the African

Methodist Episcopal Zion Church ordained Julia Foote and Mary Small as, first, deacons and then elders in the 1890s. In 1892, ongoing debates in the Methodist Protestant Church over the autonomy of the Women's Foreign Mission Society, female laity rights, and women's ordination culminated in a victory for the women: four women, including one who had been ordained in a participating conference, were accepted as full delegates at the General Conference. As with other nineteenth-century landmark victories for women's ordination, though, practical results of women's leadership were quite limited. As William T. Noll notes, "Equal opportunities for women in leadership and service thereafter were a possibility, but seldom a reality. . . . Those Methodist Protestant annual conferences that wished to ordain women or elect them to General Conference were free to do so. Although few women subsequently would be elected, their right to be seated was never again questioned [after 1896]."[30]

Women sought but failed to achieve permanent rights to preach and be delegates in the Methodist Episcopal Church, North, in the nineteenth century. At the General Conference in 1920, a member conference again raised the ordination question; it was referred to a commission whose report, passed in 1924, affirmed the right of women to be ordained as local preachers but recommended against their being admitted as members of annual conferences. Given Methodist polity and deployment practices, the distinction was a crucial one. Annual conferences assign their clergy members to churches on a rotating basis; thus if a woman, ordained to preach, were also a member of the annual conference, she would be assured of a church placement. Male Methodist leaders no longer publicly or formally questioned the theological or biblical validity of women preachers, but they feared "forcing" a woman minister upon an unwelcoming congregation, and they did not see the need for women ministers in most cases. Only a few home and foreign mission stations, they felt, would need to accept women. Thus, in effect, a woman could be ordained as a Methodist minister, but she would then have to find a church position on her own, after the more desirable posts were filled by men through the conferences. In practice, then, women generally ended up in small, poor, often rural or mission churches that could not afford or attract a male pastor.

The 1939 merger of Methodist Protestants, northern Methodists, and southern Methodists included the extension of women's right to be ordained as local preachers to the southern Methodists and allowed those women in the Methodist Protestant churches who already held membership in its General Conference to keep that status, but it was not until 1956 that the unified Methodist Church granted full ministerial status, including membership in the General Conference, to women. When the Evangelical United Brethren Church (EUB), itself the product of a union in 1947 between the Church of the United Brethren in Christ, which did ordain women, and the Evangelical Church, which did not, joined with the

Methodist Church in 1968, all of the participating groups accepted women's ordination.[31] In the meantime, the other two major black Methodist churches had also granted full ordination rights to women, the African Methodist Episcopal Church in 1948, and the Colored Methodist Episcopal Church in 1954.[32] A final landmark was reached among Methodists when, in 1984, Marjorie Matthews was elected to be a bishop, the first such woman in a mainline denomination that practices episcopal polity.

### *Presbyterians*

American Presbyterian women's push for ordination parallels in some ways the Methodist experience: both groups voted for full ordination rights for most members in 1956 and each had a smaller, more radical branch that allowed female preaching and ordination before 1900. In the case of the Presbyterians, a presbytery in the Cumberland Presbyterian Church ordained Louisa L. Woolsey in 1889. The move caused considerable controversy, because the ordination was declared invalid by the General Assembly in 1894, but the Cumberland Presbytery stood firm.[33] The issue emerged more broadly in the early twentieth century among northern Presbyterians (the Presbyterian Church in the U.S.A.). In 1923, the General Assembly agreed to allow women to be ordained as deacons, but they could not be ordained as either ruling elders (lay leaders in local churches) or teaching elders (ministers, having the right to preach and administer sacraments). Concern for further change in the 1920s was fueled in part by women's distress at the denomination's takeover of their mission board and by the 1927 *Causes of Unrest* report by Hodge and Bennett, so the General Council set up a commission and called a conference to study the issue. Eventually, the committee brought its recommendations to the General Council, which in turn proposed three "overtures" to the General Assembly and its member presbyteries in 1929. Overture A, granting full equality to women, was defeated; Overture B, which allowed women to be ordained as ruling elders, passed; Overture C, which would have licensed women as evangelists, was narrowly defeated. Thus male leaders offered Presbyterian women some compensation for the power and organizational independence they had lost in the mission board mergers, but women's status in the denomination was still clearly subordinate.

The situation remained essentially the same for the next quarter century, although few women were actually elected as ruling elders and in 1938 the General Assembly proposed a new official, though clearly unordained, status for women as "commissioned church workers." Finally, in 1955 the General Assembly responded to requests from some member presbyteries and proposed that women be granted full ordination rights, and the overture was passed rather easily the next year. There was, of course (as there had been with the Methodists) still opposition, and many of the arguments echoed similar debates over women's preaching in the nineteenth century. Biblical passages were cited by both sides, although by the mid-twentieth century, the impact of biblical criticism was widespread in mainline denominations and thus undercut for many theologically trained leaders the importance of literal adherence to Pauline strictures on women's leadership. Practical or social arguments were also raised: women would not be able to fulfill ministerial and familial duties at the same time, or they would leave the profession when they married; men (and many women) simply would not accept a woman minister; churches wanted to maintain the advantages of the informal, unpaid work of the minister's wife; women's voices didn't carry well; or women would not be able to go out at night for emergency calls. Finally, there was the recurring fear of feminization (which had surfaced earlier during the mission board mergers and as women sought representation on governing bodies of the church): women already constituted the majority of members in most churches, and if they were allowed to be ordained, not only would laymen be more likely to leave, but fewer men might be attracted to the ministry if the profession became feminized.

But conditions had changed by midcentury. Women entered traditionally male jobs during World War II (as they had in earlier wars), and the professional opportunities open to them were wider. The experiences of some European churches during the war and the impact of the World Council of Churches' major study of women's status in Christian churches helped the women's cause. In the 1950s American churches were growing, and there was a greater demand for clergy, so it seemed less likely that women would "take jobs away" from men. Finally, most church leaders assumed, correctly at that time, that few women would actually seek ordination, and those who did would be satisfied with positions in smaller, poorer churches or as assistant ministers. Indeed, Margaret Towner, the first Presbyterian woman to be ordained after the 1956 decision, explicitly repudiated any personal interest in having a pulpit and assumed that women would best serve as assistant ministers who could also cover religious education. (Towner later changed her mind, remarking in 1978 about her earlier opinions, "At that time, I guess, I didn't know better and that statement has come back to haunt me.")[34]

Other Presbyterian bodies followed the PCUSA over the next decade. The more conservative United Presbyterian Church of North America had approved the ordination of women as deacons in 1906 but took no further steps until it merged with the PCUSA in 1958, when it reluctantly accepted women's full access to ordained ministry. Southern Presbyterians defeated an overture to ordain women as ruling elders and deacons in 1956, but by 1964 they passed women's ordination as deacons, ruling elders, and teaching elders all at the same time.

### *Lutherans*

While Methodists and Presbyterians debated and studied the question of women's ordination for decades before their respective 1956 decisions, American Lutherans, although they did have deaconesses, appear to have had little interest in the question of ordination for women before the second half of the twentieth century. Indeed, Lutherans in the United States were slower than their European counterparts to address the issue. Norwegian Lutherans approved female ordination in 1938, and the Church of Sweden did the same in 1958, aided by the positive arguments of prominent theologian and biblical scholar Krister Stendahl.[35] When the issue arose for American Lutherans, the process was less prolonged and relatively less bitter and divisive than it had been earlier for Methodists and Presbyterians and would soon be for Episcopalians. Among Lutherans, the debates focused primarily on biblical and theological questions, and during the 1960s, American Lutherans produced numerous studies, reports, and articles on both sides of the issue. Opponents cited not only biblical prohibitions but also the concept of "orders of creation," those structures, including the subordination of women, decreed by God for humans' earthly and community life. Thus, they insisted, for a woman to assume the authority of a pastor was to go against divine orders and her own nature. Opponents also raised the "ecumenical argument"—that is, concern that ordination of women would impede dialogue with Anglicans and Roman Catholics—and worried about the impact of women's ordination on internal Lutheran unity.

Yet other Lutherans, including a number of prominent theologians and the Lutheran Church Women, supported a change that would open full ordination rights to women. Particularly influential were reports produced by Lutheran seminary faculty or commissioned by governing bodies of the Lutheran Church in America (LCA), the American Lutheran Church (ALC), and the Lutheran Council in the U.S.A. (LCUSA, which included the Lutheran Church–Missouri Synod (LCMS) in its membership.) These commissions drew on the services of trained Lutheran biblical scholars, historians, and theologians. For example, the faculty of Luther Theological Seminary issued a report in 1968 that noted the potential areas of objection (biblical, theological, practical, and ecumenical), suggested that the last was the most problematic, but still concluded: "In view of the considerations above, we can see no valid reason why women candidates for ordination who meet the standards normally required for admission to the ministry should not be recommended for ordination."[36] Thus in 1970, two of the three major Lutheran bodies in America voted to open ordained ministry to women. The Lutheran Church in America passed it on a voice vote after minimal debate in June, while the American Lutheran Church voted in favor in October, though by a narrower margin.[37] For those members of the LCA and ALC who could not accept the change, there was the alternative of the LCMS, still adamantly opposed to women's ordination, and it may be that this option helped to minimize the potential divisiveness of the change among Lutherans in the United States.

### *Episcopalians*

A common characteristic of the gradual movement toward women's ordination among American Protestant denominations was the tendency of governing bodies to appoint numerous commissions to study (and often effectively postpone) the issue, and Episcopalians were no exception. The reemergence of deaconesses in the nineteenth century raised the question of their status: Were they, in some sense, ordained? ordered? set apart? A 1919 report from a commission appointed by the archbishop of Canterbury studied the issue, and in 1920, the Lambeth Conference (a regular meeting of bishops from the worldwide Anglican communions) decided that the office of deaconess was a form of Holy Orders (though not comparable to male deacons); however, ten years later, the bishops changed their minds. The next few decades produced no broad movement in favor of women's ordination, but did see a few dramatic events: in 1944, the bishop of Hong Kong, faced with a need for clergy, ordained a woman, Li Tim Oi, to the priesthood, but that ordination was rejected by Anglican leadership as invalid; in 1965, Bishop James Pike of the United States precipitated a controversy (and another study) by liturgical actions that implied that a deaconess, Phyliss Edwards, had authority parallel to that of a male deacon.

In the meantime, during the 1960s, Episcopal women began to take the full course, intended to lead to ordination, at denominational seminaries, so that when in 1970 the General Convention of the American Episcopal Church voted in favor of ordaining women to the diaconate, a number of candidates were ready to seek such ordination. (That convention vote effectively ended the distinct office of deaconess for women.) But a resolution to ordain women as priests lost at the 1970 General Convention, for though it passed among the laity in the House of Deputies, it was defeated by the male priests in that House. In 1973, women's ordination to the priesthood was again defeated, this time due to a voting process that effectively counted a divided vote among a diocesan delegation, lay or clerical, as a negative. The loss, coupled with the election of John Allin, a known opponent of women's ordination, as presiding bishop, further galvanized proponents of female ordination, including some male leaders, as well as the women deacons themselves and a substantial number of female Episcopalians. (The Women's Triennial, the national organization of Episcopal churchwomen that meets at the same time as General Convention, in 1970 voted resoundingly in favor of women's ordination; their vote, however, had no standing at General Convention.)

Before the next General Convention could meet, three retired bishops ordained eleven women as priests at a special service in Philadelphia on July 29, 1974, thus gaining national publicity as well as raising a tremendous furor within the Episcopal Church in America. Supporters of the women agreed that the ordinations were irregular but insisted they were valid; opponents decried them as not only irregular but invalid, and each side could call on theological scholars to support its views. Heated debate, charges and countercharges continued, but in 1976, the issue was effectively resolved when the General Convention passed a resolution opening both the priesthood and the episcopate to women. Nevertheless, significant bitterness and deep-seated opposition to women priests lingered, and some individuals and parishes broke away from the church rather than accept the change, and the House of Bishops later passed a "conscience clause" that permitted a bishop to refuse access to the ordination process to women within his own diocese.

Over the next dozen years, many women were ordained to the Episcopal priesthood, and the vast majority of parishes and dioceses accepted their ordination. Yet individuals and organizations were still bitterly opposed to women priests, an opposition that intensified with the prospect that a woman might be elected and consecrated to the final clerical order: bishop. In September 1988, it happened: the Diocese of Massachusetts elected as its suffragan bishop (a kind of assistant bishop to the main, or diocesan, bishop) Barbara Clementine Harris. Despite vigorous work by horrified traditionalists—Harris was not only a woman, she was also an African-American, divorced, and a political and social liberal—the necessary consents from the rest of the church were obtained, and she was consecrated as bishop on February 11, 1989—a little less than fifteen years after she, as a lay leader at the Church of the Advocate, had carried the cross in procession at the irregular ordination of the "Philadelphia Eleven."[38]

The story of the drive for female religious leadership among American Protestants includes not only the culmination of ordination but also the foundational gains of laity rights and professional church work, as well as women's leadership in their own denominational and interdenominational organizations. But questions remained. Although women had a formal right to ordination, would women ministers be accepted? Would they bring a different approach to ministry? (We will turn to these first questions in the last chapter.) What would become of all-women's church groups, once women had access to all positions of lay and ordained leadership? Here, the evidence is mixed, and it is too soon to venture a definitive answer. On the one hand, fewer younger and middle-aged women appear to participate in all-female church organizations, especially those that meet during weekdays, since more of them work outside the home. Others see little attraction in leadership of a woman's group when they can serve on their church's governing board and as delegates to regional and national meetings. On the other hand, many church women's organizations at both the local and national level are vibrant and effective. They have adjusted to new female career patterns; they fund and support extensive religious and humanitarian projects; many women still appreciate the atmosphere and mutual support of all-women's organizations.

### *Judaism*

Protestant groups showed striking parallels as each went through the process of winning female ordination. Despite other very real differences between American Protestants and American Jews, some of these same patterns are found in the story of Jewish women in their search for leadership and religious identity in twentieth-century America. When immigration restrictions sharply reduced the numbers of Jews coming to America after the first two decades of the twentieth century, Jews living in the United States continued to "Americanize" but were also concerned to maintain a distinctive identity and culture. By the 1920s and 1930s, more Jewish women found in organizations like the National Council of Jewish Women, Hadassah, and the temple sisterhoods significant scope for activities that affirmed their identity as women and as Jews. Many of these groups, like some Protestant mission organizations, had strong female leadership and autonomy. As Ellen Umansky notes, "The National Council of Jewish Women . . . was unusual in its independence from any male-dominated religious movement."[39] In other cases, like B'nai Brith, a Jewish mutual aid society, women's participation was more the "auxiliary" type: raising money but having little say on how it was spent or in other organizational decisions.[40] Formal leadership of synagogues and temples was male-dominated, and as with American Protestants, the achievement of female laity rights, let alone ordination, was a slow process over the course of the twentieth century.

Many Jewish women (and Jewish men) became secularized, leaving traditional or even liberal observance behind while, perhaps, retaining a sense of Yiddish culture or sympathy for Jews as a people. A few articulate Jewish women writers openly criticized the male-dominated faith of their ancestors. Anzia Yezierska, for example, was author of a number of successful novels and short stories about eastern European immigrant life. Sara Smolinsky, the heroine of *Bread Givers,* Yezierska's semiautobiographical novel, is the youngest of four daughters. Sara rejects and actively fights the religion she sees as so unfair to women in order to "make herself for a person"—that is, to succeed in America, gaining an education and a respectable profession as a schoolteacher. Elizabeth Stern, who wrote *I am a Woman—and a Jew* under the pseudonym Leah Morton, also rejected the Jewish faith of her parents and its androcentrism. Even as she realized she could never entirely shed her Jewishness, she chose not to practice it, ultimately joining the Quakers instead.

Yet few Jewish women who chose to remain observant expressed much overt dissatisfaction with their place as Jewish women. For one thing, the gains for women in Reform and, to a lesser degree, Conservative Judaism were sufficiently recent and dramatic in comparison with Orthodox tradition that most women were quite content with the pace of change. Second, women had their own organizations, and as long as these were permitted to function and develop with relative autonomy, women were unlikely to question their position in separate spheres. Third, Jews in America, like other minorities excluded from the dominant cultural establishment, understood their need for group solidarity and hence were less likely than white Protestant women to raise critiques that might be internally divisive. Finally, the marriage of American cultural expectations and a Jewish heritage of separate, if not quite equal, spheres produced a situation in which many Jewish women embraced their unique female role as nurturers and preservers of the hearth—for in their case, this included the preservation of Jewish identity through the home at a time when many Jewish men's relationship to synagogue and temple was becoming increasingly pro forma and tangential.

That most Jewish women were far from radical feminists did not, however, prevent some male Jewish leaders, writers, and rabbis, from criticizing Jewish women. Charlotte Baum, Paula Hyman, and Sonya Michel in *The Jewish Woman in America* trace the changing literary image of Jewish women among (predominantly) male authors. In early literature the Jewish immigrant woman appears as a strong and admirable figure, but as Jews "made it," socially and economically, she is replaced by more negative images: first, "the foolish, overdecorated wife of the parvenu . . . [who] is a caricature of a 'real' lady, her pretensions to refinement laughable, and her shallowness and materialism contemptible"; ultimately, the stock characters of the Jewish Mother and the Jewish American Princess emerge.[41] While literary stereotypes are not applied solely to Jewish women, they were nonetheless influential and painful for the real Jewish women who were often unsure of their roles and goals in a culture in transition.

Furthermore, criticism was not confined to literature. Male Jewish religious leaders, even as prominent and otherwise liberal a man as Mordecai Kaplan, the founder of Reconstructionism, sometimes blamed Jewish women for the loss of Jewish faith and identity in America. The charge, however, seems ill-founded, as Norma Fain Pratt argues.[42] For one thing, fewer Jewish women married Gentile men than vice versa. In addition, women were active not only in their own female organizations but also disproportionately in the synagogue (though not its leadership), and Jewish mothers took their roles as preservers of the faith very seriously indeed. A Reform Jewish woman wrote in 1924 of her search for faith and identity and concluded that these were to be found neither in replication of Old

World traditions nor the emptiness of secular modernity but in dedication to a renewed Judaism.

> The sound and humble vigor of the Jewish faith was responding to her two needs; it was answering her heart's queries; it was imposing a duty upon her—a duty for the future.
>
> Under this awakened impulse, she drew understanding strength from her Synagogue; and she breathed into it a warmth and an exhilaration. Steadied after her stormy struggle, she became the calm and forward-looking ally of the spiritual leaders in their public work. And then she turned with mature conviction and unpretentious devotion, to the greatest of her tasks—the work in which she is at this moment earnestly engaged—the work that falls to her as the grandchild of her grandmother: the beautifying and consecrating of a Jewish home; for in the end she is the guardian of the future—at the same time providing the men of the morrow and saving for them their noblest treasures.[43]

While the great majority of Jewish women did not seek further rights of religious leadership in the first half of the twentieth century, a few did, just as a relatively small number of Protestant women personally carried on the struggle for ordination. In 1921, Martha Neumark, a student at Hebrew Union College (HUC) who was taking rabbinic courses, petitioned to be allowed to lead the High Holy Day services, thus raising the issue of a woman rabbi. A study committee was appointed and returned a report that saw "no logical reason why women should not be entitled to receive a rabbinical degree," but for practical reasons, the committee discouraged it. The report was referred to the faculty, who came to a similar conclusion. It was then sent to the Central Conference of American Rabbis who also declared, on a split vote, that "woman cannot justly be denied the privilege of ordination." Nevertheless, HUC's board decided not to change its male-only policy at that time, and Martha Neumark never became a rabbi. The pattern of study commissions and multiple committees with split votes is similar to the experiences of some Christian denominations, as were the objections raised by opponents even when no theoretical basis for denial of female ordination was found: women, as wives and mothers, could not devote themselves fully to the calling in the way men could; the situation would result in tensions between a woman rabbi's leadership role in the synagogue and her appropriately subordinate role in the family.[44]

Soon after the Neumark case, a woman in New York, Irma Lindheim, began rabbinic studies at the Jewish Institute of Religion, but later withdrew for personal reasons.[45] Subsequently, the issue was raised by another woman, Helen Hadassah Levinthal, in 1939. Again, there was debate; again, the issue was postponed, only to be raised again with similar results in 1956. In the meantime, however, Paula Ackerman had actually functioned as a lay rabbi for a few years in the early 1950s. When Ackerman's husband, William, died, Temple Beth Israel, the congregation he had served in Meridian, Mississippi, asked his widow to assume his position of spiritual leadership. Though initially reluctant, Paula Ackerman came to believe that God was calling her to the position, and she served successfully, finding acceptance from some other Reform rabbis. Finally, in 1972, half a century after Martha Neumark's petition, Sally Priesand became the first Jewish woman to be formally ordained as a rabbi by a theological seminary.[46]

Two years later, Sandy Sasso was ordained a rabbi as part of one of the early graduating classes of the Reconstructionist Rabbinical College. Although Reconstructionism had existed as a movement within American Judaism since the early decades of the twentieth century, it was not until the late 1960s that it became a distinctive denomination; its rabbinical college was founded in 1968 and was open equally to men and women from the start.[47] Although Reconstructionism is much smaller than Reform, Conservative, or Orthodox Judaism in America, its acceptance of women's equal leadership as rabbinical students was not its first contribution to increased roles for American Jewish women. In 1922, Mordecai Kaplan's daughter, Judith, celebrated a Bat Mitzvah, when she was called up to read from the Torah during a Sabbath morning service. The ceremony celebrated a young woman's religious coming of age, just as the Bar Mitzvah did for young men. Over the next decades, many Reform and some of the more liberal Conservative congregations adopted a form of Bat Mitzvah, sometimes nearly parallel to the traditional young man's Bar Mitzvah, sometimes an adapted but still formal occasion to mark the same religious landmark for girls. Today, a Bat Mitzvah equivalent to a Bar Mitzvah is celebrated in virtually all Reform and Reconstructionist congregations and in a majority of Conservative synagogues; other Conservative congregations, however, hold the ceremony on Friday evening rather than Saturday morning and have the young woman read from the Prophets rather than the Torah.[48]

During the same decade that the first female rabbis were ordained in Reform and Reconstructionist Judaism, a group of Conservative Jewish women began to raise more insistent questions about their status within that branch of Judaism. In 1974, they formed a group known as Ezrat Nashim and presented a call for change on several fronts to Conservatism's Rabbincal Assembly. They wanted women to be given synagogue membership and counted in a *minyan,* to be able to serve as valid witnesses in Jewish law and to initiate divorce, and to be admitted to appropriate training so that they could become cantors and rabbis. In response, the rabbis' Committee on Jewish Law and Standards encouraged (but did not require) member congregations to allow women to assume positions of lay leadership, to be counted in the *minyan,* and to be called up to read from the Torah. The next year, that same committee registered its rejection of female rabbis and cantors, but in 1977, the Rabbinical Assembly appointed a study commission on the question of female ordination. The commission presented its report on January 30, 1979, recommending by a vote of 11 to 3 that the Jewish Theological Seminary admit women to its rabbinic course. While the commission considered a range of arguments, it stated clearly that the decisive issue was Jewish law or *halakhah*.

> The *halakhic* objections to the ordination of women center around disapproval of the performance by a woman of certain functions [e.g., being a legal witness]. Those functions, however, are not essentially rabbinic, nor are they universally disapproved, by the accepted rules governing the discussion of *halakhah* in the Conservative Movement. *There is no direct halakhic objection to the acts of training and ordaining a woman to be a rabbi, preacher, and teacher in Israel.*[49]

At first, the seminary's faculty was divided, and they tabled the recommendation, but it was revived in 1983 and passed. The first women entered in the fall of 1984, and in 1985, Amy Eilberg became the first woman to be ordained as a Conservative rabbi. Thus by the closing years of the twentieth century, three of the four major Jewish groups in the United States, like the majority of mainline Protestant bodies, granted women full formal religious equality and ordination.

# 19

# *Women's Religious Leadership in the Twentieth Century:*

## Ambiguity among Evangelicals and Mormons

In the early 1970s, a small group of Christians, heirs to a theologically conservative Protestant tradition, began to question the limitations placed on women in their churches. Calling themselves "evangelical feminists," they argued that the exclusion of women from public leadership in the churches, rather than being an unbroken tradition, was in fact a betrayal of the nineteenth-century roots of evangelical Christianity, which was more open to women, their rights, and their religious leadership than the general culture of the day. Thus they set about rediscovering an evangelical heritage of forefathers and foremothers to support their contention that conservative theology did not necessarily mandate female subordination and silence.[1] At about the same time, small groups of Mormon women in Utah and Massachusetts began to meet and to question their church's current ideas about and treatment of women. They, too, found a contrast between the late nineteenth and the late twentieth centuries as they rediscovered a history of pioneer Mormon women.[2]

The historical case made by these evangelical feminists, Mormon women, and other scholars over the next years was convincing, but it also raised the question, Why? Why did certain Protestant groups in America who were more open to women's religious leadership in the late nineteenth and early twentieth centuries start to "back off" that precedent by the 1920s, either sharply restricting or denying altogether opportunities for female religious leadership? And despite the general trend, why were some evangelical women exceptions, achieving a substantial fame and following as preachers in the first half of the twentieth century? In this chapter I address the history, changes, and exceptions to trends regarding female religious leadership in those Protestant movements known as fundamentalism, evangelicalism, the Holiness tradition, and Pentecostalism, as well as in the Church of Jesus Christ of Latter-day Saints, over the course of the twentieth century.

### Evangelicalism

Twentieth-century evangelical churches have important roots in nineteenth-century American evangelical Protestantism, but unlike the

Christians with similar roots who came to dominate twentieth-century mainline denominations, they rejected modern intellectual developments like Darwinism, biblical criticism, and some aspects of the social sciences. Instead, many of them embraced a theological position known as premillennial dispensationalism. Premillennialism is the conviction that conditions on earth will deteriorate until Jesus Christ appears dramatically to inaugurate his thousand-year reign (an interpretation of Revelation 20) and stands in contrast to the more optimistic postmillennialism, which characterized most of nineteenth-century American Protestantism, that is, the belief that Christ would return after a period of progressive improvement in human society. Dispensationalism is the idea that history is divided into particular periods or dispensations by God, a concept associated with the Englishman John Nelson Darby, brought to America by popular revivalists like Dwight L. Moody, and given enduring influence in the Scofield Reference Bible, first published in 1910. Furthermore, these evangelical Christians were frequently appalled by changes in American culture, changes that seemed to validate their premillennialism. Thus theological concerns like premillennial dispensationalism and an understanding of the Bible as inerrant, verbally inspired, and literally true in every word distinguished them from the liberal Christians of their own time. Yet they retained the strong emphasis on a personal conversion experience and the activity of the laity that was at the heart of nineteenth-century evangelical Protestantism.[3]

Before turning to an account of the place of women in these movements, however, some clarification of the term "evangelical" in American religious history may be helpful. First, "evangelical" applies broadly in the nineteenth century to most American Protestants and is sometimes used in contrast to more "churchly" Christian denominations like Lutherans, Episcopalians, or Roman Catholics (though some Lutherans and some Episcopalians were more evangelical than churchly in their sympathies.)

"Evangelical" took on a somewhat different meaning by mid-twentieth century. Heirs of these nineteenth-century evangelicals were divided in the early twentieth century between "liberal" Protestants who, not without struggle, came to control most mainline denominations, and theologically conservative Protestants, sometimes known as fundamentalists. But as the result of a split in midcentury within American fundamentalism, "evangelical" was claimed as a name by churches or Christians who were theologically conservative but resisted the designation of "fundamentalist" because they rejected fundamentalist militancy and insistence on sharp separatism; evangelicals also wanted to avoid a term that seemed to carry derogatory associations for many Americans. The split was symbolized and formalized in 1942 with the formation of the National Association of Evangelicals (NAE). "Evangelical" in this sense is not a denomination per se, but it does have identifiable schools and seminaries, organizations, and leaders such as Billy Graham and Carl Henry.

At the same time, many contemporary observers and scholars of American religion use the term "evangelicalism" in a third, broader sense, including under that tent a range of Christian bodies from black pentecostalists to strict separatist fundamentalists. Although these groups differ in important ways, they share a common heritage and core convictions about the supernatural and authoritative nature of the Bible, the centrality of conversion, often understood as a "born-again" experience that results in a changed life, and the importance of evangelism and missions. With the exception of Mormons, the groups discussed in this chapter fit within this third definition of evangelicalism.[4]

## Women's Roles

Some Christians and churches who rallied to the fundamentalist cause, notably the strand of nineteenth-century Old School Presbyterianism associated with Princeton Seminary, had never been open to women's rights or female religious leadership and had self-consciously resisted any "feminization" of religion.[5] But other individuals and groups had, around the turn of the century, been sympathetic to some exercise of public religious activity and leadership for women. Women were very much a part of the Bible schools and institutes that appeared on the American educational and religious scene from the 1880s on. Theologically, Bible institutes were sympathetic to conservative evangelicalism in the late nineteenth century and, by the twentieth century, to an emerging and self-conscious fundamentalism, and they were important centers for fundamentalist education and popularization. These schools, the most famous of which was Moody Bible Institute (MBI) in Chicago, were often nondenominational and operated at a less rigorous educational level than seminaries, because their particular goal was training lay people for religious service in a range of roles: missionaries, evangelists, revivalists, Sunday school teachers, musicians, and other church workers. Partly because of their emphasis on lay ministry, partly because of their newness and admission standards that were less stringent than those of seminaries or colleges, the Bible schools attracted large numbers, even majorities, of female students. The women students were then encouraged by female role models on the faculty and evangelical women missionaries, preachers, and revivalists. This is not to say that the schools advocated radical gender equality even in their early days (few endorsed women's ordination), but they did provide practical opportunities and important, although limited, sanction for female religious leadership.[6]

Spurred on by the opportunities to train for religious work offered by the Bible institutes, evangelical women were visible and active in revivals and churches that identified themselves with traditional views of biblical authority. Premillennialism, combined with observation of American culture and of the opportunities for worldwide evangelism, convinced many protofundamentalists that when the harvest was so great, the laborers so few, and the time so short, female contributions should not be despised. Thus several important male leaders of the movement encouraged women's activity. A. B. Simpson, the founder of the earliest Bible school, eventually located in Nyack, New York, and of the Christian and Missionary Alliance, supported women's evangelistic work, as did A. J. Gordon and William Bell Riley, both of whom founded Bible schools in Boston and Minneapolis respectively and became prominent leaders of the fundamentalist movement. And while some other leaders and schools were more hesitant to endorse prominent leadership roles for women, the example of Moody Bible Institute was highly influential. In its early years, MBI's focus was on lay leadership, and women were well represented among the evangelists and revivalists who sought its training and endorsement. When MBI began a pastor's course, women were admitted, and in 1929, the first woman graduated from that course. Janette Hassey argues in her study of evangelical women at the turn of the century that not only did MBI allow women to attend, it continued to bless their activities by reports in its journal about alumnae who were evangelists, revivalists, supply preachers, and even pastors. To be sure, women were most often called as pastors to small, poor, or rural congregations, churches less likely be able to attract and afford a male minister, but the women's work was nonetheless accepted, even praised.[7]

Support for women's leadership was never unanimous among conservative schools and churches, but female work was defended on theological as well as practical grounds by prominent male and female leaders, who combined belief in the literal authority of the Bible with interpretations that supported women's preaching. Classic negative passages like 1 Corinthians 14 and 1 Timothy 2 were understood to be related to specific contexts in the early church rather than taken as universal prohibitions, while the prophesying activities of biblical women and the action of the Holy Spirit were highlighted. Indeed, citing Joel 2:28, some found in women's prophesying a sign of the last days, reinforcing their premillennial convictions.[8]

## Fundamentalism

In the period between the world wars, the situation gradually changed for evangelical women. As Bible institutes became more focused on training ministers and more concerned about academic standing, the percentage of women students dropped and their opportunities were significantly restricted. For example, MBI began to channel women students into more appropriately "female" courses, and in 1930 Gordon College's trustees limited the percentage of women students to one-third.[9] Fundamentalist opposition to women's leadership became the more dominant note, support a rarer tone, as the perceived need for women revivalists declined.

Several other factors contributed to fundamentalists' growing opposition to female religious leadership. As theological battle between liberals or "modernists" and fundamentalists became more heated in the early decades of the twentieth century, fundamentalist defenses of biblical inerrancy emphasized the absolute and unchanging nature of Pauline prohibitions on women's preaching and assuming positions of religious authority over men. At the same time, dispensationalist premillennialism provided a second theological source for rejections of female religious leadership. As Margaret Lamberts Bendroth has argued:

> Although dispensationalism by no means set out to resolve the issue of woman's place, its clear, consistent logic played a powerful role in the rising debate. Dispensationalist premillennialism embedded the principle of masculine leadership and feminine subordination in salvation history itself and, perhaps more important, uplifted order as the highest principle of Christian life and thought.[10]

A second factor in the growing opposition to female leadership was a series of power struggles during the 1920s within certain Protestant denominations, most notably northern Presbyterians and northern Baptists, between liberals and fundamentalists. The fundamentalists' growing sense of frustration and alienation was exacerbated by their perception that at the same time they were losing power and status in the denominations, being forced into the position of "unwilling outsiders," women (those perennial "outsiders") were gaining more access to denominational leaders and power structures through mission board mergers and debate on the question of female ordination. That women's gains in real power were minimal had little effect on fundamentalists' perception of them as rivals for status and influence in denominational establishments increasingly dominated by male liberals. Furthermore, the female-liberal alliance reinforced fundamentalist suspicions of the nineteenth-century image of women as more naturally religious and moral than men. Not only were both genders equally subject to sin, they argued, but feminized religion, like liberalism, undercut doctrinal rigor and theological truth.[11] When many fundamentalists gave up the struggle to shape existing Protestant denominations, withdrew, and formed their own churches and organizations, they were unlikely to make room for female leadership. For example, the American Conference of Undenominational Churches (later the Independent Fundamental Churches of America) accepted as members at the time of its founding in 1923 women who had been previously ordained, but by 1930 it denied membership to women entirely.[12]

Third, conservative Protestant retreat from women's religious leadership was closely related to concern with women's roles in family, church, and society.[13] Male fundamentalist leaders deplored changes in female images and activities, symbolized by the "new woman" and, worst of all, the flapper. Such females were clearly not true women. They flouted traditional sexual morality; instead of serving as guardians and exemplars of purity, their dress and activities displayed their own immodesty and tempted vulnerable young men into sin. They scorned women's natural roles and appeared to have lost any sense of responsibility to the home. Their acceptance of divorce undermined the sacred bond of marriage. They even tried to avoid motherhood through birth control. When their concerns were not immoral, materialistic, self-indulgent, or frivolous, women were trying to invade the public world and professions of men. In the face of such disruption and disaster, fundamentalist spokesmen argued vehemently for a return to a Victorian gender ideology of separate spheres, with women firmly planted in the home as self-sacrificing wives and mothers; for home was the absolutely necessary foundation for a moral society and America's Christian destiny, both of which were being undermined by women's stepping out of their place.

Fundamentalists in the 1920s and 1930s thus had to deal with ambiguous, even conflicting, views of women. Within the churches, women were unwelcome rivals for status and power, yet their presence and support, including financial support and service as foreign missionaries and Bible teachers, were critical to those churches' survival. Within the culture, women seemed to be betraying their responsibilities. Idealized Victorian gender ideology implied that women were naturally purer, more spiritual, and more moral than men, and women's conscientious fulfillment of their divinely ordained duties in their proper sphere of the home was necessary for America's well-being. Yet by denying their "proper" roles but retaining their cultural power, these "naturally moral" women were responsible for the current breakdown of morality. Women out of their sphere, throwing off the authority of husbands in the home and ministers in the churches, were undermining the moral fiber and stability of the nation. They also posed the threat of heresy, manifest in such female-founded or female-led religious alternatives as Christian Science, Spiritualism, and Theosophy. In short, alongside and in tension with the image of the ideal woman was a renewed image of Eve, woman as suspiciously immoral, a sexual temptation for men, with a weaker intellect that left her vulnerable to theological errors and heresy.

The female sphere idealized by fundamentalists was even more rigidly limited than it had been in the nineteenth century, because male leaders opposed the kind of female participation in reform and religious activities that had been condoned by their fathers and grandfathers. At the same time as they urged women to get back to their proper sphere, the home, male leaders tried to reclaim and remasculinize what they saw as a dangerously feminized church. The image of Christ and Christians had been, they felt, sentimentalized and softened; that image would have to be revised to protect their own masculine identities and to restore male dominance and attract other men back to the churches. As one male religious leader wrote:

> Christianity emasculates no man, makes no man effeminate, depreciates no manly virtue. There is nothing that puts so much iron in the blood; nothing that tones and builds up the manly nature; . . . nothing that emphasizes and exalts manliness, as does Christianity. The purpose, the incarnate idea of Christianity is to make magnificent manhood; to make men like Christ, the manliest of all men.[14]

Concern over feminine domination of the churches was by no means confined to theologically conservative Christian men in the late nineteenth and early twentieth centuries, but the rhetoric and the criticism of women were particularly vehement and uncompromising among fundamentalists. Where twentieth-century mainline Protestantism gradually came to accept, even endorse, women's changing roles, including an increased place for formal leadership in the churches, fundamentalists and their heirs maintained their insistence on a Victorian gender ideology of separate spheres and imposed greater restrictions on women's public religious activity and leadership than had most of their nineteenth-century ancestors.

## The Holiness Movement

Like fundamentalism, Holiness churches emerged from late nineteenth-century conservative evangelicalism, but their distinctive heritage came through Methodism and the nineteenth-century movement in America in which Phoebe Palmer was such an influential leader. Central to that heritage is an emphasis on the second blessing of sanctification or holiness. During the last third of the century, the National Camp Meeting Association for the Promotion of Holiness was formed to encourage holiness among all Christians and particularly to reassert the doctrine of sanctification among Methodists. Although holiness advocates were initially reluctant to establish separate denominations, by the later years of the century, tensions with established Methodism reached the breaking point. Advocates of holiness deplored the cold formality and worldliness they saw in the churches and especially their clergy and insisted that the second blessing was *the* distinctive mark of Christians. Methodist leaders were appalled by the emotionalism of Holiness revivals, and while they could not deny sanctification as part of their Wesleyan doctrinal heritage, they preferred to relegate it in a more subordinate position. Thus informal Holiness groups and missions grew into separate denominations, including the

Church of the Nazarene, the Pilgrim Holiness Church, and the Church of God (Anderson, Indiana).

In their early years, Holiness churches were relatively open to women's religious leadership, since the work of the Holy Spirit in sanctification was a more important qualification than formal education for preaching the gospel. Thus there were numerous female evangelists in the Church of God (organized in 1881), though there was also considerable male criticism of their activities; the Church of the Nazarene accepted women's right to preach in its 1894 constitution and had ordained women by 1908; as many as 30 percent of ministers in the Pilgrim Holiness Church in the 1930s were women. The Salvation Army, a group that became part of the Holiness movement, drew upon the tradition of its cofounder, Catherine Booth, to uphold the right of women to preach and to hold leadership positions. In 1934, Evangeline Booth was named the worldwide general of the Salvation Army, having already led the United States branch of the Army for some thirty years.[15] But over time, these groups modified their positions on public religious leadership for women. Some bodies rejected women's ordained leadership altogether; others, like the Church of the Nazarene and the Salvation Army, while maintaining female ordination, saw the percentage and status of women clergy gradually decline from their former highs. Even though the percentage of women clergy in some Holiness groups was significantly higher in the late twentieth century than the percentage in mainline denominations that had begun ordaining women after midcentury, that percentage was holding steady or declining while the mainline percentages of women clergy were increasing.

### Alma Bridwell White

Still, the Holiness movement had many strong women preachers, and one of the most colorful was a woman who not only preached widely and effectively but also founded her own denomination and functioned as its first bishop, Alma Bridwell White (1862–1946). Born in Kentucky, Alma managed to get an education despite her family's poverty. Although she was raised in a religious family and joined the Methodist Church, she did not experience a personal conversion until she was sixteen. At the same time, she felt God had called her to preach but, like many women before her, doubted the possibility of such a call for herself since the Methodists of her day forbade it, and she considered foreign mission work instead. After supporting herself for several years as a teacher in schools from Kentucky to Montana, in 1887 she married Kent White, a Methodist minister, and their two sons were born in 1889 and 1892. As she shared Kent's work in Colorado, Alma prayed and exhorted as often as she could, yet she felt frustrated by her inability to experience the full second blessing of sanctification. Finally, in 1893, she experienced sanctification and was called anew to a preaching vocation, leading revival meetings and taking an active role in the Colorado Holiness Association. Methodist authorities approved of neither her gender, the emotionalism of her meetings, nor her insistence on the absolute necessity of sanctification and the possibility of faith healing. She, in turn, dismissed them as cold and unworthy of the name of Christian: "I saw that the Church that had been raised up under John Wesley to spread scriptural holiness had become like a corpse and that my relationship with it would jeopardize my soul's eternal interests."[16]

Despite her success as a revivalist, Alma White experienced tensions not only with the Methodist leadership in Colorado but also with her husband, Kent. In part, these tensions were due to Kent's disapproval of Alma's typological interpretation of scripture, but at least as important was her greater success as a preacher and her growing independence. As her biographer notes:

> By this phase in her ministry, Alma considered Kent her assistant rather than an equal partner. Alma revealed at one point that she did not expect Kent to attend all her services "but it was a great help to have him present occasionally to preach or take part." During their courtship, Alma and Kent had both assumed she would perform the traditional role of a minister's wife and support Kent in his ministry. Now the roles were reversed, but Kent never adjusted to the change.[17]

By 1901, she severed her ties to the Methodists and founded her own organization, the Pentecostal Union Church (later the Pillar of Fire Church), in which she was formally ordained in 1902. In 1906, she began a community called Zarephath (see 1 Kings 17) on a farm in New Jersey that had been given to her church. She transferred her headquarters there in 1908, though she retained a strong branch in Denver. The Pillar of Fire Church grew over the next years, adding branches in other parts of the United States and in London, England, and sponsoring schools, missions, publications, and eventually two radio stations.

Kent White had joined Alma's new church, giving up his Methodist ministerial credentials, but tensions between husband and wife continued and came to a head when he was attracted to the new pentecostalist revival, while Alma adamantly opposed its speaking in tongues.[18] Kent left Alma and the Zarephath community and, despite Alma's attempts at reconciliation as long as it did not compromise her church work, the couple remained separated until his death in 1940. In the meantime, Alma was consecrated as a bishop in 1918, making her the first woman bishop in America. As such, she led the Pillar of Fire Church with an extremely firm hand until her death in 1946, when she was succeeded by her son Arthur and, subsequently, her granddaughter Arlene White Lawrence.

Alma White's religious leadership was unusual but not unique in her day (except for her episcopal status), and her defense of women preachers was similar to Holiness arguments from Phoebe Palmer on. Two further factors make Alma White an unusual and complex figure: she was a radical feminist and at the same time a self-proclaimed fundamentalist; and she had a long and close association with the Ku Klux Klan. Susie Cunningham Stanley argues that she was only a moderate fundamentalist, for while she strongly opposed modernism (especially biblical criticism and Darwinism) and embraced premillennialism, she was not a dispensationalist and did not speak in terms of biblical "inerrancy." And she was clearly a feminist. Not only did she proclaim and act upon women's religious equality, she insisted that women should be socially, economically, and politically equal to men. To that end, she promoted woman suffrage and endorsed the radical wing of the suffrage movement, the National Woman's Party, including its militant tactics and its support of an equal rights amendment to the Constitution. In 1924, she founded *Woman's Chains*, a journal that was uncompromising in its stand on full equality for women.[19]

Modern students may find "fundamentalist feminist" a hard enough combination to imagine, without trying to put together Alma White's deep concern for justice for women with her support of the Ku Klux Klan. For White, though, that support was based on her perception that the KKK opposed modernism, just as she did, and she agreed with its anti-Catholicism (far more central to her than its anti-black and anti-Semitic agenda.) To a woman who sharply criticized most Protestant churches of her time, the Roman Catholic Church did not even merit the title of Christian. Moreover, Alma White, an ardent patriot to the point of nativism, viewed Catholic immigration as a threat to America, if not a conscious takeover plot by the pope. Finally, she saw in the Catholic Church a bastion of hostility to women's rights and assumed (incorrectly) that the KKK opposed it on similar grounds. In her biography, Stanley tries to explain but not to justify White's bigotry: "Alma's association with the Ku Klux Klan was an unholy alliance. In light of their mutual concerns, the coalition is understandable, though regrettable."[20] Stanley presents Alma White in all her complexity: a strong woman who could be both brave and authoritarian, intolerant and creative, who inspired deep loyalty in her followers—a fundamentalist feminist.

## The Pentecostalist Revival

At the dawn of the twentieth century, a new movement appeared on the American religious scene, Pentecostalism. In one sense, of course, its origin lay in the biblical account of Pentecost: when Jesus ascended into heaven, he promised that God would send a Comforter to his followers gathered in Jerusalem. On the day of Pentecost, the Holy Spirit descended on the disciples, enabling them to speak in other tongues to spread the gospel message to those gathered in Jerusalem for the Jewish festival. Subsequently, this and other "gifts of the Spirit" were a mark of early Christian congregations. Twentieth-century pentecostalists believed that the Christians of their own day could and, indeed, must experience similar gifts of the Spirit, especially speaking in tongues and healing.

The pentecostalist revival formally began after the turn of the twentieth century, but the ground was prepared in numerous places in late nineteenth-century America. Among its immediate roots were the Wesleyan/Holiness tradition with its emphasis on the second blessing of sanctification, and a Reformed theological tradition with manifestations in both America and England in the Keswick movement, which also pointed to a second decisive religious experience after conversion, but spoke of it in terms of "enduement of power for service" rather than sanctification. Two further influences were the premillennial dispensationalism already prominent in evangelical/protofundamentalist circles and interest in the power and possibilities of faith healing among a number of small groups, particularly one led by John Alexander Dowie in Zion, Illinois.[21]

Most contemporary scholars locate the effective birth of modern American Pentecostalism in the Azuza Street revival of 1906 under the leadership of William J. Seymour, a black minister. A little earlier, Charles H. Parham, a white man, founded the Apostolic Faith movement and established a Bible school in Topeka, Kansas. There, according to pentecostalist tradition, the first student to speak in tongues on January 1, 1901, was a woman, Agnes N. Ozman. Soon thereafter, Parham moved on to found a Bible school in Houston, and though he was not one of the movement's most prominent leaders, he influenced others who were. In 1905 William J. Seymour attended Parham's Houston school for several weeks. While Seymour failed to experience the baptism of the Holy Spirit in Houston, he carried Parham's ideas back to Los Angeles. There he and a few followers, meeting in an old warehouse on Azuza Street, received Spirit baptism, spoke in tongues, and ignited a pentecostalist revival.

Initially open to leadership by anyone anointed by the Spirit, male or female, black or white, the movement spread rapidly from Azuza Street. Missionaries and visitors took its message of Christ's imminent return, of which baptism by the Holy Spirit and speaking in tongues were signs, to Holiness congregations and other groups that were ripe for conversion. Many of pentecostalism's early adherents came out of the Holiness churches, although some Holiness groups and leaders, like Alma White, were highly critical of this new movement, as were fundamentalists. Pentecostalism was split by many minor and some major divisions, particularly over the issue of sanctification. Some (those most influenced by the Reformed tradition) saw sanctification not as a distinct second action of grace but as a process initiated at conversion, insisting that baptism by the Spirit with the sign of tongues was the second decisive act of God's grace. Others (those with more of a Wesleyan heritage) maintained their belief in sanctification as the second blessing and saw the gift of the Spirit as a third stage. Another division occurred over the issue of whether baptism should be in the name of the Trinity or of Jesus only.[22] Nevertheless, pentecostalists were united in their belief in the necessity of baptism by the Holy Spirit as part of a full gospel, their hope that they were living in the last days before Christ's triumphant return, their practice of spiritual gifts, especially speaking in tongues, and their highly negative view of other Christians and churches.

## Open Leadership

The early stage of the movement, prophetic pentecostalism, was both interracial and open to women's religious leadership. Charles H. Barfoot and Gerald T. Sheppard identify three factors that made the pentecostalism of this early period "prophetic" and, consequently, more open in its leadership:

1. The importance of "a calling" as the only difference between ministers and laity,
2. The confirmation of the call through the recognition of charisma by the community, and
3. The community's eschatological belief that they were experiencing the "latter rain" (Joel 2:23), in which "your sons *and your daughters will prophesy*" (Joel 2:28).[23]

We might add a fourth factor: the demonstrable success of women evangelists, such as Maria Woodworth-Etter and Marie Burgess Brown, who embraced and promoted pentecostalism. Woodworth-Etter had already had an extraordinary career as an evangelist before she joined the pentecostalist movement. Born in 1844, she experienced a call to preach shortly after her conversion at the age of thirteen, but like many of her nineteenth-century sisters with a similar experience, she deferred action on that call due to her church's disapproval of women preachers, marrying and raising a family instead. She began preaching around 1880 and by 1885 had become extremely successful as an evangelist, drawing crowds in the thousands for extended revivals. By 1890, she had purchased a tent seating 8000, and as her biographer notes, "often the tent was too small to accommodate the faithful and the curious."[24] Until 1904, she was associated with a Holiness group, the Churches of God (Winebrenner); her dismissal from that body did not, however, slow her work or popularity. Although she never formally associated herself with another denomination, groups like the Assemblies of God supported her work, as would pentecostalist leaders later. If anything, her status as an independent evangelist may have enhanced her broad appeal and protected her from the restrictions that might have been imposed by a male-led organization. In the years before the Azuza Street revival, Woodworth-Etter already endorsed many of the perceptions and practices, with the exception of speaking in tongues, that would come to mark Pentecostalism: healings, the conviction that Christians were living then in the end times and experiencing a new Pentecost, and encouragement of physical manifestations at revivals, especially trances, as signs of the Spirit's power in believers. Thus she seemed a natural candidate to sympathize with the early pentecostalist revival, and by 1912, she emerged as a popular and successful pentecostalist preacher. Sixty-eight years old in 1912, Woodworth-Etter nevertheless "hit the sawdust trail with the vigor she demonstrated in her campaigns of the 1880s" and continued an active ministry until her death in 1924.[25]

Considerably younger than Woodworth-Etter, Marie Burgess Brown lived out her career within the context of the pentecostalist revival. Marie Burgess was a member of Dowie's faith healing community in Zion, Illinois, when she met Charles Parham in 1906 and was converted to Pentecostalism. At Parham's urging, Burgess went to New York City to try to establish Pentecostalism there, eventually founding a mission known as Glad Tidings Hall. There she met a young Irish immigrant, Robert Brown, who also converted to Pentecostalism, and the two were married in 1909. Together they pastored the Glad Tidings Tabernacle, which expanded rapidly and affiliated with the Assemblies of God. The church was a center for Pentecostalism in the eastern United States, especially active in support of foreign missions. After Robert died in 1948, Marie carried on as pastor of Glad Tidings Tabernacle until her own death in 1971, a ministry of over sixty years.[26] Although Marie Brown was unusual in having begun her ministry before her marriage, so that her husband joined her in a copastorship, her experience of carrying on pastoral responsibilities as a widow was repeated by other pentecostalist women, including a few in the black Church of God in Christ, which otherwise does not allow full female ordination.[27]

## Diminishing Openness

The striking interracial character of the pentecostalist movement was short-lived, and by the 1920s, congregations split and denominations were formed as predominantly either white or black, though there continued to be a few pentecostal churches that counted substantial numbers of both black and white members. Openness to women's leadership also diminished over time, and even in the early days, there were some gender restrictions. In the Church of God in Cleveland, Tennessee, a major white pentecostal denomination, only men could perform certain administrative functions. During the 1920s, as the denomination became more organized and its ministry more formal in terms of education, official sanction, and hierarchical structure, women were increasingly excluded from the higher ranks of leadership and from more "priestly" functions. The Assemblies of God, another large, white pentecostal group, initially allowed women to function as ordained evangelists and missionaries, but not as elders (pastors). (Marie Brown was an exception here, condoned perhaps because of her copastorship and undeniable success.) In 1935, their General Council passed a resolution opening the role of elder to women, a more liberal position than most pentecostal groups took, but even though thereafter women could formally seek ordination, very few did.[28] Despite the spiritual leadership and activities of black women during the Azuza Street revival and in the early days of the movement, most black pentecostal denominations rejected female ordination and preaching, though some allowed for alternative positions like evangelist or missionary. The Church of God in Christ (COGIC), the largest black pentecostal church body—indeed, currently the second largest black denomination in America, with a membership of some 3.5 million—did not ordain women.[29] Yet the multiplicity of groups within Pentecostalism meant that occasionally a black woman who felt called by the Spirit to ministry and who could convince others of her call could found her own church. Such was the case with Ida Robinson.

Ida Robinson was born in Georgia in 1891, converted during her teens, and moved to Philadelphia in 1917. She began her ministerial career by assisting a male pastor at a small mission, moved to her own church as pastor, and was formally ordained in the United Holy Church of America. But in 1924, when that body moved to restrict female ordination, Ida Robinson had a vision in which she believed God called her to "come out on Mount Sinai" and found her own church. This she did, also serving as first bishop of the Mount Sinai Holy Church of America, Inc. By the time of her death in 1946, the group included some eighty-four churches located along the eastern coast of the United States, plus missions in Cuba and Guyana. Theologically and in much of its practice, Mount Sinai was pentecostal: members were expected to experience the gift of the Holy Spirit, usually manifest in speaking in tongues but also in healings, as a second distinct event after conversion; the dramatic second coming of Christ was anticipated in these "latter days." Members were also expected to abide by a very strict moral code, which prohibited divorce, membership in secret societies, military service, and the use of alcohol, tobacco, showy clothing, and worldly amusements. But the stance of Mount Sinai toward women was unusual. As founder and first bishop, Robinson remained closely involved with all the activities of the church.

> Ida Robinson was available to her congregation. Her seemingly ceaseless schedule of services virtually assured not only the churches she pastored, but also the denomination she shepherded, the opportunity to experience her as a real presence; . . . Her style of preaching and singing in the aisles of the church, where she could "get out with her people"; her multiple services, where she would preach several times a week at Mount Olive [the "mother" church in Philadelphia]; and her frequent episcopal visits to other churches were all parts of her "presence," her "visibility."[30]

Ida Robinson asserted her own divine call, endorsed equal religious leadership roles for other women, and actively promoted their preaching, and her successors as bishops were women.

### Aimee Semple McPherson

Women like Maria Woodworth-Etter, Marie Brown, and Ida Robinson were successful pentecostalist preachers, although their achievements were largely overlooked by historians until very recent times. But there was another "exception," a woman preacher who was as successful in attracting wide publicity and followers in the broader society as she was among pentecostalists: Aimee Semple McPherson.[31] Aimee Elizabeth Kennedy was born on October 9, 1890, in Ontario; her father was a faithful Methodist and her mother's background was Salvation Army. Although Aimee reports a period of doubt in her teens, she experienced a personal conversion at the age of seventeen under the preaching of a young pentecostalist minister, Robert Semple; several months later, in August 1908, they were married. The young couple spent a brief period in evangelistic work in the United States and Canada, including ordination for both in January 1909 by the Full Gospel Assembly,[32] but by 1910, they set out for China as foreign missionaries. There, tragedy struck: Robert died of malaria or typhoid fever in August, when Aimee was eight months pregnant.

Aimee Semple returned to the United States after her daughter Roberta was born, living for a time with her mother, who had resumed Salvation Army work in New York City, then marrying Harold McPherson in October 1911. This marriage was not a happy one, and Aimee suffered from serious illness after the birth of their son Rolf, in March 1913, which she interpreted as God's way of forcing her back to her preaching vocation during a period of backsliding. As Aimee recounts in her autobiography, she was on the point of death after an operation when she finally gave in:

> Just before losing consciousness, as I hovered between life and death, came the voice of my Lord, so loud that it startled me:
>
> "NOW—WILL—YOU—GO?" And I knew it was "Go," one way or the other: that if I did not go into the work as a soul-winner and

> get back into the will of God, Jesus would take me to Himself before He would permit me to go on without Him and be lost.
>
> Oh, don't you ever tell me that a woman can not be called to preach the Gospel! If any man ever went through one hundredth part of the hell on earth that I lived in, those months when out of God's will and work, they would never say that again.
>
> With my little remaining strength, I managed to gasp:
>
> "Yes—Lord—I'll—go." And go I did![33]

First she went back to Canada with her children and began preaching again. Harold joined her for a time in her revivals, but they had separated by 1918 and were divorced in 1921. In the meantime, Aimee began a career as an itinerant preacher all over the eastern United States, joined by her mother, Minnie Kennedy—not the preacher Aimee was, but a more efficient organizer and administrator. In 1918, she moved to Los Angeles, though she continued to make national and international revival tours for the rest of her life. It was in Los Angeles that she built the Angelus Temple (dedicated January 1, 1923) and organized the International Church of the Foursquare Gospel. (The name, Aimee insisted, was the result of a divine inspiration and based on Ezekiel 1:4–10, a vision of four cherubim with four faces. These she interpreted as Jesus Christ as Savior, Baptizer, Healer, and Coming King.) Aimee Semple McPherson built her church during the 1920s to include numerous branches and institutions, including a Bible college, a radio station, a tower for continuous prayer where the faithful volunteered two-hour shifts, and a commissary, which opened in 1927, supplying enormous amounts of food and clothing to the needy through the depression.

The center of it all, though, was Aimee Semple McPherson herself. To say her preaching style was dramatic is a significant understatement; it was also sufficiently effective to inspire thousands of devoted followers. And it was not unprecedented, for Edith L. Blumhofer shows the roots of her "illustrated sermons" and dramatic presentations in the Salvation Army techniques she observed in her youth. The Salvation Army also provided for the young Aimee successful examples of women preachers, not only her mother, Minnie, but especially Evangeline Booth, who was at that time Commissioner of the Canadian Army. Later, Aimee would meet both Marie Brown and Marie Woodworth-Etter, successful women pentecostalist leaders. Nevertheless, part of Aimee's appeal may have been the relative novelty of a female revivalist; surely the dramatic style contributed to her fame; but at least as important to her success was the content of her message. She was indeed a pentecostalist, endorsing premillennialsim, faith healing, and baptism of the Holy Spirit as evidenced by speaking in tongues, but she was not theologically rigid or denominationally narrow. Insisting that her creed was simple "Bible Christianity," she preached an "old-fashioned gospel" that evoked deeply rooted strains of evangelical revivalism, at the same time she was a master of "modern" techniques like the radio. When she held revivals in cities across the United States and Canada, she welcomed support from ministers across denominational lines and encouraged her hearers to support their own churches. Moreover, hers was a joyous gospel, emphasizing the happiness of heaven far more than the terrors of sin and hell, and accessible to anyone and everyone, regardless of gender, class, or race. Not only was Aimee's gospel "user-friendly," as Blumhofer calls it,[34] but she herself seemed accessible, a Canadian farm girl who had made good, a person like the common people who flocked to hear the one they could identify as nurturing mother and "Sister."

The loyalty of thousands of her devoted followers remained unshaken through an alleged kidnapping in 1926, another brief and disastrous marriage, and a series of lawsuits and breaks between Aimee, her mother, her daughter, and various colleagues—all these events the subjects of intense publicity. After her death in September 1944 of an overdose of sleeping pills (ruled accidental), the funeral held for her in Los Angeles was one of the largest the city had ever seen. Her son Rolf succeeded her as president of a church organization that included some four hundred branches in the United States and Canada, with "almost 200 Foursquare missionaries stationed throughout Africa, Asia, South America, and the Philippines. Her Bible College had graduated over 3000 ministers, missionaries, and evangelists who ministered to the 22,000 members of her unique denomination."[35] By 1993, the International Church of the Foursquare Gospel had more than 200,000 members in North America and some one and a half million worldwide.[36]

While Aimee Semple McPherson was denounced in her own time as a self-seeking charlatan, and she surely had her share of human frailties, she was, as McLoughlin concludes, "a simple and sincere pietist who tried to fight fire with fire in the Jazz Age."[37] Not only did she set an example for other women (and men), effectively combining traditional evangelical revivalism with upbeat, modern methods, the church she founded extended the office of ministry to other pentecostal women. That ordination is still available, but over time, fewer women took advantage of it. The pattern is similar to one found among other pentecostal groups, and students of pentecostal women ministers in the late twentieth century have found that: (1) women ministers do, indeed, still exist, but (2) they face a good deal of opposition, and (3) they themselves do not identify female religious leadership with general support for feminism. Most pentecostalist women preachers self-consciously repudiate what they regard as "radical" feminism. Elaine J. Lawless concludes:

> Within the religious community there exist clear directives for female pastors: they must be compassionate, caring loving mothers for their congregations, and they must be biological mothers as well. As pastor of a church, a woman's strength in that capacity will lie in her ability to apply all the maternal aspects of her female being to the care and guidance of her symbolic family, or as one woman pastor puts it, her "babes in Christ." . . . These women must be loving and tough, but they must deny that they have or seek equal footing with men.[38]

Susan Kwilecki in her study of both black and white pentecostal clergywomen does not mention an implicit requirement for biological motherhood, but she does note that most of the women fit a pattern long set in American evangelicalism: religious leadership is based on a divine call and hence "overrules" cultural gender expectations, but gender equality is limited and does not extend to familial or other societal relationships.[39]

## The Church of Jesus Christ of Latter-day Saints

Although the Church of Jesus Christ of Latter-day Saints quickly developed into a distinctive, separate religious body with its particular sacred texts and prophets, its early roots were in the same evangelical Protestantism as the Holiness and pentecostal movements, and like them, it exhibited during the twentieth century a pattern of retreat from its original acceptance of some female religious leadership and women's rights. Gradually, Mormon women lost the right to exercise spiritual gifts, particularly healings and blessings, that had flourished in the nineteenth century, and the activities of the women's Relief Society were limited. At the same time, the role of motherhood, which had been highly valued among pioneer Saints but only as one of several important functions fulfilled by women, was more and more held up as the only legitimate female role.

While early Mormon women never held equal religious leadership with men, they were encouraged to express spiritual gifts, including healings. They administered blessings, largely though not exclusively to women and children, and in particular they followed the tradition of women blessing another woman about to undergo childbirth. The first women leaders of the reorganized Relief Society—Eliza R. Snow, Zina D. H. Young, and Bathsheba W. Smith—were also priestesses, presiding over women's work in the temple in Salt Lake City. That dual function ended with the death of Bathsheba Smith in 1910; a few years later, male leaders insisted that healings and blessings were first and foremost a function of the male priesthood and should be exercised by women only in a secondary and supplemental fashion. Women did not give up their traditions overnight, but by 1946, a directive from the church's head, Joseph Fielding Smith, prohibited women from anointing for illness or childbirth.[40] The priesthood remains today strictly male, although in contrast to most Christian groups, priesthood is extended to all men who are full members of the church, not just to a smaller group among them. (For many years, Mormon priesthood was denied to black men, but in 1978 the First Presidency of the church announced that a divine revelation had opened the priesthood to "every faithful, worthy man in the Church." At the same time, President Kimball made it very clear that no such revelation should be expected about women and the priesthood.)[41]

Even if nineteenth-century Mormon women did not have the same leadership in the church as men, they, like many Protestant women, developed an independent and powerful organization. The Relief Society involved women in charitable work, economic ventures, and classes. It promoted female autonomy, being organizationally and financially separate from the male leadership. And its journal, the *Woman's Exponent,* provided a public voice for women. But at about the same time as the men began to restrict women's spiritual gifts and blessings, President Joseph F. Smith made other organizations, including the Relief Society, auxiliaries clearly functioning under the priesthood. Over the next half century, the distinctive role of the Relief Society for Mormon women was gradually eroded. As Mormon society became less isolated, its women began to look to other outlets like women's clubs for expression and activity, even though the trend, which seemed to weaken the Relief Society and the women's exclusive loyalty to the church, was not particularly welcomed by male or female Mormon leaders. Meanwhile, some of the Relief Society's functions in the social service area were taken over by other agencies or by the state. In 1936, the church set up a Church Security Committee (later renamed the Welfare Committee) to consolidate internal benevolence. The Relief Society continued to function, but as Jill Mulvay Derr notes:

> Introduction of a new churchwide welfare program eventually lessened Relief Society involvement in the work for which it had been named. . . . Erosion of the Relief Society's participation in welfare work was hastened by the professionalization and governmentalization of services which had once been the responsibility of volunteer organizations. . . . Charitable work remained central to Relief Society's ideological identity, but the real time spent on it shrank steadily from the 1940s through the 1960s as women spent a greater proportion of Relief Society time in lesson work, fundraising, and socials, all typical of non-Mormon groups as well.[42]

In 1971, the *Relief Society Magazine,* the successor to the *Woman's Exponent,* was discontinued, and the women were "forbidden to have separate fundraising activities or budgets."[43]

## Changing Roles of Women in Mormon Society

As was the case with the consolidation of mission boards in some Protestant denominations in the early decades of the twentieth century, the changes in the Mormon Relief Society were not *simply* attempts by male leaders, jealous and suspicious of female autonomy, deliberately to restrict women. Starting in the 1960s, there was in the LDS Church a broad movement, known as correlation, to develop a more effective and efficient organization to meet the needs of rapid, worldwide growth of the church, and that process partially explains the fate of the Relief Society. Nevertheless, it seems clear that male concern over female independence was also an issue, as it was for the Protestant mission boards, for as Mormon women lost some of the spiritual functions they had once exercised, as the female sphere of the Relief Society was taken over and restricted, the image of woman as mother came in the twentieth century to be the exclusive ideal held up to LDS women.

The glorification of motherhood among Mormons that began in the early decades of the twentieth century represented both a departure from the image and realities of nineteenth-century pioneer Mormon women and a reaction to changes in the relationship of Mormon society to American culture. In the early days, women were needed to fill a range of economic and social functions and to defend the Mormon practice of polygamy against a hostile world, but by the twentieth century Mormons had dropped their unpopular marriage practices as the price of political acceptance and had achieved a fair degree of economic stability and prosperity. Far less isolated than they previously had been in Utah, Mormons reacted to more immediate pressures of mainstream American culture in two ways: first, they adopted, if a little belatedly, the idealization of Victorian womanhood; second, they resisted certain twentieth-century trends affecting women. Women working outside the home and changing standards of female morality, especially as manifest in rising divorce rates and birth control, were seen by Mormons, as they were by fundamentalists, as threats to home and family and thus by extension to the whole Mormon culture and faith.

Many religious groups have idealized mothers as the epitome of purity, piety, and sacrifice and have cited religious justifications for restricting women to the domestic sphere. Yet two particular points of Mormon theology reinforce the religious significance of motherhood and make it more difficult to challenge its traditional features. First, Mormons believe that having children provides bodies for preexistent, waiting spirits, who can then in Mormon families have the best opportunity to work out their eternal salvation; thus birth control is discouraged, though it is not forbidden so long as it is not used to avoid having children altogether. Second, in the Mormon vision, the highest level of eternal life is reserved for married men and women, where each man is the priest and ruler of his own family kingdom and where biological motherhood continues for women for eternity.[44] Thus in Mormon belief, explicit, gendered family roles are not confined to this temporal existence but are an intrinsic part of eternal spiritual reality.

An ideal of glorified motherhood among Mormons remained strong into the second half of the twentieth century, when a resurgent women's movement seemed to threaten that ideal. Issues like birth control and working mothers continued to cause tensions, which then came to a head in 1972 with congressional passage of the Equal Rights Amendment. In December 1974, Barbara B. Smith, president of the Relief Society, voiced her opposition to the amendment, and a month later, an unsigned but influential editorial in the *Church News* rejected the ERA and reiterated a stance of separate gender spheres. The ERA, it said, is "so broad that it is inadequate, inflexible, and vague. . . . Men and women are different, made so by a Divine Creator. Each has his or her role."[45] Over the next few years, the Mormon Church became one of the most outspoken and effective opponents of the ERA and of a feminist agenda in meetings for the International Women's Year in 1977. Not all Mormons, however, agreed with this position or with the church's political activities to oppose the ERA. Sonia Johnson, a self-described Mormon "housewife" and ERA supporter, became the most famous female dissenter when she was excommunicated by the church in 1979,[46] but other women within the church had already been raising questions about the role of women beyond the particular issue of the ERA. These women insisted they were loyal to the church but argued that the more limited activities and restricted roles allowed for twentieth-century Mormon women betrayed a rediscovered heritage of strong Mormon foremothers, who had filled a range of roles and firmly supported women's rights. Not only did the dissenting women publish their scholarly studies of that heritage, they also started journals like *Dialogue, Exponent II,* and *Mormon Women's Forum* to express their views and provide a voice for other Mormon women.

Even though these protests are voiced from within the church, and they do not attack motherhood per se, only its exclusivity and idealization, the ideas and activities have not met with unqualified approval in some official church circles.[47] Indeed, the historical work of these women, and some men, raised further tensions within the church. In September 1993, five Mormons, two women and three men, were excommunicated, and a third woman was disfellowshiped. The excommunicated included Lavina Fielding Anderson and Maxine Hanks, editor of a 1993 collection, *Women and Authority: Re-emerging Mormon Feminism,* and Paul Toscano, a longtime supporter of Mormon feminism. Since significant portions of the records are not public, it is hard to say with certainty what caused the church hierarchy's actions in each case. Yet Jan Shipps, prominent scholar and observer of Mormonism, suggests that the actions are less a reaction to feminist or intellectual activity beyond the sphere of good wives and mothers than "a reflection of concern about how Mormon women's history is being used to call into question the church's conservative stance on the role of women, and also how history seems to be driving the development of an LDS feminist theology centered on the Mormon concept of a Mother in Heaven . . . ."[48] Church leaders cannot prevent scholars' rediscovery and publication of parts of Mormon history when women had greater freedom and more leadership roles than are available to LDS women in the late twentieth century, but they seem to want to avoid any official acknowledgement or sanction of such history, lest it raise too many questions within the church today.

## The New Religious Right

The Church of Jesus Christ of Latter-day Saints was not the only religious group in America during the last third of the twentieth century to enter the mix of national politics with a politically and socially conservative agenda. That combination of individuals, organizations, and techniques known as the New Religious Right or New Christian Right seemed to some observers to burst onto the scene from nowhere. Its rise and influence were quickly embraced, decried, or analyzed, and its putative triumph or decline almost as quickly predicted or asserted. While many Americans might identify the New Christian Right with a famous televangelist like Jerry Falwell, a political aspirant like Pat Robertson, or fallen heroes like Jim Bakker and Jimmy Swaggart, the movement was and is significantly broader and more complex than its most visible leaders.[49]

By the mid-1970s, skilled conservative activists recognized that the cultural shocks of the 1960s and early 1970s, from Supreme Court bans on prayer and devotional Bible reading in public schools to drastic changes in sexual morality to legalized abortion, had provoked growing dismay among conservative Christians, who felt with a sense of frustration that their voices were being ignored. Men like Richard Viguerie, Howard Phillips and his Conservative Caucus, and Paul Weyrich and the Committee for the Survival of a Free Congress tapped into this unhappiness as a new and potent political force. By the 1980 election, the coalition of conservative political activists and Christians had a presidential candidate in Ronald Reagan and a religious leader of growing national visibility in Jerry Falwell and his Moral Majority, with other leaders and groups quickly following. Its organizations formed what Hill and Owen term "a virtual labyrinth of political action committees, lobbies, educational and research foundations, publications, television programs, and churches."[50] The apparent political clout of the New Religious Right brought rejoicing in some quarters, consternation in others. That clout seemed to peak, at least at the national level and in terms of media attention, in the mid-1980s. A changing political mood and highly publicized scandals about two of its leaders, Jim Bakker and Jimmy Swaggart, hurt the image and the national political credibility of the New Religious Right. But localized grassroots campaigns continued with modest success into the 1990s, and the mid-90s saw a resurgence of the Christian Right's visibility and political clout, especially through the "Christian Coalition" led by Ralph Reed.

Whether pursued at a national or a local level, the agenda of the New Religious Right usually included a vociferous patriotism and support for a strong American military posture and for the state of Israel; endorsement of economic capitalism and suspicion of government intervention into business and industry, which was sometimes associated with incipient socialism; and an adamant anticommunism. "Secular humanism" was perceived as an equally dangerous threat to America, its influence manifest not only in "liberal control" of government and media but also in public education, as God was "taken out" of the schools and sex education put in. Another area of deep concern was changing sexual morality: America seemed to be turning into a society that condoned promiscuity, homosexuality, pornography, and abortion. Such issues were perceived as morally problematic in themselves but also linked to still another major concern, the decline of the family, which was seen as a threat to the very survival of America as a nation and as a consequence of rapidly changing roles for women and the emergence in the 1960s and 1970s of a reinvigorated feminist movement. Thus issues affecting women as women were not the only concerns of the New Religious Right, but they were surely among the high priorities on its agenda.

## Distinctions from Other Groups

Before we proceed to further analysis of these issues, however, it is important to note that the New Religious Right was not identical with conservative Protestant Christianity in general or evangelicalism in particular during the last decades of the twentieth century. The New Religious Right drew upon an evangelical constituency with marked success, and the concerns on its agenda were shared by many, though not all, conservative Protestant Christians. Yet on the one hand, the most visible leaders of the New Religious Right, while themselves conservative Protestants, made common cause with groups like Mormons and Roman Catholics on certain issues (especially "family" ones), even though historically fundamentalists had regarded those groups as singularly heretical in their theology.[51] Furthermore, the New Religious Right attracted the support of significant numbers of Americans who lacked a strong, distinctive religious identity but who agreed with their conservative stance on certain political and moral issues. On the other hand, not all evangelicals agreed with everything on the political, social, and moral agenda of the New Religious Right. (To cite but one of the most obvious examples, black pentecostalists were unlikely to embrace a movement that virtually identified itself with the Republican party.) Other evangelicals remained indifferent or were suspicious of its methods, particularly its overt and vigorous political activity. Since the early decades of the twentieth century, many evangelicals had eschewed public politics both as a sign of worldliness and as an arena in which evangelical convictions were ignored, repudiated, or mocked. Still others, who agreed that evangelicals, like other Americans, could and should act politically from their religious convictions, distrusted the tendency of the New Religious Right to present every issue as having a single, clear, "Christian" response.[52] Thus outsiders at times overestimated the impact, particularly the political clout, of the New Religious Right (aided, to be sure, by inflated claims of membership by the movement's leaders), while they underestimated and misunderstood the significance, diversity, and pervasiveness of evangelicalism.[53] Nevertheless, the New Religious Right as an organized movement drew heavily upon evangelical constituencies and shared common concerns with many of them. Prominent among the agenda items so shared were issues of sexual morality and gender definition, issues that were seen as critical to the survival of the institution of the family in America.

## Views on the Family

Increased legal and cultural acceptance of abortion and homosexuality aroused some of the strongest passions and most vigorous activity within the New Religious Right. In their view, both are wrong, simply and definitively immoral. Homosexuality is unnatural and perverted; abortion is murder of innocent and helpless victims. Moreover, in their interpretation both are forbidden by the Bible, the ultimate authority for Christians. Finally, both loom as threats to the traditional family and its values, as defined and understood by the New Religious Right, for homosexuality mocks the sacred institution of monogamous marriage, and the easy availability of abortion promotes sexual permissiveness and promiscuity and undermines the natural, divinely intended connection of sexual intercourse with procreation and responsible parenthood.[54] Such "family"-connected arguments were not the only reasons for the New Religious Right's condemnation of homosexuality and abortion, but they were important, and they connected these issues with a central public agenda concern, the preservation of the traditional family.

That traditional family is very closely tied to women's roles and nature. Thus serious threats to the family were identified by the New Religious Right not only in homosexuality and abortion, and in the perceived attack on parental control through the public schools' "rejection" of God and promotion of "secular humanist," "anti-family" values, but also in the rapidly changing roles of American women in general and the feminist movement in particular. Women, it appeared, were forsaking the joys and responsibilities of marriage and motherhood for careers and self-fulfillment, to the detriment of husbands and children. By the mid-1970s and into the early 1980s, a constitutional amendment granting equal rights to women, the ERA, came to symbolize the new feminist movement for both its advocates and its opponents, among whom the forces of the New Religious Right were prominent. Over and over, these religious opponents insisted in public statements that it was not that they viewed women as intrinsically inferior ("unequal") as human beings; rather, it was that the ERA threatened the family and the social and legal protections needed by women. Some examples of the predicted and horrifying consequences of the ERA were new—unisex bathrooms, co-ed football teams, women in combat, loss of protective legislation and of alimony/child support for divorced women—but behind the particulars was an old debate on the shape and image of Christian marriage and, indeed, of the relationship between men and women in society. Should the pattern be one of equality or hierarchy? Was the image of an idealized Victorian family with its distinctive roles for men and women not simply a product of a particular time, class, and culture, but an eternal reality set by God and nature?

### *John R. Rice*

While the issue was not new in twentieth-century America, neither was the answer of conservative Christians. Earlier in this chapter, we saw how fundamentalists of the first third of the twentieth century defended the Victorian family image against the perceived threat of changing female roles. That affection for hierarchical structure and sharply differentiated roles continued in the decades between the heyday of the flapper and the rise of the new feminism. One widely popular fundamentalist work from that period is illuminating, not because all its ideas are new but because the connections among "women's issues" and the theological rationale behind the author's pronouncements are particularly clear. In 1941, John R. Rice published *Bobbed Hair, Bossy Wives and Women Preachers*. The three images of the title are not random phrases, calculated merely to catch a reader's attention; rather, each represents a dangerous and unbiblical practice. A modern reader should not conclude that the "bobbed hair" of the title was no more than a reflection of passing fashions. For Rice it defied a biblical command and was a significant symbol:

> [Bobbed hair] is the symbol of the wicked fashion of rebellion of wives to their husbands' authority or of wicked daughters who rebel against their fathers. . . . Do not confuse the subject of

> bobbed hair with the general subject of woman's dress and use of cosmetics. The question of whether a Christian woman bobs her hair is of infinitely more importance than whether she paints her face or her lips or her fingernails. . . . Men wear short hair as a sign that they take their responsibilities as made in the image of God and as rulers over their households. Women are to wear long hair as symbols of their submission to husband and father, taking their place with meekness as women surrendered to the will of God and subject to the authority God places over them.[55]

While some protofundamentalists around the turn of the century embraced both an inerrant Bible and some public roles of religious leadership for women, by 1941 Rice could not. Yet throughout his book it is clear that he is not simply defending a literal, universal, and eternal applicability of such familiar passages as Genesis 3:16, 1 Corinthians 14:34–35, and 1 Timothy 2:9–15; he is also defining a core theology of sin and salvation. Women preachers and bossy wives are both examples of the "heart of all sin . . . rebellion against authority."[56] Nor is sin defined only (or in this work, discussed most frequently) as rebellion directly against the authority of God; equally reprehensible is rebellion against what Rice sees as God's ordained earthly authorities. For all women as women, that authority is the husband or father, absolute and in all things. No woman can hold authority over an adult male in the family or in the church, and thus women cannot preach, pastor, teach adult Bible studies, or take any position of authority over men; and Rice cites the biblical Miriam's leprosy as "an appalling object lesson to all women who would seek to take authority or leadership over men or alongside men."[57] In clear and related concerns, Rice endorses obedience of citizens to government and workers to bosses. He is insistent that the pastor rules the church as the husband rules the wife, and he deplores contemporary "feminine" influences in the churches that drive away "real" men.

### *Larry Christenson and Jerry Falwell*

By the last third of the century, few evangelical writers were as concerned about female hair length or as absolutist in their language as Rice, but they were very concerned about the family, and most continued to insist on the need for order and the divine origin of a pattern of hierarchy along gender lines.[58] Larry Christenson, a neocharismatic Lutheran who in 1970 published a popular guide, *The Christian Family,* avoided Rice's rhetoric of wicked rebellion and discussed instead woman's need for protection: submission is for her own good, as well as an act of obedience to God. Other authors, like Jerry Falwell, placed concern for the family in the context of a broad New Religious Right agenda and a call for political involvement. For example, not only did Falwell decry the ERA as an attack on religion and the family, he deplored governmental intrusion into the family via the public schools and federally funded day care centers and shelters for battered women. At the same time he faulted the government for its omissions: "The most notable example of government malfeasance in its family obligations is in the area of defense. . . . Our American government is providing its families far less protection from nuclear attack than is the Soviet Union providing its families."[59] Yet both Christenson and Falwell agreed: a hierarchical pattern of gender relations is a divine and eternal command; wives should be submissive and husbands should be in authority. This arrangement included men's spiritual authority over wives, often coupled with a now-familiar plea for men to reverse feminization in the churches and to reclaim spiritual leadership of the family. Both further agreed that the growing tendency of married women to work outside the home was a threat to the family and, in most cases, unnecessary. Yes, in a few cases there might be genuine economic need (the preferred examples were widows), but more often materialism drove married women to seek paid employment (and thereby to undermine the husband's divine role as provider and protector).

> That cases of genuine necessity exist no sensible person would deny. But it is also evident that in many, perhaps the great majority of cases, the income of the wife goes toward luxuries which a family could do without. A working wife also tends to employ fewer habits of thrift in her management of the household, thus narrowing the actual margin of economic advantage which her income provides. And no amount of income can counter-balance the loss to the family in having the wife and mother spend her energies outside the home.[60]

### *Other Conservative Voices*

Concern for traditional families and hierarchical gender roles was not confined to religiously conservative spokesmen; women, too, joined the chorus. Phyllis Schlafly, conservative activist (also a lawyer and Roman Catholic, and cited approvingly and at length by Falwell), was one of the most prominent and successful opponents of the ERA. Beverly LaHaye, the wife of pastor and New Religious Right leader Tim LaHaye, founded a group in 1979 known as Concerned Women of America (CWA) to protest passage of the ERA and the "secular humanism" of a feminist movement that claimed to speak for American women. A grassroots movement that grew to national proportions by the mid-1980s, CWA combined local prayer groups with political activism to oppose abortion and pornography and to defend religious expression in the public schools. Elisabeth Elliot, an evangelical author less directly associated with the New Religious Right, in her popular 1976 work, *Let Me Be a Woman*, defended gender hierarchy in the family as the divine order. But perhaps the best-known advocate of the rewards of female submission was Marabel Morgan, whose best-selling book, *The Total Woman,* included a liberal sprinkling of Bible verses along with suggestions about how sexy costumes could put the "sizzle" back in a marriage and ended with a written "altar call" to "Plug yourself into the One, the only One, who can give you life."[61]

### *Minority Protests*

Some evangelicals voiced a minority protest, advocating instead a pattern of equality and partnership within marriage.[62] In 1974, Letha Scanzoni and Nancy Hardesty, both evangelicals, published a book that explicitly rejected hierarchy in marriage and promoted instead a model of partnership. They defended the choice of some married women to work outside the home; they called their churches to task for underutilizing or rejecting women's leadership gifts and promoted women's ordination. Well aware of opposing viewpoints in their own ecclesial communities, they addressed not only those familiar biblical passages that seemed to prohibit female religious leadership (as had their foremothers for more than a century) but also took on the question of biblical interpretation and authority. They never directly challenged the doctrine of inerrancy, but they did insist that it is legitimate for the evangelical Christian to address issues of context, interpretation, and consistency.[63]

The following year (1975) saw the publication of a major work on women's issues by an established male evangelical theologian, Paul K. Jewett, who was at the time professor of systematic theology at Fuller Theological Seminary. Jewett's work was intentionally scholarly and theological, surveying classic theologians like Aquinas, Luther, and Karl Barth as well as biblical texts, but his conclusions were similar to those of Scanzoni and Hardesty in defending partnership rather than hierarchy as a paradigm of male-female relationships and in advocating female ordination. As a result of his study, Jewett also rejected a Barthian "compromise" popular among late twentieth-century evangelicals that tried to insist that female subordination did not imply inherent female inferiority. One cannot have hierarchy, he said, *without* inferiority. "My own conclusion is that the case for hierarchy, in the last analysis, requires one to argue not only for the priority but also the superiority of the male."[64] The two books raised considerable controversy among evangelicals, attracting both like-minded support and bitter criticism. As Nancy Hardesty wrote in a preface to a revised edition of *All We're Meant to Be* in 1986:

> I have been challenged and chastised, defended and denounced. One woman who had been my role model from the time I was twelve years old informed me, after a lecture I gave at a theological seminary, that I was teaching "pure blasphemy." Some in the

student body there were so abusive in their responses that the faculty voted to extend me an apology.[65]

*Division in the Southern Baptist Convention*

Division of opinion on women's issues was also reflected in the Southern Baptist Convention (SBC), the largest evangelical denomination in the United States. Traditionally more conservative than their northern Baptist counterparts, Southern Baptists had nevertheless followed an American Protestant pattern of increasing activity and leadership for women in the churches, albeit more slowly than most, forming women's groups and allowing women voice and vote at the local church level, and supporting home and foreign missions through women's societies that gradually developed national organization and leadership. Because of Baptists' congregational polity, female ordination was theoretically possible all along, but it was not until 1964 in Durham, North Carolina, that the first woman, Addie Davis, was formally ordained in a Southern Baptist church. Only a few women followed Davis's example over the next years, but by 1986, there were at least 232 ordained women in the SBC, though only a small percentage of these were pastoring churches.[66]

In the meantime, however, tensions were growing within the SBC between "moderates" and "fundamentalists," and a major power struggle erupted in the 1980s. Furthermore, the New Religious Right had attracted significant support from the SBC for its religious and political agenda, especially from the SBC's fundamentalist wing.[67] Through the 1980s, the balance of power swung decisively in favor of the fundamentalist forces, which adamantly opposed female ordination. At its 1984 national convention in Kansas City, the SBC passed a resolution "that endorsed 'the service of women in all aspects of church life and work other than pastoral functions and leadership roles entailing ordination' . . . Women were excluded from pastoral roles, the resolution noted 'to preserve a submission God requires because the man was first in creation and the woman was first in the Edenic fall' "[68] Such a resolution could not absolutely stop a local congregation from ordaining a woman, but the atmosphere was hardly encouraging. Local and regional associations dismissed churches who ordained a woman, and an effective staff takeover of the SBC's Home Mission Board enabled the conservatives to cut off that agency's usual aid to a mission church with a female pastor.[69] Clearly the issue of inerrancy and literal interpretation of key biblical passages was part of the fundamentalists' rejection of female ordination, but their position was also rooted in acceptance of that hierarchical paradigm of male over female in the church, marriage, and society in general; hence the agreement of the fundamentalist party of the SBC with the New Religious Right on such issues as the ERA, abortion, homosexuality, and the traditional male-headed family.

## An Analysis: Why Did They Back Off?

As the end of the twentieth century approaches, American evangelicalism encompasses a range of views on issues of women's nature, roles, and leadership. Nevertheless, advocates of a partnership paradigm and female ordination appear to be in the minority (in the case of the SBC, a very embattled minority), unlikely to become a majority in the immediate future. Most evangelical churches that still allow female ordination are not moving to expand the proportion, visibility, or authority of women clergy, and some actively discourage women from seeking such positions. We are then left with the question, Why did some religious groups in America that allowed, even encouraged, female leadership at the turn of the twentieth century back off from that position, rather than maintaining or even expanding it?

No single theory can account for the changes, especially given the diversity of race and class in American evangelicalism, and different explanations fit better with different groups. Scanzoni and Setta in their study of women in evangelical, holiness, and pentecostal traditions suggest three major factors for the changes.[70] First, the equality advocated by turn-of-the-century evangelicals was a limited one. Women were permitted to function in "prophetic" roles—that is, in roles whose authority was linked to a special call from God, such as evangelist or preacher—much more often than in "priestly" roles that carried sacramental or administrative power. That pattern has been typical of women's religious leadership in Judaism and Christianity since biblical times. Furthermore, the relative religious equality of evangelical churches was not extended to the family; with rare exceptions, even women preachers insisted that the husband remained the head of the household.[71] Finally, acceptance of women's preaching in earlier decades was a pragmatic decision, fueled by the perception that Americans were living in the last days, that laborers for the harvest were too few, and thus even the "second-best choice" of women preachers was justified. For many women clergy in Holiness and pentecostal churches today, a similar situation prevails: women serve "less desirable" churches (or have to found their own), and limited equality in religious leadership does not necessarily affect other spheres of gender relationships. Susan Kwilecki, in her study of contemporary pentecostal clergywomen, describes a theological resolution of this apparent tension that some of them offered:

> From the standpoint of eternity, in heaven, . . . there is no gender. Nevertheless, for his own reasons, God ordained a patriarchal order for creation, which must be upheld. Eternity and creation meet in the church—an earthly institution in which some order must prevail, but also the prototype of heaven. As a foretaste of the parity of the Kingdom, women can lead in the church, but they must also serve and obey in the home. . . .[72]

Second, social changes in the broader culture drew mixed reactions from evangelicals, who more deplored than welcomed the changes. Women's suffrage, changing fashions and moral habits, and increased female participation in the labor force (and not simply at the lowest levels) were deeply unsettling to many conservative Christians. Margaret Bendroth's assessment of the appeal of fundamentalism for women in the mid-twentieth century is equally suggestive for the continued appeal of conservative evangelicalism to women in the century's last decades:

> Women, like men, found in the fundamentalist movement a clear, though perhaps narrow, call to Christian vocation and a language of cultural critique that simplified the daunting range of choices in a secular lifestyle. Women perhaps especially appreciated the movement's high standard for family life, still the primary area of concern for most mid-twentieth-century women. Fundamentalist churches upheld women's role in the family and, even more important, provided a forum for like-minded women to air common fears and hopes for their children.[73]

Nor was a certain degree of self-interest absent from male clerical opposition to women preachers, for they feared their profession might be devalued, symbolically and literally, by having too many women in it. To be fair, such concerns were not limited to conservative male clergy but were shared by mainstream ministers, too. Like evangelicals at the turn of the century, the male establishment of mainline groups like Presbyterians and Methodists was more open to women's preaching/ordination in midcentury, when demand exceeded supply for ministers. And status concerns came from the pew, as well as the pulpit, as Hassey notes: "Some [evangelicals] considered the presence of a female pastor a tacit acknowledgement of a church's poverty."[74]

A third reason for the change in attitude about women's ordination was "*conservative evangelicalism's penchant for order* . . . a prescribed place for everything and everything in its place—especially in the case of women. . . ."[75] That place, of course, was ever more narrowly in the home. To these three main factors, Scanzoni and Setta add a number of other possibilities.

> The growing professionalization of the ministry, the bureaucratization and institutionalization of groups formerly more open and flexible, the move toward increased cultural accommodation and concern over "respectability" and greater acceptance in established ecclesiastical circles, and other factors associated with the classic sect-to-church transition no doubt played a significant part. Likewise, a rigid, mechanistic approach to Scripture and a zealous commitment to a particular understanding of verbal inerrancy came to be viewed as a badge of orthodoxy. Biblical criticism and interpretations that took into account the Bible's human element

> and culturally specific applications were viewed with alarm and suspicion of apostasy.[76]

Janette Hassey cites similar reasons in her own study of evangelical women and backlash, noting the irony of a literal approach to the Bible and a premillennialism that, at the turn of the century, found in prophesy by sons *and daughters* (see Joel 2:28; Acts 2:17) a positive sign of the last days before Christ came, while later dispensationalists "began to interpret women's leadership as an *evil* sign of the end times, identifying such women with the whore of Babylon."[77] Hassey further notes geographical as well as chronological shifts as factors in the impact of culture.

> Significantly, Fundamentalism widened geographically during the same decades in which it narrowed denominationally. Whereas early Fundamentalist strength lay in the urban North, the welcoming of southern conservative cousins like the Southern Baptists into their fold produced a shift of strength to the southern Bible belt. . . . Southern conservative social values, which traditionally included the subordinate place of women in society and church, typified an increasingly larger segment of the Fundamentalist controversy.[78]

## Theological Assumptions

Such factors underlying the shift in evangelical attitudes toward female religious leadership are interrelated; they also reflect theological assumptions beyond matters of literal biblical interpretation. Early evangelical equality was limited in its scope in part because evangelicals failed to address the underlying paradigm of hierarchy. They were thus content to view the woman preacher as the exception, the one whose direct call from God overrode the usual authorities and traditions in a religious setting, without questioning the hierarchical family model. The whole nature of an "orderly" universe, perceived as necessarily hierarchical, remained untouched. Cultural threats, especially the "loss" of traditional families and gender roles, challenged the paradigm and the orderly universe, and thus female religious leadership was closely linked to other changes. Bobbed hair, bossy wives, and women preachers were symptomatic of the fundamental sins of disorder and rebellion against authority. God's authority was so closely identified with the intermediate, temporal authorities of this world that rebellion against one was hard to distinguish from rebellion against the others.

Because a view of sin as primarily disorder and rebellion against authority marked American evangelicalism as it developed in the twentieth century, it is hardly surprising that the 1960s, that chaotic decade of rebellion on virtually every front, helped to trigger the rise of the New Religious Right and to confirm the direction in which evangelicals—and

Mormons—were moving in regard to female religious leadership and social change. Moreover, by the 1960s and 1970s, "outsiders"—minorities and women—were actively questioning hierarchical patterns of social order and demanding equality. They called for *real* and not token equality—political, economic, religious, social, and cultural—and for equality on their own terms, not just acceptance based on emulation of white male values and standards. In short, they wanted power.

Thus rebellion, or perceived rebellion, against God-given earthly authorities was easily linked to issues of power, especially when power is understood as a finite, limited commodity of control. Margaret Bendroth's argument, noted earlier in this chapter, that battles within certain mainline denominations in the 1920s and 1930s were, in part, struggles for power between conservatives and women, both outsiders, suggests that power was a key issue in evangelical shifts in views on women. The shrinking roles permitted to women in new fundamentalist churches, coupled with reassertion of a "masculine" identity of Christianity and the church, can be seen as further signs of a power struggle. Yet if retreat among evangelicals on female religious leadership was, even in part, a sign of a male leadership that felt its power was threatened by women's gains, why was there not a similar backlash within the male establishment of the mainline denominations?

In the first place, there *was* a good deal of male opposition within the mainstream to women's ordination, even though those opponents ultimately lost the formal battle among most Protestants. Second, white men in mainstream Protestantism, despite the real, growing pluralism of twentieth-century America, were still the closest thing to a "cultural establishment," and hence power, as could likely be found. They may have felt beleaguered by the clamorous voices of the sixties, but cultural outsiders they were not. Evangelical leaders were outsiders, at least in comparison to men of the Protestant mainstream. Third, those women and men who supported female ordination in mainline Protestant denominations were generally open about their sympathy for the new women's movement and felt comfortable using many of its arguments and accepting many of its consequences. This moderate level of comfort with cultural change, specifically about gender roles, may have helped mainline denominations to break the more typical pattern in which women's leadership is confined to "prophetic" (as opposed to "priestly") leadership or confined to an early period of a group's existence. In contrast, a good number of evangelical men and women were more wary of tying women's religious leadership to an explicit feminist stance because of the cultural image evangelicals had of the women's movement as dominated by atheistic, man-hating, bra-burning radicals. Thus cultural images and their baggage often meant evangelical women were forced to demonstrate that their desire to serve

God in positions of religious leadership was not part of "that kind" of "radical" feminism.

Finally, there were significant theological differences between conservative and mainstream Protestants by the last third of the twentieth century. Acceptance or rejection of the methods of biblical criticism and consequent interpretation of the Bible was one difference, but so was a core assumption about the basic nature of sin. Evangelicals, especially fundamentalists, were more likely to speak of sin in terms of disobedience and rebellion, an understanding of sin that fit well with a paradigm of hierarchy, but many mainstream Protestant theologians, embracing a kind of neosocial gospel and influenced by liberation theology, came to identify sin more with injustice, dehumanization, and oppression. Others, less sympathetic to "political" theology, might use the personal language of sin as a lack of self-acceptance or self-realization. In the last two cases, the theology of sin was more compatible with a paradigm of partnership and equality than one of hierarchy. And such a paradigm shift, however imperfectly realized, was significantly more open to the emergence of female religious leadership and female equality in general.

# 20

# *Women's Religious Leadership in the Twentieth Century*

## Affirming Traditional Roles

"I declare that the church has no authority whatsoever to confer priestly ordination on women and that this judgment is to be definitively held by all the church's faithful."[1] In the waning years of the twentieth century, Pope John Paul II thus made it clear that the official Catholic position forbidding women's ordained leadership in the church would not change in the foreseeable future. Although there was considerable internal Catholic dissent in the United States about this decision, Roman Catholicism remained an example of a religious group that neither moved toward and approved female ordination, nor had ever endorsed preaching or formal leadership roles for women, other than those in religious orders. Three other major religious groups followed a similar pattern in twentieth-century America on female leadership and ordination but, unlike the Catholics, evidenced little significant internal dissent, even by women, to that position: Lutheran Church–Missouri Synod, Eastern Orthodox Christians, and Orthodox Jews.

Why did these groups resist the changes of the twentieth century concerning women's roles in the broader society and especially in religious organizations, when several major Protestant Christian and Jewish groups ultimately endorsed full religious leadership for women? One reason was that all four retained a strong ethnic component well into the twentieth century. Ethnic identity and religious faith were closely related and were guarded as bulwarks against too much Americanization. In general, these groups felt that capitulation to American values entailed acceptance of cultural trends, especially those concerning women and the family, which they did not endorse. They also feared that Americanization would dilute both their ethnic identity and their religious faith.

The first half of the twentieth century was a period of growth and consolidation for Roman Catholics with significant gains in numbers and in construction of schools and churches. Gradually, and at different times for different ethnic groups whose migration began in the nineteenth century, Catholics moved into the economic and cultural mainstream of the United States. Yet as many "ethnic Catholics" became more Americanized, there was a major increase in the number of Hispanic Catholics, particularly

Mexicans and, later, Puerto Ricans, coming to the United States. Mexican Catholics practiced a family- rather than church-centered faith. As Jay P. Dolan notes, "domestic family rituals and the public celebration of a saint's feast day were much more important than regular attendance at Sunday mass."[2] And there was a problem with clergy: few followed the immigrants from Mexico, and American Catholics were often prejudiced, more than willing to encourage Hispanic Catholics to form their own separate parishes. By the middle decades of the century, as Puerto Rican Catholics flocked to the United States and especially New York City, the church was showing increased sensitivity to issues of social justice and was more intentional in its efforts to integrate Hispanic Catholics into the American church. Nevertheless, by the closing decades of the century, Hispanic Catholics were distressed that so few of their number were named to the Catholic hierarchy, just as, in their turn, nineteenth-century Catholics like Germans, Italians, and Poles had resented Irish domination of the hierarchy. At the same time, Hispanic women were speaking out in their own distinctive voice. Inspired by other liberationist movements and concerned to preserve and defend their ethnic ties and traditions in a culture that too often devalued or trivialized them, they criticized the women's movement for its insensitivity to women of color and Hispanic men for their sexism.[3]

Currently the second-largest Lutheran body in the United States, the Missouri Synod of the Lutheran Church was founded in 1847 by German immigrants. They and their descendants made up the vast majority of members in the Lutheran Church–Missouri Synod (LCMS) throughout the nineteenth and well into the twentieth century. Like other religious groups dominated by immigrants, the LCMS endorsed quite traditional views of women and their roles in the home and in the church. Here, they differed little from the majority of Americans; however, unlike many other Protestant groups, the LCMS had no "discoverable feminist minority."[4] Nor was the LCMS notably feminized in either membership or ethos, despite its importance, along with the home, for LCMS women.

Eastern Orthodox Christianity was a relative latecomer to the United States. Despite a few earlier, ultimately unsuccessful attempts at settlement, the Eastern Orthodox presence essentially began with Russian explorers and missionaries to Alaska in the nineteenth century. This Russian center moved to San Francisco after the Civil War and to New York in 1905. In the meantime, immigrants from places like Greece, the Balkans, Russia, and eastern and central Europe began to arrive in the United States in significant numbers starting in the 1880s, came in greater numbers during the first two decades of the twentieth century, but then were effectively halted by immigration restrictions until a renewed flow after the Second World War. Eastern Orthodox numbers in America were also augmented by the alliance of Uniate Christians, churches that had, historically, entered unions with the Roman Catholic Church while retaining many of their

Eastern Orthodox customs and rituals. In America, Roman Catholic authorities showed little toleration of Uniate practices, especially their tradition of married clergy, and so significant numbers of these Christians defected to Eastern Orthodoxy.

Eastern Orthodox immigrants, like ethnic Roman Catholics and Jews, found that Americans of the dominant culture regarded them as suspiciously "strange" in both nationality and religion, and they were equally determined to preserve a culture and a religious faith that were closely intertwined. Furthermore, they, too, evidenced internal divisions as ethnic loyalties were reinforced by jurisdictional differences among the "mother" churches from which they came. (The family of Eastern Orthodoxy within Christianity is made up of several autocephalic ("self-headed"), geographically oriented churches. They hold in common their roots in the early Christian church of the eastern Roman Empire and a theological tradition expressed particularly in the seven great ecumenical councils of the church, from 325 to 787, but they also prize their independent authority within that family.) The situation in America was further complicated by internal and interethnic disputes and divisions, often rooted in political conflicts in mother churches that came under communist control during the twentieth century. The history of Eastern Orthodox struggles and divisions in America is both bitter and complicated, but the 1970s began to see movement toward greater cooperation and consolidation. Currently, the Greek Orthodox form the largest body in the United States, followed by the Orthodox Church in America (largely Russian but now autocephalic) and by other Russian groups, as well as Albanian, Antiochian, Bulgarian, Rumanian, Serbian, and Ukranian churches.[5]

Not all the Jews in the major wave of immigration to the United States that began in the 1880s retained a religious identity and practice, but those who did were predominantly Orthodox. Virtually all of them, religious or secularized, had to struggle to survive in a strange, new, often hostile environment, and those who were religious clung tenaciously to their faith and culture. But while some in the second and third generations retained their Orthodoxy, many others shifted their allegiance to Conservative or even Reform congregations (or maintained only tenuous ties to Jewish communities) as part of the process of Americanization, upward economic mobility, and cultural acceptance. In the meantime, immigration restrictions in the 1920s cut back drastically on the number of Jews entering America and were not significantly loosened even during Hitler's rise to power in the 1930s. It was thus not until the years after World War II that Orthodox Judaism saw a serious resurgence in America. In part, this was due to renewed immigration, including a number of distinguished European rabbis and heads of *yeshivot* (Jewish rabbinic schools) and their followers and students. But Orthodox Judaism also reaped benefits from a broad religious revival in America in the postwar years and from the heightened awareness of American Jews of their own responsibilities to represent and preserve Judaism after the Holocaust. A new generation of rabbis attracted former and newly Orthodox Jews; more Jewish day schools were founded and built; new congregations appeared not only in the East but also in the American West and South.

By the 1970s, immigration had slowed considerably and many Jews drifted away from membership in a synagogue and active religious practice. Nevertheless, other Jews in America, among them Jews attracted to Orthodoxy, were drawn in the last three decades of the century to increased observance of their Judaism. Contrary to some pessimistic predictions at midcentury, Orthodox Judaism not only held its own but grew in America. Among the most important reasons for the growth were the establishment and spread of day schools and the economic success finally experienced by Orthodox Jews, which allowed them to give greater attention to carrying out strict observance of Jewish law: for example, Orthodox Jews, lifted above a struggle for sheer survival, no longer had to accept jobs that demanded that they work on the Sabbath. Jack Wertheimer identifies two major trends that have developed since the mid-1960s: "First, Orthodoxy has achieved an unprecedented degree of respectability in the eyes of both non-Orthodox Jews and non-Jews. . . . The second trend that characterizes Orthodoxy is the shift to the right in the thinking and behavior of Orthodox Jews."[6]

Orthodox Jews are distinguished from those in the Conservative or Reform movements by their approach to the Torah and to Jewish law. They view the Torah, in its modern text, as given directly and literally by God to Moses and believe that oral tradition is implicitly included in that revelation. Jewish *halakhah* or law, including matters of ritual and ceremony, is fully binding for modern observant Orthodox Jews. Thus most continue to observe separated seating for men and women in synagogues and construct a *mikveh* (ritual bath) as soon as possible in new communities. Orthodox Jews frequently gather in close proximity, partly in an effort to preserve their religious heritage and faith, but also for practical reasons.

> An observant Jew needs a variety of institutions, within the neighborhood, to make his or her observance possible. This explains why Orthodox Jews are usually found close to each other, within walking distance of the synagogue (driving is prohibited according to Jewish law on the Sabbath and certain holidays), and within reasonable proximity of a kosher butcher, kosher baker, and ritual bath (*mikveh*). Increasingly, too, observant Orthodox use the growing network of day schools, including the studying of Torah under the obligatory "ceremonies" of Judaism.[7]

A need for ethnic/religious identity among all four of these groups is a partial but not sufficient explanation for their concern to defend women's domestic responsibilities as practically necessary and as a way to preserve and pass on their heritage to future generations. Each group also had theological reasons that, to them, mandated distinctive and traditional roles for women and that precluded women's assuming public religious leadership, whatever was happening among other Christians or Jews in twentieth-century America.

## Attitudes about Women's Religious Leadership

### Roman Catholicism

Catholic views and attitudes toward women for most of the twentieth century remained very much what they had been in the nineteenth: women were by nature and divine decree subordinate to men; except for religious sisters, their natural place was in the family as upholders of piety and purity; women who did not thus emulate Mary were to be regarded as dangerous and rebellious daughters of Eve. Not only were such images promoted by the pope and male hierarchy, they were also endorsed by leading Catholic women and their organizations. Yet church leaders tried to respond to some changing conditions with sympathy, even as they deplored other new trends. Leo XIII (pope from 1878 to 1903) and his immediate successors promoted a traditional, male-headed family, insisted that the family remained the most important concern for women not called to a religious vocation, and condemned "immoral" practices like birth control and divorce, as well as immodest fashions. They conceded, however, that women could and should engage in charitable works, and they expressed genuine concern about the low wages and poor working conditions endured by women workers. Although few male Catholic leaders were outspoken in their support of votes for women, when female suffrage passed, they urged women to exercise that new right to support family and morality. In 1930, Pope Pius XI's definitive encyclical, "Casti Connubii," reiterated the Roman Church's traditional opposition to any form of artificial birth control, commended a wife's submission to her husband, and articulated an image of "balance" in the family, a position that later came to be known as "complementarity" as church leaders tried to retain gender differences without blatant assertions of female inferiority. "For if man is the head, the woman is the heart, and as he occupies the chief place in ruling, so she may and ought to claim for herself the chief place in love."[8] Pius XII continued his predecessors' praise of motherhood, arguing in 1945 that in the absence of biological motherhood, single women (whether or not they were in religious orders) should exercise a spiritual motherhood. Assuming that a single laywoman must be in that state solely through force of circumstances, the pope advised her, "In the impossibility of marriage she discerns her own vocation and, sad at heart, though resigned, she too [like the woman religious] devotes herself entirely to the highest and most varied forms of beneficence."[9]

Catholic leadership in America was in full accord with papal directives in its praise of motherhood and its suspicion of any changes in women's activities that seemed to undermine the centrality of the family and female purity. Such concerns were expressed not only by male clerics but also by a significant number of Catholic women, especially those involved in the National Council of Catholic Women (NCCW). The NCCW was founded in 1920 at the initiative and under the direction of American bishops as a national organization for Catholic women. Like the bishops, women leaders of the NCCW were highly critical of cultural trends that they believed threatened the stability of the family: in particular, birth control, divorce, and the newly introduced Equal Rights Amendment. But also like the bishops and their National Catholic Welfare Conference, the NCCW was not simply a "conservative" organization, despite its views on woman and her place. Opposition to the ERA, for instance, was motivated in part by concern that it would invalidate the protective labor legislation that many "liberals" had worked so hard to pass. Over the decades of the twentieth century, the NCCW attracted many Catholic women to its work and presented an agenda in which relatively traditional views on women and the family were mixed with progressive views in other areas of social welfare and national concerns. Thus, for example, in the post-Vatican II era, the NCCW opposed the ordination of women as priests and ratification of the ERA (which, for many Catholics, was associated with support for abortion, just as suffrage and birth control had been linked early in the century), but it also issued in 1981 a strong resolution on disarmament and the abolition of nuclear weapons, and did so before the publication of the American bishops' pastoral letter on that topic.[10]

Given their concern for the well-being and future of the family, a concern that approached "hysteric proportions," according to Jay Dolan, by the 1930s, Catholic leaders began programs to promote family life, including a Family Life Bureau, the popular Cana Conferences (married couples' retreats begun in the 1940s), and the Christian Family Movement.[11] Motherhood was still, of course, crucial, but Catholic authorities also emphasized the importance of the father's religious leadership. Yet ironically, for many American Catholics in the 1950s the old ethnic/religious identity was fading; economic achievement made it possible for families to move to the suburbs, where women and children were more separated not only from men but from the old urban neighborhoods that had shaped and preserved Catholic identities and traditions. Clergy might urge men to reassume leadership, but it was, in fact, women who directed and organized family religion, even to the point of explaining to a husband how and when he was to step in as "leader."[12]

## John XXIII and Vatican II

John XXIII, the "dark horse" elected pope in 1958, and the Second Vatican Council, which he convened, were not completely unprecedented or revolutionary, for there had been important reformers, reform movements, and changes within the Roman Catholic Church before them, some of which had led to gradual changes for women, both lay and religious. Nevertheless, the pope and the council *were* a significant turning point on many issues. Statements about women, their rights and roles, were sufficiently radical that it is hardly surprising that many Catholic women at the time paid less attention to the qualifications in those statements. In his 1963 encyclical, "Pacem in Terris," Pope John XXIII affirmed woman's equality in marriage and society:

> Human beings have the right to choose freely the state of life which they prefer, and therefore the right to set up a family, with equal rights and duties for man and woman, and also the right to follow a vocation to the priesthood or the religious life. . . . It is obvious to everyone that women are now taking a part in public life. . . . Since women are becoming ever more conscious of their human dignity, they will not tolerate being treated as mere material instruments, but demand rights befitting a human person both in domestic and in public life.[13]

Similarly, the last official document promulgated by Vatican II, "Gaudium et Spes" ("Pastoral Constitution on the Church in the Modern World"), included a strong statement on the equality of women and men:

> With respect to the fundamental rights of the person, every type of discrimination, whether social or cultural, whether based on sex, race, color, social condition, language, or religion, is to be overcome and eradicated as contrary to God's intent. For in truth it must still be regretted that fundamental personal rights are not yet being universally honored. Such is the case of a woman who is denied the right and freedom to choose a husband, to embrace a state of life, or to acquire an education or cultural benefits equal to those recognized for men.[14]

Yet along with the ringing statements of equality there were qualifications. In "Pacem in Terris," John XXIII insisted that "[w]omen have the right to working conditions in accordance with their requirements and their duties as wives and mothers."[15] "Gaudium et Spes" affirmed that women "should be able to assume their full proper role [in culture] *in accordance with their own nature*" (emphasis added), and, like the pope, stated that a person's productive work should be adapted to his or her needs and responsibilities: "Such is especially the case with respect to mothers of families, but due consideration must be given to every person's sex and age.

. . . The children, especially the younger among them, need the care of their mother at home. This domestic role of hers must be safely preserved, though the legitimate social progress of woman should not be underrated on that account."[16] Moreover, in another document, the "Declaration on Christian Education," the council fathers argued that persons have an "inalienable" right to education, but one corresponding with one's "native talents, . . . sex, . . . cultural background, and . . . ancestral heritage," and that parents and teachers should give due attention "to the social role which divine Providence allots to each sex in family life and in society."[17] Qualifications on female equality expressed in Vatican II documents were reinforced by the council's actions: It was not until halfway through the council, in 1964, that a few women were permitted to be present at its formal deliberations, and then they had neither voice nor vote.

Finally, two issues of particular importance to women were virtually ignored by the Second Vatican Council: birth control and female ordination. The council's statements on population and family planning may have been intentionally vague and limited because a commission had been appointed to study the question. Three years after the close of the council, Pope Paul VI chose to ignore the majority report of that commission and in "Humanae Vitae" condemned all "unnatural" forms of birth control as contrary to natural law and deemed only the "rhythm" method as acceptable. The pope's conclusion evoked widespread disagreement and disobedience, especially in the North American church, and in the judgment of many observers seriously undermined respect for the pope's teaching authority in matters of morals. In addition, "Humanae Vitae" contained a significant shift back to traditional language on marriage, reversing the change of Vatican II. A comparison of marriage with the union of Christ and the church goes back to the New Testament, with the man identified with Christ and the woman with Christ's bride, the church. In "Gaudium et Spes," a subtle but important change was suggested: Husband and wife are urged to "render mutual help and service to each other" and reminded that "just as He [Christ] loved the Church and handed Himself over on her behalf, the *spouses may love each other* with perpetual fidelity through *mutual self-bestowal*."[18] But in "Humanae Vitae," Pope Paul VI returned to the older image, citing Ephesians 5: " . . . let each one of you *love* his wife as himself, and let the wife see that she *respects* her husband."[19]

Ordination of women to the priesthood was not an issue for the fathers of Vatican II; indeed, it was hardly a concern even for liberal Roman Catholic women before the 1960s. But in 1962 a Swiss lawyer, Gertrud Heinzelmann, presented a petition to the Vatican on behalf of the St. Joan's Alliance. (St. Joan's had been founded in 1911 in England to promote female suffrage and had grown to an international organization of and for Catholic women; its U.S. branch, however, was not founded until 1965.)

However radical its content, the words of the petition were extremely polite and deferential: "St. Joan's International Alliance reaffirms its loyalty and filial devotion and expresses its conviction that should the Church in her wisdom and in her good time decide to extend to women the dignity of the priesthood, women would be willing and eager to respond."[20] In the wake of Vatican II, women in the United States, lay as well as religious, began to question traditional biblical interpretations, the church's treatment of women throughout its history, and the current status of women in the church in works like Sidney Callahan's *The Illusion of Eve* (1965), Sally Cunneen's *Sex: Female; Religion: Catholic* (1968), and Mary Daly's *The Church and the Second Sex* (1968).

Encouraged by the egalitarian statements of Pope John XXIII and the Second Vatican Council and aware of Protestant women who had already gained official access to ordination or whose denominations were in the process of debate, Roman Catholic women began to raise the question of priesthood more frequently by the 1970s. In 1974, the Leadership Conference of Women Religious passed a resolution to support "the principle that all ministries in the Church be open to women and men as the Spirit calls them. . . ."[21] Late in that same year, a laywoman, Mary Lynch, called a conference on women's ordination for 1975. The conference, held in Detroit, attracted some twelve hundred people and turned away hundreds more for lack of space. As Rosemary Ruether, herself a participant in the conference, concludes:

> The conference accomplished several things. First, it brought together a fine display of the Scriptural and theological studies already developed to support the ordination of women. . . . Second, it created a powerful experience of solidarity in the pursuit of priesthood for women who had previously felt isolated and unsupported. . . . Third, the organizing staff was mandated by the conference to continue as a network center to help promote local conferences and local support groups in as many communities as possible.[22]

Even before the Detroit conference, Catholic supporters of women's ordination realized that the current pope, Paul VI, had little sympathy for the cause. Paul VI had issued in 1972 an apostolic letter, "Ministeria Quaedam," which excluded women not only from the ordained priesthood but also from the lay liturgical roles of lector and acolyte. (Compliance with such restrictions on leadership roles for the laity was not universal, especially in the United States.) At the time of the Detroit Conference, Archbishop Joseph L. Bernardin, then president of the National Conference of Catholic Bishops, issued a statement opposing the ordination of women, primarily on the theological basis of an unbroken tradition of male priesthood.[23]

## Roman Catholic Rejection of Female Ordination

Then in 1976 the Vatican's Sacred Congregation for the Doctrine of the Faith issued a formal "Declaration on the Question of the Admission of Women to the Ministerial Priesthood." The primary reason women could not be priests, it argued, was the church's tradition of male priesthood, based on Jesus' example: "By calling only men to the priestly Order and ministry in its true sense, the Church intends to remain faithful to the type of ordained ministry willed by the Lord Jesus Christ and carefully maintained by the Apostles."[24] Even though the document's authors admitted that some arguments used in the past against women are no longer defensible, they insisted that the tradition is clear and cannot be changed. A second argument advanced in the declaration is the necessity for the priest, who represents Christ during the Eucharist, to resemble the male person Jesus: "When Christ's role in the Eucharist is to be expressed sacramentally, there would not be this 'natural resemblance' which must exist between Christ and his minister if the role of Christ were not taken by a man: in such a case it would be difficult to see in the minister the image of Christ."[25] Finally, the document insisted that denial of ordination does not infringe women's equal human rights because ordination is not a "right" for any person and encouraged women (but with little specific elaboration) to fulfill their particular role "for the renewal and humanization of society and for the rediscovery by believers of the true face of the Church."[26]

While some Catholic leaders welcomed and praised the Vatican's declaration, others were seriously distressed at what they saw as its insensitivity and the weakness of its theological arguments, its biblical exegesis, and its patristic citations. Such were the grounds cited by virtually the entire faculty of the Jesuit School of Theology at Berkeley (California), who signed an open letter to the pope's apostolic delegate in America criticizing the declaration and warning the church not to make the same kind of mistake it had with Copernican science![27] Rosemary Ruether has suggested that this declaration, like "Humanae Vitae," had repercussions on the church's authority beyond the specific issues addressed:

> The attempt of the declaration to replace the traditional basis of exclusion [woman's natural inferiority and subjection] with a theological construct that links maleness, Christ and priesthood astonished those who had previously had little interest in the subject. One might say that if the Vatican lost its credibility for "infallibility" in matters of morals with the birth-control controversy, it lost its credibility for "infallibility" in matters of faith with the declaration on the admission of women to the priesthood.[28]

In the meantime, supporters of women's ordination to the priesthood were becoming more insistent that their goal was not merely "adding" women to existing offices but a challenge to the very image and nature of "priesthood" as it had been traditionally understood and practiced. They continued to press their case through conferences, papers, and local organizations. In the decades that followed Vatican II, Catholic women did not gain access to the diaconate or the priesthood, but they did begin to function in other administrative and liturgical leadership roles, at least in some United States dioceses and parishes. In 1983, a new canon (517.2) responded to the growing scarcity of priests by opening the possibility for laypersons (including women) to exercise a kind of pastoral, though not sacramental, ministry in parishes.[29] While few members of the clerical hierarchy in the United States openly supported female ordination, United States bishops did take official positions denouncing sexism and discrimination.[30]

Yet Pope John Paul II made his opposition to women priests very clear, culminating in 1994 in "Ordinatio Sacerdotalis." The reasons cited were familiar, principally Christ's *action* in choosing twelve men (and not Mary) as apostles and the unbroken tradition of male sacerdotal ministry thereafter. (Interestingly, the pope's letter does not specifically mention the need for a "natural resemblance" between the priest and Christ during the Eucharist.) Rather than suggesting new arguments, the apostolic letter was noteworthy for its vehemence and insistence on an authority little short of infallible. No further debate on the question is to be allowed. The issue of *Origins* that printed an English text of the letter also included several responses from American bishops. Some obviously welcomed the adamant papal statement; others noted the decision with little comment and instead emphasized and elaborated upon the pope's affirmation of women's equal dignity and honor, encouraging the church more effectively to recognize and use women's talents. Yet Archbishop Rembert Weakland of Milwaukee, while clearly stating his intention to obey the papal command, admitted that his obedience would come only after "inner turmoil" and "much sacrifice and inner searching." He expressed further concern about the letter's impact on faithful American Catholics, theologians, and ecumenical Christian dialogue.[31] Other American Catholics demonstrated the same range of responses, though the tone of dissenters was much more openly critical than the archbishop's.

## Lutheran Church–Missouri Synod

Although the Roman Catholic Church, the Lutheran Church–Missouri Synod (LCMS), Eastern Orthodox Christians and Orthodox Jews enunciate quite similar positions at the level of official leadership about women's ordination, there is far less internal dissent among the latter three groups. In the nineteenth century, the ideal LCMS woman embodied the virtues of the "cult of True Womanhood." In that, she was hardly different than the majority of her American sisters. But the LCMS, with a very high view of clerical authority, offered the laity (men or women) far fewer opportunities for power and responsibility than did many nineteenth-century Protestant churches. Shortly after the turn of the twentieth century, laymen in the LCMS began to take a more prominent role in parishes and synodical structures, but LCMS views on women remained highly traditional. Woman's proper sphere was the domestic one; indeed, until the early twentieth century, young immigrant women who had to work outside the home were directed to positions in domestic service rather than factory work.[32] With rare exceptions, women were expected to find their vocation in marriage in a family whose head was the husband. Thus LCMS leaders of the time were adamantly opposed to woman suffrage and to birth control, which was seen as a threat to the family and much too closely allied with the "modern woman," who supposedly scorned subordination to her husband and the duties of motherhood. Over time, however, the LCMS came to accept both women's voting and birth control, though always within a context of strong support for the family.[33]

Changing experiences and opportunities for women in the twentieth century modified the ways in which marriage was described by the Missouri Synod but did not challenge official LCMS views of marriage's basic pattern. In 1981, a synodical report on human sexuality insisted that marital hierarchy was divinely instituted and thus must "remain in effect until the close of this age regardless of the social customs, civil laws, or ecclesiastical rites which may come to surround it."[34] The report insisted that male headship is a hierarchy of function, not of merit, and is meant to preserve distinctive gender roles and promote mutual service. The husband's authority is not due to personal superiority and should not be construed as rule, and the wife's subordination connotes no inferiority and is not to be equated with subservience.

The pattern of male headship and female subordination applied just as firmly in the church. In the twentieth century, as many other Protestant bodies began to extend laity rights and positions of public leadership to women, the LCMS resisted change. Some LCMS churches refused to permit returning women missionaries to speak to mixed audiences, and "sexually segregated seating and communion attendance could still be found well into the thirties."[35] By 1969, however, the LCMS's convention passed a resolution that permitted women to vote and hold office in congregations, as long as the male membership in each individual parish agreed to the change. But ordination was another matter. Even though the Lutheran Church in America and the American Lutheran Church, the two other large Lutheran bodies in the United States, voted to permit female ordination in 1970, the LCMS continued its opposition and in 1985 reiterated its position in a synodical statement. In the document's scriptural analysis, the familiar biblical passages on women that had been cited for centuries are noted and found to contain no conclusive endorsement for female ordination, although the discussion reflects more recent social and exegetical developments in its insistence on women's spiritual worth and equality and its acceptance of women's active roles and service in the earliest churches. The main argument advanced against women's ordination, however, is the order of creation,

> the particular position which, by the will of God, any created object occupies in relation to others. God has given to that which has been created a certain definite order which, because it has been created by Him, is the expression of His immutable will. These relationships belong to the very structure of created existence.[36]

The same ideas of distinctive male and female natures and of headship and subordination that were applied to the family were seen as equally decisive for the church, yet the specific applications drawn for church roles reflected changes in scriptural interpretation and in practice from the nineteenth and much of the twentieth century. Thus the report argued that 1 Corinthians 14 does not mean "absolute" silence for women in public worship; the statements in 1 Timothy 2 on female teaching and holding authority over men should not be taken to preclude women's teaching in Sunday schools, Bible studies, and the like, nor their "authority" in congregational meetings and committees. Rather, it is strictly the "pastoral office," the "public ministry . . . of teaching the Word and administering the sacraments" that is forbidden to women. "The creational pattern of male headship requires that women not hold the formal position of the authoritative public teaching office in the church, that is, in the office of pastor."[37]

## The Eastern Orthodox Church

Very few Eastern Orthodox Christian women see female ordination to the priesthood as either desirable or defensible; rather, the issue has been addressed by Eastern Orthodox leaders and theologians in recent decades primarily because of the revived women's movement in America and, specifically, the ecumenical implications of Protestant (especially Episcopal) decisions to ordain women. Alexander Schmemann, in a preface to a collection of essays on the topic, emphasizes three essential points to consider: the role of tradition; the need to see women's ordination in the context of "the scriptural doctrine of man and woman"; and ecclesiology, ". . . the understanding of the Church and the mystery of salvation."[38]

To Eastern Orthodox Christians, there are no precedents in scripture or tradition for female priests: While there were prophetesses in both the Old and New Testaments, Israel had no female priests. Christ neither called women as apostles nor entrusted them with priestly office, and neither did the church for the next nineteen centuries.[39] Scripture, particularly Genesis 1, is also decisive in the second consideration cited by Schmemann:

Man and woman are essentially distinctive from the time of creation. To Thomas Hopko, the theological reason for sexuality is found in humanity's creation *imago Dei,* specifically in the image of the Trinity. Just as the three hypostatically different persons in one God share a relationship of community, so man and woman are created to be distinctive beings in relationship at the same time that they share a common humanity. "As the Son and the Holy Spirit are not the same and are not interchangeable in their unique forms of their common divinity, so the male and female are not the same and are not interchangeable in the unique forms of their common humanity."[40] Yet Hopko repeatedly insists that differentiation does not imply superiority and inferiority, just as it does not in the Trinity: "Because the Holy Spirit is not the Father or the Son but the 'third person' of the Holy Trinity, and because the Spirit does not do what the Father and the Son do, this in no way lessens the dignity and equality of the Holy Spirit as being divine."[41] Hopko compares man with Christ and woman with the Holy Spirit, though he insists that he does not mean to apply "masculine" or "feminine" qualities internally to persons of the Trinity, for God is beyond sexuality:

> According to the catholic tradition of the Christian faith, there is a direct analogical, symbolic and epiphanic relationship between Adam and the Son of God, and between Eve and the Spirit of God. As Adam is the *typos* of him "who was to come" as the final Adam, the "high priest of our confession" and the "pastor and bishop of our salvation," so Eve is the *typos,* as the "mother of all living," of the "life-creating" Spirit, who "proceeds from the Father and rests in the Son" as the personal power and life of all that exists, both human and divine.[42]

While Hopko is firm in his conviction about the theological and essential difference between man and woman, masculine and feminine ways of being, he is less specific about the practical implications of that difference beyond the exclusion of women from the priesthood. George Barrois, however, applies the difference to particular life roles: "By biblical charter, the woman is normally thought of as the companion of man and the mother of his children. Accordingly, the function of the woman as mother shall take exclusive precedence over any secondary avocation or individual circumstances."[43]

Schmemann's third essential point is also developed by Hopko. The church is an organic reality, divinely instituted as "the sacrament par excellence" and the body of Christ, who is, in one sense, her only priest. Preeminently in the Eucharist, male priests are then sacramental images of Christ. "The ordained priest 'presents' Christ's body and bride to the Father because he first 'presents' Christ to his body and bride." Again, Hopko argues that ontological and functional difference means that "a uniquely feminine manner of human being and life" is "incompatible" with priesthood but does not imply female defect or weakness, any more than the Holy Spirit's not being Logos and Christ, the high priest, means inferiority or defect in the Spirit.[44] Yet Hopko wants to differentiate his argument from that found in the Vatican declaration on women and priesthood in the matter of "natural resemblance."

> The priest does not bear a "natural resemblance" to Jesus in his biological and anatomical maleness. But to be the proper sacramental presence of Jesus the priest must be a once-married or celibate man, a sound Christian, whole in body and soul, without scandal and of good reputation both within and without the community of the faithful; a masculine person capable of heading the body with the compassionate wisdom and sacrificial love of a husband and father. Such a position, obviously, is based on the conviction that there is such a reality as fatherhood and husbandship, and that to be father and husband in and to an ecclesial community is a masculine spiritual activity that a woman, by nature and vocation, cannot and should not be expected to fulfill. The point is not about "natural resemblance." It is rather about *natural competence*.[45]

Finally, Mary, Theotokos (God-bearer or Mother of God), plays an important role in Eastern Orthodox Christian discussions of the theological meaning of women's nature and roles. Jesus' intent about apostolicity and priesthood is reinforced in Orthodox belief by the fact that he did not call his mother to this role. Yet Mary has long been understood in Christian tradition as the "new Eve," and she, like women, is specially related to the Holy Spirit. "The central person in the special ministry of women in the divine plan of salvation is the Mother of God, the Theotokos. In her is fulfilled the special work of the Holy Spirit for the Incarnation of the Son and Word of God."[46] Mary is also the premier representative of the new humanity and the "royal priesthood" that all Christians share as a result of baptism.

> Jesus Christ is the saviour of all persons, both men and women. Yet, in the typological and iconic experience of worship and the pastoral life of the Church, Christ as the High Priest is presented to us appropriately and fittingly only by a male in the High Priestly image. Conversely, the Theotokos, the Mother of God, represents all humanity, both female and male in the divine act of the Incarnation, giving to the eternal Son of God his human nature. She is the Mother of all, especially the members of the Body of the Church. As such, the Theotokos, in the typological and iconic experience of worship and the whole experience of the Christian life, presents us before the Lord's throne in a way which uniquely speaks for us as creatures of God.[47]

Militza Zernov, an Eastern Orthodox woman, further claims that veneration of Mary is directly related to the honor women receive in Eastern Orthodox churches, a situation that, in her view, is not exemplified in Western men's attitudes toward women.[48]

## Orthodox Judaism

Since Orthodox Jews hold Jewish law and tradition as normative, their views on women and their roles in twentieth-century America are in many ways similar to the views of eastern European Jewish immigrants described in chapter 15. Some events and trends of the twentieth century, however, have focused attention on the Jewish family and the Jewish woman's role therein. On the one hand, the Nazi Holocaust decimated European Jewry and made Jews living in America (as well as Israeli Jews) acutely aware of their critical role in the survival of the Jewish people. On the other, trends within American Judaism, especially in the last third of the twentieth century, were toward more assimilation in general and intermarriage in particular. "A survey conducted under the auspices of the Council of Jewish Federations in the early 1970s indicated that American Jewry had entered an era of demographic stagnation: Jews were having fewer children relative to the American population; immigration had virtually ceased; and rates of intermarriage had been spiraling since the mid-1960s." By the period 1985–1990, less than half the Jews who married chose a Jewish partner.[49] Couples in such "mixed" marriages were significantly less likely than Jewish couples to provide a clear, active Jewish upbringing for their children. Furthermore, the more liberal branches of American Judaism witnessed more mixed marriages with a resultant dilution of Jewish faith and identity. Thus Orthodox Jews felt compelled to discourage if not forbid mixed marriages and to promote the formation of actively observant Jewish families.

Here the role of Jewish women was crucial. Mothers most often passed on ethnic and religious traditions to future generations; moreover, the maintenance of "traditional" families and gender roles was associated with observance and hence Jewish survival. For practical as well as religious reasons, then, Orthodox Jews have resisted anything more than minimal changes in women's roles in worship or traditional laws about women. In this situation, many Jewish women raised as Orthodox have left that identification behind as adults, but others have maintained and defended their tradition. Furthermore, the closing years of the century have seen the accession of men and women not raised as Orthodox who have returned to an Orthodox expression of Judaism, the *ba'alei* (male) and *ba'alot* (female) *teshuvah*.

*Ba'alot teshuvah* have been the subject of two recent sociological studies by Debra Renee Kaufman, who concentrated on married women who had been part of their new Orthodox communities for several years, and by Lynn Davidman, who focused on single women recently attracted to Orthodoxy or in a process of conversion. In addition, *ba'alot teshuvah* themselves, like Tamar Frankiel, have added their perspectives on their choices.[50] Both types of report illuminate not only *that* such return is occurring but also *why* it is. Two central attractions of Orthodox Judaism for these women are its clear connection with an ancient tradition and its emphasis on the value of the family, with definite roles for men and women. Kaufman notes that the women in her study "reported a common experience: that their lives had been spiritually empty and without purpose before their return."[51] Davidman describes a similar perceived lack of roots and purpose, although the two groups of women she studied, one at the Modern Orthodox Lincoln Square Synagogue and the other at Bais Chana, a residential female school of Hasidic Lubavitch Jews, differed from each other in their social and economic situations. Orthodox Judaism provided a stable, long-standing religious identity with clear and authoritative answers for the meaning and practice of the person's life. Distinctive gender roles in an honored family unit were also a major attraction of Orthodox Judaism to the *ba'alot teshuvah*. The women in Davidman's study freely admitted their desire to marry and form families, and those in Kaufman's study valued their roles as wives and mothers and the community's support for those roles. In both cases, the women contrasted what they hoped to find or had found with their perception of the disintegration and devaluation of the family in modern American society and, in many cases, their own personal unhappy experiences. Such focus on traditional families and gender roles did not preclude the women's working outside of the home, but they generally agreed that such work was secondary in importance to the family. Furthermore, they appreciated the degree of familial involvement demonstrated by Orthodox men and encouraged by the communities.

Within such a context, the women not only accepted but defended some of the gender-distinct practices criticized by many Jewish feminists in Reform or Conservative congregations. Male leadership in synagogue worship was seldom questioned, nor was use of the *mehitzah,* the partition separating men and women during worship. Blu Greenberg, an observant Orthodox Jew, though not a "newly returned" one, argues:

> The *mehitzah* does not inherently demean women, nor must it fall away as women assume new roles, nor is "separate" in every last instance synonymous with "unequal." The *mehitzah* serves more than the spiritual and social functions . . . [of enhancing] an intimate aloneness with God and male and female bondings. It also undeniably highlights sex differentiation, no small feat in a society that sometimes confuses equality with androgyny.[52]

Indeed, the *mehitzah* has become a symbol of the distinction between Orthodox and non-Orthodox Jews; its use affirms halakhic loyalty and traditional values. Thus Orthodox congregations are more adamant about its use now than they were earlier in the twentieth century.[53]

Orthodox Jewish women also do not appear to rebel against the laws of family purity (*niddah*), which necessitate a married couple's abstaining from sexual intercourse during and for seven days after the wife's menstrual period and her use of the *mikveh* (ritual pool) at the end of that time. Some women, indeed, are critical of the language of "uncleanness" associated with women's ritual impurity, but they see this as correctable and peripheral. Most basically, the practice is part of the *halakhah* that observant Jews honor, and Rachel Adler has argued that its original religious intent was related to the experience of the cycle of death and resurrection.[54] Furthermore, family purity and the *mikveh* are defended on practical grounds: they acknowledge female biological cycles and prevent a woman's husband from regarding her as simply an ever-available sex object. They also heighten women's sense of autonomy during the period of abstinence and increase sexual satisfaction when intercourse is resumed: " . . . it is really like being a bride again . . . well, almost."[55]

In sum, these Orthodox Jewish women insist that, for them, "separate" does not mean "unequal" in a community that honors men's and women's inherent differences, differences they embrace with enthusiasm. Tamar Frankiel's conclusions seem consistent with the convictions of "born" and "newly returned" Orthodox women:

> In its ritual dimension the synagogue is a spiritual manifestation, not a political one. This means that communal worship expresses an archetype, an essential statement about human community, and this takes precedence over other functions the synagogue might have. . . . [This archetype is a male-female polarity which is] basic to the construction of the universe. . . . Partners with different functions, different life realities, women and men also have different spiritual needs and purposes, and the synagogue is the place where those manifest in community.[56]

When surveying the views of Roman Catholics, Missouri Synod Lutherans, Eastern Orthodox Christians, and Orthodox Jews on women's religious leadership, we find some common themes but also distinctive emphases. All four groups cite scripture in their rejection of female ordination, but where the Lutherans and Orthodox Jews understand scripture as literally true and inerrant, Roman Catholics and Orthodox Christians do not, though they certainly regard scripture as divinely inspired and authoritative. The voice of tradition, that is, that women have not been ordained to the priestly ministry or the rabbinate in the past, is especially important for Catholics, Eastern Orthodox Christians, and Orthodox Jews, less decisive for Lutherans (not surprising, given the Lutheran emphasis on *sola scriptura*, "scripture alone"). All four groups also cite theological reasons for their position, including a basic, essential, created difference between men and women that precludes female ordination. For Eastern Orthodox Christians, this difference plus the weight of tradition appear to be the central arguments. Roman Catholic documents put more emphasis on tradition, especially Jesus' example in not calling women, not even Mary, to be apostles, and on the "natural resemblance" between male priests and Jesus Christ during the Eucharist. Missouri Synod Lutherans highlight the "order of creation" in their arguments, while Orthodox Jews focus on tradition and the Law. Yet a striking feature of modern statements by each of the four groups is the way they de-emphasize female inferiority, implicitly or explicitly repudiating past "errors" when such inferiority was assumed. Rather, they self-consciously promote a "separate but equal" or complementary understanding of male and female humanity and insist that it is these essential differences that make women's ordination impossible.

## Affirming Traditional Roles and Encouraging New Roles Today

Why is there so little internal dissent by women in all of the groups except Roman Catholics now, when they have examples, especially in America, of other Jews and Christians who ordain women and when women have greater freedom and more choices, social and professional, in the larger culture? First, we cannot discount the role of religious conviction, of agreement with each group's theological arguments. Second, those who are seriously unhappy with the exclusion of women from ordination in their own tradition can move with relative ease. This is especially true for Missouri Synod Lutherans and Orthodox Jews, for whom there are other branches of their traditions that do ordain women. It is more problematic, however, for Roman Catholic or Eastern Orthodox Christian women who feel strongly about their particular religious tradition. Third, all four groups seem to promise stability, security, and a clear and ancient truth in the face of bewildering changes in cultural practices and values and in the light of an apparent decline in morality within American society, especially but not only in the area of "family" values. This attraction is often related to a perception of feminism as "radical," a threat to morality, to core religious truths, and to the family. While some contemporary feminists would argue that the woman's movement is not incompatible with morality, family, and faith, there are enough "radical" voices within the broad diversity that is modern feminism to confirm the suspicions of critics, and this impression is reinforced by the tendency of the American media to publicize and define feminism through its more "radical" statements and events. In particular, the women in these four groups perceive feminists as devaluing both traditional female roles and the women who choose them; their reaction is therefore, not surprisingly, critical and defensive.

Thus all four groups offer, in addition to arguments for the theological validity of their position, an affirmation of traditional roles and morality as an alternative to what they see as modern American chaos, role confusion, and moral disintegration. Moreover, each of the four offers additional, alternative roles for women beyond the central, religiously valued ones of wife and mother. Catholics have sisters; Missouri Synod Lutherans offer positions as pastor's wife, parochial school teacher, and deaconess; Eastern Orthodox Christianity encourages women to pursue and use higher theological education and proposes a revived diaconate for women. While Orthodox Judaism does not offer as distinctive an alternative, some current leaders endorse more study of Torah and Jewish *halakhah* than was the practice in the past for Orthodox Jewish women.

## Roman Catholicism

Roman Catholic women at the turn of the twentieth century lacked the important if limited access to formal religious leadership enjoyed by some evangelical Protestant women, and they would not see a movement over the course of the century toward acceptance of female ordination, as would many mainline Protestants. What Roman Catholic women did have was that religiously and personally significant alternative to marriage and motherhood: the religious life of a sister. Yet when compared with women religious in nineteenth-century America, many Catholic sisters in the first decades of the twentieth century found their lives more restricted and their vocational choices more limited. Why?

In part, the situation of the sisters reflected the situation of the Roman Catholic Church in America at that time. Not only had it begun to achieve a kind of stability, which decreased the need for unorthodox solutions demanded by a pioneer church, but it had also grown more cautious and conservative after papal rebukes directed at the Americanist movement and modernist theology. It was a period of "brick and mortar" Catholicism when growing numbers of Catholics needed many more buildings—especially churches and schools—and demonstrated an increased feeling of satisfaction and acceptance as American Catholics. The schools also had a direct impact on American sisters. When the Third Plenary Council made the support of parochial education obligatory for each parish, not every parish or Catholic leader agreed with the decision, and implementation was often slowed by the practical realities of personnel and finances. But the ideal remained, and as school enrollments grew in the twentieth century, so too did the demand for teachers. At the same time, American standards for teacher certification increased, leaving women superiors and the sisters whom they led caught between the pressures of bishops and priests who wanted—needed—cheap and plentiful labor for the parochial schools and external and internal concerns for more adequate education. Too often novices were thrown into teaching before they were ready, spiritually or intellectually. Those nuns who obtained higher education often had to do so over a long period of time and on top of already heavy workloads.

The need for teachers restricted vocational choices for many sisters, but this was not the only kind of limitation they experienced in the early twentieth century. The papal bull "Conditae a Christo," which recognized American sisters as "real" religious, also imposed stricter standards for their partial cloistering, and, as Mary Ewens notes, with the 1918 New Code of Canon Law, "such a 'cloister mentality' became even more pronounced. In the 1920s, 1930s, and 1940s, sisters were warned to restrict contact with the outside world as much as possible."[57] Papal pronouncements were reinforced by the American hierarchy, for reasons both cultural and practical. James J. Kenneally argues that stricter regulations were intended to protect nuns from the changing—and to the hierarchy, dangerous—images and practices of turn-of-the-century women,[58] while Mary J. Oates suggests that financial considerations reinforced cultural fears: "The economic constraints facing women's communities no doubt contributed to the stringency of the rules regulating their members' behavior. . . . The clearest evidence of the importance of financial considerations is the imposition by Church authorities from without of many regulations with little observable 'religious' significance."[59]

## *New Directions*

While large numbers of American sisters went into education in the first half of the twentieth century, some vocational alternatives, particularly nursing and charitable work, continued from the nineteenth century, and a few new directions developed. Until the twentieth century, the United States was largely a recipient of Catholic "foreign" missions as European priests and sisters emigrated to serve the rapidly growing Catholic immigrant population; indeed, the nation was formally classified as "mission status" within the Roman Catholic Church until 1908. In America, Roman Catholic attention was directed almost entirely to "home" missions, serving American Catholics and reaching out, if at all, to blacks and Native Americans. But by the early years of the twentieth century, United States Catholics began to show more interest in the foreign mission fields that had been attracting American Protestants for a century. Mary Josephine Rogers (1882–1955), a student and later a teacher at Smith College, observed the Protestant women's interest and enthusiasm for foreign missions and wanted to promote similar concerns among Catholic women;

when she met Father James A. Walsh, she found a priest with similar missionary concerns, and the two worked in partnership for many years. In 1911, Fathers Walsh and Thomas Price received American and Vatican approval to found the Catholic Foreign Mission Society of America (better known as the Maryknoll Fathers and Brothers) and a seminary to train foreign missionaries. The next year, Mary Rogers gathered a small group of women to work at Maryknoll as lay "secretaries" who took charge of domestic duties in support of the seminary and of much of the publication work for a missionary journal, *The Field Afar*. By 1920, Rogers was able to persuade male Catholic leaders in America and Rome that, contrary to their assumptions, women could be foreign missionaries, and thus she gained approval for the founding of the Foreign Mission Sisters of Saint Dominic (better known as the Maryknoll Sisters.) Two years later, Maryknoll sisters were working in China. The order grew rapidly and was a major source of twentieth-century Catholic missionaries, with a reputation for unusual cultural sensitivity and for promoting indigenous Christian leadership in the countries they served.

A second new direction for American Catholic sisters combined their tradition of health care with the emerging interest in foreign missions. While some of the nineteenth-century women's orders had ignored clerical disapproval to work as nurses with maternity cases, the early twentieth-century changes in canon law were stricter, insisting that such work was inappropriate for nuns. Yet Roman Catholic women interested in foreign missions discovered, as had their Protestant counterparts, that only female physicians would be accepted to treat women in places like India. In 1936, Anna Dengal (1892–1980) was finally able to get a change in that restrictive canon and found the Medical Mission Sisters. (She and her mentor, Agnes McLaren, had tried earlier to get around the dilemma by recruiting lay women to become missionary physicians, and in fact, the Medical Mission Sisters were preceded by Dengel's Society of Catholic Medical Missionaries, a lay group founded in 1926 who would voluntarily but not officially function as a community.) In time, the order expanded to include medical services to poor communities in the United States.[60]

By the 1950s, more widespread changes were beginning to occur for American sisters. In 1950, Pope Pius XII called an international meeting in Rome for superiors of women's orders and encouraged them to consider and submit to Rome changes in their constitutions that would enhance their effectiveness and service. Two years later, American superiors met in a national meeting, as orders began to propose and enact changes in customs, rules, and training. In 1956, they formed the Conference of Major Superiors of Women (CMSW), later known as the Leadership Conference of Women Religious (LCWR). The Sister Formation Conference (SFC) was established in 1954 under Sister Mary Emil Penet, who wanted "to promote the idea that young sisters should be fully prepared for their work before they embark on it."[61] Born out of the National Catholic Education Association, the SFC initially focused on teaching sisters but soon came to include women religious in nursing and social work as well, arguing that all these sisters needed a rigorous and integrated preparation that was spiritual, intellectual, professional, and apostolic. Thus American sisters had already begun to "modernize" when Pope John XXIII announced his plans to call a major council, Vatican II, to bring the Roman Catholic Church "up to date."

The general spirit of the Second Vatican Council seemed to endorse change and modernization, as did its specific statements about religious life. In perhaps the most obvious and visible change, sisters were no longer required to wear a full habit. More significantly, the council encouraged women's orders to go back and study their own roots and history in light of the central message of the Christian gospel and with an eye to changing practices and ideas that had strayed from those roots or were no longer functional.[62] Sisters responded enthusiastically to the challenge, as they did to the Vatican's request that ten percent of United States sisters volunteer for service in Latin America. But Vatican II and the 1960s had other results for American sisters, not always positive or intended. Many sisters left their orders for a variety of reasons, while others were deeply distressed by the nature and rapid pace of change. Still other sisters became newly aware that their authority and influence were limited under a male hierarchy; for example, it was not until halfway through the Council that a few women were even permitted to attend its deliberations, and then with neither voice nor vote, and sisters found that all too often they were neither represented nor even listened to by church commissions that affected their lives and work. Some male clergy were indifferent or hostile to changes proposed by sisters for their own orders. Many of the sisters who responded to the call to Latin America were "radicalized" by the experience and the emerging liberation theology they encountered there.[63]

Tensions increased in the 1970s, as many in the Roman Catholic Church's male hierarchy began to move away from some of the "liberal" positions or implications of Vatican II at the same time that sisters in the United States increasingly and publicly identified with an emerging women's liberation movement. While sisters in the nineteenth century often enjoyed the substance of opportunities sought by the woman's movement—challenging work, independence, and a life not defined by familial relationships—they generally ignored or even avoided identification with that movement. By the 1970s, such identification was self-consciously embraced by many Catholic sisters. American sisters became more vocal and insistent in their calls to the church to open further leadership roles for women and were among the most visible supporters of priestly ordination for women.

## Lutheran Church–Missouri Synod

Not only does the Lutheran Church–Missouri Synod currently forbid female ordination, it has only in the relatively recent past allowed laity rights and some congregational leadership to women. Nevertheless, women have found in the LCMS, as in so many other religious bodies, parallel or auxiliary roles in which they could express a religious identity and serve the church. The nineteenth-century LCMS pastor's wife held an important role in the congregation. Not only was she to be a "model wife and mother," she was also regarded as the "mother of the congregation, [who] shared more directly in her husband's ministry."[64] Of course that role was found in other Protestant churches, but in the LCMS, it continued to be an especially distinctive and demanding role into the mid-twentieth century. Moreover, since the mid-1800s women had their *Frauenverein* or ladies aid societies for charitable activities and fellowship, well before significant male lay activity developed in LCMS parishes. In other areas, however, women of the LCMS claimed female activity and leadership later than many other Protestant groups. Not until the twentieth century did Sunday school teaching, by either men or women, develop significantly, and the first attempts to form a national women's organization around 1930 were unsuccessful. Instead, women in the St. Louis area formed a regional organization which gradually expanded. As Alan Graebner notes, "Having failed in an assault on the center of the line, the women were attempting a ladylike, but determined, end-run."[65] At the same time, women organized to support foreign missions (though under close clerical control), and by 1942, a national organization, the Lutheran Women's Missionary League, was founded, acceptable to the church's hierarchy since it kept its focus on missions and avoided controversial topics.

Women's organizations in the LCMS were thus later in forming, less independent in structure, and less powerful than those in many Protestant bodies, but LCMS women had two distinctive alternative roles in the church that developed especially in the twentieth century: parochial school teaching and deaconess work. The LCMS was one of the most active Protestant bodies in supporting parochial education, and from the middle of the nineteenth century, a few women were involved in such schools, teaching younger children and girls. These female teachers were not, however, equal to male parochial school teachers: Unlike men, women were not required to receive training at synodical colleges, nor were they considered "called." In the twentieth century, women were given permission to attend synodical teachers colleges in Seward, Nebraska, and River Forest, Illinois, but relatively few were regular students at these schools, although some attended special courses or summer institutes, and many congregations and male church leaders continued to regard women teachers as less desirable and more temporary than men. In

1941, a committee report to the LCMS convention conceded that women teachers designated by a congregation indeed carried out "a function of the ministry" and therefore occupied "one of the auxiliary offices of the ministry as does the male teacher," but the report quickly added that women were still subordinate and could not hold "the ministry proper" or assume public leadership of a congregation. By 1965, another committee report to convention allowed that certified appointments of women teachers "should properly be regarded as a call," though women were still forbidden to attend voters' meetings or assist at Communion.[66] After the mid-twentieth century, the number of female teachers increased and eventually surpassed the number of male parochial school teachers.[67] Even though women parochial school teachers still hold a secondary status to their male counterparts, the role provides a respectable, church-sanctioned and church-based option for LCMS women.

The second distinctive church role was as a deaconess, although an official female diaconate in the LCMS did not emerge until the twentieth century, well after such developments among Methodists, Episcopalians, and other American Lutherans. Perhaps even more than other Protestants, Missouri Synod Lutherans were wary of an institution that smacked of Roman Catholicism or seemed to compete with woman's primary vocation of motherhood. Only after reassurances that Lutheran deaconesses would not take permanent vows of celibacy—that is, they could leave for marriage—was the Lutheran Deaconess Association (LDA) founded in 1919 under male initiative and leadership. Initially associated with a Lutheran hospital in Fort Wayne, Indiana, the LDA's goal was "to educate and train Lutheran deaconesses for the care of the sick and poor in the congregations of the Evangelical Lutheran Synodical Conference and for the administering of charity and mercy in the charitable institutions and in home and foreign mission work of said Synodical Conference."[68] In its first two decades, the Lutheran Deaconess Association coordinated and helped to staff deaconess training and services at hospitals and other institutions in Indiana, Wisconsin, and South Dakota; it also published a journal and sponsored deaconess conferences. In 1935, the separate training programs were consolidated in Fort Wayne, and in 1943, the deaconess program was associated with Valparaiso University. The training period was lengthened, more rigorous professional standards were promoted, and appeals for financial support were coordinated. By the mid-1970s, the Valparaiso program and the Association were admitting women who were not members of the LCMS, a situation sufficiently distressing to some deaconesses and synodical authorities who disagreed with the theology and practices (especially women's ordination) of other American Lutherans that they broke from the Lutheran Deaconess Association in 1979 to support a strictly LCMS deaconess program in River Forest, Illinois.

## The Eastern Orthodox Church

While there is virtually no support among Eastern Orthodox Christians for female ordination to the priestly ministry, women and their roles have received greater attention in the last quarter of this century. In 1976, the Consultation of Orthodox Women, sponsored by the World Council of Churches, was held at the women's monastery of Agapia in Roumania, and in 1988, the Interorthodox Consultation on the Place of Women in the Orthodox Church took place in Rhodos, Greece. Both consultations proposed greater attention to the place of women in the church, insisted on women's inherent dignity and human equality as persons and Christians, and suggested specific roles that could be more honored, expanded, or revived for women in the church. American Orthodox participated in both consultations, and individual American Orthodox women have added their voices to support similar activities.

Not surprisingly, the consultations emphasized woman's role of motherhood, "spiritual" as well as biological, as crucial for the church and the larger society and praised the traditional charitable work of women. The role of female monastics was noted and commended, although this is not a tradition that has been particularly active among American Orthodox. Reports from both consultations encouraged Orthodox women to pursue theological education, including advanced work, not only because greater religious knowledge would better equip women for familial education but also so that they might exercise their talents in institutional teaching and as contributors to Orthodox and ecumenical administrative organizations. Such training would further enable more women to hold appropriate volunteer or paid positions at the parish level and to use their talents and training to write and publish educational materials for use within Orthodox churches and to represent Orthodoxy to outsiders. Women should be permitted to take certain liturgical roles in Orthodox worship, like readers, acolytes, and choir directors. Finally, beyond the consultations, almost every Orthodox group or writer who addresses the topic of women and the church calls for study and revival of the ancient order of deaconess. Here is an ordained role for women with undeniable roots in the Bible and the early church and in which women continued to serve for centuries in the Byzantine church.[69]

Official encouragement for new or revived women's roles is indeed significant, but implementation is another matter, and even though Orthodox women generally agree with the church's position on male priesthood, they encounter mixed reactions to more modest changes. They are thus caught at times between their non-Orthodox Christian sisters who assume they must want full ordination and some male leaders who fear and resist any change. Stephanie Yova Yazge, an Orthodox woman with a master's degree from St. Vladimir's Seminary, expresses both frustrations:

> Many Orthodox women who are seminary-educated face the same situation that I do. The messages we receive are mixed. Many of my contemporary male counterparts, mostly clergy, have accepted me. My seminary professors have encouraged me. But the Orthodox Church is a hierarchical church with male-only clergy. There are those within that structure who do not look kindly on a woman who wants to be *too* involved, especially if she wants to be involved in liturgical theology. To be involved in liturgical theology is to step into a province that has usually been reserved for priests and bishops. . . . When a woman questions or dares to urge the modification (or correction) of liturgical practice, some priests and bishops have been known to rather righteously imply or reply that a woman should mind her own business. . . Too often we Orthodox women are the object of our ecumenical partners' pity. This attitude, which does not recognize and respect the experience and perspective of Orthodox women, must be addressed during the Ecumenical Decade if the decade is to be in solidarity with Orthodox women.[70]

## Orthodox Judaism

Where Roman Catholicism, Missouri Synod Lutheranism, and Eastern Orthodox Christianity offered distinctive alternative roles for women (even if the numbers of Lutheran and Orthodox Christian women involved were fairly small), Orthodox Judaism presented no substantive alternative role for women. Nevertheless, even while Orthodox Jews criticized contemporary feminism, the women's movement has had an impact on them. At a practical level, married women work outside the home and can cite not only the example of other American women of their own time but also the precedent of their grandmothers and great-grandmothers in eastern Europe and early twentieth century America. Orthodox Jewish women have also shared in the widespread interest among modern feminists to discover and celebrate their roots and heritage: strong, admirable women in Hebrew Scriptures and Jewish history who made significant contributions to the Jewish people and their faith.[71]

Moreover, Orthodox Judaism has had to look more intentionally and self-consciously at women and their roles. If some male leaders and women seem to reject feminism in toto, other women strive to reconcile some of its insights with their commitment to Judaism. The work of Blu Greenberg is especially notable here, because she insists that she is Jewish first and foremost, but she is also sympathetic to feminism as an ethical movement and thus seeks ways to affirm certain feminist concerns without "diminishing . . . the divine essence of Judaism and *Halakhah*."[72] She acknowledges that changes must come within *halakhah* but believes that they can. First, she calls for halakhic solutions to Jewish women's problems with family law, especially a divorce law that allows only the husband to initiate a divorce. Such legal study and change is not unprecedented, she argues, because earlier rabbis modified the conditions surrounding legal divorce to accommodate women's needs by "increasing the number of cases in which the absolute prohibition against divorce applies, embellishing and encumbering the divorce proceedings, expanding the financial responsibilities of the husband, and enlarging the wife's opportunity to assent or dissent, giving her some mastery over her fate as a married woman."[73]

Second, Greenberg calls for better Jewish education for women and an expansion of women's rights and responsibilities in communal prayer. She argues that women need not only permission but greater opportunities and encouragement for further religious study. Indeed, she concludes that "Halakhic education is the single most important area in reaching for the equalization of women in the Jewish community."[74] In the area of communal prayer and worship, women's exemption from timebound commandments could be reconsidered, perhaps becoming more function-related (as, for instance, when mothers have the care of young children.) Women might be counted in their own *minyan* for services. While the full obligations of *kaddish* (eleven months of ritual mourning for a dead parent through public prayer in a *minyan*) might be difficult for most women to assume, those who can and want to should not be denied the experience. Greenberg makes it clear that she is not asking for identical *mitzvot* for men and women, but she believes that "prayer, like study, is such a large and significant part of a traditional Jew's life that to foster a climate that inhibits the flowering of a woman's prayer and learning is to cut off the nurturing forces in the life of a Jew, to reduce one's wholeness as a Jew, to weaken the links to past and future."[75] In short, many Orthodox Jewish women are quite willing to accept a "separate but equal" status, but they insist that the "separate" for women must command genuinely equal respect and include expanded opportunities for development of their Jewish understanding and identity.

For some Orthodox women, this has meant forming women's *tefillah* (prayer) groups to enhance their Jewish spirituality through fuller and more direct participation in public, communal prayer without challenging *halakhah*. Rivka Haut describes the groups:

> Women's *tefillah* groups are communities of women who meet regularly, usually once or twice a month, to pray together. Sometimes they meet for Shabbat *minhah* (afternoon prayers, during which a Torah portion is read); sometimes for *Rosh Hodesh* (the New Moon); and, most often, on Shabbat mornings. They conduct a full service, with the exception of prayers for which a *minyan* of men is necessary, which are therefore omitted. The prayer groups conduct a complete Torah and *haftarah* [prophets] reading. Men are not present. In the absence of men, women are

> halakhically permitted to lead prayers, to receive Torah honors, and to read from a Torah scroll.[76]

These services may also be used as occasions for celebrating a young woman's Bat Mitzvah, engagements or marriages, or the naming of a baby. Yet despite the Orthodox women's care not to break *halakhah,* the reaction of most Orthodox rabbis has been very negative. A few, however, have been supportive, and the movement itself has continued to grow, forming its own network for information and mutual encouragement.

Finally, women in Orthodox Judaism, like their Catholic, Lutheran, and Orthodox Christian sisters—and indeed, like the women in evangelical Protestant and mainline American religious groups—have continued to form and support their own sisterhoods and church organizations. These have not only provided untold amounts of work and funding for internal projects, but have also offered charitable service for those in need and often been advocates of social justice. It is to this aspect of women and religion in twentieth-century America that we will turn in the next chapter.

# 21

# *Women, Religion, and Reform in the Twentieth Century*

Religion and reform were closely connected in nineteenth-century America: religious convictions motivated many Americans not only toward charitable, "benevolent" activities but also into more controversial social action. Church and synagogue groups were often the vehicles for such work. For American women, benevolence and reform provided an entree into a more public sphere, even as some of them justified their actions as a necessary defense of woman's "natural" sphere of home and family. But charity or benevolence is not the same thing as reform. Both make substantial contributions to genuine human need, but charity focuses more on individuals and raises few questions about the social order; hence its enemy is indifference rather than outright opposition. Reform addresses social justice with its insistence that structures, as well as individual hearts, must change and thus frequently generates significant controversy. Yet while there is a legitimate distinction between charity and reform, the two often overlap. Moreover, some people who begin with charity discover through personal experience with actual conditions that charity is inadequate, and they are pushed into reform, as were many of the deaconesses and settlement house workers in the late nineteenth century. And what may at first look like irreproachably respectable charity—providing food and shelter for the poor, for example—can become quite a hot political issue in certain circumstances.

The tradition of religiously based benevolence and reform continued in the twentieth century but with some modifications. As American women gained more options and more acceptance in public and professional roles, they could more easily choose from a wider range of avenues to engage in such work, and they were less dependent on the sanction of religion to gain social approbation. At the same time, most Christian and Jewish groups continued to limit women's leadership roles, not only by denying ordination but more broadly in substantive professional and voluntary positions. We could interpret the change as evidence that nineteenth-century women were not so much religiously driven as they were cognizant that they had few other respectable choices, that they, in a sense, "used" religion for personal and political ends.

On the other hand, it could also be argued that many twentieth-century women participated in charitable and reform work for religious reasons, but they found less overtly church-connected means more effective ways to act on their convictions. Given the range and complexity of human motivation, both explanations are probably valid. Gradually, women were able to work more often with men in common organizations and movements. This gave them more options and potentially expanded their impact, but women found that such cooperation was often bought at the price of tokenism and a loss of genuine power, for men seldom yielded their monopoly on leadership easily. So women also continued to work through distinctively female groups, whether or not these were overtly religious. "Secular" groups had a further attraction in allowing Americans to work across denominational or religious boundaries, or indeed, with nonreligious persons, for a common cause at a time when religious prejudice was slowly subsiding and religious pluralism was acknowledged, if not embraced.

## Mainline Protestant Churches

Of course not every woman who worked for social justice in the twentieth century was religiously motivated, nor were all religious Americans advocates of social justice. Far from it. But neither had this been the case in the nineteenth century. Even though many women in twentieth-century America found arenas outside the churches to pursue personal growth, charitable work, or social justice concerns, the religious women's groups that had been so central for women in the nineteenth century as a bridge between the domestic and public spheres continued to appeal to significant numbers of women. Most of these groups had a history of benevolent activity, from local outreach to societal concerns like "moral reform" or temperance to foreign missions, and that tradition continued into the twentieth century. Just as it had in the nineteenth century, women's support of foreign missions exhibited a high degree of concern for humanitarian issues, as well as evangelism, and focused especially on women and children of other lands. Charitable activities, from fund-raising for institutions like schools, hospitals, or homes for girls to local community projects, were relatively noncontroversial yet provided genuine help to many persons in need. During the twentieth century, both conservative and mainline Protestant groups supported charitable work, most often directed to individuals' problems, but conservative churches tended to be suspicious of reform or political causes. Two exceptions should be noted to this generalization: first, certain "moral" issues like abortion or prayer in the schools have indeed generated church-based and religiously motivated political action in conservative Protestantism; second, a minority movement among evangelicals in the last half of the twentieth century has supported not only women's ordination but also "liberal" causes related to race relations, peace, and economic justice.

Among mainline churches, some women's groups have maintained a Social Gospel tradition by speaking out on political issues of reform. There have been general denominational differences in this area—for example, Lutherans were usually more conservative, while Methodists were more likely to take a liberal stand—as well as divisions within the church women's groups themselves and, often, differences between the leadership's public statements and the sentiments of many of the rank and file. Nevertheless, Protestant women's groups did speak out on peace and justice issues. Although the problems of labor that had been so central in the classic Social Gospel movement still drew considerable concern, two other issues became especially prominent after 1920: peace and race relations.

### Methodists

In the 1920s and 1930s, Methodist women in the Wesleyan Service Guild were encouraged to practice "Christian citizenship" and support a child labor amendment (never ratified), prohibition, the World Court, and the Kellogg-Briand Pact to outlaw war except in cases of self-defense.[1] In an essay addressed to the Methodist Woman's Home Missionary Society in 1928, Ada Townsend sounded a Social Gospel note by looking beyond charity to structural change:

> Active participation in all matters which relate to government and public welfare, through the use of the ballot, is the patriotic duty of every woman of voting age. . . . Our objective as home missionary women is the winning of America to Christ. This objective can be reached only by purifying the political, social and economic conditions of our country. . . . Our missionary task is not alone the establishment of settlements, the alleviation of suffering and distress, and the care of underprivileged women and children; it is also to discover what gives rise to poverty, inefficiency, child-labor and kindred conditions, and to abolish the cause.[2]

Nor was Methodist women's activism confined to the North. Because of the more rigidly maintained gender roles of a generally conservative South, church women there were later in gaining their own organizations. But as they did so, they found in them a bridge to broader public activity and an arena for the development of skills, self-confidence, and interest in social causes, just as their northern sisters had earlier. Indeed, John Patrick McDowell has argued that the Woman's Home Mission Movement of the southern Methodists was one of the most important voices of the Social Gospel in the South.[3] They sponsored charitable endeavors like kindergartens, boarding houses for women, and settlement houses, but they also endorsed child labor laws and better wages and conditions for women workers. And Methodist women were prominently represented in white Southerners' tentative but important steps toward racial justice in that region. After two white Methodist women, Carrie Johnson and Estelle Haskin, attended a groundbreaking interracial meeting at Tuskegee, they called an interracial women's conference for Memphis in 1920 and urged support of the Commission on Interracial Cooperation (CIC). At that conference, white southern churchwomen, the majority of them Methodists, were addressed by four prominent black women.

> Confronted by proud and articulate black women, exhorted passionately, yet in acceptable generalities and in the language of a shared religious tradition, to accept responsibility for the plight of women whose aspirations were so much like their own, the white women present responded with an outpouring of emotion that would become the paradigm for—and often the only accomplishment of—interracial meetings for a decade.[4]

Measured by the need for change in race relations, the Methodist women's activities were timid and tentative, yet in the context of their culture the activities were sufficiently radical to incur considerable condemnation. After 1920, local women's committees of the CIC were gradually formed across the South. Formally inter- or nondenominational, the groups were in fact dominated by Methodist women, and Methodist women provided the lion's share of support when Jessie Daniel Ames founded in 1930 the Association of Southern Women for the Prevention of Lynching, a white women's movement dedicated to protesting the immorality of lynching and to repudiating the "chivalry" that claimed lynching was a gallant southern male response to protect white female honor. In 1934, the Southern Methodist Woman's Missionary Council voted unanimous support for a federal anti-lynching law, a position more progressive than that of Ames herself or of the women's Methodist brothers.

## Quakers

Quaker women, with their historic tradition of nonviolence and social activism, continued their witness of word and action, even when these were not socially popular. They were prominent in the formation of the Women's International League for Peace and Freedom, and three Quaker women were among the founders of the American Friends Service Committee (AFSC) in 1917, while others served as relief workers for the AFSC. As Margaret Bacon notes, in the period between World Wars I and II, "it became traditional for younger Quaker women to offer a year or two of service. After the worst of the postwar emergency was over in Europe, AFSC opened service opportunities in settlement houses, southern schools for blacks, and Indian reservations throughout the United States."[5]

## Presbyterians

In the 1940s and 1950s, several white Protestant women's groups expressed their concern for international peace through support of the United Nations. Some also began, slowly, to act more openly on a growing realization that white racism was incompatible with a profession of Christianity. For example, in the 1940s the Presbyterian Women's Organization refused to hold meetings in hotels that would not accept black guests equally, a policy the women implemented before the Presbyterian General Assembly itself did.[6] In 1952, the Methodist Woman's Division (including southern Methodists since the 1939 merger) established a Charter of Racial Policies that opposed discrimination and urged that Methodist schools and hospitals be opened to all persons, regardless of race. Two years later, the Assembly of Methodist Women was meeting in Milwaukee when the *Brown v. the Board of Education* decision was handed down; they immediately drafted and passed a resolution of support, "the first public statement to affirm the court's action."[7] Despite widespread public opposition, Methodist women at the national and grassroots levels worked for integration of public schools and, later, housing through the 1950s. Presbyterian women also expressed firm support for the historic *Brown* decision in 1954, and during the late 1950s and 1960s, they and other white Protestant women took part in the civil rights movement. When so doing, they were, like their male counterparts, a significant minority—and both those terms are important. Active support for the cause of blacks' civil rights never commanded a majority within white American Protestantism in the 1960s, any more than abolition had in the nineteenth century; yet the minority was not insignificant and the level of some individuals' commitment was impressive.

## Ecumenical Groups

Ecumenical Christian organizations like the Young Women's Christian Association (YWCA) and Church Women United were also active in charitable work and reform causes. In the early decades of the twentieth century, the American YWCA promoted "missions" at home and abroad and recruited young college women with a commitment to Christian service for such work. At home, the YWCA provided residences and educational and recreational opportunities for young women in the cities and supported public health work through classes and clinics. Other recruits became secretaries (the YWCA administrative position) abroad, with a strong emphasis on humanitarian aid for women and children, though less overt evangelism than church-sponsored missionaries. Through its national board and conventions, the "Y" voiced support for progressive causes, endorsing in 1920 the Federal Council of Churches' Social Creed with its strong prolabor position, and advocating United States cooperation with the League of Nations, the World Court, and the International Labor Organization. The YWCA took progressive political stands through the 1930s and 1940s, a tradition that earned the organization an attack during the McCarthy era. A 1948 pamphlet, "Beyond the Lace Curtains of the YWCA," suggested that the YWCA's support for causes like a world health organization, an anti-lynching bill, and the labor movement made it a "fellow traveler" with communism.[8]

Over the first half of the twentieth century, the YWCA moved steadily, if slowly, toward racial justice in its pronouncements and activities. The "Y" supported some "colored" branches in the North and Midwest starting in the late nineteenth century and began to set up black branches in the South after 1906. Until the first World War, the YWCA was more "biracial" than "interracial":[9] white women's approach was clearly discriminatory and paternalistic as they insisted on maintaining control over black work and workers; yet the black branches under the leadership of Eva Bowles provided significant services for black women and children, as well as opportunities for black women's professional leadership. Prodded insistently by black women through the 1920s, 30s, and 40s, the YWCA gradually moved toward a more genuinely interracial position in its own work and spoke out more courageously on racial issues. Thus, for example, the YWCA in the South, along with white Methodist women, was a major source of support for interracial dialogue and activities and for the anti-lynching campaign led by Jessie Daniel Ames, and the Boston "Y" worked to get young black women admitted to nurses' training at Boston schools and hospitals.

> Two factors played a role in this change [slow but steady progress toward integration]. First, the national organization, in pushing the local YWCAs to become more inclusive, constantly provided support and justification to those in the local association who wished to move in that direction. They could use the national policy to bolster their arguments. . . . The second force was the moral power of the argument that the YWCA was a Christian organization, and that Christian principles of equality, love for all, the oneness of all under Christ were compelling reasons for action.[10]

By 1946, the National Convention adopted an interracial charter, and the YWCA was a significant training ground for civil rights activists, both black and white, culminating in 1970 when "the elimination of racism became its 'one imperative.'"[11] Surely, the pace of change for the YWCA was slow when measured by the demands of justice, yet its record compares favorably with many other organizations, secular or religious.

Formed in 1941, the United Council of Church Women (later Church Women United) immediately launched a tradition of activism with a variety of war relief efforts and a protest against the internment of Japanese

Americans. By no means free of racism, the council did take stands against racial discrimination, modest in retrospect but relatively radical in its time. In the 1940s, the United Council of Church Women refused to meet in segregated facilities; they later supported the *Brown* decision and a number of CWU leaders joined Coretta Scott King, herself a board member, on the Selma march. The organization worked to decrease its white American members' prejudice and increase racial sensitivity through a global focus. Fund-raising was one major concern, along with education about women's lives and culture in others lands. But over time, Church Women United came to emphasize an international sisterhood and shifted its perspective from working "for" foreign women to working "with" them as partners. Slowly they learned to let women in other nations define their own needs and set priorities, and then to work with them rather than imposing an American agenda. Despite slow and often painful progress, these American women were intentional about the process and tried to increase their self-awareness and sensitivity as they reached out to help an international sisterhood.

## Georgia Harkness

This concern for economic and racial justice and for international peace and understanding as a necessary outgrowth of a person's Christian faith was epitomized in the career of one of the most prominent women church leaders of the twentieth century, Georgia Harkness. At one level, Harkness is notable as a pioneer woman theologian. Her life began modestly in rural northeastern New York, where she was born in 1891 to a Methodist family, although her more distant ancestors were Quakers. Enabled by a scholarship to attend Cornell University, she graduated in 1912 and taught high school for several years before returning to school at Boston University, where she earned a master's degree at the School of Religious Education and Social Service and later a Ph.D. in philosophy. She taught at two women's colleges, Elmira and Mount Holyoke, until 1940, when she accepted an appointment to a Methodist seminary, Garrett Biblical Institute in Evanston, Illinois. Her appointment there as professor of applied theology made her the first woman to teach full time at an American seminary in a field other than religious education. In 1950, she moved to the Pacific School of Religion in Berkeley, California, where she taught until her retirement in 1961. In the course of her professional career, she combined teaching with an impressive output of publications, books and articles that were most often addressed to a broad audience, for her particular genius was to take theological ideas and express them accessibly and effectively for pastors and lay Christians. Though she never sought ordination herself, Harkness was a lifelong advocate of women's full status in her own Methodist church, and her influence was acknowledged at the convention in 1956 that finally granted women full conference membership.

Georgia Harkness's words and example inspired women who struggled for equality in theology and the church, but Harkness also, like her older contemporary Vida Scudder, combined a deep personal spirituality and loyalty to the church with lifelong social activism. While at Boston University, she embraced the Social Gospel; for Harkness, opposition to injustice in its varied but interrelated forms was a Christian imperative, and she consistently called on her fellow Christians to live out their faith in radical action. In a 1937 article, "Wanted—Prophets!" she wrote:

> If the church is to have a prophetic function, Christian leaders must be willing to challenge comfortable, traditional modes of thought, and do it in terms not glossed over with vague generalities. Such challenge is imperative in the areas of economics, of militaristic nationalism and of race, and because in these areas we are now least Christian, it is in these most dangerous to be prophetic. It is safe to talk of social justice in general, but not to be a socialist; to read Isaiah's vision of a warless world and preach an eloquent sermon from it, but not to be a pacifist; to quote, "God hath made of one blood all nations of the earth," but not to invite a Negro to one's home or to one's pulpit.[12]

Although Harkness supported many social justice issues and insisted on their interrelation, peace was, perhaps, her most central lifelong concern. In 1924, she was part of a seminar of religious leaders who visited post-World War I Europe, and what she observed there made her a pacifist. She maintained that stance through World War II when other American religious leaders who endorsed pacifism in the 1920s and 1930s felt compelled to abandon that position. Subsequent world events, wars, and the development of nuclear weapons only strengthened her resolve, and her 1966 essay, "The Churches and Viet Nam," was read into the *Congressional Record* by one of her former students, Senator George McGovern.[13]

Her experiences in the ecumenical movement in which she was an early and, as a woman, unusual participant at international conferences only reinforced her pacifism. Moreover, her opposition to war was intimately tied to her convictions about the equal worth of all persons and hence her active opposition to any form of racism. Thus she was unwilling to demonize America's enemies, from the Germans in World War I to the Viet Cong, and while she acknowledged the need to take a stand on issues, she refused to give uncritical support to American claims of righteousness in war. She was equally adamant in her criticism of racism at home, whether manifest in the churches or in society at large. She castigated her own Methodist Church when it set up a separate jurisdiction for blacks in its 1939 merger; she publicly condemned the internment of

Japanese Americans during World War II; and she firmly supported African Americans' struggle for civil rights.

Although Georgia Harkness retired from teaching in 1961, she continued writing and speaking—and working as a social activist—for the rest of her life. In *Biblical Backgrounds of the Middle East Conflict,* the last of her many books and incomplete at her death in 1974, she drew on her experiences visiting in the Middle East to plead with American Christians to promote peaceful solutions to the conflict there and to recognize the justice in the positions of both Arabs and Israelis. After her death, a tribute from one of her colleagues at Pacific School of Religion underlined the close connection she made between faith and social action: "No one in my acquaintance combined such a genuine Christian commitment to God as revealed through Jesus Christ; a life of prayer and devotion; and a commitment to the great Christian social concerns which were so much a part of her own compassion."[14]

## African-American Churches

African-American churches were among the most consistently and conspicuously committed to charity and social reform. Black women were involved in both through specific church groups and through organizations that, although not overtly church-oriented, attracted people with deeply spiritual motives and frequently used religious language and images in the organizations' public statements. Indeed, Mary R. Sawyer has argued that one reason secular organizations drew some black women was the greater opportunity for leadership roles that the groups offered at a time when many black churches denied women substantive leadership outside specifically female groups.

> Heretofore scholars have tended to examine these arenas of political and religious intersection by focusing on the role of clergy and lay church leaders, who more often than not were men. As is increasingly being acknowledged, women, because of the patriarchal structure of the church, have historically been compelled to take their organizing skills and social consciousness into secular avenues without the benefit of church identity and authority. These extra-church involvements were sometimes in exclusively female organizations, sometimes in male-dominated organizations, and sometimes fiercely independent of any organization.[15]

Yet for many black women, the choice was "both/and," not "either/or," as they joined local, regional, or national church groups *and* worked through secular organizations. Several prominent black women leaders of the twentieth century were deeply religious people who might well have sought ordination had it been available; since it was not, they found other fields where they could act on their convictions and carve out significant careers, even as they remained active in their churches. Mary McLeod Bethune (1875–1955) initially hoped to be a foreign missionary, but despite her training at Presbyterian schools and Moody Bible Institute, she was turned down by the Presbyterian Mission Board because of her race. So she turned instead to education, founding a girls' school in Daytona, Florida, which eventually became a coeducational college, Bethune-Cookman. Along with her educational work, Bethune served as president of the National Association of Colored Women and founded the National Council of Negro Women in 1935 to advance a more national and political agenda than the NACW's more local, club-oriented work, a political agenda she was in an unusual position to forward when she became part of Franklin Roosevelt's administration.

Nannie Helen Burroughs (1878–1961) combined the careers of educator and paid (though not ordained) church professional. Elected in 1900 as corresponding secretary of the National Baptist Convention's new Women's Convention, she served in that post for over fifty years. Her relationships with male Baptist leaders were seldom submissive and thus frequently stormy, but time after time she could count on the women's financial and moral support. Such support was crucial in helping her to found the National Training School for Women and Girls in Washington, D.C., to offer *both* industrial and classical education and to build racial pride in young black women. Burroughs brought her religious convictions into her educational work and her support of organizations like the NAACP, but equally, she helped to lead black Baptist women into political action. For example, in 1913, the Woman's Convention formulated a manifesto, "What We Want and What We Must Have," which ranged in its demands from equal treatment in housing, education, and the courts to the vote and an end to lynching and the convict lease system.[16] Throughout her life, Burroughs was uncompromising in her calls for justice and economic opportunity for black people, especially black women, and in her insistence on greater equality for women in American society and the black church. For Burroughs, to work actively for justice was nothing less than an imperative of Christian faith.

Individual leaders who combined faith and social responsibility made a critical contribution to the African-American community, yet at least as important was the work of thousands of little-known black women throughout the twentieth century. While there were notable examples of white Christians working to provide educational and social services for newly freed blacks in the post-Civil War period, black Americans soon found that they would have to carry the larger burden for such services themselves, especially after the growing problems of urbanization and industrialization diverted the attention of many Christians in the North from racial issues, and southern whites worked to reestablish white supremacy and strict segregation. Women in the black churches played a crucial role by filling immediate needs in the black community, from education to care of the poor and elderly. For the next century, local churches would provide for the needs of the black community. Although the forms that service took might change, some needs remained constant, like the need for better educational opportunities or food and shelter for the poor; in other cases, new problems, like AIDS and drug addiction, called forth new programs in black urban churches.[17] Often unremarked and underappreciated by the larger society, local church work was nevertheless a clear indication of the linkage between faith and action.[18]

By the dawn of the twentieth century, black women were turning to other forms of social service as well. They helped to found and staff black settlement houses and black branches of the YWCA, complementing and extending the work of the churches. They came together in black women's clubs with their dual focus of self-improvement and social service. Black women also joined predominantly male-led groups like the National Association for the Advancement of Colored People (NAACP) and the National Urban League. Two prominent black women, Ida B. Wells-Barnett and Mary Church Terrell, signed the original call for a conference out of which would come the NAACP, and a few other women were included in the national leadership, but the most important contribution by women in the early years of the movement was at the local level. They raised money, wrote articles, investigated cases of discrimination, and gave speeches, "but the most significant role played by black women during these early years was in the organization of branches. Their activities as field workers determined the ultimate survival and expansion of the NAACP in the black communities."[19] When the National Urban League was founded in 1911, it brought together organizations that had been focused on employment issues and social service needs in the black community, including the National League for the Protection of Colored Women, a group formed to aid black women migrating to the cities. As the National Urban League tried to coordinate social services for blacks, it drew heavily on existing local programs, many of which "had been developed by and remained under the control of black women."[20] The League relied on female grassroots work and fund-raising, often from women's church groups or clubs, even though few women were represented at the higher levels of leadership.

## Confronting Racism

While the reform efforts of African-American women were not confined exclusively to racial issues—for example, some joined the Women's International League for Peace and Freedom—it is hardly surprising that their primary concerns continued to be addressing the needs of the black community, promoting interracial cooperation, and protesting against unjust laws or—in the case of the most brutal form of racism, lynching—the lack of laws. Their efforts were critical not least because white Americans were so slow to acknowledge either the needs or their own racism. With the emergence of the Civil Rights movement in the mid-twentieth century, the more progressive white churches and women's groups had grown more sensitive and willing to translate concern into action, making significant contributions. Nevertheless, black women and men gave the most sustained and widespread support to the movement.

Black women's contributions to the Civil Rights movement began long before the 1950s in their consistent commitment to education and in their work through organizations like the NAACP, the NUL, and the YWCA. They also formed new organizations, like the Women's Political Council in Montgomery, Alabama. Founded in 1946 to promote political action, including voter registration, to protest against segregated public facilities, and to offer educational opportunities for both children and adults, the Women's Political Council provided the initial idea and organization for the Montgomery bus boycott that catapulted a young black minister, Martin Luther King Jr., into national prominence.[21] As the pace of protest and hard-won accomplishment accelerated in the 1950s and 1960s, black women played an invaluable role in the struggle. Some were acknowledged leaders, though they seldom gained the national fame of male leaders. Rosa Parks's refusal to give up her seat sparked the Montgomery bus boycott. Septima Clark, called by King "the Mother of the Movement,"[22] began civil rights work in the 1920s; her particular contribution was in citizenship education—through schools that taught adult literacy (imperative for voter registration) and pride, first in the 1930s in her own community of Columbia, South Carolina, then at the Highland Folk School in Tennessee, and finally as director of the Citizenship Education Program of the Southern Christian Leadership Conference (SCLC), so critical to the voter registration drives of the early 1960s. Ella Baker worked as a field organizer for the NAACP in the 1930s and 1940s and for the SCLC in the late 1950s, then founded and served as the guiding spirit of the Student Non-Violent Coordinating Committee (SNCC). Fannie Lou Hamer was a fearless worker for voter registration and uncompromising leader in the Mississippi Freedom Democratic Party, whose inspirational song and oratory echoed the black religious tradition of applying biblical words and stories to black experiences and hopes.

At least as important as the work of the leaders was the contribution of the many women at the grassroots. They provided food and shelter for civil rights workers and volunteers; registered to vote themselves and encouraged others to do so; took part in the public demonstrations of marches, boycotts, and sit-ins; provided behind-the-scenes organizational work and served as conduits to the rest of the black community, particularly in rural areas; and were especially active in educational work, like their mothers and grandmothers before them. Leaders and grassroots workers alike, black women were a critical part of the Civil Rights movement, and yet their contributions were often overlooked at the time and in early histories of the movement. Why? There is no single or simple answer, but several factors may have been at work. First, there were not as many prominent women as men in the ranks of the movement's leadership, and the contributions of "foot soldiers," those in the field, both men and women, traditionally receive less publicity. Second, the situation is little different in the case of white movements and activities. Typically, women's leadership has been restricted and their roles minimized, while male leadership and contributions have been emphasized by participants and historians.

There are also factors particular to African-American women in mid-twentieth-century America. Fully aware of their people's history in America, the vast majority of black women perceived racism as a more immediate and debilitating threat than sexism. Quite simply, they faced greater injustice and more obstacles to freedom on account of their race than their gender. Furthermore, while the close connection of the movement with black churches and the religious themes that pervaded its rhetoric make it a particularly clear example of the link between faith and social action, black churches were traditionally pastored and led by men. The male ministers who were so prominent in the movement were comfortable with women's working in the background and under their direction but not as peers. Thus when Septima Clark became the first woman to serve on the SCLC's executive board, male clergy like Ralph Abernathy questioned her right to that position, although she was defended by King because of her effective work; and Ella Baker likewise had her share of clashes with what she saw as unnecessarily authoritarian male leadership. The complex and destructive heritage of gender and racial roles from the time of slavery and Reconstruction, when black men were denied any respected role other than that of a minister, played a part, too. Knowing only too well how white society treated black men, many black women were proud to see their men emerge as strong leaders and understandably reluctant to hurt or criticize them. Nor were they anxious to give ammunition to their white opponents by an open display of discord in the ranks. Fannie Lou Hamer was sometimes at odds with more educated black women but insisted that middle-class or poor, men or women were ". . . still in this bag together. Not to fight to liberate ourselves from the men—this is another trick to get us fighting among ourselves—but to work together with Black men."[23]

## Roman Catholicism

Protestant Christians in twentieth-century America held no monopoly on either charity or social action, of course. Roman Catholic women, both sisters and laywomen, maintained and at times expanded the kind of work they had done in the nineteenth century and also participated in new programs directed toward social justice issues. Sisters served both Catholics and non-Catholics through schools, orphanages, hospitals, and relief work, especially in times of crisis like disease, natural disasters, or economic depressions. A particular focus on African Americans and Native Americans animated the work of some orders, like the Sisters of the Blessed Sacrament for Indians and Colored People, founded in 1891 by heiress Katherine Drexel. She and the sisters of her order founded missions and schools throughout the United States, including in 1925 Xavier University as a Catholic college for blacks. Although Drexel died in 1955, her order still staffs schools and centers for health care and social services, with "a special ministry among black and native Americans to foster unity and justice among all the people of God and to enrich the Church with the diverse and beautiful exuberance of the black and native American cultures."[24]

During the twentieth century, some sisters moved from charity to social activism, in part as a result of firsthand experiences with the poor and marginalized, in part as a result of their own formal education, which included more sophisticated study in the social sciences. As Mary Ewens notes:

> Sisters who pursued advanced study in such fields as economics, sociology, or political science gained new insights into social problems that they had been encountering for decades on an experiential level. Their personal experience of the trauma of war, the sufferings caused by economic depressions, the struggle of the poor, and the evils of racism was supplemented by a knowledge of historical trends, the national and international extent of social ills, and various theories about ways to correct or alleviate them.[25]

Of course not all Catholic sisters in the first half of the twentieth century became social activists, given the new restrictions on their activities, budget problems, and heavy demands by the hierarchy for their services, especially in parochial schools. But those who did become activists not only incorporated activism into their own direct work but also tried to pass on to their female students a greater understanding and a higher level of commitment to social action.

By the middle of the twentieth century, however, many more sisters became more self-conscious and assertive about their roles and identity, a process that was accelerated by the impact of Vatican II with its mandate for religious orders to reclaim their roots and, where necessary, revise their constitutions, and by the growing influence of Latin American liberation theology with its insistence that the church exercise a "special option for the poor." At the same time, the security and acceptance provided by a Catholic "coming of age" in America and the greater ecumenical openness that followed Vatican II encouraged sisters to engage in more cross-denominational cooperative action. Individual sisters protested against the Viet Nam War and United States policies that buttressed repressive regimes in Latin America; they spoke, marched, and worked for civil rights for minorities and better treatment of migrant workers and refugees. "In 1971, an organization called Network was formed in Washington, D.C., as a social justice lobby through which sisters and others could influence legislation. It also attempted to raise the consciousness of sisters regarding the political process and mobilize their energies and numbers to support key issues."[26] The church's hierarchy, however, was frequently distressed by such newly visible activism, especially when a few sisters decided to run for—and won—political office, and tensions were exacerbated by some sisters' outspoken support of ordination of women to the priesthood, and of feminism in general.

As Catholic sisters gradually became more activist during the twentieth century, so too did Catholic laywomen. During the first few decades of the twentieth century, the church began to emphasize a more active role for the laity, a "lay apostolate." In contrast to the previous century, when laypeople had been counseled to accept a relatively passive role and to obey the clergy, now they were urged to cooperate in Catholic work and witness to the world, and this included women as well as men. Catholic laywomen had already done impressive charitable work during the First World War and supported the National Catholic Service School for Women. The bishops of the National Catholic Welfare Conference, however, which had grown out of the National Catholic War Council of World War I, created national groups for laymen and laywomen (although the National Council of Catholic Women (NCCW) became more active and successful than its male counterpart).[27] The NCCW was then expected to work with (and under) those bishops particularly committed to social activism to promote study and action on social concerns. Yet the NCCW had a somewhat ambivalent approach to social issues in the twentieth century, perhaps because of its close ties with—and indeed, subordination to—the male hierarchy, perhaps because of the views of its middle-class constituency. On the one hand, the NCCW firmly advocated traditional "family values" and women's role in upholding them, deploring modern trends like divorce and birth control; on the other, the women, like their episcopal mentors, were relatively progressive on economic and labor issues, speaking out and working on behalf of immigrants, working women, and the poor.

## Three Key Movements

Three particular movements in the first half of the twentieth century—the Grail Movement, Friendship House, and the Catholic Worker Movement—took advantage of the church's encouragement of a lay apostolate by involving lay women in social service and action. All three tied faith to social responsibility: just as the gospel mandates Christians actively to love their neighbors and to do justice in this world, so too social activism should be rooted in and nourished by faith. A person's spirituality was best developed not only by the personal disciplines of prayer, meditation, and sacrifice but also through the benefits of life within a community offering opportunities for service and frequent, active, liturgical worship.

### *The Grail*

The Society of the Women of Nazareth was founded in the Netherlands in 1921 for laywomen—*not* as a religious order—to integrate intense Catholic spirituality with religious witness and action in the world. It spread throughout Europe in the 1930s and, under a new name, the Grail, was brought to the United States in 1940 by two Catholic laywomen, Lydwine van Kersbergen and Joan Overboss. The women initially settled near Chicago, where they tried to recruit members and otherwise develop the movement while also providing social services, like a summer camp for poor children, advocated by Chicago's Catholic hierarchy. In 1944 they moved to Loveland, Ohio, to a farm known as Grailville. Women of the Grail criticized communism, capitalism, and the secularism and materialism of Western society; they associated these and other social problems with excessive masculinization of culture and believed that part of the solution was reaffirmation of distinctive female identity and gifts of charity, nurturing, and spirituality. (The women of the early Grail movement were thus not very sympathetic to feminist women, whom they saw as misguidedly trying to be like men.) By the 1950s, the Grail had moved into foreign missions work and a range of educational and social services, through centers in American cities, including the promotion of interracial dialogue, ministry with foreign students, and service to the poor of the inner cities. In the 1960s, the Grail continued to focus on economic injustice, and some members were active in civil rights and peace issues; but it shifted to other areas of emphasis, promoting personal freedom over commitment to the movement itself,[28] opening its membership to non-Catholics, and evidencing increasing sympathy for feminism. As a result, its membership and Catholic identity declined, even as the Grail became a center for religious feminism.

### *Friendship House*

Unlike the Grail, Friendship House was open to both men and women, but like the Grail, it welcomed the opportunities and responsibilities of a lay apostolate. It was founded by a woman, Catherine de Hueck, and many women were attracted to the movement by opportunities for leadership, as well as the chance to live out a religious commitment to racial justice. De Hueck founded the first Friendship House in Toronto in 1930 in outrage over racial discrimination, and in 1938, she was invited by some Catholic clergy in New York to begin a similar establishment in Harlem. The men and women who joined her combined Catholic spirituality and an intense community liturgical life with social activism, focusing especially on African Americans. Eventually other branches were established in Chicago; Portland, Oregon; Washington, D.C.; and Shreveport, Louisiana, and the movement supported several farms for study and retreats. The workers at Friendship Houses tried to better American race relations in three ways: the direct charitable work of providing food, clothing, and help in finding shelter to the needy; publications, lectures, and workshops to try to change the racial attitudes of white Americans, especially Catholics; and investigation and nonviolent demonstrations to bring about political change.[29] At a time when racial issues were not a high priority for most American Catholics, Friendship House was one of the few Catholic organizations to challenge Catholic apathy and prejudice, helping to pave the way for Catholic involvement in the civil rights movement. By the 1960s, while most of the movement's urban centers had closed, Friendship House shifted its headquarters to Chicago, where it promoted publications, education, and political action for interracial justice.

### *Catholic Worker Movement*

The Catholic Worker Movement was the most successful of these three lay movements, and its founder, Dorothy Day (1897–1980) was one of the best known and most influential Catholic laypersons of the twentieth century. Although Dorothy displayed some interest in religion as a child (despite her father's hostility to organized religion), she "gave it up" during her two years of study at the University of Illinois at Urbana, and when she subsequently moved to New York to work as a journalist, she became deeply involved with the communities of young socialists, communists, and bohemian artists that she found there. Following a love affair that ended after she had an abortion, and a brief, unhappy marriage, she entered a common-law marriage in the mid-1920s with Forster Batterham. Even though she had repudiated religion in college, she continued to read the Bible and visit Catholic churches, and when her daughter, Tamar Teresa, was born in March 1927, she had her baptized as a Catholic. But Day's growing interest in Catholicism puzzled and alienated Batterham, and she finally concluded that she had to choose between her love for him and her love for God. She chose God and was baptized a Catholic on December 28, 1927. Yet she retained her radical social ideas and carried her passionate concern for the poor into her now equally passionate Catholicism. Although Day could be critical of certain aspects of the church, especially of wealthy clergy who ignored the gospel mandate to serve others, she remained a devout and loyal Catholic until her death.

After a few more years of searching for her vocation, she met Peter Maurin, a radical French peasant and philosopher, and together they founded the Catholic Worker Movement. Its initial venture drew on Day's journalistic skills: the publication of a newspaper, the *Catholic Worker*, first sold on May Day, 1933. The date was no accident, for Day's purpose was to counter the appeal of communism and its paper, the *Daily Worker*. Day was sympathetic to communism's idealism and concern for the poor, but she rejected its atheism, its materialism, and its vision of an ideal community confined to this world. Rather, she hoped to inspire a Catholicism that was equally committed to the poor but that recognized the spiritual values that communism mocked. Sold for a penny a copy, the *Catholic Worker*'s circulation increased rapidly, reaching at its peak well over 100,000 copies. In addition to explaining the philosophical base of the movement and promoting its activities, the paper took unusually radical stands on issues of the day, for example, denouncing the Scottsboro trial in 1933, in which nine young black men were accused of rape, or condemning the popular "radio priest," Charles Coughlin, for his anti-Semitism.

Besides the newspaper, the movement's most successful and effective venture was the establishment of houses of hospitality, first in New York but ultimately all over the United States and even abroad. The purpose of the houses was simple: to offer food, shelter, and a Christian community to anyone who needed them (and in the depression, there were many who did). Day was convinced that personal, self-sacrificial action was the best response a person could make to the needs of the poor, for she believed that state programs were far too impersonal and should be used only as a last resort in times of crisis. Many idealistic young men and women were attracted to the movement, joining the communities to help others and to live in *voluntary* poverty (very different from the destitution imposed on people by social and economic conditions). Voluntary poverty was also to be a witness against the overwhelming materialism of the day, exalted by both capitalism and communism, and a way of lifting up spiritual values instead.

Dorothy Day was an absolute pacifist, basing her position on the teachings of Christ. During World War II, her consistent stance caused tensions within the movement and drew sharp criticism from outsiders. Many young male Catholic Workers left to join the armed services (or were drafted), and many of the houses of hospitality were forced to close when workers left and financial support dried up because of Day's uncompromising and unpopular position. But both the paper and the movement began to grow again after the war, and Day not only continued her own pacifism (to the point of being jailed in the 1950s for refusing to participate in air raid drills) but inspired other Catholics to protest against war and look more generously on conscientious objectors. In the later years of her life, Day strongly endorsed the Civil Rights movement and particularly admired Martin Luther King Jr. and his nonviolent tactics; she also applauded the young men and women who opposed the Viet Nam war but was deeply distressed by their sexual morality and rejection of religion. In 1973, she was jailed for the last of numerous occasions over the years, this time for joining Cesar Chavez and his United Farm Workers in a protest against the terrible conditions endured by migrant workers.[30]

While none approached the prominence of Dorothy Day, other Catholic laywomen, like women religious, became more outspoken and more activist in the wake of Vatican II. To the degree that they took fairly liberal positions on concerns related to women's rights, the family, and sexuality, Catholic women found that most of the male hierarchy had little sympathy for change. But in other areas of a justice agenda, they received inspiration and approval from official church voices, including a long and important series of papal social teachings starting with Leo XIII's *Rerum Novarum* in 1891, and formal statements by United States Catholic bishops in letters on racism, peace, and the economy. Although many Catholic women, lay and religious, were uninvolved in social ministry, an important minority performed valuable work by serving the poor and the outcast, responding to newly critical problems like homelessness in late twentieth-century America, and speaking out against injustice. That same conclusion can be drawn not only about American Protestant women but also about American Jewish women.

## Judaism

Active social concern, particularly for other Jews, was always a part of American Judaism. For one thing, it was a basic religious duty for all Jews, men and women: "In the Hebrew language, there is no word for charity; the closest word is *tzdakah,* meaning 'righteousness.' It was not an act of good-will for a Jew to help another Jew; it was his obligation."[31] Furthermore, Jewish women focused their charitable work first on their own community (as did African-American women) because the white Christian establishment often discriminated against or neglected the poor and needy among both blacks and Jews. Thus nineteenth-century Jewish women helped to found and support hospitals, homes for the elderly, and orphanages. Not only did these basic institutions respond to the community's needs, but being Jewish, they could be sensitive to issues of religious observance, diet, and custom in a way that Christian institutions would not be, even when they accepted Jews. The wave of eastern European immigration that began in the 1880s accelerated the need for more extensive social services. As the Jewish community as a whole responded, women played critical roles in fund-raising and staffing. These "volunteer activists," as June Sochen calls them,[32] could take advantage of the economic security of a middle-class status (and often their husbands' support) to give time and money, to provide real help to others, and to find personal fulfillment and accomplishment—all without challenging American or Jewish cultural expectations for appropriate female roles. Such volunteer work for identifiably Jewish institutions continued throughout the twentieth century, although it was gradually devalued and challenged by the rise of professionally trained and paid social workers, often men.

A cause that was uniquely important for Jews was Zionism, combining religious, benevolent, and political concerns; the dominant Jewish women's organization that dealt with this issue was Hadassah. Its founder, Henrietta Szold, was born in 1860, the daughter of a Baltimore rabbi who encouraged her education. She became a teacher and later an editor for the Jewish Publication Society; she was also unusual among American Jewish women in showing an interest in Zionism in the early twentieth century. In 1909, she visited Palestine and was appalled at the lack of medical care and facilities available to its people, so a few years later, she gave up her other careers and devoted herself solely to Zionism. Meanwhile, in 1912, she and a group of Jewish women in New York founded Hadassah with the dual purpose of promoting the cause of Zionism among American Jews and raising funds to address medical needs of Palestine, initially by sponsoring visiting nurses there. From that modest beginning the work expanded significantly to include hospitals, training schools, work in hygiene and nutrition, and youth work. Szold herself lived in Palestine, with brief return visits to America, from 1920 until her death in 1945. She not only directed Hadassah work there but was also an internationally prominent leader of the Zionist movement, an unusual post for a woman and a clear recognition of her contributions. In the 1930s, she joined with other Jewish leaders to form the Youth Aliyah, an organization that brought Jewish youth to Palestine from Germany, thus rescuing them from the Holocaust that soon claimed many of their parents. As important as Szold's individual accomplishments were, however, she was supported by the thousands of women who joined Hadassah, where they raised money for medical work in Palestine, learned more about Zionism, and built support for that cause at home. Eventually, Hadassah became the single largest Jewish women's organization in the world, with over 350,000 members in 1980.[33]

## Turning to Broader Causes

The needs of the Jewish community continued to have a particular claim on the time and resources of Jewish women, but they also turned their attention in the twentieth century to broader causes. Many Jewish young people were drawn to the settlement house movement in nondenominational houses that served both a Jewish and a Gentile clientele, as well as specifically Jewish establishments. Perhaps the best-known Jewish settlement worker was Lillian Wald (1867–1940), the founder of the famous Henry Street Settlement in New York. Its initial focus, and Wald's lifelong concern, was public health and providing nurses and medical care for the poor, but the settlement soon expanded its range of services, and Wald herself engaged in a range of social reform activities from child welfare to peace work. Although Wald's family was Jewish, she was not herself a practicing Jew, but other Jewish women in the settlement movement maintained their Jewish faith along with progressive social concerns. One such woman was Lizzie Black Kander (1858–1940), whose interest was initially aroused by the plight of Jewish immigrants. Kander was the first president of the Milwaukee Jewish Mission, formed in 1896 by a small group of Jewish women; in 1900, the mission merged with another Jewish women's service organization to found the Milwaukee Jewish Settlement House, and Kander served as president until 1918.

The work of Jewish women in the labor movement, especially in the cities of the north, was, of course, extremely significant and has been mentioned before. Northern urban Jewish women were also vocal and enthusiastic supporters of Margaret Sanger, helping her to spread illegal information about birth control especially to the poor women for whom multiple pregnancies spelled economic and physiological disaster.[34] Jewish communities in the South were generally smaller than those in northern cities, yet women there, too, engaged in benevolent and reform work within and beyond their Jewish communities. For example, Jewish women in Atlanta, particularly concerned for the Jewish community, affiliated with the Georgia Federation of Women's Clubs, which addressed issues like child labor and the establishment of city playgrounds and parks. "As Jews and as women, [National] Council [of Jewish Women] members came to view their duties as including the needs of both the Jewish community and the larger society. The Council valued both realms of activity and, in fact, seldom differentiated between the two when establishing priorities."[35] Across the South, Jewish women, spurred by their leaders in the National Council of Jewish Women, supported a broad interracial movement, the Association of Southern Women for the Prevention of Lynching, and a federal antilynching law.[36]

In the second half of the twentieth century, Jewish women continued to connect faith and social responsibility at both practical and theoretical levels. One focus was still specifically Jewish organizations, whether the traditional women's groups or the broader Jewish ones in which women's work, although seldom their leadership, was welcomed. They also joined their Christian and secular sisters in reform causes like civil rights, women's

# 22

# *Women and Religion in America*

## Looking toward the Twenty-first Century

Both continuity and change characterize the situation of women and religion in the United States as we approach a new millennium. Women have entered the ranks of ordained and lay leadership of many Christian and Jewish groups in unprecedented numbers, and it is a leadership exercised for men and women together, not simply leadership by women for women. Yet access to such leadership roles is not universal, and where it is formally open, women continue to encounter overt and subtle resistance and discrimination. Feminist theologians challenge not only the patriarchal practices of Judaism and Christianity but also formulations of basic beliefs. They criticize the androcentric bias of traditional orthodoxy and insist that women's voices be heard and women's experiences considered in the formulation of common beliefs and practices. Yet other women find themselves engaged in some of the same battles fought by their mothers, grandmothers, and great-grandmothers on interpretation of scripture and gender roles. Women in late twentieth-century America have discovered widely shared concerns like domestic violence and the ecological crisis at the same time they continue the concern of their foremothers for their children's needs and for the nation and the world that their children will inherit.

Yet serious divisions surface among American women, even among those who accept the name of feminist. Some differences are rooted in racial and ethnic diversity; these in turn are an important but not comprehensive source of ideological differences. Is the goal to be equal to men in the sense of each individual's having equal opportunities for success and self-fulfillment? But does that classic liberal goal implicitly devalue the traditional roles and contributions of women in an unspoken affirmation that white male goals and values are indeed the "best" and most desirable? Can women affirm what the vast majority of their foremothers did and claim traditional roles, if in modified form, for themselves? In short, is it possible to both step out of woman's traditional places and to rejoice in what women have done, and still may choose to do, in those places? The tensions are real and the obstacles formidable for women who want to insist that human worth is not determined by a person's place in a society that continues to be hierarchically structured, despite feminist critiques. Resistance to change comes not only from men but also from women, women whose goal is to share equally with men in the rewards of the status quo without challenging its structures, as well as women who perceive change and feminism as threats to the values of home, family, and culture, and to a stable society.

Common concerns and internal tensions exist alongside growing religious and cultural pluralism among American women. To be sure, religious pluralism characterized the North American continent before the arrival of Europeans and most assuredly with their advent, even though the dominant white culture was generally unwilling to acknowledge, let alone appreciate, that pluralism. Nevertheless, it is still fair to say that the twentieth century has witnessed a significant increase in pluralism, both in the diversity of religious groups with substantial representation on American soil and in the greater willingness of many Americans to accord respect to others' religious beliefs and practices. Growth in Hindu, Buddhist, and Muslim communities in the United States through both immigration and conversion is one important manifestation of pluralism, as is the revitalization of the oldest religious traditions on the American continent, those of the Native Americans.

## Native American Women and Religion

During the last third of the twentieth century, Native Americans displayed more public militance than they had since the "Indian wars" of the previous century. Inspired by the Civil Rights movements of African Americans, Indians appeared on the surface to endorse contrary goals: where blacks under the leadership of people like Martin Luther King Jr. called for integration, Native Americans condemned assimilation and exalted separation. Yet there were divisions about goals and tactics within both groups, and, at a deeper level, both sought self-determination and respect. Differences were at least partly attributable to different historical experiences, in particular, the nearly constant pressure on Native Americans from white Americans, including sympathetic reformers, to assimilate, to adopt white customs, values, and religion. Despite their devastating effect on Indian landholding, the allotment policies of the federal government lingered well into the twentieth century until John Collier became Commissioner of Indian Affairs under Franklin D. Roosevelt. An opponent of assimilation, Collier wanted to revitalize traditional Indian cultures. This goal was to be implemented in the Indian Reorganization Act of 1934, which gave tribes more governing rights, promoted a revival of Indian arts and culture, and restored religious freedom—no longer would Christian teachings and practice be forced upon Native Americans with government approval. Collier was not without his critics: implementation of the policy was problematic at times; the United States government retained powers of approval and veto that limited tribal sovereignty; for all his sympathy, Collier failed to consult Indians themselves as much as he might have and thus continued the tradition of whites telling Native Americans what was best for them. Nevertheless, the act and Collier's leadership marked a turning point for Native Americans.

In the 1950s, however, the United States government's approach changed, and it now promoted compensation, termination, and relocation—in other words, assimilation again. Native American people could be financially compensated by the government for their losses if they were willing to terminate the legal existence of their tribe (and hence the government's protection and support). At the same time, Indians living on reservations, which often suffered from severe economic depression, were encouraged to relocate to urban centers. The policies, like allotment before them, failed in their goal of assimilation and were more often destructive for those they were designed to help. They were formally ended in 1958, but urban migration continued through the sixties and seventies. Such migration often undercut traditional tribal identities, but it also provided the setting for renewal of pan-Indian movements and the new militancy that demanded the right to self-determination.[1]

## Religious Diversity

As they have been throughout their history, Native American religions—and women's roles therein—are central in the movement for cultural revitalization. Yet "religion" has a range of meanings for contemporary Native Americans. Religion is the distinct, traditional tribal religions of the people. It is also the Christianity promoted by white missionaries and embraced (and adapted) by some Indians. Pan-Indian religions like the Native American Church cross traditional tribal lines. Finally, a broad "Indian spirituality" can exist alongside any or all of these.[2] As contemporary Native Americans reaffirm and even rediscover their particular tribal cultures, religion is an inseparable part of those identities, and women's participation is critical. Contemporary Indian women emphasize the respect shown for women in a tribe's cultural pattern of complementarity and the presence of important female figures in tribal creation accounts and ongoing spirituality, figures like Corn Mother or Selu among the Cherokees, Blue Corn Woman and White Corn Maiden among the Tewa Pueblo people, the Iroquois's Grandmother Turtle and the Three Sisters, the Apaches' White-Painted Woman, and White Buffalo Calf Woman among the Sioux (Lakota).[3] Some Indian women today, following in the footsteps of their grandmothers, seek to preserve tribal languages and to pass on Indian beliefs and practices through the oral tradition that has been so central to Indian culture.[4] The crafts and artwork that wed symbolic meaning to practical use are frequently created by women. While male and female roles in religious ritual are seldom identical, women have signficant parts in male-led rituals, as well as specific female ritual activities, and women function in religious leadership roles like shaman and in the political leadership of many tribes. Far from being mere nostalgia, contemporary efforts to revitalize tribal beliefs and practices represent an important way of reclaiming an individual's or a whole tribe's very identity and at the same time resisting unwelcome cultural pressures and intrusions from the dominant culture. For example, Beatrice Medicine suggests that recovery of traditional child-rearing practices, social roles, and sense of communal responsibility among the Sioux might help to counter current problems of child abuse. Women's roles and rituals are particularly important, she argues, since women are the culture-bearers and "primary socializers of children."[5]

At the same time, many Indian people today embrace some form of the Christianity offered or, often, imposed upon their forebears by missionaries. In areas like the Southwest, native people were given no choice about accepting Catholic Christianity, but they also maintained their own tribal practices, secretly if necessary, so that the religion of many of their twentieth-century descendents combines Christian and tribal elements. Roman Catholic and Episcopal missionaries were generally more open to some form of syncretism, while other Protestant churches tended to dismiss any and all native beliefs and practices as "pagan" and to be repressed. Today, however, when about 15 percent of Native Americans identify themselves as Christians,[6] most mainline Protestants (like Methodists, Lutherans, Presbyterians, and Episcopalians) as well as Catholics encourage Native Americans to incorporate Indian song, art, and practices into worship. With conscious denominational support, Indian leadership (both male and female) is growing. The experiences of seminary training and interchurch activity are not without tensions and cultural misunderstandings on both sides, but the commitment to native leadership seems unlikely to be reversed. In addition, fundamentalist Christians and Mormons have increased evangelism to Native Americans in the twentieth century, with Mormons particularly active in the Southwest and Oklahoma. For some Native Americans, the ability to select from two cultures, specifically the combination of Christianity with traditional beliefs and practices, is religiously satisfying, but others find it ultimately insufficient.

> No matter how tolerant or how inclusive Christian sects may be—for example, using the Sacred Pipe in their rituals, and Indian designs in their churches and priestly garb—there is always something lacking for American Indian people, who are searching not

> so much for identity as for a viable, believable system—an orientation to something that will guide them through their lives. The sacred sphere of native life must be restored.[7]

Diversity of belief is hardly new among Native Americans, as inter- and even intratribal tensions at times erupted into open hostility, but the pressures of white encroachment, dishonesty, and violence sometimes called forth alliances across tribal lines, which in turn produced practices like the Ghost Dance of the late nineteenth century. Movements that crossed tribal lines and appealed to a broader Indian identity grew in the twentieth century, resulting in some actions that were political, others that were more specifically religious, like the Sun Dance and especially the formation of the Native American Church. In the second half of the nineteenth century, the practice of using peyote in a communal religious ritual entered the United States from Mexico. Peyote use spread, attracting adherents especially in the southwestern and south central states, but also eliciting opposition from whites, who generally condemned it as a drug, and from Indians who saw its use and its association with Christianity as a threat to traditional tribal ways. When the government tried to outlaw peyote, a group of Indians formally incorporated in 1918 as the Native American Church. Its articles of incorporation explicitly connected Christianity and the "practice of Peyote Sacrament" and announced the group's intention to "teach the Christian religion with morality, sobriety, industry, kindly charity and right living and to cultivate a spirit of self-respect among the members of the Native Race of Indians. . . ."[8] By the late twentieth century, the Native American Church had a substantial membership (estimated between 100,000 and 225,000)[9] in a loose federation of churches. As a national religious movement, it both crosses tribal boundaries and is compatible with Christian practice, with its distinctive, all-night meetings where use of peyote is combined with prayer, song, and dance, using traditional Indian and Christian symbols.

The choice of selective adaptation is strikingly illustrated in the life of Mountain Wolf Woman, a Winnebago woman who was born in 1884 and died in 1960, and whose life story was told with relatively minimal editorial intrusion by anthropologist Nancy Lurie. In many areas, Mountain Wolf Woman retained traditional ways, including religious activities, becoming a medicine woman as an adult and participating in various tribal ceremonies. Yet she also identified herself as a church member, and in 1908 she joined the peyote movement, when she had a peyote-induced vision of Jesus. (Mountain Wolf Woman's account also clearly illustrates the intratribal tensions precipitated by the spread of the peyote movement.) Thus it was fitting, if to some eyes incongruous, that after her death, she was mourned at a traditional Winnebago wake and at a peyote meeting, and was then buried at the mission cemetery after Christian services.[10]

Finally, the twentieth century has witnessed the emergence of what Sam Gill calls "Native American spirituality," a self-consciously anti-Western set of values and traits held to be common to all Native Americans. Its tenets include reverence for the land and for nature, stress on community and traditions, and suspicion of materialistic, individualistic capitalism. It is practiced in sweat lodges, pipe ceremonies, and powwows. Because its advocates use the written word rather than primarily oral tradition, Native American spirituality has helped to introduce Indian ways to a much wider range of people, appealing to others in American society who are critical of certain aspects of modern American life and Western religions.[11] While many Native Americans justifiably fear superficial appropriation and commercialization by outsiders of what is most sacred to them, there is also hope that the popularity of Native American spirituality may result in more respect for the oldest examples of American religious pluralism.

## Women and Hinduism in America

Among examples of traditions that have contributed more recently to American religious pluralism are two Asian religious traditions, Hinduism and Buddhism, whose numbers have grown as a result of immigration and through conversion, mostly by white Americans.[12] Some nineteenth-century Americans, like transcendentalists or followers of Madame Blavatsky's Theosophy, developed an interest in oriental religions, spirituality, and the occult. In 1893, Swami Vivekananda, a disciple of the mystic Ramakrishna and himself a spiritual leader and reformer, introduced Hinduism directly to Americans at the World's Parliament of Religions and later organized the Vedanta Society in America, associated with his Ramakrishna Mission in India. Other Indian emissaries appeared during the twentieth century, seeking converts among Euro-Americans as well as Asian Americans, with the 1960s and 70s witnessing a particular explosion of interest and popularity. Among these are the Self-Realization Fellowship, introduced in the 1920s by Paramahamsa Yogananda, and two groups brought to the United States in the 1960s: Transcendental Meditation, founded by Maharishi Mahesh Yogi, and the International Society for Krishna Consciousness (ISKCON) or Hare Krishnas. These examples of "export Hinduism" or "neo-Hinduism"[13] generally give great authority and reverence to a particular *guru* or spiritual leader, who helps followers to resolve personal dilemmas, as well as to find spiritual enlightenment. In addition, they typically emphasize devotion and meditation through the practice of yoga, repetition of a mantra, or other spiritual disciplines. Most of the religious leaders of these groups are men, though many disciples are women. For example, in ISKCON, while both men and women work as missionaries and recruiters, the great majority of leadership positions are held by men. In marriage, women are seen as subordinate and in need of protection, while for a man, marriage may be perceived as an act of self-sacrifice, delaying his progress to a higher spiritual state of celibacy.[14] There are some female spiritual leaders in ISKCON, however, and other neo-Hindu groups have women *gurus*. Such is the case with the Siddha Yoga movement, brought to the United States in 1970 by Swami Muktananda. When he died in 1982, he was succeeded by a brother and sister as co-*gurus*, but the brother withdrew in 1985, leaving a woman, Swami Chidvilasananda, as sole leader. Because devotion to the *guru*, who reveals and personifies the divine, is so central in Siddha Yoga, Swami Chidvilasanada is an object of tremendous reverence to her followers and is credited with miraculous powers. Some members, though not the majority, of a secondary tier of leaders are women, and Catherine Wessinger concludes, "Although Siddha Yoga has no explicit teachings on the proper social role of women, the egalitarian relationship of the divine masculine and feminine in its philosophy, as well as the presence of women as religious specialists, strongly implies an acceptance of women in roles not confined to the domestic sphere."[15]

Groups like Siddha Yoga or ISKCON have attracted both Asian Americans and European Americans in recent decades, but the Hindu community has also grown through immigration from India and the Hindu diaspora. Most groups settled on the east and west coasts, or in major urban centers like Chicago or Houston. Unlike many other immigrant groups in American history, however, they tend to be unusually well educated, well represented in professional and managerial occupations, and reasonably prosperous. While some Indian Americans have become secularized and others follow "neo-Hindu" religious movements, many maintain a broad Hindu practice or devotion to a particular divine figure or tradition, especially through family worship and the celebration of holidays and festivals.

Worship in the home has traditionally been central in Hinduism; indeed, while many Hindus participate in temple worship, a person need not do so to be considered a "good" Hindu. The tradition continues among Hindus in North America: most homes have a room or part of a room where icons are kept and daily family worship is performed, morning and evening. (Given the realities of a typical American work week, Saturdays and Sundays are opportunities for longer, more elaborate worship.) Women take an important part in family worship, though not necessarily in specific gender-determined ways because ritual activity tends to depend more on competence and interest than a tradition of gender-linked roles.

While temple ritual flourished in India, it was secondary to home worship, and temples, unlike Christian churches, were not built for corporate worship. In the United States and Canada, however, where Hindus are a religious and cultural minority, temples are becoming more significant as centers for communal identity, teaching, and corporate worship. Purchased from other groups or sometimes built to accommodate congregations, temples are the setting for more regular patterns of worship, frequently held on Sunday morning. (Although Sunday morning gathering has no particular religious significance in Hinduism, the timing of worship has more to do with the pragmatic realities of the American work/school week than any intentional patterning on Christian practice.) In a place like India or Trinidad where Hinduism permeates the culture, little self-conscious attention to children's religious education is necessary, but since Hindus are a very small minority in America, more explicit means are needed to preserve a cultural and religious tradition. Along with the family, temples are therefore playing a larger role in children's religious education. For example, the Hindu Mandir of Minneapolis has recently begun "Sunday school" classes and sponsors an annual camp for children of the community to teach the tradition and supplement home training.

Holidays and festivals celebrate past and present religious realities as they pass on traditions to future generations. Particularly important in Hinduism is Divali, the Festival of Light, which takes place in November or December. In the spring, Holi is celebrated with music, song, and dance. Special days honor different incarnational figures, or avatars, like the birthday of Krishna or the birthday of Rama. In Hinduism, Ishta Deva, the doctrine of the chosen deity, reflects religious belief in one God who yet has multiple representations or manifestations, any of which can totally embody the divine, so that the believer may choose a particular form of God as his or her "lens" for the whole. For example, Shiva Ratri (Night of Shiva) is the major celebration for that manifestation of God. Among the manifestations, too, are female figures who fully embody the divine and have their own devotees; for example, Nava Ratri (Nine Nights of Durga) in October or November honors Durga, one of the more popular forms of the mother goddess in India and the wife of Shiva. In these, as in many other festivals and in home worship, women play significant roles.

In terms of religious leadership, Hinduism traditionally has had two kinds of religious authorities: first, priests, either temple priests who live in a temple compound, perform the rituals there, and help visitors to make offerings, or family priests, who do not live at the temple but serve families by coming to their homes and providing ritual help for events like marriages or funerals if the family itself does not have the expertise; and second, teachers (or *gurus*), who are not generally involved in doing rituals for others but rather are spiritual guides in the search for liberation. Of the two roles, the second, teacher, has the higher status and has always been open to women, though in fact, far fewer women than men have sought the position. Traditionally, priests have been male, and while some groups in Hinduism today permit women to train to be family priests, others exclude women from these ritual specialist roles. This does not, however, appear to be an issue for most Hindu women, given the many other roles in home and temple practice that they can and do fulfill. Furthermore, the broader social roles open to Hindu women in America reflect their relative socioeconomic position: girls are encouraged in their education as boys are, and women hold positions of paid and professional work outside the home. Yet they continue to play active roles in the work and administration of Hindu temples, as well as in home worship.[16]

## Women and Buddhism in America

Like Hinduism, Buddhism formed part of the "oriental wisdom" that intrigued some white Americans in the nineteenth century, but Buddhism's introduction to the United States was more dependent on immigrants, particularly Chinese people who worked and settled on the West Coast in the mid-nineteenth century. These settlers had little interest in proselytism, however, and it was once again the World's Parliament of Religions that sparked a movement to spread Asian religious teachings to Americans, this time a version of Zen Buddhism brought by Japanese masters. During the twentieth century, Buddhists from other areas of Asia like Korea, Vietnam, and Tibet joined Chinese and Japanese people in coming to the United States, each bringing one or more distinctive traditions within Buddhism. (There are two main traditions within Buddhism, Mahayana and Theravada; some scholars add a third, Vajrayana, which developed in Tibet. Mahayana Buddhism flourished in places like China and Japan and fostered subtraditions like Zen and Shinshu ("Pure Land"). Theravada Buddhism was more dominant in Southeast Asia, and thus more often brought to America by Thai, Cambodian, and Laotian immigrants.) The second half of the twentieth century saw more rapid growth of Buddhism among Western Americans, to the point that Charles Prebish concluded in the late 1980s:

> Today, there are clearly more non-Asian Americans in the Buddhist movement than Asian-Americans. Nearly all non-Asian Buddhists are white, middle class, and between twenty and forty-five years old; as a group they have an unusually high level of education. Individuals rather than families seem to be attracted to Buddhism.[17]

While there have been changes relating to women during the twentieth century in the Buddhism of Asian countries—for example, interest in reestablishing full monastic ordination for women in areas where it no longer exists or the emergence of a few women spiritual leaders[18]—non-Asian Buddhist women in the West have been particularly active in raising questions about the role of women in Buddhist thought and practice. Although an explicit feminist voice is still a minority even among those Buddhist groups in America, like various forms of Zen Buddhism, that are dominated by non-Asians, a feminist voice is more likely to be found there than among traditional, Asian-American Buddhists. Sandy Boucher's book, *Turning the Wheel: American Women Creating the New Buddhism,*[19] introduces the reader to the variety as well as the common concerns of these (primarily Euro-American) women. Just as Buddhism itself in America is manifest in multiple traditions, so these women embrace a range of practices, especially Theravada, Zen, and the Vajrayana Buddhism of Tibet. Yet many of them share a basic attraction to what they perceive as Buddhism's nondualist, nonsexist philosophy and the opportunity for full female participation, even leadership.

> But the more basic appeal of Buddhist practice to women resides in the fact that Buddhism posits no god, creates no I-Thou relationship with an all-powerful father figure. A central tenet is that one must trust one's own experience above all else. Nothing—no tradition, belief, or direction from a teacher—must be accepted unless it can pass the test of experience.[20]

While some have criticized these women's departures from traditional Buddhist ideas and ways, Boucher is unabashedly positive about the creation of a "new" and "American" Buddhism that will meet the needs of contemporary Americans, especially women, and she points out that historically Buddhism was adapted to the countries and cultures to which it spread. Indeed, some advocates of this new Buddhism argue that the United States situation may allow Buddhism to reclaim what they believe is its essential, nonsexist, nondualist, and nonhierarchical core.[21] Thus the women work for change in various ways: some study to recover a "usable" Buddhist past (paralleling the efforts of Christian and Jewish feminists); some combine Buddhism and political activism; still others join Buddhist monastic orders or function as spiritual teachers, like Roshi Jiyu Kennett, who founded and leads a rigorous and fairly traditional Zen monastery of men and women, Shasta Abbey, in northern California.

Probably the largest Buddhist group in America made up of Asian Americans is the Japanese Jodo Shinshu tradition, known in the United States as the Buddhist Churches of America. The group was begun in 1899 by two missionary-priests from Japan to serve Japanese immigrants in America—and to counter Christian pressures of evangelism. Nearly 100 years later, the tradition is stable, though not growing rapidly, with approximately 100,000 members and sixty-two temples or churches, most of which are located on the West Coast.[22] The Jodo Shinshu tradition is part of "Pure Land" Buddhism, which emphasizes "salvation by *tariki* (other-power), rather than by *jiriki* (self-power)." Through faith in the Amida Buddha, or Buddha of Eternal Light and Infinite Life, a person can be reborn into the Pure Land and attain nirvana from there, that is, release from the cycles of existence and suffering.[23] Although clearly Buddhist in belief, affirming the "Four Noble Truths" on suffering and the overcoming thereof, the Buddhist Churches of America have adapted certain forms that appear more Christian or Western, including the name "church," regular worship services on Sunday (as well as on traditional festivals), and buildings that often resemble Christian churches except that the central figure on the altar is the Amida Buddha. Flowers, candles, incense and food-offerings also contribute to the services, which are generally held in Japanese, though there may also be an English service. In addition, the Buddhist Churches of America, like Christian or Jewish groups, have affiliated organizations like Sunday schools and women's auxiliaries. It is possible for women to be ordained and serve temples in the Buddhist Churches of America, but instances of such female religious leadership are fairly rare.[24]

While other Asian-American Buddhists share some basic beliefs with the Buddhist Churches of America, they exhibit equally important differences. Although Buddhism has a common historical root, its development in Asia led to significant cultural and religious differences, not only between major traditions like Theravada and Mahayana but also among ethnic groups within these traditions. In a sense, Buddhism in America is similar to Native American religion: just as we must be aware of different tribal traditions and wary of generalizing about a univocal "Native American religion," so there are several "Buddhisms" in America. Furthermore, Asian-American Buddhists are found in a larger socioeconomic spread than American Hindus, ranging from the very poor, like recently arrived Laotian immigrants, to the quite prosperous, like some third-generation Japanese or some recent Chinese immigrants. Consequently, we also find a range in their responses to social and gender roles and to issues like female education and women working outside the home.

Yet like American Hindus—and many other ethnic immigrant groups in the centuries before them—Asian-American Buddhists find in the home the primary setting to practice and retain a religious and cultural identity. Thus for most Buddhists in a Mahayana tradition, a Buddha altar is found in the home, and the wife/mother of the family is particularly responsible for maintaining the altar, making offerings, burning incense, and so forth. In these groups, the altar is also the focus for ancestor rituals. Ancestor veneration proceeds along patrilineal lines—that is, fathers and their wives are the objects of veneration, and a daughter-in-law "joins" this line rather than that of her biological family. In Theravada groups, by way of contrast, one would still find the central Buddha altar and the woman's role in burning incense or offering flowers, but the altar is not used for ancestor rituals. Instead, an important religious role for Theravada Buddhist women is to provide food for the monks, who are regarded as living symbols of the Buddha. For a woman to bring food offerings to the temple helps both the monks and her own religious development and prospects for a better rebirth. Women play a similar role in Theravada festivals, like the Buddha's birthday: they prepare and bring the food to the temple, but the chanting and ritual are carried out by men, while women are primarily observers.[25]

## Women and Islam in America

The majority of Muslims in the United States are immigrants or descendents of immigrants, not only from Arab countries but also from places like Pakistan and eastern Europe. In addition, a substantial number of African Americans and a smaller number of white Americans have converted to some form of Islam. The numbers are growing rapidly—indeed, scholars predict that by the early part of the twenty-first century, Islam will be the second largest religious group in America (after Christianity and passing Judaism).[26] Yet Muslims are little known by many Americans or are classed indiscriminately with "terrorists," an association understandably resented by American followers of Islam.

Historically, Muslims have argued that Islam holds women in high regard. Men and women are religiously equal in terms of basic responsibilities and of accountability on Judgment Day. Those parts of the Qur'an that portray women as subordinate—a step below men and in need of male protection and support—are closely tied to Muslim concerns for the family. Hence Muslim apologists "affirm that it is precisely because men are invested with the responsibility of taking care of women, financially and otherwise, that they are given authority over the females of their families. And that, affirm many Muslim women today, is exactly the way it should be."[27] Women are expected to fulfill the five "Pillars of Islam"—professing faith in the singularity of God and Muhammad's role as prophet; worshiping five times daily; almsgiving; fasting during daylight hours during the month of Ramadan; and making the pilgrimage to Mecca at least once in a lifetime—though there are some modifications for women, often related to their family responsibilities in a situation similar to that of traditional Judaism. For example, women generally pray in their homes rather than attend communal prayer services in the mosque on Friday, as men would, and women who are menstruating, pregnant, or nursing are excused from the most rigorous demands of fasting during Ramadan.[28]

American Muslims are a diverse group. A significant number are secularized or at least "unmosqued,"[29] practicing Islam to whatever degree they do in their homes, while others are very strict and traditional in their observation of Islamic law. So, too, Muslim women vary in the degree to which they follow a traditional Islamic dress code, one of the most obvious signs of religious identification: while some practice full veiling, others are content with modest street clothes or don traditional dress only for worship and other religious occasions. For both women and men in America, the mosque has taken on special importance, not only in its classic role as a place for worship but also, in a country where Muslims are relatively few and often misunderstood, as a kind of community center. Some mosques allow mixed worship; others have separate areas for women's prayer. Some even discourage female attendance for worship, but generally Muslim women in America are more likely to attend mosques than women in Islamic countries, sometimes for the Friday worship but more often on Sundays and certainly on major festivals.[30] In addition, Muslim women in America have taken on roles in connection with their mosques that parallel in many ways the activities of Jewish women in synagogues and Christian women in churches: raising money; organizing social activities; teaching the young; exerting indirect influence and, occasionally among more acculturated Muslims, direct leadership. Women cannot, however, be *imams*, the traditional leaders of worship who have, in America, taken on some of the other functions of Christian and Jewish religious leaders. The following quotation from an American Muslim from Pakistan, with just a few adjectival changes, could as well describe Jewish or Christian women in the earlier years of this century:

> The sisters have an equally important role to play in the activities of the Islamic center as do the men. Sometimes I feel that without them we probably wouldn't exist. They are the ones who essentially are planning the day-to-day activities and are a lot of help in bringing their families to the mosque functions and activities. They do perform a significant help in making sure that the social aspects are a full part of the Center's activities. We do not have any female members on the board this year, but we have had some in the past, and they have been a lot of help. The Islamic School was really started by the women.[31]

Like many immigrants before them, especially those who were religiously, ethnically, or culturally "different," Muslims in America have had to try to balance the benefits and attractions of acculturation with the potential loss of a distinctive religious and cultural identity and heritage. The dilemma is intensified for women because both Islam as a religion and many of the cultures from which the immigrants come have expectations for male and female roles and relationships that are significantly different from modern American cultural norms. As Yvonne Yazbeck Haddad and Adair T. Lummis note, "The issue of dating between young Muslim men and women is a particularly sensitive one in this country. Dating is generally discouraged and often forbidden for both sexes, largely as a holdover of customs in Islamic countries and because of a concern for the apparent license in sexual relations among many American youth."[32] While dating is accepted by some American Muslims, most tend to be stricter with daughters than sons. In part, this may be due to the fact that in Islamic law, a male Muslim may marry a Christian or a Jew, as well a Muslim, but a female Muslim can only marry another Muslim. While arranged marriages are not common among American Muslims, there is strong feeling that a person should marry within the faith. Again, the pattern is hardly unique to American Muslims: immigrants in other ethnic and religious minorities in the United States have discouraged intermarriage in order to try to retain a strong cultural and religious identity. Yet religion may be even more important than ethnic identity here, as Marcia K. Hermansen notes:

> For the new generation of Muslims, the first growing up in America, patterns of marriage include more intercultural marriage across Muslim ethnic lines (e.g., Pakistani-Arab) as degree of religious commitment and socio-economic level have become more important criteria than ethnic background.[33]

The family functions as a center for religious practice and for transmission of religious and ethnic identity, as a resource for resisting too much acculturation, and as a bulwark of traditional gender roles. Muslims in America often agree with the criticism of many people in Islamic countries who see Western and especially American culture as degenerate, pervaded by sexual license, crime, drugs, pornography, and the like. Thus some Muslim women in America voluntarily assume a form of veiling, traditional Islamic dress, as a way of preserving their modesty, protesting American sexual immorality, and affirming a Muslim identity.

## Black Muslims

In 1993, African Americans accounted for roughly two-fifths of Muslims in America.[34] While some of the Africans brought to America as slaves were Muslim, the major growth of Islam among black Americans has occurred in the twentieth century through the Black Muslim movement. Whether the Nation of Islam was or is fully Islamic is another question, since its adherents regarded Wallace Fard Mohammed as an appearance of Allah and Elijah Muhammad as Allah's messenger. Founded in Detroit in the early 1930s, the Nation of Islam (or Black Muslims) spread first to Chicago, expanding slowly but steadily until midcentury, when the dynamic leadership of its most famous convert, Malcolm X, spurred more rapid growth. In these years, the Nation of Islam's appeal to many African Americans lay in its repudiation of whites and Christianity, the "white man's religion," and its affirmation of black dignity and destiny. After Elijah Muhammad's death in 1975, the movement split, with his son Wallace (later Warith) Deen Muhammad moving toward a less separatist and more Islamically orthodox position, named the American Muslim Mission in 1980. Minister Louis Farrakhan, who replaced Malcolm X as second-in-command to Elijah Muhammad after Malcolm X's defection and subsequent assassination, maintained the religious and racial positions of Elijah Muhammad and retained the name, though not the resources, of the Nation of Islam, insisting that worldwide orthodox Islam, as well as Christianity, was racist.[35]

An unusual feature of the Nation of Islam as it emerged in mid-twentieth century America was the number of young males it attracted, and men were to be leaders in the home as well as the movement. Women's role was honored but distinctive, to be found primarily in the home or in supportive, not directive, positions. While women might help in the temples or businesses of the Nation of Islam, men held the roles of responsible leadership.[36] Girls' education was separate from that of boys, and the ethic that C. Eric Lincoln has called "Black Puritanism" included hard work and strict sexual morality for faithful Muslims.

> Courtship or marriage outside the group is discouraged, and unremitting pressure is put on non-Muslim spouses to join the Black Nation. Divorce is frowned upon but allowed. No Muslim woman may be alone in a room with any man except her husband; and provocative or revealing dress and most cosmetics are absolutely forbidden. Any Muslim who participates in an interracial liaison may incur severe punishment, even expulsion, from the Movement. Clear lines are drawn to indicate the behavior and social role appropriate to each sex; and Muslim males are expected to be constantly alert for any show of interest in a Muslim woman on the part of a white man, for whom sex is alleged to be a degrading obsession.[37]

Yet Black Muslim women responded to the sense of black pride fostered in the movement, and rather than resenting gender roles that appear to go counter to those evolving in American culture, seemed to welcome the stability, the encouragement of male responsibility, and the respect for women and the family found within the movement. Under Farrakhan, the Nation of Islam maintains similar roles and standards, and while there has been some relaxation in the American Muslim Mission, standards of female modesty, male leadership, and the centrality of the family are like those in many orthodox Islamic communities.

## Women in Churches and Synagogues

By the late twentieth century, American women could be ordained as ministers, priests, and rabbis in most mainline Protestant denominations and in three of the four major Jewish groups. That this was a historic development was clear; what was less clear was its long-term meaning for women, lay and ordained, and for the churches and synagogues and their concepts of ministry and religious leadership. Meanwhile, "feminist theology" burst upon the scene, challenging Christianity and Judaism from within and breaking away into new religious forms.

Even those groups that had begun ordaining women in the mid-twentieth century or earlier witnessed sharply increased numbers of women entering seminary and seeking ordination in the 1970s and 1980s. As ordained women became more than a token few, a number of questions were raised, some with hope, some with horror, some simply in curiosity: Would women "take over" the profession, completing the so-called feminization of the church and driving men out? Would women be accepted by more than a few congregations, and would they rise to denominational leadership positions? And one of the most intriguing questions—Would women, as a group, bring different gifts, styles, and goals to the ordained ministry? By the early 1990s, the numbers of ordained women were substantial but hardly indicative of a female takeover. A few seminaries had as many or more women students than men; some had only a few women; overall, not quite a third of the students in American seminaries were women.[38] In no Christian group were women more than a minority of ordained ministers, but their numbers were large enough to make a visible impact. Overall, women made up 11 to 12 percent of all clergy (including groups which do not ordain women).[39] By 1993, there were over 200 women rabbis in Reform Judaism, plus 52 in Reconstructionism and 50 in Conservatism.[40]

In the early 1980s, after the first major wave of ordained women had made their way into parishes and denominational structures, Jackson W. Carroll, Barbara Hargrove, and Adair T. Lummis published a study, *Women of the Cloth,* based on extensive interviews with clergywomen and clergymen in nine mainline Protestant denominations. On the one hand, they discovered that women did not have too difficult a time getting ordained and finding a first job placement, most often as an assistant or associate minister. While most Americans' image of a minister continued to be a male one, when people actually met and experienced the ministry of ordained women, they were more accepting of the idea and the women themselves. Clergywomen saw themselves and were seen by the laity as doing a good job at levels comparable to clergymen. However, the authors also discovered some "bad news." Some people—laity, clergy, and denominational officials—refused to accept women as ministers even if their denomination had formally endorsed female ordination. That resistance was rooted not only in the traditional biblical, theological, and social arguments that had been advanced for many years, but also in a concern that the innovation of women clergy might prove especially disastrous at a time when mainline Protestant bodies had experienced significant decline in membership and financial support. Furthermore, the "good news" about first placements was not matched by subsequent job mobility and advancement for women.

> Men and women find it relatively easy to find first positions, but the kinds of positions differ, with more women than men serving in assistant or associate pastor positions or as part-time pastors.

> Likewise, the career lines of women seem to be more 'flat' than those of men. It appears that women continue to serve as pastors of smaller churches or in assistant or associate positions in second, third, and subsequent positions. Also, there are salary inequities between men and women, although women are more likely than men to report that their current salary is sufficient.[41]

The same differences between male and female career lines were found among Jewish rabbis. To try to account for that pattern, some have hypothesized that women make different choices than men and are less willing to sacrifice other aspects of their lives to single-minded pursuit of a career. Others have suggested that the "glass ceiling" impacts female clergy, as well as women in business and the professions.[42]

Carroll, Hargrove, and Lummis noted two further developments that continued throughout the 1980s and into the 1990s: women and men seeking ordained ministry as a second career and hence entering seminaries at an older age than had been the tradition for young men; and team or co-pastorates, situations where both marriage partners were ordained and sought to share a single or perhaps a one-and-a-half-time position at a church. Women clergy advanced more slowly than most of their male counterparts, but they did advance. By 1995, there were women at the highest clergy levels of some major Christian denominations: Lutherans had elected two women bishops, and there were four women bishops in the Episcopal Church in the United States. Numerous Presbyterian women served as moderators of presbyteries or executive presbyters and on the national staff. Methodists had an especially strong record: by 1992, eight women had been elected as bishops and over eighty as district superintendants.[43]

Were women "different" as ministers or rabbis, once they had moved beyond token positions? Here the debate was internal, that is, among those who supported ordained women rather than simply between supporters and opponents. The claim that women would be different, if not better, as ordained ministers was hardly a new one: in 1889, Frances Willard argued:

> The mother-heart of God will never be known to the world until translated into terms of speech by mother-hearted women. Law and love will never balance in the realm of grace until a woman's hand shall hold the scales. . . . Men preach a creed; women will declare a life. Men deal in formulas, women in facts. Men have always tithed mint and rue and cummin in their exegesis and ecclesiasticism, while the world's heart has cried out for compassion, forgiveness, and sympathy.[44]

Carroll, Hargrove, and Lummis identified a desire to "transform" the profession and, indeed, the church itself as one motivation of women clergy,[45] and the assertions of individual ordained women and anecdotal evidence seemed to argue that women, whether for reasons of "nature" or social conditioning and experience, were less hierarchical and authoritarian and more democratic and nurturing than male clergy. In a recent survey of women ministers and women rabbis, the authors found that not only were there differences between Christian and Jewish ordained women, but that nearly all of the rabbis and a substantial majority of the ministers believed that they approached their positions and functioned differently than their male colleagues.[46] Others disagreed, insisting that differences among women clergy were just as great as those between men and women ministers and that to posit a normative female style or approach simply perpetuated stereotypes, and hence limits, for both men and women. Sociologist Edward C. Lehman Jr. set out to explore the issue more systematically, characterizing the two sides as "maximalists" and "minimalists." The results of his extensive survey of mainline Protestant men and women were, perhaps not surprisingly, ambiguous. For one thing, he discovered that "As a group, then, *the clergy tend to manifest feminine styles of interpersonal relations.*"[47] Whether or not it is a result of women's greater visibility or of other cultural changes, the old stereotype of the authoritarian "Herr Pastor" finds little public acceptance in mainline Protestantism in the late twentieth century: clergy, male or female, are expected by their parishoners to be open, supportive, and caring individuals. In terms of ministry style, Lehman found statistically significant gender differences on four characteristics: "willingness to use power over the congregation"; "desire to empower the congregation to manage its own life"; "preference for rational structure in decision making"; and "legalistic tendencies when dealing with ethical issues." On the other hand, he found little gender difference on five characteristics: "desire for positions of formal authority"; "openness and vulnerability in interpersonal style"; "approach to preaching"; "acceptance of traditional criteria of clergy status"; and "involvement in social issues beyond the congregation." Indeed, Lehman found that racial/ethnic identity had more impact on ministry style than gender. Among minorities, both male and female clergy tended to display more "masculine" characteristics in their ministerial style than white clergy, and they were more involved in social issues.[48] Hence the "evidence" is mixed, and it seems likely that both sides to the debate will continue to find reasons to argue for or against a distinctively female style of ministry.

## Feminist Theology

In 1979, Carol P. Christ and Judith Plaskow published an anthology of recent writings about women and religion called *Womanspirit Rising: A Feminist Reader in Religion*. Along with a range of diverse, sometimes groundbreaking, articles, the editors presented a typology of feminist theology: reformists and revolutionaries. Both groups agreed that the Western religious traditions of Judaism and Christianity were patriarchal and had frequently oppressed, ignored, or denigrated women; both agreed that change was necessary. But where the reformists wanted to work within their respective traditions, convinced that there were resources and themes there that could support equality and liberation for women, the revolutionaries concluded that Judaism and Christianity were irredeemably sexist and that women's best and healthiest option was to abandon them and seek a new source of spiritual experience and religious expression. Ten years later, Plaskow and Christ published another anthology, noting both the explosion of literature on women and religion and the important refinements and correctives within the field that had appeared during the 1980s, especially the "increasing chorus of minority voices [that] has been the single most important development in feminist work in religion in the last ten years."[49] The editors acknowledged that new voices and more sophisticated and nuanced analyses raised questions about the adequacy of their twofold typology. Nevertheless, while Christ and Plaskow themselves, along with many scholars and teachers of feminist theology, recognize the dangers of oversimplification, they still find the basic distinction a helpful one, and I follow it here.

## Common Themes

Some of the themes and arguments found among reformists had been developed during many years of debate over women's right to preach and be ordained, but feminist theologians' concerns went far beyond those two issues. Indeed, some of the most creative and influential feminist theologians come out of a tradition, Roman Catholicism, that does not yet ordain women, and some Catholics question the desirability of women's access to the priesthood without serious revision of the structure and conception of ordained ministry.[50] Common to all the analyses is recognition and critique of patriarchy as an enormously powerful historical and cultural reality that should never be ignored or underestimated. Nevertheless, the critique of patriarchy has been accompanied by a project of retrieval and reconstruction of positive elements within Judaism and/or Christianity in the attempt to find a "usable past" in scripture and tradition. As the work of literally hundreds of scholars and teachers, the results of retrieval, reinterpretation, and reconstruction over the last quarter-century are impressively complex, rich, and sophisticated. The project is important for its own sake, that is, for the much fuller picture of the past that it has made possible, but also practically as resource and argument for change today.

A third commonality among reformist feminist theologians, in addition to the critique of patriarchy and the search for a usable past, is a stress on the role of experience in theology. Of course, human experience of the divine, of self, and of others has always shaped theology, even if its influence was not acknowledged, but what was often presumed to be "universal" experience was, in fact, privileged male experience. Thus feminist theologians insist we must look at women's experience, recognizing at the same time other previously excluded groups' experiences as these have been articulated recently in various forms of liberation theology. But when examining views on "experience," we also find significant diversity, even disagreement. While feminist theologians agree on the foundational, nonnegotiable premise that women and men are equal—in the sense that they are fully human, equally created in the image of God and deserving of equal opportunities for personal, social, and religious leadership and spiritual development—they disagree about whether women and men have the same "nature." Early in the current women's movement, this seemed obvious to many feminists: equal rights and opportunities and the rejection of gender roles could only be grounded in the presumption that women and men share the same human nature. Yet other voices within the women's movement questioned that assumption, suggesting that women were different than men, not only as a result of incredibly powerful historical and social conditioning but also in some intrinsic way that was related to but not comprehended by biological difference. The problem, they insisted, was that women's contributions, women's perspectives, and women's very ways of being had been devalued by patriarchy. The solution was not to deny but to appreciate those differences. As each side of the debate argued persuasively, many contemporary feminist theologians claimed a "both/and" position, though some leaned more to one side than the other.

### Womanist Theology

How women's experience was defined depended to some extent on where one stood in the "nature" debate, yet an even more critical issue of diversity surfaced as women of color called white, middle-class feminists to account for a false universality that may have been unintentional but was still destructive. Just as male theologians had presumed to speak for all people, so white feminists had projected their own experiences to all women. As a result, recent writings by feminist theologians are more self-conscious about the author's experiential base, and particular feminist theologies have been articulated from the perspectives of women of color. One such perspective, termed "womanist,"[51] comes from African-American women like Delores S. Williams. While Williams agrees that there are commonalities between white feminist theologians and African-American womanist theologians, she cites four areas of difference on which she invites dialogue: the understanding of what is "acceptably female" behavior in various cultural contexts; the need for greater attention to the interstructuring of race, class, and gender and the degree to which women oppress other women; the biblical hermeneutic that is emphasized (and here there are differences among womanist theologians); and the perception and interpretation of God's response to the oppressed in history.[52]

Yet Williams is also critical of black male liberation theology and the male-led African-American denominational churches on at least two levels. First, she decries their sexism, whether that is manifested in the denial of women's call to preach, in patriarchal theology and biblical interpretation, in the exploitation of largely female congregations by some black ministers, or in black men's buying into white cultural gender roles and expectations to the detriment of African-American women. Second, Williams argues that there are two distinctive traditions of African-American biblical interpretation. First, there is the more familiar liberation tradition, whose paradigm is the Exodus. This has functioned both critically and constructively in the black church since the days of slavery and has been decisively highlighted in the work of black liberation theologians of the second half of the twentieth century. Williams by no means rejects this tradition; indeed, she commends it and the black voices who have kept it alive. Nevertheless, she urges its advocates to be in dialogue with a second tradition, which she calls the "survival/quality of life tradition of African-American biblical appropriation."[53] This tradition has been especially meaningful to African-American women, and its central biblical paradigm is not the Exodus but the story of Hagar. Hagar, the slave from Egypt/Africa, had no choice about bearing a son for her master Abraham, yet she was despised and exiled, twice, by her slave mistress, Sarah; many African-American women, too, endured similar experiences of slavery and sexual exploitation. But Hagar is also a paradigm of survival, for herself and her child. Driven into the wilderness first while she is pregnant and later when Sarah perceives Hagar's son, Ishmael, as a threat to her own son, Isaac, Hagar turns to God, and God answers her, not with liberation but with help for survival for herself and her child. So, too, black women have demonstrated a risk-taking faith, meeting God in a time of trouble when there seemed to be no other help. For Hagar, wilderness was both positive and negative, and Williams traces both aspects of a "wilderness experience" in African Americans' history. During the time of slavery, wilderness was a positive symbol, a refuge for fugitives and a place to encounter God. After the Civil War, however, wilderness took on a more negative connotation: the economically, socially, physically, and psychologically hostile world outside faced by former slaves, men and women. Thus Williams argues that a Hagar tradition of survival and the symbol of the wilderness experience bring together men and women, just as they join the spiritual and the political.[54] Yet finally the tradition is especially meaningful to black women because it resonates so closely with their particular experience; as such, it has much to contribute to dialogue with other women and African-American men. As Williams concludes:

> The greatest truth of black women's survival and quality-of-life struggle is that they have worked without hesitation and with all the energy they could muster. Many of them, like Hagar, have demonstrated great courage as they resisted oppression and as they went into the wide, wide world to make a living for themselves and their children. They depended upon their strength and upon each other. But in the final analysis the message is clear: they trusted the end to God. Every important event in the stories of Hagar and black women turns on this trust.[55]

## Classic Doctrinal Issues

### *God-Language*

Womanist theologians like Williams raise classic doctrinal issues, particularly where they impact African-American women's experiences, but these issues have been even more central in the work of white Christian feminist theologians, for whom gender is the primary category of analysis. Put in blunt form: Is God male, and if so, what has "he" to do with women? Can women be redeemed by a male savior? The "language question" surfaced early in the current phase of feminist religious thought, and it was soon evident that far more was involved than a "simple" change to generic language for human beings. What about God-language? Feminist theologians' basic assumption is that all language about God is metaphorical or symbolic. On the one hand, this is nothing new: the notion that language about God is not to be taken literally or comprehensively is as old as the Christian tradition and found in male theological giants from Clement of Alexandria to Thomas Aquinas to Paul Tillich. Yet since the vast majority of language about God in the Bible and in Jewish and Christian tradition has been male, the overwhelming psychological impression has been that God is, indeed, male. Feminist theologians questioned that assumption and asked what changes were possible. One suggestion was the use of neutral language, like (the early) Mary Daly's image of God as Verb or Being; an alternative proposal was the addition of female images to male ones.[56] Such proposals quickly drew an intense backlash: while of course God was not literally male, some critics argued, traditional images were invested with a certain sacrality and biblically sanctioned, and the use of female metaphors was unacceptable, even heretical.

At the same time, feminist theologians themselves questioned the "simplicity" of the issue. Some, like Sallie McFague, argue that it is not merely a matter of male pronouns and images that can be balanced by female pronouns and images; rather, the problem is the whole triumphalist, monarchical, and patriarchal imagery of God as king and conqueror, and the world as God's realm. The question, she insists, is not whether such imaginative constructs are true or false; they are inappropriate and destructive *in our day,* and other similarly imaginative models may better serve Christian faith now. Our age has, she believes, come to a new appreciation of holistic, relational approaches (rather than atomistic, individualistic images of existence), and we know we must take seriously human beings' potential to bring about ecological and nuclear disaster. Thus McFague proposes to speak of the world as God's body and develops three heuristic models for God: God as Mother (or Father, if that is understood in a parental rather than a patriarchal sense); God as Lover; God as Friend. Each model is associated with a particular aspect of God's love: Mother with *agape,* or love that creates and nurtures *all* of creation with impartial and inclusive justice; Lover with *eros* and its passionate care that affirms the "valuableness" of the beloved, the world and all that is in it; Friend with *philia,* love freely chosen, reciprocal, welcoming the other's companionship in mutual concerns. Yet the metaphors are never to be taken literally or seen as mutually exclusive: "in our models of God as mother, lover, and friend we see different aspects of God's one love, the destabilizing, nonhierarchical, inclusive love of all."[57]

### *Christology*

Christology is a second crucial area of discussion for Christian feminist theologians. There is, of course, no question that Jesus of Nazareth was a male human being. That unavoidable fact coupled with the early church's tendency to equate normative humanity with male humanity and to see the *imago dei* reflected more excellently in men than in women, despite Jesus' own iconoclastic egalitarianism, has appeared to some women too great an obstacle, and they conclude that this male savior cannot save women. Others, however, concede that there may have been practical, historical, and sociological reasons that God chose to become incarnate in a male human being in the context of first-century Palestine, but that the choice had no ontological necessity. There is nothing in the very nature of God or of salvation that made incarnation in a man rather than a woman intrinsically necessary. Yet not only has the tradition consistently identified males more closely with the divine in a hierarchical order of creation, there are arguments emerging in the modern period that do seem to rest on an ontological necessity of maleness: for example, one of the major arguments of the 1976 Roman Catholic "Declaration on the Question of the Admission of Women to the Ministerial Priesthood" is that the priest, especially as he represents Christ in the Eucharist, must bear a "natural resemblance" to Christ (in the matter of gender, not of age, ethnicity, race, or any other human category).[58] But if this is so—if maleness, not humanity, is the critical element for incarnation—what impact does that claim have on women's salvation?

It denies it, respond the critics. Ironically, theological emphasis on the ontological necessity of maleness for incarnation is not in accord with foundational theological formulations of the early church, which emphasized Christ's humanity, not his maleness, as necessary for human salvation. In the late fourth century, toward the end of an Arian challenge to Christ's full divinity and in the early stages of subsequent Christological controversies, Gregory of Nazianzus insisted that "what has not been assumed has not been redeemed." He was building on a much longer tradition of Christian theologians' repudiation of docetism (the belief that Jesus Christ was not truly or fully human but only appeared to be such) as well as Arianism (the belief that Jesus Christ, while greater than human, is subordinate to and not consubstantial with God the Father). What is not assumed by God in a true, full incarnation—human nature—is not redeemed. If Christ has not taken on *human* nature, *human beings* (both male and female) cannot be saved. While it is highly unlikely that Gregory ever anticipated modern feminist theologians citing his work to defend, for example, women's ordination, it is a relevant response to those who insist that God had to assume specifically male humanity in the incarnation; indeed, Elizabeth A. Johnson insists that it is those who hold the latter position who invite charges of heresy and even blasphemy. "While Jesus was indeed a first-century Galilean Jewish man, and thus irredeemably particular, as we all are, what transpires in the Incarnation is inclusive of the humanity of all human beings of all races and historical conditions and both genders."[59]

### *Wisdom Tradition*

A third development related to images of God and Christology is the retrieval of the Hebraic and Christian concept of divine Wisdom or Sophia (a term that is feminine in both Hebrew and Greek). It is also a development that has set off significant controversy among some mainline Christians, because its advocates are perceived as "inventing" a female God and claiming her as Christian.[60] Sophia is not, however, so much "a" God in female form as a metaphor, rooted in the Hebrew Scriptures and in early Christian theology, which uses female imagery as one perspective on God. In Hebrew Scriptures, Wisdom appears as a personification of God, the first of God's works and present at the creation, one who invites humans to seek her and hear her instruction (Proverbs 8). The Wisdom tradition, including a female personification, continued in Jewish literature of the intertestamental period and was picked up by the Jewish scholar Philo and identified with the philosophical concept of the Logos, functioning in a similar way in God's creation of and manifestation in the world. Wisdom influences are also present in the New Testament, where Jesus is portrayed in parts of the gospels as a teacher of wisdom and in the identification of Sophia, the Logos, and Jesus Christ.

> Most influential of all for the later Christian tradition, the prologue of the Gospel of John uses the language of Sophia to describe the Word (Logos). Everything John says of the Logos could be said of Sophia except for the identification of the Logos as God. The substitution of the masculine "Logos" for the feminine "Sophia" may have been inspired by the maleness of Jesus, by the desire to parallel Genesis 1:1, or by an effort to communicate with Hellenistic philosophy.[61]

Sophia, as a female personification of God's wisdom but also identified with the second person of the Trinity, continued as a theme, albeit a controversial one, in the theological debates of the early church and remained in common usage in the Eastern tradition, though her image was gradually dropped in the Western church in favor of more unambiguously male models of the divine. Thus contemporary feminist theologians who seek to retrieve and explore the image find Sophia attractive for her ancient roots and for her modern potential to "open up" gendered God language and the normative maleness of Jesus as savior. Whether such imagery will be both theologically defensible and widely accepted in the worship of the church, however, remains to be seen.

## Other Issues and Revolutionary Feminist Responses

Though highly significant, the nature of God, Christology, and God-language are only a few of the topics on which reformist feminist theology challenges traditional doctrinal interpretations. Taking account of women's experiences and a broad range of women's voices impacts other issues, from theological anthropology, what it means to be human, to sacraments to the nature of the church and of salvation. Nor should it be surprising that feminist theologians differ among themselves as well as with the tradition on such topics as the meaning of the atonement. Nevertheless, virtually all agree in rejecting the dualism and hierarchy that have been so integral a part of Christian and Western tradition. Revolutionary feminist theologians agree with reformists on that rejection; however, they believe dualism and hierarchy are so intrinsic to Judaism and Christianity that attempts to purge them from the traditions are futile.

### *Religion of the Goddess*

Having come to the conclusion that Judaism and Christianity were hopelessly sexist, some women were quite comfortable simply dropping "religion" in the sense of an organized community or even personal practice. Others, however, felt a need to find an alternative, and the most self-consciously feminist was the creation or recovery of a religion of the Goddess. There was historical precedent for the attempt: in the late nineteenth and early twentieth centuries, women like Matilda Joslyn Gage and Charlotte Perkins Gilman picked up anthropological theories of an ancient matriarchy, including female images of the divine, and interpreted it as a "golden age" with values of peace, harmony, and female ascendency. Nearly a century later, revolutionary feminists are equally fascinated with the goddess figures of ancient civilizations and what they believe was a peaceful, harmonious matriarchal society preceding the rise of warlike and hierarchical patriarchies.[62] Considerable controversy has been generated over the historicity of such arguments—not in the sense of questioning the existence of significant female images of the divine in numerous ancient cultures, but over the legitimacy of movement from the existence of goddesses to assertions about female roles and power and the peaceable nature of these societies. (To be sure, projection and romanticism about a distant past are not unique to radical feminist historians. As Carol Christ notes, "While there is no convincing evidence to support the theory that the transition from God the Mother and the Goddess to God the Father and King reflects a simple transition from matriarchy to patriarchy, the widely held theory that the transition was from the orgiastic excesses of nature religion to the higher morality of a religion of covenant and history seems tainted with apologetic pleading."[63])

Similar disagreements about historicity emerge in connection with the feminist religion known as Wicca. Some of its advocates, who identify themselves as modern-day witches, believe that they have recovered a self-conscious and distinctive religious tradition of Western culture. Worshiping the divine in female form and looking to nature as the primary locus of spiritual meaning, Wicca's advocates believe that this ancient craft survived the domination of a hostile and patriarchal Christianity by going underground and has been reclaimed openly by twentieth-century feminists.[64]

Historicity is a serious issue, not only between critics and defenders of a religion of the Goddess but also among advocates of Goddess religion. Nevertheless, "historical facts" are ultimately less important to revolutionary feminists than the resources Goddess traditions offer for contemporary women's spirituality. Similarly, practitioners are comfortable with varying interpretations of the nature or even separate existence of the Goddess.

> If the simplest meaning of the Goddess symbol is an affirmation of the legitimacy and beneficence of female power, then a question immediately arises, "Is the Goddess simply female power writ large, and if so, why bother with the symbol of the Goddess at all? Or does the symbol refer to a Goddess 'out there' who is not reducible to a human potential?" The many women who have rediscovered the power of the Goddess would give three answers to this question: (1) The Goddess is divine female, a personification who can be invoked in prayer and ritual; (2) the Goddess is

> symbol of the life, death, and rebirth energy in nature and culture, in personal and communal life, and (3) the Goddess is symbol of the affirmation of the legitimacy and beauty of female power (made possible by the new becoming of women in the women's liberation movement).[65]

### *Common Themes in Revolutionary Feminst Theology*

Despite the multiplicity of the forms of Goddess religion, a multiplicity that is welcomed and celebrated by participants rather than decried, there are several common themes among revolutionary feminist theologians. First, they emphasize a female image of the divine, insisting that women can identify with the Goddess and feel affirmed by her in a way that they never can with a male deity. The Goddess further endorses female power, female creativity, female strength, and female sexuality, all of which have been denigrated or repressed in traditional patriarchal religions. Second, they encourage religious communities and rituals that are led by women, if not composed entirely of women. Some groups worship male God images as well as the central Goddess figure and allow men to join; others do not. Carol Christ argues that such diversity is understandable, as is the need many women find for a temporary or permanent female "space" in the midst of patriarchy.

> As long as patriarchal culture continues to exist, women will still need to find spaces where we can be somewhat free of patriarchal attitudes. Whether we like it or not, it remains true that in mixed groups men will often try to dominate or diffuse women's creative energy. . . . Few feminists would deny the validity of women forming groups in which women can share and articulate our spiritual visions with other women. On the other hand, I believe most women in the spirituality movement would be uncomfortable with a *purportedly universal* religion that excluded men or gave them only a subordinate role.[66]

A third common theme in revolutionary feminist theology is a strong connection to nature. Most of these writers reject or minimize ideas of divine transcendence and an otherworldly afterlife in favor of emphasis on the presence or immanence of the divine in human beings and all of nature.[67] Consequently, they have marked ecological and antinuclear concerns that, they think, are more compatible with a religion of the Goddess than with patriarchal—and fearfully heedless and destructive—Western culture. (Similar strong commitment to ecological concerns marks the work of reformist theologians like Rosemary Radford Ruether and Sallie McFague.) Finally, revolutionary feminist theologians stress the importance of personal experience for theology and spirituality and rejoice in a subsequent plurality of approaches. They are very wary of "institutionalization," understood as set structures that might duplicate the hierarchy and rigidity they rejected in Judaism and Christianity, stifle creativity and diversity, and invalidate differences of experience.

As we recover the story of women and religion in America, it is clear that change did not begin in the 1960s, that issues like biblical injunctions on women's place and female preaching have been raised (if not widely heeded) for centuries. Numerous parallels emerge: the maternal societies of the early nineteenth century that functioned in ways not unlike the women's support groups of the late twentieth century; fear of "feminism" by men and women in the nineteenth and the twentieth centuries for its perceived anti-male and anti-family "radicalism." As debates were passionately serious and divisive before, so they are now, because mainline Christian denominations in America are torn by bitter differences over sexuality, abortion, and women's roles. Nevertheless, the women's story is one of movement (if sometimes two steps forward and one step back), a movement out of the subordinate female places enjoined on Anne Hutchinson. Even those who see themselves as anti-feminist have accepted some of the gradual changes that have occurred during America's history. Rare today would be the critic who rejected women's speaking in mixed gatherings, higher education for women, or woman suffrage. Opposition to women's religious leadership remains, but the language has changed as divinely enjoined "subordination" is replaced by arguments about "complementarity." At the same time, modern feminists have come to embrace and appreciate what their foremothers accomplished in and through traditional female roles. They are more willing to value those places, so long as these are chosen by women, not imposed upon them. Thus one central issue for the future is choice; a second is pluralism, as the diverse ideological and racial/ethnic voices within Judaism and Christianity are joined by a revitalized Native American voice and by representatives of other religious traditions, old and new.

# Notes

**Notes for chapter 1: Anne Hutchinson**

1. John Winthrop, *The History of New England from 1630 to 1649,* ed. James Savage (Boston: Phelps & Farnham, 1825), 201 (hereinafter Winthrop, *Journal*).

2. Ibid., 213–14.

3. Thomas Weld, Preface to "A Short Story of the rise, reign, and ruine of the Antinomians, Familists and Libertines, that infect the Churches of New-England" by John Winthrop, in David D. Hall, ed., *The Antinomian Controversy: 1636–1638: A Documentary History* (Middleton, Conn.: Wesleyan University Press, 1968), 203 (hereinafter Winthrop, *Short Story*).

4. Winthrop, *Journal,* 213.

5. Ibid., 240.

6. Winthrop, *Short Story,* 262.

7. "A Report of the Trial of Mrs. Anne Hutchinson before the Church in Boston," in Hall, *Controversy,* 382–83.

8. "Proceedings of the Boston Church against the Exiles," in Hall, *Controversy,* 221.

9. Richard L. Greaves, "The Role of Women in Early English Nonconformity," in Greaves, ed., *Triumph over Silence: Women in Protestant History* (Westport, Conn.: Greenwood, 1985).

10. Mary Maples Dunn, "Saints and Sisters: Congregational and Quaker Women in the Early Colonial Period," in Janet Wilson James, ed., *Women in American Religion* (Philadelphia: University of Pennsylvania Press, 1980), 30.

11. Anne Hutchinson and the Antinomian controversy have been a continuing source of fascination and controversy for American religious historians. For a good sampling of a range of views and approaches, see Francis J. Bremer, ed., *Anne Hutchinson: Troubler of the Puritan Zion* (Huntington, N.Y.: Krieger, 1981).

**Notes for chapter 2: Quakers in Colonial America**

1. For the text of Mary Dyer's letter, see George Bishop, *New England Judged by the Spirit of the Lord,* rev. ed. (London: T. Sowle, 1703), 377–80; also reprinted in part in Gerda Lerner, *The Female Experience: An American Documentary* (Indianapolis: Bobbs-Merrill, 1977), 472–74.

2. Mary Maples Dunn, "Women of Light," in Carol Ruth Berkin and Mary Beth Norton, eds., *Women of America: A History* (Boston: Houghton Mifflin, 1979), 120. See also Dunn, "Saints and Sisters: Congregational and Quaker Women in the Early Colonial Period," in Janet Wilson James, ed., *Women in American Religion* (Philadelphia: University of Pennsylvania Press, 1980). Another excellent source on Quaker women in America is Margaret Hope Bacon, *Mothers of Feminism: The Story of Quaker Women in America* (San Francisco: Harper & Row, 1986).

3. Dunn, "Women of Light," 123.

4. Bacon, *Mothers of Feminism,* 46–47.

5. Ibid., 52–53.

6. See ibid., 35–37, 68–69, for examples of Quaker women who left children behind to travel in ministry.

**Notes for chapter 3: Puritanism in America**

1. For a perceptive essay on the two images of women and a selection of primary documents, see Rosemary Skinner Keller, "New England Women: Ideology and Experience in First-Generation Puritanism (1630–1650)," in Rosemary Radford Ruether and Rosemary Skinner Keller, eds., *Women and Religion in America, vol. 2, The Colonial and Revolutionary Periods* (San Francisco: Harper & Row, 1983).

2. Carol F. Karlsen, *The Devil in the Shape of a Woman: Witchcraft in Colonial New England* (New York: W. W. Norton, 1987), 20. Besides Karlsen's excellent work, see John Putnam Demos, *Entertaining Satan: Witchcraft and the Culture of Early New England* (New York: Oxford, 1982) for another recent and comprehensive study that puts Salem in a broader context.

3. See Keller, "New England Women," 140–43, for further examples. Keller also includes an excerpt from Hibbens's church trial, 176–83.

4. Karlsen, *Shape of a Woman,* 5.

5. Ibid., 46ff; Demos, *Entertaining Satan,* 59ff.

6. Karlsen, *Shape of a Woman,* 118, 119, 128. Demos also addresses the gender issue, but his conclusion is more psychological.

7. Laurel Thatcher Ulrich, *Good Wives: Image and Reality in the Lives of Women in Northern New England, 1650–1750* (New York: Knopf, 1982) is an excellent study of the everyday lives of New England women.

8. John Cotton, "Singing of Psalms a Gospel-Ordinance, 1650," excerpted in Keller, "New England Women," 191.

9. Mary Maples Dunn, "Saints and Sisters: Congregational and Quaker Women in the Early Colonial Period," in Janet Wilson James, ed., *Women in American Religion* (Philadelphia: University of Pennsylvania Press, 1980), 33–34. The Wenham church was unusual in other practices that acknowledged women's individuality, but after Fiske moved in the mid-1650s, neither he nor the Wenham church continued such practices.

10. Ulrich, *Good Wives,* 217ff.

11. Jeannine Hensley, ed., *The Works of Anne Bradstreet,* The John Harvard Library (Cambridge, Mass.: Belknap Press of Harvard University Press, 1967), 225, 294–95.

12. Gerald F. Moran, " 'Sisters' in Christ: Women and the Church in Seventeenth-Century New England," in James, *Women in American Religion,* 60–61; Martha Tomhave Blauvelt and Rosemary Skinner Keller, "Women and Revivalism: The Puritan and Wesleyan Traditions," in Ruether and Keller, eds., *Women and Religion,* vol. 2., 317.

13. Ben Barker-Benfield, "Anne Hutchinson and the Puritan Attitude Toward Women," in Francis J. Bremer, ed., *Anne Hutchinson: Troubler of the Puritan Zion* (Huntington, N.Y.: Krieger, 1981). 110.

14. Margaret W. Masson, "The Typology of the Female as a Model for the Regenerate: Puritan Preaching, 1690–1730," *Signs* 2 (Winter 1976), 304–07.

15. Dunn, "Saints and Sisters," 35–40.

16. Barbara Leslie Epstein, *The Politics of Domesticity: Women, Evangelism, and Temperance in Nineteenth-Century America* (Middletown, Conn.: Wesleyan University Press, 1981), 27–28.

17. Moran, "'Sisters' in Christ," 55–60.

18. Cotton Mather, *Ornaments for the Daughters of Zion, or The Character and Happiness of a Vertuous Woman,* 3d ed. (Boston: 1741); facsimile reproduction (Delmar, N.Y.: Scholars' Facsimiles and Reprints, 1978), 49.

19. Cotton Mather, *Tabitha Rediviva, An Essay to Describe and Commend the Good Works of a Vertuous Woman,* excerpted in Blauvelt and Keller, "Women and Revivalism," 339. For Cotton's biblical allusion, see 1 Tim. 2:15.

20. Quoted in Lonna M. Malmsheimer, "Daughters of Zion: New England Roots of American Feminism," *The New England Quarterly* 50 (September 1977): 495.

21. See Laurel Thatcher Ulrich, "Virtuous Women Found: New England Ministerial Literature, 1668–1735," in James, *Women in American Religion;* Masson, "Typology;" Malmsheimer, "Daughters of Zion."

22. Mather, *Ornaments,* 3.

23. Ibid., 10–19.

24. John Winthrop, "A Modell of Christian Charity," excerpted in *American Christianity: An Historical Interpretation with Representative Documents,* vol. 1, *1607–1820,* eds. H. Shelton Smith, Robert T. Handy, and Lefferts A. Loetscher (New York: Charles Scribner's Sons, 1960), 99–100.

**Notes for chapter 4: Religious Diversity in Colonial America**

1. Julia Cherry Spruill, *Women's Life and Work in the Southern Colonies.* (1938; reprint, New York: W. W. Norton, 1972), 246–47.

2. Ibid., 345.

3. Joan R. Gundersen, "The Non-Institutional Church: The Religious Role of Women in Eighteenth-Century Virginia," *Historical Magazine of the Protestant Episcopal Church* 51 (December 1982): 351; Patricia U. Bonomi, *Under the Cope of Heaven: Religion, Society, and Politics in Colonial America* (New York: Oxford, 1986), 112–13.

4. Gundersen, "The Non-Institutional Church," 348.

5. Alice E. Mathews, "The Religious Experience of Southern Women," in Rosemary Radford Ruether and Rosemary Skinner Keller, eds., *Women and Religion in America,* vol. 2, *The Colonial and Revolutionary Periods* (San Francisco: Harper & Row, 1983), 194ff.

6. Gundersen, "The Non-Institutional Church," 347–49.

7. Mathews, "Southern Women," 197.

8. Jay P. Dolan, *The American Catholic Experience: A History from Colonial Times to Present* (Garden City, N.Y.: Doubleday, 1985), 94.

9. Ibid., 86–87.

10. Asuncion Lavrin, "Women and Religion in Spanish America," in Ruether and Keller, eds., *Women and Religion,* vol. 2, 43–44.

11. Ibid., 46.

12. Christine Allen, "Women in Colonial French America," in Ruether and Keller, eds., *Women and Religion,* vol. 2, 81. Allen gives both biographical sketches and excerpts from primary sources for six important individual women.

13. Laurel Thatcher Ulrich, *Good Wives: Image and Reality in the Lives of Women in Northern New England, 1650–1750* (New York: Knopf, 1982), 208–13.

14. Mary Ewens, *The Role of the Nun in Nineteenth Century America* (New York: Arno Press, 1978), 22–24. See also Cyprian Davis, *The History of Black Catholics in the United States* (New York: Crossroad, 1990), 72.

15. For Indian religion, see Jacqueline Peterson and Mary Drake, "American Indian Women and Religion," in Ruether and Keller, eds., *Women and Religion,* vol. 2. For African religion, see Albert J. Raboteau, *Slave Religion: The "Invisible Institution" in the Antebellum South* (New York: Oxford, 1978), 5–16.

16. Peterson and Drake, "American Indian Women," 6.

17. Ibid., 3–8; Lillian Ashcraft Webb, "Black Women and Religion in the Colonial Period," in Ruether and Keller, eds., *Women and Religion,* vol. 2, 223–34.

18. *Le Clercq: New Relation of Gaspersia,* excerpted in Peterson and Drake, "American Indian Women," 29.

19. See Raboteau, *Slave Religion,* 48–55, for a summary of the debate.

20. Excerpted in Edwin S. Gaustad, ed., *A Documentary History of Religion in America: To the Civil War* (Grand Rapids, Mich.: Eerdmans, 1982), 187.

21. Webb, "Black Women," 235–37; Gundersen, "The Non-Institutional Church," 351.

22. Quoted in Raboteau, *Slave Religion,* 104.

23. Webb, "Black Women," 237.

24. Excerpted in Allen, "Colonial French America," 123.

25. The conclusion that Wheatley "sold out" her blackness is reported but not shared by John C. Shields, preface to *The Collected Works of Phillis Wheatley* (New York: Oxford, 1988), xxvii. (Hereinafter *Works.*) See also Charles W. Akers, "'Our Modern Egyptians': Phillis Wheatley and the Whig Campaign against Slavery in Revolutionary Boston," in Darlene Clark Hine, ed., *Black Women in United States History,* vol. 1 (Brooklyn, N.Y.: Carlson Publishing Co., 1990), 1–14; and R. Lynn Matson, "Phillis Wheatley—Soul Sister?" in Hine, *Black Women,* vol. 3, 913–21.

26. Shields, *Works,* 18.

27. See, for example, the poem "On the Death of General Wooster" (*Works,* 149–50) and "Letter to Samson Occam," 1774 (*Works,* 176–77).

28. Pocahontas, the young Indian girl whose dramatic intervention to save Captain John Smith made her one of the most famous women in the folklore of American colonial history, was later instructed in Christianity and baptized before her marriage to a Virginia colonist, John Rolfe. Like Kateri Tekakwitha and Phillis Wheatley, her acceptance by white colonists and subsequent historical recognition were gained at the price of separation from much of her cultural heritage, but it is less clear how important Christianity as a religion was to her personally, beyond the fact that she was baptized, married, and buried in the Church of England.

## Notes for chapter 5: The Great Awakening

1. Sydney E. Ahlstrom, *A Religious History of the American People* (New Haven, Conn.: Yale University Press, 1972), 315.

2. Donald G. Mathews, *Religion in the Old South*, (Chicago: University of Chicago Press, 1977), 20. In New England, on the other hand, the Great Awakening does not appear to have followed class lines in any significant or consistent way.

3. Albert J. Raboteau, *Slave Religion: The "Invisible Institution" in the Antebellum South* (New York: Oxford, 1978), 149.

4. See Lillian Ashcraft Webb, "Black Women and Religion in the Colonial Period," in Rosemary Radford Ruether and Rosemary Skinner Keller, eds., *Women and Religion in America*, vol. 2, *The Colonial and Revolutionary Periods* (San Francisco: Harper & Row, 1983), 251–52.

5. See Raboteau, *Slave Religion*, 133–35.

6. Martha Tomhave Blauvelt and Rosemary Skinner Keller, "Women and Revivalism: The Puritan and Wesleyan Traditions," in Ruether and Keller, eds., *Women and Religion*, vol. 2, 319; Donald Mathews, *Religion*, 37; Joan R. Gundersen, "The Non-Institutional Church: The Religious Role of Women in Eighteenth-Century Virginia," *HIstorical Magazine of the Protestant Episcopal Church* 51 (December 1982): 355; William L. Lumpkin, "The Role of Women in 18th Century Virginia Baptist Life," *Baptist History and Heritage* 8 (1973): 158, 160.

7. Barbara Leslie Epstein, *The Politics of Domesticity: Women, Evangelism, and Temperance in Nineteenth-Century America* (Middletown, Conn.: Wesleyan University Press, 1981), 14.

8. Ibid., 37–41; see also Blauvelt and Keller, "Women and Revivalism," 320.

9. Blauvelt and Keller, 327; Gerald F. Moran, "'The Hidden Ones': Women and Religion in Puritan New England," in Richard L. Greaves, ed., *Triumph over Silence: Women in Protestant History* (Westport, Conn.: Greenwood, 1985), 132–33.

10. See Lumpkin, "The Role of Women," 161–64.

11. Quoted in Frank Baker, "Susanna Wesley: Puritan, Parent, Pastor, Protagonist, Pattern," in Rosemary Skinner Keller, Louise L. Queen, and Hilah F. Thomas, eds., *Women in New Worlds: Historical Perspectives on the Wesleyan Tradition*, vol. 2 (Nashville: Abingdon, 1982), 125.

12. Excerpted in Blauvelt and Keller, "Women and Revivalism," 346. Emphasis added.

13. *The Life of the Reverend Devereux Jarratt*, excerpted in Alice E. Mathews, "The Religious Experience of Southern Women," in Ruether and Keller, eds., *Women and Religion*, vol. 2, 215.

14. Lumpkin, "The Role of Women," 161–63; Gundersen, "The Non-Institutional Church," 355.

15. Sarah Osborn to the Reverend Joseph Fish, February 28–March 7, 1767, reprinted in Mary Beth Norton, "'My Resting Reaping Times': Sarah Osborn's Defense of Her 'Unfeminine' Activities, 1767," *Signs* 2 (Winter 1976): 523. Norton's article emphasizes Fish's criticism, while Barbara E. Lacey, "The Bonds of Friendship: Sarah Osborn of Newport and the Reverend Joseph Fish of North Stonington, 1743–1779," *Rhode Island History* 45 (November 1986): 127–36, argues that in the

light of the entire correspondence, Fish was generally supportive of Osborn and her activities, and that he accepted her defense of what she did. Charles E. Hambrick-Stowe, "The Spiritual Pilgrimage of Sarah Osborn (1714–1796)," *Church History* 61 (December 1992): 408–21, gives less attention to Osborn's "conflicts" with Fish and her neighbors, focusing instead on her theology, which was rooted in classic Puritan themes, affirmed the Great Awakening's contribution, and looked forward to developments of the Second Great Awakening.

16. Osborn, reprinted in Norton, "Reaping Times," 528.

17. *Seasonable Thoughts on the State of Religion in New England*, quoted in Raboteau, *Slave Religion*, 129.

18. Webb, "Black Women," 239.

19. Alice E. Mathews, "Southern Women," 200, 228–30.

## Notes for chapter 6: The Ideal American Woman

1. Judith Sargent Murray, "On The Equality of the Sexes," excerpted in Rosemary Radford Ruether and Rosemary Skinner Keller, eds., *Women and Religion, in America*, vol. 2, *The Colonial and Revolutionary Periods* (San Francisco: Harper & Row, 1983), 399–400.

2. Two major and illuminating studies of women in this period are Linda K. Kerber, *Women of the Republic: Intellect and Ideology in Revolutionary America* (Chapel Hill, N.C.: University of North Carolina Press, 1980); and Mary Beth Norton, *Liberty's Daughters: The Revolutionary Experience of American Women, 1750–1800* (Boston: Little, Brown and Co., 1980).

3. Kerber, *Women of the Republic*, 200.

4. Barbara Welter, "The Cult of True Womanhood, 1820–1860," *American Quarterly* 18 (Summer 1966): 151–74. Since 1966, there has been a burst of scholarship on the "cult of true womanhood" or "cult of domesticity" that has expanded and modified the concept, but the main lines of Welter's formulation remain valuable. See, for example, Nancy F. Cott, *The Bonds of Womanhood: 'Woman's Sphere' in New England, 1780–1835* (New Haven, Conn.: Yale University Press, 1977); Barbara Leslie Epstein, *The Politics of Domesticity: Women, Evangelism, and Temperance in Nineteenth-Century America* (Middletown, Conn.: Wesleyan University Press, 1981). Barbara J. Berg, *The Remembered Gate: Origins of American Feminism. The Woman and the City, 1800–1860* (New York: Oxford, 1978); Mary P. Ryan, *Cradle of the Middle Class: The Family in Oneida County, New York, 1780–1865* (Cambridge: Cambridge University Press, 1981).

5. James Fordyce, "Sermons to Young Women," excerpted in Rosemary Radford Ruether and Rosemary Skinner Keller, *Women and Religion in America*, vol. 1, *The Nineteenth Century* (San Francisco: Harper & Row, 1981), 13.

6. Donald G. Mathews, *Religion in the Old South* (Chicago: University of Chicago Press, 1977), 111.

## Notes for chapter 7: The Second Great Awakening

1. See Mary P. Ryan, "A Women's Awakening: Evangelical Religion and the Families of Utica, New York, 1800–1840," in Janet Wilson James, ed., *Women in*

*American Religion,* (Philadelphia: University of Pennsylvania Press, 1980), 90–91. Ryan's study in this and her longer work, *Cradle of the Middle Class: The Family in Oneida County, New York, 1780–1865* (Cambridge: Cambridge University Press, 1981), is outstanding in its detailed demographic evidence from a specific time and place, but virtually every account of the Second Great Awakening that acknowledges gender in converts agrees on the preponderance of women.

2. Nancy F. Cott, "Young Women in the Second Great Awakening in New England," *Feminist Studies* 3 (Fall 1975): 19–29.

3. Martha Tomhave Blauvelt, "Women and Revivalism," in Rosemary Radford Ruether and Rosemary Skinner Keller, *Women and Religion in America,* vol. 1, *The Nineteenth Century* (San Francisco: Harper & Row, 1981), 4.

4. Ryan, "A Woman's Awakening," 91.

5. Donald G. Mathews, *Religion in the Old South* (Chicago: University of Chicago Press, 1977), 102–4.

6. See Dickson D. Bruce Jr., *And They All Sang Hallelujah: Plain-Folk Camp Meeting Religion, 1800–1845* (Knoxville, Tenn.: University of Tennessee Press, 1974), 61–95, for a detailed study of the structures of a camp meeting.

7. Leonard I. Sweet, *The Minister's Wife: Her Role in Nineteenth-Century American Evangelicalism* (Philadelphia: Temple, 1983), 161.

8. Ryan, *Cradle of the Middle Class,* 89. Maternal associations were not unique to upstate New York, but across the nation they left fewer records in general than many other female associations.

9. See Anne M. Boylan, "Evangelical Womanhood in the Nineteenth Century: The Role of Women in Sunday Schools," *Feminist Studies* 4 (October 1978): 62–80.

10. Margaret Hope Bacon, *Mothers of Feminism: The Story of Quaker Women in America* (San Francisco: Harper & Row, 1986), 80–81.

11. Nancy A. Hewitt, *Women's Activism and Social Change: Rochester, New York, 1822–1872* (Ithaca, N.Y./London: Cornell University Press, 1984), 17. In a careful study of a specific but important locale, Rochester, Hewitt distinguishes three groups of female reformers: the pioneer elite women with their benevolent approach; the "perfectionist" evangelicals influenced especially by Finney and the Second Great Awakening; and the "ultraists," made up of Quakers and other radicals, who insisted on the interrelationship of the various reforms, including women's rights.

12. Suzanne Lebsock, *The Free Women of Petersburg: Status and Culture in a Southern Town, 1784–1860* (New York/London: W. W. Norton, 1984), 196ff. Lebsock notes a number of other formal female benevolent organizations in the South of the early nineteenth century, 301.

13. Ibid., 210.

14. Carroll Smith-Rosenberg, *Religion and the Rise of the American City: The New York City Mission Movement, 1812–1870* (Ithaca/London: Cornell University Press, 1971), 43.

15. Boylan, "Evangelical Womanhood," 71.

16. Julie Roy Jeffrey, *Frontier Women: The Trans-Mississippi West, 1840–1880* (New York: Hill and Wang, 1979), 98.

17. L. DeAne Lagerquist, *From Our Mothers' Arms: A History of Women in the American Lutheran Church* (Minneapolis: Augsburg, 1987), 41.

18. Sweet, *The Minister's Wife,* 159.

19. Jeffrey, *Frontier Women*, 97–100.

20. Joan R. Gunderson, "The Local Parish as a Female Institution: The Experience of All Saints Episcopal Church in Frontier Minnesota," *Church History* 55 (September 1986): 310.

21. See Leon McBeth, *Women in Baptist Life* (Nashville: Broadman, 1979), 101–2, for a similar story of women's central role in founding the First Baptist Church of Dallas, Texas.

22. Opposition to any form of women's organization in the nineteenth century was more frequent in the South or among immigrant groups like the Lutherans in the midwest, but even there opposition was not universal. See Anne Firor Scott, *The Southern Lady: From Pedestal to Politics, 1830–1930* (Chicago: University of Chicago Press, 1970), 139–40; Lagerquist, *Mother's Arms*, 32; Lois A. Boyd and R. Douglas Brackenridge, *Presbyterian Women in America: Two Centuries of a Quest for Status* (Westport, Conn.: Greenwood, 1983), 8, 207ff.

23. Sweet, *The Minister's Wife*, 3.

24. See ibid., 3–11, for a summary of the four models.

25. Ibid., 99.

26. See Julie Roy Jeffrey, "Ministry Through Marriage: Methodist Clergy Wives on the Trans-Mississippi Frontier," in *Women in New Worlds*, vol. 1, ed. Hilah F. Thomas and Rosemary Skinner Keller (Nashville: Abingdon, 1981), 146ff, for the contrast between what male authorities saw as the limits of wifely activities and the actual conduct of ministers' wives. Jeffrey concludes, "The boundary between female 'lay' and male 'clerical' efforts was, in practice, often hazy . . . [and] some clergy wives encroached upon . . . male prerogatives" (153).

## Notes for chapter 8: The Foreign Missionary Movement

1. Rosemary Skinner Keller, "Lay Women in the Protestant Tradition," in Rosemary Radford Ruether and Rosemary Skinner Keller, *Women and Religion in America*, vol. 1, *The Nineteenth Century* (San Francisco: Harper & Row, 1981), 242.

2. R. Pierce Beaver, *All Loves Excelling: American Protestant Women in World Mission* (Grand Rapids, Mich.: Eerdmans, 1968), 47–48.

3. On Ann Hasseltine Judson, see Joan Jacobs Brumberg, *Mission for Life: The Story of the Family of Adoniram Judson*. (New York: Free Press/Macmillan, 1980), especially chap. 4, "The Apostolate of Women."

4. Elizabeth Alden Green, *Mary Lyon and Mount Holyoke: Opening the Gates* (Hanover, N. H.: University Press of New England, 1979), 252.

5. Ibid., 264.

6. Jane Hunter, *The Gospel of Gentility: American Women Missionaries in Turn-of-the-Century China* (New Haven, Conn.: Yale University Press, 1984), 112. See also Patricia Grimshaw's discussion of missionary mothers in Hawaii, "'Christian Woman, Pious Wife, Faithful Mother, Devoted Missionary': Conflicts in Roles of American Missionary Women in Nineteenth Century Hawaii," *Feminist Studies* 9 (Fall 1983): 489–521.

7. Helen Barrett Montgomery, *Western Women in Eastern Lands: An Outline Study of Fifty Years of Woman's Work in Foreign Missions* (1910; reprint, New York: Garland, 1987), 24.

8. Ann White cites nearly 100 single women sent out by mission boards before 1870, still far fewer than missionary wives but more than the "handful" identified by earlier historians. "Counting the Cost of Faith: America's Early Female Missionaries," *Church History* 57 (March 1988): 22.

9. Ibid., 26.

10. Mary Sudman Donovan, *A Different Call: Women's Ministries in the Episcopal Church, 1850–1920* (Wilton, Conn.: Morehouse-Barlow, 1986), 68.

11. Beaver, *All Loves Excelling*, 101.

12. Montgomery, *Western Women*, 38.

13. Ibid.

14. Elaine Magalis, *Conduct Becoming to a Woman: Bolted Doors and Burgeoning Missions* (New York: United Methodist Church, Board of Global Ministries, Women's Division, 1973), 35.

15. Excerpted in Ruether and Keller, *Women and Religion*, vol. 1, 285. Although the article's author was surely not conscious of the implications, the choice of roles ("sister" and "wife") rather than "a person" to epitomize female dignity is a telling sign of assumptions.

16. See Patricia R. Hill, *The World Their Household: The American Women's Foreign Mission Movement and Cultural Transformation, 1870–1920* (Ann Arbor, Mich.: University of Michigan Press, 1985), especially chap. 5; and Ann White, "Counting the Cost of Faith," 19–30, for interpretations that stress a change of focus within the women's movement.

17. For a thorough discussion of Lottie Moon's career and impact on Southern Baptists, see Irwin T. Hyatt Jr., *Our Ordered Lives Confess: Three Nineteenth-Century American Missionaries in East Shantung* (Cambridge, Mass.: Harvard University Press, 1976), 63–136.

18. Beaver, *All Loves Excelling*, 173.

19. Barbara Welter, "She Hath Done What She Could: Protestant Women's Missionary Careers in Nineteenth-Century America," in Janet Wilson James, ed., *Women in American Religion* (Philadelphia: University of Pennsylvania Press, 1980), 121.

20. Shirley S. Garrett, "Sisters All: Feminism and the American Women's Missionary Movement," in *Missionary Ideologies in the Imperialist Era, 1880–1920*, ed. Torben Christensen and William R. Hutchinson (Arhus, Denmark: Aros, 1982), 225. See also Joan Jacobs Brumberg, "The Ethnological Mirror: American Evangelical Women and their Heathen Sisters, 1870–1910," in *Women and the Structure of Society*, ed. Barbara J. Harris and JoAnn K. MacNamara (Durham, N. C.: Duke University Press, 1984); Adrian A. Bennett, "Doing More Than They Intended: Southern Methodist Women in China, 1878–1898" in *Women in New Worlds*, vol. 2, eds. Hilah F. Thomas and Rosemary Skinner Keller (Nashville: Abingdon, 1981); and Jane Hunter, *The Gospel of Gentility*, on the cultural imperialism of women missionaries.

21. For analyses of these reforms that cover both missionary and indigenous contributions, see S. Cromwell Crawford, *Ram Mohun Roy: Social, Political and Religious Reform in 19th Century India* (New York: Paragon House Publishers, 1987), 101–15, 222–30, on female infanticide and sati (suttee); Bernice J. Lee, "Female Infanticide in China," in *Women in China: Current Directions in Historical Scholarship*, ed. Richard W. Guisso and Stanley Johannesen, *Historical Reflections/Réflectiones Historiqus* 8 (Fall 1981): 163–77; and Alison R. Drucker, "The

Influence of Western Women on the Anti-Footbinding Movement, 1840–1911," in Lee, *Women in China,* 179–99.

22. Welter, "She Hath Done What She Could," 124.

23. Magalis, *Conduct Becoming to a Woman,* 29–30.

24. Quoted in Barbara Brown Zikmund and Sally A. Dries, "Women's Work and Woman's Boards," in *Hidden Histories in the United Church of Christ,* ed. Barbara Brown Zikmund (New York.: United Church Press, 1984), 148.

25. Brumberg, "The Ethnological Mirror," 115.

26. Marjorie King, "Exporting Femininity, Not Feminism: Nineteenth-Century U.S. Missionary Women's Efforts to Emancipate Chinese Women," in *Women's Work for Women: Missionaries and Social Change in Asia,* ed. Leslie A. Flemming (Boulder, Co./San Francisco/London: Westview Press, 1989), 124.

27. Garrett, "Sisters All," 228.

28. See, for example, Hunter, *The Gospel of Gentility,* especially chap. 7, on China; and Leslie Flemming, "New Models, New Roles: U.S. Presbyterian Women Missionaries and Social Change in North India, 1870–1910," in *Women's Work for Women.*

29. See articles cited above by Flemming on India and King on China.

30. Jane Hunter, "The Home and the World: The Missionary Message of U.S. Domesticity," in *Women's Work for Women,* 164.

31. Ibid., 165.

## Notes for chapter 9: Reform Movements

1. See, for example, Phillida Bunkle, "Sentimental Womanhood and Domestic Education, 1830–1870," *History of Education Quarterly* 14 (Spring 1974): 13–30.

2. Catharine E. Beecher, *Suggestions Respecting Improvements in Education, Presented to the Trustees of the Hartford Female Seminary, and Published at Their Request* (Hartford, Conn.: Packard and Butler, 1829), 4–6.

3. Catherine E. Beecher, *The Duty of American Women to Their Country* (New York: Harper and Brothers, 1845), 61–62.

4. Anne Firor Scott, "The Ever-Widening Circle: The Diffusion of Feminist Values from the Troy Female Seminary, 1822–72," in *Making the Invisible Woman Visible* (Urbana, Ill.: University of Illinois Press, 1984), 73ff; Elizabeth Alden Green, *Mary Lyon and Mount Holyoke: Opening the Gates* (Hanover, N.H.: University of New England, 1979), 264ff.

5. Polly Welts Kaufman, *Women Teachers on the Frontier* (New Haven, Conn.: Yale University Press, 1984), 17.

6. Julie Roy Jeffrey, *Frontier Women: The Trans-Mississippi West, 1840–1880* (New York: Hill and Wang, 1979), 93.

7. Mary P. Ryan, "The Power of Women's Networks: A Case Study in Female Moral Reform in Antebellum America," *Feminist Studies* 5 (Spring 1979): 67.

8. Carroll Smith-Rosenberg, *Religion and the Rise of the American City: The Rise of the New York City Mission Movement, 1812–1870* (Ithaca and London: Cornell University Press, 1971), 111. See also Smith-Rosenberg's article, "Beauty, the Beast, and the Militant Woman: A Case Study in Sex Roles and Social Stress in Jackson-

ian America," *Disorderly Conduct: Visions of Gender in Victorian America* (New York: Alfred A. Knopf, 1985), 109–29.

9. See, for example, Margaret Prior's account of her visits with New York's unfortunate "fallen women" in her diary, excerpted in Rosemary Radford Ruether and Rosemary Skinner Keller, eds., *Women and Religion in America,* vol. 1, *The Nineteenth Century* (San Francisco: Harper & Row, 1981), 322–24. The female moral reformers' image of the prostitute as victim had elements of accuracy, insofar as women were more limited in their options for economic self-support and more vulnerable to social condemnation for sexual activity outside marriage than men, yet the image could also be overly narrow and misleading, overlooking the complexity of motives and experiences among prostitutes. See Barbara Meil Hobson, *Uneasy Virtue: The Politics of Prostitution and the American Reform Tradition* (New York: Basic Books, Inc., 1967), 49–76.

10. Quoted in Smith-Rosenberg, *Religion and the Rise of the American City,* 106.

11. Smith-Rosenberg, "Beauty, the Beast, and the Militant Woman," 118.

12. Ibid., 115–16.

13. Quoted in ibid., 125.

14. Ibid., 126.

15. Ryan, "The Power of Women's Networks," 73–74.

16. Smith-Rosenberg, *Religion and the Rise of the American City,* 203ff.

17. See David J. Pivar, *Purity Crusade: Sexual Morality and Social Control, 1868–1900* (Westport, Conn.: Greenwood, 1973) for an account of the postwar movement.

18. Ibid., 167, 169.

19. Ibid., 172.

20. Ibid., 115, 165.

21. Ibid., 104–5.

22. Jed Dannenbaum, *Drink and Disorder: Temperance Reform in Cincinnati from the Washingtonian Revival to the WCTU* (Urbana, Ill./Chicago: University of Illinois Press, 1984), 34.

23. Ibid., 188.

24. Alice Felt Tylor, *Freedom's Ferment: Phases of American Social History from the Colonial Period to the Outbreak of the Civil War* (New York: Harper & Row, 1944), 448–49.

25. Elizabeth Cazden, *Antoinette Brown Blackwell: A Biography* (Old Westbury, N.Y.: Feminist Press, 1983), 80.

26. Jack S. Blocker Jr., *"Give to the Wind Thy Fears": The Woman's Temperance Crusade, 1873–1874* (Westport, Conn./London: Greenwood, 1985), challenges the "myth" that Hillsboro was the "cradle" of the crusade as Frances Willard and most subsequent historians have asserted. Rather, he argues, the crusade began in Fredonia, Ohio, a week earlier under similar circumstances (11, 27).

27. In one incident in 1854, a lawyer named Abraham Lincoln defended nine women from Marion, Ohio, against charges of saloon destruction by arguing that the Boston Tea Party was "a moral precedent for their action." Dannenbaum, *Drink and Disorder,* 198.

28. Ibid., 204.

29. Susan Dye Lee, "Evangelical Domesticity: The Woman's Temperance Crusade of 1873–1874," in Rosemary Skinner Keller, Louise L. Queen, and Hilah F. Thomas, eds. *Women in New Worlds: Historical Perspectives on the Wesleyan Tradition,* vol. 1, (Nashville: Abingdon, 1982), 299–300.

30. Ruth Bordin, *Women and Temperance: The Quest for Power and Liberty, 1873–1900* (Philadelphia: Temple University Press, 1981), 29.

31. In analyzing "why women marched," Blocker concludes that a primary cause of the crusade was exactly what the women said it was: "They were directly threatened by the sale of liquor to their husbands, brothers, and sons" (Blocker, *"Give to the Wind,"* 93). Barbara Epstein, on the other hand, argues that consumption of alcohol had in fact declined since the earlier decades of the nineteenth century and that few women crusaders had been directly hurt by male drinking. *The Politics of Domesticity: Women, Evangelism, and Temperance in Nineteenth-Century America* (Middletown, Conn.: Wesleyan University Press, 1981), 101–7. However widespread the women's immediate suffering from drinking men may have been, it did exist. Nor need their suffering have been due to a male family member's intemperance. Matilda Carse, who later was a leader of the WCTU in Chicago, lost a young son when he was run over by a drunken cart driver (Bordin, *Women and Temperance,* 143).

32. Epstein, *The Politics of Domesticity,* 100–14. Dannenbaum also sees elements of ethnocentrism and social control in the crusade (*Drink and Disorder,* 222–6) but is more skeptical about whether women's anger at liquor dealers and sympathy for women victims should be generalized to broad "anti-male·feelings" (185).

33. Bordin, *Women and Temperance,* 32–33.

34. Ibid., xviii.

35. See ibid., 78–88, on the WCTU and black and immigrant women.

36. Ibid., 52.

37. Ibid., 61.

38. Ibid., 103.

39. In this section the focus is primarily on white women, and the story of black women and the antislavery cause will be told later. It is important, nevertheless, to emphasize that black men and women were actors in the movement, not merely the passive objects of white benevolence or abuse.

40. Blanche Glassman Hersh, "To Make the World Better: Protestant Women in the Abolitionist Movement," in Richard L. Greaves, ed., *Triumph over Silence: Women in Protestant History* (Westport, Conn.: Greenwood, 1985), 176–77.

41. Quoted in Eleanor Flexner, *Century of Struggle: The Woman's Rights Movement in the United States* (New York: Athenaeum, 1973), 46.

42. Sarah M. Grimké, *Letters on the Equality of the Sexes and the Condition of Women* (1838; reprint, Source Book Press, 1970), 4, 16.

43. Hersh, "To Make the World Better," 186.

44. See ibid., 188ff.

45. Quoted in Elizabeth Clark and Herbert Richardson, *Women and Religion: A Feminist Sourcebook of Christian Thought,* (New York: Harper & Row, 1977), 207.

46. Angelina Emily Grimké, *Appeal to the Christian Women of the South* (1836; reprint, New York: Arno Press, 1969), 16, 26.

47. Charles Edward Stowe, *Life of Harriet Beecher Stowe, Compiled from Her Letters and Journals* (Boston/New York: Houghton, Mifflin and Company, 1889), 145.

48. Ibid., 198–99.

49. *Uncle Tom's Cabin,* chap. 9. For a thoughtful discussion of this chapter, see Jeanne Boydston, Mary Kelley, and Anne Margolis, *The Limits of Sisterhood: The Beecher Sisters on Women's Rights and Woman's Sphere* (Chapel Hill, N.C./London: University of North Carolina Press, 1988), chap. 6.

50. *Uncle Tom's Cabin,* chap. 45, "Concluding Remarks."

51. Anne Firor Scott, "Women's Perspective on the Patriarchy in the 1850s," in *Making the Invisible Woman Visible,* 182.

52. Ibid., 180ff. Donald G. Mathews, *Religion in the Old South* (Chicago: University of Chicago Press, 1970), 184, also argues that women were more critical of slavery than were men, and Suzanne Lebsock, testing that thesis against the records of Petersburg, discovered that women were more likely than men to free slaves or restrict the break-up of slave families (Lebsock, *The Free Women of Petersburg: Status and Culture in a Southern Town, 1784–1860* [New York and London: W. W. Norton, 1984], 137).

53. See Thomas F. Gossett, *Uncle Tom's Cabin and American Culture* (Dallas: Southern Methodist University Press, 1985), 185–211, for Southern reaction to *Uncle Tom's Cabin.*

54. See Dorothy C. Bass, "'In Christian Firmness and Christian Meekness': Feminism and Pacifism in Antebellum America," in Clarissa W. Atkinson, Constance H. Buchanan, and Margaret R. Miles, eds., *Immaculate and Powerful: The Female in Sacred Image and Social Reality.* Harvard Women's Studies in Religion Series. (Boston: Beacon Press, 1985), 201–25, for the interrelationship of abolitionism, women's rights, and pacifism.

55. Margaret Hope Bacon, *Mothers of Feminism: The Story of Quaker Women in America* (San Francisco: Harper & Row, 1986), 123.

56. Jacqueline Jones, *Soldiers of Light and Love: Northern Teachers and Georgia Blacks, 1865–1873,* (Chapel Hill, N.C.: University of North Carolina Press, 1980), 14.

57. Ibid., 9, 153ff.

58. Evelyn Brooks Higginbotham, *Righteous Discontent: The Women's Movement in the Black Baptist Church, 1880–1920* (Cambridge, Mass.: Harvard University Press, 1993), 119. See Higginbotham's chap. 4, "Unlikely Sisterhood," for the story of the cooperation and tensions between northern white and southern black Baptist women during this period.

### Notes for chapter 10: Women's Religious Leadership in the Nineteenth and Early Twentieth Centuries

1. William L. Andrews, ed., "Introduction," in *Sisters of the Spirit: Three Black Women's Autobiographies of the Nineteenth Century* (Bloomington, Ind.: Indiana University Press, 1986), 6. Jarena Lee's autobiography is one of those included in this volume, along with Zilpha Elaw and Julia A. J. Foote. Because black women preachers' experiences were both similar to and different from those of white

Protestant women in nineteenth-century America, they will be covered more fully in chapter 13.

2. Almond H. Davis, *The Female Preacher, or Memoir of Salome Lincoln, afterwards the Wife of Elder Junia S. Mowry* (1843; reprint, New York: Arno, 1972).

3. Palmer frequently described the events of 1837 in her later writings. See, for example, selections from her memoirs in Thomas C. Oden, ed., *Phoebe Palmer: Selected Writings* (New York: Paulist, 1988), 107–30.

4. Charles Edward White, *The Beauty of Holiness: Phoebe Palmer as Theologian, Revivalist, Feminist, and Humanitarian* (Grand Rapids, Mich.: Francis Asbury Press, Zondervan, 1986), 23. The congruence of Palmer's altar theology with traditional Wesleyan doctrine was a matter of debate in her own time and since by historians and theologians, but she believed she was being true to Wesley, and her preaching convinced many others of the effectiveness of her theological formulations. See White, chap. 5, "Phoebe Palmer as Theologian," for a summary and assessment of her theology and its roots.

5. Oden, *Phoebe Palmer,* 165.

6. White, *The Beauty of Holiness,* 177.

7. Phoebe Palmer, "Tongue of Fire on the Daughters of the Lord," in Oden, *Phoebe Palmer,* 33–34. "Tongue of Fire" is Palmer's own shorter version of *Promise of the Father; or, A Neglected Specialty of the Last Days* (1859; reprint, Salem, Ohio: Schmul Publishers, 1981). Published first in 1869, ten years after *Promise of the Father,* "Tongue of Fire" is included in its entirety in Oden.

8. Palmer, "Tongue of Fire," in Oden, *Phoebe Palmer,* 38.

9. Ibid., 42.

10. White, *The Beauty of Holiness,* 196. Palmer's status as a "feminist" is thus assessed differently by contemporary scholars, in part because of different definitions of feminism. See, for example, White, 187–206; Theodore Hovet, "Phoebe Palmer's 'Altar Phraseology' and the Spiritual Dimension of Woman's Sphere," *Journal of Religion* 63 (July 1983): 264–80; Nancy A. Hardesty, "Minister as Prophet? Or as Mother?" in Rosemary Skinner Keller, Louise L. Queen, and Hilah F. Thomas, eds., *Women in New Worlds: Historical Perspectives on the Wesleyan Tradition,* vol. 1, (Nashville: Abingdon, 1982), 88–101.

11. Elizabeth Cazden, *Antoinette Brown Blackwell: A Biography* (Old Westbury, N.Y.: Feminist Press, 1983), 41.

12. Luther Lee, "Woman's Right to Preach the Gospel," in *Five Sermons and a Tract,* ed. Donald W. Dayton (Chicago: Holrad House, 1975), 80.

13. Ibid., 99.

14. Cazden, *Antoinette Brown Blackwell,* 52.

15. Frances Willard, *Woman in the Pulpit* (Chicago: Woman's Temperance Publication Association, 1889), 94. Willard failed to include the women "officers" of the Salvation Army, who preached and functioned as clergy, following in the footsteps of the Army's cofounder, Catherine Booth. Booth herself was emboldened to preach by the example of Phoebe Palmer and wrote "Female Ministry: Woman's Right to Preach the Gospel" in 1859. The Salvation Army came to America in 1880.

16. See Bacon, *Mothers of Feminism: The Story of Quaker Women in America* (San Francisco: Harper & Row, 1986), chap. 11.

17. Virginia Lieson Brereton and Christa Ressmeyer Klein, "American Women

in Ministry: A History of Protestant Beginning Points," in Janet Wilson James, ed., *Women in American Religion* (Philadelphia: University of Pennsylvania Press, 1980), 183.

18. Antoinette Brown's ordination was questioned by some Congregational authorities at the time, and Luther Lee later refused to give her a certificate of ordination, whereas Olympia Brown was ordained with "full denominational authority." See Cazden, *Antoinette Brown Blackwell,* 83–84; and Russell E. Miller, *The Larger Hope: The First Century of the Universalist Church in America, 1770–1870* (Boston: Unitarian Universalist Association, 1979), 551.

19. Several other women who were ordained Universalist ministers became prominent public figures, including Augusta Jane Chapin, Phoebe Hanaford, and Caroline Soule. See Miller, *The Larger Hope,* 546–59, on Universalist women ministers. Brief biographies can also be found in David Robinson, "Part Two: A Biographical Dictionary of Unitarian and Universalist Leaders," *The Unitarians and the Universalists* (Westport, Conn.: Greenwood, 1985); and in the volumes edited by Edward T. James, Janet Wilson James, and Paul S. Boyer, *Notable American Women, 1607–1950: A Biographical Dictionary* (Cambridge, Mass.: Belknap Press of Harvard University Press, 1971).

20. Janet S. Everhart, "Maggie Newton Van Cott: The Methodist Episcopal Church Considers the Question of Women Clergy," in Keller, et al., eds., *Women in New Worlds,* vol. 2, 309–10.

21. See Barbara Brown Zikmund, "Winning Ordination for Women in Mainstream Protestant Churches," in Rosemary Radford Ruether and Rosemary Skinner Keller, eds., *Women and Religion in America,* vol. 3, *1900–1968* (San Francisco: Harper & Row, 1986), 340–42, on Methodists. Several articles in Keller, et al., eds., *Women in New Worlds,* vol. 1, deal with the institutional status of women, including laity rights and ordination, in various branches of American Methodism.

22. For an excellent summary of pro and con arguments in the nineteenth century, as well as a selection of illuminating primary sources, see Barbara Brown Zikmund, "The Struggle for the Right to Preach," in Rosemary Radford Ruether and Rosemary Skinner Keller, *Women and Religion in America,* vol. 1, *The Nineteenth Century* (San Francisco: Harper & Row, 1981).

23. Willard, *Woman in the Pulpit,* raises such arguments on several occasions. See, for example, 46ff. and 65–67, and chap. 7, where Willard includes a critique by one male authority, L. T. Townsend, of the attack by another male minister, Henry J. Van Dyke (chap. 6), on an earlier publication of Willard's arguments in chap. 2.

24. Hardesty's comparison of Palmer and Willard in "Minister as Prophet? Or as Mother?" in Keller, et al., eds., *Women in New Worlds,* clearly favors Palmer's prophet model. Yet Palmer herself frequently endorsed domestic roles for women, despite her insistence on the exception of preaching, and she was not an advocate of ordination or the pastoral ministry as a profession for women, as Willard was.

25. Willard, *Woman in the Pulpit,* 96.

26. For example, four women were elected locally as delegates to the General Convention of the Methodist Episcopal Church, North in 1888, including Frances Willard, but they were not accepted as such. Leon McBeth notes that some local Southern Baptist churches allowed women to vote in the late nineteenth century,

but they were not allowed to be delegates to conventions (*Women in Baptist Life* [Nashville: Broadman, 1979], 107). The Episcopal Diocese of Minnesota allowed women to vote in parish meetings in 1896, but they could not serve on the vestry. Joan R. Gundersen, "Parallel Churches?: Women and the Episcopal Church, 1850–1980," *Mid-America: An Historical Review* 69 (April–July 1987): 91. Lois A. Boyd and R. Douglas Brackenridge report some local exceptions in the nineteenth century, especially among Cumberland Presbyterians (*Presbyterian Women in America: Two Centuries of a Quest for Status* [Westport, Conn.: Greenwood, 1983], 96–97, 114–17).

27. Brereton and Klein, "American Women in Ministry," 182.

28. See Boyd and Brackenridge, *Presbyterian Women*, 109–12, on Presbyterians. Ruth W. Rasche, "The Deaconess Sisters: Pioneer Professional Women," in Barbara Brown Zikmund, ed., *Hidden Histories in the United Church of Christ* (New York: United Church Press, 1984), 95–109, discusses deaconesses in the Evangelical Synod and the German Reformed Church, two roots of the present United Church of Christ. C[hristian] Golder, *History of the Deaconess Movement in the Christian Church* (Cincinnati: Jennings & Pye; New York: Eaton & Mains, 1903), gives a comprehensive survey of deaconess institutions among Protestants in the United States at the turn of the twentieth century.

29. Frederick S. Weiser, *Serving Love: Chapters in the Early History of the Diaconate in American Lutheranism* (B. D. thesis, Lutheran Theological Seminary, Gettysburg, Penn.: May 1960), 73.

30. Ibid., 82–83.

31. L. De Ane Lagerquist, *From Our Mothers' Arms: A History of Women in the American Lutheran Church* (Minneapolis: Augsburg, 1987), 67.

32. The conference was in some ways typical of the deaconess movement among American Lutherans: Until 1914, all of the formal papers were given by men (Weiser, *Serving Love*, 132). Similarly, men initiated and directed the establishment of the diaconate in every case except Brooklyn under Sister Fedde (Weiser, 76).

33. A 1910 conference report shows 220 out of 275 deaconesses working as nurses (Ibid., 143).

34. Ibid., 121, 133.

35. Ibid., 128–40.

36. Mary Sudman Donovan, *A Different Call: Women's Ministries in the Episcopal Church, 1850–1920* (Wilton, Conn.: Morehouse-Barlow, 1986), 43. See 43–47 for a list of "Episcopal Religious Orders for Women, 1900, with Institutions Committed to Their Care."

37. Ibid., 105.

38. Lucy Rider Meyer, the leading figure in the Methodist deaconess movement in America, not only insisted on the importance of the distinction as she observed the Episcopalians, she was rather critical of the sisterhoods' "retired, and, we believe, sometimes sentimental and morbid, life possible therein; . . ." *Deaconesses, Biblical, Early Church, European, American, with the Story of How the Work Began in the Chicago Training School, for City, Home, and Foreign Missions, and the Chicago Deaconess Home*. 3d ed. (Cincinnati: Cranston and Stowe; New York: Hunt & Eaton, 1889), 58.

39. Donovan, *A Different Call*, 89.

40. Ibid., 90.

41. Meyer, *Deaconesses,* 235.

42. For the perspective of the Robinson side, see "The Early History of Deaconess Work and Training Schools for Women in American Methodism, 1883–1885," published in 1912, reprinted in *The American Deaconess Movement in the Early Twentieth Century,* ed. Carolyn DeSwarte Gifford (London: Garland, 1987). While the report takes pains to defend its "unprejudiced, impartial attitude," it is equally concerned to insist that the deaconess movement in American Methodism began before Meyer's Chicago Training School and that the "Deaconess Work of the Woman's Home Missionary Society has developed on original lines in no wise related to the Chicago Work, and the large success of the Deaconess Work of the Woman's Home Missionary Society is due alone to the earnest, devoted labors of the many noble, consecrated workers of the Society" (28).

43. Catherine M. Prelinger and Rosemary S. Keller, "The Function of Female Bonding: The Restored Diaconessate of the Nineteenth Century," in Keller, et al., eds., *Women in New Worlds,* vol. 2, 326.

44. See Keller, "Lay Women in the Protestant Tradition" in Ruether and Keller, *Women and Religion,* vol. 1, 277–81, for two excerpts from such exceptional male leaders.

## Notes for chapter 11: The Social Gospel

1. Dorothy Bass Fraser, "The Feminine Mystique: 1890–1910," *Union Seminary Quarterly Review* 27 (Summer 1972): 234–37; Walter Rauschenbusch, *Christianizing the Social Order* (New York: Macmillan, 1912), 131, and "Some Moral Aspects of the 'Woman Movement'," *Biblical World* 42 (October 1913): 196.

2. For Social Gospel concern with the manliness of religion, see Susan H. Lindley, "Women and the Social Gospel Novel," *Church History* 54 (March 1985): 65–66; Janet Forsythe Fishburn, *The Fatherhood of God and the Victorian Family: The Social Gospel in America* (Philadelphia: Fortress, 1981), 28–33.

3. Lindley, "Social Gospel Novel"; Rauschenbusch, "Some Moral Aspects of the 'Woman Movement'," 197–99.

4. Rauschenbusch, *Christianizing the Social Order,* 128. Fishburn details the centrality of the Victorian family for six Social Gospel leaders and concludes that their loyalty to that cultural ideal ultimately "crippled" their theology (175).

5. See, for example, Rauschenbusch, *Christianity and the Social Crisis* (New York: Macmillan, 1907), 276–79; Lindley, "Social Gospel Novel," 61.

6. A partial exception to this generalization can be found in leaders like Graham Taylor, whose work with the Chicago Commons brought him into close working relationship with women leaders in the settlement movement like Jane Addams.

7. Vida D. Scudder, *On Journey* (New York: E. P. Dutton, 1937), 127. Her lectures were published in 1898 as *Social Ideals in English Letters* (Boston/New York: Houghton Mifflin).

8. Not only was *A Listener in Babel* noteworthy among Social Gospel novels for its less simplistic approach to theological and social issues, it also offered, along with a few other Social Gospel novels by women authors, more diverse and

realistic images of women than did most male Social Gospel novelists. See Lindley, "Social Gospel Novels."

9. Scudder, *On Journey*, 163.

10. Scudder herself identified *Socialism and Character* (Boston/New York: Houghton, Mifflin, 1912) as "my favorite though forgotten book" (*On Journey*, 168).

11. On the SCHC, see Mary Sudman Donovan, *A Different Call: Women's Ministries in the Episcopal Church, 1850–1920* (Wilton, Conn.: Morehouse-Barlow, 1986), chap. 10; Sister Theresa Corcoran, "Vida Dutton Scudder: The Progressive Years" (Ph.D. diss., Georgetown University, 1973), 82–98; Miriam U. Chrisman, *"To Bind Together": A Brief History of the Society of the Companions of the Holy Cross* (Byfield, Mass.: The Society of the Companions of the Holy Cross, 1984).

12. For Scudder's distinctive contributions, see Corcoran, "Vida Dutton Scudder"; Susan H. Lindley, "'Neglected Voices' and *Praxis* in the Social Gospel," *Journal of Religious Ethics* 18 (Spring 1990): 76–84.

13. Mary E. Frederickson uses the term in "Shaping a New Society: Methodist Women and Industrial Reform in the South, 1880–1940" in Rosemary Skinner Keller, Louise L. Queen, and Hilah F. Thomas, eds., *Women in New Worlds*, vol. 1 (Nashville: Abingdon, 1982), 348, to contrast the position of the women she studied with the more typical image of southern piety and individualism, but it can also suggest a contrast between the approach of many women to the Social Gospel and the more theoretical, self-consciously theological approach of some of the movement's male leadership.

14. In addition to Scudder's *A Listener in Babel*, see two novels written by her close friend and coworker, Florence Converse: *The Burden of Christopher* (Boston: Houghton Mifflin, 1900) and *The Children of Light* (Boston: Houghton Mifflin, 1912).

15. An "institutional church" in this time period was located in a city and consciously expanded its services to address the physical and social needs of its neighbors, while still retaining its traditional religious functions. Some institutional churches were interdenominational, while others maintained a specific Protestant affiliation. In 1894, the Open or Institutional Church League was founded to promote cooperation and expansion. See Aaron Ignatius Abell, *The Urban Impact on American Protestantism, 1865–1900* (Cambridge, Mass.: Harvard University Press, 1943), chap. 6, "The Institutional Church Movement."

16. See, for example, Graham Taylor, *Pioneering on Social Frontiers* (Chicago: University of Chicago Press, 1930), 331–36.

17. Ronald C. White Jr. and C. Howard Hopkins, *The Social Gospel: Religion and Reform in Changing America* (Philadelphia: Temple University Press, 1976).

18. Ruth Bordin, *Woman and Temperance: The Quest for Power and Liberty, 1873–1900* (Philadelphia: Temple University Press, 1981), xviii. See chap. 9 for a fuller discussion of Willard and the WCTU.

19. White and Hopkins, *The Social Gospel*, 80–97.

20. See Frederickson, "Shaping a New Society"; and John Patrick McDowell, *The Social Gospel in the South: The Woman's Home Mission Movement in the Methodist Episcopal Church, South, 1886–1939* (Baton Rouge, La.: Louisiana State University Press, 1982).

21. McDowell, *The Social Gospel*, 15.

22. Ibid., 20.

23. On Scarritt, see Virginia Lieson Brereton, "Preparing Women for the Lord's Work: The Story of Three Methodist Training Schools, 1880–1940," in Keller, et al., eds., *Women in New Worlds*, vol. 1, 178–99.

24. On Bennett, see Rosemary Radford Ruether and Rosemary Skinner Keller, eds., *Women and Religion in America, 1900–1968* (San Francisco: Harper & Row, 1986), vol. 3, 269–71, 287–94.

25. Isabelle Horton, *The Burden of the City* (New York: Fleming H. Revell, 1904), reprinted in Carolyn DeSwarte Gifford, ed., *The American Deaconess Movement in the Early Twentieth Century* (London: Garland, 1987), 135.

26. Ibid., chap. 2, "Settlement Work."

27. Quoted in Mary Agnes Dougherty, "The Social Gospel According to Phoebe: Methodist Deaconesses in the Metropolis," in Keller, et al., eds., *Women in New Worlds*, vol. 1, 214.

28. Ibid., 215, 203.

29. Part of the problem in historical conclusions about settlements and the Social Gospel lies in the difficulty of defining the line between a settlement and religious missions whose workers lived in the city alongside those they served, a definitional problem addressed by leaders at the time. Judith Ann Tolander concludes that prior to World War I, there were about four hundred settlement houses, about half of which had religious sponsorship "and, depending on the individual house, may have functioned like a church mission. The National Federation of Settlements, founded in 1911, denied membership to houses that proselytized extensively" (*Professionalism and Social Change: From the Settlement House Movement to Neighborhood Centers, 1886 to the Present* [New York: Columbia University Press, 1987], 3).

30. Allen Davis, *Spearheads for Reform: The Social Settlements and the Progressive Movement, 1890–1914* (New York/London/Toronto: Oxford University Press, 1967), 15, 27.

31. Just as it is difficult to divide urban institutions—missions, institutional churches, and especially settlements—into religious or secular categories, so, too, it is hard to say when particular settlement workers, especially female residents, can legitimately be included in the Social Gospel. Ordination made such identification easier for men, as Davis notes: "The settlement idea was especially appealing to a number of Protestant clergymen, who had been influenced by the social gospel movement, or by what William Jewett Tucker called 'a stirring progressive movement in religion and social ethics'" (*Spearheads for Reform*, 12–13; see also 27). But what of laymen and women? Not all the women who were active in settlements self-consciously identified with the Social Gospel, but Scudder and Dudley surely did, and a good case can be made for strong religious motivation in women like Ellen Gates Starr, Eleanor McMain, Mary Simkhovitch, Mary McDowell, and Cornelia Bradford.

### Notes for chapter 12: Native American Women and Religion in Nineteenth-Century America

1. Katherine Weist, "Beasts of Burden and Menial Slaves: Nineteenth Century Observations of Plains Indian Women," in Patricia Albers and Beatrice Medicine, eds. *The Hidden Half: Studies of Plains Indian Women* (Lanham, Md.: University Press of America, 1983), 43.

2. I am indebted to Richard A. Grounds for insight into the religious dimension of gendered division of labor among Eastern tribes in particular.

3. Historians have a similar problem when attempting to get back to what Native American women of the nineteenth century "really" did and thought, especially those women who retained traditional ways and beliefs. Written sources from the time by both whites and Native Americans do exist and can be supplemented by more recent work by anthropologists, ethnographers, and contemporary Native Americans who speak from within a tradition. Nevertheless, most sources are still filtered by time, cultural assumptions, or even language.

4. Sam D. Gill warns against reading a single figure of the "Great Spirit" back into tribal religion before Christian contact. See Gill, "Native American Religions," in *Encyclopedia of the American Religious Experience: Studies of Traditions and Movements,* vol. 1, ed. Charles H. Lippy and Peter W. Williams (New York: Charles Scribner's Sons, 1988), 140. Gill's article is a very helpful and balanced introduction to a complex topic. Paula Allen Gunn, *The Sacred Hoop: Recovering the Feminine in American Indian Traditions* (Boston: Beacon Press, 1986), notes important female deities among Native Americans and the significant leadership roles played by women, and she contrasts this with the white colonizers' patriarchy. Carolyn Niethammer, *Daughters of the Earth: The Lives and Legends of American Indian Women* (New York: Macmillan, 1977) is a good general introduction. Rayna Green, *Native American Women: A Contextual Bibliography* (Bloomington, Ind.: Indiana University Press, 1983) suggests both the wealth and the limitations of writings by and about Native American women. For this chapter, I have drawn not only on such general sources but also on a number of "autobiographies" of individual Indian women who lived a good part of their lives in the nineteenth century before white contact significantly altered traditional ways of their tribe. As old women in the early twentieth century, they told their stories to ethnographers and anthropologists. While the filters of translators and editors must be recognized, the stories provide a genuine glimpse into traditional women's lives at that time.

5. Ruth M. Underhill, ed., *Papago Woman* (New York: Holt, Rinehart, and Winston, 1979, copyright 1936), 50.

6. Frank B. Linderman, ed., *Pretty-shield, Medicine Woman of the Crows* (Lincoln, Nebr.: University of Nebraska Press, 1972, copyright 1932), 155–56, 166.

7. See Niethammer, *Daughters of the Earth,* 37–55.

8. Underhill, *Papago Woman,* 58.

9. Gilbert L. Wilson, ed., *Waheenee, An Indian Girl's Story Told by Herself* (1921; reprint, Occasional Publication No. 4, Bismarck; N. Dak.: State Historical Society of North Dakota, 1981), 8.

10. Norma Kidd Green, *Iron Eye's Family: The Children of Joseph La Flesche.* Sponsored by the Nebraska State Historical Society. (Lincoln, Nebr. : Johnsen Publishing Co., 1969), 46. For a fuller description of the "turning of the child," see Alice C. Fletcher and Francis LaFlesche, *The Omaha Tribe* (1911; reprint, New York: Johnson Reprint Co., 1970), 117–22.

11. Sarah Winnemucca Hopkins, *Life Among the Piutes: Their Wrongs and Claims,* ed. Mrs. Horace Mann. (1883; reprint, Bishop, Calif.: Sierra Madre, Inc., 1969), 54–55. In the "Editor's Preface," Mary Mann insists that her editing has been minimal and that the work is indeed the firsthand account of Sarah herself.

12. Underhill, *Papago Woman,* 39–40. Underhill herself was able to accompany

Maria Chona for these events when Underhill went to study the Papago and describes them in an introduction to Maria Chona's story, 19–27. Maria Chona later made it very clear that she did not see the tribal tradition in the same light as white drinking: "There were white men here and there on our land by that time, as there had never been. So our men began to learn to drink that whiskey. It was not a thing that you must drink only once a year like our cactus cider. You could drink it any time, with no singing and no speeches, and it did not bring rain" (74).

13. Niethammer, *Daughters of the Earth*, 146.

14. Niethammer, ibid, 158–63. See also Henry Warner Bowden, *American Indians and Christian Missions: Studies in Cultural Conflict* (Chicago: University of Chicago Press, 1981), 29–30, on witches among the Pueblos.

15. Underhill, *Papago Woman*, 52.

16. Ibid., 83.

17. Gill, "Native American Religions," 144ff. Bowden, *American Indians*, describes variations among Native American groups before white contact and suggests some correlation between the strength and institutionalization of communal identity and the tribe's ability to resist white culture (Chapters 2–4).

18. Niethammer, *Daughters of the Earth*, 109.

19. The accounts of Waheenee and Pretty-shield raise no objections to polygyny. Maria Chona was unusual in that she left her first husband when he took a second wife, but even she admits that he was doing nothing that was not customary (Underhill, *Papago Woman*, 76.) Moreover, she was able to return to her family and subsequently married again.

20. Hopkins, *The Piutes*, 50.

21. Wilson, *Waheenee*, 127–55.

22. Niethammer, *Daughters of the Earth*, 165–85. See also Beatrice Medicine, "'Warrior Women'—Sex Role Alternatives for Plains Indian Women," in Albers and Medicine, *The Hidden Half*, 267–80.

23. Linderman, *Pretty-shield*, 227–31 and 38.

24. Wilson, *Waheenee*, 54.

25. See Annemarie Shimony, "Women of Influence and Prestige among the Native American Iroquois," in Nancy Auer Falk and Rita M. Gross, eds., *Unspoken Worlds: Women's Religious Lives*, 2d ed. (Belmont, Calif.: Wadsworth, 1989), 201–11. Maps in Harold E. Driver, *Indians of North America* (Chicago: The University of Chicago Press, 1961) are helpful in illustrating in which areas of the North American continent lived tribes that were matrilineal or matrilocal. Other maps indicate how in different geographical areas, such tasks as horticulture or house construction were divided by gender. Nancy Bonvillain, "Gender Relations in Native North America," *American Indian Culture and Research Journal* 13 (1989): 1–28, focuses on five North Amerindian groups to illustrate the variety and complex interplay of gender roles and status, as well as the impact of contact with whites on traditional ways.

26. Wilson, *Waheenee*, 175–76. Waheenee's poignant but sweeping statement about the end of Indian culture represents the historical perspective of one woman who had seen devastating changes and inroads into traditional ways. In their fullest, integrated form, the "old ways" were indeed gone; however, Native American culture, religion, and values did not disappear, although their vitality was sometimes carried in altered forms into the new contexts of the twentieth century.

27. Annemarie Shimony, "Iroquois Religion and Women in Historical Perspective," in Yvonne Yazbeck Haddad and Ellison Banks Findly, eds., *Women, Religion and Social Change* (Albany, N.Y.: State University of New York Press, 1985), 397–418, focuses on women and religion before and after white contact with one important eastern tribal family. For white-Indian contact in the colonial period with a particular focus on missions and religion, see Bowden, *American Indians*, 25–163; Jay P. Dolan, *The American Catholic Experience: A History from Colonial Times to the Present* (Garden City, N.Y.: Doubleday, 1985), 15–68; and Margaret Connell Szasz, *Indian Education in the American Colonies, 1607–1783* (Albuquerque, N. Mex.: University of New Mexico Press, 1988).

28. An allotment policy had, in fact, been tried before the Dawes Act, especially with the four so-called civilized tribes of the Southeast (Chickasaws, Choctaws, Creeks, and Cherokees), but it failed. See Mary Elizabeth Young, *Redskins, Ruffleshirts, and Rednecks: Indian Allotments in Alabama and Mississippi, 1830–1860* (Norman, Okla.: University of Oklahoma Press, 1961). By 1934, more than 60 percent of tribal Indian lands had been lost to whites through allotment policies (Bowden, *American Indians*, 194.) For a thorough discussion of the presumptions underlying allotment policies and the varied motives of different groups who supported the Dawes Act, see Frederick E. Hoxie, *A Final Promise: The Campaign to Assimilate the Indians, 1880–1920* (Lincoln, Nebr.: University of Nebraska Press, 1984).

29. Virginia Driving Hawk Sneve, *That They May Have Life: The Episcopal Church in South Dakota, 1859–1976* (New York: Seabury Press, 1977), argues that Episcopal missionaries were far more tolerant of traditional Dakota practices than "the more puritanical Calvinist creeds . . ." (9). Sneve is both a Dakota woman and an Episcopalian writing an official diocesan history, so her clearly positive assessment of Episcopal openness is hardly surprising, yet it is confirmed in other, less interested sources. See, for example, Kay Parker, "American Indian Women and Religion on the Southern Plains," in Rosemary Radford Ruether and Rosemary Skinner Keller, *Women and Religion in America*, vol. 3, [1900–1968 (San Francisco: Harper & Row, 1986), 52.

30. Zitkala-Sa (Gertrude Simmons Bonnin), a Dakota activist, wrote four articles for the *Atlantic Monthly* at the turn of the twentieth century, including "The School Days of an Indian Girl," *Atlantic Monthly* 85 (February 1900): 185–94, a very critical account of white insensitivity. She ultimately earned a college degree but was clearly bitter at the cultural price she had to pay to obtain an education.

31. Stephen R. Riggs, *Mary and I: Forty Years with the Sioux* (copyright 1880; reprint, Williamstown, Mass.: Corner House Publishers, 1971), 286.

32. Riggs, "Introduction," n. p.

33. Ibid., 24, an excerpt from Mary's diary.

34. Quoted in Michael C. Coleman, "Christianizing and Americanizing the Nez Perce: Sue L. McBeth and her Attitudes to the Indians," *Journal of Presbyterian History* 53 (Winter 1975): 346–47. Coleman further argues that while McBeth lacked any appreciation for Nez Perce culture, she did at least reject the idea that Indians were, as human beings, racially inferior and hence inherently incapable of achieving "higher" civilization. The distinction she drew was thus consistent with the broad presumptions that Hoxie sees in the reformers who supported allotment and acculturation until the turn of the twentieth century. After that, Hoxie sees a shift,

so that by 1920 most whites, including the government, assumed that Indians' failure to assimilate fully to white culture was evidence of inherent racial inferiority. "Because they believed that Native Americans would take generations to 'appreciate' modern ways, politicians and policy makers grew more tolerant of traditional practices." Ironically, this shift gave Native Americans needed "space." "Defined as marginal Americans, tribal members could take advantage of their peripheral status, replenish their supplies of belief and value, and carry on their war with homogeneity" (Hoxie, *A Final Promise,* 243–44).

35. Glenda Riley, *Women and Indians on the Frontier, 1825–1915* (Albuquerque, N.Mex.: University of New Mexico Press, 1984) is an extensive study of white women's images of themselves and of Indians, although it is not intended to present Native American perspectives. Valerie Sherer Mathes, *Helen Hunt Jackson and Her Indian Reform Legacy* (Austin, Tex.: University of Texas Press, 1990) describes Jackson as something of an exception among women who supported Indian reform, because most of the women reformers who carried on Jackson's work after her death endorsed the "cult" and assumed that Native American women needed to change to achieve it.

36. *Memoirs of Catharine Brown, A Christian Indian of the Cherokee Nation* contains letters and diary entries from Brown herself, but they date from after her conversion. Her earlier life is "transcribed" by Rufus Anderson and is, at least in part, an attempt to raise funds by presenting a successful and exemplary convert. Thus it is hard to determine Brown's motives in seeking out a white, Christian education, though there is no reason to doubt that she did so, travelling a considerable distance from her home to enroll at the mission school (1825; reprint, 1832 ed., with introduction by William Stanley Hoole, ed., University, Ala.: Confederate Publishing Co, 1986).

37. Theda Perdue, "Southern Indians and the Cult of True Womanhood," in Walter J. Fraser Jr., R. Frank Saunders Jr., and Jon L. Wakelyn, eds., *The Web of Southern Social Relations: Women, Family, and Education* (Athens, Ga.: University of Georgia Press, 1985.) Perdue argues that Cherokee women had "the highest degree of power and personal autonomy" among Southern Indians, and thus posed the greatest contrast to the whites' cult of True Womanhood (38).

38. Bowden, *American Indians,* 175–76.

39. Riggs, *Mary and I,* 189.

40. Sneve, *The Episcopal Church,* 3.

41. Riggs, *Mary and I,* 32, 51, 65.

42. Hopkins, *The Piutes,* 5–7.

43. Ibid., 178.

44. Ibid., 118.

45. Ibid., 247. The Malheur land was never restored.

46. For a description of the 1882 article and a brief but balanced biography, see Catherine S. Fowler, "Sarah Winnemucca, Northern Paiute, 1844–1891," in Margot Liberty, ed., *American Indian Intellectuals* (St. Paul, Minn.: West Publishing Co., 1978), 33–42.

47. Green, *Native American Women,* 2. Most of the following account is derived from Green's book on the La Flesche family.

48. Ibid., 62.

49. Ibid., 76.

50. Kristin Herzog, "The La Flesche Family: Native American Spirituality, Calvinism, and Presbyterian Missions," *American Presbyterians* 65 (Fall 1987): 222–32, sees in the La Flesche family an example of successful and constructive syncretism.

51. Helen Hunt Jackson, *A Century of Dishonor: A Sketch of the United States Government's Dealings with Some of the Indian Tribes* (New York: Harpers, 1881); reprinted as *A Century of Dishonor: The Early Crusade for Indian Reform*, ed. Andrew F. Rolle (New York: Harper & Row, 1965).

52. Mathes, *Helen Hunt Jackson*, 36.

53. Ibid., 77–83.

54. Ibid., xvi.

## Notes for chapter 13: African-American Women and Religion in Nineteenth-Century America

1. Albert J. Raboteau, *Slave Religion: The "Invisible Institution" in the Antebellum South* (New York: Oxford, 1978), 227.

2. Cyprian Davis, *The History of Black Catholics in the United States* (New York: Crossroad, 1990), 35.

3. Ibid., 103. On black women religious in the nineteenth century, see Davis, *Black Catholics*, chap. 4; and Theresa A. Rector, "Black Nuns as Educators," *Journal of Negro Education* 51 (1982): 238–53.

4. Sister M. Reginald Gerdes, "To Educate and Evangelize: Black Catholic Schools of the Oblate Sisters of Providence," *U.S. Catholic Historian* 6 (Spring/Summer 1986): 184.

5. For an analysis of this devastating mix of images and realities, see Rosemary Radford Ruether, "Between the Sons of White and the Sons of Blackness: Racism and Sexism in America," in *New Woman, New Earth: Sexist Ideologies and Human Liberation* (New York: Seabury Press, 1975), 117–20.

6. The whole issue of the interplay of religion, family and sex roles among black Americans in a dominant and repressive white culture is a complex and controversial one. See J. Deotis Roberts, *Roots of a Black Future: Family and Church* (Philadelphia: Westminster, 1980), 57–79, for a brief survey of changing interpretations.

7. See, for example, Linda M. Perkins, "The Impact of the 'Cult of True Womanhood' on the Education of Black Women," in Darlene Clark Hine, ed., *Black Women in United States History*, vol. 3 (Brooklyn, N.Y.: Carlson Publishing Co., 1990), 1065–76.

8. Raboteau, *Slave Religion*, 266.

9. Jarena Lee, "The Life and Religious Experience of Jarena Lee, A Coloured Lady, Giving an Account of her Call to Preach the Gospel. Revised and Corrected from the Original Manuscript, Written by Herself," originally published in Philadelphia, 1836; reprinted in William L. Andrews, ed., *Sisters of the Spirit: Three Black Women's Autobiographies of the Nineteenth Century* (Bloomington, Ind.: Indiana University Press, 1986), 29.

10. Jean M. Humez, "'My Spirit Eye': Some Functions of Spiritual and Visionary Experience in the Lives of Five Black Women Preachers, 1810–1880," in Barbara J. Harris and JoAnn K. McNamara, eds., *Women and the Structure of Society: Selected Research from the Fifth Berkshire Conference on the History of Women* (Durham, N.C.: Duke University Press, 1984), 134.

11. Amanda Berry Smith, *An Autobiography: The Story of the Lord's Dealings with Mrs. Amanda Smith, the Colored Evangelist* (Chicago: Meyer, 1893); reprinted with an introduction by Jualynne E. Dodson in The Schomburg Library of Nineteenth-Century Black Women Writers (New York: Oxford University Press, 1988), 49.

12. Benjamin Quarles, "Harriet Tubman's Unlikely Leadership," in Hine, *Black Women*, vol. 4, 1135; Humez, "'My Spirit Eye,'" 136.

13. Lee, *The Life*, 36. Julia Foote describes a similar resistance to God's call in "A Brand Plucked from the Fire: An Autobiographical Sketch by Mrs. Julia A. J. Foote," published in 1879 and also reprinted in Andrews, ed., *Sisters of the Spirit*, 200ff.

14. The resistance in the A.M.E. Church at this time to female preaching may well have been related to an internal struggle over how much education should be required for ministers. Daniel Payne, an important church leader, both advocated higher educational standards for ordination and opposed women's preaching, perhaps in part because women like Jarena Lee had minimal formal education, basing their authority to preach on God's direct call instead. See David W. Wills, "Womanhood and Domesticity in the A.M.E. Tradition: The Influence of Daniel Alexander Payne," in David W. Wills and Richard Newman, eds., *Black Apostles at Home and Abroad: Afro-Americans and the Christian Mission from the Revolution to Reconstruction* (Boston: G. K. Hall, 1982), 136–38; and Humez, "'My Spirit Eye,'" 130.

15. Jualynne Dodson, "Nineteenth-Century A.M.E. Preaching Women: Cutting Edge of Women's Inclusion in Church Polity," Rosemary Skinner Keller, Louise L. Queen, and Hilah F. Thomas, eds., in *Women in New Worlds: Historical Perspectives on the Wesleyan Tradition*, vol. 1, (Nashville: Abingdon, 1982), 285.

16. C. Eric Lincoln and Lawrence Mamiya, *The Black Church in the African American Experience* (Durham, N.C.: Duke University Press, 1990), 285–87.

17. Ibid., 278. See also Perkins, "The 'Cult of True Womanhood,'" 1071–72.

18. Lincoln and Mamiya, *The Black Church*, 278.

19. It may well be, as Jean M. Humez has suggested (132) that some of these women were personally unhappy or unfulfilled in marriage and that an identity or career as evangelist offered an attractive alternative, sanctioned by God. Yet such explanations should be seen as supplementary, not exhaustive.

20. Wills, "Womanhood and Domesticity," 139.

21. Hallie Q. Brown, *Homespun Heroines and other Women of Distinction* (Xenia, Ohio: Aldine Publishing Co., 1926); reprinted with an introduction by Randall K. Burkett in The Schomburg Library of Nineteenth-Century Black Women Writers (New York: Oxford University Press, 1988), 12.

22. Kathleen C. Berkeley, "'Colored Ladies Also Contributed': Black Women's Activities from Benevolence to Social Welfare, 1866–1896," in Hine, *Black Women*, vol. 1, 63.

23. Theressa Hoover, "Black Women and the Churches: Triple Jeopardy," in Alice L. Hageman, ed., *Sexist Religion and Women in the Church: No More Silence!* (New York: Association Press, 1974), 64–67.

24. For black Americans' work in African missions, see Sylvia M. Jacobs, ed., *Black Americans and the Missionary Movement in Africa* (Westport, Conn.: Greenwood Press, 1982); Walter L. Williams, *Black Americans and the Evangelization of*

*Africa, 1877–1900* (Madison, Wis.: University of Wisconsin Press, 1982); and Sandy D. Martin, *Black Baptists and African Missions: The Origins of a Movement, 1880–1915* (Macon, Ga.: Mercer University Press, 1989).

25. James Thoburn, "Introduction," to Smith, *Autobiography,* vi, x.

26. Walter L. Williams, "The Missionary: An Introduction," in Jacobs, ed., *Black Americans,* 132.

27. Albert J. Raboteau, "'Ethiopia Shall Soon Stretch Forth Her Hands': Black Destiny in Nineteenth-Century America," The University Lecture in Religion at Arizona State University, January 27, 1983 (Tempe, Ariz.: Department of Religious Studies, Arizona State University.)

28. For a helpful survey of times and denominations, see Sylvia M. Jacobs, "The Historical Role of Afro-Americans in American Missionary Efforts in Africa," in *Black Americans,* 5–29.

29. Smith, *Autobiography,* 423–34.

30. For further information on individual women, see Sylvia Jacobs, "Three Afro-American Women Missionaries in Africa, 1882–1904," in Hine, *Black Women,* vol. 2, 693–707; "Their 'Special Mission': Afro-American Women as Missionaries to the Congo, 1894–1937" in Jacobs, ed., *Black Americans,* 155–76; "Give a Thought to Africa: Black Women Missionaries to Southern Africa," in Nupur Chaudhuri and Margaret Strobel, eds., *Western Women and Imperialism: Complicity and Resistance* (Bloomington, Ind./Indianapolis, Ind.: Indiana University Press, 1992), 207–28.

31. Jacobs, "Three Afro-American Women," 701.

32. Jacobs, "Give a Thought to Africa," 211.

33. Jacobs, "Their 'Special Mission,'" 156–57.

34. Berkeley, "Colored Ladies," 76.

35. Stewart's Boston speeches are reprinted in Bert James Loewenberg and Ruth Bogin, *Black Women in Nineteenth-Century American Life: Their Words, Their Thoughts, Their Feelings* (University Park, Pa./London: Pennsylvania State University Press, 1976), 186.

36. Ibid., 198–99.

37. Ibid., 229.

38. Janice Sumler-Lewis, "The Forten-Purvis Women of Philadelphia and the American Anti-Slavery Crusade," in Hine, *Black Women,* vol. 4, 1339.

39. See Linda M. Perkins, "The Black Female American Missionary Association Teacher in the South, 1861–1870," in Hine, *Black Women,* vol. 3, 1049–63; and Judith Weisenfeld, "'Who Is Sufficient for These Things?' Sara G. Stanley and the American Missionary Association, 1864–1868," *Church History* 60 (December 1991): 493–507.

40. Linda M. Perkins, "'Heed Life's Demands: The Educational Philosophy of Fanny Jackson Coppin," in Hine, *Black Women,* vol. 3, 1039.

41. Loewenberg and Bogin, *Black Women,* include brief biographies of Laney, Coppin, and Cooper, along with selected examples of their writings, 296–331.

42. Quoted in Ida B. Wells, "Lynch Law in All Its Phases," an address given in 1893 at the Tremont Temple in Boston, reprinted in Mildred I. Thompson, *Ida B. Wells-Barnett: An Exploratory Study of an American Black Woman, 1893–1930,* in Hine, *Black Women,* vol. 15, 177.

43. Paula Giddings, *When and Where I Enter: The Impact of Black Women on*

*Race and Sex in America* (New York: William Morrow and Co., 1984), 83. See also chap. 1 for Church's and Wells's response to the Memphis lynchings.

44. Lincoln and Mamiya, *The Black Church*, 281–85.

45. Wills, "Womanhood and Domesticity," 140.

46. Quoted in ibid., 141–42.

47. William Jeremiah Moses, "Domestic Feminism Conservatism, Sex Roles, and Black Women's Clubs, 1893–1896," in Hine, *Black Women*, vol. 3, 959.

48. Ibid., 969.

49. Evelyn Brooks Higginbotham, *Righteous Discontent: The Women's Movement in the Black Baptist Church, 1880–1920* (Cambridge, Mass.: Harvard University Press, 1993), chap. 7, "The Politics of Respectability."

50. For "feminization," see Barbara Welter, "The Feminization of American Religion, 1800–1860," originally published in William O'Neill, ed., *Insights and Parallels: Problems and Issues of American Social History* (Minneapolis: Burgess, 1973); and Ann Douglas, *The Feminization of American Culture* (New York: Knopf, 1977).

51. Higginbotham, *Righteous Discontent*, 142.

52. Ibid., 147.

53. Anna Julia Cooper, *A Voice from the South* (Xenia, Ohio: Aldine Printing House, 1892); reprinted with an introduction by Mary Helen Washington in The Schomburg Library of Nineteenth-Century Black Women Writers (New York: Oxford University Press, 1988), 75.

54. Ibid., 254–55; for criticism of racism in the women's movement, see Anna Julia Cooper, "Woman Vs. the Indian," *A Voice from the South*, 80–126.

55. Ibid., 143–44.

## Notes for chapter 14: Roman Catholic Women in Nineteenth-Century America

1. Jay P. Dolan, *The American Catholic Experience: A History from Colonial Times to Present* (Garden City, N.Y.: Doubleday, 1985), 160–61.

2. Quoted in Karen Kennelly, "Ideals of Catholic Womanhood," in Karen Kennelly, ed., *American Catholic Women: A Historical Exploration* (New York: Macmillan, 1989), 4.

3. James J. Kenneally, "Eve, Mary, and the Historians: American Catholicism and Women," in Janet Wilson James, ed., *Women in American Religion* (Philadelphia: University of Pennsylvania Press, 1980), 194–95.

4. Dolan, *American Catholic Experience*, 250.

5. James J. Kenneally, *The History of American Catholic Women* (New York: Crossroad, 1990), 33.

6. Ibid., 26.

7. Margaret Quinn, "Sylvia, Adele, and Rosine Parmentier: 19th Century Women of Brooklyn," *U. S. Catholic Historian* 5 (Summer/Fall 1986): 345–54. For other examples of Catholic women philanthropists, see Kenneally, *The History of American Catholic Women*, 61–64.

8. Dolan, *American Catholic Experience*, 326.

9. Debra Campbell, "Reformers and Activists," in Kennelly, ed., *American Catholic Women*, 165.

10. See Dolan, *American Catholic Experience,* 127–57, for a helpful overview of Catholic immigration in the nineteenth century.

11. See Robert Anthony Orsi, *The Madonna of 115th Street: Faith and Community in Italian Harlem, 1880–1950* (New Haven, Conn.: Yale University Press, 1985), for an excellent study of a particular ethnic Catholic community and its faith.

12. Colleen McDannell, "Catholic Domesticity, 1860–1960," in Kennelly, ed., *American Catholic Women,* 66.

13. Dolan, *American Catholic Experience,* 231–32.

14. Marie Hall Ets, *Rosa: The Life of an Italian Immigrant* (Minneapolis: University of Minnesota Press, 1970). Ets was a young social worker at Chicago Commons just after the First World War when she met Rosa and recorded her story. Expectation of "favors" such as cures, conversions, and help in family difficulties from the "supernatural" members of the "household of faith"—Jesus, Mary and the saints—was an integral part of the devotional Catholicism of nineteenth-century America. See Ann Taves, *The Household of Faith: Roman Catholic Devotions in Mid-Nineteenth-Century America* (Notre Dame, Ind.: University of Notre Dame Press, 1986), 47–69.

15. Quoted in Taves, *Household of Faith,* 83.

16. See Orsi, *The Madonna,* and McDannell, "Catholic Domesticity," for more extended descriptions of family shrines and festivals.

17. Ets, *Rosa,* 82.

18. Orsi, *The Madonna,* 216.

19. McDannell, "Catholic Domesticity," 54.

20. Dolan, *American Catholic Experience,* 140–55. See also Timothy J. Meagher, "Sweet Good Mothers and Young Women Out in the World: The Roles of Irish American Women in Late Nineteenth Century and Early Twentieth Century Worcester, Massachusetts," *U. S. Catholic Historian* 5 (Summer/Fall 1986): 325–44.

21. Philip S. Foner, *Women and the American Labor Movement: From Colonial Times to the Eve of World War I* (New York: The Free Press, Macmillan, 1979), 202.

22. Ibid., 200.

23. Ibid., 290.

24. James J. Kenneally, "Catholicism and Woman Suffrage in Massachusetts," *The Catholic Historical Review* 53 (April 1967): 48.

25. Kenneally, *American Catholic Women,* 87.

26. Kenneally, "Catholic and Feminist," 245–53.

27. Kennelly, "Ideals of American Catholic Womanhood," 14.

28. Eileen Mary Brewer, *Nuns and the Education of American Catholic Women, 1860–1920* (Chicago: Loyola University Press, 1987), 124.

29. Quoted in Mary Ewens, *The Role of the Nun in Nineteenth Century America* (New York: Arno Press, 1978), 17. Shorter versions of Ewens's excellent work on nineteenth-century sisters can be found in "Women in the Convent," in Kennelly, ed., *American Catholic Women,* 17–47, and "The Leadership of Nuns in Immigrant Catholicism," in Rosemary Radford Ruether and Rosemary Skinner Keller. *Women and Religion in America* vol. 1, *The Nineteenth Century* (San Francisco: Harper & Row, 1981), 101–49.

30. Eleanor Commo McLaughlin has argued that restrictions on the lives of women religious and active discouragement of women who sought entrance into orders were based not only on concern about abuses but also on the male lead-

ership's ambivalent response to women who responded in large numbers to new modes of monasticism at that time. The "frailer" sex "ought" not to be demonstrating so much spiritual superiority, and besides, too many women religious would put unacceptable demands on the church's resources of money and personnel. "Equality of Souls, Inequality of Sexes: Woman in Medieval Theology," in Rosemary Radford Ruether, ed. *Religion and Sexism: Images of Woman in the Jewish and Christian Tradition* (New York: Simon & Schuster, 1974), 238–45.

31. Ewens, *The Role of the Nun*, 19. Technically, the terms "nun" for the religious woman and "order" for a group apply only to situations where solemn vows are taken, whereas the parallel terms "sister" and "congregation" apply where simple vows are involved, but following the precedent of scholars like Ewens and Kenneally, I use the terms interchangeably.

32. Ibid., 32–64, for descriptions of these early orders.

33. Ibid., 68.

34. Dolan, *American Catholic Experience*, 121.

35. Dolan comments that for putting up with the harassment of French male superiors like John Baptist David, Mother Seton "deserved canonization!" Ibid.

36. Ewens, *The Role of the Nun*, 69. Benedictine nuns who came to America after midcentury also struggled with the question of how much adaptation to an American environment was possible without compromising their central, traditional monastic identity, involving such issues as praying the Divine Office and simple versus solemn vows. The dispensations granted by Rome (and initiated more by male clerical authorities than by the nuns themselves) were necessary for their work in America, given the stricter enclosure rules imposed on Benedictine nuns than on their male counterparts, but they left the women with an anomalous canonical status. See Judith Sutera, O.S.B., *True Daughters: Monastic Identity and American Benedictine Women's History* (Atchison, Kans.: Mount Saint Scholastica, 1987), 33–39.

37. Ruether and Skinner, "The Leadership of Nuns," 107.

38. Excerpts from Gerhardinger's letters are included in ibid. 122–28.

39. See documents about Mother Caroline Friess in Barbara J. MacHaffie, *Readings in Her Story: Women in Christian Tradition* (Minneapolis: Fortress Press, 1992), 166–71.

40. Ewens, *The Role of the Nun*, 156.

41. An excerpt from a newspaper account of the trial of the rioters is included in "The Leadership of Nuns," 132–35.

42. Quoted in Ewens, *The Role of the Nun*, 236–37.

43. For excerpts from records of the Satterlee Military Hospital in Pennsylvania, see Ruether and Keller, *Women and Religion*, vol. 1, 138–41; and MacHaffie, *Her Story*, 171–77.

44. Dolan, *American Catholic Experience*, 289. See also Mary J. Oates, "Organized Volunteerism: The Catholic Sisters in Massachusetts, 1870–1940," in James, *Women in American Religion*, 154.

45. Brewer, *Nuns and Education*, 137.

46. Ibid., 41.

47. Ewens, *The Role of the Nun*, 267.

48. Ibid., 267–74.

49. Ibid., 274.

50. Anne M. Butler, *Daughters of Joy, Sisters of Misery: Prostitutes in the American West, 1865–90* (Urbana, Ill./Chicago: University of Illinois Press, 1985), 66–67.

51. Kenneally, *American Catholic Women*, 53.

52. Dolan, *American Catholic Experience*, 286.

53. Kenneally, *American Catholic Women*, 78.

54. Ibid., 15.

55. Quoted in Brewer, *Nuns and Education*, 32. Unable to recruit other sisters, Mazzuchelli then founded the Sinsinawa Dominicans as a women's order.

56. Dolan, *American Catholic Experience*, 289.

57. Ewens, "Women in the Convent," 29.

58. Ibid., 32.

59. Kenneally, *American Catholic Women*, 78.

60. Dolan, *American Catholic Experience*, 265. For a biography of Mother Joseph, see Sister Mary McCrosson, *The Bell and the River* (Palo Alto, Calif.: Pacific Books, 1957).

### Notes for chapter 15: Jewish Women in Nineteenth-Century America

1. There were a few scholarly women in Hasidic Judaism, but they were rare exceptions indeed. See Sally Priesand, *Judaism and the New Woman* (New York: Behrman House, Inc., 1975), 28–29.

2. See Judith Plaskow, *Standing Again at Sinai: Judaism from a Feminist Perspective* (San Francisco: Harper & Row, 1990), 170–85, on the ambiguity of traditional Jewish attitudes toward sexuality.

3. Chava Weissler, "The Traditional Piety of Ashkenazic Women," in Arthur Green, ed., *Jewish Spirituality: From the Sixteenth Century Revival to the Present* (New York: Crossroad, 1987), 245–75.

4. See Rebecca Samuel's letters in Jacob R. Marcus, ed., *The American Jewish Woman: A Documentary History* (New York: KTAV Publishing House, 1981), 42–46.

5. Tradition holds that as a young woman she was in love with a Christian, but she did not marry him lest she lose her Jewish identity; see Anita Libman Lebeson, *Recall to Life: Jewish Women in American History* (New Brunswick, N.J.: Thomas Yoseloff, 1970), 75–77. Jacob Marcus, on the other hand, rejects the tradition of the Gentile suitor and suggests it was the lack of a socially suitable Jewish mate that led to her spinsterhood, while Linda Gordon Kuzmack argues that Gratz remained single by her own positive choice. Jacob R. Marcus, *The American Jewish Woman, 1654–1980* (New York: KTAV Publishing House, 1981), 24; Linda Gordon Kuzmack, *Woman's Cause: The Jewish Woman's Movement in England and the United States, 1881–1933* (Columbus, Ohio: Ohio State University Press, 1990), 20.

6. Excerpted in Ellen M. Umansky and Dianne Ashton, eds., *Four Centuries of Jewish Women's Spirituality: A Sourcebook* (Boston: Beacon Press, 1992), 85.

7. Kuzmack, *Woman's Cause*, 19–22.

8. Umansky and Ashton, *Four Centuries*, 5.

9. Ann Braude, "The Jewish Woman's Encounter with American Culture," in Rosemary Radford Ruether and Rosemary Skinner Keller, *Women and Religion in America*, vol. 1, *The Nineteenth Century* (San Francisco: Harper & Row, 1981), 153.

See also Riv-Ellen Prell, "The Vision of Woman in Classical Reform Judaism," *Journal of the American Academy of Religion* 50 (December 1982): 575–89.

10. Quoted in Priesand, *The New Woman,* 32.

11. Prell, "Vision of Woman," 579–81.

12. For a brief and helpful summary of the history, ideology, and institutions of Reform Judaism from 1810 to 1983, see Marc Lee Raphael, *Profiles in American Judaism: The Reform, Conservative, Orthodox, and Reconstructionist Traditions in Historical Perspective* (San Francisco: Harper & Row, 1984), 1–78.

13. Braude, "Jewish Woman's Encounter," 155.

14. Isaac M. Wise, "Women as Members of Congregations," in David Philipson and Louis Grossman, eds., *Selected Writings of Isaac M. Wise, with a Biography* (1900; reprint, New York: Arno Press and the New York Times, 1969), 398–99.

15. Kuzmack, *Woman's Cause,* 23.

16. Excerpted by Braude, "Jewish Woman's Encounter," 175.

17. For a firsthand account of conditions within the Pale, see Mary Antin, *The Promised Land* (Boston/New York: Houghton Mifflin Co., 1912), chap. 1.

18. Ibid., 37.

19. Bella Chagall, *Burning Lights* (New York: Schocken Books, 1946), 48–49. Chagall's reminiscences give a particularly vivid picture of the Jewish holidays she celebrated as a child. Beyond the accounts of shtetl life found in individual autobiographies like Chagall's and Antin's, see Mark Zborowski and Elizabeth Herzog, *Life Is With People: The Culture of the Shtetl* (New York: Schocken Books, 1952) and Sydney Stahl Weinberg, *The World of Our Mothers: The Lives of Jewish Immigrant Women* (Chapel Hill, N.C.: University of North Carolina Press, 1988).

20. Weinberg, *World of Our Mothers,* 72.

21. Chagall, *Burning Lights,* 96–105.

22. Antin, *The Promised Land,* 34.

23. Weinberg, *World of Our Mothers,* 94.

24. Paula E. Hyman, "Gender and the Immigrant Jewish Experience in the United States," in Judith R. Baskin, ed., *Jewish Women in Historical Perspective* (Detroit: Wayne State University Press, 1991), 230. For a glimpse of the personal pain of such poor women, see selections from the *Bintel Brief,* an advice column in the *Jewish Daily Forward,* excerpted in Ann Braude, "Jewish Women in the Twentieth Century: Building a Life in America," in Rosemary Radford Ruether and Rosemary Skinner Keller, eds., *Women and Religion in America,* vol. 3, *1900–1968* (San Francisco: Harper & Row, 1986), 152–57.

25. Hyman, "Immigrant Jewish Experience," 226.

26. Philip S. Foner, *Women and the American Labor Movement: From Colonial Times to the Eve of World War I* (New York: The Free Press, 1979), 328. Foner's study is an extensive account. For a briefer summary of the role of Jewish women in the early twentieth-century labor movement, see Charlotte Baum, Paula Hyman, and Sonya Michel, *The Jewish Woman in America* (New York: The Dial Press, 1976), 121–62.

27. See Weinberg, *World of Our Mothers,* 202; Hyman, "Immigrant Jewish Experience," 228.

28. Alice Kessler-Harris, "Organizing the Unorganizable: Three Jewish Women and Their Union," in Milton Cantor and Bruce Laurie, eds., *Class, Sex, and the*

*Woman Worker* (Westport, Conn.: Greenwood Press, 1977), 149. See also Hyman, "Immigrant Jewish Experience," 229–30.

29. Weinberg, *World of Our Mothers*, 263.

30. On Conservative Judaism in the United States, see Raphael, *Profiles in American Judaism*, 79–123.

31. Excerpted in Braude, "Jewish Woman's Encounter," 190.

32. Excerpted in Umansky and Ashton, *Four Centuries*, 130–36.

33. Excerpted in ibid., 136–38.

34. Julia Richman, "Women Wage-Workers: With Reference to Directing Immigrants," excerpted in Marcus, *The American Jewish Woman*, 421–27.

35. Rebekah Kohut, the widow of a famous traditionalist rabbi, became the president of the New York chapter of the NCJW. Although she devoted her early years to her husband, Alexander, and her eight stepchildren, after his death she became an active speaker and educator and was prominent in Jewish women's circles. See Rebekah Kohut, *My Portion (An Autobiography)* (1925; reprint, New York: Arno Press, 1975.) Rebekah was to be on the program at the Jewish Women's Congress in 1893, but Alexander persuaded her that he could not survive her absence for a week, so she stayed home and her sister read her paper instead.

36. See Kuzmack, *Woman's Cause*, 63–78.

37. Excerpted in Braude, "Jewish Woman's Encounter," 169–71.

38. Kuzmack, *Woman's Cause*, 40.

39. Marcus, *The American Jewish Woman, 1654–1980*, 93.

40. Kuzmack, *Woman's Cause*, 38–40, 143–47.

41. Elinor Lerner, "Jewish Involvement in the New York City Woman Suffrage Movement," in Barbara J. Harris and JoAnn K. McNamara, eds., *Women and the Structure of Society* (Durham, N.C.: Duke University Press, 1984), 191–205, argues that Jewish contributions to the suffrage cause have been historically underrated. Nevertheless, Jews, like other Americans, had their share of opponents of female suffrage, including some prominent women. See Kuzmack, *Woman's Cause*, 149–51.

## Notes for chapter 16: Alternative Religions in Nineteenth-Century America

1. Shakers have fascinated Americans since the nineteenth century, and the literature about them is enormous. Best known to the public for their architecture and crafts and for the hymn, "Simple Gifts," they have also intrigued students of utopian experiments. Stephen J. Stein, *The Shaker Experience in America: A History of the United Society of Believers* (New Haven, Conn./London: Yale University Press, 1992) is a fine comprehensive study, especially since he carries his narrative into the late twentieth century. Other recent works have studied the significance of Shaker ideas and practices for women. See, for example, Barbara Brown Zikmund, "The Feminist Thrust of Sectarian Christianity," in Rosemary Ruether and Eleanor McLaughlin, eds., *Women of Spirit: Female Leadership in the Jewish and Christian Traditions* (New York: Simon and Schuster, 1979), 205–24; Mary Farrell Bednarowski, "Outside the Mainstream: Women's Religion and Women Religious Leaders in Nineteenth-Century America," *Journal of the American Academy of Religion* 48 (June 1980): 207–31; Rosemary Radford Ruether, "Women in Utopian

Movements," in Rosemary Radford Ruether and Rosemary Skinner Keller, *Women and Religion in America,* vol. 1, *The Nineteenth Century* (San Francisco: Harper & Row, 1981), 46–100; Marjorie Procter-Smith, *Women in Shaker Community and Worship: A Feminist Analysis of the Uses of Religious Symbolism* (Lewiston, N.Y.: Edwin Mellen Press, 1985); and Lawrence Foster, *Women, Family, and Utopia: Communal Experiments of the Shakers, the Oneida Community, and the Mormons* (Syracuse, N.Y.: Syracuse University Press, 1991).

2. Foster, *Women, Family, and Utopia,* 6, argues that one of the four lived until age six.

3. For further discussion of Mother Ann's work and its significance for women, see Stein, *The Shaker Experience,* 165–200; Foster, *Women, Family, and Utopia,* 37–38, 43–56; Procter-Smith, *Community and Worship,* 180–208.

4. Foster, *Women, Family, and Utopia,* 25–27; Procter-Smith, *Community and Worship,* 100–105.

5. Stein, *The Shaker Experience,* 195.

6. Procter-Smith, *Community and Worship,* 47.

7. As Ruether notes, the Shakers practiced "the division of labor of the preindustrial village, not that of average middle-class Americans of that period." That is, Shaker women's work was more varied, directly productive, and economically necessary than that of typical middle-class True Women ("Women in Utopian Movements," 52).

8. Procter-Smith, *Community and Worship,* 199–200.

9. Ibid., 162–63.

10. Stein, *The Shaker Experience,* 256–72.

11. Eldress Polly Reed to Winniford Aspinwall, April 24, 1881, New York State Library. My thanks to Professor Jane F. Crosthwaite of Mount Holyoke College for calling to my attention this letter, transcribed by her former student, Glendyne Wergland.

12. Not only was complex marriage controversial in its own time, but that system, the practice of birth control known as "male continence," and the status of women at Oneida draw divergent assessments from contemporary scholars. Ira L. Mandelker, *Religion, Society, and Utopia in Nineteenth-Century America* (Amherst, Mass.: University of Massachusetts Press, 1984), 93–162, and Foster, *Women, Family, and Utopia,* 73–120, are generally positive though not uncritical, while Louis J. Kern, *An Ordered Love: Sex Roles and Sexuality in Victorian Utopias—the Shakers, the Mormons, and the Oneida Community* (Chapel Hill, N.C.: University of North Carolina Press, 1981), 205–79, presents a Freudian and largely negative analysis.

13. Quoted in Robert Allerton Parker, *A Yankee Saint: John Humphrey Noyes and the Oneida Community* (1935; reprint, Hamden, Conn.: Archon Books, 1973), 25–26.

14. Quoted in ibid., 44.

15. *Bible Communism: A Compilation of the Annual Reports and Other Publications of the Oneida Association and Its Branches* (1853; reprint, New York: AMS Press, 1973), 26–31.

16. See ibid., 42–53.

17. Foster, *Women, Family, and Utopia,* 82–83.

18. "First Annual Report of the Oneida Association, January 1, 1849," in

Constance Noyes Robertson, ed., *Oneida Community: An Autobiography, 1851–1876* (Syracuse, N.Y.: Syracuse University Press, 1970), 297–98.

19. See ibid., 294–310.

20. For a recent biography of the complex woman who supported her husband and his religion and yet bitterly opposed his ideas on polygamy, see Linda King Newell and Valeen Tippetts Avery, *Mormon Enigma: Emma Hale Smith—Prophet's Wife, "Elect Lady," Polygamy's Foe, 1804–1879* (Garden City, N.Y.: Doubleday and Co., 1984).

21. Foster, *Women, Family, and Utopia,* 182.

22. Quoted in ibid., 188.

23. Stephanie Smith Goodson, "Plural Wives," in Claudia L. Bushman, ed., *Mormon Sisters: Women in Early Utah* (Salt Lake City, Utah: Olympus Publishing Co., 1976), 89–111, covers a range of responses to plural marriages among Mormon women.

24. Estimates about how many Mormon marriages were polygamous vary: Foster, *Women, Family, and Utopia,* 189, suggests that 15 to 20 percent of marriages were polygamous, and two-thirds of these involved only two wives, while Jill Mulvay Derr, "Strength in Our Union: The Making of Mormon Sisterhood" in Maureen Ursenbach Beecher and Lavina Fielding Anderson, eds., *Sisters in Spirit: Mormon Women in Historical and Cultural Perspective* (Urbana, Ill./Chicago: University of Illinois Press, 1987), 166, cites a figure of 25 to 50 percent of marriages involving polygamy and, given the nature of polygamy (actually polygyny), perhaps 80 percent of the women. The authors in *Sisters in Spirit* are themselves Mormon, and while they are by no means uncritical of particular practices and beliefs, their assessments of nineteenth-century Mormon women and their roles are generally positive. For a more negative view of Mormon ideas, especially polygamy and the place of women, see Kern, *An Ordered Love,* 137–204.

25. Claudia Lauper Bushman, "Mystics and Healers," in Bushman, ed., *Mormon Sisters,* 1–23; Linda King Newell, "Gifts of the Spirit: Women's Share," in Beecher and Anderson, *Sisters in Spirit,* 111–50.

26. Carol Cornwall Madsen, "Mormon Women and the Temple: Toward a New Understanding," in Beecher and Anderson, *Sisters in Spirit,* 80–110.

27. Newell and Avery, *Mormon Enigma,* 106.

28. Ibid., 106–18.

29. Judith Rasmussen Dushku, "Feminists," in Bushman, *Mormon Sisters,* 177–97, criticizes interpretations of female suffrage in Utah as *simply* a ploy by male Mormons to increase the church's power, focusing instead on Mormon women's views.

30. Quoted in ibid., 194–95.

31. Early biographies of Eddy were either extremely critical or highly laudatory; recent works are more balanced but hampered by the inaccessibility of Christian Science archives to general scholars. For a helpful biographical summary, see Sydney E. Ahlstrom's entry on Eddy in Edward T. James, Janet Wilson James, and Paul S. Boyer, eds., *Notable American Women 1607–1950: A Biographical Dictionary,* vol. 1 (Cambridge, Mass.: Belknap Press or Harvard University Press, 1971), 551–61. For a brief survey of secondary literature, see Susan Hill Lindley, "The Ambiguous Feminism of Mary Baker Eddy," *Journal of Religion* 64 (July 1984): 318–19.

32. Mary Baker G. Eddy, *Science and Health with Key to the Scriptures* (Boston: Joseph Armstrong, 1905), 517.

33. Lindley, "Ambiguous Feminism," 322–25.

34. Eddy, *Science and Health*, 534.

35. Denial of the ultimate reality of matter did not, however, imply for Eddy and Christian Scientists denial of the comforts and rewards of this life. As Ahlstrom notes, Eddy's "religion could in a sense be described as a this-worldly, man-centered, health-oriented immaterialism" (*American Women*, 559).

36. In a poem titled "Woman's Rights," Eddy summarized those "rights" as the female right to be religious, charitable, and nurturing through nursing and education in a "happy home." Quoted in Lindley, "Ambiguous Feminism," 326.

37. Eddy, *Science and Health*, 59.

38. Linda P. Wilcox, "The Mormon Concept of a Mother in Heaven" in Beecher and Anderson, *Sisters in Spirit*, 64.

39. Eliza R. Snow, "O My Father," hymn 292 in *Hymns of the Church of Jesus Christ of Latter-Day Saints: 1985* (Salt Lake City, Utah: The Church of Jesus Christ of Latter-day Saints, 1985).

40. Ruether, "Women in Utopian Movements," 47–48, 60–61.

41. Ibid., 50.

42. Ann Braude, *Radical Spirits: Spiritualism and Women's Rights in Nineteenth-Century America* (Boston: Beacon Press, 1989), 83. This fine study chronicles opportunities for female religious leadership in Spiritualism and explores its widespread theological appeal to many nineteenth-century American women as it offered "empirical evidence of the immortality of the soul," a liberal alternative to the Calvinism that could damn helpless and innocent infants, and comfort and assurance for those who had lost loved ones in death (33ff.). Indeed, many Americans who participated in Spiritualism did not feel compelled to break with their own more orthodox churches.

43. Ibid., 85.

44. Braude, *Radical Spirits*, 117–41; Ruether, "Women in Utopian Movements," 49.

45. Braude, *Radical Spirits*, 117–41.

## Notes for chapter 17: A Nineteenth-Century Feminist Critique of Religion

1. Elizabeth Cady Stanton, et al., *The Woman's Bible* (New York: European Publishing Co., 1895, 1898); reprinted as *The Original Feminist Attack on the Bible (The Woman's Bible)*, with introduction by Barbara Welter (New York: Arno Press, 1974), 2:185.

2. Celia Morris Eckhardt, *Fanny Wright: Rebel in America* (Cambridge, Mass.: Harvard University Press, 1984) is a sensitive and balanced biography of this controversial woman.

3. Frances Wright D'Arusmont, *Life, Letters, and Lectures: 1834/1844* (New York: Arno Press, 1972), 70.

4. See, for example, ibid., 68, 98–100.

5. Ibid., 67.

6. Ibid., 45.

7. Ibid., 25.

8. Ibid., 31ff.

9. Quoted in Eckhardt, *Fanny Wright,* 279–80.

10. Ibid., 156–57.

11. Elizabeth Cady Stanton, Susan B. Anthony, and Matilda Joslyn Gage, eds., *History of Woman Suffrage,* vol. 1, *1848–1861* (1881; reprint, New York: Arno and the New York Times, 1969), 692.

12. Yuri Suhl, *Ernestine L. Rose and the Battle for Human Rights* (New York: Reynal & Co., 1959), 10.

13. Stanton, et al., eds., *History of Woman Suffrage,* 1:100.

14. Ibid., 1:376.

15. Ernestine Rose, Speech at the Second National Woman's Rights Convention, Worcester, Mass., October 15, 1851, reprinted in the appendix of Suhl, *Human Rights,* 283. Ernestine Rose does not appear to have mixed her arguments appealing to natural rights and to woman's finer-and-different nature as justification for change, but since relatively few of Rose's speeches and writings are preserved, such a conclusion must remain tentative.

16. See Suhl, *Human Rights,* 127–32, 164–66; and Stanton, et al., eds., *History of Woman Suffrage* 1:376–86, 1:539–40.

17. Ernestine Rose, Speech at the Infidel Convention, New York, May 4, 1845, reprinted in the appendix of Suhl, *Human Rights,* 279–80.

18. Letter quoted in Suhl, *Human Rights,* 221–22.

19. Suhl, *Human Rights,* 224.

20. Ibid., 252.

21. Bell Gale Chevigny, *The Woman and the Myth: Margaret Fuller's Life and Writings* (Old Westbury, N.Y.: The Feminist Press, 1976), 38.

22. See ibid., 400n40 for a brief summary of the controversy.

23. Paula Blanchard, *Margaret Fuller: From Transcendentalism to Revolution* (New York: Delacorte Press/Seymour Lawrence, 1978), 147.

24. Margaret Fuller, *Woman in the Nineteenth Century* (1855; reprint, New York: W. W. Norton & Co., 1971), 119ff.

25. Ibid., 174–75.

26. Ibid., 35.

27. Ibid., 115–16; see also 168ff.

28. Ibid., 25, 105, 171–72.

29. Margaret Fuller, "Credo," in Frederick Augustus Braun, *Margaret Fuller and Goethe* (New York: Henry Holt & Co., 1910), 252–54.

30. Ibid., 257.

31. Ibid., 253.

32. Arthur B. Fuller's preface to Margaret Fuller, *Woman in the Nineteenth Century,* 8–9.

33. Evelyn A. Kirkley, "'The Female Peril': American Freethinkers and Woman Suffrage," 6–8, a paper delivered at the national meeting of the American Academy of Religion, Kansas City, Missouri, November, 1991. Used by permission of the author.

34. Stanton, et al., eds., *History of Woman Suffrage,* 2:353.

35. Two recent biographies of Cady Stanton are Lois W. Banner, *Elizabeth Cady Stanton: A Radical for Women's Rights* (Boston: Little, Brown and Co., 1980) and Elisabeth Griffith, *In Her Own Right: The Life of Elizabeth Cady Stanton* (New York/Oxford: Oxford University Press, 1984). There is no full-length biography of Gage, but helpful summaries of her life and contributions can be found in Elizabeth B. Warbasse's entry on her in Edward T. James, Janet Wilson James, and Paul S. Boyer, *Notable American Women, 1607–1950: A Biographical Dictionary*, vol. 2 (Cambridge, Mass.: Belknap Press of Harvard University Press, 1971), and Sally Roesch Wagner's introduction to a reprint edition of Matilda Joslyn Gage, *Woman, Church, and State* (Watertown, Mass.: Persephone Press, 1980). For a recent thoughtful analysis of Stanton's religious and ethical ideas, see Mary D. Pellauer, *Toward a Tradition of Feminist Theology: The Religious Social Thought of Elizabeth Cady Stanton, Susan B. Anthony, and Anna Howard Shaw* (Brooklyn, N.Y.: Carlson Publishing Inc., 1991).

36. Stanton, et al., eds., *History of Woman Suffrage*, 3:124.

37. *The Woman's Bible*, 1:7.

38. Ibid., 1:14–15.

39. Quoted in Banner, *Elizabeth Cady Stanton*, 155.

40. Quoted in Pellauer, *Feminist Theology*, 35.

41. Stanton, et al., *The Woman's Bible*, 1:66.

42. Ibid., 2:25.

43. Ibid., 2:125–26.

44. Ibid., 2:114.

45. Ibid., 2: 214.

46. Griffith, *In Her Own Right*, 212.

47. Gage, *Woman, Church, and State*, 9, 21.

48. Ibid., 245–46.

49. See Rosemary Radford Ruether, "Radical Victorians: The Quest for an Alternative Culture," in Rosemary Radford Ruether and Rosemary Skinner Keller, eds., *Women and Religion in America*, vol. 3, *1900–1968* (San Francisco: Harper & Row, 1986), 1–10. Other women through the last years of the nineteenth century and into the early decades of the twentieth would make similar use of anthropological discoveries and theories about matriarchy, including Charlotte Perkins Gilman, the ideological heir of Gage but a biological descendent of the Beechers, who published in 1923 a book titled *His Religion and Hers* in which she asserted that "his" religion focused on death and the world to come, while "hers" was concerned with birth, nurturing, and growth in this life.

50. Cady Stanton not only took opportunities to speak in churches when she could, she made extensive use of the exegetical work of liberal bishop John Colenso in her commentaries on the Pentateuch, finding him to be one of the few Anglicans she admired. See Barbara Welter's introduction to the reprint of Stanton, et al., *Woman's Bible*, vii.

51. Mary Farrell Bednarowski cites "a tempering or denial of the doctrine of the Fall" as one of four key characteristics of Shakerism, Christian Science, and Theosophy ("Outside the Mainstream: Women's Religion and Women Religious Leaders in Nineteenth-Century America," *Journal of the American Academy of Religion* 48 [June 1980]: 209). Braude argues that a major appeal of Spiritualism was its

rejection of Calvinism, including the ideas of a fall, original sin, hell, and the need for a Savior, as "inconsistent with the benevolence of God and the essential goodness of human beings . . ." *Radical Spirits*, 38.

## Notes for chapter 18: Women's Religious Leadership in the Twentieth Century: Movement in the Mainline

1. Gail Bederman, "'The Women Have Had Charge of the Church Work Long Enough': The Men and Religion Forward Movement of 1911–1912 and the Masculinization of Middle-Class Protestantism," *American Quarterly* 41 (September 1989): 436.

2. Ibid., 434. Presumably, the contemporary movement Promise Keepers is another example.

3. R. Pierce Beaver, *All Loves Excelling: American Protestant Women in World Mission* (Grand Rapids, Mich.: Eerdmans, 1968), 178–80.

4. Helen Barrett Montgomery, *Western Women in Eastern Lands: An Outline Study of Fifty Years of Woman's Work in Foreign Missions* (1910; reprint, New York: Garland, 1987), 269.

5. Mary Sudman Donovan, *A Different Call: Women's Ministries in the Episcopal Church, 1850–1920* (Wilton, Conn.: Morehouse-Barlow, 1986), 128.

6. Ernest Trice Thompson, *Presbyterians in the South*, vol. 3, *1890–1972* (Richmond, Va.: John Knox Press, 1973), 386.

7. Ibid., 389. For Southern Presbyterian women, see also Lois A. Boyd and R. Douglas Brackenridge, *Presbyterian Women in America: Two Centuries of Quest for Status* (Westport, Conn.: Greenwood, 1983), 207–24.

8. See Sharon Klingelsmith, "Women in the Mennonite Church, 1900–1930," *The Mennonite Quarterly Review* 54 (July 1980): 163–207.

9. Lorraine Lollis, *The Shape of Adam's Rib: A Lively History of Women's Work in the Christian Church* (St. Louis: Bethany Press, 1970), 99–111.

10. Beaver, *All Loves Excelling*, 184–85.

11. Ibid., 186.

12. Theressa Hoover, *With Unveiled Face: Centennial Reflections on Women and Men in the Community of the Church* (New York: Women's Division, General Board of Global Ministries, The United Methodist Church, 1983), 23.

13. Evelyn Brooks Higginbotham, *Righteous Discontent: The Women's Movement in the Black Baptist Church, 1880–1920* (Cambridge, Mass.: Harvard University Press, 1993), 159.

14. Quoted in Rosemary Skinner Keller, "Patterns of Laywomen's Leadership in Twentieth-Century Protestantism," in Rosemary Radford Ruether and Rosemary Skinner Keller, *Women and Religion in America*, vol. 3, *1900–1968* (San Francisco: Harper & Row, 1986), 270.

15. Report excerpted in Barbara J. MacHaffie, *Readings in Her Story: Women in Christian Tradition* (Minneapolis: Fortress, 1992), 194.

16. Bennett's speech is excerpted in Keller, "Patterns of Laywomen's Leadership," 287–90.

17. L. DeAne Lagerquist, *From Our Mother's Arms: A History of Women in the American Lutheran Church* (Minneapolis: Augsburg, 1987), 29, 112–13.

18. Donovan, *A Different Call*, 173; Pamela W. Darling, *New Wine: The Story of*

*Women Transforming Leadership and Power in the Episcopal Church* (Cambridge, Mass.: Cowley Publications, 1994), 51–98. It is not within the scope of this work to try to identify dates for the granting of different female laity rights for the many Christian denominations in America; however, a helpful appendix of the "Legal Status of Women in the Denominations" as of midcentury is included in Inez M. Cavert, *Women in American Church Life* (New York: Friendship Press, published for the National Council of Churches of Christ in America, 1949), 87–91. Cavert includes information for 105 denominations on three points: whether women can serve on local church boards; whether they can serve as representatives in the highest denominational body; and whether they can be ordained or licensed as ministers.

19. Quoted in Margaret Shannon, *Just Because: The Story of the National Movement of Church Women United in the U. S. A., 1941–1975* (Corte Madera, Calif.: Omega Books, 1977), 19. See also Cavert, *Women in Church Life*, 57ff.; and Virginia Lieson Brereton, "United and Slighted: Women as Subordinated Insiders," in William R. Hutchison, ed., *Between the Times: The Travail of the Protestant Establishment in America, 1900–1960* (Cambridge: Cambridge University Press, 1989).

20. Shannon, *Just Because*, 34.

21. Brereton, *United and Slighted*, 150.

22. Dorothy Jean Furnish, "Women in Religious Education: Pioneers for Women in Professional Ministry," in Ruether and Keller, eds., *Women and Religion*, vol. 3, 310–11. For women and religious education in the Presbyterian Church, see Elizabeth Howell Verdesi, *In But Still Out: Women in the Church* (Philadelphia: Westminster Press, 1973), 109–37.

23. Furnish, "Religious Education," 312.

24. Keller, "Patterns of Laywomen's Leadership," 271.

25. Sophia Fahs's ordination sermon, excerpted in Furnish, "Religious Education," 325.

26. Virginia Lieson Brereton and Christa Ressmeyer Klein, "American Women in Ministry: A History of Protestant Beginning Points," in Rosemary Radford Ruether and Eleanor McLaughlin, eds., *Women of Spirit: Female Leadership in the Jewish and Christian Traditions* (New York: Simon and Schuster, 1979), 316.

27. Quoted in ibid., 316–17.

28. C. Eric Lincoln and Lawrence Mamiya, *The Black Church in the African American Experience* (Durham, N.C.: Duke University Press, 1990), 287.

29. Ibid., 44.

30. William T. Noll, "Laity Rights and Leadership: Winning Them for Women in the Methodist Protestant Church, 1860–1900," in Rosemary Skinner Keller, Louise L. Queen, and Hilah F. Thomas, eds., *Women in New Worlds: Historical Perspectives on the Wesleyan Tradition* vol. 1, (Nashville: Abingdon, 1982), 230–31.

31. See Barbara Brown Zikmund, "Winning Ordination for Women in Mainstream Protestant Churches," in Ruether and Keller, eds., *Women and Religion*, vol. 3, 339–83, for a helpful summary of the processes among Methodists, Presbyterians, Lutherans, and Episcopalians, as well as excerpts from key source documents. For more detail on the predecessors of the EUB, see Donald K. Gorrell, "'A New Impulse': Progress in Lay Leadership and Service by Women of the United Brethren in Christ and the Evangelical Association, 1870–1910," in Keller, et al., eds., *Women in New Worlds*, vol. 1, 233–45; and James E. Will, "Ordination of Women: The

Issue in the Church of the United Brethren in Christ," in *Women in New Worlds,* vol. 2, 290–99.

32. See Lincoln and Mamiya, *The Black Church,* 285–89, for a summary of the progress of women's ordination in black denominations.

33. Boyd and Brackenridge, *Presbyterian Women,* 113–17.

34. Quoted in ibid., 183.

35. For an account of the debates in Sweden and a translation of Stendahl's essay, see Krister Stendahl, *The Bible and the Role of Women* (Philadelphia: Fortress, 1966).

36. Quoted in Gracia Grindal, "Getting Women Ordained," in Todd Nichol and Marc Kolden, eds., *Called and Ordained: Lutheran Perspectives on the Office of the Ministry* (Minneapolis: Fortress, 1990), 166.

37. For a helpful summary of the events and issues among American Lutherans, see Grindal, "Getting Women Ordained," 161–79.

38. Darling, *New Wine,* 99–180. For contemporary accounts of the Episcopal actions and arguments, see Emily C. Hewitt and Suzanne R. Hiatt, *Women Priests: Yes or No?* (New York: Seabury Press, 1973); Norene Carter, "The Episcopalian Story," in Ruether and McLaughlin, eds., *Women of Spirit,* 356–72; Heather Huyck, "Indelible Change: Woman Priests in the Episcopal Church," *Historical Magazine of the Protestant Episcopal Church* 51 (December 1982): 385–98. While all three of these authors support female ordination, they also summarize the principal arguments raised against it.

39. Ellen M. Umansky, "Spiritual Expressions: Jewish Women's Religious Lives in the Twentieth-Century United States," in Judith R. Baskin, ed., *Jewish Women in Historical Perspective* (Detroit: Wayne State University Press, 1991), 271.

40. Norma Fain Pratt, "Transitions in Judaism: The Jewish American Woman Through the 1930s," in Janet Wilson James, ed., *Women in American Religion* (Philadelphia: University of Pennsylvania Press, 1980), 225.

41. See Charlotte Baum, et al., *The Jewish Woman in America* (New York: The Dial Press, 1976), 187–261, for a provocative survey of Jewish female literary types, their historical roots and distortions.

42. Pratt, "Transitions in Judaism," 220ff.

43. A. Irma Cohen, "Judaism and the Modern Woman," excerpted by Ann D. Braude, "Jewish Women in the Twentieth Century," in Ruether and Keller, eds., *Women and Religion,* vol. 3, 161.

44. For accounts of the events and arguments about women's ordination as Reform rabbis, see Sally Priesand, *Judaism and the New Woman* (New York: Behrman House, 1975), 62–67; and Umansky, "Spiritual Expressions," 278–81. Jacob R. Marcus, ed., *The American Jewish Woman: A Documentary History* (New York: KTAV Publishing House, 1981), gives some excerpts from the 1922 discussion of the rabbis of the Central Conference, 739–44, while Ann Braude, "The Jewish Woman's Encounter with American Culture," provides an excerpt from Neumark's own arguments in favor of female ordination in Ruether and Keller, *Women and Religion,* vol. 3, 165.

45. Pamela S. Nadell, "The Women Who Would Be Rabbis," in T. M. Rudavsky, ed., *Gender and Judaism: The Transformation of Tradition* (New York: New York University Press, 1995), 127ff.

46. Regina Jones was ordained by another rabbi in the 1930s in Germany and

practiced until 1940, when she was sent to a concentration camp. Sally Priesand, *Judaism and the New Woman* (New York: Behrman House, Inc., 1975), 67.

47. Mordecai M. Kaplan, the founder of Reconstructionism, wanted it to be an organic approach permeating American Judaism and emphasizing Judaism as a total civilization, not as a supernaturalistic religion. See Marc Lee Raphael, *Profiles in American Judaism: The Reform, Conservative, Orthodox, and Reconstructionist Traditions in Historical Perspective* (San Francisco: Harper & Row, 1984), 179–94, for a helpful summary of the growth, ideas, and institutions of Reconstructionist Judaism.

48. Ellen M. Umansky and Dianne Ashton, eds., *Four Centuries of Jewish Women's Spirituality: A Sourcebook* (Boston: Beacon Press, 1992), 22.

49. "Final Report of the Commission for the Study of the Ordination of Women as Rabbis," in Simon Greenberg, ed., *The Ordination of Women as Rabbis: Studies and Responsa* (New York: The Jewish Theological Seminary of America, 1988), 20–21.

## Notes for chapter 19: Women's Religious Leadership in the Twentieth Century: Ambiguity among Evangelicals and Mormons

1. See, for example, Donald W. Dayton, *Discovering an Evangelical Heritage* (New York: Harper & Row, 1976), 85–98; and Nancy A. Hardesty, *Women Called to Witness: Evangelical Feminism in the 19th Century* (Nashville: Abingdon Press, 1984).

2. These women's ideas and the results of their research were published in new journals, like *Dialogue* and *Exponent II*, and in books: Claudia L. Bushman, ed., *Mormon Sisters: Women in Early Utah* (Salt Lake City: Olympus Publishing Company, 1976); Maureen Ursenbach Beecher and Lavina Fielding Anderson, *Sisters in Spirit: Mormon Women in Historical and Cultural Perspective* (Urbana, Ill./ Chicago: University of Illinois Press, 1987).

3. Letha Dawson Scanzoni and Susan Setta, "Women in Evangelical, Holiness, and Pentecostal Traditions," in Rosemary Radford Ruether and Rosemary Skinner Keller, eds., *Women and Religion in America*, vol. 3, *1900–1968* (San Francisco: Harper & Row, 1986), 223–65, is a very helpful and accessible introduction to this topic.

4. At this point, I have followed a modified version of one definition of modern evangelicalism proposed by George Marsden in his introduction to *Evangelicalism and Modern America* (Grand Rapids, Mich.: Eerdmans, 1984), ix–x. Both "evangelicalism" and "fundamentalism" are terms that have been used loosely in popular discussions; in addition, scholars have defined "evangelicalism" in different ways and related the term to different historical periods. Similarly, they have defined "fundamentalism" differently and disagree about the appropriate historical context in which it should be used. Marsden's introduction is a helpful road map for the confused student of "evangelicalism." An appendix titled "Defining Fundamentalism" in Virginia Lieson Brereton, *Training God's Army: The American Bible School, 1880–1940* (Bloomington, Ind.: Indiana University Press, 1990), 165–70, is a concise survey of historical and contemporary meanings of American "fundamentalism."

5. Ronald W. Hogeland, "Charles Hodge, The Association of Gentlemen and Ornamental Womanhood," *Journal of Presbyterian History* 53 (Fall 1975): 239–55.

6. Brereton, *God's Army,* 129–31.

7. Janette Hassey, *No Time for Silence: Evangelical Women in Public Ministry Around the Turn of the Century* (Grand Rapids, Mich.: Zondervan, 1986), 11–45.

8. See ibid., 95–121, for analyses of evangelical defenses of women's preaching.

9. Brereton, *God's Army,* 132.

10. Margaret Lamberts Bendroth, *Fundamentalism and Gender, 1875 to the Present* (New Haven, Conn.: Yale University Press, 1993), 41.

11. Ibid., 54–72. See also Bendroth, "Fundamentalism and Femininity: Points of Encounter Between Religious Conservatives and Women, 1919–1935," *Church History* 61 (June 1992): 221–25.

12. Hassey, *No Time for Silence,* 79.

13. See Bendroth, *op cit.;* and Betty A. Deberg, *Ungodly Women: Gender and the First Wave of American Fundamentalism* (Minneapolis: Fortress, 1990). Deberg draws extensively on popular literature to demonstrate the deep and pervasive uneasiness of fundamentalists with changing gender roles. She further argues that fundamentalism's outspoken opposition to cultural change in gender identities formed a significant, though historically neglected, source of its appeal to many Christians.

14. Quoted in DeBerg, *Ungodly Women,* 92.

15. Nancy Hardesty, Lucille Sider Dayton, and Donald W. Dayton, "Women in the Holiness Movement: Feminism in the Evangelical Tradition," in Rosemary Radford Ruether and Eleanor McLaughlin, *Women of Spirit: Female Leadership in the Jewish and Christian Traditions* (New York: Simon and Schuster, 1979) 234–40; Hassey, *No Time for Silence,* 52–55.

16. Alma White, *Looking Back from Beulah* (Zaraphath, N.J.: Pillar of Fire, 1902); reprinted in *Women in American Protestant Religion, 1800–1930,* ed. Carolyn DeSwart Gifford (New York: Garland, 1987), 237.

17. Susie Cunningham Stanley, *Feminist Pillar of Fire: The Life of Alma White* (Cleveland: Pilgrim Press, 1993), 43.

18. The "Pentecost" of her original church title should not be confused with the pentecostal revival of the twentieth century. In 1910, she published a bitter attack on the new pentecostalism, *Demons and Tongues.*

19. Stanley, *Pillar of Fire,* 98–114. Scanzoni and Setta include a brief selection from one of White's sermons on women's equality in their section in Ruether and Keller, *Women and Religion,* vol. 3, 248–51.

20. Stanley, *Pillar of Fire,* 98.

21. Grant Wacker, "Pentecostalism," in Charles H. Lippy and Peter W. Williams, *Encyclopedia of the American Religious Experience: Studies of Traditions and Movements,* vol. 2, (New York: Charles Scribner's Sons, 1988), 935–36.

22. See Robert Mapes Anderson, *Vision of the Disinherited: The Making of American Pentecostalism* (New York: Oxford University Press, 1979), 153–94, on the divisions within the pentecostal movement.

23. Charles H. Barfoot and Gerald T. Sheppard, "Prophetic vs. Priestly Religion: The Changing Role of Women Clergy in Classical Pentecostal Churches," *Review of Religious Research* 22 (September 1980): 4. The authors argue that white pentecostalism, especially the Church of God, supports the contention of sociologist Max Weber that religions of the disinherited are often initially open to women's equal-

ity but that female religious leadership rarely lasts into a subsequent period of "routinization and regimentation," a period they designate "Priestly Pentecostalism."

24. Wayne Warner, "Maria B. Woodworth-Etter and the Early Pentecostal Movement," *Assemblies of God Heritage* 6 (Winter 1986/87): 11.

25. Ibid., 12. See also Warner's full-length study, *The Woman Evangelist: The Life and Times of Charismatic Evangelist Maria B. Woodworth-Etter* (Metuchen, N.J.: Scarecrow Press, 1986).

26. Edith L. Blumhofer, "A Woman Used by the Spirit," *Paraclete* 21 (Summer 1987): 5–9.

27. C. Eric Lincoln and Lawrence Mamiya, *The Black Church in the African American Experience* (Durham, N.C., Duke University Press, 1990), 88.

28. Edith Waldvogel Blumhofer, *The Assemblies of God: A Popular History* (Springfield, Mo.: Gospel Publishing House, 1985), 137–38.

29. Denial of full ordination to women in most black Holiness and pentecostal denominations, known collectively as the Sanctified Church, did not mean women exercised no power in those groups. They could be missionaries and, sometimes, revivalists or evangelists; they had a significant ministry through music; the women's departments of churches like COGIC developed considerable strength and autonomy in a range of interests, some of which will be dealt with more fully in chapter 21. See Cheryl Townsend Gilkes, "'Together and in Harness': Women's Traditions in the Sanctified Church," *Signs* 10 (Summer 1985): 678–99.

30. Harold Dean Trulear, "Reshaping Black Pastoral Theology: The Vision of Ida B. Robinson," *The Journal of Religious Thought* 46 (Summer–Fall 1989): 28–29. While Trulear's perspective is particularly on Robinson's potential contribution to black pastoral theology, as his title suggests, his article includes valuable biographical information on Robinson. Arthur Huff Fauset, *Black Gods of the Metropolis: Negro Religious Cults of the Urban North* (Philadelphia.: University of Pennsylvania Press, 1944) provides information about Mount Sinai and a contemporary's verbal portrait of its founder, but Fauset's identification of Mount Sinai as a "cult" is questionable.

31. The publication of Edith L. Blumhofer's *Aimee Semple McPherson: Everybody's Sister* (Grand Rapids, Mich.: William B. Eerdmans Publishing Company, 1993) fills a long-standing need for a balanced, critical biography of this important woman. Unlike some earlier biographies, which focused almost entirely on the more sensational aspects of McPherson's public career, like the alleged kidnapping and legal battles with relatives and one-time followers, Blumhofer's volume, while never uncritical, surveys the whole of her life, appreciates her contributions, and sets "Sister" in the broad historical context of evangelicalism in the early decades of the twentieth century. Two helpful articles are William G. McLoughlin, "Aimee Semple McPherson: 'Your Sister in the King's Glad Service,'" *Journal of Popular Culture* 1 (Winter 1967): 193–217; and Susan M. Setta, "Patriarchy and Feminism in Conflict: The Life and Thought of Aimee Semple McPherson," *Anima* 9 (Fall 1983): 128–37.

32. This "ordination" was primarily a confirmation of a person's call for preaching and mission work; it did not, as Blumhofer notes, "automatically translate into access to the pastorate or confer the right to preside over the ordinances of the church . . ." (80). Subsequently, McPherson received other religious credentials, including another pentecostal ordination, formal recognition by the Assemblies of

God as an evangelist (which she later returned over intra-pentecostalist differences), a Methodist exhorter's license, and a Baptist preaching license—plus, of course, her authority in the church she herself founded.

33. Aimee Semple McPherson, *This Is That: Personal Experiences, Sermons, and Writings* (1919; reprint, in Donald W. Dayton, ed., *"The Higher Christian Life": Sources for the Study of the Holiness, Pentecostal, and Keswick Movements,* vol. 27 (New York: Garland, 1985), 102. Aimee's resistance to God's call fit a long-standing pattern for women preachers in America; and she was not unique in her preception that God used a serious illness finally to get her attention.

34. Blumhofer, *Everybody's Sister,* 390.

35. McLoughlin, *Aimee Semple McPherson,* 215.

36. Blumhofer, *Everybody's Sister,* 384.

37. McLoughlin, *Aimee Semple McPherson,* 215.

38. Elaine J. Lawless, *Handmaidens of the Lord: Pentecostal Women Preachers and Traditional Religion* (Philadelphia: University of Pennsylvania Press, 1988), 152.

39. Susan Kwilecki, "Contemporary Pentecostal Clergywomen: Female Christian Leadership, Old Style," *Journal of Feminist Studies in Religion* 3 (Fall 1987): 57–75.

40. Linda King Newell, "Gifts of the Spirit: Women's Share" in Beecher and Anderson, *Sisters in Spirit,* 138.

41. Lavina Fielding Anderson, "Landmarks for LDS Women: A Contemporary Chronology," *Mormon Women's Forum* 3 (December 1992): 6.

42. Jill Mulvay Derr, "'Strength in Our Union': The Making of Mormon Sisterhood," in Beecher and Anderson, *Sisters in Spirit,* 187–88.

43. Anderson, "Landmarks," 4.

44. Linda P. Wilcox, "Mormon Motherhood: Official Images," in Beecher and Anderson, *Sisters in Spirit,* 216–20.

45. Quoted in Anderson, "Landmarks," 4.

46. Sonia Johnson, *From Housewife to Heretic* (New York: Doubleday & Co., 1981) is Johnson's account of her personal journey to feminism and her battle with the male Mormon leadership.

47. The volumes edited by Bushman (*Mormon Sisters*) and by Beecher and Anderson (*Sisters in Spirit*) are examples of such recent work by Mormon women. The authors may be critical of some modern Mormon practices, but they clearly see a positive heritage in their Mormon foremothers, whom they regard as feminist. On the other hand, Marilyn Warenski, a non-Mormon, is less impressed by the "feminism" of early Mormon women, arguing that the nineteenth-century Mormon women who supported female suffrage are similar, not a contrast, to twentieth-century Mormon women rallying against the ERA: both groups of women carried out the agenda and goals of the male leadership of the church (*Patriarchs and Politics: The Plight of the Mormon Woman* [New York: McGraw-Hill, 1978]).

48. Jan Shipps, "Dangerous History: Laurel Ulrich and her Mormon Sisters," *The Christian Century* 110 (October 20, 1993): 1013. See also a special edition of *Mormon Women's Forum* 4 (September 1993) for a chronology of events and statements by some of the disciplined Mormons and their supporters.

49. The New Religious Right has precipitated an enormous literature of attack, defense, and analysis. Among many works, Samuel S. Hill and Dennis E. Owen,

*The New Religious Political Right in America* (Nashville: Abingdon, 1982) is a readable and helpful introduction to the movement, its goals, methods, and critics, and its context in American religious history. Matthew C. Moen, *The Transformation of the Christian Right* (Tuscaloosa, Ala.: University of Alabama Press, 1992) takes up the story a decade later, arguing that the movement had grown both more politically sophisticated in its methods and more "secular" in its public rhetoric if not in the motivations of its followers. For a brief summary of the agenda of the New Religious Right from the perspective of its proponents, see Jerry Falwell, ed., with Ed Dobson and Ed Hindson, *The Fundamentalist Phenomenon: The Resurgence of Conservative Christianity* (Garden City, N.Y.: Doubleday, 1981), 186–223. Frances FitzGerald, "Reflections: Jim and Tammy," *The New Yorker* 66 (April 23, 1990): 45–50, 67–87, is a fascinating account of the Bakkers' rise and fall set in the context of the 1980s. Finally, I want to acknowledge with thanks my debt to my friend and colleague, Professor Erling Jorstad, for his patient help in sorting through and understanding the figures, organizations, and progress of the New Religious Right.

50. Hill and Owen, *Political Right,* 51.

51. DeBerg notes a similarly incongruous—and historically unremarked—earlier alliance between fundamentalists and "their sworn enemy, Roman Catholicism, against divorce" (*Ungodly Women,* 70).

52. See Hill and Owen, *Political Right,* 77–99, for religious critiques of the New Religious Right from leading conservative as well as mainline theologians.

53. See, for example, Randall Balmer's fascinating pilgrimage into what he calls the subculture of American evangelicalism, *Mine Eyes Have Seen the Glory: A Journey into the Evangelical Subculture in America* (New York: Oxford University Press, 1989).

54. It is not my intention to enter here into description, let alone evaluation, of the bitter arguments in late twentieth-century America over these two issues, homosexuality and abortion, beyond identifying their centrality for the New Religious Right and suggesting their connection with its views on women. Nevertheless, two further points should be noted briefly. First, there are religious persons and institutions in America on both sides of both issues, and on both sides they draw upon religious convictions and arguments. Second, there is a minority religious voice within the broad ranks of the "prolife" or "anti-abortion" movement whose agenda does not "fit" other parts of the New Religious Right. Some Roman Catholics and some evangelicals, for example, express what they call a "consistent" life ethic: anti-abortion but also anti-capital punishment, pro-gun control, and pro-peace.

55. John R. Rice, *Bobbed Hair, Bossy Wives, and Women Preachers: Significant Questions for Honest Christian Women Settled by the Word of God* (Wheaton, Ill.: Sword of the Lord Publishers, 1941), 15, 66, 71. Uncut hair continues to hold religious significance for some conservative American Christians. Elaine J. Lawless, "'Your Hair Is Your Glory': Public and Private Symbology of Long Hair for Pentecostal Women," *New York Folklore* 12 (1986): 33–49.

56. Ibid., 13.

57. Ibid., 55.

58. This discussion will refer to only a few representative works, which far from exhaust the genre. Edith L. Blumhofer and Joel A. Carpenter provide two very helpful chapters of annotated bibliography, one on marriage and family and one on

women's roles, in their *Twentieth Century Evangelicalism: A Guide to the Sources* (New York: Garland, 1990), 345–60. Recent scholarly studies have begun to set the relationship of fundamentalism and gender roles in cross-cultural perspective. See, for example, John Stratton Hawley, ed., *Fundamentalism and Gender* (New York: Oxford University Press, 1994). Randall Balmer's case study on American fundamentalism in that collection raises the provocative and intriguing suggestion that late twentieth-century American fundamentalism is so obsessed with abortion because the fetus symbolizes purity, innocence, and vulnerability, qualities that embattled fundamentalists also see in themselves ("American Fundamentalism: The Ideal of Femininity," 57–58).

59. Jerry Falwell, *Listen, America!* (Garden City, N.Y.: Doubleday & Co., 1980), 132.

60. Larry Christenson, *The Christian Family* (Minneapolis: Bethany Fellowship, 1970), 128; see also Falwell, *Listen America!* 126.

61. Marabel Morgan, *The Total Woman* (New York: Fleming Revell, 1973; Pocket Book edition, 1975), 238.

62. The distinction between evangelicalism and the New Religious Right here is significant: I have found no public, identifiable advocate of the New Religious Right who explicitly endorses partnership rather than hierarchy as the model for male-female relationships.

63. Letha Scanzoni and Nancy Hardesty, *All We're Meant to Be: A Biblical Approach to Women's Liberation* (Waco, Tex.: Word Books, 1974).

64. Paul K. Jewett, *MAN as Male and Female: A Study in Sexual Relationships from a Theological Point of View* (Grand Rapids, Mich.: Eerdmans, 1975), 14.

65. Scanzoni and Hardesty, *All We're Meant to Be*, rev. ed. (Nashville: Abingdon, 1986), 9.

66. Carolyn DeArmond Blevins, "Patterns of Ministry among Southern Baptist Women," *Baptist History and Heritage* 22 (July 1987): 45.

67. Ellen M. Rosenberg argues that what occurred was a "New Right takeover attempt" and that the "ostensible battleground" of biblical inerrancy was a "cover ideology" for New Right political issues, including the status of women. "Serving Jesus in the South: Southern Baptist Women under Assault from the New Right," in Holly F. Mathews, ed., *Women in the South: An Anthropological Perspective* (Athens, Ga.: University of Georgia Press, 1989), 122–23. Nancy Tatom Ammerman's study, *Baptist Battles: Social Change and Religious Conflict in the Southern Baptist Convention* (New Brunswick, N.J.: Rutgers University Press, 1990), focuses more on the internal power struggle and the theological battle over inerrancy, and argues that while the views of the fundamentalist wing in that struggle are overwhelmingly supportive of the leaders and agenda of the New Religious Right, the moderate wing was more split in its endorsement of particular New Religious Right issues and more than a little suspicious of Jerry Falwell and his Moral Majority (100ff.).

68. Ammerman, *Baptist Battles*, 223–24.

69. Blevins, "Patterns of Ministry," 47; Ammerman, 224.

70. Scanzoni and Setta, "Traditions," 229–32.

71. Scanzoni and Setta cite only Katharine C. Bushnell and Jessie Penn-Lewis as rare exceptions (230), yet Stanley's work on White suggests that she too argued for full male-female equality.

72. Kwilecki, "Pentecostal Clergywomen," 67.
73. Bendroth, *Fundamentalism and Gender*, 11.
74. Hassey, *No Time for Silence*, 139.
75. Scanzoni and Setta, "Traditions," 232.
76. Ibid., 233.
77. Hassey, *No Time for Silence*, 143.
78. Ibid., 138.

## Notes for chapter 20: Women's Religious Leadership in the Twentieth Century: Affirming Traditional Roles

1. Pope John Paul II, "Apostolic Letter on Ordination and Women (*Ordinatio Sacerdotalis*)," May 22, 1994. Reprinted in *Origins: CNS Documentary Service* 24 (June 9, 1994): 51.

2. Jay P. Dolan, *The American Catholic Experience: A History from Colonial Times to the Present* (Garden City, N.Y.: Doubleday, 1985), 371.

3. See, for example, Ada Maria Isasi-Diaz and Yolanda Tarango, *Hispanic Women: Prophetic Voice in the Church* (San Francisco: Harper & Row, 1988).

4. James W. Albers, "Perspectives on the History of Women in the Lutheran Church–Missouri Synod during the Nineteenth Century," *The Lutheran Historical Conference: Essays and Reports* 9 (1982): 139.

5. Despite their historic importance and their growing numbers, Eastern Orthodox Christians in the United States have received far less scholarly attention than Protestants, Catholics, Jews, and even proportionately much smaller groups like the Shakers, although that neglect is slowly being remedied as American Orthodox Christians themselves have become more confident and less divided than they were. For a helpful summary of Eastern Orthodoxy in America, see Paul D. Garrett, "Eastern Christianity," in Charles H. Lippy and Peter W. Williams, eds., *Encyclopedia of the American Religious Experience: Studies of Traditions and Movements* vol. 1, (New York: Charles Scribner's Sons, 1988), 330–44.

6. Jack Wertheimer, *A People Divided: Judaism in Contemporary America* (New York: Basic Books, 1993), 114. For Orthodox Judaism in twentieth-century America, see also Reuven P. Bulka, ed., *Dimensions of Orthodox Judaism* (New York: KTAV Publishing House, 1983).

7. Marc Lee Raphael, *Profiles in American Judaism: The Reform, Conservative, Orthodox, and Reconstructionist Traditions in Historical Perspective* (San Francisco: Harper & Row, 1984), 159.

8. See *The Woman in the Modern World*, papal teachings selected and arranged by the Benedictine Monks of Solesmes (Boston: St. Paul Editions, 1959), 36.

9. Ibid., 131.

10. Mary Jo Weaver, *New Catholic Women: A Contemporary Challenge to Traditional Religious Authority* (San Francisco: Harper & Row, 1986), 121.

11. Dolan, *American Catholic Experience*, 394ff.

12. Colleen McDannell, "Catholic Domesticity, 1860–1960," in Karen Kennelley, ed., *American Catholic Women: A Historical Explanation* (New York: Macmillan, 1989), 77ff.

13. Pope John XXIII, "Pacem in Terris," ed. William J. Gibbons (New York: Paulist Press, 1963), 10, 17.

14. Walter M. Abbott, ed., *The Documents of Vatican II* (New York: America Press, 1966), 227–28.

15. Pope John XXIII, "Pacem in Terris," 11.

16. "Gaudium et Spes," in Abbott, *Documents*, 267, 276, 257. Like protective labor legislation for women in the first decades of the twentieth century and a so-called mommy track in its closing years, issues of employment, child care, and differentiated treatment are complex and divide even self-identified feminists.

17. Abbott, *Documents*, 639, 647.

18. Emphasis added. "Gaudium et Spes," in Abbott, *Documents*, 250, 251.

19. Emphasis added. From Vincent P. Mainelli, *Official Catholic Teachings: Social Justice*, Consortium Books (Wilmington, N.C.: McGrath Publishing Co., 1978), 250.

20. Quoted in Rosemary Ruether, "Entering the Sanctuary: The Roman Catholic Story," in Rosemary Ruether and Eleanor McLaughlin, eds., *Women of Spirit: Female Leadership in the Jewish and Christian Traditions* (New York: Simon and Schuster, 1979), 374.

21. Ibid., 375.

22. Ibid., 378–79. For a fuller description of the conference, see Anne Marie Gardiner, ed., *Women and Catholic Priesthood: An Expanded Vision. Proceedings of the Detroit Ordination Conference* (New York: Paulist Press, 1976).

23. See "Archbishop Bernardin's Statement," in Gardiner, *Proceedings*, 194–97.

24. Sacred Congregation for the Doctrine of the Faith, *Declaration on the Question of the Admission of Women to the Ministerial Priesthood* (Washington, D.C.: Publications Office, U.S. Catholic Conference, 1977), 5.

25. Ibid., 12.

26. Ibid., 17.

27. For the text of the open letter, see *Commonweal* (1 April 1977): 204–6.

28. Ruether, "Entering the Sanctuary," 380.

29. See Ruth A. Wallace, *They Call Her Pastor: A New Role for Catholic Women* (Albany, N.Y.: State University of New York Press, 1992).

30. See, for example, statements quoted in Antoinette Iadarola, "The American Catholic Bishops and Woman: From the Nineteenth Amendment to ERA," in Yvonne Yazbeck Haddad and Ellison Banks Findly, eds., *Women, Religion and Social Change* (Albany, N.Y.: State University of New York Press, 1985), 467.

31. Archbishop Weakland's comments, *Origins* 24 (June 9, 1994): 55.

32. Alan Graebner, *Uncertain Saints: The Laity in the Lutheran Church–Missouri Synod, 1900–1970* (Westport, Conn.: Greenwood Press, 1975), 25.

33. Alan Graebner, "Birth Control and the Lutherans: The Missouri Synod as a Case Study," in Janet Wilson James, ed., *Women in American Religion* (Philadelphia: University of Pennsylvania Press, 1980), 229–52, describes the LCMS journey from condemnation to silence to approval by the mid-twentieth century.

34. Excerpt from "Human Sexuality: A Theological Perspective" (1981), in J. Gordon Melton, ed., *The Churches Speak on Sex and Family Life. Official Statements from Religious Bodies and Ecumenical Organizations* (Detroit: Gale Research Inc., 1991), 96.

35. Graebner, *Uncertain Saints*, 87.

36. "Women in the Church: Scriptural Principles and Ecclesial Practice" (1985), in J. Gordon Melton, ed., *The Churches Speak on Women's Ordination: Official*

*Statements from Religious Bodies and Ecumenical Organizations* (Detroit: Gale Research Inc., 1991), 134.

37. Ibid., 142.

38. Thomas Hopko, ed., *Women and the Priesthood* (Crestwood, N.J.: St. Vladimir's Seminary Press, 1983), 7–8.

39. Kallistos Ware, "Man, Woman, and the Priesthood of Christ," 14–15; George Barrois, "Women and the Priestly Office According to the Scriptures," 39–60; and Nicholas Afanasiev, "Presbytides or Female Presidents: Canon 11, Council of Laodicea," 61–74, all in Hopko, *Women and the Priesthood*. See also "Conclusions of the Interorthodox Consultation on the Place of the Woman in the Orthodox Church and the Question of the Ordination of Women," Rhodos, Greece, 30 October–7 November 1988, reprinted in *St. Vladimir's Theological Quarterly* 33 (1989): 394.

40. Thomas Hopko, "On the Male Character of Christian Priesthood," in Hopko, *Women and the Priesthood*, 107.

41. Ibid., 105.

42. Ibid., 106.

43. Barrois, "The Priestly Office," 46.

44. Hopko, "On the Male Character of Christian Priesthood," 113–27. Deborah Belonick, a woman theologian and Eastern Orthodox Christian, not only agrees with Hopko's major arguments, she is more pointed than he in attacking the feminist theology that, she believes, has been formulated to support female priesthood. Such theology, she argues, is simply not Christian, for it is opposed to traditional Christian understandings of creation and the church, of Christology and soteriology. "The Spirit of the Female Priesthood," in Hopko, *Women and the Priesthood*, 135–68.

45. Hopko, "Women and the Priesthood: Reflections on the Debate," in Hopko, *Women and the Priesthood*, 186.

46. "Conclusions of the Interorthodox Consultation," 395.

47. Ibid., 397.

48. Militza Zernov, "Women's Ministry in the Church," *Eastern Churches Review* 7 (1975): 37–38.

49. Wertheimer, *A People Divided*, 33, 59.

50. Debra Renee Kaufman, *Rachel's Daughters: Newly Orthodox Jewish Women* (New Brunswick, N.J.: Rutgers University Press, 1991); Lynn Davidman, *Tradition in a Rootless World: Women Turn to Orthodox Judaism* (Berkeley, Calif.: University of California Press, 1991); Tamar Frankiel, *The Voice of Sarah: Feminine Spirituality and Traditional Judaism* (San Francisco: HarperCollins, 1990).

51. Kaufman, *Rachel's Daughters*, 7.

52. Blu Greenberg, *On Women and Judaism: A View from Tradition* (Philadelphia: Jewish Publication Society of America, 1985), 94–95.

53. Norma Baumel Joseph, "*Mehitzah:* Halakhic Decisions and Political Consequences," in Susan Grossman and Rivka Haut, eds., *Daughters of the King: Women and the Synagogue: A Survey of History, Halakhah, and Contemporary Realities* (Philadelphia: The Jewish Publication Society, 1992), 117–34.

54. Rachel Adler, "Tum'ah and Toharah: Ends and Beginnings," *Response* 7 (Summer 1973): 117–27.

55. Quoted in Kaufman, *Rachel's Daughters*, 77. See Jody Myers and Jane

Rachel Litman, "The Secret of Jewish Femininity: Hiddenness, Power, and Physicality in the Theology of Orthodox Women in the Contemporary World," in T. M. Rudavsky, ed., *Gender and Judaism: The Transformation of Tradition* (New York: New York University Press, 1995), 51–77, for an analysis of Orthodox women's defense of *niddah*.

56. Frankiel, *Voice of Sarah*, 123–24.

57. Mary Ewens, "Women in the Convent," in Karen Kennelley, ed., *American Catholic Women: A Historical Explanation* (New York: Macmillan, 1989), 33.

58. James J. Kenneally, *The History of American Catholic Women* (New York: Crossroad, 1990) 172.

59. Mary J. Oates, "Organized Volunteerism: The Catholic Sisters in Massachusetts, 1870–1940," in Janet Wilson James, ed., *Women in American Religion* (Philadelphia: University of Pennsylvania Press, 1980), 167.

60. Weaver, *New Catholic Women*, 32ff.

61. Ewens, "Women in the Convent," 40. See also Marjorie Noterman Beane, *From Framework to Freedom: A History of the Sister Formation Conference* (Lanham, Md.: University Press of America, 1993).

62. See especially the "Decree on the Appropriate Renewal of the Religious Life (*Perfectae Caritatis*)," in Abbott, *Documents*.

63. Weaver, *New Catholic Women*, 83.

64. Albers, "Perspectives," 145.

65. Graebner, *Uncertain Saints*, 138.

66. George J. Gude Jr., "Women Teachers in the Missouri Synod," *Concordia Historical Institute Quarterly* 44 (November 1971): 168–69.

67. Gude gives figures of 3,951 women teachers and 2,539 men teachers in Lutheran parochial schools in 1968 (163).

68. Quoted in Wilma S. Kucharek, "A History of the Lutheran Deaconess Association," unpublished paper at Valparaiso University, 1976, 6.

69. See "Conclusions of the Interorthodox Consultation"; Constance J. Tarasar and Irina Kirillova, eds., *Orthodox Women: Their Role and Participation in the Orthodox Church* (Geneva, Switzerland: World Council of Churches, 1977); Zernov, "Women's Ministry," 34–39; and Kyriaki Karidoyanes FitzGerald, "The Characteristics and Nature of the Order of the Deaconess" in Hopko, *Women and the Priesthood*, 75–95.

70. Stephanie Yova Yazge, "From One Orthodox Woman's Perspective," in Melanie A. May, ed., *Women and Church: The Challenge of Ecumenical Solidarity in an Age of Alienation* (Grand Rapids, Mich.: William B. Eerdmans Publishing Co.; New York: Friendship Press, 1991), 65, 68.

71. See, for example, Frankiel, *The Voice of Sarah*.

72. Greenberg, *Women and Judaism*, x. On the other hand, Wertheimer argues (*A People Divided*, 132ff.) that more rabbis, even from "modern" or "centrist" orthodoxy, are hostile to any changes in the official religious status or roles of women.

73. Ibid., 128.

74. Ibid., 9. See also Chana K. Poupko and Devora L. Wohlgelernter, "Women's Liberation—An Orthodox Response," in Bulka, *Dimensions of Orthodox Judaism*.

75. Greenberg, *Women and Judaism*, 101.

76. Rivka Haut, "Women's Prayer Groups and the Orthodox Synagogue" in Grossman and Haut, *Daughters of the King*, 135.

## Notes for chapter 21: Women, Religion, and Reform in the Twentieth Century

1. Ann Fagan, *This Is Our Song: Employed Women in the United Methodist Tradition* (Cincinnati: The Women's Division of the General Board of Global Ministries, 1986), 29ff.

2. Quoted in Walter G. Muelder, *Methodism and Society in the Twentieth Century* (New York: Abingdon Press, 1961), 287.

3. John Patrick McDowell, *The Social Gospel in the South: The Woman's Home Mission Movement in the Methodist Episcopal Church, South, 1886–1939* (Baton Rouge, La.: Louisiana State University Press, 1982).

4. Jacquelyn Dowd Hall, *Revolt Against Chivalry: Jessie Daniel Ames and the Women's Campaign Against Lynching* (New York: Columbia University Press, 1979), 94, a compelling study of Ames herself and the complex mixture of racism and sexism behind lynching.

5. Margaret Hope Bacon, *Mothers of Feminism: The Story of Quaker Women in America* (San Francisco: Harper & Row, 1986), 213.

6. Lois A. Boyd and R. Douglas Brackenridge, *Presbyterian Women in America: Two Centuries of a Quest for Status* (Westport, Conn.: Greenwood, 1983), 85–86.

7. Alice G. Knotts, "Methodist Women Integrate Schools and Housing, 1952–1959," in Vicki L. Crawford, Jacqueline Anne Rouse, and Barbara Woods, eds., *Women in the Civil Rights Movement: Trailblazers and Torchbearers, 1941–1965*, in Darlene Clark Hine, *Black Women in United States History*, vol. 16 (Brooklyn, N.Y.: Carlson Publishing, Inc., 1990), 253.

8. Nancy Boyd, *Emissaries: The Overseas Work of the American YWCA, 1895–1970* (New York: The Woman's Press, 1986), 156–57.

9. Dorothy Salem, *To Better Our World: Black Women in Organized Reform, 1890–1920*, in Hine, *Black Women*, vol. 14, 121, makes this distinction.

10. Sharlene Voogd Cochrane, "'And the Pressure Never Let Up': Black Women, White Women, and the Boston YWCA, 1918–1948," in Crawford, et al., eds., *Women in the Civil Rights Movement*, 267.

11. Mary R. Sawyer, "Black Religion and Social Change: Women in Leadership Roles," *The Journal of Religious Thought* 47 (Winter–Spring 1990–1991): 22.

12. Quoted in Rosemary Skinner Keller, *Georgia Harkness: For Such a Time as This* (Nashville: Abingdon Press, 1992), 183–84.

13. Martha L. Scott, "Georgia Harkness: Social Activist and/or Mystic," in Rosemary Skinner Keller, Louise L. Queen, and Hilah F. Thomas, eds., *Women in New Worlds: Historical Perspectives on the Wesleyan Tradition*, vol. 1, (Nashville: Abingdon, 1982), 122.

14. Harland Hogue, quoted in Keller, *Georgia Harkness*, 301.

15. Sawyer, *Black Religion*, 18.

16. Evelyn Brooks, "Religion, Politics, and Gender: The Leadership of Nannie Helen Burroughs," *The Journal of Religious Thought* 44 (Winter–Spring 1988): 14–15.

17. Cheryl Townsend Gilkes, "'Until My Change Comes': In the African-American Baptist Tradition," in James D. Davidson, C. Lincoln Johnson, and Alan K. Mock, *Faith and Social Ministry: Ten Christian Perspectives* (Chicago: Loyola University Press, 1990), 198–200.

18. While local church-related activism, especially by women, has traditionally been overlooked by scholars, more recent work has begun to remedy that neglect. See Delores C. Carpenter, "Black Women in Religious Institutions: A Historical Summary from Slavery to the 1960s," *The Journal of Religious Thought* 46 (Winter–Spring 1989–1990): 7–27.

19. Salem, *To Better Our World,* 158.

20. Ibid., 181.

21. Mary Fair Burks, "Trailblazers: Women in the Montgomery Bus Boycott," in Crawford, et al., eds., *Women in the Civil Rights Movement,* 71–83.

22. Grace Jordan McFadden, "Septima P. Clark and the Struggle for Human Rights," in Crawford, et al., eds., *Women in the Civil Rights Movement,* 85.

23. Quoted in Bernice Johnson Reagon, "Women as Culture Carriers in the Civil Rights Movement: Fannie Lou Hamer," Crawford, et al., eds., in *Women in the Civil Rights Movement,* 214.

24. *Images of Women in Mission: Resource Guide and National Directory of Catholic Church Vocations for Women* (Ramsey, N.J.: Paulist Press, 1981), 149. This guide provides brief descriptions of the work of over 180 Catholic women's orders in the United States.

25. Mary Ewens, "Women in the Convent," in Karen Kennelly, ed., *American Catholic Women: A Historical Explanation* (New York: Macmillan, 1989), 35.

26. Ibid., 44.

27. Aaron I. Abell, *American Catholicism and Social Action: A Search for Social Justice, 1865–1950* (Notre Dame, Ind.: University of Notre Dame Press, 1963), 223.

28. Alden V. Brown, *The Grail Movement and American Catholicism, 1940–1975* (Notre Dame, Ind.: University of Notre Dame Press, 1989), 136.

29. Jay P. Dolan, *The American Catholic Experience: A History from Colonial Times to Present* (Garden City, N.Y.: Doubleday, 1985), 413.

30. Among many useful sources on Dorothy Day and the Catholic Worker Movement are her own autobiographical accounts, *From Union Square to Rome* (1938) and *The Long Loneliness* (1952); two works by William B. Miller: *A Harsh and Dreadful Love: Dorothy Day and the Catholic Worker Movement* (New York: Liveright, 1973) and *Dorothy Day: A Biography* (San Francisco: Harper & Row, 1982); and Mel Piehl, *The Catholic Worker and the Origin of Catholic Radicalism in America* (Philadelphia: Temple University Press, 1982).

31. June Sochen, *Consecrate Every Day: The Public Lives of Jewish American Women, 1880–1980* (Albany, N.Y.: State University of New York Press, 1981), 4.

32. Ibid., 45–83.

33. Ibid., 80.

34. Jacob R. Marcus, *The American Jewish Woman, 1654–1980,* (New York: KTAV Publishing House, 1981), 96.

35. Beth S. Wenger, "Jewish Women of the Club: The Changing Public Role of Atlanta's Jewish Women (1870–1930)," *American Jewish History* 76 (March 1987): 321.

36. Hall, *Revolt Against Chivalry,* 178, 242.

37. Judith Plaskow, *Standing Again at Sinai: Judaism from a Feminist Perspective* (San Francisco: Harper & Row, 1990), 214.

## Notes for chapter 22: Women and Religion in America: Looking toward the Twenty-first Century

1. For helpful introductions to Native American history in the modern period, see James S. Olson and Raymond Wilson, *Native Americans in the Twentieth Century* (Urbana, Ill.: University of Illinois Press, 1984) and Frederick E. Hoxie, ed., *Indians in American History: An Introduction,* D'Arcy McNickle Center for the History of the American Indian, The Newberry Library (Arlington Heights, Ill.: Harlan Davidson, Inc., 1988).

2. Sam Gill, "Native Americans and their Religions," in Jacob Neusner, ed., *World Religions in America: An Introduction* (Louisville, Ky.: Westminster John Knox Press, 1994), 11–30.

3. Rayna Green, *Women in American Indian Society* (New York: Chelsea House Publishers, 1992), 21.

4. Beverly Hungry Wolf brings together an account of her own appreciative search for the wisdom and traditional ways of her "grandmothers" (literal and communal) and an offering to a younger generation of girls who will "miss out on meeting some of these fine old women. . . . This is my tribute to them." *The Ways of My Grandmothers* (New York: William Morrow and Co, 1980), 16.

5. Beatrice Medicine, "Indian Women and the Renaissance of Traditional Religion" in Raymond J. DeMallie and Douglas R. Parks, eds., *Sioux Indian Religion: Tradition and Innovation* (Norman, Okla.: University of Oklahoma Press, 1987), 169–70.

6. Howard Meredith, "Christianity and Native Americans," in Duane Champagne, ed., *The Native North American Almanac: A Reference Work on Native North Americans in the United States and Canada* (Detroit: Gale Research Inc., 1994), 661.

7. Medicine, "Indian Women," 164.

8. Quoted in Arlene Hirschfelder and Paulette Molin, *The Encyclopedia of Native American Religions* (New York: Facts on File, 1992), 193.

9. Ibid., 194.

10. Nancy Lurie, ed., *Mountain Wolf Woman, Sister of Crashing Thunder: The Autobiography of a Winnebago Indian* (Ann Arbor, Mich.: University of Michigan Press, 1961), 107.

11. Gill, *Native Americans,* 28–30.

12. For helpful introductions to Hinduism in America, see John Y. Fenton, "Hinduism," in Charles H. Lippy and Peter W. Williams, *Encyclopedia of the American Religious Experience,* vol. 2 (New York: Charles Schribner's Sons, 1988), 683–98; and Gerald James Larson, "Hinduism in India and in America" in Neusner, *World Religions in America,* 177–202.

13. Fenton uses the former term, Larson the latter.

14. Susan Jane Palmer, *Moon Sisters, Krishna Mothers, Rajneesh Lovers: Women's Roles in New Religions* (Syracuse, N.Y.: Syracuse University Press, 1994), 15–31.

15. Catherine Wessinger, "Woman Guru, Woman Roshi: The Legitimation of Female Religious Leadership in Hindu and Buddhist Groups in America," in Catherine Wessinger, ed., *Women's Leadership in Marginal Religions: Explorations Outside the Mainstream* (Urbana, Ill.: University of Illinois Press, 1993), 128.

16. I am deeply indebted to my friend and colleague, Professor Anantanand Rambachan, for information about contemporary Hinduism in America.

17. Charles S. Prebish, "Buddhism," in Lippy and Williams, *Encyclopedia of the American Religious Experience,* vol. 2, 676.

18. Nancy J. Barnes, "Women in Buddhism," in Arvind Sharma, ed., *Today's Woman in World Religions* (Albany, N.Y.: State University of New York Press, 1994), 156–69.

19. Sandy Boucher, *Turning the Wheel: American Women Creating the New Buddhism,* updated and expanded edition (Boston: Beacon Press, 1993).

20. Ibid., 2.

21. Ibid., 22; see also Barnes, "Women in Buddhism," 167–69.

22. William B. Williamson, ed., *An Encyclopedia of Religions in the United States: One Hundred Religious Groups Speak for Themselves* (New York: Crossroad, 1992), 57.

23. Emma McCloy Layan, *Buddhism in America* (Chicago: Nelson-Hall, 1976), 33–51.

24. Tetsuden Kashima, "The Buddhist Churches of America: Challenges for Change in the 21st Century," *The Pacific World: Journal of the Institute of Buddhist Studies,* n.s., 6 (Fall 1990): 36.

25. I am grateful to my friend and colleague, Professor Barbara Reed, who generously shared bibliography and insights about Buddhism with me.

26. Yvonne Yazbeck Haddad and Adair T. Lummis, *Islamic Values in the United States: A Comparative Study* (New York: Oxford University Press, 1987), 3.

27. Jane I. Smith, "Islam," in Arvind Sharma, ed., *Women in World Religions* (Albany, N.Y.: State University of New York Press, 1987), 236.

28. Ibid., 243.

29. Haddad and Lummis, *Islamic Values,* 8.

30. Ibid., 46, 130.

31. Quoted in ibid., 131.

32. Ibid., 135.

33. Marcia K. Hermansen, "Two-Way Acculturation: Muslim Women in America Between Individual Choice (Liminality) and Community Affiliation (Communitas)," in Yvonne Yazbeck Haddad, ed., *The Muslims of America* (New York: Oxford University Press, 1991), 198.

34. Steven Barboza, *American Jihad: Islam after Malcolm X* (New York: Doubleday, 1993), 9.

35. C. Eric Lincoln, *The Black Muslims in America,* rev. ed. (Queens, N.Y.: Kayode Publications, Ltd., 1973) is a classic study of the movement. Two articles in Earle H. Waugh, Baha Abus-Laban, and Regula B. Qureshi, eds., *The Muslim Community in North America* (Edmonton, Alberta: The University of Alberta Press, 1983) carry the story into the 1980s: C. Eric Lincoln, "The American Muslim Mission in the Context of American Social History," 215–33; and Lawrence H. Mamiya, "Minister Louis Farrakhan and the Final Call: Schism in the Muslim Movment," 234–55.

36. Lincoln, *The Black Muslims in America,* 25.

37. Ibid., 84.

38. Kenneth B. Bedell, *Yearbook of American and Canadian Churches: 1995* (Nashville: Abingdon Press, 1995), 280.

39. *Statistical Abstract of the United States*, 1994, 407; United States Bureau of Labor Statistics, *Employment and Earnings*, 42, 1 (1995): 176.

40. Laura Geller, "From Equality to Transformation: The Challenge of Women's Rabbinic Leadership," in T. M. Rudavsky, ed., *Gender and Judaism: The Transformation of Tradition* (New York: New York University Press, 1995), 244.

41. Jackson W. Carroll, Barbara Hargrove, and Adair T. Lummis, *Women of the Cloth: A New Opportunity for the Churches* (San Francisco: Harper & Row, 1983), 138.

42. Geller, "Equality to Transformation," 246ff.

43. Barbara B. Troxell, "Honoring One Another with Our Stories: Authority and Mutual Ministry Among United Methodist Clergywomen in the Last Decade of the Twentieth Century," in Rosemary Skinner Keller, ed., *Spirituality and Social Responsibility: Vocational Vision of Women in the United Methodist Tradition* (Nashville: Abingdon Press, 1993), 289.

44. Frances E. Willard, *Woman in the Pulpit* (Chicago: Woman's Temperance Publication Association, 1889), 46–47.

45. Carroll, et al., *Women of the Cloth*, 44–47.

46. Rita J. Simon, Angela J. Scanlon, and Pamela S. Nadell, "Rabbis and Ministers: Women of the Book and the Cloth," in William H. Swatos Jr., ed., *Gender and Religion* (New Brunswick, N.J.: Transaction Publishers, 1994), 50.

47. Edward C. Lehman Jr., *Gender and Work: The Case of the Clergy* (Albany, N.Y.: State University of New York Press, 1993), 39.

48. Ibid., 84–95, 183.

49. Judith Plaskow and Carol P. Christ, eds., *Weaving the Visions: New Patterns in Feminist Spirituality* (San Francisco: Harper & Row, 1989), 1.

50. Mary E. Hines, "Community for Liberation: Church," in Catherine Mowry LaCugna, ed., *Freeing Theology: The Essentials of Theology in Feminist Perspective* (San Francisco: HarperCollins, 1993), 170.

51. The term comes from Alice Walker, *In Search of Our Mothers' Gardens* (San Diego: Harcourt Brace Jovanovich, Publishers, 1983), xi–xii.

52. Delores S. Williams, *Sisters in the Wilderness: The Challenge of Womanist God-Talk* (Maryknoll, N.Y.: Orbis Books, 1993), 179–99. I have focused on one example of womanist theology, recognizing that a few brief paragraphs cannot do justice to a complex and provocative full-length study but convinced that briefer coverage of several voices would be even more superficial. Readers may wish to consult other works like Jacquelyn Grant, *White Women's Christ and Black Women's Jesus: Feminist Christology and Womanist Response* (Atlanta: Scholars Press, 1989); Ada Maria Isasi-Diaz and Yolanda Tarango, *Hispanic Women: Prophetic Voice in the Church* (San Francisco: Harper and Row, 1988); and Chung Hyun Kyung, *Struggle to Be the Sun Again: Introducing Asian Women's Theology* (Maryknoll, N.Y.: Orbis, 1990).

53. Williams., *Sisters in the Wilderness*, 6.

54. On Hagar and the wilderness symbol, see especially chap. 5, "Sisters in the Wilderness and Community Meanings."

55. Ibid., 238–39.

56. Rita Gross, "Female God Language in a Jewish Context," in Christ and Plaskow, eds., *Womanspirit Rising: A Feminist Reader in Religion* (San Francisco: Harper & Row, 1979), 167–73, is a brief but excellent early introduction to the God-language issue, including both theological grounding and practical alternatives.

57. Sallie McFague, *Models of God: Theology for an Ecological, Nuclear Age* (Philadelphia: Fortress Press, 1987), 169.

58. Sacred Congregation for the Doctrine of the Faith, "Declaration on the Question of the Admission of Women to the Ministerial Priesthood" (Washington, D.C.: United States Catholic Conference, 1977), 11–15.

59. Elizabeth A. Johnson, "Redeeming the Name of Christ: Christology," in LaCugna, *Freeing Theology*, 131. This is a particularly helpful anthology, not only because of its excellent individual articles but also for its extensive notes and annotated bibliographies.

60. Charges that participants prayed to a female God, Sophia, were central in the controversy that broke out in the wake of a "Re-Imagining" conference held in Minneapolis in November 1993. Indeed, the popular mainline journal, *The Christian Century*, cited the controversy, especially among Presbyterians, as its number two religious news story of 1994 (*The Christian Century* 111 [December 21–28, 1994]: 1211).

61. Leo D. Lefebure, "The Wisdom of God: Sophia and Christian Theology," *The Christian Century* 111 (October 19, 1994): 954. Lefebure's article is a brief but balanced introduction to the topic. Elizabeth A. Johnson, *She Who Is: The Mystery of God in Feminist Theological Discourse* (New York: Crossroad, 1992); and Elisabeth Schüssler Fiorenza, *Jesus: Miriam's Child, Sophia's Prophet: Critical Issues in Feminist Christology* (New York: Continuum, 1994) are two recent works by feminist theologians that include more developed treatments of Sophia.

62. See, for example, Merlin Stone, *When God Was a Woman* (New York: Dial Press, 1976) and Riane Eisler, *The Chalice and the Blade: Our History, Our Future* (San Francisco: Harper & Row, 1987).

63. Carol P. Christ, *Laughter of Aphrodite: Reflections on a Journey to the Goddess* (San Francisco: Harper & Row, 1987), 156.

64. Perhaps the best-known spokesperson for Wicca is Starhawk. Her first book, *The Spiral Dance: A Rebirth of the Ancient Religion of the Great Goddess* (San Francisco: Harper & Row, 1979), focused especially on the practice of modern Wicca. A second, *Dreaming the Dark: Magic, Sex and Politics*, 2d ed. (Boston: Beacon Press, 1988), also includes an account of her participation in the anti-nuclear movement and a long historical appendix on witch persecution in the West. A third work appeared in 1987: *Truth or Dare: Encounters with Power, Authority, and Mystery* (San Francisco: Harper & Row).

65. Christ, *Laughter of Aphrodite*, 122.

66. Ibid., 70.

67. Both Jewish and Christian theological traditions have insisted that God is both "other" and "present," both transcendent and immanent, but different times, movements, and thinkers have emphasized one side substantially more than the other. Thus as revolutionary feminist theologians, most of whom have Jewish or Christian roots, essentially reject transcendence in favor of immanence, so critics

of feminist theology seem to exalt God's transcendence, which they believe is threatened by radical and heretical feminists, and minimize or ignore the theological tradition of divine immanence. See, for example, Elizabeth Achtemeier, "Why God Is Not Mother: A Response to Feminist God-Talk in the Church," *Christianity Today* 37 (August 16, 1993): 17–23.

# Index

Index

Index

# Index

## Index

Printed in the United States
92427LV00003B/113/A

9 780664 257996